The Seventies in America

The Seventies in America

Volume III

Room 222—Zodiac killer
Appendices
Indexes

Editor
John C. Super
West Virginia University

Managing Editor
Tracy Irons-Georges

SALEM PRESS, INC.
Pasadena, California
Hackensack, New Jersey

Editorial Director: Christina J. Moose
Managing Editor: Tracy Irons-Georges
Copy Editor: Sarah M. Hilbert
Assistant Editor: Andrea E. Miller
Photo Editor: Cynthia Beres
Production Editor: Joyce I. Buchea
Acquisitions Editor: Mark Rehn
Graphics and Design: James Hutson
Layout: William Zimmerman

Title page photo: *On November 17, 1973, President Richard M. Nixon answers questions about his alleged illegal actions.* (AP/Wide World Photos)

Cover images: *Saturday Night Fever* (Hulton Archive/Getty Images)
"Sorry no gas until the 1st" (Hulton Archive/Getty Images)
President Richard Nixon (Hulton Archive/Getty Images)

∞ The paper used in these volumes conforms to the American National Standard for Permanence of Paper for Printed Library Materials, Z39.48-1992 (R1997).

Library of Congress Cataloging-in-Publication Data

The seventies in America / editor, John C. Super ; managing editor, Tracy Irons-Georges.
p. cm.
Includes bibliographical references and index.
ISBN-10: 1-58765-228-5 (set : alk. paper)
ISBN-13: 978-1-58765-228-8 (set : alk. paper)
ISBN-10: 1-58765-231-5 (vol. 3 : alk. paper)
ISBN-13: 978-1-58765-231-8 (vol. 3 : alk. paper)
1. United States—Civilization—1970—Encyclopedias. 2. Nineteen seventies—Encyclopedias.
I. Super, John C., 1944- II. Irons-Georges, Tracy.
E169.12.S447 2006
973.924—dc22

2005023549

First Printing

PRINTED IN THE UNITED STATES OF AMERICA

Table of Contents

Complete List of Contents

Volume I

Volume II

Volume III

The Seventies in America

■ Room 222

Identification Television comedy-drama
Date Aired from 1969 to 1974

Room 222 *pioneered the combination of television comedy with drama and realistically addressed social concerns within entertainment television.*

Though not as well known as *All in the Family* and *The Mary Tyler Moore Show*, *Room 222* was not only their peer but also their predecessor. The American Broadcasting Company (ABC) network aired 112 half-hour episodes beginning September 17, 1969, and ending on January 11, 1974. A final episode was written but not aired. Though never a ratings success, the show received awards and nominations within the entertainment industry and recognition from educators and civil rights groups.

In the series, the teachers, principal, and students of Walt Whitman High School confronted timeless issues of emotions and ethics as well as contemporary issues, including gender stereotypes, drug use, the Vietnam War, and sexually transmitted disease. The protagonist, African American history teacher Pete Dixon (played by Lloyd Haynes), shared the show's focus with a strong ensemble cast, which included strong nonwhite characters, such as the black guidance counselor, Liz McIntyre (Denise Nicholas), who became Pete's love interest. Students included a young militant African American man named Jason (Heshimu) who wore an Afro (referred to as "a natural"). Other main characters were teacher Alice Johnson (Karen Valentine) and the sarcastic but caring principal, Seymour Kaufman (Michael Constantine).

Most important, none of the characters became racial stereotypes. The teachers were caring and effective but showed human frailties and gave realistic responses to their students. Good acting and scripting, as well as the show's mixture of comedy and drama, helped create the show's realism. Moreover, *Room 222* was primarily filmed in Los Angeles High School, which added to its realistic approach.

Humor punctuates each episode, yet it was widely recognized as a drama. Its first season featured a laugh track, but later seasons did not. Thus, *Room 222* may be the first example of a "dramedy" although this terms was not coined for several more years. In fact, the creators behind *Room 222* later helped established the dramedy genre, taking key roles in producing two notable programs in the genre, *The Mary Tyler Moore Show* (first aired in 1970) and the television show *M*A*S*H* (first aired in 1972).

Various influences on *Room 222* included *Mr. Novak*, a short-lived series about a caring English teacher that aired from 1963 to 1965, and *The Mod Squad*, with its biracial cast and interest in social justice, which aired from 1965 to 1973. Other important influences included several films, such as *Up the Down Staircase* (1967) and *To Sir with Love* (1967), which served as stories of teaching in difficult, underprivileged schools. *To Sir with Love* features a black protagonist, teacher Mark Thackeray, played by Sidney Poitier.

Impact Episodes of *Room 222* provide a time capsule of fashions, ideas, and controversies of the time and served as a forward-looking treatment of race. It also introduced the dramedy genre, which would be pervasive on television from the 1970's onward.

Further Reading

MacDonald, J. Fred. *Black and White TV: Afro Americans in Television Since 1948.* Chicago: Nelson-Hall, 1992.

Newcomb, Horace, and Robert Alley, eds. *The Producer's Medium: Conversations with the Creators of American TV.* New York: Oxford University Press, 1983.

Bernadette Lynn Bosky

See also African Americans; *All in the Family*; *Mary Tyler Moore Show, The*; *M*A*S*H*; Sitcoms; Television in the United States.

■ Roots

Identification Landmark television miniseries
Date Aired January 23-30, 1977

Roots *helped shape racial attitudes, furthered changes already underway in the television industry, and promoted an interest in genealogy among Americans.*

The hardback edition of African American author Alex Haley's *Roots: The Saga of an American Family*, published in 1976, sold more than 1.6 million copies in the first six months. By 1977, *Roots* was the number-one nonfiction book. The American Broadcasting Company (ABC) produced a miniseries based on the book that ran on eight successive nights in early

1977. *Roots* starred many prominent African American and white actors, including Leslie Uggams, Louis Gossett, Jr., Ben Vereen, Lloyd Bridges, and Ed Asner. The series introduced LeVar Burton as its most memorable character, Kunta Kinte. The television audience was enormous, with more than 100 million viewers seeing the final episode.

Haley's Research and Plot Line Haley's inspiration was family lore passed down from his maternal grandparents, including some African words and mentions of a slave ancestor named Toby. Over a period of eleven years, Haley researched his background by calling on resources such as slave ship records and African language experts. He visited Juffure, Ghana, and met with a native oral historian. Haley wove his findings into a smoothly flowing narrative with memorable characters. He described *Roots* as combining fact and fiction; while the book's events may not be entirely true to historic record, they broadly recounted what happened to many African slaves and their progeny.

The miniseries covered many generations of Haley's ancestors, beginning with Kunta Kinte. He was born in 1750 and was captured by slave hunters at age fifteen. He endured terrible conditions while chained below the deck of a slave ship, and he was humiliated at the Annapolis slave market, where he was sold to John Waller. Waller named him "Toby." Typical of his defiance of slavery in all its aspects, Kunta Kinte refused to accept his slave name, and he attempted escape many times. He had a daughter, Kizzy, to whom he taught pride in her African heritage. Each succeeding generation passed on this oral tradition. In a traumatic scene, Kizzy was sold away from her parents and was raped repeatedly by her new owner, Tom Lea. Kizzy's son, George, had cockfighting skills, which led to his nickname "Chicken George." George and his slave wife had eight children before he was sold to cover his owner's gam-

Athlete-turned-actor O. J. Simpson (left) and LeVar Burton in a scene from the groundbreaking miniseries Roots. (Capital Cities/ABC, Inc.)

bling debts. George eventually became a free man. He and his son Tom, a blacksmith, worked to achieve freedom and a better life for the rest of the family.

Promoting Change *Roots* reinforced some of the trends in American society during the mid-1970's, when advances in civil rights for African Americans were occurring. Consistent with this trend, *Roots* highlighted that black Americans had endured great discrimination in the past and deserved respect and fair treatment in the present.

It portrayed African Americans as dignified, noble people, contrasting with the negative Uncle Tom stereotype. The show brought about a new understanding among white Americans of the immorality of slavery and racial discrimination, since the characters were portrayed vividly as real people with gut-wrenching experiences. White Americans could begin to empathize with the "interior life" of African Americans. The show dispelled some myths commonly believed by white Americans: that the slaves were docile, that they accepted their fate, and that slavery was no worse than the difficulties encountered by European immigrants.

Roots also represented a continuation of trends in television programming during the mid-1970's. Americans had witnessed serious topics depicted on television, such as the Watergate hearings, and they were becoming accustomed to seeing previously taboo topics on the small screen with programs such as *Saturday Night Live* and *All in the Family*. Network television featured several African Americans in leading roles, and race became a theme in programs such as *Good Times* and *Sanford and Son*.

Impact American television was never the same after *Roots*. The networks previously had aired only one miniseries, *Rich Man, Poor Man*, in 1976. *Roots* was a blockbuster success and proved that Americans appreciated the miniseries format. Networks began to produce many miniseries, such as *Holocaust* (1978), *Shogun* (1980), and *War and Remembrance* (1988). *Roots* also developed the "docudrama" form, a presentation of historic fact using the melodramatic style of a soap opera. Violence and sex permeated the story line, and the emotional scenes captured viewers' interest. A sequel to the miniseries, *Roots: The Next Generations*, aired in 1979.

Moreover, the series led to an enormous growth of interest in popular genealogy. Americans realized that they too could research their family backgrounds. This interest was awakened especially in African Americans, who learned to investigate linkages with their homelands, and many traveled to Africa as tourists.

Further Reading

Bogle, Daniel. "*Roots* and *Roots: The Next Generation*." In *Blacks in American Film and Television*. New York: Taylor & Francis, 1988. Provides plot synopses of the two miniseries and critical analyses of the shows' impact.

Fiedler, Leslie. *The Inadvertent Epic: From Uncle Tom's Cabin to "Roots."* New York: Simon & Schuster, 1979. Discusses important works that shaped American cultural attitudes about race.

Tucker, Lauren R., and Hemant Shah. "Race and the Transformation of Culture: The Making of the Television Series *Roots*." *Critical Studies in Mass Communication* 9 (1992): 325-336. Highlights how *Roots* brought race to the forefront of American television viewing.

Nancy Conn Terjesen

See also African Americans; *All in the Family*; Book publishing; Literature in the United States; Miniseries; Racial discrimination; *Sanford and Son*; Television in the United States.

■ Rose, Pete

Identification American baseball player
Born April 14, 1941; Cincinnati, Ohio

Rose, the iconic leadoff hitter for "the Big Red Machine" Cincinnati Reds of the 1970's, thrilled fans and infuriated opponents with energetic play that earned him the nickname "Charlie Hustle."

Pete Rose grew up in a working-class family, the son of Harry Rose, a gifted amateur athlete. He signed with the hometown Reds and was in the major leagues by 1963. Rose collected many hits playing in the pitching-dominated 1960's, but only in the following decade did the Reds begin winning consistently under manager Sparky Anderson, featuring Rose along with catcher Johnny Bench and second baseman Joe Morgan.

Rose had little power and no fixed defensive position—he played most infield and outfield positions during his career—but his ability to put the bat on the ball and his capacity to stretch his talent as far as possible made him one of the premier players of the

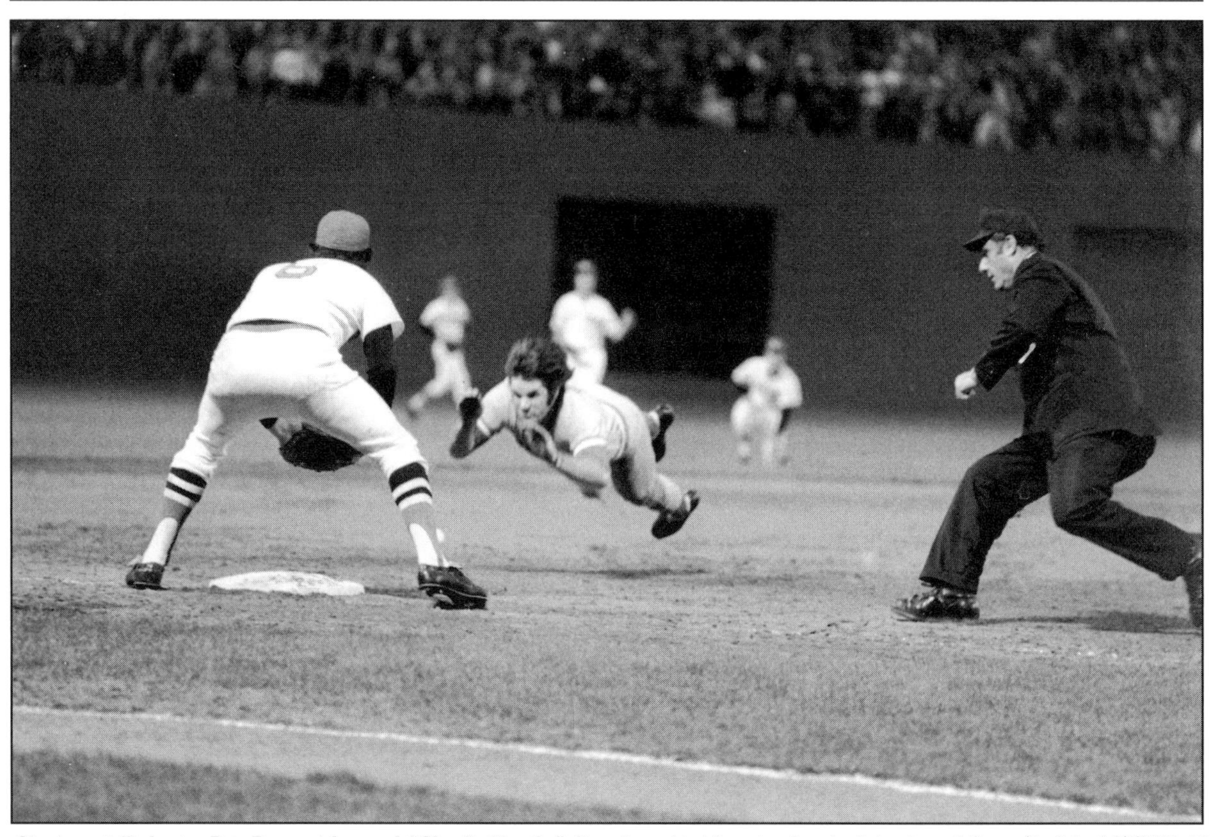

Cincinnati Reds star Pete Rose, nicknamed "Charlie Hustle," dives into third base in the ninth inning of Game 7 of the 1975 World Series. (AP/Wide World Photos)

game. In the 1970 All-Star Game, Rose bowled into Cleveland catcher Ray Fosse while sliding into the plate, injuring Fosse to an extent that marred his career. This incident, along with a fight that Rose had with New York Mets shortstop Bud Harrelson after Rose slid into Harrleson at second base during the 1973 playoffs, raised questions over whether Rose played all-out or simply "played dirty."

Although he was a gritty player praised for his blue-collar ethic, Rose's long hair and love for publicity and a lavish lifestyle made him one of the baseball players, along with Reggie Jackson and Steve Garvey, who most represented the individualism of the 1970's. After winning two championships with Cincinnati, Rose signed as a free agent with the Philadelphia Phillies in 1979. The next year, the Phillies won their first championship in many decades.

Impact Pete Rose's in-your-face attitude and unabashed self-glorification heralded the rise of a new kind of athlete in the 1970's, one that did not conform to the model of the "organization man" from previous decades. With Rose and his contemporaries, the counterculture, in its own way, had at last come to sports.

Subsequent Events In 1981, Rose broke Stan Musial's National League hit record of 3,630. Rose played with the Montreal Expos in 1984 and then returned to Cincinnati until his retirement in 1986, by which time he had broken Ty Cobb's major league hit record of 4,191. Three years later, while serving as manager of the Cincinnati Reds, Rose was found to have gambled on many sports, including baseball games in which his own team was involved. A lifetime ban was imposed on him by Baseball Commissioner A. Bartlett Giamatti, an action that remained controversial decades later.

Further Reading

Reston, James, Jr. *Collision at Home Plate: The Lives of Pete Rose and Bart Giamatti.* New York: HarperCollins, 1991.

Sokolove, Michael. *Hustle: The Myth, Life, and Lies of Pete Rose.* New York: Simon & Schuster, 1990.

Nicholas Birns

See also Baseball; Bench, Johnny; Jackson, Reggie; Palmer, Jim; Ryan, Nolan; Sports.

■ Roy, Gabrielle

Identification French Canadian novelist
Born March 22, 1909; Saint-Boniface, Manitoba, Canada
Died July 13, 1983; Quebec City, Quebec, Canada

Popular with both French- and English-language readers and critics, Roy continued her successful career as a novelist of French Canadian life during the 1970's.

Gabrielle Roy repeated in the 1970's the pattern that she established with her first two books of alternating realistic with pastoral stories. Her first novel, *Bonheur d'occassion* (1945; *The Tin Flute,* 1947), was a realistic account of life in the Montreal slums that contrasted sharply with previous French Canadian literature featuring saccharine stories about pious peasants in rural Quebec. It was a best-seller that received several prizes, including France's prestigious Prix Fémina and the Canadian Governor General's Award for Fiction. It also established Roy's reputation as a leading French Canadian novelist, in France as well as Canada. Her second book, *La Petite poule d'eau* (1950; *Where Nests the Water Hen,* 1951), painted a nostalgic portrait of French Canadian life in rural northern Manitoba.

La Rivière sans repos (1970; *Windflower,* 1970), set in an Inuit settlement in northern Quebec, describes the difficulties experienced by an Inuit woman, raped by an American soldier, in bringing up her half-breed son. The novel explores the tension between tradition and the modern world faced by Inuit in the twentieth century. In 1971, the Quebec government awarded Roy the Prix David. Roy's next volume, *Cet été qui chantait* (1972; *Enchanted Summer,* 1976), contains nineteen lyrical sketches remembering a summer spent in northern Quebec.

Un Jardin au bout du monde (1975; *Garden in the Wind,* 1977) turned toward realism. Four stories sympathetically convey the experiences of different minority communities in rural Manitoba. In each tale, the lead character struggles to survive in an often hostile human and natural environment. The title story explores the significance of a flower garden on the prairie to an embittered Ukrainian housewife. Roy's final work of fiction, *Ces enfants de ma vie* (1977; *Children of My Heart,* 1979), won Roy her third Governor General's Award. Set in the rural Manitoba community where Roy had taught as a newly fledged schoolteacher, each story celebrates a student's attempt to achieve excellence.

Roy's only nonfiction book, *Fragiles lumiéres de la terre* (1978; *The Fragile Lights of Earth,* 1982), collects essays dealing with urban Montreal and the people of rural Manitoba who inspired her novels.

Impact In the 1970's, Gabrielle Roy extended her compassionate narratives beyond urban poor to other oppressed groups: the Inuit of northern Quebec and immigrants faced with the daunting task of building new lives on Manitoba's prairies. Roy's nostalgic accounts of French Canadian life on the prairies were marked by vivid detail, reminding readers that the Francophone community extended over all of Canada, not just the province of Québec.

Further Reading

Clemente, Linda M., and William A. Clemente. *Gabrielle Roy: Creation and Memory.* Toronto: ECW Press, 1997.
Hesse, M. G. *Gabrielle Roy.* Boston: Twayne, 1984.
Mitcham, Allison. *The Literary Achievement of Gabrielle Roy.* Fredericton, N.B.: York Press, 1983.

Milton Berman

See also Francophonie, La; Immigration to Canada; Literature in Canada; Minorities in Canada.

■ Rubik's cube

Identification A three-inch square and multicolored mechanical puzzle game
Date Invented in 1977

Solving this challenging puzzle became a worldwide fad during the late 1970's and early 1980's.

In late 1974, the Hungarian inventor of the Rubik's cube, Erno Rubik, conceptualized a cube made up of twenty-six smaller cube pieces. Each of the cube's six sides (colored red, orange, yellow, green, blue, and white) exposed nine separate square faces. Rubik, a math professor and sculptor, struggled to find a way to make the blocks move independently yet remain connected to the main cube. He solved the problem by adding small extensions to the blocks and connecting them to a central base. He then placed colorful stickers on each of the fifty-four exposed faces, realizing quickly that once the puzzle was twisted randomly, it was very difficult to return to its original appearance.

In 1977, the invention, initially called the Magic Cube, was patented in Hungary. A small toy company produced the toy, but commercial success was slow in coming. Finally, in 1979, a toy expert noticed the unusual puzzle at a toy fair and made arrangements for Ideal Toy Company to manufacture one million cubes. Later that same year, the puzzle caught the attention of mathematician David Singmaster whose interest led to a cover picture and feature article in *Scientific American*. After the publication of this article, U.S. sales began to take off.

Erno Rubik, inventor of the Rubik's cube, surrounded by his puzzles. (Hulton Archive/Getty Images)

Impact By 1981, the demand for the Rubik's cube had exceeded capacity and a veritable craze had begun. It soon became the best-selling puzzle in history. The success of the toy spawned a host of copycat puzzles of varying shapes. Rubik's cube solution books proliferated the market and sold well. Devotees to the challenging game organized international speed contests and Rubik's cube clubs. Although sales diminished after the initial craze faded, the Rubik's cube experienced moderate commercial success well into the ensuing decades.

Subsequent Events Rubik's cube became a trademark of Seven Towns Limited, and although Rubik held a Hungarian patent for the mechanism, he had not taken out an international patent. This oversight opened the market for imitation puzzles. Rubik himself released similar puzzles, including a four-inch version called Rubik's Revenge.

Further Reading

Rubik, Erno, et al. *Rubik's Cubic Compendium.* Oxford, England: Oxford University Press, 1987.

Singmaster, David. *Notes on Rubik's Magic Cube.* Hillside, N.J.: Enslow, 1981.

Taylor, Don. *Mastering Rubik's Cube: The Solution to the Twentieth Century's Most Amazing Puzzle.* New York: Holt, Rinehart and Winston, 1981.

Valerie Brown

See also Fads; Toys and games.

■ Rush

Identification Canadian rock trio
Date Formed in 1969

Rush formed in the early 1970's and proved to be one of Canada's most successful and long-standing bands.

Alex Lifeson and Geddy Lee played together first in 1968, but their band underwent a number of personnel (and name) changes until reforming under the name Rush in 1969. Lee and Lifeson were Canadian. Lee was born Gary Lee Weinrib in 1953, and he changed his name to Geddy in honor of his mother, who was Polish and pronounced Gary that way. Lifeson was born in 1953 to Yugoslavian immigrants, who named him Alexander Zivojinovich.

The band released "Not Fade Away" (a Buddy Holly cover) in 1973, with their own song "You Can't Fight It" on the B side. It then released the album *Rush* on Moon Records in 1974, which, after it did well, was picked up by Mercury. After *Rush,* the band changed drummers, going from John Rutsey—who had diabetes and did not want to tour as much as Lifeson and Lee did—to Neil Peart. In 1975, the band released *Caress of Steel,* which sold poorly. However, the 1976 follow-up, *2112,* went platinum.

Rush often was individualistic. For instance, the first half of *2112* is one song that tells a story. Its record company did not want the band to do this, since the last album, similarly structured, had not sold well. Rush did it anyway and sold millions, and it became the first very successful album for the band. In 1976, it also released a live album *All the World's a Stage,* and in 1978, it released *Archives* and *Hemispheres.*

Rush often played two hundred dates a year. After joining the band, Peart wrote most of the lyrics for its albums, as Rutsey did on the first record. Lifeson wrote the music and played guitar, while Lee sang and played bass. Science fiction and fantasy serve as themes for many of the band's songs, and its music continually evolved, even though its music has roots in "Working Man," a song from the band's first album. Further, the band's lyrics have always inspired analysis. For instance, the songs on *2112* worked from a theme inspired by author Ayn Rand, although Peart later denied agreeing with Rand's philosophy. Rush was also inspired by J. R. Tolkien's *Lord of the Rings* trilogy, with songs titled "Necromancer (Caress of Steel)" and "Rivendell (Fly By Night)."

Impact Rush is one of the most successful Canadian rock bands of all time, and the band members' ability to reinvent themselves during the 1970's, while still holding true to what they wanted, indicated that their band would be a long-term success.

Further Reading

Nutall, Carrie. *Rhythm and Light.* Landham, Md.: Rounder Books, 2005.

Peart, Neil. *Ghost Rider: Travels on the Healing Road.* Toronto: ECW Press, 2002.

_______. *Traveling Music: Playing Back the Soundtrack to My Life and Times.* Toronto: ECW Press, 2004.

Popoff, Martin. *Contents Under Pressure: Thirty Years of Rush at Home and Away.* Toronto: ECW Press, 2004.

Scott A. Merriman

See also Hard rock and heavy metal; Music; Progressive rock.

■ RVs

Definition Recreational vehicles, or motor homes, that are motorized or towable, combine transportation with temporary living quarters, and are generally used for vacation travel

During the 1970's, RVs evolved from do-it-yourself converted vans and buses to manufactured vehicles that came complete with every modern convenience that a vacationing family needed. Rising gas prices, however, limited their use for some consumers.

One of the most popular RV models to come out of the 1970's was the van. It was more than likely copied from the Volkswagen bus. The van had a boxy shape and was roomy inside. Vans and converted buses became popular with hippies, a generation of rebellious young Americans who purchased these low-cost vehicles to travel in caravans and promote their message of peace, love, and togetherness. These vans and buses were often painted in psychedelic colors, reminiscent of images created by the use of drugs such as LSD. The hippie movement was short-lived, but the hippie van became a lasting part of American culture.

By the early 1970's, RVs had become a major part of the American vacation industry. With their mobility and easy access to scenic areas, motor homes were perfect for getaways. The development of superhighways gave motorists the opportunity to travel greater distances in ease and comfort. In order to accommodate these travelers, campgrounds began to appear along highway routes. Rental sales increased, making motor home travel more affordable for the average American. As motor homes grew bigger in size and quantity, however, naturalists voiced their concerns about the effect that these vehicles were having on the environment. National park roads became so congested with RV traffic that the National Park Service limited automobiles in high-use areas, such as Yosemite, California.

Motor home living also became popular with Americans who wanted to get away from their hectic lifestyles. Some of these people traveled across the nation in cabin trucks, which were literally a cabin on wheels, made with wood shingles and fashioned in Victorian style. These truck owners were often artists, silversmiths, or jewelry makers who lived between the hippie culture and mainsteam America, selling their wares. Retirees also discovered the benefits of motor home living. RVs could be parked semipermanently at a campground and used as a vacation home or be made into a permanent residence, allowing the retirees to spend their time "on the road."

Impact Prior to 1970, interest in RVs had increased to such a degree that manufacturers and retailers were certain that the upward trend would continue. No one, however, foresaw the toll that the fuel crises of the 1970's would take on the industry. The gas shortages of 1973-1974 and 1979 created long lines at the pump and soaring prices. The production of motor homes fell from 65,300 vehicles in 1973 to 26,700 vehicles in 1974. Many manufacturers went out of business, and those who survived did so by redesigning their products. Vehicles became smaller and lighter in weight and more aerodynamic in design.

Despite the fact that by 1975 fuel had once again become plentiful, the shortages of the 1970's had a deep, long-lasting effect on the RV industry. Sales did not rebound again until the mid-1980's.

Further Reading

White, Roger B. *Home on the Road: The Motor Home in America.* Washington, D.C.: Smithsonian Institution Press, 2000.

Wood, Donald F. *RVs and Campers, 1900-2000: An Illustrated History.* Hudson, Wis.: Iconografix, 2002.

Maryanne Barsotti

See also Automobiles; Energy crisis; Gas shortages; Hobbies and recreation; Transportation.

■ Ryan, Claude

Identification French Canadian politician
Born January 26, 1925; Montreal, Quebec, Canada
Died February 9, 2004; Montreal, Quebec, Canada

Although Ryan was the principal representative of the nationalist movement in Quebec in the mid-1970's, he switched his stance in the late 1970's and, by opposing initiatives for the secession of Quebec, became best known as a pro-federalist politician.

Claude Ryan, one of three children, was brought up as a traditional Roman Catholic. Despite his family's Irish surname, he was of thoroughly French Canadian cultural background. At age twenty, he almost became a Benedictine monk. He took sociology courses in college but did not finish his degree, instead becoming involved in Catholic Action, a religious organization that worked for social justice, and he later became one of the leaders of it. However, by the time Ryan turned forty during the 1960's, Quebec was changing as a result of the Quiet Revolution, a time when the province became more modernized and secularized. Ryan became editorial director of the Montreal newspaper *Le Devoir*, encouraging a new generation of Québécois journalists, and he became a major force in the more nationalistic Quebec that was emerging.

Though Ryan became best known as the leader of antiseparatist forces for most of the 1970's, he was sharply opposed to politicians, such as Prime Minister Pierre Trudeau, who later became his allies. He opposed Trudeau's invocation of the War Measures Act during the 1970 October Crisis and, in 1976, threw the weight of *Le Devoir* behind the Parti Québécois in the crucial election in which the nationalist party won power.

In 1978, however, Ryan switched sides and came out in defense of a unified Canada and against the concept of "sovereignty-association" espoused by René Lévesque. He replaced former premier Robert Bourassa as the leader of the Quebec Liberal Party (not formally linked with the Federal Liberals, though aligned with them on the referendum issue), and in 1979, he became a member for Argenteuil for the Quebec National Assembly.

Despite his intellectual, aloof style, and notwithstanding his lack of closeness to Trudeau, during the late 1970's, Ryan effectively rallied a coalition of French- and English-speaking Quebec citizens in the fight against the 1980 referendum that called for Quebec's secession from Canada. The "No" side won nearly 60 percent in the referendum, and Ryan for the moment was a hero across much of Canada.

Between 1978 and 1982, during his leadership of the Quebec Liberal Party, he promoted an ambitious agenda that sought the return of the Liberals to power in Quebec, a new constitutional agreement with the provinces, and a diminution of the increasingly statist and technocratic orientation that had taken over Quebec politics in the previous two decades. Ryan was far less of a socialist than either his ally Trudeau or his opponent Lévesque, and his Catholic political roots always informed his thinking.

Impact Claude Ryan showed that one could be committed to the distinct identity of Quebec and yet not be a nationalist or seek sovereignty. On his death in 2004, he was widely lauded as the man who kept Canada together.

Subsequent Events The provincial Liberals were decisively defeated by the Parti Québécois in the April, 1981, election. Though Ryan later served with distinction in a variety of provincial, municipal, and advisory positions, he was never again a national political figure.

Further Reading

Leclerc, Aurelien. *Claude Ryan: A Biography*. Toronto: NC Press, 1978.

MacDonald, Ian. *From Bourassa to Bourassa: A Pivotal Decade in Canadian History*. Montreal: Harvest House, 1984.

Nicholas Birns

See also Charter of the French Language; Elections in Canada; Francophonie, La; Lévesque, René; Minorities in Canada; October Crisis; Trudeau, Pierre.

■ Ryan, Nolan

Identification American baseball player
Born January 31, 1947; Refugio, Texas

Ryan established major league records for most career strikeouts, walks, no-hit games, and seasons pitched.

Nolan Ryan was drafted by the New York Mets in 1965 and spent his first full season in the major leagues with New York in 1968, striking out 133 batters in 134 innings. He possessed a blazing fastball and a devastating curveball, but he battled control problems. The six-foot, two-hundred-pound right-hander was used sparingly by the Mets between 1969 and 1971 and pitched seven innings in relief against the Atlanta Braves in Game 3 of the 1969 National League Championship Series to clinch the Mets' first pennant. He hurled 2.5 innings of scoreless relief against the Baltimore Orioles to earn a save in Game 3 of the 1969 World Series. The Mets captured the 1969 World Series in five games, giving Ryan his only World Series ring. He finished 7-11 with 97 walks in 132 innings in 1970 and 10-14 with 116 walks in 152 innings in 1971. In December, 1971, the Mets traded him to the California Angels.

Ryan, who had an insatiable work ethic that stressed arm conditioning, improved as a pitcher with the Angels from 1972 through 1979. During the 1970's, he paced the American League in strikeouts seven times, walks six times, shutouts three times, and once each in innings pitched, losses, and complete games. He compiled a 19-16 record with a 2.28 earned run average (ERA) and 329 strikeouts in 1972 and achieved his first twenty-game victory season with a 21-16 record and a 2.87 ERA in 1973. He set a major league record with 383 strikeouts in 1973 and recorded at least 300 strikeouts in five seasons. His best season with the Angels came in 1974, when he finished 22-16 with a 2.89 ERA and league-leading 367 strikeouts. Arm injuries limited him to twenty-eight starts and a 14-12 record with a 3.45 ERA in 1975. After struggling with a 17-18 mark with a 3.36 ERA in 1976, Ryan fared 19-16 with a 2.77 ERA in 1977. He won just 10 of 23 decisions with a 3.71 ERA in 1978 but rebounded with a 16-14 slate and a 3.59 ERA in 1979.

Ryan set Angels records for most shutouts (40), complete games (56), strikeouts (2,416), and walks (1,302), and he held franchise records for most victories (138), starts (288), and innings (2,182). He averaged more than one strikeout per inning, but he walked more than five batters per game. He hurled no-hitters against the Kansas City Royals on May 15, 1973; the Detroit Tigers on July 15, 1973; the Minnesota Twins on September 24, 1974; and the Baltimore Orioles on June 1, 1975.

Impact Nolan Ryan is arguably the best pitcher never to win a Cy Young Award. During twenty-seven major league seasons, he won 324 and lost 292 for a .526 winning percentage, struck out 5,714 batters and walked 2,795 batters in 5,387 innings, hurled sixty-one shutouts, threw twelve one-hitters, and compiled a 3.19 ERA. He was selected to the American

League All-Star team five times and the National League All-Star team twice.

Subsequent Events In November, 1979, the Houston Astros signed Ryan. He pitched with Houston from 1980 through 1988 and with the Texas Rangers from 1989 through 1993. He hurled three more no-hitters and became the twentieth major leaguer to win 300 games when he defeated the Milwaukee Brewers on July 31, 1990. In 1999, Ryan was elected to the Hall of Fame in his first year of eligibility and was selected for baseball's All-Century Team.

Further Reading

Ryan, Nolan, with Harvey Frommer. *Throwing Heat.* New York: Doubleday, 1988.

Ryan, Nolan, with Jerry B. Jenkins. *Miracle Man: Nolan Ryan, the Autobiography.* Nashville: W Publishing Group, 1993.

Trujillo, Nick. *The Meaning of Nolan Ryan.* College Station: Texas A&M University Press, 1994.

David L. Porter

See also Baseball; Bench, Johnny; Jackson, Reggie; Palmer, Jim; Rose, Pete; Sports.

S

■ Safe Drinking Water Act of 1974

Identification U.S. federal legislation
Date Signed on December 16, 1974

During the early 1970's, growing public awareness and media coverage of deteriorating water quality throughout the country led to the passage of the Safe Drinking Water Act of 1974, a landmark environmental and human health law that regulated certain contaminants in public drinking water systems.

The Safe Drinking Water Act (SDWA) of 1974 is the primary legislation at the federal level that protects the public drinking water system. Public water systems that supply drinking water are defined as those systems that serve more than twenty-five people. Discovery of organic chemical compounds in public drinking water systems, as well as the variance in regulations from state to state, prompted the passage of the SDWA.

The initiation of national drinking water standards as specified in the SDWA called for a two-part implementation process. Interim regulations were established immediately after the passage of the act. The interim regulations, put into effect in 1975, were based upon United States Public Health Service guidelines established in 1962. The second step of the process outlined in the act was to revise those standards, which was done after a thorough scientific study conducted by the National Academy of Science. The study assessed the effects on human health by drinking water contaminants and the toxicology of those contaminants.

Maximum contaminant levels (MCLs) as defined by the Environmental Protection Agency (EPA) were set as interim standards in 1975. These standards included guidelines for six organic compounds, ten inorganic compounds, the cloudiness of the water (turbidity), and total coliform bacteria. MCLs were set for chemicals such as the herbicide 2,4-D, as well as for arsenic and mercury. The act also required the EPA to set guidelines for contaminants that affect the aesthetic nature of drinking water but are not harmful to humans.

The SDWA of 1974 also delegated certain powers of enforcing the drinking water standards to the states. The federal-state arrangement allows states, U.S. territories, or tribes that meet specific requirements to have primary authority in enforcing the standards set by the national government for public drinking water systems. The SDWA authorized the EPA to offer grants to states for the purpose of regulating drinking water contaminants.

Under the SDWA, public water systems are required to collect water samples at specified times and locations. The results of these tests are reported to the state government, which has the primary authority to enforce the water quality standards. Besides setting and enforcing standards for drinking water contaminants, the act also required the EPA to protect wells and collection systems, to establish the integrity of distribution systems, and to ensure that qualified operators are employed to treat drinking water; it also stipulated that the information about the public water supply be made available to the individuals who use that particular water supply.

Impact The far-reaching effects of the Safe Drinking Water Act of 1974 helped improve the quality of the nation's public water supply and protect the health of those living in the United States.

Further Reading

DeZuane, John. *Handbook of Drinking Water Quality.* 2d ed. Hoboken, N.J.: John Wiley & Sons, 1996.

Dunlap, Riley E., and Angela G. Mertig, eds. *American Environmentalism: The U.S. Environmental Movement, 1970-1990.* Philadelphia: Taylor & Francis, 1992.

Kegley, Susan, et al. *The Chemistry of Water.* New York: University Science Books, 1997.

Trey Watson

See also Earth Day; Environmental movement; Environmental Protection Agency (EPA); Leaded gasoline ban; Water pollution.

■ Sagebrush Rebellion

Definition Popular movement aimed at returning control of Western federal lands to the states

The Sagebrush Rebellion reflected frustration toward federal land policies among ranching, mining, and logging interests in Western American states. The rebellion achieved some of its power from a widespread perception that environmental regulations were damaging to economic growth.

The Sagebrush Rebellion was a movement within the American West to transfer control of federal lands to individual states. Drawing strength from a conservative backlash against environmental regulations implemented in the 1960's and 1970's, the rebellion was popularized by romantic images of ranchers and cowboys standing up to Washington bureaucrats.

Origin of the Rebellion Roots of the rebellion can be traced to federal land-use policies of the nineteenth century. Western lands at the center of controversy came under federal control as a result of the 1846 Oregon Compromise with Great Britain through areas ceded by Mexico after the Mexican-American War in 1848 and through territory acquired as a result of the Gadsden Purchase in 1853. Until the establishment of federal forest reserves (later national forests), private use of public lands for mining, logging, and grazing was mostly unregulated. However, a shift in control over forested lands following passage of the Forest Reserve Act in 1891 was perceived as a direct challenge to Western ranchers and their sense of autonomy. Under pressure from the grazing industry, state and local officials in Western states opposed the establishment of forest reserves on the grounds that herd owners would be prevented from grazing sheep, cattle, and horses in alpine pastures during summer months. Although the issue was soon resolved by opening the reserves to regulated grazing, opposition to federal control of public lands began to stiffen. The conflict was brought to a head again in 1907, when President Theodore Roosevelt set aside additional acreage in advance of a law that barred the creation of new national forests without congressional approval.

The controversy simmered quietly for several years until the enactment of changes in grazing fees following World War II. Until this time, mining, logging, and grazing operations using public lands enjoyed generous subsidies, including below-market rates for mineral development, timber rights, and grazing permits. Outrage over grazing-fee changes culminated in a Senate bill to privatize federal lands in Western states. The bill died quietly, but only after Congress approved new spending for rangeland improvement and restoration.

Implementation of federal environmental legislation in the 1960's and 1970's brought the next major face-off between government and private interests in Western states. The National Environmental Policy Act (NEPA), the Clean Air and Clean Water Acts, and the Endangered Species Act stipulated new roles for land managers in the protection of water, air quality, and wildlife. At the same time, the 1973 oil embargo and subsequent economic downturn brought fears that newly implemented environmental laws would lead to lost jobs.

The Sagebrush Rebels Angered by their perception that the new regulations were damaging to economic growth, local lawmakers initiated steps to bring a larger proportion of federal lands under state control. In 1970, the state of Nevada was unsuccessful in its petition to the Federal Land Law Review Commission for additional land grants. The denial, coupled later with a decision by the Carter administration to increase grazing fees, prompted the Nevada State legislature to form the Select Committee on Public Lands in an attempt to change public land policies and encourage other Western states to join their efforts toward state control of public lands.

By the late 1970's, state legislatures in Nevada, Arizona, Utah, Wyoming, and New Mexico had passed bills calling for state control of lands managed by the U.S. Department of the Interior's Bureau of Land Management. Dubbed the Sagebrush Rebellion Bill, Nevada's Assembly Bill 413 called for 48 million acres of federal lands to be turned over to the state. Thereafter, the entire movement was called the Sagebrush Rebellion.

Impact The Sagebrush Rebellion grew from local objections to outsiders dictating public land policy and became a popular movement aimed at returning control of federal lands to Western states. The principal factor leading to the end of the rebellion was a failure to establish that land in the public domain belongs to the states. Although no federal land was transferred to state or private control, the rebellion helped to mobilize both environmental organizations seeking to toughen environmental regulations and "wise use" organizations working to strengthen property rights through state laws.

Subsequent Events As a presidential candidate late in the decade, Ronald Reagan became an important proponent of the rebellion, pledging to reduce the size and regulatory activities of the federal government. His presidency was marked by the relaxation of environmental standards and regulatory enforcement. Some cabinet members, notably Secretary of the Interior James Watt, furthered Reagan's deregulatory agenda with unsuccessful attempts to implement large-scale sales of federal lands. However, Watt's 1983 resignation curtailed White House support for the rebellion. Within a short time, the movement began to fade with weakening public support and a failure in the courts to demonstrate legal claim to federal lands.

Further Reading

Cawley, R. McGreggor. *Federal Land, Western Anger: The Sagebrush Rebellion and Environmental Politics.* Lawrence: University Press of Kansas, 1993. An in-depth look at the origins of the rebellion and an appraisal of James Watt's tenure as secretary of the interior.

Graf, William L. *Wilderness Preservation and the Sagebrush Rebellions.* Savage, Md.: Rowman & Littlefield, 1990. This book focuses on federal land policy, particularly as it relates to conflicts between environmental groups seeking to protect wilderness lands and developers.

Mollison, Richard M., and Richard Eddy, Jr. "The Sagebrush Rebellion: A Simplistic Response to the Complex Problems of Federal Land Management." *Harvard Journal on Legislation* 19 (1982): 97-142. Provides an overview of state laws passed in Nevada, Wyoming, New Mexico, Utah, and Arizona that called for state control of federal lands.

Switzer, Jacqueline. *Green Backlash.* Boulder, Colo.: Lynne Rienner, 1997. Provides a provocative overview of antienvironmentalism, including a review of the wise use movement.

Thomas A. Wikle

See also Clean Air Act of 1970; Endangered Species Act of 1973; Environmental movement; Reagan, Ronald; Tax revolt.

■ SALT I and SALT II treaties

Identification Nuclear arms control agreements
Date SALT I signed May 26, 1972; SALT II on June 18, 1979

SALT I was the first agreement between the United States and the Soviet Union limiting offensive nuclear weapon systems, and SALT II was an attempt to expand that agreement.

Following the end of World War II, most of the world was affected by the Cold War, with the United States and the Soviets as the leaders of the rival blocs. A race for superiority in the types and numbers of nuclear weapon systems formed part of this rivalry. By the end of the 1960's, leaders of the two countries believed it was in their mutual interest to control this growth. Representatives of the two countries met in November, 1969, to begin what became called the Strategic Arms Limitation Talks (SALT).

SALT I The SALT I treaty is formally called the "Interim Agreement Between the United States of America and the Union of Soviet Socialist Republics on Certain Measures with Respect to the Limitation of Strategic Offensive Arms." The initial round of discussion in Helsinki was to allow the two sides to clarify the objectives that each had for the negotiations. The main bargaining sessions began in April, 1970, in Vienna. The Soviets initially wanted to include any type of weapon system capable of carrying a nuclear weapon, while the United States wanted a more limited treaty dealing only with intercontinental ballistic missiles (ICBMs). The United States got its way on this point. Before and during the negotiations, research on antiballistic missile systems (ABMs) was ongoing, and simple systems were being deployed. The United States wanted to include discussion of these systems, while the Soviets wanted to deal only with offensive weapons. While the outcome of SALT I dealt only with offensive weapons, a separate agreement, the Anti-Ballistic Missile Treaty, was signed the same day as the SALT I agreement. The agreement was adopted by both nations, with President Richard M. Nixon presenting it to the U.S. Senate, where it received only two negative votes. The agreement entered into force on October 3, 1972.

Although it took two and a half years to negotiate, the SALT I agreement was a fairly simple document,

The SALT II treaty is signed by U.S. president Jimmy Carter (left) and Soviet president Leonid Brezhnev in 1979. (AP/Wide World Photos)

about two pages in length. However, by the time it was signed, there were five additional pages of agreed statements, common understandings, and a protocol. This was to be a five-year agreement with a more comprehensive agreement to be negotiated during that period of time. It prohibited the construction of new fixed, land-based ICBM launchers; the conversion of light systems into heavy systems; and an increase in the number of submarine-launched ballistic missiles. However, replacements for old systems could be constructed. No specific numbers were included in the agreement, as it was assumed that each side knew what the other had. Compliance with the treaty was to be by "national technical means"; that is, spy satellites and any other technology allowing observations from outside the country.

SALT II The SALT II treaty is formally called the "Treaty Between the United States of America and the Union of Soviet Socialist Republics on the Limitation of Strategic Offensive Arms, Together with Agreed Statements and Common Understandings Regarding the Treaty." Article VII of the SALT I agreement stated "The parties undertake to continue active negotiations for limitations on strategic offensive arms." In November, 1972, the United States and the Soviets began the SALT II talks. SALT I had not mandated any cuts in the number of nuclear weapon systems. Therefore, the goal of the SALT II negotiations was to reduce the number of weapon systems. Once again, the early discussions focused on which systems would be included in the treaty. Discussion also occurred regarding qualitative differences between the systems of the two countries. Two years later, at a summit meeting, President Gerald R. Ford outlined the basic points of the treaty. However, it would be almost another five years before the treaty would be complete and signed by President Jimmy Carter.

In its final form, the treaty is about four times longer than SALT I and its related documents. Within the treaty, specific names and descriptions of the weapons systems are listed, as are specific numbers for each type of weapon. It allowed 2,400 delivery systems, to be decreased to 2,250 in 1981. Missiles with multiple independent reentry vehicle (MIRV) warheads were not to number more than 1,320, and only 820 of these could be on ICBMs. It allowed the development of only one new light ICBM system by each country and banned the conversion of old light ICBM systems to heavy systems. It limited the number of warheads on each type of system and the number of missiles to be carried by bombers. The two sides agreed that once a system was tested with an MIRV, then it would be assumed that all systems of that type had MIRV warheads. All these limits were to be verified by national technical means, and the treaty was to have been in effect through 1985.

Impact The impact of the SALT I agreement was tremendous. Until that agreement was signed, each year had seen growth in the number of weapon systems owned by the two superpowers. In the late 1960's, this growth amounted to more than two hundred new delivery systems a year. That the two countries recognized their mutual interest in controlling this growth was an important turning point in the Cold War. During this period, the level of trust between the United States and the Soviets was the highest it had been since the Cold War began. Moreover, the negotiation of the much more complex SALT II treaty was also a monument to the rivals' relative openness in strategic military matters. However, Cold War politics—for example, the Soviet invasion of Afghanistan—forced President Carter to delay the Senate's consideration of the treaty. Even though it was not a formal treaty, during most of the years after it was signed, both the United States and the Soviet Union voluntarily agreed to abide by its provisions.

Further Reading

Clift, Arthur Denis. *With Presidents to the Summit.* Fairfax, Va.: George Mason University Press, 1993. Written by a former member of the National Security Council during this era, the book details the summits held by and related foreign policy decisions of presidents Nixon, Ford, and Carter.

Garthoff, Raymond. *Détente and Confrontation.* Rev. ed. Washington, D.C.: Brookings Institution, 1994. Offers a discussion that explains diplomatic negotiations and various crises of the 1970's through the lens of U.S.-Soviet relations.

Goldblat, Jeff. *Arms Control: The New Guide to Negotiations and Agreements.* Thousand Oaks, Calif.: Sage Publications, 2002. This text places the SALT agreements within the context of all Cold War arms agreements.

Donald A. Watt

See also Anti-Ballistic Missile (ABM) Treaty; Antinuclear movement; Carter, Jimmy; Cold War; Détente; Ford, Gerald R.; Neutron bomb; Nixon, Richard M.; Soviet invasion of Afghanistan; Soviet Union and North America.

■ Sanford and Son

Identification Television situation comedy
Date Aired from 1972 to 1977

Along with The Jeffersons, Good Times, *and* What's Happening, Sanford and Son *demonstrated both the commercial viability of television programming centered around specifically black social situations and the power of frank, often misanthropic, humor to defuse the more combustible aspects of America's racial tensions.*

When *Sanford and Son,* a licensed adaptation of the British comedy series *Steptoe and Son,* debuted on American television in 1972, few in the mainstream television audience had experienced the humor of Redd Foxx firsthand. Foxx had spent much of his career up to that point earning a cult following as a stand-up comedian specializing in "after hours," or raunchy, humor. As Fred G. Sanford, the malingering sixty-five-year-old coordinator of a South Central Los Angeles junkyard that he runs with his son Lamont (played by Demond Wilson), Foxx's nightclub humor was, to some extent, whitewashed for mass consumption. His blunt, insulting style remained, however, making him not only a kind of black counterpart to *All in the Family*'s equally bigoted Archie Bunker but also a worthy participant in the bare-knuckled comedic tradition popularized by the likes of Don Rickles.

The rest of the show's regular characters—Lamont, Fred's buddies Grady Wilson (Whitman Mayo) and Bubba Hoover (Don Bexley), and police officers "Smitty" Smith (Hal Williams) and "Hoppy" Hopkins (Howard Platt)—were primarily foils for Fred's one-liners. Aunt Esther Anderson (LaWanda Page) was the purse-swinging, "holy roller" sister of Fred's late wife Elizabeth and provided many memorable comic (and sometimes literal) counter-punches. The function of such ethnically identified stock characters as the Latino Julio Fuentes (Gregory Sierra) and the Asian Ah Chew (Pat Morita) was more complex: As the butts of Fred's explicitly racist put-downs, they served as vehicles for the controversial implication that racism was not solely a white man's burden.

The show's overriding tone, however, was light. Each episode ended with a more-or-less happy resolution, and the filial affection between Fred and Lamont, though hidden beneath a veneer of mutual antagonism and always a work in progress, was never seriously in question.

Impact Although the squalor and social disenfranchisement that served as the setting and context of *Sanford and Son* was not one with which the majority of its viewers were well acquainted, the series was able to universalize its dramatic situation and ultimately serve as a microcosm of American life, endearing it to millions of viewers and paving the way for Redd Foxx's late-life entry into the mainstream of American entertainment.

Further Reading

Foxx, Redd. *The Redd Foxx Encyclopedia of Black Humor.* Pasadena, Calif.: W. Ritchie Press, 1977.

MacDonald, J. Fred. *Blacks and White TV: Afro-Americans in Television Since 1948.* Chicago: Nelson Hall, 1993.

Ross, Robert, Ray Galton, and Alan Simpson. *Steptoe and Son.* London: BBC Consumer, 2002.

Arsenio Orteza

See also African Americans; *All in the Family*; *Chico and the Man*; Comedians; *Fat Albert and the Cosby Kids*; *Jeffersons, The*; Sitcoms; Television in the United States.

■ Sanitary napkins with adhesive strips

Definition Personal hygiene product for women

As a result of the invention of hot-melt adhesives, hygiene products for women were revolutionized.

By the mid-1960's, hot melt glues were used with hygiene products, and the first self-adhesive napkin was introduced to the public. New adhesive sanitary napkins were protected by silicone paper strips attached to undergarments. Personal Products introduced the Stayfree beltless pads in 1970, while Kimberly-Clark sold New Freedom, another beltless pad. The introduction of these products made the sanitary belt obsolete. Prior to the adhesive strip, women work bulky sanitary belts to which sanitary napkins attached. Besides the bulk, this method was uncomfortable and messy, as napkins twisted into a rope as women moved throughout the day.

New Freedom advertised its product as requiring no belts or pins and touted that it would not slip. Easy disposal was an additional perk, as the product was flushable. Adhesive strips were revolutionary because the napkin self-attached to women's panties. Women peeled off the backing and placed the adhesive side against the crotch of the panty or panty girdle. Once used, the pad peeled away from the panty easily. Adhesive strips were secure, comfortable, and invisible.

Beginning in 1970, television and radio advertisements for sanitary napkins soared despite the National Advertising Board's (NAB) stringent guidelines, which prohibited any instructions or graphic references for use or application, or shots of sanitary napkins, tampons, or other sanitary products. In 1974, more than seven million dollars was spent on promoting feminine hygiene products. The use of television to promote the product resulted in increased sales for new products as well as for old ones. Excited by the increased sales, manufacturers researched and developed new products and revamped old ones, and new companies entered the field for the first time.

In the spring of 1975, Kimberly-Clark overhauled its sanitary napkin line by bringing out Kotex Lightdays, improving New Freedom maxipads and minipads, and repackaging other products. Its efforts were rewarded with a 17 percent jump in sales between 1970 and 1974. Further advances by manufacturers included anatomically shaped pads in 1975 and the introduction of panty shields, a thin product with reduced absorbent capacity, in 1976.

Impact Adhesive strips that were added to sanitary napkins provided women with freedom from the problematic sanitary belt. Women gained confidence in their physical movements and worried less about menstrual stains and embarrassment. Manufacturers continued to improve upon their products through the decade and beyond.

Further Reading

Delaney, Janice. *The Curse: A Cultural History of Menstruation.* Urbana: University of Illinois Press, 1988.

Golub, Sharon, ed. *Lifting the Curse of Menstruation: A Feminist Appraisal of the Influence of Menstruation on Women's Lives.* New York: Haworth, 1983.

Rebecca Tolley-Stokes

See also Advertising; Inventions; *Our Bodies, Ourselves*; Toxic shock syndrome.

■ *Saturday Night Fever*

Identification Motion picture
Director John Badham (1939-)
Date Released in 1977

Saturday Night Fever *captured the ethos of the 1970's when young people faced a changing social, cultural, and economic landscape and shifting values.*

The 1970's was a transitional decade—one in which young people tried to find new values to replace the traditional ones that they had abandoned. *Saturday Night Fever* reflects this search for identity and a better life in the person of Tony Manero (played by John Travolta), a nineteen-year-old man from a working-class family in Brooklyn. The film, based on a 1975 article by Nik Cohn titled "Tribal Rites of the New Saturday Night," tells of the struggle that Tony undergoes in trying to reconcile the traditional values of his family, friends, and community with the shifting cultural territory of American life and values. As Tony attempts to release himself from the mediocrity of everyday life, he finds self-fulfillment in his talent for dancing. Although Tony has a rather pedestrian job as a clerk in a paint store, he is intelligent, charming, and self-confident. His quest is the quintessential American quest to become better off through his own efforts and talents. It is dancing that helps Tony negotiate this terrain.

Family, Traditional Values, and Loyalties It was in the 1970's that the American family began to change, with the traditional two-parent household giving way to households with one parent and the proliferation of single people. Tony's family is a traditional one in which Tony's father assumes dominance over the other members of the household—Tony's mother, little sister, grandmother, and Tony himself.

Tony is comfortable with his friends at the beginning of the film. However, as he becomes embroiled in an ethnic war with some Puerto Ricans and then sees that a talented Puerto Rican couple is denied the top prize at the disco dance contest, he begins to see that traditional values can no longer guide him in the world but instead result in aggression and self-deception.

Economic Recession Economic recession was the backdrop of the 1970's—the condition that defined and constrained what was possible for American families to achieve. Tony is the only wage earner in his family. His father is an unemployed construction worker whose place as head of his family is put in jeopardy by his failure to provide. The tension created by the father's situation and consequent negative assessment of Tony's achievements underscores the difficulties of the decade.

Tony works hard, and his boss makes note of how Tony charms his customers and offers him permanent employment for the rest of his life—an offer that underscores the possible fate that Tony could end up living a life not notably different from that of his father or his friends. When Tony is offered a raise, his news is met with his father's sarcasm at the dinner table, and this kind of response becomes one more incentive for Tony to try to make a change. Another opportunity for change comes when Tony's fortunes within his family and his view of himself begin to shift as a result of the return of his older brother, Frank, Jr., a priest.

Changing Religious Values and Sex Roles The 1970's were a time of religious disaffection. Church attendance plummeted as young people considered establishment religion irrelevant to their needs and to the solution of social problems. One aspect of this disaffection was the exodus of many young priests from the Roman Catholic Church. When Frank, Jr., arrives home and announces that he has left the priesthood, he sends his family into a tailspin.

The film also demonstrates the dilemma of young people trapped by traditional religious values in a changing world when Tony's friend Bobby can find no way out of marriage when he gets his girlfriend pregnant and is forced to marry her because of the dictates of his family and church. Unable to resolve the problem on his own, Bobby turns to Tony for a solution, but Tony fails him. It is Bobby's fall from the Verrazano Narrows Bridge that opens Tony's eyes to the futility of trying to hold on to outdated values.

One of the profound changes to emerge in American society in the 1970's was the shift in sex roles as a result of the rise of the women's movement. There was a constant clash between traditional relationships and the as-yet-undefined new relationships between women and men. Perhaps the most profound change in Tony's way of seeing the world comes from his association with Stephanie, a twenty-year-old woman whom he sees dancing at the disco on Saturday nights.

At the disco, Tony is a celebrity and a hero because of his dancing abilities, and he is courted by many different women. The most persistent is Annette, whom he rebuffs. It is clear from his interchanges with Annette that Tony holds very traditional views about women—they are either for marrying or for having sex. It is Stephanie who changes Tony's view about women.

At the end of the film, when Stephanie has made the move from Brooklyn to Manhattan permanently, Tony seeks her out and asks to be friends. The idea of being friends with a "girl" represents Tony's willingness to see women in a different light and to move toward values more in line with the realities of the changing world.

For some, this image of John Travolta striking a disco pose in the film Saturday Night Fever *symbolizes the 1970's.* (Hulton Archive/Getty Images)

Impact Perhaps because it dealt so intimately with many of the decade's issues, *Saturday Night Fever* became a top-grossing film in 1977. It launched the film career of John Travolta, who was nominated for an Academy Award for Best Actor, and reinforced the fame of the Bee Gees, whose original score brought disco dancing to nationwide prominence. The film also influenced fashion, making popular the white polyester suit that Travolta wore in the film. *Saturday Night Fever* remained an emblem of the 1970's because of the careful integration of so many themes emerging from that decade.

Further Reading

Grau, Andree. "*Saturday Night Fever*: An Ethnography of Disco Dancing." In *Dance, Gender, and Culture*, edited by Helen Thomas. New York: St. Martin's Press, 1993. A critical paper emphasizing the film's approach to disco dancing.

Jordan, Chris. "Gender and Class Mobility in *Saturday Night Fever* and *Flashdance*." *Journal of Popular Film and Television* 24, no. 3 (Fall, 1996): 116-122. Explores the tension between the sexes in the light of the American value of success and the role of middle-class models in the success of working-class people.

Keeler, Greg. "*Saturday Night Fever*: Crossing the Verrazano Bridge." *Journal of Popular Film and Television* 7 (1979): 158-167. A critical study of the film.

Stewart, Gail. *The 1970's*. San Diego, Calif.: Lucent Books, 1999. This book explores the issues and movements of the 1970's, such as the Vietnam War, environmentalism, feminism, and racism—issues that are central to *Saturday Night Fever*.

Susan Love Brown

See also Academy Awards; Bee Gees, The; Blockbusters; Dance, popular; Disco; Discotheques; Fashions and clothing; Film in the United States; Leisure suits; Music; Sexual revolution; Travolta, John.

■ Saturday Night Live

Identification Late-night television comedy-variety series
Producer Lorne Michaels (1944-)
Date Premiered in 1975

Saturday Night Live *ushered in a new style of television comedy built on irreverence, improvisation, and an almost total lack of inhibition, completely rewriting the standards of late-night home entertainment.*

In the mid-1970's, late-night television was defined by the National Broadcasting Company (NBC) network's *Tonight Show* and Johnny Carson, its affable host, which dominated the ratings during the week. However, reruns of his program that aired on Saturday failed to generate much of an audience, and it was generally assumed that most viewers—especially young adults—were finding their weekend entertainment away from their television sets. In a move to create a reason for these viewers (who were especially attractive to advertisers) to tune in, NBC executive Dick Ebersol hired writer-comedian Lorne Michaels to put together a program geared to this youthful demographic.

Michaels took on the challenge with enthusiasm and assembled a program that had little to do with the traditional *Tonight Show* model. Each week, the program revolved around a guest host, usually someone with "hip" credentials such as George Carlin, Richard Pryor, or Lily Tomlin. These hosts, in addition to their opening monologue, would perform in sketches, supported by a repertory troupe dubbed the Not Ready for Prime Time Players. Each program also featured a musical guest, often chosen for their offbeat or underground appeal as opposed to success on the pop charts. Early on, sketches featuring Jim Henson's Muppets (though not the lovable characters from *Sesame Street*) and short films by Gary Weis and Albert Brooks were also recurring elements of the show. Much of the tone of the program was set early on by head writer Michael O'Donoghue, whose dark and twisted sense of humor imbued the show with a strong dose of sinfulness.

One key aspect of *Saturday Night Live*, perhaps the component that gave it its greatest edge, was that it was broadcast live each week, providing audiences with the sensation that almost anything might happen. This made network executives nervous, especially once it became clear that Michaels, O'Donoghue, and the cast were intent on pushing the limits of acceptable television fare. This risk factor generated considerable interest in the show from the start, and within just a few weeks, it developed into a full-fledged media phenomenon. Suddenly, people had a reason to stay home on Saturday night, and the program attracted a large, devoted following.

A Star Vehicle While Michaels held off the network censors, his writers and performers blossomed. Very quickly, members of the regular cast began to emerge from their support roles and supplant the guest hosts as the true stars of *Saturday Night Live.* Chevy Chase was the first breakout figure, largely because of his solo spot as host of the news show parody "Weekend Update" and his patented pratfalls that opened each episode. Despite the often black elements of his material, his good looks and boyish charm caused many to imagine him as the heir to Carson's chair on *The Tonight Show.* Before the end of the second year, he left the cast for a shot at Hollywood, proving very early that *Saturday Night Live* could be a launching pad for more substantial entertainment careers.

With Chase's departure, other cast members moved to the forefront. John Belushi and Dan Aykroyd were masterful satirists who recognized few boundaries in picking the targets of their incisive barbs. Their characterizations were often intense and menacing. Even superficially affectionate tributes, such as their Blues Brothers musical act, reflected an attitude that all show business was marked by an underlying sordidness.

Gilda Radner was a more lovable performer. Her Emily Litella and Roseanne Roseannadanna characters retained a basic sweetness, even as they innocently stomped on their share of sacred cows. Jane Curtin replaced Chase on "Weekend Update" and naturally projected an air of professionalism that added extra sting to her barbs on current events and prominent figures. Bill Murray was the glib goofball who was expert at projecting slimy insincerity in his portrayals of Nick the Lounge Singer and the quintessential nerd, Todd DiLamuca. Larraine Newman and Garrett Morris were less associated with recurring characters, but their versatility allowed them to inject any character that they played with the requisite comic bite that was a hallmark of the program.

By 1979, the original cast and writing team ran out of steam. Aykroyd and Belushi had already followed Chase to Hollywood, and Murray was soon to follow. Michaels felt that he could no longer maintain the grind of a weekly live show and turned his creation over to the network, which retooled and relaunched the program with an entirely new cast in the fall of 1980.

Impact *Saturday Night Live* turned a group of essentially underground performers into mass media stars. As the Not Ready for Prime Time Players (and frequent guests such as Steve Martin and Andy Kaufman) branched out into other media, most notably film, they carried the show's innovative satiric pulse with them. By the end of the 1970's, their biting form of humor, which acknowledged virtually no limits in targets or comic weapons employed, helped redefine the comedy landscape across American popular culture.

Subsequent Events Over the years the program continued to evolve, with performers coming and going. Many, such as Eddie Murphy, Julia Louis-Dreyfus, and Mike Myers, went on to substantial success in film or prime-time television. In 1985, Michaels returned to his creation as producer, and although the program's popularity and cultural cachet have waxed and waned over the years, it remained a mainstay of late-night programming and a valuable venue for the nurturing of comic talent into the twenty-first century.

Further Reading

Cader, Michael, ed. *"Saturday Night Live": The First Twenty Years.* Boston: Cader Books, 1994. A commemoration of the program's first two decades.

Hill, Doug, and Jeff Weingard. *Saturday Night: A Backstage History of "Saturday Night Live."* New

Football star and actor O. J. Simpson appears with Gilda Radner (left) and Jane Curtin on an episode of Saturday Night Live *in 1978.* (AP/Wide World Photos)

York: Vintage Books, 1987. As the title suggests, a behind-the-scenes look at the personalities and process that contributed to making the show a success. While occasionally focusing on lurid details of the performers' lifestyles, it is essential for its insight into how the program was constructed each week and the battles that occurred with network officials over certain material.

Shales, Tom, and James Andrew Miller. *Live from New York: An Uncensored History of "Saturday Night Live."* Boston: Little, Brown, 2002. An oral history, drawing on the recollections of cast and crew members, writers, and guests.

John C. Hajduk

See also Belushi, John; Carlin, George; Comedians; Kaufman, Andy; Martin, Steve; Monty Python; *National Lampoon's Animal House*; Pryor, Richard; Television in the United States; Variety shows.

■ Saturday Night Massacre

The Event The resignations of Attorney General Elliot Richardson and Deputy Attorney General William Ruckelshaus

Date October 20, 1973

During the Watergate scandal, Richardson and Ruckelshaus resigned rather than obey President Richard M. Nixon's order to dismiss Watergate special prosecutor Archibald Cox. The public reaction forced Nixon to surrender tapes of White House conversations.

Immediately after the resignations of President Nixon's senior staff at the end of April, 1973, a Senate resolution was passed that called for the appointment of a special prosecutor to investigate the Watergate burglary and cover-up. The special prosecutor would be given broad power to investigate the matter, including the power to subpoena documents or bring to court anyone but the president himself. On May 18, 1973, Elliot Richardson appointed Cox, a professor at Harvard Law School, to the post. Cox, a former solicitor general of the United States, was known both for his integrity and for his legal acumen. By June, 1973, he had recruited his staff and begun operations in a guarded office on K Street in Washington, D.C.

On July 16, 1973, Alexander Butterfield, a member of the White House staff, testified before the Senate Watergate Committee. He revealed that President Nixon had a voice-operated taping system installed in his offices in the White House and the Executive Office Building. A week later, Cox's staff issued a subpoena for nine of the tapes on which crucial Watergate evidence might be present. The president's lawyer rejected the subpoena and refused to produce the tapes, claiming that they were protected by executive privilege, or the president's traditional power to deny certain information to Congress and the public.

After a United States district court ordered enforcement of the subpoena, the president's counsel appealed to the Court of Appeals. On October 12, 1973, this court upheld the district court's order and gave the president seven days in which to either comply or appeal the decision to the U.S. Supreme Court. Six days of negotiations between the special prosecutor, Attorney General Richardson, and the president's lawyers produced no agreement.

On Friday night, October 19, Richardson received a letter from the president directing him to order the special prosecutor to take no action to obtain the tapes. Richardson refused to transmit this order to Cox as it violated assurances that he had given the Senate that the special prosecutor would be able to operate independently.

On Saturday, October 20, Cox held a press conference at which he announced that he would move to enforce the court order on the following Monday. President Nixon instructed his new chief of staff, General Alexander Haig, to order Richardson to dismiss Cox. Richardson again refused and sought and received an interview with the president, at which he tendered his resignation. Just as he was arriving back at the Justice Department, Haig telephoned Deputy Attorney General William Ruckelshaus, now the acting attorney general, and ordered the dismissal of Cox. Ruckelshaus also refused and resigned. By prearrangement with Richardson and Ruckelshaus, Solicitor General Robert Bork then accepted the president's order and dismissed Cox.

Public Reaction In the early evening, the White House Press Office announced the resignations of Richardson and Ruckelshaus, the dismissal of Cox, and the abolition of the special prosecutor's office. An astonishing display of public fury erupted immediately. General Haig called it a "firestorm." Fueled in part by news reports that Federal Bureau of Investigation (FBI) agents had sealed off the special prosecutor's offices, it seemed to many that the rule of law had been abolished—that the president had put himself above the law and worse, that he had something to hide. To some it appeared like a *coup d'état.*

Telegrams of protest began to descend on the White House and congressional offices in huge numbers—nearly half a million within a week. Significant numbers of telephone calls and letters also arrived, only a few of them supporting the president. Many notable Republicans joined in the protest. Nixon and his lieutenants had completely misunderstood the public mood and the outrage that the Watergate scandal had engendered. The pressure continued to grow over the next week until it could no longer be resisted. The president's lawyer announced that the tapes would be made available since "this president does not defy the law."

Impact The public reaction to the Saturday Night Massacre sealed the doom of Nixon's presidency. A new special prosecutor, Leon Jaworski of Texas, was quickly appointed. The investigation continued, and additional tapes were subpoenaed and obtained. The House Judiciary Committee began a parallel investigation of Watergate to determine whether impeachable offenses had occurred. Three impeachment counts were eventually recommended. The final batch of subpoenaed tapes contained conversations that showed clearly that President Nixon had inspired and participated in the cover-up. Within a few days of public disclosure of that conversation, Nixon preempted the ongoing impeachment procedure by resigning from office. Gerald R. Ford succeeded to the presidency on August 9, 1974.

Further Reading

Ben-Veniste, Richard, and George Frampton. *Stonewall: The Real Story of the Watergate Prosecution.* New York: Simon & Schuster, 1977. Ben-Veniste and Frampton were senior staff members of the special prosecutor's office. This book provides an insider's view of the struggle over Nixon's tapes and the dismissal of Archibald Cox.

Sirica, John J. *To Set the Record Straight.* New York: W. W. Norton, 1979. Sirica was the United States district court judge in most of the Watergate cases. Chapters 7 through 10 contain a detailed account both of the legal maneuvering that produced the Saturday Night Massacre and of its immediate aftermath.

White, Theodore H. *Breach of Faith: The Fall of Richard Nixon.* New York: Atheneum, 1975. Excellent history of the Watergate affair; the Saturday Night Massacre and the public response to it are discussed in detail.

Woodward, Bob, and Carl Bernstein. *The Final Days.* New York: Simon & Schuster, 1976. Informed account of the last year of the Nixon administration by the two *Washington Post* reporters who first uncovered the crucial links between the burglary and the White House.

Robert Jacobs

See also Cox, Archibald; Nixon, Richard M.; Nixon tapes; Nixon's resignation and pardon; Watergate.

■ Scandals

Definition Activities that are illegal or deemed morally offensive

During the 1970's, a series of scandals topped the news and led to the resignation of a president, reforms of the political process, and changes in the private sector.

Scandals, both private and public, dominated the news during the 1970's. Without a doubt, the decade will be best remembered for the Watergate scandal and the subsequent resignation of President Richard M. Nixon in 1974. The scandal dated back prior to the 1972 presidential reelection campaign. The Nixon White House, following the lead of its predecessor presidents, engaged in various levels of political espionage and "dirty tricks." During the 1968 presidential election, President Lyndon B. Johnson had bugged candidate Nixon's campaign plane in an attempt to get inside information about Nixon's political plans. Wiretapping and harassment of political opponents by the president had become a staple of the political process by the 1970's. Nixon's White House added to this record by hiring people to break into the office of a psychiatrist treating antiwar dissenter Daniel Ellsberg. Nixon had also ordered widespread wiretapping of White House aides' phones. In addition, the Nixon reelection campaign had intimidated wealthy supporters into providing illegal cash donations to the president's campaign. However, in June, 1972, members of the White House staff approved the placing of wiretaps in the phones at the Democratic National Headquarters located in the Watergate complex in Washington, D.C. When the burglars were captured and arrested, Nixon and his staff attempted to cover up their connection to the plot. The cover-up led to a congressional investigation during which Nixon's top aides were questioned about their knowledge and the president's knowledge of the break-in plan.

The investigation was foundering until it was revealed that Nixon had approved the taping of all Oval Office conversations. Those tapes were expected to provide evidence that Nixon had known about the cover-up and had aided it. When Nixon refused to turn over the tapes to Congress or a special prosecutor, the dispute went to the Supreme Court, where the justices ruled that the president had to release the tapes. Once the contents of conversations were revealed, Nixon was shown to have committed several crimes, including obstruction of justice. Faced with likely impeachment and removal by Congress, Nixon resigned on August 9, 1974. This followed the resignation of Vice President Spiro T. Agnew in 1973 for taking bribes while serving as governor of Maryland.

CIA Scandals The Watergate scandal affected other parts of the executive branch long after President Nixon had left office. Emboldened at having forced a president to resign, Congress went after other institutions that it associated with the Nixon administration and the Vietnam War. A published story charging the Central Intelligence Agency (CIA) with spying on American citizens drew an immediate response from Congress. Two select committees were created to investigate the CIA and its activities both inside and outside the United States. The House Committee was embroiled in controversy immediately as Democrats and Republicans fought over which member would be chairman. Democrat Otis Pike of New York was chosen. On the Senate side, Democrat Frank Church of Idaho became the chairman of the Church Committee.

The committees began their work in June, 1975. Many of the committees' members were vocal opponents of the CIA and stated their desire both to hammer the agency for any abuses found and to write legislation taking powers away from the agency. The committees did uncover CIA plans for overthrowing and assassinating foreign leaders, such as Cuban dictator Fidel Castro. However, the disagreements among the members caused problems for the committee. The Pike Committee could not even issue an official report. Instead, it was leaked to the newspapers in February, 1976. The Church Committee issued a report, but the hearings were more dramatic. Senator Church had announced his candidacy for the Democratic presidential nomination and used the media to attack the CIA and to improve his own image and name recognition with Democratic voters. Church would not win another election after his committee actions, losing the presidential nomination and his own reelection campaign in 1980. The CIA suffered considerable damage to its public image and saw its own powers severely limited.

Congress Congressional scandals during the 1970's included groups of congressmen taking bribes and individual scandals involving some of the most powerful and senior members of the House of Representatives. One of those members was Arkansas Democrat Wilbur Mills, who was chairman of the Ways and Means Committee, which wrote tax laws. Mills had sought the Democratic nomination for president in 1972 but had failed badly. In the fall of 1974, Mills's car was pulled over by Washington, D.C., police. In the car was a stripper by the name of Fannie Foxe, who subsequently fled the scene by diving from a bridge into the water below. Mills was not charged, but rumors soon spread that the elderly congressman was romantically involved with a stripper. Mills did not deny it, instead appearing publicly with Foxe and having his picture taken with her. His bizarre behavior was blamed on alcoholism, and his political career came to a swift end in 1974.

Another longtime congressman, Democrat Wayne Hays, was involved in another sex scandal when it was found that his administrative assistant, Elizabeth Ray, was a salaried employee while lacking typing and telephone skills. Their involvement soon became public, and Hays was investigated by the Federal Bureau of Investigation (FBI) for improper use of federal funds. This ended his career in the House.

The late 1970's saw one of the largest congressional scandals of the twentieth century. The FBI initiated a sting operation known as Abscam, an abbreviation for Arab Scam, to investigate whether members of Congress were taking bribes. An FBI informant disguised himself as an Arab sheikh and offered certain members of Congress money for favors. These meetings were taped by the FBI during 1978 and 1979 and captured one senator, New Jersey Democrat Harrison Williams, along with five other Democratic congressmen taking bribes from the impersonator. Only one member, Republican senator Larry Pressler of South Dakota, rejected the bribes, noting that what was being proposed was illegal. Indictments of the members were not handed down until 1980, and each member charged was either forced to resign or lost his bid for reelection.

Governmental scandals were not limited to Congress or to the White House. In 1972, Judge Otto Kerner was indicted and later convicted of taking bribes and of tax evasion. Kerner, part of the Mayor Richard Daley political machine in Chicago, was best known for heading a commission that blamed violent riots on racism and white Americans. Kerner was a judge on the prestigious Seventh Circuit Court of Appeals and had used his position as a state and federal judge to take bribes from racetrack operators looking for favors. Upon his conviction, Kerner was sentenced to the federal penitentiary for three years, where he died in disgrace.

Business Scandals One of the largest financial scandals of the 1970's came to light in 1973 with the collapse of the Equity Funding Corporation of America. The company engaged in a complicated strategy whereby investors bought mutual funds and used their gains to also purchase life insurance. The company was founded by Gordon McCormick, but he was replaced by Stanley Goldblum, a former salesman who would take Equity Funding in the wrong direction.

During the 1960's, the company grew dramatically, drawing in thousands of investors. However, when profits began to sag, Goldblum kept the company afloat by using a series of complex accounting maneuvers that included creating fake clients and false insurance policies. Those insurance policies were sold to other insurance companies for a profit. Dummy corporations were formed to hide debt and losses, and accounting tricks were used to fool auditors and investors. By the early 1970's, the company was losing hundreds of millions of dollars a year while claiming on its financial reports to be making hundreds of millions in profit. The situation became so bad that when a group of employees was discovered embezzling from the company by writing fake life insurance policies of their own, these employees were given the assignment to write fake insurance policies to bilk investors and make money for Equity Funding.

Nearly one hundred employees were aware of the company's scam, and eventually one spoke publicly after becoming upset with Equity Funding. A Wall Street analyst, Raymond Birk, broke the story of the fraud, turning over his information to the Securities and Exchange Commission (SEC). This prompted closer examination of Equity Funding's dealings, and by 1973, auditors and investors were looking closely at the company's books and found the fraud. The collapse came quickly, and investors found that their Equity Funding stock was worthless.

Perhaps the best remembered of the 1970's financial scandals involved Robert Vesco. Vesco was a high-ranking executive in a company known as Investors Overseas Services, which sold mutual funds to individuals in Europe. Vesco joined the company in the 1960's and quickly rose in the ranks. In 1972, as the company was having financial difficulties, Vesco was being investigated by the SEC. Facing questions from within the company and from both investors and the government about money that had disappeared, Vesco left the United States for Costa Rica. He was charged with embezzling more than 200 million dollars from the company but did not return to the United States to face trial. Instead, he became the "fugitive financier" who was tied to the Watergate scandal because of $200,000 that he gave to President Nixon's reelection campaign. Vesco became a legendary figure during the 1970's, evading law enforcement by traveling through the Caribbean, attempting to buy an island and establish a sovereign country of his own, then landing in Cuba, where he was safe from extradition back to the United States.

University Scandals College sports were not immune from scandals during the 1970's. The worst one was a point shaving operation run by members of the Boston College men's basketball team. Starting in December, 1978, and continuing until March of the next year, players were found to have manipulated scores of games in order to allow gamblers to make money betting on the games. The scheme was allegedly hatched by infamous mobster Henry Hill. While the games were fixed during the 1978 season, the point shaving was not made public until the early 1980's, when one Boston College player, Rick Kuhn, was convicted and sentenced to ten years in prison, though that sentence was later reduced.

Even the U.S. military academy at West Point could not escape scandal during the 1970's. One of the courses taken by cadets was electrical engineering. When a take-home test was returned to the course instructors in March, 1976, the instructors noted similar answers. In April, a full-fledged investigation was launched and found that more than one hundred cadets who had taken the test had cheated. These findings led to hearings before honor code boards, and cadets found guilty of cheating were either suspended or expelled from the academy.

The widespread cheating injured the academy's public image, and an outside commission was created, headed by Frank Borman, United Airlines chairman and former West Point graduate. The Borman Commission examined the entire honor code structure of the academy and the cheating scandal. In December, 1976, it issued a report that supported the academy and made a few recommendations on improving knowledge and teaching of the code.

Impact The scandals of the 1970's led to real attempts to reform the public and private sectors. At the same time, Americans began to adopt a more negative perspective of public and private institutions after coming to view officials as mostly corrupt.

Further Reading

Dirks, Raymond, and Leonard Gross. *The Great Wall Street Scandal.* New York: McGraw-Hill, 1974. Details the Equity Funding scandal of the early 1970's and how one of the largest investment scams in history was discovered.

Emery, Fred. *Watergate.* New York: Touchstone Books, 1995. A detailed analysis of the Watergate scandal from the original break-in to the resignation of President Nixon.

Porter, David. *Fixed: How Goodfellas Bought Boston College Basketball.* New York: Taylor Trade, 2002. This book examines the Boston College point shaving scandal of the late 1970's and the involvement of mobsters in one of the decade's worst sports scandals.

Ross, Shelley. *Fall from Grace.* New York: Ballantine, 1988. A wide-ranging book that examines political scandals in American history up to the 1990's.

Wells, Joseph. *Frankensteins of Fraud.* New York: Obsidian, 2000. This fast-paced book examines a variety of frauds and scandals with a focus on business and investment scandals.

Douglas Clouatre

See also Agnew, Spiro T.; Basketball; Business and the economy in the United States; Central Intelligence Agency (CIA); Congress, U.S.; Nixon, Richard M.; Nixon tapes; Nixon's resignation and pardon; Sports; Watergate.

■ *Schoolhouse Rock!*

Identification Children's television programming comprising short animated segments

Date Aired from 1973 to 1985

In the early 1970's, amid a climate of mounting concern over violence and lack of good content in children's television programming, Schoolhouse Rock! *brought an element of education to Saturday morning cartoons, teaching American children about history, math, science, and grammar.*

In 1971, when advertising executive David McCall saw his son struggling with multiplication tables, he came up with a unique idea to help him learn the information. Knowing that the child could sing countless pop songs verbatim, McCall decided to link contemporary music with math concepts. He used his own agency's creative team to execute his idea and, together with Texas jazz musician Bob Dorough, came up with the project's first song, "Three Is a Magic Number," which explained multiplication by threes using a soothing melody. The song and several more about math were combined on the record album *Multiplication Rock,* released by Capitol Records. The creators then decided to make animated adaptations of the songs. The American Broadcasting Company (ABC) network, already worried about parental and political pressure to decrease the commercialization and violence in children's programs, agreed to air "Three Is a Magic Number" and gave the green light for the development of more segments.

Following the success of the math-related segments, *Grammar Rock* was introduced and used the same formula: silly characters, catchy songs, and repetition. American children learned that "A Noun Is a Person, Place, or Thing" and sang along to "Conjunction Junction" and "Lolly, Lolly, Lolly, Get Your Adverbs Here," among others. The 1976 bicentennial celebration prompted *America Rock,* a new set of segments that related to American history, including "I'm Just a Bill," "The Shot Heard 'Round the World," and "Sufferin' Till Suffrage." *Science Rock* followed, and among its memorable contributions were "Telegraph Line," which explained the human

America Rock
"No More Kings" (colonization of the New World)
"The Shot Heard 'Round the World" (American Revolution)
"Fireworks" (Declaration of Independence)
"The Preamble" (U.S. Constitution)
"Elbow Room" (westward expansion)
"The Great American Melting Pot" (immigration)
"Mother Necessity" (inventions)
"Sufferin' Till Suffrage" (women's right to vote)
"Three-Ring Government" (three branches of government)
"I'm Just a Bill" (lawmaking process)

Grammar Rock
"A Noun Is a Person, Place, or Thing"
"Verb: That's What's Happening"
"Rufus Xavier Sarsaparilla" (pronouns)
"Lolly, Lolly, Lolly, Get Your Adverbs Here"
"Unpack Your Adjectives"
"Conjunction Junction"
"Interjections!"

Multiplication Rock
"Elementary, My Dear" (two)
"Three Is a Magic Number"
"The Four-Legged Zoo"
"Ready or Not, Here I Come" (five)
"I Got Six"
"Lucky Seven Sampson"
"Figure Eight"
"Naughty Number Nine"
"The Good Eleven"
"Little Twelvetoes"
"My Hero, Zero"

Science Rock
"The Body Machine"
"Do the Circulation" (circulatory system)
"Them Not-So-Dry Bones" (skeleton)
"Telegraph Line" (nervous system)
"Electricity, Electricity"
"A Victim of Gravity"
"Interplanet Janet" (solar system)
"The Energy Blues" (energy)

nervous system, and "Interplanet Janet," which explained the solar system.

Impact In all, forty-one segments of *Schoolhouse Rock!* were created during its run. The series won four Emmy Awards for Outstanding Children's Programming, and it earned the respect of parents and educators for the way in which it made learning palatable and memorable with its fun characters and catchy melodies.

Subsequent Events *Schoolhouse Rock!* experienced a revival during the mid-1990's, beginning in 1994 with the musical production of *Schoolhouse Rock Live!* by Chicago-based Theater BAM. Original fans of the series reacted with a mixture of nostalgia and amusement, and the production gained national attention. In 1996, a new generation of musicians contributed their own versions of *Schoolhouse Rock!* classics to a compilation compact disc (CD) box set, released by Rhino Records.

Further Reading

Burke, Timothy, and Kevin Burke. *Saturday Morning Fever: Growing Up with Cartoon Culture.* New York: St. Martin's Griffin, 1999.

Yohe, Tom, and George Newall. *"Schoolhouse Rock!" The Official Guide.* New York: Hyperion Books, 1996.

Sarah M. Hilbert

See also Bicentennial celebration; Children's television; Education in the United States; *Sesame Street*; Television in the United States.

■ Schreyer, Edward

Identification Premier of Manitoba, 1969 to 1977; governor-general of Canada, 1979 to 1984

Born December 21, 1935; Beausejour, Manitoba, Canada

Schreyer presided over the first socialist government in the province of Manitoba. His appointment as governor-general broke the long-established tradition of alternating French- and English-speaking appointees.

Edward Schreyer entered politics in 1958 at the age of twenty-two under the banner of the Co-operative Commonwealth Federation (CCF), becoming the youngest member of the Manitoba Legislative Assembly. Concurrently, he taught political science at the University of Manitoba. Schreyer moved to federal politics in 1965 and served as a CCF (later New Democratic Party, NDP) member until June, 1969, when he returned to provincial politics with a resounding win as Manitoba's NDP leader. Later that month, Schreyer's party swept to an unprecedented victory in Manitoba. While the NDP was a socialist party, Schreyer's more centrist political approach was appealing to voters.

Upon assuming office, Schreyer announced his belief that government could be used to achieve a more equitable distribution of worldly goods. This would mean readjustment of taxation to emphasize "progressive" rather than "regressive" taxes and greater government intervention through ownership of crown corporations. The NDP government introduced Autopac, a publicly owned automobile insurance program; Manitoba Hydro; Manitoba Telephone; and Pharmacare, which would pay most family drug expenses. Medical insurance premiums were eliminated. Perhaps the most lasting legacy was the 1972 amalgamation of the city of Winnipeg with eleven smaller suburban communities. Schreyer's NDP was defeated in 1977 by the Progressive Conservatives under Sterling Lyon.

In 1978, Liberal prime minister Pierre Trudeau appointed Schreyer governor-general of Canada, breaking with the precedent of alternating French- and English-speaking governors-general. Schreyer assumed office in January, 1979, succeeding Jules Léger. The appointment of someone whose ethnicity was neither French nor English was a tangible recognition of Canada's multicultural landscape. Schreyer's ethnic background was German Austrian, and he was a multilingual Roman Catholic. Schreyer's appointment was also clearly a nonpartisan one. The governor-general, as the monarch's representative, is meant to be an impartial arbiter of Canadian political affairs, guided only by constitutional precedent and not political inclinations. Cynics have suggested, however, that this prestigious appointment was a way for Trudeau to remove a serious threat from the sphere of active politics.

At forty-three, Schreyer was considerably younger than most governors-general, and his socialist views—and image as a rumpled academic—seemed at odds with the regal atmosphere of Government House. He and his wife, Lily, inaugurated a less formal approach to their official duties.

Impact The election of Schreyer's socialist NDP government in Manitoba, a province long associated with leftist politics and social activism, was greeted with wide interest and, in some quarters, alarm. The comparatively modest scope of reforms that were introduced reveal the compromises required for practical politics. Schreyer's term as governor-general helped to shape the evolution of that office in the age of multiculturalism and democracy.

Further Reading

Beaulieu, Paul, ed. *Ed Schreyer: A Social Democrat in Power.* Winnipeg, Man.: Queenston House, 1977.

McAllister, James A. *The Government of Edward Schreyer: Democratic Socialism in Manitoba.* Montreal: McGill-Queen's University Press, 1984.

Mowat, Claire. *Pomp and Circumstances.* Toronto: McClelland and Stewart, 1989.

Barbara J. Messamore

See also Health care in Canada; Elections in Canada; Léger, Jules; Michener, Roland; Minorities in Canada; Trudeau, Pierre.

■ Science and technology

Definition The physical, biological, earth, and computer sciences and the practical technological innovations developed from scientific advances

In the 1970's, almost every field of science saw profound progress, often made by scientists in the United States and Canada, while new technologies, especially those related to computers, presaged significant changes in social behavior.

During the 1970's, science in the United States and Canada made astonishing leaps in understanding the structures of nature, both at very small scales and at very large scales. For instance, physicists proposed a theory that accounted for the bewildering array of subatomic particles that had been discovered over the previous twenty years, while biologists and geneticists began to unravel and imitate the processes in cells that sustain life. New telescopes and robot space probes afforded astronomers greatly enhanced views of phenomena beyond Earth. Meanwhile, engineers were making available new products that revolutionized how people could be treated for diseases or use information.

At the same time, a growing backlash of unease about science and technology characterized the decade. Revelations that pollution could threaten public health accounted for much of this reaction, which intensified following highly publicized events such as the groundwater pollution scandal at Love Canal, New York, in 1978 and the partial meltdown of a commercial nuclear reactor the next year at Three Mile Island in Pennsylvania. Moreover, recession and budgetary pressures led to the curtailment of some high-profile projects. In the face of declining public interest in lunar exploration, President Richard Nixon cut back the number of Apollo missions and redirected the National Aeronautics and Space Administration (NASA) away from crewed planetary exploration and toward a reusable orbital vehicle, the space shuttle; between 1975 and 1981, there were no American human spaceflights at all, the longest hiatus since crewed missions began. In 1974, biologists and geneticists from the U.S. National Academy of Sciences announced a moratorium on research in genetic engineering while they studied its implications, in part to assess the danger that it might inadvertently create hazardous new organisms.

The Physical Sciences In 1972, Murray Gell-Mann, Harald Fritzsch, and William Bardeen proposed a theory called quantum chromodynamics (QCD) to explain the strong interaction that holds together particles in the atomic nucleus. When QCD was added to earlier theories concerning electromagnetism and the weak interaction, physicists came to believe that they had a single, comprehensive, general understanding of the three fundamental forces that control atoms. This knowledge was first summarized as a unity in 1974 in a lecture by John Iliopoulos and became known as the Standard Model.

The Standard Model theory rested upon on the existence of quarks, infinitesimal particles with fractional charges predicted earlier by Gell-Mann. Experiments in particle accelerators such as the immense new machine at the Fermi National Accelerator Laboratory in Illinois, which first became operational in 1974, produced evidence for quarks and QCD. These experiments included the discovery of the J/psi particle in 1974, quark jets in 1975, the tau lepton in 1975, the D0 meson in 1976, and the bottom quark in 1977. By the end of the decade, the Standard Model was considered among the most successful scientific theories ever.

However, the Standard Model could not reconcile its conceptual foundation, quantum mechanics, with the remaining fundamental force of nature, gravity, and the theory describing it, the general theory of relativity. In order to merge these two master theories into a grand unified theory (GUT), scientists began proposing a series of radical ideas, including supersymmetric string theory (1976) and eleven-dimensional supergravity (1978), which influenced work on cosmological theories thereafter.

Other physicists and chemists were at work on more specific, concrete projects, some with long-reaching effects. Robert Woodward synthesized vitamin B_{12} in 1972, and in 1974 Lawrence Livermore National Laboratory created a new element, seaborgium (atom number 106). In 1977, lasers were used for the first time to cool trapped atoms, a technique that later enabled scientists to study the strange properties of ultracold matter, including superconductivity.

Outer Space After a harrowing voyage that returned Apollo 13 to Earth after an equipment failure in 1970, Apollo 14 and Apollo 15 in 1971 and then Apollo 16 and 17 in 1972 took crews of scientists to the Moon to study its terrain and bring back rocks for analysis, but it was NASA's robot probes that really expanded astronomers' knowledge of the solar system. Mariner 9 orbited Mars in 1971. Pioneer 10 passed close to Jupiter in 1973, followed by Pioneer 11 the next year. Mariner 10 took pictures of Venus on its way to Mercury, photographing both planets in 1974. Helios 1 and Helios 2 flew by the Sun in 1975 and 1976. Also in 1976, Viking 1 and Viking 2 landed on Mars. In 1978, two Pioneer Venus probes went into orbit. In 1979, Voyager 1 and Voyager 2 visited Jupiter, while Pioneer 11 slipped through the rings of Saturn. The close-up photographs and other data sent back by these various missions revealed rings and more moons around Jupiter and Saturn; suggested that the Sun is slowly shrinking; showed Venus, Mercury, and Mars to have harsh, barren landscapes; and suggested that life does not now exist on Mars.

New telescopes, ground-based or in orbit around earth, fostered further discoveries. Rings were detected around Uranus in 1977, and a moon, Charon, was discovered around Pluto in 1978. During the decade, NASA launched a series of satellites that could sense X rays and gamma rays, and they showed the universe beyond the solar system to be an unimaginably violent place of marvels. A special type of neutron star that emits explosions of X rays, called a burster, was identified, and whirling pulsars were found to exist in pairs. Astronomers found giant clouds of hydrogen, organic molecules, and a gravitational lens (whereby the image of a distant object is magnified by the gravitational field of a nearer object). In 1972, Canadian C. T. Bolton demonstrated the existence of a black hole, which had been hitherto only theoretical. American astronomer Vera Rubin calculated that the Milky Way is moving through space at 500 kilometers per second relative to cosmic background radiation, and R. Brent Tully and J. Richard Fisher developed a technique enabling astronomers to measure the distances to galaxies outside the Milky Way. In 1979, the Canadian-American team of Robert Dicke and James Peebles questioned the basic assumption in big bang cosmological theory that the universe is flat—that is, has no overall gravitational curvature—as lacking experimental verification.

Earth Sciences In addition to infamous examples of pollution, such as Love Canal and Three Mile Island, new types of environmental damage came to public attention during the 1970's. In 1974, F. Sherwood Rowland and Mario Molina published a landmark study demonstrating that chlorofluorocarbons (CFCs) damage the ozone layer in Earth's atmosphere, which protects living organisms from ultraviolet radiation. The same year, scientists found that acid rain created in the U.S. Midwest has international effects, crossing into Canada and then back into the U.S. Northeast, damaging forests and freshwater bodies.

New technology helped scientists scrutinize Earth on a broad scale in order to assess its resources. In 1972, NASA launched the first of five Landsat satellites in order to study the patterns of crops, timber, vegetation, water sources, and geological indications of mineral and oil deposits worldwide. In the oceans, a new generation of submarines enabled scientists to explore features previously hidden in the murky depths. In 1977, a team led by Robert Ballard aboard the submersible *Alva* examined volcanic vents that spew sulfur-laden hot water in an abyss near the Galápagos Islands.

Earth sciences also revealed clues about the origin of humanity and its diaspora. In 1974, a team in Africa led by Donald Johanson unearthed the remains of a new human ancestor, *Australopithecus afarensis.* One skeleton, which they named Lucy, dated from more than three million years ago and proved that hominids walked upright before large brains evolved. In 1970, archaeologists explored a rock shelter at Meadowcroft, Pennsylvania, where evidence indicated that people lived in North America nineteen thousand years ago, eight thousand years earlier than previously thought.

Meanwhile, other, much more ancient species came to light. In 1971, *Quetzalcoatlus northropi*, the largest flying animal ever found, was uncovered in Texas; it had an estimated wingspan of thirty-nine feet. The next year, Robert Bakker published a controversial paper arguing that dinosaurs were warm-blooded, and in 1975 Mary-Claire King and Allan Wilson revealed findings that human and chimpanzee deoxyribonucleic acid (DNA) sequences differ by only 1 percent. Various geological and paleontological lines of evidence prompted Stephen Jay Gould and Niles Eldredge in 1972 to publish the theory of punctuated equilibrium, which holds that bursts of rapid evolution interrupt long periods of biological stability.

Life Sciences The 1970's saw rapid developments in biological sciences, especially genetics, that promised both greater understanding of the basic processes of life and new therapies for human disease. In 1970 came the discovery of retroviruses, which can copy the DNA of the infected host on a ribonucleic acid (RNA) template; retroviruses were later found to cause some cancers and acquired immunodeficiency syndrome (AIDS). In 1974, biologists first detected the internal structure of cells, a network of microtubules within the cytoplasm, and in 1978 Stephen C. Harrison discerned the structure of a virus (the tomato bushy virus) in high resolution for the first time. On a more general scale, Edward O. Wilson published *Sociobiology* (1975), a seminal but controversial study of the biological basis of social behavior, and in 1977 Carl Woese proposed a new taxonomic domain of microorganisms, Archaebacteria, adding it to the traditional domains of prokaryotes (which have no nucleus) and eukaryotes (with a nucleus).

Advances in genetics appeared to hold the promise of great benefit and great harm. In 1970, the first restriction enzyme for cutting DNA into specific lengths was isolated, and Indian American microbiologist Har Gobind Khorana constructed the first artificial gene. In 1972, Paul Berg and Herbert W. Boyer produced recombinant DNA molecules—foreign DNA inserted into a bacterium so that it makes foreign proteins, a process also known as gene splicing. A year later, Annie Chang, Stanley Cohen, and Boyer showed that recombinant DNA molecules can be made to replicate in the host bacterium. These achievements inaugurated the discipline of genetic engineering. In 1975, after a year's moratorium on genetic engineering research, an international meeting of biologists issued guidelines to help scientists avoid unleashing deadly biological innovations. That year, the first biotechnology company, Genentech, was founded, and the burgeoning industry soon produced medical benefits from recombinant DNA techniques. In 1978, somatostatin became the first human hormone produced by this new technology, followed in 1979 by artificial insulin.

New discoveries continued in the mechanisms of DNA. In 1974, gyrase was found to be the agent that causes DNA to curl into supercoils. In 1974, Harold E. Varmus and J. Michael Bishop isolated oncogenes, which participate in starting cancers inside otherwise normal cells. In 1977, Phillip A. Sharp and Richard J. Roberts separately identified introns, sections of DNA that do not code for proteins and at the time were thought to be simply junk, and the same year Walter Gilbert introduced a method for rapidly reading the long sequence of codes along the DNA molecule—both fundamental discoveries that hastened the search for disease-causing genetic abnormalities. The complete genetic structure of a virus was also deciphered in 1977.

Medical researchers made progress in treating and understanding heart disease, one of the leading killers in North America. In 1973, Michael S. Brown and Joseph L. Goldstein isolated the cell receptor that takes low-density lipoproteins out of the bloodstream, a discovery that was fundamental to understanding atherosclerosis (hardening of the arteries). In 1978, Robert K. Jarvik introduced the Jarvik-7 artificial heart, which was invented to keep patients alive until a human heart became available for transplant.

In 1977, a deadly new disease that attacks the immune system was first described in American hospitals and later named AIDS. That year, a team led by Raymond V. Damadian conducted the first body scan using nuclear magnetic resonance imaging (MRI), which became a sensitive tool for detecting tumors. Progress in the treatment of behavioral disorders came in 1970 when lithium received government approval for treatment of bipolar disorder. In 1974, Stanley Milgram published *Obedience to Authority*, in which he described studies that led him to a shocking conclusion: People tend to obey authority figures even to the point of obvious immorality, such as inflicting unjust punishment.

Technological Innovations As transistors were to the technology of the 1960's, so were microprocessors to the technology of the 1970's. Microprocessors, also called computer chips, are integrated complexes of transistors that serve as the data processing units for computers, and the first of them, the Intel 4004, was introduced in 1971. They soon saw a host of diverse applications. Texas Instruments marketed the first pocket calculator in 1971. The first video games, *Pong* and *Odyssey*, came out in 1972. With the creation of the floppy disk, introduced in 1970, small, inexpensive computers became possible. The first mass-produced personal computer (PC), the Altair 8800, was a kit for home assembly with 256 bytes of memory; it was offered to the public in 1975. The first ready-built PC to be a commercial success was the Apple II, which appeared on the market in 1977. In 1978, Apple Computer introduced the first disk drive for a PC, and VisiCalc put out the first spreadsheet software. To accompany the new computers, a variety of printers appeared: the daisy-wheel printer in 1970, the dot-matrix printer in 1971, the laser printer in 1975, and the ink-jet printer in 1976. Meanwhile, Seymour Cray developed powerful supercomputers for complex industrial and research uses, bringing out the Cray I in 1976.

Among the later developments that PCs made possible was the Internet, which had its origins in the 1970's as well. The first cross-country link for the U.S. Department of Defense's Advanced Research Projects Agency Network (ARPANET), an Internet precursor, was set up in 1970, and the first international connection, between the United States and Norway, occurred in 1973, the same year that Robert Metcalf of Xerox invented Ethernet technology for local networks. In 1975, Telnet, the first publicly available packet data service, was started as the commercial equivalent of ARPANET. In 1971, Ray Tomlinson invented the first e-mail program. In an attempt to bring human touches to Internet communications, Kevin Mackenzie introduced in 1979 the first of the typographical symbols called emoticons, such as ":-)" and ";-|."

Communications grew swifter, more profuse, and easier thanks to yet more new technologies. Corning Glass fabricated the first light-transmitting glass fibers in 1970, and fiber-optic cables were first used to carry live telephone traffic in 1977 in the United States and a year later in Canada. Charles A. Burrus devised light-emitting diodes in 1970, Westinghouse brought out liquid crystal displays (LCDs) in 1974, and cell phones were invented in 1979. In 1970, the Department of Defense began development of the global positioning system (GPS), a satellite network that made it possible to identify exact locations anywhere on Earth's surface.

Lasers became a basic part of industry and commerce. Powerful carbon-dioxide lasers were first used for welding and cutting metal in 1970, and in 1973 Bell Laboratories produced tunable, continuous-wave lasers, which had greater flexibility than did other lasers. In the next year, the first shipments of bar-coded products reached stores; read by lasers, the bar codes simplified accounting and inventory recordkeeping. Among other major developments, Boeing 747 jumbo jets began transatlantic service, the first electricity-producing nuclear reactor cooled by ordinary water started up in Canada, and Sony began selling videocassette recorders (VCRs)—all in 1971.

Impact Environmental research had the most immediate and practical effects on 1970's science by exposing human-made threats to the environment, which led to legislative action. In 1970, many Canadians joined Americans in celebrating the first Earth Day on April 22. The U.S. Congress passed the Endangered Species Act in 1973 and prohibited the use of CFCs as propellants in 1978, a decision inspired by the work of Rowland and Molina. The U.S. Environmental Protection Agency (EPA) banned the insecticide DDT in 1972.

The physical and life sciences advanced the theoretical understanding of the universe on a broad scale during the decade. The creation of the Standard Model was a turning point in particle physics, and new clarity in imaging violent X-ray and gamma-ray sources contributed to astrophysical theories about the origins of stars and galaxies. The discoveries of a black hole and a gravitational lens and measurements of time dilation verified the implications of Albert Einstein's special and general theories of relativity, while supersymmetry and string theory brought new vitality to cosmological theory.

In genetics, the understanding of how DNA and RNA produce substances for bodily metabolism made several crucial advances, but it was the techniques of genetic engineering that created the most excitement. Researchers began to give medical and agricultural scientists tools with which to create wholly novel biological agents or old molecules in new, faster ways. Artificial insulin reduced the cost of treating diabetes, and the promise of new medicines, even gene replacement therapy, was within reach and foods genetically modified to resist frost or pests were at hand. Some of these developments, especially genetically modified foods, sparked controversy, fear, and protest, but the potential to improve the food supply and cure seemingly intractable inherited diseases invigorated medical research.

Communications technology and computers inaugurated profound changes in behavior. Fiber optics, cell phones, and satellite communications intensified telephone traffic worldwide. Personal computers and the ARPANET created the basis for electronic commerce, electronic recordkeeping and finance, and the borderless social nexus of the World Wide Web: The 1970's fostered the birth of the information age. Acquiring the plethora of new consumer goods and services grew ever easier and cheaper. As science writer and philosopher James Gleick observed, everyday life began to move faster and faster.

Further Reading

Bunch, Bryan, and Jenny Tesar. *Discover Science Almanac.* New York: Hyperion, 2003. Organized by scientific discipline, this book contains time lines, summary articles, biographical sketches, and listings of books and Web sites.

Calder, Nigel. *Magic Universe: The Oxford Guide to Modern Science.* New York: Oxford University Press, 2003. Drawing on more than two hundred interviews with scientists, Calder, a renowned science writer, traces the cross-connections among recent scientific discoveries.

Crease, Robert P., and Charles C. Mann. *The Second Creation: Makers of the Revolution in Twentieth-Century Physics.* New York: Macmillan, 1986. An eminently readable, thorough account of developments in particle physics that concentrates on the discoveries of the 1960's and 1970's.

Rothenberg, Marc, ed. *The History of Science in the United States*. New York: Garland, 2001. Articles about science topics and American scientists from throughout U.S. history are presented in an alphabetical format.

Roger Smith

See also Anik communication satellites; Apollo space program; Apple Computer; Archaeology; Astronomy; Automatic teller machines (ATMs); Bar codes; CAT scans; Closed captioning; Communications in Canada; Communications in the United States; Computer networks; Computers; Dolby sound; 8-track tapes; Genetics research; Inventions; LED and LCD screens; Medicine; Microprocessors; Microsoft; Pioneer space program; Quadraphonic sound; Skylab; Space exploration; Ultrasonography; Videocassette recorders (VCRs); Viking space program; Voyager space program; Walkman.

■ Science-fiction films

Definition Motion pictures that focus on the impact of actual or imagined science on society or individuals

The science-fiction films of the 1970's offered advancements in special-effects technology. Their plots tended to reflect contemporary concerns about dehumanizing technology and deteriorating natural environments.

The two most popular and influential science-fiction films of the 1970's repeat the genre's prior history of being stronger in sensational images than in story or ideas. Lavishly produced, George Lucas's *Star Wars* (1977) is at heart an old-fashioned Flash Gordon space opera emphasizing lengthy combat scenes as young Luke Skywalker helps rescue Princess Leia from evil Darth Vader. No less militaristic and basic in story line, Ridley Scott's *Alien* (1979) revisits Howard Hawks's *The Thing* (1951) as a spaceship commander and her crew battle a rapidly adapting and voracious creature adept at concealment. Although having a woman commander in *Alien* gestures toward 1970's feminist awareness, neither of these visually stimulating films with enhanced special effects invites serious reflection on 1970's social issues.

Technology and the Human Spirit If combat equipment simply is flaunted in *Star Wars* and *Alien*, other science-fiction films registered the decade's anxieties about the dehumanizing impact of such technology. *The Andromeda Strain* (1971), with a plot taken from a novel by Michael Crichton about a plaguing alien microorganism, cautions against a growing dependence on computers. Another Crichton creation, *Westworld* (1973), warns against naïvely relying on robots, which turn against their human creators in the film. The hazards of technology likewise are dramatized in Crichton's *The Terminal Man* (1974), which features a protagonist who paradoxically murders precisely because of a brain-embedded computer designed to repress violence. In the same vein, a malfunctioning computer and a crew's increasing mental instability drive the apocalyptic plot of John Carpenter's *Dark Star* (1974).

Technological dehumanization is the theme of *Coma* (1978), based on Robin Cook's best-selling medical thriller that updates the mad-doctor scenario of typical older science fiction. In *The Stepford Wives* (1975), a version of Ira Levin's satirical book, women are reprogrammed into emotionless, socially conforming robots. Love is outlawed in *THX 1138* (1971), an early Orwellian production by Lucas that portrays a heavily policed and economics-driven future. As if commenting both on the underlying trait of science-fiction stories and on his own 1970's world, a psychiatrist in the remake of *Invasion of the Body Snatchers* (1978) observes that people "are becoming less human."

In contrast, *Star Trek: The Motion Picture* (1979) celebrates emotion and reason as safeguards against the tyranny of machinery. When he rebels against a mind-controlled future governed by six cartels, the hero of *Rollerball* (1975) similarly exhibits indomitable survival instincts. Widely viewed in the United States, Stanley Kubrick's 1971 British film adapted from Anthony Burgess's 1962 novel *A Clockwork Orange* also celebrates the triumph of human will, despite its perversity, against futuristic technological efforts to control it. Woody Allen's *Sleeper* (1973), another film critiquing robotlike social conformity and despotic authority, suggests that "rebellious" laughter is an insuppressible expression of human freedom.

The Limits of Nature and Civilization 1970's fears about dehumanization included anxieties concerning the techno-industrial impact on nature. The ef-

The film and television industries tried to capitalize on the phenomenal success of Star Wars *with an explosion of science-fiction motion pictures and series—and even special television programming such as* The *Star Wars* Holiday Special, *with Carrie Fisher as Princess Leia and Anthony Daniels as C3PO, broadcast in 1977.* (CBS/Landov)

fects of radiation depicted in *The Giant Spider Invasion* (1975) recall a 1950's tradition evident in *Them!* (1954) and *Tarantula* (1955). However, most revenge-of-nature films during the 1970's tended not to specify the causes of biological disruption. Given the prominence of environmental issues during the decade, 1970's audiences of these B-films were expected to understand that, for example, the rampant amphibians of *Frogs* (1972), the fire-starting insects of *Bug* (1975), the voracious canine packs in *Dogs* (1976), and the gargantuan animals of *The Food of the Gods* (1976) punish humanity for abusing nature.

In *Soylent Green* (1973) and *Logan's Run* (1976), contemporary fears about the decline of natural resources extended to civilization. In the uncomfortably overpopulated world of *Soylent Green*, synthetic food is made from the corpses of people who are encouraged to volunteer for a government-managed, pleasant death. In contrast, the subterranean world of *Logan's Run* is beautiful but maintained by a state-mandated death sentence at the age of thirty.

Nuclear Holocaust and Redemption The decade's science-fiction films, such as the three sequels to *Planet of the Apes* (1968), also mirrored Cold War anxieties about worldwide nuclear destruction that was typical of previous decades. *Damnation Alley* (1977), an adaptation of Roger Zelazny's novel, dramatizes the efforts of a West Coast team to deliver a plague antidote to the East Coast of a devastated United States. Subterranean sterile males represent the hopelessness of the postnuclear future in *A Boy and His Dog* (1975), based on Harlan Ellison's prize-winning novella. In this brutal, thoroughly unsentimental story, a scavenger kills his girlfriend in order to feed his telepathic dog.

The world likewise is ruined but is not as hopeless in *Glen and Randa* (1971), featuring a postnuclear Adam-and-Eve couple wandering through ruins in search of a legendary place called Metropolis. A small postnuclear Garden of Eden is highlighted in *Silent Running* (1972), the story of an act of disobedience that sends the world into deep space so that humanity might have a second chance.

The meaning of second chance is very different in Steven Spielberg's *Close Encounters of the Third Kind* (1977), one of the decade's most notable science-fiction films. Depicting human salvation by benevolent aliens, this nearly spiritual work reverses the apocalyptic stereotypes of first-contact films while nonetheless delivering superb special effects and an elemental sense of wonder. This film ends optimistically with humans ascending with aliens into a heaven of possibilities in outer space.

Impact Although *Close Encounters of the Third Kind* was appreciated for its salient revision of science-fiction film stereotypes, it did not change the direction of the genre. Instead, the popular traditional science-fiction patterns of *Star Wars* and *Alien* were copied in less adept imitations such as the television series *Battlestar Galactica* (1978-1979) and *Buck Rogers in the Twenty-fifth Century* (1979-1981) and various film sequels to *Alien*. Overall, 1970's science-fiction films recycled 1950's characters, plots, and themes pertaining to the perils of technology, the decline of nature and civilization, and the possibility of nuclear annihilation. The decade's replay of these themes, however, also reflected the era's Cold War politics, antinuclear sentiment, environmental concerns, and computer-dependence anxieties.

Further Reading

Hardy, Phil. *The Encyclopedia of Science Fiction Movies*. Minneapolis: Woodbury Press, 1986. Provides chronological entries, photos, and brief commentaries.

King, Geoff, and Tanya Krzywinska. *Science Fiction Cinema: From Outer Space to Cyberspace*. London: Wallflower Press, 2000. Outlines major themes and cultural implications.

Telotte, J. P. *Science Fiction Film*. Cambridge, England: Cambridge University Press, 2001. Emphasizes filmic attitudes toward science and technology.

William J. Scheick

See also *Alien*; Allen, Woody; Antinuclear movement; *Battlestar Galactica*; *Clockwork Orange, A*; *Close Encounters of the Third Kind*; Disaster films; Environmental movement; Horror films; Special effects; Spielberg, Steven; *Star Trek*; *Star Wars*.

■ Scientology

Identification American religious group
Founder L. Ron Hubbard (1911-1986)
Date Established in 1952

During the 1970's, Scientology seemed to be more a system of therapy than a religion, and the church experienced a complete reorganization as a result of legal battles.

Formerly known as the Hubbard Association of Scientologists International and based on the ideas of its founder, L. Ron Hubbard, the Church of Scientology was one of the few new religions to originate in the United States in the twentieth century. Scientology was at first a chain of therapy groups based on a popular self-help system called Dianetics until Hubbard announced that it was a religion. Scientology has been embroiled in controversies in Great Britain, Australia, and the United States and has been criticized by such groups as the psychiatric profession and the Internal Revenue Service (IRS).

History and Beliefs Established in the 1950's, the Church of Scientology spread quickly in the United States and Great Britain and, by the late 1960's, throughout Europe. A special office, called the Guardian's Office (GO), was established in 1966 to deal with attacks upon the church. One of the major controversies surrounding Scientology was whether it is really a religion.

Scientologists believe that spiritual knowledge is of primary importance in human purpose and salvation, and communities of the faithful gather at certain times to discuss their beliefs and conduct rituals. Certain believers are given the role of providing spiritual leadership. At these gatherings, Scientologists affirm their devotion to the belief that human beings can become optimum individuals by reaching Clear, a state of being cleared of false information and traumatic memories. Beyond Clear, they may advance to being Thetans, immortal beings trapped in the bodies of mortals. One of the spiritual discoveries of Scientology is that humans are all Thetans. Another concept of Scientology is the combination of technological precision and spiritual progress. An electric instrument called an E-meter is used to assist in spiritual counseling, which must be done in strict accordance with a format that practitioners term "auditing."

Scientology is based on fees for services, as opposed to being financed through donations from members. Scientology attempts to use scientific research to measure results by encouraging members to record and evaluate their experiences. It has several branches that perform specialized functions. The educational branch offers courses and exercises at hundreds of "missions" or "churches" that members must take. Each site offering this education is a franchise that pays a certain percentage to the top level of bureaucracy.

The Sea Organization The Sea Organization—or Sea Org, as it came to be called—was founded in 1967 and took its name from the fleet of ships, primarily the *Apollo*, where Hubbard and some senior associates had located in order to develop the advanced teachings of the church. In 1971, this group decided that the church's Executive Council World Wide was not performing its function well, and the council was disbanded. The management of Scientology's offices and churches was taken over by the Sea Org, which also assumed responsibility for the Saint Hill Organizations, the equivalent of seminaries and graduate schools.

Joining the Sea Org was the ultimate commitment to Scientology. Sea Org members believed that they had worked together in previous lives and were now together again, forming an elite group. New arrivals had to sign a one-billion-year contract, and they were required to give up their passports, which made it hard to escape the *Apollo* as it sailed internationally. Once aboard, the new arrivals went through an "internship" from 8:30 A.M. to 10:30 P.M., and, if they did well, they were allowed one day off every two weeks. They spent their time studying materials or auditing preclears (PCs), those who had not yet reached the state of Clear. If the auditing did not go well, then the auditor was to blame and was sent back to review previous folders on the PC. If an auditor made too many mistakes, then he or she was punished, sometimes by being locked up in the chain locker, sometimes by performing ceremonies to Kali, goddess of death and destruction, and sometimes by cleaning the ship. In 1974, a Rehabilitation Task Force was created for those who committed breaches of ethical policies, emphasizing physical work such as building maintenance, furniture making, and grounds upkeep. The task force is largely run by its participants.

In 1979, Scientology suffered a major setback, largely brought about by the GO, which had formed a secret Intelligence Bureau. The bureau was conducting illegal activities such as attempting to gather files from the IRS and the Federal Bureau of Investigation (FBI), breaking into the offices of people who opposed Scientology, and destroying the credibility of its critics. Many officers of the GO faced criminal charges and lawsuits, and the church conducted its own investigation, which led to a complete reorganization at the national and international levels. The GO was disbanded, and new structures of organization were created. These new structures were placed in the hands of the Sea Org, whose members assumed leadership roles at the national and international levels.

Impact By dissolving the secret, and often illegal, Guardian's Office and by recognizing a certain amount of improper conduct among church leaders in the 1970's, Scientology restructured its organization and subsequently moved toward more traditional, mainstream religions. It became increasingly successful in accommodating the enthusiasm of committed members as well as reintegrating members who had difficulties with their original commitment.

Further Reading

Bromley, G. David, and L. Mitchell Bracey, Jr. "The Church of Scientology: A Quasi Religion." In *Sects, Cults, and Spiritual Communities*, edited by William Zellner and Marc Petrowsky. Westport, Conn.: Praeger, 1998. An excellent explanation of Scientology's rituals, organization, and operation.

Melton, J. Gordon. "A Contemporary Ordered Religious Community: The Sea Oranization." In *New Religious Movements and Religious Liberty in America*, edited by Derek H. Davis and Barry Hankins. Waco, Tex.: Baylor University Press, 2002. This essay was presented at a symposium at Baylor University and is helpful in understanding Scientology in the context of other religions.

_______. "The Newer Cults." In *Encyclopedic Handbook of Cults in America*. New York: Garland, 1986. A good source of information about the history of Scientology and its difficulties during the 1970's.

Sheila Golburgh Johnson

See also Cults; Religion and spirituality in the United States.

■ Sears Tower

Identification Skyscraper in downtown Chicago
Date Completed on May 4, 1973

The Sears Tower stood as the world's tallest building for twenty-three years, and it is still considered one of the architectural wonders of the world.

The Sears Tower is a skyscraper, a tall inhabitable building usually taller than five hundred feet. Skyscrapers are supported by a skeletal frame instead of being supported by walls, like shorter buildings.

The building was designed by chief architect Bruce Graham and structural engineer Fazlur Khan in the late 1960's. It was named for Richard Sears, who brought Sears and Roebuck, a retailer and the largest catalog order company in the world, to Chicago in 1887. The Sears Tower was built by the engineering and construction company of Skidmore, Owings & Merrill (SOM) in less than two and a half years. It took fifteen hundred workers to assemble the bronze-tinted and stainless steel 110-story structure. The construction of the Sears Tower cost $150 million, an enormous amount of money in the 1970's. According to the May 4, 1973, issue of the *Chicago Tribune*, "a final twenty-five hundred pound girder was lifted a quarter of a mile into the sky to make the Sears the world's tallest building."

The Sears Tower covers two city blocks in downtown Chicago on South Wacker Drive. It was constructed of seventy-six thousand tons of steel. The building rises 1,450 feet into the air and boasts 4.5 million square feet of office and retail space.

One of the interesting facts about the Sears Tower is that, on a clear day, four states—Illinois, Indiana, Wisconsin, and Michigan—can be seen from its Skydeck. Also, the elevators of the Sears Tower are the fastest in the world, capable of operating at 1,600 feet per minute. About two thousand miles of electrical cable and approximately forty-three thousand miles of telephone cable run through the building.

Impact The Sears Tower was the tallest building in the world until 1996, when the Petronas Towers in Kuala Lumpur, Malaysia, were completed; its spires are thirty-three feet taller than those of the Sears Tower. The Sears Tower, however, was awarded the title for tallest occupied floor in 1997. The building is still visited frequently by native Chicagoans and tourists alike. Approximately 25,000 people enter the Sears Tower each day, and about 1.5 million tourists visit the Skydeck each year.

Further Reading

Graham, Bruce. *Bruce Graham of SOM.* New York: Rizzoli, 1989.

Pridmore, Jay. *Sears Tower: A Building Book from the Chicago Architecture Foundation.* San Francisco: Pomegranate, 2002.

Sears Tower. Http://www.thesearstower.com/index.html.

Starletta Barber Poindexter

See also Architecture.

The topping ceremony takes place on the roof of the Sears Tower in Chicago on May 3, 1973, making the skyscraper the tallest building in the world. (AP/Wide World Photos)

■ Secretariat

Identification American thoroughbred racehorse
Born March 30, 1970; Meadow Stable, Doswell, Virginia
Died October 4, 1989; Claiborne Farm, Paris, Kentucky

Secretariat won the 1973 Triple Crown and set racing records that helped boost morale during the socioeconomic concerns and political scandals of the early 1970's.

Secretariat's athleticism amazed people worldwide. His breeder and owner, Christopher T. Chenery, hired trainer Lucien Laurin to develop Secretariat's innate talent and physique. Secretariat's twenty-five-foot stride gave him a natural advantage over most of his peers. As a two-year-old, Secretariat won seven races in nine starts. His 1972 earnings totaled more than $456,000. He ran record-setting races, and at season's end, he was named champion two-year-old colt. Designated Horse of the Year, he was the first two-year-old racehorse to receive the honor.

Secretariat repeated his stellar performances in 1973, winning nine races and placing second twice and third once. He earned more than $860,000 in twelve starts. When Chenery died, his estate taxes resulted in his daughter, Helen (Penny) Tweedy, syndicating Secretariat in February, 1973. Thirty-two shares were created, totaling $6.08 million, which historically was the most expensive value for a racehorse to date.

No horse had won the Triple Crown since Citation's victories in 1948. Jockey Ron Turcotte guided Secretariat around the 1.25-mile Kentucky Derby course at Churchill Downs on May 5, 1973. Secretariat won in record track time, 1:59.40. At the Preakness at Pimlico on May 19, 1973, Secretariat again surged ahead of the pack and won with a time of 1:54.40. Secretariat probably set another record, but track representatives disagreed about the accuracy of the track's timer.

Secretariat then led the five-horse pack in the Belmont Stakes on June 9, 1973. He dashed thirty-one lengths ahead of his competitors to set a world

Secretariat. (AP/Wide World Photos)

dirt track record, 2:24 minutes, for the 1.5-mile race. Secretariat bested his Kentucky Derby record for that race's distance on Belmont Park's track. Officials declared Secretariat the ninth Triple Crown winner.

After the Belmont, Secretariat won four races before retiring in November, 1973, to stud at Claiborne Farm. He repeated Horse of the Year honors, and his accolades included being named champion three-year-old colt. The National Museum of Racing's Hall of Fame inducted Secretariat in 1974.

Impact During his career, Secretariat enchanted people who were awed by his athleticism, and he set standards for racing. He provided Americans with a hero to be proud of and celebrate when national leaders were exposed for corruption during Watergate—Secretariat won honestly and did not disappoint his supporters. His successes represented optimism during the bleakness of the Vietnam War, energy shortages, and social turmoil. Moreover, Secretariat became a cultural phenomenon. People bought Secretariat merchandise, and magazine covers and television programs featured him. Finally, his progeny significantly improved the quality and value of American racehorses. Breeders and trainers aspire to produce champions superior to Secretariat with the goal of challenging his long-standing records.

Further Reading

Kierman, Thomas. *The Secretariat Factor: The Story of a Multimillion-Dollar Breeding Industry.* Garden City, N.Y.: Doubleday, 1979.

Nack, William. *Secretariat: The Making of a Champion.* Cambridge, Mass.: Da Capo Press, 2002.

Woolfe, Raymond G., Jr. *Secretariat.* Rev. ed. New York: Derrydale Press, 2001.

Elizabeth D. Schafer

See also Horse racing; Sports.

■ Segal, George

Identification American sculptor
Born November 26, 1924; New York, New York
Died June 9, 2000; South Brunswick, New Jersey

During the 1970's, Segal continued to be one of the United States' most influential figurative sculptors. He began making powerful social and political statements in outdoor public sculpture.

As the 1970's began, George Segal was producing white plaster sculpture by wrapping live models in plaster-soaked bandages, a unique technique he had invented. Although he was considered a pop artist for using imagery from contemporary consumer culture, Segal's art was also intensely personal and poetic.

In 1971, he developed the new technique of double-casting. From the original plaster cast, Segal made a more refined positive cast in hydrostone, a durable industrial plaster, which could further be cast in bronze. This inside casting resulted in more delicate and realistic details in skin textures and clothing. His new figures, such as those in his first bronze sculpture, *The Dancers,* showed more fluid movement than his frozen, introspective figures of the 1960's. Casting in bronze enabled Segal to construct permanent outdoor sculptures. In 1976, Segal installed his first outdoor sculpture, *The Restaurant,* outside the Federal Office Building in Buffalo, New York.

In the mid-1970's, Segal also began using color more frequently. He experimented with solid primary colors, as in *Red Girl Behind Red Door* (1976), *Couple on Black Bed* (1976), and *Magenta Girl on Green Door* (1977).

In 1970, the National Guards killed four students during antiwar demonstrations at Kent State University in Ohio. In May, 1978, the Cleveland-based Mildred Andrews Fund commissioned Segal to create a commemorative outdoor sculpture. Segal's work, *In Memory of May 4, 1970, Kent State: Abraham and Isaac,* portrays Abraham about to stab a kneeling Isaac. Segal chose this biblical story because he felt that both events involved incredible contradictions and conflicts of values. An angel of God had asked the aged Abraham to kill his beloved only son. At Kent State University, the right to protest clashed with opposing stances on patriotism. Although there was support for the sculpture at Kent State, the university's official position was that this depiction of an imminent act of violence was inappropriate. In 1979, the sculpture went to the John B. Putnam, Jr., Memorial collection at Princeton University.

In 1979, the Andrews Fund commissioned Segal to create public art at Sheridan Square, New York, to commemorate the 1969 Stonewall Inn riots, in which gays fought police harassment. This event signaled the beginning of the modern gay liberation movement. Segal's sculpture, *Gay Liberation,* was finished in 1980, but controversy and protests delayed its intended installation.

Impact During the 1970's, commissioned public art became mandatory for new government buildings, and public artwork helped promote contemporary artists. George Segal made the transition to public sculptures, which, like his other work, were eloquent expressions of a deep humanism. However, his public artwork also created intense public debate and controversy that continued after the decade.

Further Reading

Hunter, Sam. *George Segal.* New York: Rizzoli, 1989.
Segal, George, Martin L. Friedman, and Graham Beal. *George Segal, Sculptures.* Minneapolis: Walker Art Center, 1978.
Tuchman, Phyllis, and George Segal. *George Segal.* New York: Abbeville Press, 1983.

Alice Myers

See also Art movements; Pop art; Kent State massacre.

■ Self-help books

Definition Popular literary works that stress the power of individuals to change themselves

Patterned on American "self-made man" literature such as Benjamin Franklin's Autobiography *(1818) and Horatio Alger's late nineteenth century fictional tales of courage and perseverance, self-help books during the 1970's also embodied postwar attitudes about individualism and ambition that seemed to appeal especially to middle-class readers. Popular titles offered inspiration and advice in a condensed and accessible format and incorporated themes of the women's movement in their examinations of issues such as body image, marriage, and motherhood.*

The American self-help movement emerged from post-World War II middle-class attitudes about individualism and upward mobility. Following the publication of Norman Vincent Peale's 1952 best-seller *The Power of Positive Thinking,* popular self-help authors described the process of improving one's circumstances as primarily a psychological one. For Peale and his literary heirs—including Crystal Cathedral pastor Robert H. Schuller—success depends not only on discipline and hard work but also on attitude and will.

Baby boomers who matured during the turbulent 1960's increasingly turned to self-help books during this decade because the genre articulated commonsense principles in a straightforward, presentational style. The works also offered inspiration and guidance in a world of confusion and change. In part because of the books' enormous popularity among lay readers—that is, those without formal training in psychology or religion—many decried the trend as symbolic of the self-indulgence of the so-called Me Decade.

Self-help literature encompassed a variety of subjects: weight loss, exercise, housekeeping, interior decorating, home repair, health, first aid, fashion, marital advice, child care and development, and spirituality. During the 1970's, the most popular titles tended to fall under one of two headings: sex and sexuality and self-esteem.

Sex and Sexuality In part because of changing social mores, many popular self-help books published during the 1970's focused on gender roles and human sexuality. Two books published in 1969—*The Sensuous Woman* by Terry Garrity under the pseudonym "J" and David Reuben's *Everything You Always Wanted to Know About Sex but Were Afraid to Ask*—became best-sellers during the early 1970's. The books' frank discussions about masturbation, oral sex, and female orgasm inspired similar discussions in women's magazines and on daytime talk shows. Other titles in this area included *The Sensuous Man* by "M" (1971), Alex Comfort's *The Joy of Sex* (1972), and *Our Bodies, Ourselves* (1973), a collection of advice from the Boston Women's Health Book Collective.

In 1973, Miami homemaker and born-again Christian Marabel Morgan published *Total Woman* with a small evangelical press. The book, aimed at women who were interested in improving their marriages, transgressed many conservative Christian boundaries about appropriate public discourse. It was named *The New York Times*' Book of the Year for 1974. *The Hite Report: A Nationwide Study of Female Sexuality* was published in 1976; Shere Hite's study of male sexuality followed five years later. Perhaps the most enduring title of the decade, however, was Gail Sheehy's *Passages* (1976), a compelling look at the previously underexamined subject of menopause. All these titles allowed readers to explore their own questions and anxieties within the private context of reading.

On the Art of Feeling Good Besides sex and sexuality, self-esteem was a popular self-help topic. The quintessential book on mental health as it affects relationship issues was Thomas A. Harris's *I'm OK, You're OK* (1974), a popular look at the psychological theory of transactional analysis. The best-selling book, which inspired many sequels and many parodies, was premised on the idea that human relationships are built on certain patterns, some healthy and some dysfunctional. The key, Harris argued, is to monitor one's own behavior within these structures.

Another best-seller in this genre was Richard Bach's popular fable *Jonathan Livingston Seagull* (1970), an inspirational story of a bird in search of freedom and discovery. Though it was an allegorical tale and offered no direct prescriptive advice to readers, this wildly popular book drew on important themes such as friendship and courage. Leo Buscaglia's *Love* (1972) and M. Scott Peck's *The Road Less Traveled* (1978) addressed life lessons through essays and anecdotes. Restless readers in search of peace and reassurance used the books as springboards for conversation in book clubs and ministry clubs.

In 1974, actor and activist Marlo Thomas partnered with the *Ms.* Foundation for Women to create *Free to Be . . . You and Me*, a book about creativity and self-expression targeted specifically at children. Popular psychologist Dr. Joyce Brothers, newspaper advice writer Ann Landers, magazine editor Helen Gurley Brown, and singer Dale Evans all produced titles of self-help and self-improvement during the 1970's.

Impact While critics continued to bemoan self-help books' sometimes trite and oversimplified solutions to complicated problems, the American reading public continued to consume these personalized guides and to view them as models for negotiating the difficult challenges and anxieties associated with everyday life, even in decades following the 1970's. The self-help genre that seemed to mature during that decade laid secure groundwork for the genre both in print media and in television. Although some of the themes changed in subsequent years, late twentieth century self-help gurus, such as popular talk-show host Oprah Winfrey and later her adviser and protegé Dr. Phil McGraw, structured their televised advice around the same principles of attitude and willpower that had dominated the genre for more than half a century.

Further Reading

Anker, Roy M. *Self Help and Religion in Modern American Culture: An Interpretive Guide.* Westport, Conn.: Greenwood, 1999. The second of a two-part set, this volume examines the lives and works of key figures in the modern self-help movement.

Simonds, Wendy. *Women and Self-Help Culture: Reading Between the Lines.* New Brunswick, N.J.: Rutgers, 1992. Countering the traditional reading of self-help books as "whiny" and self-indulgent, Simonds argues that they are accessible and empowering.

Starker, Steven. *Oracle at the Supermarket: The American Preoccupation with Self-Help Books.* New Brunswick, N.J.: Transaction, 1989. A general overview of popular themes.

Jennifer Heller

See also Book publishing; *Everything You Always Wanted to Know About Sex but Were Afraid to Ask*; *Free to Be . . . You and Me*; *Hite Report, The*; *I'm OK, You're OK*; *Jonathan Livingston Seagull*; *Joy of Sex, The*; Literature in the United States; "Me Decade"; Miss Manners column; New Age movement; *Our Bodies, Ourselves*; *Passages.*

■ *Sesame Street*

Identification Children's television series
Date Debuted in 1969

Called "the largest educational experiment ever," Sesame Street *changed the concept of educational television and children's programming with its innovative content and style.*

Produced by Children's Television Workshop and aired on the newly established Public Broadcasting Service (PBS), *Sesame Street* was designed to teach preschool-age children, especially in inner cities, the basic knowledge of letters and numbers as well as social skills. It was a response to political and social concerns regarding a widening gap between the haves and have-nots in American society—a gap that became increasingly visible after the rise of the Civil Rights movement. In its initial years, the program was primarily funded by the Carnegie Corporation, the Ford Foundation, and the U.S. Department of Education.

Prior to *Sesame Street*, educational television programs were produced on a small and local basis and were shown in classrooms as part of instruction. However, as a product of a close collaboration between educators and television professionals who made up Children's Television Workshop, *Sesame Street* proved to be entertaining and high quality and was able to compete with other programs on commercial television.

Sesame Street's style and content were innovative. The show adopted the "kaleidoscope" approach—a succession of short sequences—that was first used in *Rowan and Martin's Laugh-In* and that was becoming popular in comedy and variety programs. In order to attract and keep children's attention, the show also used a variety of techniques, such as humor, slapstick, animation, and music and sound effects, all of which made segments resemble commercials. *Sesame Street*'s regular characters included the Muppets, which were puppets created by Jim Henson and given distinctive personalities. The Muppets not only made possible the portrayal of exaggerated roles and functions but also were likable enough to popularize the show. The human characters were also diverse. From the beginning, there were as many African American actors as there were white ones; Latino and Asian characters were later added to the regulars. In the mid-1970's, the show introduced a deaf librarian played by a deaf actress. The traditional gender role of passive females was broken by both the human characters and the Muppets.

Various educational groups, including the Educational Testing Service, measured the effectiveness of *Sesame Street* as a teaching tool and consistently proved that children who were regular viewers scored higher on tests than those who were not. *Sesame Street* thus broke the stereotype that educational instruction and entertainment were not compatible. By its second year, the program secured its place on a majority of PBS stations across the country and later became one of the few PBS programs that was able to sustain itself through the sale of merchandise and international coproductions, which began in 1971.

Impact *Sesame Street* convinced people that educational television did not have to be dull; there were ways to make televised teaching entertaining and effective. It also proved that television could be used as an effective teaching tool. Moreover, *Sesame Street* changed the popular perception of public broadcasting as "highbrow" fare.

Further Reading

Borgenicht, David. *Sesame Street Unpaved: Scripts, Stories, Secrets, and Songs.* New York: Hyperion, 1998.

Howe, Michael J. A. *Television and Children.* London: New University Education, 1977.

Palmer, Edward L. *Television and America's Children.* New York: Oxford University Press, 1988.

Yasue Kuwahara

See also Children's television; Education in the United States; Muppets, The; Public Broadcasting Service (PBS); *Schoolhouse Rock!*; Television in the United States; Variety shows.

■ Sexual revolution

Definition Period of significant change in cultural sexual values and practices

The sexual revolution was an era of broad changes in cultural attitudes toward sex, gender, and traditional values. It is generally defined as beginning during the 1960's and continuing into the 1970's and beyond.

In the early part of the twentieth century, the Western world witnessed developments that dramatically changed the lives of most people. Improvements in economies, changes in social customs, and shifting gender roles were transforming life in Western Europe and in North America. For the first time, women were going to work in factories, offices, and retail stores or going to college in order to pursue professional careers. The new freedom from parental supervision and tradition marked changing norms about sex and gender.

Growing numbers of opportunities for young unmarried adults to interact without the chaperonage of their elders evolved, and unsupervised interactions in the form of dating became popular. Sex was discussed more openly, young people were finding greater freedom from parental control, men and women could interact openly in public settings, love became a legitimate pursuit, and leisure became an acceptable goal at the end of a long workweek for both genders. These changes were not enthusiastically supported by everyone. The unprecedented freedom of middle-class youth was a threatening development to an older generation largely accustomed to traditional values.

Progress in birth control methods in particular was most controversial because it signaled a shift away from sex for procreation toward sex for pleasure. For the first time ever, during the 1960's, the contraceptive pill allowed women the freedom to explore sexuality without concerns for pregnancy.

Older generations lamented these threats to traditional values and to such institutions as marriage, the family, and religion. Prostitution and pornography were partly blamed for the breakdown of traditional morality. Prostitutes in particular became the symbol of degradation and sin, a belief that was only strengthened by medical advances in understanding sexually transmitted infections, or "social diseases" as they were euphemistically called. All these changes challenged existing sexual norms and signaled the beginning of a new era: the rise of "sexual liberalism."

Sexual Liberalism By the mid-1970's, cultural views of sex in North America were characterized by a growing emphasis on openness, freedom, and experimentation. Free love became a rallying call for a generation of young adults disillusioned with the system and with tradition. They challenged the existing rules as well as the government and authority, and they proclaimed the importance of unrestricted love. Moreover, along with love, they heralded uninhibited sexual experimentation. The growing availability and accessibility of contraception forcefully emphasized sex for fun instead of sex for a family. Other cultural trends, such as the greater freedom and independence of women, the increased availability of automobiles, and better economic conditions, played important roles in the shifting sexual norms.

The trends in the media, especially in films, novels, and theater, revealed that for the first time, sex was a daily staple of popular culture. The circulation of *Playboy* magazine reached one million copies by the late 1950's and peaked at six million by the early 1970's. On college campuses, students campaigned for an end to visiting hours in the dormitories, against college health centers' policies that withheld contraceptives from unmarried students, and against policies that prohibited female students from living off campus with males. Most universities eventually gave in, and it was during this time that coeducational, or "coed," dormitories were introduced.

Young adults were postponing marriage but not sexual initiation. Some married couples were even experimenting with open marriages and "swinging." For the first time, the double standard about acceptable sexual behavior for men and women was shifting toward more equality. In fact, the new sexual freedom changed the lives of women much more than it did for men.

Feminism, popularly known as the women's liberation movement, was also very influential in challenging the traditional gender roles. Mainstream feminism advocated political, social, and sexual equality for men and women. More radical feminists called for women to distance themselves from men, whom they perceived as the root of all problems for women. The other significant movement centered on gay rights: The gay liberation movement was born in New York City from a riot in 1969 following a police raid. Within a decade of the riot, it became the most visible and best organized homosexual movement in the world. Both of these movements powerfully challenged traditional morality and popular views of sex, love, and marriage.

Impact By the late 1970's, several disillusioned critics lamented the end of the sexual revolution. Clearly, the revolution had lost much of its momentum. The double standard was never completely eliminated, and many of the ideals about sex, gender, and sexual orientation never materialized. Some of the changes fostered by the sexual revolution became entrenched in American society, however. Premarital sex became viewed as acceptable under certain circumstances by the majority of people in Western cultures. Alternatives to marriage, including cohabitation, remained popular, while sexual themes continued to serve a significant part of a popular culture and media.

Further Reading

Allyn, David. *Make Love, Not War: The Sexual Revolution—An Unfettered History*. New York: Little, Brown, 2000. This book addresses the turbulence of the sexual revolution and the ensuing reexamination of values.

D'Emilio, John, and Estelle B. Freedman. *Intimate Matters: A History of Sexuality in America*. 2d ed. Chicago: University of Chicago, 1997. A detailed survey of sexual trends in the United States from 1600 to the present. The book is replete with excerpts from representative writings of different periods in history. One chapter is devoted to the "sexual revolutions."

Heidenry, John. *What Wild Ecstasy: The Rise and Fall of the Sexual Revolution*. New York: Simon & Schuster, 2002. The author, who was the *Penthouse* Forum editor for thirty years, offers a detailed overview of some of the events and trends prior to, during, and following the sexual revolution. With an admittedly prosexuality slant, Heidenry chronicles the trends in pornography, popular culture, and sexual minorities.

Richard D. McAnulty

See also Abortion rights; Cohabitation; *Everything You Always Wanted To Know About Sex but Were Afraid To Ask*; Feminism; *Hite Report, The*; Homosexuality and gay rights; *Joy of Sex, The*; Marriage and divorce; National Lesbian and Gay Rights March of 1979; Open marriage; Pornography; Swingers; White Night Riots; Women's rights.

■ Shange, Ntozake

Identification African American poet, dramatist, and novelist

Born October 18, 1948; Trenton, New Jersey

During the 1970's, Shange served as an influential woman writer who was inspired by the Black Arts Movement and who dramatized the difficult lives experienced by many African American women.

Ntozake Shange was born Paulette Williams to a well-to-do black family. Despite the advantages of her childhood, she was outraged by the discrimination against black women in the dominant white society, as well as by the often troubled relationships between African American men and women. Her African name, which translates as "she who brings her own thing" and "one who walks with lions," was chosen in 1971 to demonstrate the independence and strength that helped her recover from a painful divorce and several suicide attempts. Her dramatic work *for colored girls who have considered suicide/ when the rainbow is enuf* was a major theatrical breakthrough when it was first staged in New York City in 1975.

for colored girls who have considered suicide . . . was a dramatic sensation that marked a departure from traditional theater. Described as a "choreopoem," the play features seven women who take the stage to recite poetry, dance, and sing, expressing outrage at the way society has treated them and anger at the violence of the black men in their lives. A follower of the Black Arts Movement that began in the 1960's, Shange created her drama as a powerful revelation of the abuse and rape of black women at the hands of black men. These were not secrets of African American life, she claimed, but rather the truth that she believed was her responsibility as an artist to expose. Rebelling against the confinement of standard English, Shange's text is rooted in the African American oral tradition, abandoning conventional dramatic structure. Despite its explosive content, the play dramatizes the black woman's discovery of her individual strength and the power and joy of sisterhood.

Although she produced an extensive collection of poetry, as well as other plays and a novel, *for colored girls who have considered suicide* . . . is the work for which she is best known. The play sparked strong reactions among African Americans, some of whom found it unjustly critical of black men. However, most critics praised it as an imaginative and creative breakthrough in the literature of the theater.

Impact Shange was the second black female dramatist (after Lorraine Hansberry) whose work was given a major production in New York City. Her feminist themes and original use of language opened new possibilities for African American women writers whom she subsequently inspired. Her play *for colored girls who have considered suicide* . . . has been produced a number of times by other theater companies, proof of its lasting significance in the history of American theater.

Further Reading

Richards, Sandra L. "Ntozake Shange." In *African American Writers: Profiles of Their Lives and Works from the 1700's to the Present*, edited by Valerie Smith, Lea Baechler, and A. Walton Litz. New York: Charles Scribner's Sons, 1993.

Tate, Claudia, ed. "Ntozake Shange." In *Black Women Writers at Work*. New York: Continuum, 1983.

Marjorie Podolsky

See also African Americans; Black Arts Movement; Feminism; Literature in the United States; Poetry; Theater in the United States; Women's rights.

■ Shaw, Irwin

Identification American writer

Born February 27, 1913; New York, New York

Died May 16, 1984; Davos, Switzerland

Shaw wrote the 1970 novel Rich Man, Poor Man, *which became the basis for the first blockbuster miniseries on television.*

A prolific playwright, screenwriter, short-story writer, and novelist for five decades, Irwin Shaw achieved his greatest popularity and commercial success during the 1970's with the novel *Rich Man, Poor Man.*

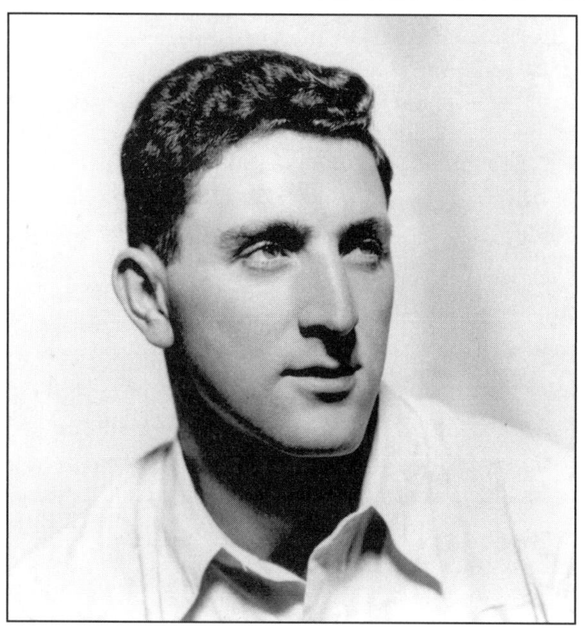

Irwin Shaw. (Library of Congress)

Published to mixed reviews, Shaw's novel nonetheless hit the best-seller list almost immediately and remained there for seven months. The work caught the attention of American Broadcasting Company (ABC) network executives who, aware of the success both of "made-for-television" shows on commercial stations and of imported British drama series on public television, began to consider the idea of an American miniseries. Shaw's novel, with its saga of the Jordache family, intense plot of sibling rivalry, and focus on the perennially popular theme of American success, seemed ideally suited for such a series. Shaw's agent, convinced that an American miniseries would never succeed, sold all rights to the novel to ABC and Universal Television for a meager sum. Universal then hired a veteran screenwriter and producer who spent two and a half years on the project, but ABC temporarily shelved the script and produced instead its first miniseries in April, 1974, based on the 1970 novel *QB VII* by Leon Uris.

Buoyed by the moderately positive reception of *QB VII*, ABC returned to Shaw's novel and reached a licensing agreement with Universal for the production of the miniseries *Rich Man, Poor Man.* The initial episode on February 1, 1976, astounded everyone by attracting approximately fifty million viewers, and subsequent episodes proved equally popular. The twelve-chapter miniseries became the second highest rated television show for the 1975-1976 television season and received twenty-two Emmy Award nominations, winning four. The impact was such that ABC immediately planned for a second season production called *Rich Man, Poor Man: Book Two,* and all of the major networks produced at least one miniseries the following year.

Although Shaw profited little from the television production of *Rich Man, Poor Man,* increased sales of the novel, as well as his other works, brought him fame and wealth. Ironically, the commercial success of Shaw in the 1970's paralleled and perhaps contributed to a lessening of his critical reputation. Acclaimed in previous decades as the author of excellent short stories as well as *The Young Lions* (1948), one of the great World War II novels, Shaw was increasingly attacked by literary critics for producing what they considered popular slick fiction.

Impact The adaptation of Irwin Shaw's novel *Rich Man, Poor Man* into a television miniseries made him one of the most popular and financially successful writers of the 1970's. More important, the miniseries earned an important place in television history by proving that the genre was economically viable in the United States. It prepared the way for the even more successful *Roots* (1977) and helped establish the miniseries as an integral part of American television.

Further Reading

Giles, James R. *Irwin Shaw.* Boston: Twayne, 1983.
Shnayerson, Michael. *Irwin Shaw: A Biography.* New York: G. P. Putnam's Sons, 1989.

Verbie Lovorn Prevost

See also Literature in the United States; Miniseries; *Roots*; Television in the United States.

■ Silkwood, Karen

Identification American union activist
Born February 19, 1946; Longview, Texas
Died November 13, 1974; near Crescent, Oklahoma

The mysterious death of Silkwood, a union activist who had protested for workplace safety, became a focus for the antinuclear and environmental movements.

In August, 1972, newly divorced Karen Silkwood took a job at oil company Kerr-McGee's Cimarron plutonium plant at Crescent, Oklahoma. She soon became active in the Oil, Chemical, and Atomic Workers (OCAW) union and took part in a strike that began in October, 1972. After the failure of the ten-week strike, only 20 of the 150 employees remained in the union.

Kerr-McGee scheduled a decertification election to strip the union of its collective bargaining status. Silkwood was elected to the union's three-person bargaining committee, assigned to study health and safety issues of which most employees had been unaware. The emphasis on health and safety issues worked: OCAW won the election by a vote of 80-61.

Kerr-McGee, behind schedule on a government contract for plutonium fuel rods, instituted twelve-hour shifts that increased the possibility of dangerous mistakes. Silkwood mysteriously became contaminated with plutonium residue in July, 1974, and she was required to submit weekly urine and fecal samples thereafter. In September, 1974, she went to Washington, D.C., to meet with OCAW officials. She disclosed that X rays showed dangerous hairline cracks in some rods and that data had been tampered with in order to conceal this fact. She was asked to work undercover to get conclusive evidence on this and other issues.

On November 5, Silkwood's hands showed a high level of contamination. The glove box she used was either leaky or had been deliberately dusted with plutonium. The hand contamination persisted, and she was subjected to painful scrubbing procedures. On November 7, it was determined that she had inhaled plutonium and that her apartment also was contaminated. A Los Alamos laboratory report confirmed a perhaps-fatal contamination.

She left a union meeting at 7 P.M., November 13, after showing a large manila folder with evidence against Kerr-McGee. On her way to meet with a reporter from *The New York Times* and a union official, her car crashed into an abutment, killing her instantly. The police ruled it an accident and said that her blood showed a high level of tranquilizers. Family and union investigators said there was no evidence that she had been asleep at the wheel. Her car had fresh dents in the rear, indicating that she may have been pushed off the road. Her evidence folder was not found.

Impact The Cimarron plant was closed the next year. All of Karen Silkwood's allegations later were confirmed by government investigations. Silkwood's father sued Kerr-McGee and was awarded a large settlement, which was later reduced on appeal and finally settled before a second trial in 1986 for $1.38 million. Meryl Streep played Silkwood in a popular 1983 film. Ultimately, Silkwood's death helped focus attention on environmental issues and of the possible dangers of nuclear power.

Further Reading

Kohn, Howard. *Who Killed Karen Silkwood?* New York: Simon & Schuster, 1981.

Rashke, Richard. *The Killing of Karen Silkwood: The Story Behind the Kerr-McGee Plutonium Case.* 2d ed. Ithaca, N.Y.: Cornell University Press, 2000.

J. Quinn Brisben

See also Antinuclear movement; Environmental movement; Environmental Protection Agency (EPA); Scandals; Streep, Meryl; Unions in the United States.

■ Simon, Neil

Identification American playwright
Born July 4, 1927; Bronx, New York

The 1970's were a decade of transition for Simon, who began the decade as a popular playwright whose work was viewed lukewarmly by theater critics. He subsequently found the theatrical formula that would ensure his critical acclaim following a period of personal turmoil and theatrical experimentation.

Neil Simon rose from humble origins as a television gag writer to become one of the best-known American playwrights of the twentieth century. Between early popularity and later critical acclaim, the plays he wrote during the 1970's were introspective, somewhat experimental, and somewhat successful.

In 1971, *The Prisoner of Second Avenue* opened on Broadway. This story of a middle-aged Manhattan married couple featured characters who were morose and disenchanted with city life. Despite positive reviews, critics rank the play low in the Simon pantheon.

The Sunshine Boys (pr. 1972) was both a tribute to vaudeville and a way for Simon to find solace as his wife succumbed to breast cancer. Shortly after *The Sunshine Boys* opened, Simon's wife died. Within a year, he married actor Marsha Mason and began an experimental phase of his career. In 1973, he adapted

Anton Chekhov's short stories to create *The Good Doctor.* Many playwrights had stumbled trying to put Chekhov onstage, and Simon did no better. The next year, he adapted the Old Testament story of Job for the stage in a play titled *God's Favorite*—another work that received lukewarm reception.

Simon followed with *California Suite* in 1976, which attempted to revive the comedic format that made his *Plaza Suite* (pr. 1968) an earlier hit. The sketches in *California Suite* deal with a variety of life situations faced by middle-aged couples. In addition to probing the humorous side of modern marriage and romance, Simon used the play to explore his attitudes toward Southern California.

Simon ended his productive decade with *Chapter Two* (pr. 1977). Simon had drawn on autobiographical topics in earlier plays, but the autobiographical references are much more numerous and serious in *Chapter Two.* The play featured a couple that was very similar to Simon and his second wife. As the play unfolds, it becomes apparent that the events of their previous marriages continue to haunt their attempts to start over and build their own loving and fulfilling marriage.

If *Chapter Two* had focused only on marriage, it would have been an important play, but not a major play. However, it reached major-play status because it was the first play in which Simon reflected extensively both on the art of writing and on his own philosophy of writing. Most important, he did so in a way that held the interest of the casual theater patron but included plenty of material for sophisticated theater critics to explicate and analyze.

Impact During the decade, Neil Simon created a lexicon of approachable American plays that depict common themes and situations with which audiences could easily relate. The plays he wrote during this period were not his best work, but they include flashes of brilliance that ensured their long-term reputation and success.

Further Reading

Bloom, Harold, ed. *Neil Simon.* Broomall, Pa.: Chelsea House, 2002.

Koprince, Susan. *Understanding Neil Simon.* Columbia: University of South Carolina Press, 2002.

Michael Polley

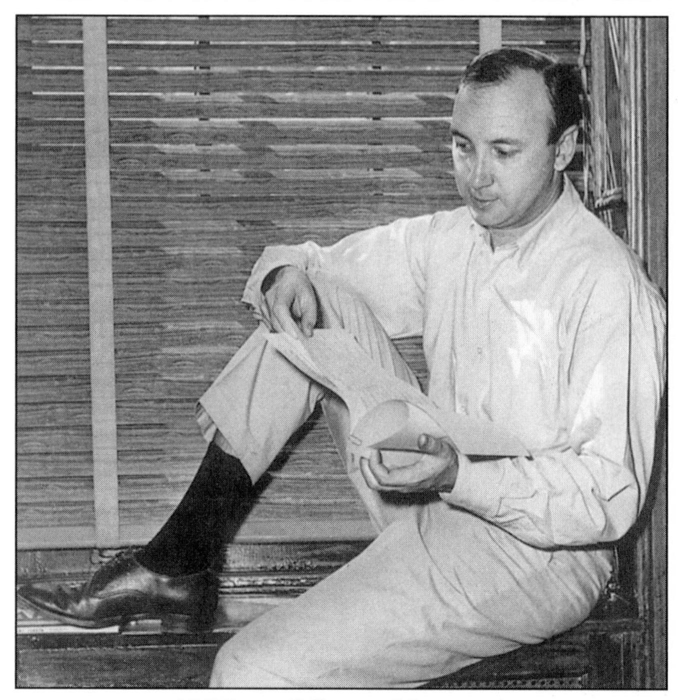

Neil Simon. (Library of Congress)

See also Broadway musicals; Theater in the United States.

■ Simpson, O. J.

Identification African American football player
Born July 9, 1947; San Francisco, California

Because of his success on the gridiron, Simpson is recognized as one of the greatest running backs in college and professional football history.

Orenthal James (O. J.) Simpson was recognized as one of the top running backs in college while playing for the University of Southern California (USC) in the late 1960's. He won the prestigious Heisman Trophy in 1968. In 1969, Simpson was the first selection in the National Football League (NFL) draft, being chosen by the Buffalo Bills. During his first three years in Buffalo, Simpson did not play a major role in the offense. When Lou Saban became the Bills head coach in 1972, however, the offense was centered around Simpson. As a result, he led the NFL in rushing in 1972, with 1,251 yards. In 1973, he became the first NFL player in history to run for more than 2,000 yards in a season, finishing the fourteen-game campaign with 2,003 yards.

In 1974, injuries slowed Simpson down, but he still ran for 1,125 yards. After healing, he ran for 1,817 yards and twenty-three touchdowns in 1975. In 1976, he led the NFL in rushing for the fourth time in five years, gaining 1,503 yards. Knee injuries limited his playing time to seven games in 1977. In 1978, he was traded to the San Francisco 49ers, where he ended his playing career in 1979. During his professional career, Simpson rushed for 11,236 yards and caught 203 passes for an additional 2,142 yards. He was selected as the most valuable player (MVP) of the NFL in 1975 and as the MVP of the American Football Conference (AFC) of the NFL in 1972, 1973, and 1975. Along with Terry Bradshaw and Walter Payton, Simpson was selected to the 1970's All-Decade Team by the Pro Football Hall of Fame Selection Committee members. In 1979, he began a successful career as a sports commentator and appeared in several television commercials.

Impact When O. J. Simpson retired from the NFL in 1979, he was number two on the all-time rushing list, with only Jim Brown ahead of him. Although Simpson's feat of eclipsing the 2,000-yard rushing mark in 1973 has been surpassed, only Simpson accomplished it in fourteen games. In 1985, he became the first Heisman Trophy winner to be elected to the Professional Football Hall of Fame. He is also a member of the College Football Hall of Fame, the Buffalo Sports Hall of Fame, and the Rose Bowl Hall of Fame.

Subsequent Events In 1994, Simpson was charged with the brutal slaying of his former wife, Nicole Brown Simpson, and her friend Ronald Goldman. Because of the circumstances and Simpson's fame, the ensuing trial was dubbed the "Trial of the Century." Simpson was found not guilty. Later, in a civil wrongful-death trial, he was found liable for the two deaths and ordered to pay $33.5 million in compensatory and punitive damages.

Further Reading

Davis, Don. *Fallen Hero: The Shocking True Story Behind the O. J. Simpson Tragedy.* New York: St. Martin's Press, 1994.

Smith, Donald R. *NFL Pro Football Hall of Fame All-Time Greats.* New York: Smithmark, 1988.

Alvin K. Benson

See also African Americans; Cosell, Howard; Football; *Monday Night Football*; Payton, Walter; Sports.

■ Singer-songwriters

Definition Artists who compose and sing reflective, lyric-based music

In the 1960's, Bob Dylan began writing and performing songs that introduced into popular music a new kind of lyrical complexity. As he continued his work during the 1970's, a generation of songwriting performers followed in his footsteps.

The singer-songwriters of the 1970's were an outgrowth of Dylan's radical transformation of songwriting in the 1960's. In an article in *Rolling Stone*, Robbie Robertson, guitarist and songwriter for the Band, wrote of Dylan, "Bob broke down the gates, opened up the sky to all of the possibilities of what a song could be." Robertson also commented on the important transformation that Dylan brought to the writing of lyrics: "His writing came directly out of a tremendous poetic influence, a license to write in images that weren't in the Tin Pan Alley tradition or typically rock and roll, either." Dylan made song lyrics vital in the same way that words were vital in poetry. As much as the Romantic poets in Great Britain during the nineteenth century became cultural icons, so too did the singer-songwriters of the decade become more than songwriters. They became important figures in the transformation of culture that began in the 1970's.

Dylan himself was the prototype for this transformation. Though he rarely gave interviews and carefully guarded his private life, the introspective quality of his lyrics fueled speculation about who and what he was. The Dylan mystique reached a fever pitch in the late 1960's because of his retreat from public life after his motorcycle wreck in July, 1966. When Dylan returned, reborn with a new country twang, his influence had created a new generation of songwriters who wrote and performed songs that chronicled their lives.

James Taylor's 1970 album *Sweet Baby James* took the music world by storm. Not only did it blend the folk music of Dylan's early material with the country sound of Dylan's present, but it also presented a life. The much-heralded song "Fire and Rain" was a biography of Taylor in three verses. The first verse disclosed the story of the death of a friend, the second verse detailed Taylor's heroin addiction, and the third verse ended with a reference to the breakup of Taylor's first band, the Flying Machine. When Taylor appeared on the cover of national magazines a year later, the word was out: His life could be read through his songs. Taylor's next album, *Mud Slide Slim and the Blue Horizon* (1971), contained a song titled "Hey Mister, That's Me up on the Jukebox," which quietly summarized the position of the singer-songwriter by including the lines "I'm the one that's singing this sad song, I'll cry every time that you slip in one more dime. . . ." It was clear to many music listeners that the music world had come many miles since Elvis Presley crooned "You ain't nothin' but a Hound Dog, cryin' all the time."

Characteristics Following the folk tradition, most singer-songwriters played acoustic instruments and wrote songs that were soft and melodic, unlike the pounding rock of the Rolling Stones or 1970's bands such as Led Zeppelin and Aerosmith. Though they used electric instruments to back up their own strumming or piano playing, the musicians never used instruments that were overpowering. Such a setting enabled the singer to place emphasis on lyrics and intonation as opposed to pounding drums and crashing cymbals.

Singer-songwriter James Taylor in 1972. (AP/Wide World Photos)

In their songs, singer-songwriters focused on personal dilemmas: the finding or losing of love, the search for meaning, or the degradation of war and injustice. Clearly etched in all these songs was the individual's attempt to confront reality in a meaningful way. A song became more than just a catchy melody, startling lyrics, or something to which people could dance. Songs began serving the function of literature or even religion. Pop songs became a source of growth and grounding for the generation of young people who came of age during the 1960's and 1970's.

Notable Performers Though there were far too many singer-songwriters during the 1970's to list all of them, some of the more important ones became significant forces in American popular music. Paul Simon left the very successful 1960's duo Simon and Garfunkel after their enormously popular album *Bridge over Troubled Water* (1970) and produced a stunning series of solo albums. Other musicians who had been important facets of 1960's rock bands also began solo careers or collaborated as singer-songwriting teams. Crosby, Stills, Nash, and Young was a merging of musicians from the Byrds, the Hollies, and Buffalo Springfield. Pooling their songwriting talents as well as their vocal and instrumental talents, the band became one of the major forces of early 1970's rock. Its multilayered harmonies added a new dimension to the vocal range of the singer-songwriter medium. Neil Young left the band to become a central figure in his own right, becoming one of the most enduring and influential singer-songwriters of the rock era.

Other musicians seemed to have been born to be singer-songwriters. Joni Mitchell had been an important part of the tradition since the mid-1960's. In songs such as "Woodstock" and "Both Sides Now," she helped to define the 1960's and the early 1970's. Jackson Browne's albums from the decade seemed to evoke every college student's encounter with the self. Browne's work brought the genre to its climax with lyrics that were so thoughtful and so poetic that they almost overpowered the vehicle of song.

Evolution of the Genre The singer-songwriter genre also contained the seeds of its own demise. Rock music fans have always valued the enormous energy implicit in rock and roll. However, a music that is based on rhythm and energy can contain only so much introspection, for introspection is, by its very nature, passive and quiet. The disco movement of the late 1970's represented a turn away from the poetic songs of the singer-songwriter. Moreover, the movement seemed to move toward mainstream rock because of the astounding success of singer-songwriter Bruce Springsteen.

A disciple of both classic rock and roll and Dylan, Springsteen could have been the new Dylan or the new Presley. When record company executives tried to market him as the classic singer-songwriter with his first album *Greetings from Asbury Park* (1973), they quickly realized the error of their ways. The next two albums created rock history, and their very titles demonstrate the return to the raw energy of rock: *The Wild, the Innocent, and the E Street Shuffle* (1973) and *Born to Run* (1975). Springsteen was as good a lyricist as anyone in the history of songwriting, but he could also tear the house down with the screaming, pulsating energy of live rock and roll. His performances were nothing short of stunning as he jumped on the piano, fell to the floor, or waltzed into the audience. It is no accident that Springsteen became one of the great singer-songwriter and rock-and-roll acts of the 1980's.

Notable Songs by 1970's Singer-Songwriters

Song	*Artist*
"Fire and Rain"	James Taylor
"Help Me"	Joni Mitchell
"Piano Man"	Billy Joel
"You've Got a Friend"	Carole King
"If You Could Read My Mind"	Gordon Lightfoot
"Tangled up in Blue"	Bob Dylan
"Wild World"	Cat Stevens
"Heart of Gold"	Neil Young
"Still Crazy After All These Years"	Paul Simon
"The Heart of Saturday Night"	Tom Waits
"The Pretender"	Jackson Browne
"Suite—Judy Blue Eyes"	Crosby, Stills, and Nash
"Anticipation"	Carly Simon
"Rocky Mountain High"	John Denver
"Year of the Cat"	Al Stewart

Impact The singer-songwriter tradition changed the nature of rock music. Into a music that had been primarily based upon pulsating energy and mindless rebellion, singer-songwriters introduced a depth and complexity of meaning that enabled music to serve the function of serious literature or even religion. Musicians such as Mitchell, Browne, Taylor, Simon, Young, Randy Newman, and others continued in subsequent decades to produce some of the finest songs in American music.

Further Reading

Charlton, Katharine. *Rock Music Styles.* Boston: McGraw-Hill, 1998. Delineates musical genres and discusses in detail the singer-songwriter category.

DiMartino, Dave. *Singer-Songwriters: Pop Music's Performer-Composers from A to Zevon.* New York: Simon & Schuster, 1994. Gives biographical information and discographies of important singer-songwriters.

Dylan, Bob. *Chronicles.* New York: Simon & Schuster, 2004. Dylan's memoirs.

H. William Rice

See also Denver, John; Joel, Billy; John, Elton; Manilow, Barry; Mitchell, Joni; Music; Progressive rock; Springsteen, Bruce.

■ Sirica, John J.

Identification Chief judge of the U.S. District Court in Washington, D.C., during the Watergate trials

Born March 19, 1904; Waterbury, Connecticut

Died August 14, 1992; Washington, D.C.

In his role as chief judge of the U.S. District Court for Washington, D.C., Sirica reinforced for the Nixon administra-

Judge John J. Sirica in 1973. (Dennis Brack/Landov)

tion and for the nation as a whole that the president was not above the law.

Judge John J. Sirica was one of several judges hearing cases related to the break-in at the Democratic National Headquarters in Washington, D.C., in June, 1972, and to the cover-up that followed. It was Judge Sirica who ruled that President Richard M. Nixon could not claim executive privilege—claiming something is necessary to protect national security—to hide from the court the substance of tape recordings from Oval Office conversations if those conversations had relevance to the trial.

Sirica grew up in a poor family in Connecticut. He never attended college but graduated from Georgetown University Law School and took the bar exam in 1926. He believed that he owed his start to the Republicans and so was a lifetime Republican who voted for Nixon in 1968.

When the first of the Watergate trials came to the U.S. District Court, Sirica, as chief judge, assigned it to himself. Although the defendants pleaded guilty to relatively minor charges, Sirica did not believe that the whole story had been revealed. Using his authority, he imposed provisional sentences and hoped that someone would decide to cooperate with the investigators, which is eventually what did occur.

The whole story came out piece by piece, both in the court and in Congress. Arguably the most significant evidence was the existence of tape recordings of Oval Office conversations. Although White House lawyers tried to keep them out of evidence on the basis of executive privilege, Sirica ordered that they be admitted into evidence. The tapes and subsequent testimony revealed that many aides in the White House had been directly involved in illegal activities related to the 1972 presidential election.

Impact John J. Sirica's interpretation of the law as it related to claims of executive privilege for the White House stood as the precedent in other cases. His conduct of the trials restored faith of a shaken country in the system of checks and balances on which the United States was established. President Nixon, in August, 1974, became the first president to resign from office.

Further Reading

Rochvarg, Arnold. *Watergate Victory: Mardian's Appeal.* Lanham, Md.: University Press of America, 1995.

Sirica, John. *To Set the Record Straight: The Break-in, the Tapes, the Conspirators, the Pardon.* New York: W. W. Norton, 1979.

Tracy E. Miller

See also Nixon, Richard M.; Nixon tapes; Nixon's resignation and pardon; Watergate.

■ Sitcoms

Definition Television comedy programs

Sitcoms of this decade commented on social and political movements, both through subject matter and through character types previously deemed taboo.

Situation comedies, or sitcoms, typically reflect and satirize the social norms and mores of everyday life. Prior to the 1970's, sitcoms primarily comprised nuclear families or fantasy scenarios, whose plots generally focused around family and the neighborhood. However, with the Vietnam War, Watergate, the Civil Rights movement, and economic uncertainty, everyday American life in the 1970's had changed. The 1970's sitcom reflected these changes through its characters and themes. The story lines of sitcoms made dramatic shifts from "safe" television family escapades to social movements actually having an impact on the country. Political criticism, gender and racial equality, the war, and the idea of what constituted a family became nightly themes on prime time.

Social Issues Perhaps the most revolutionary show of the 1970's was Norman Lear's *All in the Family*. Videotaped each week before a live studio audience, the show was set in blue-collar Queens, New York, and it became the first situation comedy to take on bigotry, prejudice, and politics in a sophisticated and satirical manner. Archie Bunker (played by Carroll O'Connor) is a reactionary bigot whom everyone loves to hate. His attentive wife, Edith (Jean Stapleton), although ditsy, seems better equipped to deal with the changing times. When Gloria (Sally

Popular Television Spin-Offs of 1970's Shows

A spin-off is a new television series that contains characters or theme elements from an old series. Spin-offs are particularly common in sitcoms.

Original program	*Spin-off(s)*	*Third-generation spin-off(s)*
Love, American Style (1969-1974)	*Happy Days* (1974-1984)	*Laverne and Shirley* (1976-1983) *Mork and Mindy* (1978-1982) *Joanie Loves Chachi* (1982-1983)
All in the Family (1971-1979)	*Maude* (1972-1978) *The Jeffersons* (1975-1985) *Archie Bunker's Place* (1979-1983) *Gloria* (1982-1983)	*Good Times* (1974-1979) *Checking In* (1981)
The Mary Tyler Moore Show (1970-1977)	*Rhoda* (1974-1978) *Phyllis* (1975-1977) *Lou Grant* (1977-1982)	
Diff'rent Strokes (1978-1985)	*The Facts of Life* (1979-1985)	
Alice (1976-1985)	*Flo* (1979-1980)	
Three's Company (1977-1984)	*The Ropers* (1979-1980) *Three's a Crowd* (1984-1985)	
The Six Million Dollar Man (1973-1978)	*The Bionic Woman* (1976-1978)	
*M*A*S*H* (1972-1983)	*After M*A*S*H* (1983-1984)	
The Carol Burnett Show (1967-1978)	*Mama's Family* (1983-1990)	

Struthers), their feminist daughter, returns home with her liberal, atheist fiancé, Mike Stivic (Rob Reiner), the political, racial, and religious slurs ensue. *All in the Family* proved that Americans were mature enough to handle a well-written topical comedy.

*M*A*S*H,* set in a military medical unit during the Korean War, showed the absurdities of war through the consternation experienced by characters in the operating tents. Through the use of experimental writing and film techniques, the series served as a comedic and honest comment on war's brutality and finality. One episode, "The Interview," simulated a 1950's documentary. For authenticity, the writers gave each cast member a question and a tape recorder. From their taped responses, the script was written. Shot in real time on black-and-white film, the camera took on the role of a wounded, scared soldier.

Minorities Prior to the 1970's, ethnic minorities were featured primarily in bit parts or cast stereotypically as servants on television. Sitcom casts of the 1970's included all ethnicities and covered topics never discussed before, such as poverty and racial inequalities in education and in the workplace. *Good Times,* a spin-off from *Maude,* depicted life for an African American family in a Chicago housing project. The father (John Amos) faces layoffs, the eldest son (Jimmie Walker) cannot find a job, and the youngest son (Ralph Carter) has difficulty in the community because he is a good student. The mother (Esther Rolle) has to hold the family together. Along with *Good Times, Sanford and Son*—featuring African American actors Redd Foxx and Demond Wilson portraying characters in the Watts neighborhood of Los Angeles—and *Chico and the Man*—featuring Freddie Prinze as Chico, a Latino car mechanic in East Los Angeles—presented a comic view of the hardships of life in the inner city.

The Jeffersons, a spin-off from *All in the Family,* depicted an African American family's assimilation into life in New York's Upper East Side though the success of their family business and the discrimination they encountered during their social climb. George Jefferson (Sherman Helmsley) is the African American version of Archie Bunker, an outspoken bigot who believes in hard work and racial segregation. George's belief system is challenged especially by neighbors Tom and Helen Willis (Franklin Cover and Roxie Roker), the first mixed-race couple to appear in a sitcom.

Feminism An explosion of sitcoms starring independent and intelligent women found their way into prime time during the 1970's. Shows such as *The Mary Tyler Moore Show* and its spin-off *Rhoda* revolved around career women (Mary Tyler Moore and Valerie Harper) who were more interested in finding their place in the world than in finding husbands. Episodes tackled workplace inequalities and social expectations.

Divorced characters became leading roles as well. *Maude,* starring Beatrice Arthur, featured a middle-age woman in her fourth marriage with an emotionally fragile alcoholic husband (Bill Macy) and a recently divorced daughter (Adrienne Barbeau), who returns home with her son. Revolutionary in its subject matter, *Maude* covered everything from abortion, to menopause, to marijuana laws. *One Day at a Time* focused on a divorced mother of two, Ann Romano (Bonnie Franklin), and her adjustment to life in the workplace.

The Family The definition of family also evolved and expanded as the decade progressed. Sitcoms featured blended families, as in *The Brady Bunch,* and extended families by marriage, as in the satiric *Soap. The Brady Bunch*'s themes were reminiscent of earlier "safe" programming, while *Soap*'s themes introduced U.S. audiences to homosexuality, senility, and criminal activity within the family.

The 1970's also introduced the workplace as a familial form, in which coworkers and friends take the place of traditional family members. Characters in sitcoms such as *M*A*S*H, The Mary Tyler Moore Show, Rhoda, Taxi,* and *Barney Miller* confide in their coworkers, and plots focus on issues in the workplace rather than those at home.

With topical commentaries, shocking plots, and outspoken characters taking over prime time, the 1970's also experienced a nostalgic throwback to the wholesome 1950's with shows such as *Happy Days* and *Laverne and Shirley.* Returning to traditional plots and characters, these shows offered familiarity and comfort during the unstable decade.

Impact Sitcoms of the 1970's changed the landscape of television. No longer restricted by social taboos, the plots of sitcoms became topical. Politics, war, gender equality, poverty, and racial struggles were given prominent focus in prime time.

The decade was revolutionary not only in what

was acceptable subject matter for comedies but also in who was acceptable as a character on the screen. There was an emergence of minorities in leading roles who faced prejudice, the struggle for equality, and economic hardships, with which families of all races found themselves confronted. Moreover, powerful modern women took on sexual inequalities in the workplace and tackled personal issues that affected real women across the country. Finally, there was a dynamic shift in the types of characters that found themselves on the networks. Viewers were introduced to homosexuals, divorcées, and nontraditional families who took taking the place of "safe" characters and nuclear families.

Further Reading

Barnouw, Erik. *Tube of Plenty.* 2d ed. New York: Oxford University Press, 1990. The ultimate resource book on the history of television.

Dow, Bonnie J. *Prime-Time Feminism: Television, Media Culture, and the Women's Movement Since 1970.* Philadelphia: University of Pennsylvania Press, 1996. Analyzes representations of women in television and covers *The Mary Tyler Moore Show* and *One Day at a Time* specifically from this decade.

Jones, Gerald. *Honey, I'm Home! Sitcoms, Selling the American Dream.* New York: Grove Weidenfeld, 1992. Provides contextual history for the rise of the sitcom and discusses the genre's influence on modern society.

Marc, David. *Comic Visions: Television Comedy and American Culture.* 2d ed. Malden, Mass.: Blackwell, 1997. Provides a critical history of situation comedies and includes a section on the 1970's.

Marc, David, and Robert J. Thompson. *Prime Time, Prime Movers: The Inside Story of the Inside People Who Made American Television.* Boston: Little, Brown, 1992. Describes the contributions to the medium made by top television producers and writers.

Marschall, Rick. *The History of Television.* New York: Gallery Books, 1986. Filled with photographs and brief descriptions of top shows from the 1970's.

Sara Vidar

See also *All in the Family*; *Brady Bunch, The*; *Chico and the Man*; *Happy Days*; *Jeffersons, The*; *Love, American Style*; *Mary Hartman, Mary Hartman*; *Mary Tyler Moore Show, The*; *M*A*S*H*; *Maude*; *Partridge Family, The*; *Sanford and Son*; *Taxi*; Television in the United States; *Three's Company.*

■ *Six Million Dollar Man, The*

Identification Television action series
Date Aired from 1973 to 1978

A popular series for much of the 1970's, The Six Million Dollar Man *combined an intriguing technological premise, based on actual cybernetic research, with story lines that evoked Cold War sensibilities by pitting the hero and the government agency he worked for against a variety of villains.*

Based on the novel *Cyborg* (1972) by Martin Caidin, *The Six Million Dollar Man* first appeared as a well-received television film in 1973, starring Lee Majors as Steve Austin, a test pilot who is rebuilt with a cybernetic arm, eye, and two legs after being critically injured in a plane crash. The original airing was followed by two additional television films later that year.

In 1974, the show was reinvented as an hour-long action series, and by the following year, it had earned a consistent spot in the top-ten Nielsen ratings. This success was fueled in part by the appearance of Lindsay Wagner as Jaime Sommers, Austin's love interest and bionic female counterpart who would later star in her own spin-off series, *The Bionic Woman*, from 1976 to 1978. The character of Oscar Goldman (played by Richard Anderson), Austin's boss, was also popular with audiences.

Audiences were very receptive to its action sequences, including the show's signature special effect of slow-motion capture with accompanying "bionic" sound to indicate when Austin was utilizing his cybernetic implants. They also liked the show's more emotional moments, such as when Austin, having difficulty adjusting to his new life, attempts suicide, or when Sommers loses her memory of her prior relationship with Austin, leaving him to deal with his now-unrequited love. This "lonely hero" characterization meshed well with the story lines in which Austin battled, or in some cases assisted, a wide variety of characters, including extraterrestrials and even Bigfoot. The contemporary rather than futuristic setting made the show accessible to more than the traditional science-fiction audience.

With gradually declining ratings and Majors's intention to leave the show, *The Six Million Dollar Man* was canceled in 1978. It remained popular enough, however, that three reunion films starring Majors, Wagner, and Anderson were aired during the 1980's and 1990's, and the show was also syndicated in both domestic and international markets.

Impact *The Six Million Dollar Man* appealed to a broad audience in the 1970's, with sympathetic characters, exciting technology, and action-oriented plots that often featured the hero defeating Cold War villains. It was particularly popular with younger viewers, many of whom regarded the bionic heroes as role models. The show eventually attained something of a cult status as evidenced by the publication of several tie-in novels, continued syndication, and follow-up television "reunion" films.

Further Reading

Muir, John Kenneth. "The Six Million Dollar Man." In *The Encyclopedia of Superheroes on Film and Television*, by John Kenneth Muir. Jefferson, N.C.: McFarland, 2004.

Phillips, Mark, and Frank Garcia. "The Six Million Dollar Man." In *Science Fiction Television Series: Episode Guides, Histories, and Casts and Credits for Sixty-two Prime Time Shows, 1959 Through 1989*, by Mark Phillips and Frank Garcia. Jefferson, N.C.: McFarland, 1996.

Amy Sisson

See also Science-fiction films; Television in the United States.

■ 60 Minutes

Identification Television newsmagazine program
Date Began airing in 1968

By the end of the 1970's, 60 Minutes *was one of the top-rated programs on network television. Its success proved television news could be popular and profitable while retaining its journalistic integrity.*

In 1970, *60 Minutes* was in its second season on the Columbia Broadcasting System (CBS) and continued to search for its identity. As conceived by producer Don Hewitt, the program was the broadcast equivalent of *Life* magazine, featuring stories that were shorter in form and more personal in tone than the typical television documentary. While critics praised the new newsmagazine program, *60 Minutes* finished last in the ratings at the end of 1970.

The show's correspondents began focusing on investigative journalism in the hope of attracting viewers. Morley Safer reported on the lack of gun control regulation and revealed how people were trying to avoid paying taxes by becoming ministers in a questionable church. Dan Rather exposed a corporation producing a toxic insecticide and a meat-packing company placing phony labels on its products. Mike Wallace showed how the Ford Pinto's gas tank could explode in a rear-end accident. The Pinto segment caused Ford Motor Company, one of the program's sponsors, to pull its ads for a week. These and other investigative reports proved popular with viewers and earned *60 Minutes* a reputation for tough, in-your-face journalism. Safer once joked that a crook did not feel he was really a crook until his story appeared on *60 Minutes.*

The program also benefited from a change in scheduling. *60 Minutes* initially aired on Tuesday nights, and in 1972, it moved to Sunday at 6 P.M. On December 19, 1976, the program began airing one hour later, competing with children's programs on rival networks. The 7 P.M. time slot gave *60 Minutes* a lock on the adult audience and a significant ratings boost.

By the end of 1979, *60 Minutes* placed among the ten highest-rated shows on television. The program was equally popular with advertisers. It became the first program in television history to retain the independence of a news show while garnering the income of an entertainment program.

Impact The commercial and popular success of *60 Minutes*, combined with the professional quality of its reporting, belied the conventional wisdom that television news shows could not be popular moneymakers and tout good journalism simultaneously. The show became a model for subsequent newsmagazine programs, such as *Dateline* and *20/20*. *60 Minutes* became the longest-running, regularly scheduled primetime broadcast in television history.

Further Reading

Blum, David. *Tick, Tick, Tick: The Long Life and Turbulent Times of "60 Minutes."* New York: HarperCollins, 2004.

Coffey, Frank. *"60 Minutes": Twenty-five Years of Television's Finest Hour.* Santa Monica, Calif.: General, 1993.

Hewitt, Don. *Tell Me a Story: Fifty Years and "60 Minutes" in Television.* New York: Public Affairs, 2001.

Jackman, Ian, ed. *Con Men: Fascinating Profiles of Swindlers and Rogues from the Files of the Most Success-*

ful Broadcast in Television History. New York: Simon & Schuster, 2003.

Rebecca Kuzins

See also Ford Pinto; Journalism in the United States; Scandals; Television in the United States.

■ Skateboards

Definition Short boards mounted on small wheels that are used for coasting

During the mid-1970's, skateboarding became an ongoing youth subculture that blended sports, music, and art. It originated in California and brought the ethos of surfing to the cityscape and suburbia.

The 1950's witnessed the introduction of a vehicle that resembled a small surfboard with four wheels mounted on an undercarriage, which allowed riders to "steer" the board by shifting their weight. By the end of the decade, these wheeled boards were associated with their waterborne counterparts, and skateboards benefited from the surf craze that swept the United States. Skateboards proved popular in the 1960's, but the use of clay wheels made them precarious to ride. Nonetheless, these early boards were the catalyst for the "sidewalk surfing" fad. The inherent instability of the design led to many accidents, however, as the wheels could disintegrate without warning, and sidewalk surfing gained a degree of infamy when some localities banned the activity. By the end of the 1960's, skateboarding had become an underground affair, and most of the companies that manufactured skateboards were bankrupt.

A California surfer, Frank Nasworthy, saw the potential for polyurethane wheels and began marketing them in San Diego in 1970. Within three years, his company, Cadillac Wheels, and the polyurethane wheel were responsible for the resurgence of skateboarding. Other companies marketed improved wheel carriages, or trucks, which enhanced rider control. Two years later, the Road Rider Company introduced the precision-bearing wheel, which com-

Young skateboarders in Los Angeles in 1975. (AP/Wide World Photos)

pleted the modern skateboard. The 1960's magazine *SkateBoarder* was brought back in 1975, and the following year saw the opening of the nation's first skate park in Florida.

Initially, skateboard competitions were timid affairs with riders judged on their ability to maneuver their boards in a fashion reminiscent of figure skating. However, the appearance of several California skateboarders in the mid-1970's would change the sport forever. At an otherwise tame competition, Jay Adams exhibited moves that outraged judges and revolutionized skateboarding. Gone was the staid riding style in which riders stood up and gently maneuvered their boards. Adams and others, such as Stacy Peralta and Tony Alva, rode their boards like surfboards and made the concrete their ocean surf.

The look of the boards changed when Dogtown boards appeared with graphics, and soon the look was de rigueur. When Alan Gelfand introduced the "Ollie," an aerial move in which the rider did not hold onto the board, in 1978, he moved skateboarding to the next level. Adams, Alva, Peralta, and others, known collectively as "Z-Boys," further revolutionized the sport with pool riding. Lacking skate parks in the Los Angeles area, they skated in empty swimming pools, often without the homeowner's consent. Their adventures were documented in the photographs of Glenn E. Friedman and the writings of C. R. Steyk III in *SkateBoarder*, which nurtured the skateboarding scene across the United States and globally.

Impact Skateboarding became one of the 1970's most lasting contributions to American youth culture. The sport mixed rebellion, creativity, and artistic expression with physical agility and created a sensation across the country. By the end of the decade, skateboarders adopted the new music and culture of punk rock and, in the process, fashioned the sport's most enduring style and image.

Further Reading

Brooke, Michael. *Concrete Wave: The History of Skateboarding*. Toronto: Warwick, 1999.

Davis, James, and Skin Phillips. *Skateboarding Is Not a Crime: Fifty Years of Street Culture*. New York: Firefly Books, 2004.

Friedman, Glenn E., and C. R. Steyk III. *DogTown: The Legend of the Z-Boys*. New York: Burning Flag's Press, 2002.

Paul D. Gelpi, Jr.

See also Fads; Hobbies and recreation; Roller skating.

■ Skylab

Identification First U.S. space station
Date Launched on May 14, 1973

The first successful space station was instrumental in studying the effects of long-term space missions on human beings, as well as providing vital information about Earth and the solar system.

The concept of a space station was discussed in the early 1960's. With the success of the moon landings in the late 1960's, the National Aeronautics and Space Administration (NASA) decided to follow up on the goal of space exploration by using spare Apollo hardware to develop an orbiting space station or workshop. Skylab would be used to study Earth and the Sun, weightlessness, and human reaction to space, among other experiments. Of special importance was the study of the long-term effects of weightlessness because the astronauts on early spaceflights had suffered bone tissue loss, and future missions would depend upon controlling or eliminating this loss.

The Missions Before 1973, only three of forty-five space missions had lasted fourteen days or more. Skylab 1, the space station, was launched crewless into orbit on May 14, 1973. Skylab 2 launched on May 25, 1973, with commander Charles "Pete" Conrad, Jr., pilot Paul J. Weitz, and science pilot Joseph Kerwin. They took pictures of Earth and the Sun and actually snapped the first good pictures of a solar flare, in addition to completing metallurgy and welding tests. After twenty-eight days in space, the crew landed safely in the Pacific Ocean on June 22, 1973. The crew took three weeks to recover and readjust to gravity, and all experienced bone loss.

On June 28, 1972, Skylab 3 launched with commander Alan Bean, pilot Jack R. Lousma, and science pilot Owen K. Garriott. Their mission lasted more than eight weeks. The crew completed forty-eight separate runs of Earth observations, filming large areas of the United States and twenty-eight countries. They also took pictures of coronal mass ejections from the Sun, the first ever seen by humans, and tested jet pack designs that were supposed to help astronauts maneuver in space. After fifty-nine days in space, twice as long as any other mission, the crew returned on September 25, 1973. Because of longer daily workouts, the crew was back to normal in about a week. However, they had lost 25 percent of their strength in the leg muscles and experienced bone loss.

Skylab 4 launched on November 16, 1973, with commander Gerald Carr, pilot William R. Pogue, and science pilot Edward G. Gibson. The crew planned to stay twelve weeks and returned on February 8, 1974, after eighty-four days in space. This record lasted worldwide for four years and for more than twenty years for an American. Although the crew recovered faster physically than the other crews, it still took them weeks to readjust mentally to gravity. They did not lose as much muscle mass in their legs, but they still had bone loss.

The three crews, totaling nine men, were on Skylab for a total of 171 days between May 25, 1973, and February 8, 1974. They accomplished nearly three hundred experiments in science, medicine, and engineering. Skylab was the last time Americans were in space until the space shuttle flew in 1981.

Skylab in orbit. (NASA)

Skylab was expected to be in orbit until 1981 or 1982, but its orbit decayed faster than planned because of high solar activity. After 34,981 orbits, the space station reentered Earth's atmosphere on July 11, 1979, scattering pieces into the Pacific Ocean and the Outback of western Australia on July 12.

Impact Experiments conducted on Skylab included astrophysics on the earth's atmosphere, comets, the Milky Way, and galaxies; material science and space manufacturing to use electrostatic and magnetic forces without contamination, the results of which were used in the electronics industry and for computer chip production applications; and engineering and technology in order to understand how people perform in space, which tools work best, and the effects of radiation. Moreover, student experiments were chosen from high school student proposals, which encouraged interest in space among young Americans. Habitability, which evaluated living and working conditions in space, was also considered, as was the way in which people adapted to low gravity for long periods of time. A major focus, however, remained how to increase the duration of spaceflight without causing irreversible damage to the astronauts' health and ability to function.

Information from the experiments during the Skylab missions transformed the study of solar astronomy. Additionally, the data from the earth observations, including ocean surfaces, erosion, ice, snow, flooding, vegetation changes, and hurricanes and storms, helped make the public more interested in the environment and the effects of pollution. The results of the experiments provided useful information on forestation and land features, which helped in mineral and resource prospecting. Furthermore, the information on the water cycle was used for forecasting floods and droughts.

Subsequent Events Information obtained during the Skylab missions was used as the basis for all subsequent space stations. The Soviets dominated space exploration from 1974 to 1986 with Salyut space stations. These stations were smaller but provided a great deal of experience, with the longest mission lasting 237 days in 1984. The Soviet Mir program lasted from 1986 to 2000. Soviets and Americans continued to cooperate on spaceflights, and seven Americans were on Mir from 1995 until 1998. The same problems encountered by Skylab astronauts were experienced during the Mir missions: scheduling crew time, maintaining adequate communications, and balancing activities such as research, repair, maintenance, exercise, sleep, and eating.

Further Reading

Crouch, Tom D. *Aiming for the Stars: The Dreamers and Doers of the Space Age.* Washington, D.C.: Smithsonian Institution Press, 1999. Provides an overall history of space exploration from the sixteenth through the twentieth centuries.

Shayler, David J. *Skylab: America's Space Station.* Bodmin, Cornwall, England: MPG Books, 2001. A very detailed account of the development, missions, and legacy of Skylab.

Zimmerman, Robert. *Leaving Earth: Space Stations, Rival Superpowers, and the Quest for Interplanetary Travel.* Washington, D.C.: Joseph Henry Press, 2003. Includes U.S. and Soviet achievements and endeavors from the 1950's to 2000.

Virginia L. Salmon

See also Apollo space program; Astronomy; Environmental movement; National Air and Space Museum; Pioneer space program; Soviet Union and North America; Space exploration; Viking space program; Voyager space program.

■ Slogans and slang

Definition Popular linguistic innovations, embraced by many speakers but not accepted as standard by language authorities

Popular terms and expressions during the 1970's revealed a holdover of 1960's speech patterns, but more important, they demonstrated the effect of popular trends in entertainment and recreation as well as various changes of attitude toward sexuality and gender on American English.

Slang and catchphrases arise primarily from three sources: adaptations (old words that have been in use in North American English for centuries and take on new or specialized meanings), cultural or social expansions (terms that have previously been popular only in certain sectors of the population and move into mainstream English), and innovations (phrases created from older words or wholly created from scratch).

Many slang terms from the 1960's were maintained during the 1970's, especially in the speech of the young. For example, "groovy" and "boss" were used as terms of approval; "bread" as a colloquial term for money; and assorted drug-related words such as "grass" for marijuana, "snow" for cocaine, and "horse" and "smack" for heroin.

However, an interesting trend began to develop during the 1970's that continued in subsequent decades: a tendency to shorten two-word phrasal verbs, or those that take two or more words to convey their primary meaning, including "to pass out," "to show up," and "to come to." A number of phrasal verbs that had developed in the 1960's began to convert to a one-word format. "To hang out," meaning to frequent or stay in a given place, became simply "to hang"; "to freak out," meaning to lose control of one's emotions, became "to freak"; and "to chill out," meaning to calm down or relax, became "to chill." This casting off of the final element of the verb may have resulted from a desire on the part of young people to sound less like their counterparts in the 1960's, when many phrasal verbs and nouns, such as "love-in" and "be-in," were used extensively.

Entertainment and Recreational Terms Fads in entertainment and more serious changes in attitudes toward sex and gender also influenced speech patterns of the decade. Two trends of the 1970's that contributed heavily to slang of the era were citizens band (CB) radio and disco music. CB radio had been employed by truck drivers and a small cult of "ham" operators for decades, but in the 1970's, a craze for these communicating devices—fueled by songs, films, and television series about truck drivers—resulted in people from all walks of life installing CB radios in their cars and spending hours chatting with people through them. Some of the expressions that flooded popular English usage from the CB subculture were "good buddy" (term of address), "handle" (pseudonym adopted by a CB user), "smokey" (uniformed official of the law, short for "Smokey the Bear"), and "10-4" (a code-number indicating a message was understood and that no problems had arisen).

From the culture surrounding music, the most important language innovation at the time was the change in the term "discotheque." Originally a French word designating a club in which people danced to records rather than to live music, the clipping derived from it, disco, came to convey something very particular—not only a shortened word but also a style of dance music that featured a very simple, very repetitive beat with lyrics that typically extolled the joys of dancing.

Changing Gender Roles Issues of gender and sexuality that concerned people of the 1970's were manifested in the colloquial language of the era as well. Influenced by feminist thought, many people attempted to use gender-neutral language—for example, "letter carrier" rather than "mailman"—and language showing greater respect for the equal role of women in society by avoiding belittling, derogatory slang terms from previous generations such as "doll," "gal," and "broad."

In the homosexual community, "buns" for "buttocks" and "hunk" for "a handsome man" had been in use for decades, but in the 1970's, these terms began to emerge into wider usage among people of all sexual orientations. Also during this period, the word "gay" as a synonym for "homosexual" first came into widespread usage after decades—some suggest centuries—of underground usage.

Slogans from the Media Since their inception, film and television have added slang to North American English and promulgated the use of new words and phrases. However, the 1970's seemed to be a decade in which media were especially influential. For example, following the hugely successful reception of the film *Star Wars* by the public in 1977, American English added the term "droid," clipped from "android," a Greek-derived word meaning a humanlike robot.

More influential, however, was television, which unleashed into contemporary usage a number of catchphrases from various popular series of the time. From *Good Times*, a comedy about inner-city life in Chicago, comedian Jimmie Walker's explosive exultation of approval, "Dy-no-mite!" was echoed by young people during the show's run. Likewise, the befuddled outcry of child-performer Gary Coleman, star of the National Broadcasting Company (NBC) network's *Diff'rent Strokes*, "Whatch you talkin' about, Willis?" was endlessly mimicked. A curious addition, however briefly, to the American slang lexicon of pejorative phrases was a coinage of the staff of the hit comedy series *Happy Days*, set in the 1950's. Unable to use earthy, authentic expressions of insulting dismissal, the scriptwriters coined the saucy imperative "Sit on it!," which entered and stayed in American colloquial usage for the length of the show's run.

Impact Slang tends to be ephemeral. CB jargon retreated quickly back into its own special interest group, and 1970's television-derived slogans faded as soon as the programs that spawned them were canceled. However, two trends from the 1970's remained in effect in the colloquial speech of Americans long after the 1970's: the one-word equivalents of phrasal verbs and the linguistic changes brought about by the impact of feminism and gay culture.

Further Reading

McCleary, John. *Hippie Dictionary: A Cultural Encyclopedia of the 1960's and 1970's.* New York: Ten Speed Press, 1985. Provides many articles that relate to language of these decades in some way.

Partridge, Eric. *A Dictionary of Slang and Unconventional English.* 8th ed. New York: Macmillan, 1985. A definitive volume on slang in English usage of any decade.

Rollin, Lucy. *Twentieth-Century Teen Culture by the Decades.* Westport, Conn.: Greenwood Press, 1999. Offers a thorough examination of the language patterns of each decade's young people.

Thomas Du Bose

See also CB radio; Disco; Fads; *Happy Days*; Homosexuality and gay rights; *Star Wars*; Television in the United States.

■ Smallpox eradication

The Event Worldwide elimination of a dreaded disease

Date Announced on October 26, 1979

Smallpox, among human history's greatest killers, was declared eliminated by the World Health Organization (WHO).

Among humanity's oldest diseases, smallpox killed some 400,000 persons each year in Europe during its peak epidemic years in the seventeenth and eighteenth centuries. It was long recognized that those who survived such illness remained immune to further infection if subsequently exposed to the disease. Near the end of the first millennium C.E., the Chinese began the practice of variolation, a procedure in which dried crusts from pocks were inhaled or inoculated under the skin. The practice subsequently made its way to Europe and Great Britain. While variolation carried its own inherent dangers, it still remained the safest method to protect against smallpox well into the eighteenth century.

In the 1790's, Edward Jenner, a country medical doctor in Great Britain, noted that women who had infections of a mild illness called cowpox appeared immune to smallpox infection. In 1796, he tested the idea by first immunizing several individuals with samples of cowpox material, followed by exposure to liquid prepared from the pocks from cases of smallpox. When the experiment proved successful, Jenner subsequently inoculated others with cowpox material. Since the material had been obtained from cows, the procedure became known as vaccination (*vacca* means "cow" in Latin).

Though the source of the material was modified in subsequent years, the procedure remained similar to that first used by Jenner. A viral disease, smallpox has no natural reservoir other than humans; consequently, both endemic and epidemic disease requires the constant movement of the virus from person to person. In 1950, Fred Soper, director of the Pan American Sanitary Bureau, proposed at a meeting of the WHO that a program be started with the goal of eliminating smallpox from the Western Hemisphere; the program proved to be successful within the decade. A similar proposal was presented to the WHO in 1958 by V. M. Zhdanov for global eradication and was accepted.

In the mid-1960's, the eradication program was begun. The procedure involved attempts to isolate and contain localized outbreaks. Rewards were offered for anyone reporting a case of the disease. Within ten years, the program proved highly successful, with the last natural case being diagnosed in Somalia on October 26, 1977, in a hospital cook named Ali Maow Maalin. In a ceremony held in Nairobi, Kenya, on October 26, 1979, the second anniversary of the last case, Dr. Halfdan Mahler, the director of the WHO, announced the eradication of the disease.

Impact When the WHO began its global campaign to eliminate smallpox, the disease had already become rare in industrialized countries—the final U.S. outbreak occurred in Texas in 1949—and throughout the Western Hemisphere—the last case was recorded in Brazil in 1971. Smallpox was endemic only in parts of Africa and India. The successful eradication of smallpox was viewed as a model and created optimism that the same result could be achieved for other diseases.

Subsequent Events The threat of bioterrorism, following the terrorist events of September 11, 2001, resulted in President George W. Bush ordering some 500,000 members of the military to undergo required smallpox vaccination. Emergency health care personnel required in the event of a biological emergency were also recommended to undergo a similar procedure.

Further Reading

Behbehani, Abbas. "The Smallpox Story: Historical Perspective." *ASM News* 57, no. 11 (1991): 571-576.

_______. "The Smallpox Story: Life and Death of an Old Disease." *Microbiological Reviews* 47, no. 4 (1983): 455-509.

Richard Adler

See also Cancer research; Genetics research; Legionnaires' disease; Medicine.

■ Smoking and tobacco

Definition A major public health issue and an important industry

During the 1970's, a nonsmokers movement demanded "no-smoking" zones and limits on advertising. The public health community also advocated greater government regulation of cigarettes while continuing to educate Americans on the health risks of smoking and offering them methods to quit.

Americans have had a long love-hate relationship with smoking and tobacco. When Christopher Columbus discovered the New World in 1492, his crew took up the Native American habit of chewing and smoking tobacco. Subsequently, physicians debated whether smoking was healthy or unhealthy. By the late nineteenth century, as cigarettes became widespread, the pendulum swung toward a massive antismoking prohibition movement. Many states banned the sale of cigarettes, although legislatures and courts later repealed or nullified these acts. Nonetheless,

U.S. surgeon general Julius B. Richmond addresses a rally to kick off the third annual Great American Smokeout, a day for quitting smoking, in 1979. (AP/Wide World Photos)

the suspicion that smoking was unhealthy gathered support when medical researchers in the 1950's linked smoking to lung cancer, heart disease, and death. The Surgeon General's Report of 1964 concluded that "cigarette smoking is a health hazard of sufficient importance in the United States to warrant appropriate remedial action."

The government and the public health community adopted measures that continued to influence smoking and tobacco policy during the 1970's, including health education, restrictions on advertising, and the development of "less hazardous," or low-tar, cigarettes. In addition, the 1970's brought an important new social trend: the rise of the militant nonsmoker. Despite these trends, the tobacco industry continued to prosper.

Health Education By the 1970's, most states already required education about the ill effects of smoking. Three voluntary health associations—the American Cancer Society, the American Lung Association, and the American Heart Association—played an active role in educating adults and youth with the help of free public service announcements on radio and television. These organizations also offered quit-smoking clinics and educational material on how to "kick the habit." In 1977, the American Cancer Society launched the first "Great American Smokeout," an annual holiday from smoking.

The federal government publicized the health risks of smoking through regular publication of Surgeon General reports. Two reports from the 1970's had an extraordinary impact: the 1972 and 1979 publications. The 1972 report suggested that "passive smoke" might endanger nonsmokers. This statement inspired nonsmoking activists to demand "Clean Indoor Air Acts"—Minnesota passed the first such law in 1975—and no-smoking zones in public spaces. Federal agencies designated no-smoking areas on airplanes in 1973, on interstate buses in 1974, and in government buildings in 1979. The nonsmoking movement also spawned militant groups inspired by the success of consumer activist Ralph Nader: Action on Smoking and Health (ASH) and Group Against Smokers' Pollution (GASP).

The 1979 report aided Health, Education, and Welfare secretary Joseph Califano's aggressive campaign against smoking. The most comprehensive report ever, the 1979 volume contained research on nicotine addiction. Califano used the report to buttress his widely publicized contention that smoking was "public health enemy number one."

Restrictions on Cigarette Advertising Starting in 1966, restrictions on cigarette advertising included mandatory warning labels on packages that read "Caution: Cigarette Smoking May be Hazardous to Your Health." In 1970, Congress changed the label to "Warning: The Surgeon General Has Determined that Cigarette Smoking is Dangerous to Your Health." This warning appeared in advertising beginning in 1972.

A 1967 ruling by the Federal Communications Commission (FCC) required radio and television stations to provide free air time to health associations to counterbalance cigarette advertising. This ruling effectively ended on January 2, 1971, when Congress banned all cigarette advertising from radio and television. Tobacco companies continued to advertise through print media and sponsorship of sports events, including the Virginia Slims Tennis Tournament, which was established in 1971 and tied smoking to the women's movement by using the slogan You've Come a Long Way, Baby.

Low-Tar Cigarettes Public health officials encouraged government- and industry-sponsored research to develop low-tar cigarettes. In 1967, the Federal Trade Commission began reporting the tar and nicotine levels of brand-name cigarettes. During the 1970's, cigarette companies aggressively marketed low-tar brands. The issue turned controversial in 1978, however, when Gio Gori, the head of the Tobacco Working Group (TWG), a government-industry body devoted to "less hazardous" research, declared that smoking ultra low-tar cigarettes posed a "tolerable" risk to health. The ensuing furor resulted in Califano shutting down the TWG. The new federal policy was "just say no" to smoking.

Impact The 1970's were watershed years for the antismoking movement. The nonsmokers movement continued to expand based on the argument that "passive smoke" hurts innocent bystanders. Politicians and public health officials advocated further regulation of cigarette advertising and other business practices.

Subsequent Events Further regulations in subsequent decades included new warning labels, more public smoking bans, a 1998 settlement that limited the marketing of cigarettes, and increased litigation. Moreover, the "just say no" philosophy continued to dominate public health discussions on the topic. The industry prospered, however, by diversifying and passing the costs of regulation, taxation, and litigation on to the consumer.

Further Reading

Fritschler, A. Lee, and James M. Hoefler. *Smoking and Politics: Policy Making and the Federal Bureaucracy.* 5th ed. Upper Saddle River, N.J.: Prentice Hall, 1996. Useful guide to changing federal policies toward smoking and tobacco.

Glantz, Stanton A., et al., comp. *The Cigarette Papers.* Berkeley: University of California Press, 1996. Compilation of internal tobacco industry documents from the 1950's to the 1980's. Provides highly polemical commentary.

Gori, Gio B. *Virtually Safe Cigarettes: Reviving an Opportunity Once Tragically Rejected.* Amsterdam: IOS Press, 2000. Chronicles the history of the Tobacco Working Group, the body responsible for developing "less hazardous" cigarettes.

Kluger, Richard. *Ashes to Ashes: America's Hundred-Year Cigarette War, the Public Health, and the Unabashed Triumph of Philip Morris.* New York: Knopf, 1996. Pulitzer Prize-winning history of the tobacco industry, discussing all aspects of smoking and tobacco.

Ross, Walter Sanford. *Crusade: The Official History of the American Cancer Society.* New York: Arbor House, 1987. Discusses the contributions of the American Cancer Society in educating Americans about the health risks of smoking.

Jonathan J. Bean

See also Advertising; Cancer research; Cigarette advertising ban; Health care in the United States; Nader, Ralph; Television in the United States; Women's rights.

■ Soccer

Definition Team sport known as football outside North America

After soccer's long and tortuous quest for popularity in North America, the mid-1970's appeared to be the era when the sport finally arrived. Soccer started to win wide acceptance during that decade, but its success was merely illusory, and it would take another two decades for soccer to grow more permanent roots.

Although soccer is perceived as relatively new to North America, its roots in the United States and Canada go back to the mid-nineteenth century. During the many decades leading up to the 1970's, soccer quietly flourished as a college, club, and semiprofessional sport throughout North America, particularly in the East. The 1960's brought two new developments that would change the face of the North American game. The first was the launching of a youth soccer movement that would eventually make soccer the most popular team sport among children and introduce to the language the term "soccer mom." The second development was a major effort to professionalize the game.

The founding of the American Youth Soccer Organization (AYSO) in Southern California in 1964 began a steadily accelerating growth of the game throughout the United States. By 1979, the AYSO could claim more than 200,000 enrolled players spread out over more than 220 regions—numbers that would triple by the end of the century. The increased participation of youths in AYSO and other soccer organizations was a sea change during the 1970's, but the impact of this new generation of native-born Americans players would not be felt until the 1990's, when American-born players began having an impact on the world game. Meanwhile,

Brazilian soccer star Pelé delivers a farewell speech to the crowd gathered at Giants Stadium on October 1, 1977, to see his final match. (DPA/Landov)

the creation of new professional leagues in during the late 1960's would have a more immediate impact on the game.

The Coming of Professional Leagues It is generally conceded that the first "international" soccer games were matches played among British teams representing England, Scotland, Ireland, and Wales in the mid-nineteenth century. Less well known is the fact that the first international matches between truly national teams were played by Canada and the United States during the mid-1880's. Over the ensuing century, soccer developed at several levels in both Canada and the United States, and both nations became full participants in the international sport.

In 1967, after decades of failing to develop beyond what were at best minor-league levels, professional soccer received a double jolt in the United States with the sudden creation of two rival leagues: the United Soccer Association (USA) and the National Professional Soccer League (NPSL). The world governing body of soccer, the International Federation of Association Football (FIFA), insisted that the leagues merge, which they did that same year. The combined body became the North American Soccer League (NASL). Aptly named, the new league included the Vancouver Canadians during its first season. Other Canadian cities later to join the league included Calgary, Edmonton, Montreal, and Toronto.

Until the league folded in 1984, it had what must have been one of the most peculiar histories of any major sports league in American history. To say that the league lacked stability would be an understatement. Over the course of its eighteen seasons, the league saw a bewildering succession of changes in team owners, locations, and names, as well as a revolving door of expansion teams and folding teams. More than forty cities saw NASL teams come and go. The league was so volatile that during its first ten seasons, ten different teams won its championship.

Boom and Bust In 1975, the NASL appeared to reach the threshold of gaining stability when its flagship team, the New York Cosmos, signed the legendary Brazilian player Pelé to a three-year contract. Pelé brought instant credibility to the league, and other international stars soon followed his example. During Pelé's three seasons with the Cosmos, league attendance rose dramatically—especially in games in which Pelé himself played. In 1977, the league signed its first major contract with a television network. The league's popularity crested that same year, when Pelé played his farewell game at Giants Stadium—an exhibition match between the Cosmos and Pelé's former Brazilian team, FC Santos. More than seventy-seven thousand people packed Giants Stadium for the game, which was televised in thirty-eight countries.

After Pelé's retirement, interest in the NASL gradually faded, and the league dissolved in 1984. Several teams hung on by joining the new Major Indoor Soccer League (MISL), but the professional outdoor game remained dead until the mid-1990's. The league's failure can be traced to shaky leadership and insufficient capitalization. Soccer suffered from something like a split personality in North America. Its historical roots were deep, but they were based primarily among immigrants, whose love of the sport reflected its popularity outside North America. Most Americans were unfamiliar with the game and saw it as something alien, possibly even un-American.

The obvious impact that Pelé had on the NASL convinced many owners that the key to success for the league would be to import foreign stars, and they brought in other top world players, such as Germany's Franz Beckenbauer, the Netherlands' Johan Cruyff, Portugal's Eusebio, and England's George Best. These stars helped to boost attendance, but they could not, even as a group, match the impact of Pelé, who as a celebrity player was in a class by himself. Moreover, the very presence of foreign stars reinforced the American perception that soccer was a foreign game. As good as those players were, they could not return value on their teams' investments. As result, the league soon folded.

Impact The success that soccer enjoyed in North America during the 1970's was not only brief but also perhaps counterproductive. During that period, professional soccer gained enough media attention for the public at large to notice its almost spectacular failure, thereby reinforcing perceptions that soccer was doomed to fail in North America. However, the sport remained strong at the club and college levels, while the youth movement was rapidly breeding a new generation of soccer players who would make noise in the world game during the 1990's and early twenty-first century.

Further Reading

Allaway, Roger, Colin Jose, and David Litterer. *The Encyclopedia of American Soccer History.* Lanham, Md.: Scarecrow Press, 2001. More than four hundred entries on soccer history through 1999, covering players, leagues, college and professional soccer, and international competitions. Detailed statistical appendices.

Cirino, Tony. *U.S. Soccer vs. the World: The American National Team in the Olympic Games, the World Cup, and Other International Competition.* Leonia, N.J.: Damon Press, 1983. Complete history of American national teams in world competitions through the early 1980's. Includes coverage of the NASL during the 1970's.

Hollander, Zander, ed. *The American Encyclopedia of Soccer.* New York: Everest House, 1980. Detailed reference book that is strong on the 1970's and easier to use than Allaway, Jose, and Litterer's encyclopedia.

Jose, Colin. *Keeping Score: The Encyclopedia of Canadian Soccer.* Vaughan, Ont.: Soccer Hall of Fame and Museum, 1998. The first comprehensive book on Canadian soccer history. Entries include detailed histories of Canadian leagues and national teams and biographies of leading players.

_______. *North American Soccer League Encyclopedia.* Haworth, N.J.: St. Johann Press, 2003. Detailed history of the NASL, with nearly exhaustive statistical records, player directory, league standings, and year-by-year narratives.

Markovits, Andrei S., and Steven L. Hellerman. *Offside: Soccer and American Exceptionalism.* Princeton, N.J.: Princeton University Press, 2001. Scholarly examination of why soccer has failed to match the popularity of baseball, basketball, football, and hockey in North America, even though it is the world's most popular team sport. The authors find the explanations primarily in American nativism and poor leadership in American soccer.

Pelé, with Robert L. Fish. *My Life and the Beautiful Game: The Autobiography of Pelé.* Garden City, N.Y.: Doubleday, 1977. Autobiography of the world's leading soccer player and the star who nearly saved the NASL. Covers his career through his years in the United States.

R. Kent Rasmussen

See also Pelé; Sports.

■ Social Security Amendments of 1972

Identification U.S. federal legislation
Date Enacted in 1972

The Social Security Amendments of 1972 represented the sixth amendment of the original 1935 Social Security Act. They established the Supplemental Security Income (SSI) benefit and introduced the concept of automatic adjustments to Social Security benefits.

The Social Security Amendments of 1972 were signed into law by President Richard M. Nixon and created the Supplemental Security Income (SSI) program in 1974 under Title XVI of the Social Security Act. While Social Security benefits for older adults and disabled individuals were an established facet of modern life, the occupational patterns of many workers limited their ability to qualify fully for Social Security benefits at retirement or to receive disability benefits. The 1972 amendments provided a special minimum benefit for those who worked in covered employment for many years but at low earnings. Unlike the already existing minimum benefit, the new minimum benefit was proportional to the number of years of covered earnings—in excess of ten and up to thirty years.

The SSI program simplified the process of qualifying for benefits in the case of older adults aged sixty-two or older and disabled persons. It replaced former federal grants to the states for lower-income, aged, blind, and disabled persons with a federal minimum-income guarantee. This new program was financed by general revenues and administered by the Social Security Administration.

The 1972 amendments also introduced the concept of automatic adjustments, or "indexing," to the Social Security system. Effective in 1975, benefit adjustments were tied directly to increases in the cost of living. Under this new procedure, benefits increased automatically through a cost-of-living allowance (COLA), when the annual consumer price index (CPI) rose 3 percent or more. In addition, effective in 1975, the earnings base and the exempt amount under the earnings test were adjusted automatically in response to increases in wage levels.

Other income-related provisions of this amendment included an increase in the annual exemption amount under the earnings test, a delayed retirement credit (beyond age sixty-five), and increases in payroll taxes beginning in 1978, with the employee rate to reach an ultimate rate of 7.3 percent in 2011. Improved benefits for disability were also added: new benefits for disabled children under age twenty-two, benefits for dependent grandchildren, and Medicare coverage for Social Security recipients in need of kidney dialysis.

The 1972 amendments established a procedure whereby male and female workers' retirement benefits were computed in the same manner; this provision was phased in to become fully effective in 1975. Prior to this legislation, a man and woman of the same age needed differing amounts of Social Security credits to qualify for retirement benefits. If a man's earnings were identical to those of a female worker, he usually received a lower benefit because his work earnings were averaged over a longer period of time.

Impact The passage of the Social Security Amendments of 1972 further asserted the expanded role of the federal government in its protective and regulatory function by supporting citizens and sharing risks. In the event of retirement or disability, concerns about income security and health care coverage played a central role. The legislation addressed these two key issues for vulnerable populations and assuaged concerns at the state-government level about the appropriate level of responsibility for addressing the needs of the growing elderly and disabled populations. Furthermore, as a result of the SSI program, more than six million Americans were able to receive benefits under SSI in the early twenty-first century—approximately 31 percent were older adults, 56 percent were disabled adults, and 13 percent were disabled children.

Further Reading

Achenbaum, W. Andrew. *Social Security: Visions and Revisions.* New York: Cambridge University Press, 1988.

Tomkiel, Stanley. *Social Security Benefits Handbook.* 3d ed. Naperville, Ill.: Sphinx, 2001.

J. B. Watson, Jr.

See also Age Discrimination Act of 1975; Disability rights movement; Equal Employment Opportunity Act of 1972; Employee Retirement Income Security Act (ERISA) of 1974; Gray Panthers; Income and wages in the United States.

■ Soledad Brothers

Identification African American prisoners charged with murder

Date Charged in January, 1970; George Jackson killed in August, 1971, and Fleeta Drumgo and John Clutchette acquitted in 1972

Racial unrest and prisoner violence in the U.S. correctional system gave the Soledad Brothers notoriety and called attention to the need for prison reform.

During the latter years of the 1960's and in the early 1970's, there was great racial tension throughout the United States. A growing prison population in California with a developing racial consciousness and related tensions put additional burdens on the system and its ability to maintain order. In the Soledad prison, three black activists were killed, and a white guard was killed in retaliation. In January, 1970, George Jackson, Fleeta Drumgo, and John Clutchette were charged with the murder. They became known as the Soledad Brothers.

Having spent most of the 1960's in California prisons serving an indeterminate sentence, Jackson had become politically aware from his study of communist and radical writers. Joining the Black Panther Party in prison, he was the best known of the three and had a wider range of contacts outside the prison. Black Panther Angela Davis became an advocate for the Soledad Brothers's cause, and in 1970, she assisted Jackson in publishing his letters in *Soledad Brother,* which brought him national attention and recognition. However, prison rights advocates believed that the Soledad Brothers were being set up for political purposes.

National attention focused on the Soledad Brothers case in August, 1970, when Jonathan Jackson, George's younger brother, drew a weapon in a Marin County courtroom and demanded freedom for the Soledad Brothers. Jonathan and three inmates tried to escape with hostages, but the police opened fire on their van. Jonathan Jackson, two of the prisoners, and the judge were killed in the gunfight.

In August, 1971, the Soledad Brothers were once more in the national spotlight because of violence. George Jackson was stopped when he was returning to his cell at San Quentin, setting off a chain of events of which there are many versions. By the end of the day, three guards and two prisoners were killed in the cellblock; a guard killed Jackson when he left the cellblock. Radical civil rights leaders and prison reform advocates saw his death as martyrdom. In an anticlimatic end to the original affair, the other two Soledad Brothers went to trial on the charge of murdering the Soledad prison guard and were acquitted in 1972.

Impact These events of the early 1970's brought to the forefront the need for prison reform. Within the prison system, the incidents at Soledad and San Quentin were the impetus for changes within the correctional facilities. Within the judicial system in California, stronger sentencing guidelines were created, rather than the indeterminate sentences that had often been used. In a related area, tighter security in courthouses was the result of the attempt to take hostages in the Marin County courthouse.

Further Reading

Carson, Clayborne. *The Eyes on the Prize: Civil Rights Reader—Documents, Speeches, and Firsthand Accounts from the Black Freedom Struggle, 1954-1990.* New York: Penguin Books, 1991.

Jackson, George. *Blood in My Eye.* Reprint. Baltimore: Black Classic Press, 1990.

_______. *Soledad Brother: The Prison Letters of George Jackson.* Reprint. Chicago: Lawrence Hill Books, 1994.

Donald A. Watt

See also African Americans; Attica prison riot; Black Panthers; Davis, Angela; Racial discrimination.

■ Sondheim, Stephen

Identification American composer for the musical theater

Born March 22, 1930; New York, New York

Through his steady compositional output, Sondheim brought innovative ideas to the unification of music and theater.

Stephen Sondheim's play *A Little Night Music* opened in 1973 and ran at the Shubert Theatre on Broadway for seventeen months and 601 performances. It proved to be one of his biggest successes. *A Little Night Music* received twelve nominations for the 1973 Tony Awards and won five awards, including Best Score and Best Musical. One of the show's highlights is the reflective song "Send in the Clowns." It was recorded by Frank Sinatra in 1973 on the album

Stephen Sondheim. (AP/Wide World Photos)

Ol' Blue Eyes Is Back and became an instant hit. Another release of this song in 1977, recorded by Judy Collins, won a Grammy Award for Song of the Year.

Sondheim's theater piece *The Frogs* opened on May 20, 1974. Produced by the Yale Repertory Theatre and performed in the Yale swimming pool, *The Frogs* ran for eight performances. A Broadway revival of *A Funny Thing Happened on the Way to the Forum,* starring Phil Silvers, began on March 30, 1972, and *Sondheim: A Musical Tribute* opened at the Shubert Theatre on March 11, 1973. A limited Broadway run of *Gypsy,* starring Angela Lansbury, occurred in the early fall of 1974.

The musical *Pacific Overtures* opened in 1976 at the Winter Garden Theatre. Based on a play by John Weidman, *Pacific Overtures* focuses on trade negotiations in nineteenth century Japan. Audiences were less than enthusiastic, and the play closed after 193 performances. *Side by Side by Sondheim,* a revue of Sondheim songs, opened on Broadway on April 18, 1977, running for 384 performances. All reviews were complimentary.

Sondheim's next project, *Sweeney Todd: The Demon Barber of Fleet Street,* would become an unqualified musical success. Based on a play by British playwright Christopher Bond, it focuses on revenge, cannibalism, and dark humor. Subtitled by Sondheim as *A Musical Thriller, Sweeney Todd* opened on March 1, 1979, at the Uris Theatre. It ran for 558 performances, won eleven Drama Desk Awards, the Drama Critics Circle Award, and eight Tony Awards, including Best Musical. Shortly after the opening of *Sweeney Todd*, Sondheim suffered a nonfatal heart attack on March 27, 1979, when he was forty-nine years old.

Impact Stephen Sondheim created a new type of musical theater with total integration of story, text, and musical treatment. Earlier generations of shows, which were generally series of musical hits interspersed with dialogue, gave way to Sondheim's new type of musical. The vocal selections aided in the plot and character development and were more integrated into the development of the show as story lines became more realistic. These musicals have provided a lasting influence and serve as models for subsequent developments in the theater, and they have provided a substantial new body of work for artists and audiences.

Further Reading

Citron, Stephen. *Sondheim and Lloyd-Webber: The New Musical.* New York: Oxford University Press, 2001.

Secrest, Meryle. *Stephen Sondheim: A Life.* New York: Alfred A. Knopf, 1998.

Zadan, Craig. *Sondheim and Co.* New York: Macmillan, 1974.

P. Brent Register

See also Broadway musicals; Film in the United States; Music; Theater in the United States.

■ Soul music

Definition Music genre that blends traditions of gospel with rhythm and blues and emphasizes black consciousness and pride

In the 1970's, soul music was as diverse as the era itself. Some artists updated the mellow sound of Motown, others emphasized social and political activism, and others used sexual or drug-related lyrics, usually with a hard-driving beat.

In the late 1960's, James Brown, dubbed the "Godfather of Soul," and Aretha Franklin, the "Queen of Soul," dominated the genre and illustrate the two sides of soul music that began the 1970's. Brown's rough vocals and relentless rhythms emphasized a dance beat, while Franklin's impassioned vocal style focused on relationships and personal communication.

As the decade progressed, soul music took new turns. Marvin Gaye's album *What's Going On?* (1971) addressed social and political issues with a percussive beat and an edgy vocal style. Stevie Wonder used socially conscious lyrics on his album *Innervisions* (1973), in which a more mellow soul style was fused with funk, rock, and jazz.

Overtly sexual lyrics also became common—notably in the music of Gaye, Brown, and Ike and Tina Turner—while drug-related lyrics were heard in the "psychedelic soul" of Sly and the Family Stone. Brown's 1970 single "Get Up (I Feel Like Being a) Sex Machine" blended soul with relentless and complex rhythmic layers, a style that soon became known as funk. While funk, especially the music of George Clinton, was marketed primarily to black audiences, both Earth, Wind, and Fire and Kool and the Gang

Popular Soul and R&B Hits of the 1970's

Song	*Artist*
"Best of My Love"	The Emotions
"We Are Family"	Sister Sledge
"Shining Star"	Earth, Wind, and Fire
"Can't Get Enough of Your Love, Babe"	Barry White
"Play That Funky Music"	Wild Cherry
"Superstition"	Stevie Wonder
"What's Going On"	Marvin Gaye
"Let's Stay Together"	Al Green
"Theme from *Shaft*"	Isaac Hayes
"It's a Family Affair"	Sly and the Family Stone
"Papa Was a Rolling Stone"	The Temptations
"Rock Steady"	Aretha Franklin

had strong crossover appeal. Funk also reached a wider audience in the soundtracks for blaxploitation films, including Isaac Hayes's *Shaft* (1971), Curtis Mayfield's *Superfly* (1972), and Gaye's *Trouble Man* (1972).

Other African American artists turned toward a more polished and romantic kind of soul, with smooth vocals accompanied by lush strings, horns, and percussion. Known as the "Philadelphia sound," this slick, mellow style was featured on the popular television dance show *Soul Train*. Groups such as MFSB (Mothers, Fathers, Sisters, Brothers), the O'Jays, the Blue Notes, the Spinners, and the Stylistics, as well as solo artists such as Roberta Flack and Barry White, epitomized this style, which helped pave the way for disco.

By the end of the decade, soul hybrids were numerous and increasingly explored the potential of synthesizers. Wonder's albums, especially *Journey Through the Secret Life of Plants* (1979) with its fusion of soul with rock, funk, jazz, synthesized sounds, and even reggae and African music, sum up the variety of soul music at the end of the 1970's.

Impact At times true to its gritty roots, at others soft and mellow with slick orchestration, and at still others uncompromisingly rhythmic, soul music always communicated a sense of black pride. During the 1970's, soul music blended with almost every other popular musical style, transforming itself and American popular music in the process.

Further Reading

Joyner, David. *American Popular Music.* 2d ed. New York: McGraw-Hill, 2003.

Stuessy, Joe, and Scott Lipscomb. *Rock and Roll: Its History and Stylistic Development.* 4th ed. Upper Saddle River, N.J.: Prentice Hall, 2003.

Werner, Craig. *A Change Is Gonna Come: Music, Race, and the Soul of America.* New York: Plume, 1999.

Mary A. Wischusen

See also African Americans; Blaxploitation films; Disco; Gaye, Marvin; Music; Wonder, Stevie.

■ Soviet invasion of Afghanistan

The Event Military action by the Soviet Union to maintain a pro-Soviet government in Afghanistan

Date December, 1979

The Soviet invasion of Afghanistan contributed to a swing to the right in American foreign policy and effectively ended the period of détente, in turn helping Ronald Reagan defeat Jimmy Carter in the 1980 presidential election.

The Soviet invasion of Afghanistan began a nine-year war that pitted the Soviet military against rural Afghan fighters known as the *mujahadeen*. It was the only time that the Soviet Union applied its Brezhnev Doctrine—a foreign policy of military intervention to prevent the establishment of an independent government in a satellite nation—to a country outside the Warsaw Pact. Coupled with communist-

sponsored martial law in Poland, the invasion of Afghanistan inspired a change in American foreign policy, as Americans increasingly saw détente as dead.

Afghanistan was unstable throughout the 1970's. In 1978, Nur Mohammad Taraki and the People's Democratic Party of Afghanistan seized power with Soviet support. However, the Soviets became increasingly dissatisfied with Taraki as opposition to his rule spread, and they plotted his removal. Taraki died mysteriously in September or October, 1978, and was replaced by Hafizullah Amin. Amin also failed to placate the Soviets. In mid-December, two Soviet infantry battalions were airlifted to Bagram Air Base in Afghanistan. On December 18, these regiments assumed control of the Salang Pass, which connected the Soviet Union to Afghanistan, while a Soviet division entered Afghanistan. Another regiment was airlifted into Bagram three days later. By December 24, the Soviets seized Afghanistan's communications centers. On December 27, the Soviets arrested most Afghan civil and military officials. That evening, three Soviet battalions assaulted the Darulaman Palace, killing Amin and his security force after several hours of fighting. The Soviets installed Babrak Karmal as president. By December 28, 1979, the Soviets had 50,000 soldiers in Afghanistan, a number that later rose to more than 135,000, in an attempt to subdue armed Afghan resistance and possibly incorporate Afghanistan into the Soviet Union.

Impact The invasion involved an increasingly unstable Soviet Union in a long, expensive, and internationally unpopular war. The United States boycotted the 1980 Moscow Olympics to protest the invasion, signaling a return of the Cold War.

Subsequent Events The war that followed the invasion cost the Soviets more than eighteen thousand dead. The number of Afghans killed exceeded one million, with another five million refugees—one-third of the prewar population. The Central Intelligence Agency (CIA) funneled more than $2.1 billion to the *mujahadeen* through Pakistan. The invasion, occurring the same year as the Iranian Revolution and the resulting standoff between the United States and the revolutionary government over the seizure of American embassy personnel, increased militant Islamic radicalism. A decade after the invasion, the Soviet Union started to collapse. Militant Islamic extremists took control of Afghanistan and increasingly saw the United States, and its allies among Arab governments, as its enemies.

Further Reading

Aspaturian, Vernon, Alexander Dallin, and Jir Valenta. *The Soviet Invasion of Afghanistan: Three Perspectives.* Los Angeles: University of California Press, 1980.

Grasselli, Gabriella. *British and American Responses to the Soviet Invasion of Afghanistan.* Brookfield, Vt.: Dartmouth, 1996.

Kakar, M. Hassan. *Afghanistan: The Soviet Invasion and the Afghan Response, 1979-1982.* Berkeley: University of California Press, 1995.

Barry M. Stentiford

See also Carter, Jimmy; Cold War; Détente; Iranian hostage crisis; Middle East and North America; Soviet Union and North America.

■ Soviet Union and North America

Definition Diplomatic relations between major world powers

The decade of the 1970's was a critical period in relations between the Soviet Union and North America because it was the time of the rise and decline of the policy of détente.

From the creation of the Soviet Union with the 1917 Russian Revolution until the Soviet Union's end in 1991, the nations of North America had troubled relations with the huge country that stretched from Eastern Europe through Asia. Opposed to the new Soviet government, the United States and several other allies sent small numbers of troops to Russia during the civil war that followed the Russian Revolution. The United States did not establish diplomatic relations with the Soviet Union until 1933, and the governments of Canada and the United States viewed the Soviets with distrust.

In World War II, after a brief period of cooperation between the Soviet Union and Nazi Germany, the United States, Canada, Great Britain, and other Western nations became allies of the Soviets. The alliance continued until about 1947, when the Cold War broke out. This introduced a period of new tension between the Soviet Union and the North American countries. This era was followed by a period of some relaxation by the end of the 1960's and begin-

The Soviet Union

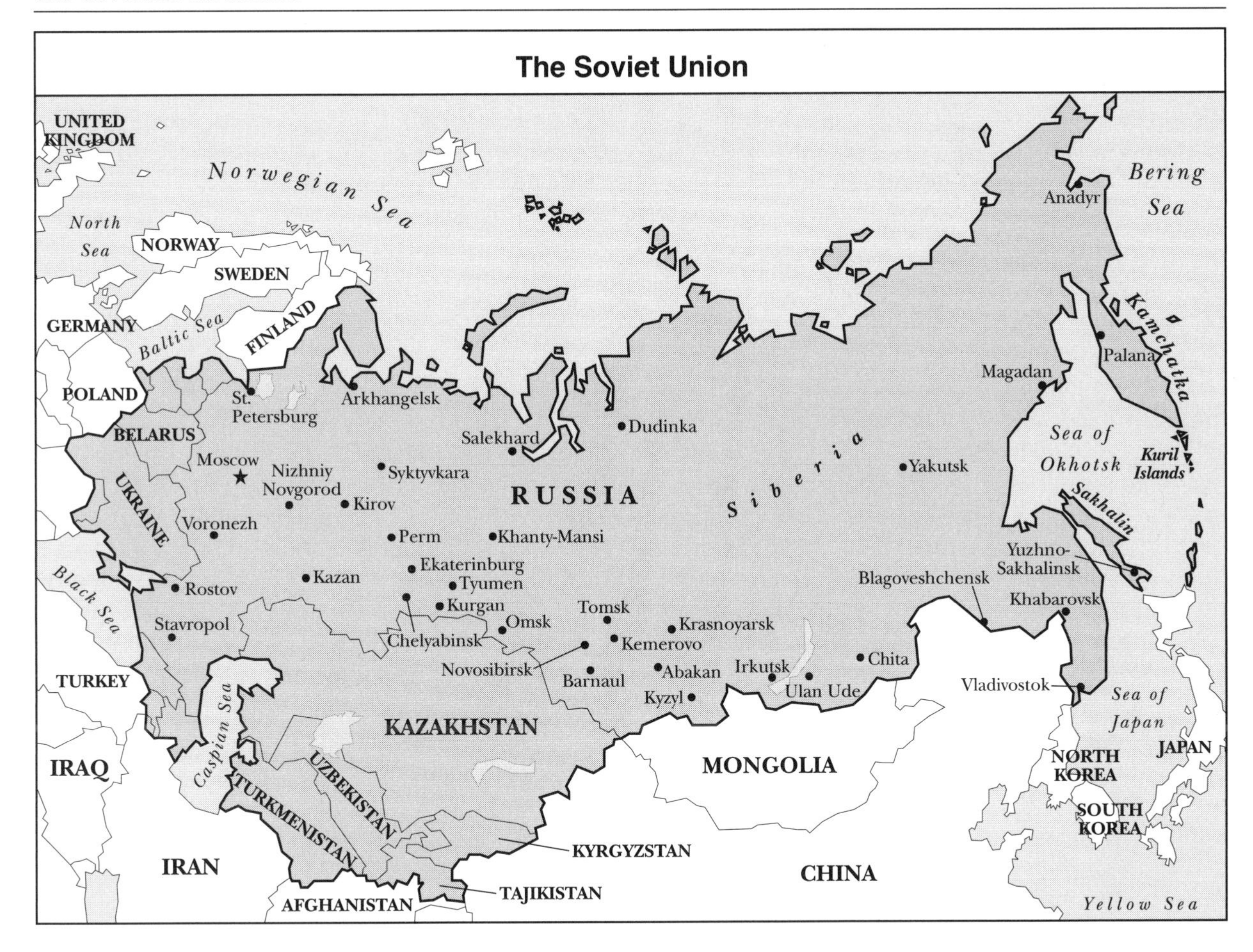

ning of the 1970's, when the era of détente began during the administrations of U.S. president Richard M. Nixon, Canadian prime minister Pierre Trudeau, and Soviet general secretary Leonid Brezhnev.

The Brezhnev Doctrine To many observers in the late 1960's, it may not have appeared that the 1970's would be a time of improved relations between the Soviet Union and North America. In early 1968, Alexander Dubcek became first secretary of the Communist Party of Czechoslovakia. Under Dubcek's administration, the Czechoslovakian government began easing travel restrictions on its citizens, experimenting with market reforms in the economy, and hinting that it would establish closer links to Western Europe. The Soviet Union became fearful that the Czechoslovakian reforms would undermine socialism and draw Czechoslovakia away from the socialist nations of Eastern Europe. Soviet leaders were concerned that this might spread to the rest of Eastern Europe. On August 21, 1968, Soviet troops invaded Czechoslovakia.

General Secretary Brezhnev declared, in justification of the intervention, that efforts to reverse the progress of socialism and restore capitalism in any socialist country posed threats to all socialist countries. Therefore, the Soviet Union and its allies reserved the right to take action whenever a state began to turn away from socialism. The Brezhnev Doctrine, as the principles of this declaration became known, guided Soviet attitudes toward countries with communist governments throughout the 1970's, and it eventually led the Soviet Union to become involved in a disastrous war in Afghanistan. However, the doctrine did not prevent the improvement of relations with North America. Trudeau, first elected in 1968, was a strong advocate of closer Soviet-Canadian relations. The United States, which elected President Nixon in the same year, was engaged in a war in Vietnam and wanted Soviet cooperation in bringing the Vietnam War to an end. Furthermore, both the North American nations and the Soviet Union were eager to bring an end to the expensive and dangerous competition in nuclear weapons.

Beginnings of Détente Détente is a French word that can be translated as "loosening" or "slackening." Although President Nixon had based much of his early political career on opposition to communism, in his first inaugural address in 1969, he declared his intention to lessen American confrontation with the Soviets through negotiation. Nixon's secretary of state, Henry Kissinger, was a celebrated negotiator and played a large part in discussions with the Soviets. Even before Nixon's inauguration, the Soviet Union, the United States, and other nations signed the Nuclear Non-Proliferation Treaty, which had the goal of stopping the spread of nuclear arms. This treaty came into force in March, 1970, beginning the decade on an optimistic note.

At the very end of 1969, the United States and the Soviet Union began the Strategic Arms Limitation Talks (SALT) in Helsinki, Finland. By May, 1972, the two sides signed SALT agreements that limited the number of intercontinental ballistic missiles (ICBMs) and antiballistic missiles (ABMs) that could be held by each country. A year later, the two superpowers signed an agreement on the Prevention of Nuclear War.

Throughout the 1970's, President Nixon and his successors, President Gerald R. Ford and President Jimmy Carter, held a series of highly publicized summit talks with the Soviet Union. Aside from the nuclear treaties, during the first half of the decade, the two powers signed a wide range of military, cultural, and economic agreements. Although Canada was not a major player in détente, Prime Minister Trudeau was a strong supporter of the détente process and established closer ties both between Canada and the Soviet Union and between Canada and Cuba, the main ally of the Soviets in the Americas.

The Helsinki Accord The policy of détente led to talks in Helsinki, beginning in July, 1973, and aimed at creating peaceful stability in Europe. Known as the Conference on Security and Cooperation in Europe, these talks involved delegates from the Soviet Union, from every European nation except Albania, from the Vatican, and from Canada and the United States. The broad agreement that these delegates signed in August, 1975, became known as the Helsinki Accord.

The Helsinki Accord established basic principles on relations among the states in Europe. It also made provisions for promoting contact between citizens of different nations and for scientific and cultural matters. The provisions of the Helsinki Accord that guaranteed human rights to people living in the nations that signed the agreement became particularly well known and influential. Dissidents in the Soviet Union saw these provisions as supporting their right to criticize their government.

Challenges to Détente In the second half of the 1970's, policies of détente began to face problems. The Soviet Union became involved in wars and rebellions in a number of countries around the world. In Africa, the Soviet Union became active in Angola and in a war between Ethiopia and Somalia. In Angola after 1975, the Soviets sent funds and supplies and encouraged Cuba to send troops to support a Marxist faction in a civil war. Further north, in 1977 and 1978, the Soviets and Cubans assisted Ethiopia after it had been attacked by neighboring Somalia. The Soviet Union also became actively involved in Afghanistan in 1978, after a communist government took power in that country and fighting broke out between the government and its Muslim opponents. Many in the United States took Soviet actions in these and other locations as evidence that the Soviet Union was an aggressive, untrustworthy power, seeking to spread its control around the world.

When President Nixon resigned his office in 1974 after the Watergate political scandal, détente lost its most important advocate, although Secretary of State Kissinger continued to serve the administration of President Ford. President Carter, who was elected in 1976, was outspoken in his criticism of human rights abuses in the Soviet Union, and this stance strained relations between the United States and the Soviets. With the failure of the U.S. Congress to ratify the second round of arms limitation talks, known as SALT II, in 1979, the era of détente came to an end.

War in Afghanistan Of all the challenges to détente, the Soviet invasion of Afghanistan was the most serious, with grave consequences for relations with North America and for the Soviets themselves. The invasion was rooted in the Brezhnev Doctrine, proclaimed just before the beginning of détente.

Two factions of the Marxist People's Democratic Party of Afghanistan had joined together to seize power in the spring of 1978. The Soviet Union supported the new government financially and sent in advisers, but the Afghan regime was plagued by internal conflict and by opposition from Muslim rebels.

By the end of 1979, Brezhnev and the other political leaders of the Soviet Union had decided that the only way to maintain a socialist government in Afghanistan was to seize control, install a new Afghan leader, and send in Soviet troops to put down the rebellion. This move proved to be the wrong decision because the Soviet Union spent the next decade fighting a costly war. The war also caused Soviet relations with North America to worsen because the Soviet Union appeared as an aggressive power invading another nation. During the Soviet occupation of Afghanistan, the United States contributed aid and supplies to the Muslim rebels.

Impact During the early 1970's, the policy of détente raised hopes in North America, the Soviet Union, and other parts of the world that the Cold War might finally be winding down. Although the Soviet Union exercised little direct control over North Vietnam, improved relations between the Soviet Union and the United States helped the United States in its negotiations with the North Vietnamese and probably contributed to the removal of American forces from Vietnam. The renewal of tensions in the second part of the decade ushered in a period of renewed distrust. In the United States, in particular, it brought back the popular image of the Soviet Union as a dangerous and aggressive power, aiming at world domination. This set the stage for a new period of confrontation during the 1980's.

Subsequent Events Although the Soviet Union appeared to be a powerful state at the end of the 1970's, its involvements around the world were placing pressures on its fragile economy. With the rise in defense spending produced by increased competition with the United States in the early 1980's, these pressures became even greater. The war in Afghanistan drained both the finances and the morale of the Soviets.

After Brezhnev died in 1982, the Soviet Union faced a leadership crisis, as well as economic difficulties. Many of Brezhnev's successors were aging men and died soon after taking office. In 1985, the Soviet Communist Party elected Mikhail Gorbachev as general secretary, and he worked toward reform and sought both to liberalize the political system and to lessen Soviet involvement in other parts of the world, including Afghanistan. As the Soviet Union loosened its hold over Eastern Europe, it became clear that the Brezhnev Doctrine had been correct. The fall of communism in some countries did lead to its fall in others. During 1989, popular demonstrations led to the collapse of communist governments throughout Eastern Europe. The Soviet Union itself lasted only a little longer, ceasing to exist in 1991.

Further Reading

Garthoff, Raymond L. *Détente and Confrontation: American-Soviet Relations from Nixon to Reagan.* 2d ed. Washington, D.C.: Brookings Institution, 1994. Uses declassified Soviet documents and U.S. government documents to examine the historical development of Soviet-American relations from 1969 to 1980.

Ouimet, Matthew J. *The Rise and Fall of the Brezhnev Doctrine in Soviet Foreign Policy.* Chapel Hill: University of North Carolina Press, 2003. A detailed examination of how the Soviet leaders decided on the Brezhnev Doctrine, and its history through the war in Afghanistan.

Roberts, Geoffrey. *The Soviet Union in World Politics: Coexistence, Revolution, and Cold War, 1945-1991.* New York: Routledge, 1999. An excellent short overview of Soviet foreign relations that provides a brief, clear summary of the rise and decline of détente.

Carl L. Bankston III

See also Africa and the United States; Anti-Ballistic Missile (ABM) Treaty; Carter, Jimmy; Cold War; Détente; Ford, Gerald R.; Foreign policy of Canada; Foreign policy of the United States; Kissinger, Henry; Nixon, Richard M.; Reagan, Ronald; SALT I and II treaties; Soviet invasion of Afghanistan.

■ Space exploration

Definition The use of manned and unmanned spacecraft to gather scientific information about space and other planets

During a decade of declining support, space officials in the United States attempted to garner public favor through such undertakings as the U.S.-Soviet Apollo-Soyuz mission. They also developed several manned and unmanned

projects—Skylab, the Viking landers on Mars, and the Voyager flybys of Jupiter—that generated important scientific results.

The successful landing of American astronauts on the Moon in the summer of 1969 was such an impressive accomplishment that it created problems for the National Aeronautics and Space Administration (NASA) in its relationships with politicians, the public, and the scientific community. During the 1970's, politicians no longer provided the ever-increasing funding to NASA that the organization had received in the 1960's. The American public's interest in the later Apollo missions steadily declined, as did interest in some of the decade's undramatic manned and unmanned spaceflights.

NASA officials did make plans for a new space delivery system (the space shuttle), and they did carry out a variety of planetary missions in the ongoing Mariner and Pioneer series and in the new Viking and Voyager ventures. Although these planetary projects did not stimulate the worldwide interest that Apollo 11 had, their scientific value far exceeded that of the Moon missions.

Final Apollo Spaceflights Apollo 13, the first Moon mission of the 1970's, created global interest not because it landed on the Moon but because it could not. During the third day of the flight, an explosion in an oxygen tank crippled the command module's capacity to generate power, water, and oxygen, but ingenious thinking by technicians on Earth and the adept implementation of their ideas by the astronauts resulted in the transformation of *Aquarius*, the lunar lander, into a life-support system. The firing of *Aquarius*'s descent rocket pushed the spacecraft around the Moon and toward Earth, where the astronauts successfully splashed down on April 17, 1970. Apollo 13's intended target, the Fra Mauro highlands, became the goal of the Apollo 14 astronauts early in 1971. With its modest scientific achievements, this mission became memorable when astronaut Alan Shepard drove a golf ball a great distance in the Moon's low gravity.

A 747 jet transports the space shuttle Columbia *to the Kennedy Space Center in Florida in 1979. In the 1980's, the shuttle program would usher in a new era of manned spaceflight.* (NASA)

The first three Moon landings had been necessarily cautious, but the final three Apollo missions involved extensive lunar exploration with sophisticated equipment. A lunar roving vehicle allowed Apollo 15 astronauts to travel several miles to explore Hadley Rille, a puzzling depression near the Appenine Mountains, where they found a 4.5-billion-year-old "Genesis Rock." The goal of Apollo 16 was to explore the Moon's volcanic activity by landing in some hills near the Descartes crater, but the sought-for volcanic rocks were not found. Apollo 17, the last mission, was notable because Harrison "Jack" Schmitt, a Ph.D. geologist, was able to explore, with Eugene Cernan, a valley near the Taurus Mountains. They spent more time on the Moon and traveled greater distances than any of the previous astronauts. After setting up various automated research stations, they left the Moon with nearly 250 pounds of rocks and soil samples. Because each Apollo mission cost about $400 million and because NASA's budget dwindled during the Vietnam War, flights 18, 19, and 20 were canceled, bringing an early end to the Apollo program.

Other Manned Space Projects NASA officials now envisioned the immediate future of manned spaceflight in terms of Earth-orbiting space stations and a space shuttle system that would make forays into orbit routine. Skylab, America's first space station, was launched on May 14, 1973, but its shield, designed to protect astronauts from meteoroids and the Sun's heat, tore loose. When astronauts arrived at the station eleven days later, they deployed a protective parasol in place of the shield. Teams of three astronauts visited Skylab three times for increasingly longer stays (twenty-eight, fifty-nine, and eighty-four days) and carried out more than a hundred experiments on Earth resources, solar radiation, and the long-term effects of weightlessness on the human body. Skylab continued to orbit the Earth unoccupied until gravity and the friction of the atmosphere caused it to break into fragments over Australia on July 11, 1979.

Although competition with the Soviet Union had been the propelling political force behind the Apollo program, the future of space exploration necessitated international cooperation for economic, scientific, and even commercial reasons. Soviet-American cooperation was the principal point of the much-publicized Apollo-Soyuz Test Project. In order to bring about the meeting of three American astronauts and two Soviet cosmonauts on July 17, 1975, much preliminary work had to be done. Despite the project's obvious symbolic value, critics questioned the cost, since little of scientific merit resulted from the flight. NASA officials realized that, if countries of the world were to cooperate in building space stations, then a reusable space transportation system was needed. Because of budgetary restrictions, the space shuttle had to be redesigned during the 1970's, and the first shuttle trip into space did not occur until 1981.

Unmanned Explorations of the Planets Planetary exploration that had begun with various probes in the 1960's continued with much more sophisticated spacecraft in the 1970's. In November, 1971, Mariner 9, the first spacecraft to orbit another planet, began sending back to Earth the first of its more than seven thousand images of Mars. Detailed pictures of Olympus Mons, a volcano three times as high as Mount Everest, and Valles Marineris, a nearly 5,000-mile-long rift valley, enhanced astronomers' understanding of the red planet.

The exploration of Mars continued with the twin Viking missions. Each Viking spacecraft contained an orbiter to map the Martian surface and a lander to explore its geology and biology. NASA scientists had planned for Viking 1's lander to touch down on July 4, 1976, the American bicentennial, but caution trumped ceremony and the Viking 1's scientific package landed on July 20 (Viking 2 landed on September 2 in another location). The Viking orbiters and landers gathered substantial data on the surface features, atmosphere, and weather of Mars, but the lander's supersensitive gas chromatograph and mass spectrometer detected no organic molecules, leading many biologists to declare the Martian surface devoid of life.

NASA missions during the 1970's also involved other planets. For example, in 1974 Mariner 10 was the first space probe to visit Mercury, which it found to be a heavily cratered world similar to Earth's Moon. Other probes, such as Pioneer 10 and its twin Pioneer 11, were sent through the asteroid belt between Mars and Jupiter to gather information on the outer planets. In 1973, Pioneer 10 became the first spacecraft to observe Jupiter directly, returning vivid pictures of the Jovian atmosphere along with data on its moons, magnetic field, and radiation belts. Pioneer 11, which traveled by Jupiter in December, 1974, became the first spacecraft to visit Saturn in 1979, discovering a new ring and two new moons.

The Pioneer probes blazed the way for the much more sophisticated Voyager missions. Some scientists called the Voyager probes' Grand Tour of Jupiter, Saturn, Uranus, and Neptune the greatest feat of space exploration in history. The spacecraft were fortunate in making the early stage of their trip in the 1970's, since these outer planets were so oriented that they could provide successive gravity assists to propel these spacecraft from one planet to another. Both spacecraft left Earth during the summer of 1977. Voyager 1 flew by Jupiter in March, 1979, while Voyager 2's encounter with the solar system's largest planet occurred in July. The cameras aboard Voyager 1 returned pictures of Jupiter's rapidly moving clouds of white, orange, and brown, and the public was particularly fascinated by images of its Great Red Spot, a gigantic storm that had been swirling for at least three hundred years. Voyager 1's cameras also detected a faint Saturn-like ring around Jupiter.

The most surprising discoveries of the Voyager spacecraft concerned Jupiter's four largest moons, as unusual and distinctive from one another as are the solar system's inner planets of Mercury, Venus, Earth, and Mars. Voyager 1's images of Io, Jupiter's innermost moon, revealed a red-and-orange volcanically active surface, and some of Io's volcanoes were still fuming four months later, when Voyager 2 flew by. In contrast, Europa, Io's nearest neighbor, was seen in Voyager 1's images as the solar system's smoothest object, but Voyager 2's much closer approach revealed an intricate network of curved and straight lines on Europa's icy crust, which floated over a water ocean kept liquid because of the satellite's interior heat.

The next of these so-called Galilean moons (because Galileo Galilei had first observed them) was Ganymede, the largest of the Jovian satellites. Its surface had cratered areas like Earth's Moon but also regions indicative of previous volcanic activity as well as features caused by the faulting of the crust. The Voyager spacecraft also studied Callisto, the Galilean moon most distant from Jupiter. Callisto's surface was the most intensively cratered in the solar system as a result of eons of meteoric impacts, and some of these craters appeared to be filled or rimmed with ice. During the 1980's, the Voyager probes continued their surprising discoveries in later encounters with Saturn, Uranus, and Neptune.

Impact Some enthusiasts compared the Apollo missions with such past attainments as construction of the Egyptian pyramids and medieval cathedrals, since the Moon landings were monumental achievements of highly trained people mastering complex technological challenges. On the other hand, some scholars interpreted Apollo and the unmanned space projects of the 1970's in terms of the Cold War, and they have criticized the technophilia of the space enthusiasts who wanted to see these accomplishments as the prelude to manned missions to Mars and the other planets. The manned and unmanned missions of the 1970's certainly had a beneficial impact on the aerospace industry, and the enormous amount of data generated by these projects kept astronomers and other specialists busy for years. However, critics pointed out that these projects sucked funds and scientists from other fields, such as medicine, to the detriment of human well-being on Earth.

The space projects of later decades evolved from and capitalized on those of the 1970's, but part of this legacy has been divided opinions over such programs as the international space station and a possible manned mission to Mars.

Further Reading

Burrows, William E. *The Infinite Journey: Eyewitness Accounts of NASA and the Age of Space.* New York: Discovery Books, 2000. This beautifully illustrated retrospective of thirty of NASA's most significant manned and unmanned missions relies heavily on the words of participants. Index.

Heppenheimer, T. A. *Countdown: A History of Space Flight.* New York: John Wiley & Sons, 1997. This comprehensive history, which makes use of archival material, has three chapters relevant to American space achievements in the 1970's. Bibliography and index.

McDougall, Walter A. *. . . the Heavens and the Earth: A Political History of the Space Age.* Baltimore: Johns Hopkins University Press, 1997. McDougall emphasizes the role that Cold War competition between the Soviet Union and the United States played in the origin, development, and marketing of many space missions, including those of the 1970's. Seventy pages of notes, with many references to primary and secondary sources. Index.

Murray, Bruce. *Journey into Space: The First Three Decades of Space Exploration.* New York: W. W. Norton, 1989. The author, a prominent space scientist, analyzes the Pioneer, Mariner, Viking, and Voyager missions. References, notes, and an index.

Reynolds, David West. *Apollo: The Epic Journey to the Moon.* San Diego, Calif.: Tehabi Books, 2002. The strength of this account of the Apollo missions is the book's detailed diagrams, many illustrations (including rare and unpublished photographs), and maps. Select bibliography and index.

Robert J. Paradowski

See also Apollo space program; Astronomy; Cold War; Pioneer space program; Science and technology; Skylab; Soviet Union and North America; Viking space program; Voyager space program.

■ Special effects

Definition Techniques used to create illusions, enhance reality, or simulate effects that are too expensive or impossible to create by normal filming methods

During the 1970's, special effects became increasingly complex and computer-generated, often replacing film stars as the main attraction. Special-effects films revived the film industry and started the summer blockbuster phenomenon.

As the 1970's began, the motion-picture industry faced a crisis. Film attendance continued to drop, as television increasingly captured the mass audience. During the late 1960's, takeovers and mergers had placed most major film studios under huge business conglomerates with holdings in television and other media. Previously, feature films were released first in major theaters and gradually in smaller venues. In the early 1970's, studios developed a new marketing strategy: a single release date and a national advertising campaign.

The success of *Airport* (1970) convinced the new management that disaster films could be popular. Using the new marketing strategy, a series of memorable and lucrative disaster films was released. Irwin Allen, the "disaster king," produced *The Poseidon Adventure* (1972) and *The Towering Inferno* (1974). Besides all-star casts, these films featured spectacular special effects such as miniature models of sinking ocean liners and burning skyscrapers. In 1972, L. B. Abbott and A. D. Flowers won the Academy Award for Visual Effects in *The Poseidon Adventure.*

In 1974, Frank Brendel, Glen Robinson, and Albert Whitlock won an Academy Award for Visual Effects in *Earthquake,* a film about the near destruction of Los Angeles from an earthquake measuring 10.5 on the Richter scale. In 1975, Whitlock and Robinson received another Academy Award for their special effects in *The Hindenburg,* the true story of the giant zeppelin that burst into flames after its final Atlantic crossing in 1937.

The special effects in these films were created using traditional mechanical, stop-motion animation and optical printing techniques. In stop-motion animation, an object or miniature model is photographed frame by frame, with changes in movement between frames. When played, the film gives a realistic illusion of movement. Optical printing combined a camera with front or rear projectors to create live action against backgrounds of matte paintings.

Blockbusters, Science Fiction, and Fantasy Although disaster films were profitable, studios also realized that traditional film genres needed revamping to draw broader audiences, especially younger crowds. In the early 1970's, Hollywood turned to a new generation of young, experimental filmmakers called the "film brats," two of whom would transform the film and special-effects industries permanently.

On June 20, 1975, Steven Spielberg released *Jaws,* a big-budget, special-effects film about a giant killer shark. Summer was normally the off-season for film releases, but *Jaws* became the first film to earn $100 million. It was the first summer "blockbuster," and $100 million became the benchmark for defining the blockbuster category. In 1978, Spielberg released *Jaws 2,* the first summer blockbuster sequel and the beginning of a trend in sequels.

Big-budget science-fiction and fantasy films also defined the 1970's and eventually made special effects more significant than a film's human stars. In 1968, Stanley Kubrick had released *2001: A Space Odyssey.* Its magnificent special effects helped inspire the young filmmaker George Lucas, who formed his own company, Industrial Light and Magic, to create original computer-generated technologies for *Star Wars* (1977), a unique combination of science fiction and fantasy. Lucas's company invented the first computer-linked camera control system. The themes of survival and the Force helping defeat evil appealed to children, as well as adult audiences, and this blockbuster earned more than *Jaws.*

In 1977, Spielberg released another hit, *Close Encounters of the Third Kind,* for which legendary visual effects pioneer Doug Trumbull created a 400-pound fiberglass model to represent the glowing alien spacecraft. Other notable special effects appeared in *A Clockwork Orange* (1971), *The Exorcist* (1973), and *Logan's Run* (1976). In 1979, *Star Trek: The Motion Picture* and *Alien* opened in theaters; both used special effects.

Impact During the early 1970's, new marketing techniques and the revival of cinematic special effects for use in popular disaster films started to pull the film industry out of its financial crisis. Complete recovery came with the birth of the summer blockbuster film trend, beginning with *Jaws* and *Star Wars,* two phenomenally profitable films by two young, risk-taking filmmakers. This led to the production of many more science-fiction, fantasy, and action-adventure blockbusters with dazzling special effects that appealed to younger audiences. Computer-generated special effects became more sophisticated to meet the increasing demands for complex animations, three-dimensional models, and realistic, textured environments. Digital effects increasingly replaced traditional methods, so that by the late 1970's, computers dominated the special-effects field. These trends continued into the following decades.

Subsequent Events Spielberg and Lucas continued directing and producing popular special-effects films, including *The Empire Strikes Back* (1980), *E.T.: The Extraterrestrial* (1982), *The Return of the Jedi* (1983), *Who Framed Roger Rabbit?* (1988), *Jurassic Park* (1993), and the Indiana Jones series. In 1999, Lucas's long-awaited *Star Wars: Episode I—The Phantom Menace* was released, twenty years after his landmark *Star Wars* film. This first Star Wars prequel featured computer-generated characters coexisting with live actors. Lucas produced the second prequel, *Star Wars: Episode II—Attack of the Clones,* in 2002, and the third, *Star Wars: Episode III—Revenge of the Sith,* in 2005.

Further Reading

Brode, Douglas. *The Films of Steven Spielberg.* New York: Kensington, 2000. Well-researched analysis of Spielberg's major films and career. Illustrated, with filmography and bibliography.

Falsetto, Mario, ed. *Perspectives on Stanley Kubrick.* New York: G. K. Hall, 1996. Includes several essays on *A Clockwork Orange.* Photos from the MOMA/Film Stills Archives. Filmography and bibliography.

Fry, Ron, and Pamela Fourzon. *The Saga of Special Effects.* Englewood Cliffs, N.J.: Prentice-Hall, 1977. Informative chapter on "The 'Disastrous' Seventies." Covers the subject through 1976. Illustrated, with bibliography.

Pollock, Dale. *Skywalking: The Life and Films of George Lucas.* New York: Da Capo Press, 1999. Full-length biography, including quotes from Lucas and discussions of his films. Illustrated, with filmography and bibliography.

Rickitt, Richard. *Special Effects: The History and Technique.* New York: Billboard Books, 2000. A comprehensive study of special effects, including ample coverage of the 1970's. Beautiful photographs, glossary, and bibliography.

Alice Myers

See also Academy Awards; *Alien*; *Battlestar Galactica*; Blockbusters; *Clockwork Orange, A*; *Close Encounters of the Third Kind*; Computers; Disaster films; Dolby sound; Dreyfuss, Richard; *Exorcist, The*; Film in the United States; Horror films; *Jaws*; Science and technology; Science-fiction films; Spielberg, Steven; *Star Trek*; *Star Wars.*

■ Speedy Trial Act of 1975

Identification U.S. federal legislation
Date Became law in January, 1975

Intended to reduce the unnecessary detention of persons accused of committing federal crimes, the act established definite time periods for the completion of various stages in the prosecution of defendants for the commission of federal crimes.

The right to a speedy trial was derived from a provision in the Magna Carta, incorporated into the Virginia Declaration of Rights of 1776 and established in the Sixth Amendment of the U.S. Constitution. The provision safeguards against undue and oppressive incarceration of persons prior to trial by minimizing anxiety and concern emanating from public accusation and limiting the possibility that undue delay will compromise the ability of accused persons to defend themselves. The passage of time may lead to loss of witnesses through death or relocation beyond the reach of the subpoena and the blurring of memories of available witnesses. Juxtaposed against these considerations is the societal interest in providing a speedy trial because incarcerated persons must be supported at public expense, and the fact that defendants incarcerated over a long period of time may be tempted to "jump" bail and may use the backlog of cases in a plea bargain for a reduction of charges or sentences. Delay is said to retard two of the goals of criminal law: deterrence and rehabilitation.

Held to be among Americans' "fundamental" liberties in the Bill of Rights made applicable to the states through the due process clause of the Fourteenth Amendment, the right to a speedy trial is activated only when a criminal prosecution has begun and extends only to accused persons. The statute of limitations protects against possible prejudice from delays between the time the government has gathered sufficient evidence to proceed and the actual instituting of proceedings.

In determining whether a time period is too long to be consistent with the speedy trial guarantee, the Supreme Court in its major case in this area, *Barker v. Wingo* (1972), identified several factors that should be assessed: length of delay, reason for the delay, and defendant's assertion of the right. A deliberate delay was deemed serious, while the absence of a witness was justifiable. Factors such as crowded dockets and negligence were to be judged individually. Finally, a court was to review the possible prejudices and disadvantages suffered by a defendant during a delay. A determination that a defendant had been denied the right to a speedy trial could result in a decision to dismiss the indictment or to reverse a conviction in order that the indictment may be dismissed.

Impact The Speedy Trial Act imposed strict time deadlines and definite time periods for bringing defendants to trial, replacing the arbitrary factors of the *Barker* decision. It was decided that the government must initiate prosecution within thirty days following arrest (sixty days if no grand jury is in session), arraign defendants within ten days after filing indictment or information, and bring defendants to trial within sixty days following arraignment. According to the act, the following delays are not counted in computing days: delays needed to determine defendant's competency to stand trial, delays due to other trials of the defendant, delays due to hearings on pretrial motions, and delays due to interlocutory (provisional) appeals that interrupt the proceedings.

The Speedy Trial Act does not apply to juvenile proceedings, which have their own speedy trial provisions. Trial courts have discretion to dismiss cases that are not brought to trial promptly. States have the authority to enact their own speedy trial deadline provisions.

Further Reading

Samaha, Joel. *Criminal Procedure.* 4th ed. Belmont, Calif.: Wadsworth, 1999.

Sundquist, James. *The Decline and Resurgence of Congress.* Washington, D.C.: Brookings Institution, 2001.

Marcia J. Weiss

See also Supreme Court decisions.

■ Spielberg, Steven

Identification American director and producer
Born December 18, 1946; Cincinnati, Ohio

During the 1970's, one of the United States' most financially and artistically successful directors in history rose to fame.

Steven Spielberg had worked in a number of areas of television production prior to 1969, when he directed one of three segments of Rod Serling's television film *Night Gallery*, which was aired again in 1970 to introduce Serling's television series of the same name. "Eyes," starring Joan Crawford, was considered by many critics to be the standout of the trio, and its success led to Spielberg directing episodes of several other television shows in the early 1970's, though he received no special public recognition for this work.

Spielberg's next notable success was the television film *Duel* (1971), a thriller chronicling an ongoing battle between a lone motorist (played by Dennis Weaver) and a homicidal truck driver whom Weaver innocently offends and who then makes repeated attempts to kill Weaver. *Duel* was highly successful both commercially and critically, and an expanded version was released overseas. The techniques used to create suspense—for example, never showing the truck driver's face, relying on the audience's imagination, and showing scenes of Weaver in apparently secure surroundings and then suddenly besieged by the monstrous truck—foreshadowed Spielberg's later work on *Jaws* (1975).

Following several less significant television films,

Spielberg directed the theatrical motion picture *The Sugarland Express* in 1974. However, it was his next film, *Jaws*, that firmly established the director's astounding reputation. Based on the 1973 Peter Benchley novel, the film lived up to its famous advertising slogan, "Just when you thought it was safe to go back into the water . . ." by terrifying American audiences and earning a place in motion-picture history. The combination of an unseen danger punctuated by brief moments of graphic shock-horror proved more effective than expected. Spielberg's talent was augmented by John Williams's menacing score and a host of talented actors, in particular Robert Shaw as the fisherman Quint. The filming of *Jaws* was extraordinarily difficult technically, but the result was a popular culture phenomenon.

Director Steven Spielberg on the set of Close Encounters of the Third Kind *in 1977.* (Hulton Archive/Getty Images)

Spielberg followed Jaws with *Close Encounters of the Third Kind* (1977), a science-fiction film that was well-received, though less enthusiastically than *Jaws*. A comedy set in World War II, *1941* (1979), was the director's most disappointing work of the decade, possibly because audiences had come to expect something different from works with Spielberg's name attached. He also served as executive producer of *I Wanna Hold Your Hand* (1978), a popular comedy about a group of young women who go to outrageous extremes to see their idols, the Beatles, on their American tour.

Impact In the 1970's, the multitalented Spielberg continuously developed creatively. With *Jaws*, he created a motion-picture phenomenon and became one of the most famous directors in the United States.

Further Reading

Gottlieb, Carl, and Peter Benchley. *The "Jaws" Log: Twenty-fifth Anniversary Edition.* New York: Newmarket Press, 2001.

McBride, Joseph. *Steven Spielberg.* New York: Simon & Schuster, 1997.

Spielberg, Steven, Brent Notbohm, and Lester D. Friedman. *Steven Spielberg: Interviews.* Jackson: University Press of Mississippi, 2000.

Charles Lewis Avinger

See also *Close Encounters of the Third Kind*; Disaster films; Dreyfuss, Richard; Film in the United States; Horror films; *Jaws*; Science-fiction films; Special effects.

■ Spitz, Mark

Identification American swimmer
Born February 10, 1950; Modesto, California

Spitz won seven gold medals and set seven world records at the 1972 Munich Olympics.

Double-jointed at his knees, Mark Spitz had a natural advantage in pools, speeding past competitors in his best strokes, freestyle and butterfly. In the early 1970's, Spitz swam for Indiana University and won several National Collegiate Athletic Association (NCAA) titles. *Swimming World* magazine twice chose Spitz as World Swimmer of Year. The Amateur Athletic Union (AAU) honored him with the 1971 Sullivan Award for best athlete and the 1972 AAU Swimming Award. Coach Sherm Chavoor conditioned Spitz for the 1972 Munich Olympics. Spitz qualified in seven events at the August, 1972, Olympic trials in Chicago, setting a new world record in the 200-meter butterfly. By the end of that month, he was ready to win races and amaze crowds at the Olympic *Schwimmhalle*.

On August 28, Spitz won his first gold medal in the 200-meter butterfly in 2:00.70 minutes, breaking his recently established world record by 2.6 seconds. He then anchored the 400-meter freestyle relay for a 3.26.42 record to secure his second gold medal. Spitz earned his third gold medal the next day in a world-record performance of 1:52.78 minutes in the 200-meter freestyle, swimming .72 seconds faster than his previous record. On August 31, Spitz won his fourth gold in the 100-meter butterfly in 54.37 seconds, setting another record, and he dove in the pool again soon after that race to anchor the 800-meter freestyle relay, which the team won in the record time of 7:35.78 minutes. At that point, Spitz matched the Olympic record of five gold medals won during an Olympiad set by Italian athlete Nedo Nadi at the 1920 Olympics. Spitz's sixth gold medal was presented after his world-record 100-meter freestyle victory of 51.22 seconds on September 3. His teammates boosted him to their shoulders after they won gold in the 400-meter medley relay swum in 3:48.16 minutes on September 4.

Although most spectators supported the swimming sensation with the distinctive mustache, the Jewish Spitz endured some anti-Semitic taunts. On the day after Spitz won his seventh gold medal, Palestinian terrorists attacked Israeli athletes at the Olympics. At a press conference that morning, Spitz, considered a possible high-profile target, spoke to reporters while surrounded by officials. Unsure whether the terrorism would escalate, Spitz departed Munich before the closing ceremonies.

Impact As a result of his Olympic success, Mark Spitz became an international hero. As the world's best swimmer in the 1970's, he popularized swimming as a sport for competition and recreation. Idolized by many Americans, Spitz represented national pride when he defeated swimmers from communist nations, particularly East Germany, in the Cold War atmosphere. Major magazines featured Spitz. Abandoning his plans to become an orthodontist, Spitz reveled in his celebrity. He accepted entertainment and endorsement contracts, posing for posters and

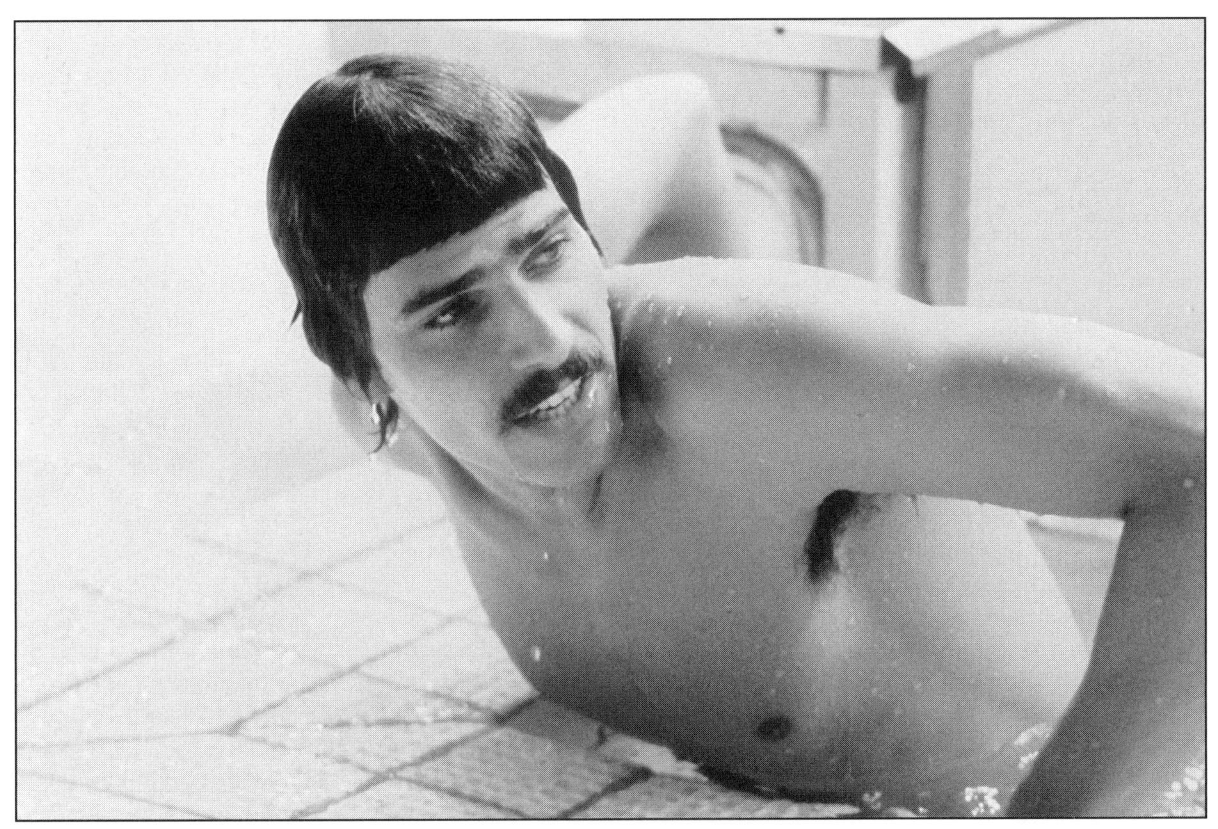

Swimming champion Mark Spitz climbs out of the pool after a race at the 1972 Olympics in Munich. (DPA/Landov)

starring in milk commercials. The International Swimming Hall of Fame inducted Spitz in 1977. Swimmers still aspire to surpass Spitz's record for most gold medals at an Olympic Games.

Further Reading

Chavoor, Sherman, with Bill Davidson. *The Fifty-Meter Jungle.* New York: Coward, McCann & Geoghegan, 1973.

Spitz, Mark, and Alan LeMond. *The Mark Spitz Complete Book of Swimming.* Photographs by Neil Leifer. New York: Thomas Y. Crowell, 1976.

Elizabeth D. Schafer

See also Advertising; Jewish Americans; Munich Olympics terrorism; Olympic Games of 1972; Sports.

■ Sports

Definition Athletic contests, both team and individual

A rich variety of athletic competitions interested and inspired Americans throughout the decade. The entry and visibility of women in sports was notable and reflected their changing role in society.

A number of professional and amateur sports were popular in North America during the 1970's, including auto racing, baseball, basketball, boxing, football, golf, hockey, horse racing, soccer, and tennis. Meanwhile, Title IX of the Education Amendments of 1972 ensured that girls and women were given opportunities in college athletics.

Auto Racing Anton "Tony" Hulman, Jr., passed away in 1977. He had purchased a near-defunct Indianapolis Motor Speedway, closed by World War II, and revived the Indianapolis 500 race, calling it "the Greatest Spectacle in Racing." If his label was overstated, there is little dispute that by the time of Hulman's death, the race had become ingrained in American popular culture. Auto racing and the Indy 500 were synonymous to many. The Unsers dominated the race this decade: Al won three times, his brother Bobby once.

Cleavage followed Hulman's passing. Dissatisfaction with the United States Auto Club (USAC), the sport's governing body, led to the creation in 1978 of Championship Auto Racing Teams (CART). The next year, CART sponsored its first race.

Meanwhile, stock car racing thrived. The National Association of Stock Car Auto Racing (NASCAR) considers these years probably the most historic for their version of the sport. Richard Petty won five Winston Cup titles. Cale Yarborough earned an unprecedented three in a row. NASCAR marks 1972 as the beginning of its modern era. Its point system was established in 1975.

Women entered professional racing during the decade. Shirley Muldowney won her first national event at Rockingham in 1971. She left funny cars for top fuel dragsters by 1974, winning the world championship in 1977. The same year, Janet Guthrie became the first woman to compete at the Indy 500, making the first of three consecutive starts. She finished ninth in 1978.

Baseball During the 1970's, two teams awed the baseball world and placed themselves squarely into contention for "best ever" status: the Cincinnati Reds and the Oakland Athletics (A's).

Between 1970 and 1976, Cincinnati's Big Red Machine won five division titles, four National League pennants, and two World Series (1975-1976). The team averaged ninety-eight wins per season and featured catcher Johnny Bench, first baseman Tony Perez, second baseman Joe Morgan, shortstop Dave Concepcion, third baseman Pete Rose, left fielder George Foster, center fielder Cesar Geronimo, and right fielder Ken Griffey, Sr. Sparky Anderson managed the club.

The A's captured five straight division titles, from 1971 to 1975, and won three consecutive World Series, the first in 1972. They did it with big hitters such as Reggie Jackson, Sal Bando, and Gene Tenace. Their pitching staff was even better. Beginning in 1971, Jim "Catfish" Hunter won more than twenty games five seasons in a row; he won twenty-five games in 1974. The 1973 team had two other twenty-game winners in Ken Holtzman and Vida Blue. Rollie Fingers waited in the bullpen with a 1.92 earned run average (ERA).

Their owner, Charley O. Finley, was as colorful as the vivid green jerseys, gold pants, and white spikes that the players donned each game. He was a cantankerous P. T. Barnum, promoting his team, the sport, and himself with many ideas, good and bad. Like Catfish's nickname, some stuck, including the designated hitter (DH) in the American League, instituted in 1973, and playing postseason games at night, which also began this decade.

U.S. president Gerald R. Ford and baseball players Hank Aaron and Pete Rose (left-right) talk before the opening day game in which Aaron hit his 714th career home run to tie Babe Ruth's record. (AP/Wide World Photos)

The game changed in other important ways. Curt Flood challenged the league's reserve clause in 1970; free agency came to professional baseball in 1975. The Senators left Washington, D.C., for Texas in 1971 and became the Rangers. In 1979, in order to preserve his arm across a long season, Cubs ace Bruce Sutter became the first pitcher to be employed as a closer.

The 1970's were marked by a number of outstanding individual achievements as well. The greatest of these occurred on April 8, 1974, in Atlanta, when Hank Aaron hit his 715th career home run, thereby breaking the mark set by Babe Ruth in 1935. He would hit another forty homers by the time that he retired in 1976.

Pitcher Nolan Ryan threw 383 strikeouts in 1973 and another 367 the following year. Although the data are sketchy, Ryan is credited with having thrown the fastest pitch ever recorded: 100.9 miles per hour. The same season, in 1974, Lou Brock stole 118 bases. In 1978, Rose hit safely in forty-four consecutive games, second only to Joe DiMaggio's fifty-six-game hitting streak in 1941. Rose became the youngest player to reach three thousand career hits, also that year. Jackson was named the World Series most valuable player (MVP) twice, with two different teams: the A's in 1973 and the Yankees in 1977. In the latter series, Jackson, nicknamed "Mr. October," became the first player since Ruth to hit three homers in one World Series game and the first ever to hit five in one World Series.

Basketball The 1969-1970 season of the National Basketball Association (NBA) was the first for Lew Alcindor (Kareem Abdul-Jabbar), who would be named league MVP six times between 1970 and 1980. The emergence of two rookies, Larry Bird and Earvin "Magic" Johnson, would redefine the sport at decade's end. The years between were marked by expansion and decline: more teams, more players, more games, and in fact more of everything except that which mattered most—fan enthusiasm, which waned. The arrival of Bird and Johnson finally reversed this slide.

Abdul-Jabbar was a product of the University of California at Los Angeles (UCLA). Coach John Wooden's Bruins were mid-dynasty as the decade opened; they would win four more consecutive national championships between 1970 and 1973 (for a total of ten in a row) and a fifth in 1975. Wooden then retired, with a record of 885-203 (an .813 winning percentage) across forty years of coaching.

During the 1970's, the NBA was emerging from a parallel universe. The Boston Celtics had won ten titles in eleven years before 1970; eight different teams would win the league trophy across this decade. (Another UCLA grad, Bill Walton, would lead the Portland Trail Blazers to one of those titles, in 1977.) The American Basketball Association (ABA) merged with the NBA in 1976, but adoption of the ABA's three-point shot would wait for three more seasons.

Four games during this decade were particularly memorable, and for very different reasons. The 1972 Summer Olympics in Munich, Germany, was forever marked by the massacre of Israeli athletes by terrorists on September 5. Five days later, the United States lost the men's basketball final to the Soviet Union, ending a winning streak dating to 1936. The team refused the silver medal, protesting the fact that the Soviets appeared to receive multiple opportunities and extra time to score the game's winning basket. Some labeled Game 5 of the 1976 NBA Finals "the greatest game ever": The Boston Celtics defeated the Phoenix Suns in three overtimes. In a game on December 9, 1977, Los Angeles Laker Kermit Washington punched Houston Rocket Rudy Tomjanovich in the face, nearly killing him. Magic Johnson's Michigan State Spartans beat Larry Bird's undefeated Indiana State Sycamores in the 1979 National Collegiate Athletic Association (NCAA) Tournament Final, with a record number of Americans tuning in.

Boxing Muhammad Ali returned to the ring in 1970. His refusal to serve in the Vietnam War had cost him his heavyweight title, his boxing license, and more than three years of his career at its prime. He lost "the Fight of the Century" to "Smokin'" Joe Frazier in 1971, but Ali won his second title from George Foreman three years later in Zaire. This "Rumble in the Jungle" was also promoter Don King's celebrity debut. Ali beat Frazier again in 1975's "Thrilla in Manila." He would go on to lose to and then regain his title from Leon Spinks in 1978. Ali shared the belt, however, as Larry Holmes held the World Boxing Council (WBC) crown.

Ali was most, but not all, of the decade's boxing story. The U.S. Boxing Team won five gold medals at the 1976 Olympics, with a squad that featured Leon and his brother Michael Spinks, along with Sugar Ray Leonard. All would go on to notable professional careers.

Football The year 1970 was a big one for football. The American Football League (AFL) merged with the National Football League (NFL). This new NFL comprised the National Football Conference (NFC) and the American Football Conference (AFC). For the sake of balance, three NFL stalwarts joined the AFC: the Baltimore Colts, Cleveland Browns, and Pittsburgh Steelers. Vince Lombardi died on September 3, and the Super Bowl trophy was renamed for the legendary Green Bay coach one week later. *Monday Night Football* debuted on September 21, and Tom Dempsey of the New Orleans Saints kicked a record sixty-three-yard field goal on November 8.

The Dallas Cowboys played in five Super Bowls during the decade, winning two, in 1972 and 1978. Led by Coach Tom Landry and quarterback Roger Staubach, the Cowboys were on television so often that Bob Ryan of NFL Films nicknamed them "America's Team."

Pittsburgh won three Super Bowls, in 1975, 1976, and 1979, with a team that featured quarterback Terry Bradshaw, running back Franco Harris, a stellar receiving corps, and the famed "Steel Curtain" defense. Two seasons prior to that first championship ring, it was Harris who took a phantom deflection (called the "immaculate reception") into the end zone against the Raiders for the Steelers' first playoff victory in forty years. They would lose their next game, the AFC Championship, to the Miami Dolphins, which were undefeated for the season. The Dolphins won the next two Super Bowls. The Minnesota Vikings would make four Super Bowl appearances in the 1970's—winning none.

The NFL changed in enduring ways. The Boston Patriots moved to Foxboro, Massachusetts, and became the New England Patriots in 1971. Two expansion teams, the Seattle Seahawks and the Tampa Bay Buccaneers, joined the NFL in 1974 and began play two years later. Referees began to use wireless microphones in 1975. Owners voted to adopt a sixteen-game regular season with a four-game preseason two years later.

In college football, each of four teams won two Associated Press (AP) national championships during the decade: Nebraska (1970-1971), Notre Dame (1973 and 1977), Oklahoma (1974-1975), and Alabama (1978-1979). The University of Southern California (USC) won in 1972, while the University of Pittsburgh claimed the title in 1976.

Golf Jack Nicklaus was golf's leading money-winner five times between 1971 and 1976; Johnny Miller interrupted the string in 1974 by winning eight Professional Golfers' Association (PGA) events. Tom Watson donned this mantle, and took PGA Player of the Year honors, for each of the last three years of the decade.

Nicklaus won eight major tournaments between 1970 and 1979, and he scored in the top five another nineteen times. Incredibly, he finished outside the top ten only five times during these ten years. He was also the only man to win each of the four major tournaments at least once during the 1970's. *Sports Illustrated* named him "Athlete of the Decade."

Lee Trevino was Player of the Year in 1971, and with good reason: He won five tournaments, including the U.S. and British Opens, and finished among the top five in four others. He beat Nicklaus in an eighteen-hole playoff to earn the U.S. Open victory. Trevino went on to win the British Open again in 1972 and the PGA Championship in 1974.

Gary Player won both the Masters and the British Open in 1974. Watson accomplished the identical feat in 1977. Player was the only other golfer to win four major tournaments during the 1970's. Having won the PGA Championship in 1972, he earned his second green jacket, presented to the winner of the Masters, at Augusta National in 1978. Watson's 1977 win at the British Open was his second; he beat Nicklaus by one stroke in the final round, having tied two rounds prior.

The United States continued its unbroken string of Ryder Cup victories, winning all four meetings.

In women's golf, Kathy Whitworth continued her reign as the leading money-winner of the Ladies Professional Golf Association (LPGA) for the first four years of the decade; she was also Player of the Year from 1971 to 1973. Sandra Haynie became the first golfer since Babe Zaharias to win the Grand Slam, taking the U.S. Women's Open and the LPGA Championship in 1974. Two years later, Judy Rankin became the first woman to surpass the $100,000 mark, earning a robust $150,734. She was both the leading money-winner and the Player of the Year during 1976 and 1977.

Then came Nancy Lopez. She won a record five straight tournaments, took the LPGA Championship and the Vare Trophy (for lowest scoring average), banked the most money, and was named Rookie of the Year and Player of the Year in 1978. She earned this last honor, and was the leading money-winner, again in 1979.

Hockey The Montreal Canadiens dominated the sport during this decade, winning the Stanley Cup six times: in 1971 and 1973 and from 1976 to 1979. A hockey dynasty, the team that won four consecutive cups included eleven future Hall of Famers: Coach Scotty Bowman, Yvan Cournoyer, Ken Dryden, Bob Gainey, Guy Lafleur, Guy Lapointe, Jacques Lemaire, Sam Pollock, Larry Robinson, Serge Savard, and Steve Shutt.

The Boston Bruins won the Stanley Cup twice, in 1970 and 1972, led by superstar Bobby Orr. In 1970, Orr was the first defenseman to score 100 points in a season, finishing with 139, and he made the decisive goal in the final.

Centerman Bobby Clarke led the Philadelphia Flyers to consecutive Stanley Cup victories in 1974 and 1975. In contrast to Montreal teams known for their skating and finesse, this team was nicknamed "The Broad Street Bullies" for its physical style of play—"goon" Dave Schultz set the record for most penalty minutes in a season (472 in 1974-1975)—but the players also had talent. Bernie Parent won both the Vezina (best goalie) and Conn Smythe (playoff MVP) trophies in each of these two years.

This was also an era of expansion for the National Hockey League (NHL), which would begin the decade with twelve teams and end it with twenty-one. The Buffalo Sabres and the Vancouver Canucks joined the league in 1970. The Atlanta Flames and the New York Islanders began play two years later. In 1974, it was the Kansas City Scouts and the Washington Capitals. The Scouts became the Colorado Rockies by 1976, the same year that the California Seals morphed into the Cleveland Barons. The Barons, in turn, merged with the Minnesota North Stars in 1978.

The World Hockey Association (WHA) began play in 1972. That it lured superstar Bobby Hull to jump over with a lucrative contract caused some controversy and trepidation. In fact, when it folded in 1979, the WHA contributed four teams to the NHL: the Edmonton Oilers, the Hartford Whalers, the Quebec Nordiques, and the Winnipeg Jets.

The U.S. Olympic hockey team earned the silver medal at the 1972 Winter Olympics, while the Soviet Union took the gold that year and again in 1976.

Horse Racing Three Triple Crown winners and two near misses meant that interest in horse racing surged during the decade. Secretariat won the Triple Crown—the Kentucky Derby, the Preakness, and the Belmont Stakes—in 1973, the first horse to do so in twenty-five years. Jockey Ron Turcotte was aboard for each race. Jean Cruguet rode Seattle Slew to the Triple Crown title in 1977. Affirmed and jockey Steve Cauthen captured the Triple Crown in 1978, a feat made all the more exciting by the fact that Alydar finished second in all three races. Cauthen was the youngest jockey ever to win the Triple Crown; in 1977, he had been named male athlete of the year by the Associated Press and "Sportsman of the Year" by *Sports Illustrated.* Two other horses came close to winning the Triple Crown during the decade before losing at Belmont: Canonero II in 1971 and Spectacular Bid in 1979.

Jockey Robyn Smith made the cover of *Sports Illustrated* in 1972. The following year, she became the first female jockey to win a stakes race, at Aqueduct. Female jockey Julie Krone was only a teenager in the 1970's, but she had begun riding at local tracks in Michigan by decade's end. The Hall of Fame lay ahead.

Soccer The North American Soccer League (NASL) grew fourfold, from six teams in 1970 to twenty-four by 1979. The New York Cosmos lured Brazilian legend Pelé out of retirement in 1974. He played his final game three years later against his old team, FC Santos, to a sold-out crowd at Giants Stadium.

That game was the sport's professional peak for the decade and also the exception: Most NASL teams had serious attendance problems, even though they had signed a series of aging European stars.

Tennis Jimmy Connors was ranked number one for five years, from 1974 to 1978. He brought attitude and intensity to the game. He grunted, yelled, and played with the crowd, especially at the U.S. Open, which he won three times: in 1974, 1976, and 1978. In 1974, Connors nearly captured a Grand Slam—Wimbledon and the U.S., French, and Australian Opens—winning all but the French Open. His use of a metal racket put him in the vanguard as well.

Björn Borg won the French Open that year, the next, and twice more in 1978 and 1979. Even more impressive were his four consecutive victories at Wimbledon beginning in 1976, where the year before Arthur Ashe became the first African American to win tennis's most prestigious event.

Women's tennis was even more amazing in the 1970's. Margaret Court retired in 1977 with sixty-two titles in Grand Slam events, more than any other man or woman by far. In fact, she won the Grand Slam in 1970 and nearly did so again three years later; Billie Jean King took Wimbledon.

King could play and was willing to speak up, making her a transcendent feminist icon and exemplar. Her own shot at the Grand Slam was foiled when Virginia Wade won the Australian Open in 1972. King was the first woman to reach $100,000 in earnings. She beat aging male player Bobby Riggs, handily, in the infamous "Battle of the Sexes" in 1973. *Time* named her "Woman of the Year" three years later.

The second half of the decade was dominated by Chris Evert and Martina Navratilova. Evert took back-to-back French Open titles (1974-1975) and won four consecutive U.S. Opens beginning in 1975. Navratilova won Wimbledon in 1978 and again in 1979, which assured her number-one ranking.

Other Olympic Notables Mark Spitz won seven gold medals in swimming at the 1972 Olympics. That he also set seven world records in the process made an unprecedented feat likely untouchable. Figure skater Dorothy Hamill won gold at Innsbruck in 1976. Bruce Jenner took the decathlon at the Montreal Summer Games that year. All became instant celebrities with lucrative endorsement deals.

Title IX Title IX under the Education Amendments of 1972 barred sex discrimination for any educational program or activity receiving federal funds, including athletics. Intended to level the playing field for women, it threatened the status quo and was therefore controversial. Prior to its passage, some states barred women from intermural competition, and women's sports constituted on the order of 15 percent of athletic programs and a mere 2 percent of athletic budgets. During the 1970's, female participation in sports exploded, no doubt in large measure the result of Title IX. However, disentangling the effect of this change in the law from the empowerment associated with the women's movement in general is quite difficult.

Impact Many athletic accomplishments from the 1970's endure, both in the record books and in the hearts and minds of fans. This decade marked a peak for some sports and the transition to a modern era for others.

Further Reading

Kilmeade, Brian. *The Games Do Count: America's Best and Brightest on the Power of Sports.* New York: HarperCollins, 2004. Notable Americans ranging from President George H. W. Bush to comedian Bernie Mac explain why sports matter.

McGovern, Mike. *The Complete Idiot's Guide to Sports History and Trivia.* Indianapolis: Alpha Books, 2002. Colorful statistics and factoids on many of the personalities and developments in sports, in an accessible format.

Sports Illustrated, eds. *Sports Illustrated Fifty Years: The Anniversary Book.* New York: Author, 2004. Photographs and stories from, arguably, the authoritative source. Coverage allows context for achievements of the 1970's, both before and after.

John Patrick Piskulich

See also Ali, Muhammad; Anthony, Earl; Ashe, Arthur; Baseball; Basketball; Battle of the Sexes; Bench, Johnny; Boxing; Canada Cup of 1976; Commonwealth Games of 1978; Connors, Jimmy; Cosell, Howard; Designated hitter; Erving, Julius; Evert, Chris; Fischer, Bobby; Football; Free agency; Golf; Hamill, Dorothy; Hockey; Horse racing; Jackson, Reggie; Jenner, Bruce; King, Billie Jean; Lafleur, Guy; Little League participation by girls; Lopez, Nancy; *Monday Night Football*; Muldowney, Shirley; Munich Olympics terrorism; Nicklaus, Jack; Olympic Games of 1972; Olympic Games of 1976; Orr, Bobby; Palmer, Jim; Payton, Walter; Pelé; Rose, Pete; Ryan, Nolan; Secretariat; Simpson, O. J.; Soccer; Spitz, Mark; Tennis; Title IX of the Education Amendments of 1972; Walton, Bill; Washington punching of Tomjanovich; Wooden, John.

■ Springsteen, Bruce

Identification American rock-and-roll singer and musician

Born September 23, 1949; Freehold, New Jersey

Springsteen was one of the most successful and influential performers and songwriters to emerge in American popular music during the 1970's.

Bruce Springsteen began playing rock-and-roll music in small clubs along New Jersey's south shore. John Hammond, the legendary artist-and-repertoire (A&R) man who discovered Bob Dylan, signed Springsteen to Columbia Records in 1972, and his first album, *Greetings from Asbury Park, N.J.*, was released in 1973. The public took little notice, but critics reacted warmly. *The Wild, the Innocent, and the E Street Shuffle* was released later the same year, but it did not enter the charts until 1975, when *Born to Run*

Bruce Springsteen performs in 1979. (AP/Wide World Photos)

came out and entered the top 30. *Born to Run* catapulted Springsteen into the major leagues. However, a legal dispute with his manager, Mike Appel, halted any other releases until the critically acclaimed 1978 album, *Darkness on the Edge of Town.* Springsteen made good use of the time between records, touring extensively with his ten-piece backing ensemble, the E Street Band.

In 1975, Springsteen appeared on the covers of *Time* and *Newsweek* and attracted the notice of rock critic Jon Landau, who became his producer, friend, and collaborator after Springsteen split with Appel. Landau grew into a trusted adviser and guided Springsteen's career over the coming decades by helping him hone his talents and focus his immense energy.

During this decade, Springsteen inspired a fiercely loyal following. His electrifying performances lasted three and four hours, and he toured almost constantly. He was compared often to Dylan because his lyrics were dense and emotionally deep. Throughout the decade, he grew tremendously both as a performer and as a songwriter. His songs were often narratives of working-class people who occupied the dark and hopeless margins of society. His audience related and reacted viscerally to songs about losing jobs, breaking up, and feeling restless. Many of the songs he released in the 1970's, such as "Born to Run" and "Thunder Road," became rock-and-roll classics.

Impact Springsteen influenced a generation of singer-songwriters and built his reputation on a foundation of personal integrity, loyalty to his working-class roots, and generosity toward his fan base.

Subsequent Events Springsteen's fame grew in the 1980's, and his 1984 album *Born in the U.S.A* produced seven top-ten singles. He became involved in many political issues, performing benefits for and raising awareness about concerns such as veterans' benefits and feeding the poor. He continued to perform and record and enjoys one of the most sustained, successful careers of any American popular music performer.

Further Reading

Alterman, Eric. *It Ain't No Sin to Be Glad You're Alive: The Promise of Bruce Springsteen.* Boston: Back Bay Books, 2001.

Goodman, Fred. *The Mansion on the Hill: Dylan, Young, Geffen, Springsteen, and the Head-on Collision of Rock and Commerce.* New York: Vintage, 1998.

Sawyers, June Skinner, and Martin Scorsese. *Racing in the Street: The Bruce Springsteen Reader.* New York: Penguin Books, 2004.

Lacy Schutz

See also Music; Singer-songwriters.

■ *Star Trek*

Identification Television series and film
Creator Gene Roddenberry (1921-1991)
Date Series aired from 1966 to 1969; film released in 1979

The 1970's witnessed the transformation of Star Trek *from a short-lived television series to an iconic media franchise.*

The last episode of *Star Trek*'s three-year run on television aired in 1969. By most accounts, that was the end of a quirky television show that had achieved moderate popularity. The cast of the show—including William Shatner (as Captain Kirk), Leonard Nimoy (as Mr. Spock), DeForest Kelley (as Dr. McCoy), Nichelle Nichols (as Uhura), James Doohan (as Scotty), George Takei (as Sulu), and Walter Koenig (as Chekov)—went on to find other work, as did the show's creator, Gene Roddenberry.

Unexpectedly, the 1970's saw an unprecedented resurgence of interest in *Star Trek* that would result in the creation of a cultural icon. The first *Star Trek* convention was held in January, 1972. These conventions became a national and later an international phenomenon, during which actors from the show made guest appearances, and fans had an opportunity to purchase merchandise. More important, the conventions created the momentum for *Star Trek*'s comeback.

In 1973, *Star Trek* returned to television as an animated Saturday morning show with most of the original cast resuming their roles in voice for the cartoon. Over two years, twenty-two animated episodes aired. Meanwhile, actors from the show made appearances on television variety shows and discussed the enduring popularity of *Star Trek*, which was then airing in syndicated reruns.

Although Paramount Studios indicated an interest in creating a *Star Trek* feature film, it did not pursue the idea seriously. In 1977, Paramount decided to launch a new television network and feature *Star*

Trek II. The plan fell through, but not before casting and production had been set in motion. However, the viability of theatrical science fiction was solidified with the success of *Close Encounters of the Third Kind* (1977), and *Star Trek II* was converted into *Star Trek: The Motion Picture*. Robert Wise directed the film, Roddenberry served as producer, and the entire television cast reprised their roles.

Released on December 7, 1979, the film cost $45 million to make and grossed $105 million domestically. Fans who had waited eleven years for their beloved characters to return were delighted, but the film had many critics for its uneven editing and slow development. Nevertheless, *Star Trek* was back.

Star Trek *creator Gene Roddenberry and actors William Shatner, DeForest Kelley, and Leonard Nimoy (left-right) reunite on the set of* Star Trek: The Motion Picture *in 1978. During the 1970's, the 1960's science-fiction series reached cult status and spawned a film franchise.* (AP/Wide World Photos)

Impact While political corruption and the Vietnam War shook the American public's faith in humanity during the 1970's, *Star Trek* offered the alternative of Roddenberry's vision of a positive future that eliminated racism and greed in return for the pursuit of growth and improvement. Fans found this vision so compelling that they brought the show back from the ashes to become an important cultural icon. The unprecedented, albeit slow, return of *Star Trek* during the 1970's would lead to a series of films, numerous television shows, novels, comic books, and casino and theme park rides as part of one of the largest media franchises that television ever created.

Further Reading

Fern, Yvonne. *Gene Roddenberry: The Last Conversation*. New York: Pocket Books, 1996.

Hise, James Van. *The Unauthorized History of Trek*. San Francisco: HarperPrism, 1995.

Maurice Hamington

See also *Battlestar Galactica*; *Close Encounters of the Third Kind*; Film in the United States; Science-fiction films; Special effects; *Star Wars*; Television in the United States.

■ *Star Wars*

Identification Science-fiction film
Director George Lucas (1944-)
Date Released in 1977

Star Wars *started as a science-fiction summer film and turned into a worldwide phenomenon that had a profound effect on the entire film industry.*

Made in the era of the Vietnam War and Watergate, *Star Wars* began as a run-of-the-mill science-fiction story to entertain audiences, but by the end of the 1970's, it had broken box-office records and spawned an entire industry. *Star Wars* became a watershed film because it blended high action with unprecedented special effects in order to create a unique filmgoing experience. The film was science fiction, but the way it was done recalled old-time cliffhanger films such as the serial *Buck Rogers* (1939). *Star Wars* also helped to usher in an era of what later came to be called "blockbuster" films—motion pictures that feature a plot that at times is secondary to action and special effects.

After his success with *American Graffiti* (1973), George Lucas began work on what was called in an early draft of the script "The Star Wars." Casting relatively unknown actors (with the exception of Sir Alec Guinness and Peter Cushing), Lucas harked back to the days of weekly film serials. He also drew from mythology and Westerns and created an experience that had not been seen before. People associated with the film wondered if it was doomed to failure, but cheering audiences quickly quenched these doubts. *Star Wars*, filmed with a budget of only eight million dollars, was a huge success.

Innovations Even though *Star Wars* was supposed to be an ordinary film, the way Lucas went about making it was unique. He founded Lucasfilm LTD, his own production company, in 1971 and Industrial Light and Magic (ILM) in 1975. ILM was one of the first companies that did visual effects outside the studio itself. Lucas wanted to make films children could see, but he did not want to lose creative control over the entire franchise. Like his mentor Francis Ford Coppola, who founded his own production company, American Zoetrope, Lucas established Lucasfilm LTD as a way to break ties with Hollywood. Twentieth Century-Fox still had ties with *Star Wars* financially, but when the film broke box-office records, Lucas used the money to break away completely from Hollywood's major studios.

Lucas also hired composer John Williams to write a symphonic soundtrack that was a throwback to cliffhanger serials: It was exciting and adventurous without being melodramatic or frightening. The theme music would soon become so recognizable that with only a few notes people all over the world would instantly think of the film.

The sound effects, under the supervision of Ben Burtt, were of organic and natural sounds instead of electronic noises; for example, R2-D2's "voice" is Burtt's synthesized voice doing baby talk. Even the opening credit was unique: All credits were placed at the end, and the camera panned across the star field instead of using a fixed, nonmoving camera. This approach was in direct violation of what the Directors Guild expected; Lucas paid a fine and gave up his membership in the Directors Guild rather than be told how his film was supposed to look.

Licensing Lucas made deals with Marvel Comics and a few others months before the film opened. He realized that traditional advertisements were not going to work because *Star Wars* might be viewed primarily as children's science-fiction material. He encouraged word-of-mouth marketing at the World Science Fiction Convention, where he was sure there would be people interested in the film he was making. Toy tie-ins were unusual in the 1970's, and only after the film's success did Kenner Toys began making the action figures. There were few ready by Christmas of 1977, so Kenner sold an "Early Bird Certificate Package" with a slip to order the actual figures, which arrived two months later.

Licensed materials for films had existed before, but the amount that was generated with *Star Wars* was unprecedented. Everything from music and food to clothing and household accessories was marketed along with the related toys. Because Lucas owned the rights to the film, all profits from merchandizing went to him rather than to the film's distributing company, Twentieth Century-Fox. That meant that the more products released with the *Star Wars* name on them, the more return Lucas could make. It was a gamble, but Lucas used the proceeds to finance his other films himself—he truly had become an independent filmmaker.

Impact *Star Wars* became one of the highest-grossing films of all time, earning more than $460 million. Moreover, Lucasfilm LTD became its own independent Hollywood, further expanding to include Skywalker Sound and LucasArts games, while ILM became the world's leading visual effects company. Lucas is recognized as one of film's true pioneers, creating new techniques and technology for the next generation of filmmakers.

Further Reading

Brooker, Will. *Using the Force: Creativity, Community, and "Star Wars" Fans.* New York: Continuum, 2002. Talks about the various aspects of being a *Star Wars* fan.

Henderson, Mary. *"Star Wars": The Magic of Myth.* New York: Bantam, 1997. This book accompanied the 1998 Smithsonian exhibit on *Star Wars* and offers insight into the symbolism of Lucas's universe.

Salewicz, Chris. *George Lucas Close Up: The Making of His Movies.* New York: Thunder's Mouth Press, 1998. A detailed account about the making of

Lucas's films; also has reprints of *Variety* reviews of Lucas's films in the back.

Sansweet, Stephen J. *Star Wars: From Concept to Screen to Collectible.* New York: Chronicle, 1992. Talks about *Star Wars* and its collectibles and offers behind-the-scene details of many *Star Wars* products, including the action figures.

Kelly Rothenberg

See also *American Graffiti*; Film in the United States; Science-fiction films; Special effects.

■ Steinem, Gloria

Identification American feminist editor, author, and lecturer

Born March 25, 1934; East Toledo, Ohio

Steinem consciously used her good looks and quick wit to popularize feminism and fight for women's rights through the media. She cofounded Ms. *magazine as well as a number of women's political action groups. She worked to promote, among other things, equality of pay and abortion rights for women.*

Gloria Steinem entered the 1970's eschewing the word "feminist" in favor of "humanist," but she rapidly became a spokesperson for feminism and the enlargement of women's rights. She was a popular role model for many women, while at the same time being attacked by other prominent feminists for her popularity with the media and her association with powerful men. Her research and work in the previous two decades positioned her well. In 1970, she received the Penney-Missouri Journalism Award for her first feminist article, "After Black Power, Women's Liberation," published in 1969 in *New York Magazine.*

The following year, she marched in the New York City Women's Strike for Equality and became friends with Dorothy Pitman Hughes, an African American woman who founded one of the first community day care centers for working mothers in the city. The two women formed the Women's Action Alliance and hatched the idea for *Ms.* magazine, which was first published as an insert in the December, 1971, *New York.* Steinem also cofounded, with Bella Abzug, Shirley Chisholm, and Betty Friedan, the National Women's Political Caucus. She was featured on the cover of *Newsweek* as the personification of women's liberation.

In 1972, Steinem worked toward making abortion legal, announcing that she was one of millions who had had an illegal abortion, and is credited by some with coining the phrase "reproductive freedom." *McCall's* magazine named her Woman of the Year in 1972. Two years later, she helped found the Coalition of Labor Union Women, in 1975 helped plan the women's agenda for the Democratic National Convention, helped plan and was a prominent participant in the 1977 National Women's Conference in Houston, and during the decade also participated in founding Voters for Choice and Women Against Pornography. She gave numerous commencement speeches and lectures on feminism throughout the United States.

Steinem's first commencement address was by invitation at her alma mater, Smith College, an occasion that highlighted for the first time what was to become an escalating rivalry between her and a fellow Smith alumna, author and activist Friedan. Because of their appearance and manner, Friedan was perceived by the media as the radical and Steinem as the more moderate feminist, but in reality, as evi-

Gloria Steinem. (Library of Congress)

denced by their speeches, writings, and political support, Steinem was the more radical of the two.

Impact From the 1970's on, Gloria Steinem has, as a writer and an activist, been a leader in the women's rights movement. Her greatest impact has come through her editorship and continuing influence at *Ms.*, her books and articles, and her connection with powerful men.

Further Reading

Cohen, Marcia. *The Sisterhood: The True Story of the Women Who Changed the World.* New York: Simon & Schuster, 1988.

Heilbrun, Carolyn G. *The Education of a Woman: The Life of Gloria Steinem.* New York: Ballantine Books, 1996.

Steinem, Gloria. *Outrageous Acts and Everyday Rebellions.* New York: New American Library, 1983.

Erika E. Pilver

See also Abortion rights; Equal Rights Amendment (ERA); Feminism; Journalism in the United States; Liberalism in U.S. politics; *Ms.* magazine; National Organization for Women (NOW); *Roe v. Wade*; Sexual revolution; Women's rights.

■ Streaking

Definition Running naked through public areas

Streaking became a popular fad during the early to mid-1970's and reflected the playfully impudent flavor of the decade.

Fads in inexplicable behavior or interests are part of the popular culture of every era, but the 1970's seemed especially rich in them, with pet rocks, mood rings, and disco music being among the most notable. The origins of streaking—joyfully racing through public places in the nude—are difficult to establish. Urban legend from the era suggests that public ordinances in various cities around the United States outlawed nakedness only if the person or persons involved were walking or standing still. If this were the case, the fad arose in part from the impulse to flout legal statutes in a playful manner. Per-

A streaker runs behind presenter David Niven at the Academy Awards ceremony in 1974. (AP/Wide World Photos)

haps adding to this impetus for baring the body in public was a revival of "mooning," or baring the buttocks, created in part by films of the 1970's that were set in the 1950's, when the practice was popular.

Whatever its source, streaking seems to have arisen on college campuses in 1973 in the Northeast and Midwest, spreading then to other institutions of higher learning around the country. For a few years, streaking was as much a part of university life in the United States as keg parties and all-night study sessions before final examinations. It was incorporated into already existing college traditions and conventions: fraternity initiations, football games, and graduation ceremonies. Occasionally, the nude sprinting was associated with political protest or solidarity with a social cause, but for the most part, it was undertaken purely in a sense of play and fun.

From college campuses, the fad spread to other public venues, including televised national events such as the 1974 broadcast of the Academy Awards, at which a streaker running across the stage in full view of cameras elicited an acidic remark from presenter David Niven that the man had just revealed his "shortcomings" to the world. However, the favorite spot for streaking, both on and off college campuses, remained sporting events of various sorts. Streaking earned the ultimate pop culture accolade in 1974 when it served as the subject for a Top 10 hit from comic-songwriter Ray Stevens, "The Streak," which included a line referring to turning "the other cheek."

Impact The height of the streaking craze was brief: the early to mid-1970's. Nevertheless, in many ways, streaking was reflective of 1970's attitudes. Just as the madness for mood rings and pet rocks gently mocked the cult of feelings and emotions in the 1960's, streaking likewise seemed to be a 1970's-era spoof of 1960's public protest and political street theater—one in which the spectacle was only mildly shocking and only rarely made a statement beyond the briefest flouting of mainstream mores. Streaking never faded completely, occurring from time to time into the twenty-first century, especially at sporting events in places such as the United States, Great Britain, and Australia.

Further Reading

Schulman, Bruce J. *The Seventies: The Great Shift in American Culture, Society, and Politics.* New York: Da Capo Press, 2002.

Skolnik, Peter L., Nikki Smith, and Laura Torbet. *Fads: America's Crazes, Fevers, and Fancies from the 1890's to the 1970's.* New York: Crowell, 1978.

Thomas Du Bose

See also Academy Awards; Fads.

■ Streep, Meryl

Identification American film, stage, and television actor

Born June 22, 1949; Summit, New Jersey

One of the most admired film actors of her generation, Streep became known during the 1970's for her careful research, her meticulous re-creation of accents and behaviors, and her dramatic range.

When Meryl Streep appeared in a minor role in her first film, *Julia* (1977), she was already an accomplished performer, with experience in more than forty productions while a student thespian at Vassar, Dartmouth, and the Yale Drama School. Her early commercial work ranged from Off-Broadway to Broadway to made-for-television films. In *Everybody Rides the Carousel* (1975), Streep voiced the struggle between intimacy and isolation in "the sixth stage" of the life cycle as understood by psychoanalyst Erik Erikson and animators John and Faith Hubley.

Streep's well-trained voice and her radiant face became known to a huge international audience through her powerful, Emmy-winning performance in the seven-hour miniseries *Holocaust* (1978), in which Streep, herself a Jewish American, plays the Gentile wife of the eldest son of the Weiss family, whose tragedy becomes emblematic of Jewish suffering. Later in 1978, Streep appeared in one of the major films of the decade, *The Deer Hunter,* Michael Cimino's story of three young working-class men whose lives are forever changed by their experiences in Vietnam. Streep's vivid portrayal of a hometown woman loved by two friends adds poignancy to a narrative of personal and national loss.

In 1979, Streep received a cluster of awards for supporting performances in three films about relationships in crisis, a common 1970's theme. Although the films differed greatly in their styles, in each Streep portrays a restless woman. In *Manhattan,* she leaves her husband (played by Woody Allen) for another woman and writes an exposé about her disastrous marriage; in *Kramer vs. Kramer,* she abandons her husband and young son, returning later to fight for child custody; and in *The Seduction of Joe Tynan*, she plays a Southern lawyer who jeopardizes a colleague's marriage. In this film, she displayed her ability with accents, a talent that became a trademark.

Impact Meryl Streep's chameleon quality more resembled theatrical traditions than the fixed persona typical of Hollywood stardom. Her range extended to comedic acting and musical performance, but she became most associated with serious drama and memorable characterizations of strong-willed women. The intelligence, care, and skill that characterized her acting helped shape standards in American film performance.

Subsequent Events Streep moved into leading roles in the 1980's that were characterized by their complexity and diversity. In 2004, she became the sixth woman to receive the American Film Institute Lifetime Achievement Award. Then only in her mid-fifties, she had amassed a record thirteen Academy Award nominations in three decades of remarkable performances.

Meryl Streep. (CBS/Landov)

Further Reading

Cardullo, Bert, et al., eds. *Playing to the Camera: Film Actors Discuss Their Craft.* New Haven, Conn.: Yale University Press, 1998.

Maychick, Diana. *Meryl Streep: The Reluctant Superstar.* New York: St. Martin's Press, 1984.

Carolyn Anderson

See also Academy Awards; Allen, Woody; *Deer Hunter, The*; Film in the United States; Hoffman, Dustin; *Kramer vs. Kramer*; Theater in the United States.

■ Studio 54

Identification Renowned discotheque
Date Opened in 1977
Place New York City

Studio 54 was a wildly successful dance club with a reputation as both a social phenomenon and a symbol of the decade's decadence and excess.

A former television studio located at 254 West 54th Street in New York City, Studio 54 was the creation of entrepreneurs Steve Rubell and Ian Schrager, who transformed the cavernous, theatrical space into the most popular disco dance club of its era. With the intention of capitalizing on the up-tempo beat of disco, an emerging form of music popular with gay and black audiences, the discotheque offered a perpetually festive party atmosphere fueled both by the presence of colorful celebrities and by flamboyant "nobodies."

Among its most famous attributes was a dance floor decorated with a neon "man-in-the-moon" inhaling cocaine from a silver spoon, a mirrored diamond-shaped main bar, strobe lights, an exclusive VIP basement party room, and balconies that became a venue for uninhibited sexual liaisons and rampant drug use. Most well-known of all its characteristics was the entrance's famed velvet ropes, behind which swarmed eager mobs of people hoping to be admitted to the club. With a selection policy that mixed a salad of racial and ethnic minorities, social classes, genders, sexual preferences, everyday people, and celebrities, Studio 54 was highly egalitarian. At the same time, the club developed a new form of exclusivity based on finding the right blend of black and white, straight and gay, along with its premium on beauty, youth, and theatricality.

Eventually Studio 54 became known for its dangerous levels of promiscuity, alcohol, and drug use, so that its magical mood of freewheeling fun gave way to a sense of dangerous hedonism that ended by giving the club a reputation for decadence and debauchery. Although a hugely prosperous enterprise, Studio 54's liberal tolerance of drugs combined with dubious financial practices led to the arrest of the club's two owners and to their sentencing to three and a half years in federal prison. Although the club continued to operate in the hands of other owners, it never again achieved the legendary status it enjoyed in the late 1970's.

Writer Truman Capote at Studio 54 in 1978. (AP/Wide World Photos)

Impact For a time the most famous nightclub in the world, Studio 54 was regarded as one of the great centers of a new, permissive morality that encouraged acceptance of recreational drug use and sexual freedom. Above and beyond its cult of celebrity, the club additionally helped make that decade's feminist, gay rights, and racial equality movements more mainstream.

Further Reading

Haden-Guest, Anthony. *The Last Party: Studio 54, Disco, and the Culture of the Night.* New York: Harper Collins, 1988.

Haden-Guest, Anthony, Niels Kummer, Domitilla Sartago, and Felice Quinto. *Studio 54: The Legend.* New York: Te Neues, 1997.

Lawrence, Tim. *Love Saves the Day: A History of American Dance Music Culture, 1970-1979.* Durham, N.C.: Duke University Press, 2004.

Margaret Boe Birns

See also Dance, popular; Disco; Discotheques; Drug use; Fashions and clothing; Homosexuality and gay rights; "Me Decade"; *Saturday Night Fever*; Sexual revolution; Summer, Donna.

■ Summer, Donna

Identification African American pop singer
Born December 31, 1948; Boston, Massachusetts

Known as the queen of disco, Summer was the most celebrated pop singer of the 1970's.

Beginning her career as a sexual icon, Donna Summer matured into a passionate singer with a distinctive vocal personality that combined elements of rock and soul and both defined the disco sound and built upon it. She was the first female artist to have three number-one singles in one year and the first to have three consecutive number-one double albums.

Summer had a strict religious upbringing and began her musical career in the church choir. At the age of nineteen, she joined a German touring company of the musical *Hair* and became active in musical theater in Germany. In 1971, she recorded her first single, "Sally Go 'Round the Roses," which was unsuccessful. However, in 1974, she teamed up with producers Giorgio Moroder and Pete Bellotte to record her first album, *Lady of the Night,* which contained two singles that became hits in Europe.

In 1975, Summer recorded "Love to Love You, Baby," which became her first major success in the United States. Although the seventeen-minute erotic single pushed the limits of decency for the time, it was an incredibly popular dance tune and was often played in its entirety on the radio. Reportedly, Summer was so embarrassed by the explicit lyrics that she insisted upon singing it for the first time in a darkened recording studio.

Summer followed the 1975 hit with two popular albums in 1976—*A Love Trilogy* and *The Four Seasons of Love*—and her 1977 album *I Remember Yesterday,* which included the single "I Feel Love," the first song to be recorded with an entirely synthesized backing track. Her critically acclaimed sixth album, *Once upon a Time,* employs a Cinderella rags-to-riches theme to tell its story. In 1979, she released the singles "Hot Stuff" and "Bad Girls," which, for the first time, brought an element of rock to the disco sound.

Donna Summer displays her American Music Awards at the 1979 ceremonies, including one in the newly created category of Best Disco Album. (AP/Wide World Photos)

Impact Donna Summer accumulated fourteen top-ten hits, four number-one singles, three platinum albums, five Grammy Awards, and twelve other Grammy nominations. Although she is strongly associated with disco, her career began before disco and continued after its demise. One of the few disco artists to be taken seriously by music critics, she is a gifted songwriter as well as performer. Unlike most disco artists, she focused on albums rather than on singles, creating well-received concept albums. Her music was enormously influential in the development of techno and electronica music as well as disco. Despite her musical accomplishments, Summer's name will always be synonymous with disco, a genre that she helped to create and raised to a new level.

Further Reading

Miller, Ernestine. *Donna Summer: Her Life and Music.* Cranberry Township, Pa.: Tiny Ripple Books, 2003.

Summer, Donna, and Marc Eliot. *Ordinary Girl: The Journey.* New York: Random House, 2003.

Mary Virginia Davis

See also Disco; Discotheques; Music; Studio 54.

■ Supreme Court decisions

Definition Rulings made by the highest court in the United States

The U.S. Supreme Court decisions in the 1970's played an important role in defining the American legal and political systems of subsequent decades.

During the 1970's, the U.S. Supreme Court was led by Chief Justice Warren Burger, who served as leader of the Court from 1969 to 1986. Burger was appointed by President Richard M. Nixon, a Republican, who campaigned for the presidency in 1968 on a platform that he would appoint conservative justices to the Supreme Court. In addition to Burger,

President Nixon appointed justices Harry A. Blackmun, Lewis Powell, and William H. Rehnquist to the Court early in the decade. Because the only other appointment during the 1970's was Justice John Paul Stevens by President Gerald R. Ford in 1975, the Supreme Court became known as the "Nixon Court" during this era.

While the Court was more conservative during the 1970's than the liberal Supreme Court of the 1950's and 1960's, the shift toward conservatism was not dramatic. During the 1970's, the Supreme Court handed down landmark decisions with both liberal and conservative outcomes in the areas of religion, free press, obscenity, the death penalty, abortion, racial desegregation, women's rights, affirmative action, presidential power, and campaign finance.

Issues of Religious Freedom During the 1970's, the Supreme Court issued two landmark rulings involving religion. According to the First Amendment, government is prohibited from establishing religion or infringing upon religious freedom. In the 1971 case of *Lemon v. Kurtzman*, the Supreme Court established the "Lemon test" to guide the Court in decisions dealing with the separation of church and state. The Lemon test contains three prongs used to judge laws where religion and government intersect: A law must have a secular purpose, a law must not advance or inhibit religion, and a law must not foster excessive entanglement between government and religion. A government law or policy must pass all three prongs to be declared constitutional. If a law fails one prong, then it violates the idea of separation of church and state grounded in the establishment clause. In the *Lemon* case, the Court ruled that government laws providing financial assistance to parochial schools violated the establishment clause of the First Amendment.

The First Amendment also contains a free exercise clause that protects the religious freedom of individuals. The Supreme Court demonstrated the importance of the free exercise clause in 1971 in *Wisconsin v. Yoder*, when the justices ruled that a state could not force Amish children to attend school because it violated their religious freedom. This case established the highest level of protection for individuals whenever government laws attempt to limit religious freedom. A government law that restricts religious freedom will more likely be struck down as a violation of the First Amendment unless the government can justify the law based upon a compelling state interest.

Freedom of the Press In regard to freedom of the press, the Supreme Court provided broader protections for newspapers during the 1970's. In 1971, in *New York Times Co. v. United States*, the Supreme Court ruled that *The New York Times* was protected in publishing classified information under the free press clause. The U.S. government had attempted to prevent *The New York Times* and *The Washington Post* from publishing a manuscript titled the Pentagon Papers, which documented the United States' foreign policy in Vietnam. The Pentagon Papers were secretly copied and sent to *The New York Times* by Daniel Ellsberg, who had worked at the Pentagon on the study. Even though the government claimed national security as a reason for censorship, the Court decided that freedom of the press was more important.

During this time, the Court also established that judicial gag orders on the press violated the First Amendment in most instances. The justices voted unanimously in *Nebraska Press Association v. Stuart* in in 1976 to strike down a gag order in a murder case because the justices argued that an unbiased jury could be selected without a gag order.

Finally, the Court recognized that advertising, or commercial speech, was protected expression. In 1975, in the case of *Bigelow v. Virginia*, the justices ruled that the *Virginia Weekly* could advertise abortion services and that a nineteenth century Virginia law that prohibited the advertising of abortion services was in violation of the First Amendment. This was a very important decision because the Court acknowledged for the first time that commercial speech was protected under the First Amendment. Because of the Court's ruling in *Bigelow*, commercial advertisements once prohibited, such as legal services and pharmaceutical drugs, were declared protected expression under the First Amendment.

Obscenity Returned to States and Localities In the area of obscenity, the Supreme Court issued a landmark ruling that was a direct result of Nixon's appointments in the early 1970's. Prior to this decade, the Court issued liberal rulings that provided broad protection under the First Amendment for sexually explicit material. Under the Court's test from the late 1950's and 1960's, material was judged obscene and unprotected by the First Amendment only if it appealed to the prurient interest, was patently offen-

U.S. Supreme Court Justices During the 1970's

Justices are nominated by the U.S. president and approved by the U.S. Senate. The table below lists the justices who served during the 1970's. The names are placed in the order in which they took the judicial oath of office and thereby started their term.

Justice	*Term*
William O. Douglas	1939-1975
John M. Harlan II	1955-1971
William Brennan	1956-1990
Potter Stewart	1962-1993
Byron White	1962-1993
Thurgood Marshall	1967-1991
Warren Burger (Chief Justice)	1969-1986
Harry A. Blackmun	1971-1994
Lewis Powell	1972-1987
William H. Rehnquist	1973-2005
John Paul Stevens	1975-

sive, and was utterly without redeeming social value. This liberal test made it very difficult for material to be judged obscene because all three criteria had to be established based upon national standards.

The conservative justices appointed by Nixon had a direct impact on the area of obscenity when the Court handed down its decision in *Miller v. California* in 1973. Whereas the liberal test from the 1950's and 1960's allowed for material to be protected if it had any isolated reference to something of social value, the Miller test focused upon the centrality of the literary, artistic, political, and scientific (LAPS) value. The Miller test applied the "prurient interest" and "patently offensive parts" of the test to applicable state laws and removed the "utterly without redeeming value" criteria with the LAPS test. The LAPS test judged a work as a whole and placed less of a burden on government prosecutors to establish obscenity. In short, the Miller test provided conservative states and localities flexibility to define obscenity from their own cultural perspective.

Death Penalty Ruled Constitutional During the 1970's, the Supreme Court addressed the death penalty by allowing states to use death as a punishment while at the same time forcing states to provide defendants facing a death sentence with special procedures and standards. In 1972, the Court ruled in *Furman v. Georgia* that Georgia had violated the Eighth Amendment's cruel and unusual punishment clause by issuing the death penalty as a mandatory sentence for murder. Because of the *Furman* decision, states were forced to rewrite their death penalty laws to provide constitutional protections for criminal defendants.

Four years later, in *Gregg v. Georgia*, the Court decided that states may use the death penalty as punishment, but a bifurcated, or two-stage, process must be employed wherein the guilt or innocence of the defendant is decided by a jury, and then death is considered as punishment at a later stage. In addition, the jury must weigh aggravating and mitigating factors at the latter stage to determine whether a defendant should receive death. For example, the murder of a child might be considered an aggravating factor in a death penalty case, while a murder judged to be a crime of passion might be considered a mitigating factor.

Privacy and Abortion Rights In 1973, the Supreme Court expanded the legal concept of privacy to include a woman's right to abortion in the *Roe v. Wade* ruling. While the Court had established the right of privacy in 1965, it was not until the *Roe* decision that the Court defined the whereabouts of privacy in the Constitution. In his majority opinion, Justice Blackmun wrote that privacy existed in the due process clause of the Fourteenth Amendment. According to Blackmun, privacy is found specifically in the word "liberty" in the phrase "no state shall deny a citizen life, liberty, or property without due process of law."

Blackmun divided the thirty-six-week pregnancy term into three stages, or trimesters. The first trimester lasted until the twelfth week of pregnancy and, during this time, a woman maintained an absolute right to privacy regarding the abortion decision. During the second trimester, from the twelfth to the twenty-fourth week, a woman could have the abortion decision regulated by the state in the interests of maternal health. In the third and final trimester, from the twenty-fourth to the thirty-sixth week, states may regulate or ban abortions to protect the unborn child because a point of viability might exist after the twenty-fourth week of pregnancy when the unborn child might be able to survive without the mother.

Racial Desegregation and School Busing The Supreme Court in the 1970's also addressed the issue of racial segregation and school busing in two landmark cases, *Swann v. Charlotte-Mecklenburg Board of Education* in 1971 and *Milliken v. Bradley* in 1974. Nearly twenty years after the Court had declared the concept of "separate but equal" unconstitutional in *Brown v. Board of Education of Topeka, Kansas* (1954), many school systems across the country, particularly in the South, remained separated by race. In 1970, 66 percent of black students in North Carolina were still attending all-black schools, and virtually no integration had occurred since the *Brown* decision. In North Carolina, a federal judge developed a plan to integrate black and white students in the Charlotte, North Carolina, school system, and a busing program was created to achieve the goal of ending segregation. In *Swann*, a unanimous Court upheld the plan as constitutional and called upon lower courts to presume racial discrimination in cases of de jure segregation, or segregation approved by law.

Three years later, the Court in *Milliken* dealt with the pressures of urban school systems attempting to desegregate in Detroit. A phenomenon called white flight had emerged whereby white residents were leaving the inner cities. The result was a number of all-black schools in cities across the country. This phenomenon caused the federal district courts to order interdistrict busing of whites from the suburbs to the inner city. Here, the Court ruled that the equal protection clause of the Fourteenth Amendment did not reach de facto segregation, or segregation that occurs naturally in a society. Therefore, school busing could be used where de jure segregation existed, but not de facto segregation. The ruling in *Milliken* was significant because it drew a distinction between de jure and de facto segregation, and it also placed serious constraints upon federal judges attempting to use cross-district busing to desegregate school systems in the inner cities. Many legal scholars cited the four Nixon appointments as a key reason for the antibusing decision in *Milliken.*

Equality for Women During the 1970's, the Supreme Court confronted the issue of equality for women. Although the Equal Rights Amendment (ERA), a constitutional amendment that would have given equality to women, failed in the 1970's, the Court handed down landmark decisions designed to address gender discrimination. In *Reed v. Reed,* a 1971 case dealing with a divorced couple fighting over the estate of their deceased son, the Court ruled that Idaho could not favor the father in such legal disputes simply because it allowed for cases to be processed more efficiently. The justices stated that the Idaho law was a clear violation of the equal protection clause of the Fourteenth Amendment. Two years later, in *Frontiero v. Richardson,* the Supreme Court ruled that the military could not deny health benefits to the spouse of an officer simply because the officer was a female.

Finally, in 1976, the Court ruled in *Craig v. Boren* that the state of Oklahoma could not prohibit the sale of alcoholic beverages to males between the ages of eighteen and twenty while allowing females within the same age group to purchase alcohol. The justification for the Oklahoma law was based upon data showing that young males were more likely to be involved in alcohol-related traffic accidents. Although the *Craig* decision did not deal directly with equality for women, the three decisions above were used by the Court to create a heightened level of equal protection against gender discrimination. Because of the discrimination historically against women, these landmark cases of the 1970's were more significant for women. In later years, the Court allowed gender discrimination only if a discriminatory law could be justified by an important governmental objective.

Affirmative Action In 1978, the Supreme Court issued a ruling on the controversial topic of affirmative action in *Regents of the University of California v. Bakke.* Affirmative action policies are designed to provide educational and employment opportunities for historically disadvantaged groups, such as women and minorities. However, some legal scholars argued that affirmative action was reverse discrimination against white men. Allan Bakke, a white male, claimed reverse discrimination when he was denied admission to the University of California

Medical School. Bakke had scored higher on the standardized test for medical school and had a higher grade point average than sixteen minority applicants who were admitted based upon a set-aside quota system.

The Court issued a divided ruling in the *Bakke* case, with the justices split on two issues. On the first issue, the justices voted 5-4 that affirmative action programs with set-aside quotas violated the equal protection clause of the Fourteenth Amendment. In short, quotas such as those used by the University of California were deemed to be reverse discrimination and therefore illegal. Secondly, however, the justices voted 5-4 that affirmative action programs such as specialized recruitment or training programs for disadvantaged groups were permissible because diversity is an important objective for universities and employers. In short, race, ethnicity, or gender can be considered a factor in the admissions process. However, it cannot be the sole factor.

Presidential Power In 1973, Congress passed the War Powers Resolution over the veto of President Nixon. The resolution limits the amount of time that presidents can send military personnel into a hostile area without approval from Congress. The resolution was a product of the abuse of war powers by Presidents Lyndon B. Johnson and Nixon in Southeast Asia. Some legal scholars argued that the resolution is consistent with the congressional power to declare war, while others stated that it violated the president's role as commander in chief. Whatever the case, the Supreme Court chose not to decide on the constitutionality of the law. The Court's inaction subsequently allowed presidents to ignore the law at times and caused some to question the power of Congress and the Court to challenge the president in the area of foreign policy.

In a landmark 1974 decision that led to the resignation of Nixon, the Supreme Court declared in *United States v. Nixon* that Nixon could not use the power of executive privilege to conceal secret tape recordings made in the Oval Office of the White House. The tape recordings revealed Nixon's involvement in the Watergate scandal, in which Republican employees had burglarized the Democratic National Committee headquarters in 1972 in an attempt to uncover damaging information against Democratic presidential candidate, George McGovern. While the decision in *United States v. Nixon* ultimately ended Nixon's presidency, the ruling also was important because the Court expanded presidential power by acknowledging that executive privilege, the power to withhold information from the public, was an inherent power of the presidency that might be permitted in future instances.

Campaign Finance Prior to the 1970's, wealthy individuals with large financial contributions dominated American politics. In 1971, Congress passed the Federal Election Campaign Act (FECA) and the Revenue Act. FECA was an attempt to limit the amount of money contributed by individuals and groups to candidates in federal elections. The law also imposed reporting requirements and spending limits as well as the creation of an executive agency with eight members called the Federal Election Commission to monitor the implementation of contributions. The Revenue Act called for public funding of presidential elections by way of citizens checking off a box on their tax returns.

In a significant but controversial ruling, the Supreme Court in 1976 upheld certain aspects of FECA but also struck down portions. In *Buckley v. Valeo*, the justices decided that limitations on contributions by individuals and political parties to a single candidate and a limitation of total contributions of any individual to various candidates were constitutional and did not violate free speech. Also, the public disclosure and reporting provisions of campaign funds and the public financing of presidential elections were declared constitutional. However, the limitations placed upon independent expenditures, or soft money, and a candidate's own personal wealth violated free speech. Therefore, a person or organization can spend an unlimited amount of money promoting a person for federal office as long as there is no direct coordination with the candidate's campaign organization. An individual candidate also is not limited in spending his or her own personal wealth to promote candidacy in a federal election. The *Buckley* ruling was controversial because some legal scholars did not equate free speech with spending money to promote a political candidate, and it subsequently allowed millions of dollars of soft money to influence federal elections.

Impact The Supreme Court of the 1970's defined the boundaries for issues that continued to be debated in later years. While the Court ruled liberally in providing more protection for religious freedoms, free press, privacy, and women's rights, it decided conservatively by allowing states and localities to impose the death penalty and to define obscenity from their own perspectives. In the areas of racial desegregation, affirmative action, campaign finance, and abortion, the Court issued complex rulings that caused confusion and controversy in subsequent cases. The Court expanded presidential power by acknowledging the existence of executive privilege, allowing presidents to conceal information in political scandals. In terms of the War Powers Resolution, the Court's inaction allowed modern presidents to operate virtually unchallenged in their foreign policy decisions to deploy military troops.

Further Reading

Berger, Raoul. *Executive Privilege.* Cambridge, Mass.: Harvard University Press, 1974. Berger demonstrates that the power of executive privilege, although exercised by several presidents throughout history, violates the Constitution. He argues that the exercise of an unconstitutional power is not justified but only dangerous in the American political system.

Lewis, Thomas T., and Richard L. Wilson, eds. *Encyclopedia of the U.S. Supreme Court.* Pasadena, Calif.: Salem Press, 2001. Serves as a guide to the U.S. Supreme Court, its justices, and the landmark decisions that have defined American legal code throughout the history of the United States.

The Pentagon Papers: The Defense Department History of United States Decisionmaking on Vietnam. 5 vols. Boston: Beacon Press, 1971-1972. This multivolume study of U. S. government policy on Vietnam illustrates the making of American foreign policy. The Pentagon Papers are significant because they show the contrast with the public statements of American leaders explaining the rationale and evolution of the war. While the deception is apparent, it also features the bureaucratic operations of the U.S. government.

Yarbrough, Tinsley E. *The Burger Court: Justices, Rulings, and Legacy.* Santa Barbara, Calif.: ABC-Clio, 2000. Yarbrough proves that the Burger Court was not as counterrevolutionary as conservatives had hoped. It was moderate and independent of political influence, as evidenced by its ruling to grant privacy for women in the abortion decision. Yarbrough demonstrates that an understanding of the Burger Court and its decisions is critical to understanding how the Supreme Court fits into the long history of the American political system.

Scott P. Johnson

See also Abortion rights; Affirmative action; Busing; Conservatism in U.S. politics; Death penalty; *Lau v. Nichols*; Liberalism in U.S. politics; Nixon, Richard M.; Nixon tapes; Pentagon Papers; *Regents of the University of California v. Bakke*; *Roe v. Wade*; *Swann v. Charlotte-Mecklenburg Board of Education*; War Powers Resolution of 1973; Watergate; Women's rights.

■ Swann v. Charlotte-Mecklenburg Board of Education

Identification U.S. Supreme Court decision
Date Decided on April 20, 1971

The Court's controversial ruling in Swann v. Charlotte-Mecklenburg Board of Education *that federal judges could order school busing to bring about racial integration caused initial turmoil and resistance in the 1970's but eventually brought about more racially balanced schools both in the North and in the South.*

Because of the history of legal, or de jure, racial segregation in much of the United States, schools had been built and school district lines drawn to accommodate segregation. Even after legal segregation was ended by *Brown v. Board of Education* (1954) and its successor cases, most schools remained substantially segregated. This was particularly noticeable in urban areas. In the Charlotte, North Carolina, metropolitan area, fully half of the black students still attended all-black schools.

In an effort to remedy this situation, the United States District Court adopted a plan that required the redrawing of some district lines and busing of elementary school students in both directions—that is, white students to all-black schools and black students to all-white schools. On appeal, the Supreme Court unanimously approved this plan in the *Swann* case. Chief Justice Warren Burger's opinion held that where the segregation was the result of previous constitutional violations, federal judges could issue court orders to correct the segregated pattern even if such orders meant transporting students away from their neighborhood schools. The opinion went on to hold that once the "duty to desegregate" had been accomplished and schools had become "unitary," neither courts nor school districts would be under any obligation to make annual adjustments of racial balance.

Impact School busing was immediately controversial, especially when courts began to hold that housing and district patterns in the North had created school segregation for which busing was an appropriate remedy. In the mid-1970's, fierce resistance to busing plans broke out. There were riots in Boston and elsewhere as traditional ethnic neighborhoods and their schools were affected. After these disturbances had subsided, the work of integrating the schools went on more peaceably, and significant racial integration had taken place by the end of the 1970's. However, a new phenomenon arose: "white flight," or the movement of large numbers of white families from cities to suburbs, thereby leaving several metropolitan areas predominantly all black demographically. Detroit, Michigan, and Camden, New Jersey, were two examples of this phenomenon.

Further Reading

Raffel, Jeffrey. *Historical Dictionary of School Segregation and Desegregation: The American Experience.* Westport, Conn.: Greenwood, 1998.

Schwartz, Bernard. *Swann's Way: The School Busing Case and the Supreme Court.* New York: Oxford University Press, 1986.

Robert Jacobs

See also Affirmative action; Busing; Education in the United States; Racial discrimination; Supreme Court decisions.

■ Swingers

Definition Couples who exchange partners for sexual encounters

The practice of swinging, also referred to as wife-swapping, coincided with wide-scale changes in social norms and values. It reflected and reinforced a shift away from traditional values toward sexual openness and experimentation.

Alternative lifestyles, including swinging, became increasingly visible during this era that witnessed fairly rapid change and dramatic tests of traditional values. Books such as Gilbert D. Bartell's *Group Sex: A Scientist's Eyewitness Report on the American Way of Swinging* (1971) and the popular 1969 film *Bob and Carol and Ted and Alice,* which was adapted as a television series in 1973, brought the topic of swinging to the mainstream. Other movements, such as women's liberation and gay pride, also served as catalysts for a close reexamination of traditional cultural values. For the first time, such social norms as sexual exclusivity were challenged, and some couples experimented with sexual sharing while maintaining emotional fidelity to their primary partners. The practice of swinging was viewed by some as a solution to the soaring divorce rates of the time.

In general, swingers were white, middle-class, professional couples in their thirties who were fairly unremarkable in most respects with the obvious exception of their sexual practices. Fearing social stigma and legal sanctions, most practitioners operated in clandestine fashion. Organizations that catered to these interests facilitated contacts between interested parties while preserving privacy.

For most participants, the practice was temporary and may have represented a way of finding sexual variety without actually cheating on one's partner. Although group sex sometimes occurred, the majority of swingers restricted their activities to partner-swapping with like-minded couples. Swingers insisted that the practice occur only by mutual consent with complete openness. Another rule was that practitioners refrain from becoming emotionally attached to anyone other than the primary partner. Common concerns among swingers included jealousy and the risk of sexually transmissible infections.

Impact In the 1970's, swinging and other alternative lifestyles represented challenges to such traditional values as marriage and monogamy. Although they remain controversial, these practices have entered the cultural consciousness and remain popular among a segment of the population.

Further Reading

Buunk, Bram P., and Barry van Driel. *Variant Lifestyles and Relationships.* Newbury Park, Calif.: Sage Publications, 1989.

Gould, Terry. *The Lifestyle: A Look at the Erotic Rites of Swingers.* Buffalo, N.Y.: Firefly Books, 2000.

Rubin, Roger H. "Alternative Lifestyles Revisited: Or, Whatever Happened to Swingers, Group Marriages, and Communes?" *Journal of Family Issues* 22, no. 6 (2001): 711-727.

Richard D. McAnulty

See also Homosexuality and gay rights; Marriage and divorce; Open marriage; Sexual revolution; Women's rights.

■ Sylmar earthquake

The Event A 6.6 magnitude earthquake also known as the San Fernando earthquake
Date February 9, 1971
Place The San Fernando Valley of Southern California, near the San Gabriel Mountains

The Sylmar earthquake caused sixty-five deaths and more than one thousand serious injuries. Many structures collapsed, particularly old, unreinforced masonry buildings.

At 6:01 A.M. on February 9, 1971, the city of San Fernando, about twenty miles northwest of Los Angeles in Southern California, was struck by a strong earthquake. Also known as the Sylmar earthquake because its epicenter was located about 10 kilometers (6 miles) from the town of Sylmar, the earthquake originated in a previously unstudied fault 12 kilometers (7.5 miles) below the surface.

Prior to 1971, the region had experienced no major earthquakes for almost four hundred years; the last recorded one occurred in Pico Canyon, 6 miles from Sylmar, in 1593. Major structures had been built over the fault, and many older buildings were designed and constructed without proper reinforcement. Another potential threat to Sylmar was the Lower San Fernando Dam upstream from the town. Built between 1912 and 1915, this 142-foot-high earth dam held 15 million tons of water in a reservoir that was 1.6 miles long and 130 feet deep. Approximately eighty thousand people lived in the San Fernando region at the time of the earthquake.

When the earthquake measuring 6.6 on the Richter scale hit, a number of older buildings collapsed. Forty-four people died when two tile masonry buildings at the Sylmar Veterans Administration Hospital were destroyed. Even at Olive View Hospital, housed in a well-engineered, reinforced modern building, serious damage killed three people. Chimneys, masonry walls, fences, about 1,700 mobile homes, and 1,300 buildings were partially or totally destroyed. Landslides and soil liquefaction were widespread. Freeways were heavily damaged, and some bridge spans were destroyed. Luckily, because the quake oc-

This freeway was heavily damaged in the 1971 Sylmar earthquake in California. (Hulton Archive/Getty Images)

curred very early in the morning, few people were on the roads or in the center of town, where dense construction could have resulted in many fatalities.

In some areas, the fault caused vertical displacement as great as 1.5 meters (5 feet) and horizontal movement of about 1.3 meters (4.5 feet), damaging utility lines and causing fires to erupt. The San Fernando Dam was damaged, as were three other dams in the region. The Van Norman Dam, which at the time was the largest provider of water for Los Angeles, suffered sufficient damage to cause concern for its stability and the evacuation of an 80-square-mile area below it. The Hansen Dam also reported minor damage and leaks, resulting in further evacuations. Fortunately, none of the dams collapsed. Had they failed, the loss of life and property would have been greatly increased, well beyond the sixty-five deaths and half billion dollars of damage that the earthquake actually caused.

Impact Because the area had been considered very stable, many buildings were designed and constructed without proper reinforcement to withstand earthquakes. Following the earthquake, building codes were strengthened. The Los Angeles Dam and Reservoir, built from 1975 to 1976 further up the valley, survived the similar 1994 Northridge earthquake with little damage.

Further Reading

Hough, Susan Elizabeth. *Earthshaking Science: What We Know (and Don't Know) About Earthquakes.* Portland, Oreg.: Book News, 2004.

_______. *Finding Fault in California: An Earthquake Tourist's Guide.* Missoula, Mont.: Mountain Press, 2004.

Denyse Lemaire and David Kasserman

See also Natural disasters.

■ Symbionese Liberation Army (SLA)

Identification Paramilitary organization
Date Active from 1973 to 1975
Place San Francisco Bay Area and Los Angeles

The Symbionese Liberation Army (SLA) was a violent organization that identified itself with an anticapitalist, antiestablishment ideology and gained national attention through a high-profile kidnapping.

In California during the late 1960's and early 1970's, there was a confluence of ideas that contributed to a growth in violence. Among these was the idea held by many "left-wing" radicals that the justice system and prisons were used to maintain the supremacy of the rich. In the Vacaville, California, correctional facility, the Black Cultural Association had as members both visiting political radicals and incarcerated criminals. It was in this organization that eight individuals became acquainted, a meeting that proved instrumental in the development of the Symbionese Liberation Army in the spring of 1973.

Donald DeFreeze, who organized the SLA and acted as its leader, escaped from prison and turned to the radicals in the Oakland-Berkeley area for a safe place to live. Three individuals, Willie Wolfe, Russell Little, and Nancy Ling Perry, who had often visited Vacaville, allowed him to move in with them. After a short time, DeFreeze moved to the apartment of Patricia Soltysik, and these two composed the initial statements that proclaimed the foundation of the SLA.

In their writing, it was explained that Symbionese was adapted from the biological term "symbiosis," which was to be the goal of the organization—for all to live in harmony seeking mutual benefit. However, to get to that utopia, the SLA was to be the vanguard of revolution with the motto Death to the Fascist Insect That Preys upon the Life of the People. Other left-wing groups rejected the SLA in large part because they had no respect for DeFreeze (who went by the name Field Marshall Cinque) and considered him dangerous to their causes. Although there is some dispute over who formally was a member of the SLA, the total membership over the two years of its activities was no more than a dozen.

Actions and Repercussions In November, 1973, the SLA undertook its first public action, the murder of Marcus Foster, the superintendent of the Oakland schools. This was followed by the release of its first public political statement to justify its activities. In January, 1974, two members of the organization, Little and Joe Remiro, were arrested for the murder, and eventually Remiro was convicted. Just after the arrest of these individuals, plans to kidnap Patty Hearst—an heir to the fortunes of newspaper magnate William Randolph Hearst—were found, but nothing was done to inform her or to offer her extra security.

Six members of the SLA died when this South-Central Los Angeles house burned down during a shootout with FBI agents and police in 1974. (AP/Wide World Photos)

In February, 1974, the SLA kidnapped Hearst. The ransom demanded the distribution of two million dollars (later increased to six million) worth of food to the poor in the San Francisco Bay Area. In mid-April, after her family met the SLA's demands, it was announced that while being held captive, Hearst had voluntarily joined the SLA. In line with the SLA practice of adopting the names of revolutionaries, she became known as Tania. The organization moved to Los Angeles to avoid arrest. In April, 1974, Hearst and the others robbed a bank in San Francisco. In May, Hearst, along with Bill and Emily Harris, went to a store to get more ammunition for the group. When the Harrises were stopped for shoplifting, Hearst fired shots into the store to allow them to escape, but they did not return to the hideout. The next day, the Los Angeles police department surrounded the hideout, and six members of the SLA were killed in the shootout.

The surviving members of the group split up, with some staying in California and others temporarily going to Pennsylvania. Eventually all returned to northern California, and they needed money to survive. In February, 1975, the remaining members robbed a bank in Carmichael, California, which resulted in the death of one customer. The last documented action by the SLA was a failed attempt in August, 1975, to kill police officers in Los Angeles.

In September, 1975, Bill and Emily Harris were arrested, as was Hearst. Hearst was convicted for her role in the SLA crimes, but her sentence was commuted in 1979 and she was pardoned for her actions in 2001.

Impact Although a violent organization, some argue that the SLA may have actually reduced the amount of politically inspired violence during the 1970's. There were many other organizations that had considered the use of violence. However, the extreme to which the SLA attempted to carry this vision and the massive backlash against the SLA by both the general public and the people in left-wing political organizations convinced others that violence was not the way to bring about societal change. The fact that Patricia Hearst was not freed after her family met the ransom demands caused many to rethink their position on negotiating with political extremists. Moreover, Hearst's cooperation with her kidnappers caused much public discussion regarding the concept of "brainwashing." Although the SLA claimed it was trying to transform society, its actions did not result in any changes.

Further Reading

Boulton, David. *The Making of Tania Hearst.* Bergenfield, N.J.: New American Library, 1975. This book deals with the SLA with a special focus on the transformation of Hearst from kidnap victim to participant.

Hearst, Patricia, and Alvin Moscow. *Patty Hearst, Her Own Story.* New York: Avalon Books, 1988. The autobiography by the best-known "member" of the SLA, which deals with the events from her perspective.

McLellan, Vincent, and Paul Avery. *The Voices of Guns: The Definitive and Dramatic Story of the Twenty-Two-Month Career of the Symbionese Liberation Army, One of the Most Bizarre Chapters in the History of the American Left.* New York: Putnam, 1977. Completed shortly after the trial of Patricia Hearst, this book gives a good overview of the SLA and the climate in which it developed.

Donald A. Watt

See also Black Panthers; Hearst, Patty; Soledad Brothers; Terrorism; Weather Underground.

T

■ Talk shows

Definition Television programs in which the audience and guests engage in topical conversations

Television talk shows of this decade responded to social and technological changes, as well as new demands from advertisers.

During the 1970's, the United States found itself in the middle of the Vietnam War, the Watergate scandal, various civil rights movements, and economic uncertainty. In addition to society's transforming, the media landscape was also in flux. Production and technological innovations such as cable, satellite, public television, and syndication threatened the networks' hold on the airwaves and their viewers. Advertisers began to emphasize demographics—what segments of the population were watching—rather than ratings—how many viewers were watching. Television talk shows of this decade had to evolve to reflect social needs and changes, compete against new technologies, and deliver target audiences to advertisers.

Social Changes The explosive cultural climate Americans experienced during the 1970's no longer permitted talk shows to ignore social controversy and the individual. After a decade of trying to change the country, Americans turned inward and focused on changing themselves. While traditional interview show hosts such as Johnny Carson and Merv Griffin and roundtable discussion shows such as *Face the Nation* and *Meet the Press* were still popular, the era introduced new talk show formats and hosts that reflected and related to a changing society.

Recognizing an inward self-help trend, the 1970's networks offered a new popular and profitable talk show genre, the participatory therapeutic talk show, which answered both the social and emotional needs of the public and the new demands of advertisers. Typically comprising a desired demographic, the studio audience became an active inquisitor, while the host served as a mediator between the audience and guest(s). Discussing social and personal issues such as affirmative action, welfare, adultery, and domestic violence, the audience and at-home callers became the "experts" by sharing personal experiences and conversing with guests. The therapy talk show served as a social broadcasting tool, a "teledemocracy," allowing minorities and those previously without a voice a vehicle through which to be heard.

Most notable in this genre was *Donahue.* Phil Donahue played the sympathetic and somewhat naïve moderator-host, sharing the microphone with audience members and callers. Donahue would ask the audience and guest panel to help him make sense of the same issues with which Americans were confronted. Opposite of *Donahue* was *The Michael Douglas Show,* which emphasized traditional American values and focused on entertainment rather than social issues. As the decade progressed, even Douglas would invite controversial guests and co-hosts to debate current affairs, arguably the most famous being John Lennon and Yoko Ono.

As the 1970's experienced the feminist movement, the networks supported an increase in women newscasters and talk show hosts; perhaps the most successful was Barbara Walters. Walters tackled tough issues through political and celebrity interviews on *The Today Show* and later as an anchor on the American Broadcasting Company (ABC) network. Conversely, Dinah Shore's *Dinah's Place* featured celebrities politely cooking and chitchatting. While Walters gave feminists an aspiration, Shore reinforced traditional gender roles.

Technological Changes and Competitors Americans during the 1970's relied more on television for their news than on periodicals, thereby resulting in decreased magazine subscriptions and increased news and roundtable discussion talk shows. Since commercial television was heavily censored and at the mercy of its sponsors, news talk shows began to find intellectual freedom on public television as evidenced by *The NewsHour with Jim Lehrer, Firing Line* with William F. Buckley, and interview talk shows such as *The Dick Cavett Show.* This new home, although not as profitable and weaker in ratings than the advertiser-supported networks, served as a springboard for new talk formats and siphoned viewers away from mainstream networks.

In addition to the public television threat, the networks found themselves competing with new technologies. Cable and satellite television were increasing their reach on American households by narrowly casting special-interest talk shows opposed to the homogenous programming broadcasted by the networks.

Censorship and contract disputes caused some talk shows, such as *The Merv Griffin Show,* to turn to syndication companies to produce and distribute their shows. Syndication took the networks out of the picture completely, and as a result, many talk shows were able to reach a competitive portion of the country.

Advertiser Demands Although celebrity guests drew huge ratings, advertisers in the 1970's began to shift their focus from concern about how many people were watching to what type of people was watching a particular show. As ratings became less important than target demographic groups to advertisers, the networks were forced to tailor their programming to attract a desired crowd. At the same time, the networks and advertisers were trying to accommodate a consuming audience that was younger, less docile, more urban, and more outspoken than that of previous decades. Participatory talk shows attracted these new audiences comprising targeted demographics. The networks thus had vehicles that could attract and deliver the desired viewing demographic to their sponsors.

Impact After the 1960's protests and social upheaval, Americans tuned into their televisions not merely for entertainment but also for news, socialization, and therapy. Participatory therapeutic talk shows provided help to those who felt helpless, gave them a voice, and elevated them to celebrity status.

To compete with the programming choices offered to the viewer through new technologies, syndication, and public television, the networks had to create issue-driven talk shows that revolved around controversy, social themes, or the individual.

Finally, advertisers during the 1970's shifted their attention from ratings to demographics. Realizing it was more profitable to hone in on desired segments of viewers, sponsors and producers created talk shows that attracted desired audiences.

Further Reading

Barnouw, Erik. *Tube of Plenty.* 2d ed. New York: Oxford University Press, 1990. Serves as an excellent resource on the history of television.

McNeil, Alex. *Total Television.* 4th ed. New York: Penguin Books, 1997. A comprehensive guide to programming from the 1940's through the 1990's.

Parish, James Robert. *Let's Talk: America's Favorite Talk Show Hosts.* Las Vegas: Pioneer Books, 1993. Explores the professional and private lives of the hosts of America's talk shows.

Scott, Gini Graham. *Can We Talk? The Power and Influence of Talk Shows.* New York: Insight Books, 1996. A thorough history of the rise of television talk shows.

Timberg, Bernard M. *Television Talk: A History of the TV Talk Show.* Austin: University of Texas Press, 2002. An excellent resource on talk shows, their hosts, and network histories.

Tolson, Andrew, et al. *Television Talk Shows: Discourse, Performance, Spectacle.* Mahwah, N.J.: Lawrence Erlbaum, 2001. An academic look at the history and impact of talk shows.

Sara Vidar

See also Advertising; *Donahue*; Journalism in Canada; Journalism in the United States; Public Broadcasting Service (PBS); Self-help books; *60 Minutes*; Television in Canada; Television in the United States; Walters, Barbara.

■ Tax revolt

Definition National, citizen-led tax reform

Following the end of the Vietnam War and the Watergate scandal, the American public, in an antigovernment mood and suffering from significant inflation and unemployment, revolted against government tax systems at both the local and the national levels.

The 1970's did not begin with a call by the American public to reform the tax structure or to limit government spending. Instead, the United States was gripped by two situations that focused the voters' attention on national crisis. The decade began in turmoil and national conflict. In April, 1970, President Richard M. Nixon began the bombing of neutral

Cambodia as the Vietnam War raged on, and at home, war protests were reaching a fever pitch. In early May, 1970, students at Kent State University demonstrated, and the National Guard opened fire, killing four students and wounding eleven. Demonstrations followed at four hundred American universities across the country. Nixon's divisive reelection in 1972 over George McGovern quickly turned into another debacle for the country as the Watergate scandal soon dominated the news. Eventually, Nixon, along with many of his top staff, resigned.

The new president, Gerald R. Ford, pardoned Nixon in an effort to bring "the long national nightmare" of Watergate to an end. Even though the country had survived the shock and scandal of Watergate, its citizens were left in a mood of cynicism and despair. Their faith in government had been put to a serious test from which they would not easily recover.

As these events were unraveling, events in the Middle East added to the world crisis. In October, 1973, Egypt and Syria launched a surprise attack on Israel, initiating the Yom Kippur War. Because of Israel's successful retaliation, the Organization of Petroleum Exporting Countries (OPEC) announced a 5 percent cut in production for each month that Israel did not return the lands that it had seized from Egypt, Syria, and Jordan in the 1967 Six Day War. This oil embargo had disastrous effects on the world and especially on the United States, which consumed 40 percent of the world's energy resources despite having only 6 percent of the world population. The price Americans paid for oil went up sixfold during the decade, weakening the American economy and leading to higher interest rates and periodic recession. Consumer spending declined considerably, causing a slowdown in manufacturing and ultimately resulting in a 9 percent unemployment rate, the highest rate since the Great Depression.

Tax Reformers Emerge In was amid these serious economic conditions and the atmosphere of despair that growing concerns began to emerge over the heavy tax burden that Americans had carried during the war and the resulting weakened economic conditions during the decade. Gerald Ford, attempting to alleviate the problem, had successfully passed a twenty-two billion dollar reduction in taxes in 1975. However, his successor, President Jimmy Carter, was again faced with another oil crisis and staggering inflation rates and was unable to turn the economy around. Americans, again faced with gasoline shortages and paying more than a dollar a gallon, were very pessimistic about the future.

It was during these mid-decade years that the modern conservative movement is believed to have begun. While Barry Goldwater had been the conservative nominee for president of the Republican Party in 1964, it was Ronald Reagan who had emerged from the party convention as the conservative hope for the future. Backed by influential businessmen in California, Reagan successfully ran for state governor in 1966 and ushered in a new conservative agenda. He quickly gauged the suburban middle-class sentiment that was concerned about wasteful welfare programs, excessive government regulations, and high taxes. As governor of the largest state in the nation, Reagan quickly became the leader of the anti-big-government movement in the country. By the end of his second term in 1974, he had spawned many disciples in his own state and across the United States who would build on his tax-cutting policies and his reduction of many government programs.

Two of these disciples were Howard Jarvis and Paul Gann. In the years following Reagan's governorship, inflation and housing shortages in California caused a significant increase in housing prices, accompanied with significant property taxes based on market value. In 1978, 40 percent of all revenue received by property taxes went to local governments, including school districts. This fact meant little to Jarvis and Gann as they capitalized on taxpayer discontent and qualified an initiative for the 1978 state elections. Proposition 13 was approved handily with more than 60 percent of the vote. It limited the amount of annual property taxes to 1 percent of the March 1, 1975, market value or selling price of the property, whichever was higher.

As a result of the passage of the Jarvis-Gann initiative, as it was popularly called, repeated demands were made in California for more tax cuts. In a special election in 1979, Gann had qualified for the ballot another initiative in "the spirit of Proposition 13" to limit government spending and require the state's budget to grow only by as much as inflation and the state's population. This initiative also passed. Jarvis then qualified an initiative for the 1980 ballot that would cut the personal income tax in half, and other groups sought to qualify an initiative to do away with the sales tax in the state.

A Tax Shift Occurs Because of the high inflation in the country, the California initiative caused a nationwide tax revolt. In the years after Proposition 13, nearly half the states passed similar legislation. Clearly the proposition had tapped a current of popular unrest not only with tax structures but also with government spending in general. The results of Proposition 13 in California and in many other states was to produce a tax shift. In California, the 57 percent reduction in property tax revenues caused a 20 percent decline in city and county revenues and even more of a loss for school districts. School districts lost more than $3 billion, while counties lost $2.2 billion.

While the proposition reduced the property tax burden by $8 billion, it shifted the burden to the sales tax and income tax. Governor Jerry Brown and the state legislature were then faced with the task of trimming government spending, while at the same time increasing the state's responsibility to fund schools and assist local governments. No wage increases were given to state employees for three years, and seventeen thousand state workers were laid off. Between 1970 and 1980, the state budget nearly doubled, and the shift in funding to the state resulted in a significant loss of local control by city and county governments and school districts. The net effect in California and nationwide was to shift considerable portions of funding from the local level to the state level.

Impact The burden of the Vietnam War and the Watergate scandal lead to cynicism and despair among American citizens. Buffeted further by the oil embargos during the decade and accompanying economic slowdown, rising inflation, and high unemployment, the public was ready for a tax revolt. Led by California's property tax reform initiative, Proposition 13, more than half the states in the nation passed similar measures. The result was a tax shift to state government, reducing local governments' tax sources and local control.

Further Reading

Bell, Charles G., and Charles M. Price. *California Government Today: Politics of Reform.* Homewood, Ill.: Dorsey Press, 1980. Presents the significant aspects of California politics from a practical and historical approach, based on academic research and the personal political participation of the authors.

Divine, Robert A., et al. *America Past and Present.* 5th ed. New York: Longman, 1999. A history of the United States that tells the unfolding story of national development. Examines each period with insights into the underlying social, economic, and cultural forces that brought about change.

Huber, Walter. *California State and Local Government in Crisis.* Covina, Calif.: Educational Texts, 1992. Examines how, after decades of prosperity, California was faced with endless population growth and how local and state government responded to this crisis.

Raymond J. Gonzales

See also Business and the economy in the United States; Education in the United States; Energy crisis; Gas shortages; Income and wages in the United States; Inflation in the United States; Oil embargo of 1973-1974; Reagan, Ronald; Unemployment in the United States.

■ Taxi

Identification Television situation comedy
Date Aired from 1978 to 1983

Taxi *introduced a harder-edged form of comedy than other Mary Tyler Moore (MTM) Productions shows of the same era, and as such, it served as a harbinger of future television trends. It also helped to elevate several of its cast members to star status, including Judd Hirsch, Danny DeVito, Tony Danza, and Andy Kaufman.*

Premiering on American Broadcasting Company (ABC) during a time of economic strife and an unsettled state of foreign affairs, millions of television viewers came to look forward to their weekly visit to the fictional Sunshine Taxi Company. *Taxi* featured an array of eccentric characters who nevertheless possessed a certain charm that fans found endearing. These characters included a strange immigrant mechanic (played by Andy Kaufman), whose perplexing accent did not seem to be of earthly origin. Only the character portrayed by Judd Hirsch seemed to accept his fate maturely and sadly acknowledge that he was a "cabby" and likely to remain one. The taxi drivers were supervised by a dispatcher played by Danny DeVito, a figure so devoid of basic human decency and kindness that the viewer was reluctantly bemused. Unlike earlier comedies that seemed to be perpetually upbeat and positive, the overall tone of *Taxi* was often surprisingly somber. These individuals were going nowhere fast, and they and the viewers understood that fact.

Excellent writing and the vividness of the characters made *Taxi* fascinating to its stalwart fans. The dialogue was alternately witty, sarcastic, thoughtful, and often incredibly funny. These people seemingly did not recognize the constraints of polite and civil behavior. Perhaps another explanation for the program's charm was the feelings and reactions it aroused from its audience. The typical viewer would most likely experience an array of emotions, including disgust and amazement, while watching a single episode.

There were many paradoxes associated with the program. Although very popular with the critics—it won an incredible fourteen Emmy Awards in only five years—it never succeeded in maintaining consistently high ratings. Despite the loyal support of its core audience, it often was assigned undesirable times and nights and eventually suffered the embarrassment of being canceled by two different networks.

Impact Although appearing late in the decade, *Taxi* is closely associated with the 1970's. The brain-damaged character played by Christopher Lloyd was often referred to as a victim of the drug culture of the late 1960's and topical references to current events were not infrequent. *Taxi* also served as a link between the popular MTM comedies of the early 1970's—*The Mary Tyler Moore Show* and *The Bob Newhart Show*, for example—and the more sophisticated Thursday night "must-see" comedies of the 1980's and 1990's, including *Cheers*, *Seinfeld*, and *Friends*. Although its network run was relatively short, it continued to appear in reruns, and its influence remained in later decades.

Further Reading

Maltin, Leonard. *Leonard Maltin's Movie Encyclopedia: Career Profiles of More than Two Thousand Actors and Filmmakers, Past and Present*. New York: Penguin Books, 1995.

Zehme, Bill. *Lost in the Funhouse: The Life and Mind of Andy Kaufman*. New York: Delacorte Press, 1999.

Thomas W. Buchanan

See also Kaufman, Andy; *Mary Tyler Moore Show, The*; *Saturday Night Live*; Sitcoms; Television in the United States.

■ Taxi Driver

Identification Motion picture
Director Martin Scorsese (1942-)
Date Released in 1976

Scorsese's critically acclaimed Taxi Driver *captured the seamy underside of New York City and probed the psyche of an alienated taxi driver whose frustration leads him to apocalyptic violence.*

Taxi Driver is the story of Travis Bickle (played by Robert De Niro), a New York City cab driver who rescues Iris Steensma, a child prostitute played by Jodie Foster, and returns her to her midwestern parents by taking the law into his own hands. Charles Bronson in *Death Wish* (1974) and Clint Eastwood both in *Dirty Harry* (1971) and in *Magnum Force* (1973) had earlier tapped into an American frustration with law enforcement and an endorsement of vigilante action, but *Taxi Driver* transcends the vigilante genre.

Jodie Foster plays a twelve-year-old prostitute in the film Taxi Driver. (AP/Wide World Photos)

Throughout the film, New York is seen as a kind of hell, with dark shadows, steaming manholes, and neon lights; it is a classic *film noir* setting. The denizens of New York—prostitutes, pimps, bums, and criminals—appall Travis, a Vietnam vet who wishes that the city could be cleansed of its scum by a redeeming rain. Travis is the typical *film noir* antihero: an alienated outsider working on the margins. His repressed sexuality finds outlet only in his visits to pornographic film houses and his idealized image of an angel in white, Betsy (Cybill Shepherd), who works for a presidential candidate. He fails to pick up the cashier at the pornographic film house, and when he cons Betsy into a date, he foolishly takes her to a pornographic film.

Travis may divide women into the categories of whores and angels, but he cannot treat the two differently. After he sees twelve-year-old Iris working as a prostitute, he attempts to take her away from "Sport" Matthews, her pimp, but she does not want to leave Sport. This failure, coupled with his thwarted attempt to kill a presidential candidate, results in a bloodbath in which he kills Sport and some of his minions and is himself wounded.

In *Taxi Driver*, sex and violence are inextricably linked. Travis wants to use violence to achieve the cleansing he only dreamed about. The cleansing is itself linked to religion, a common theme in the work of Martin Scorsese and Paul Schrader, the scriptwriter. Travis's act, however, is not redemptive, and despite the media adulation that he receives, he remains an outsider, much like the John Wayne character of John Ford's *The Searchers* (1956), a Western film with which *Taxi Driver* is often compared.

Impact Martin Scorsese's portrait of the New York that Americans love to despise and his creation of an individual lost in the post-Watergate and post-Vietnam United States earned the film four Academy Award nominations, and Foster won Best Supporting Actress. Ironically, in 1981, John Hinckley, citing his love for the Foster he saw in *Taxi Driver*, attempted to assassinate President Ronald Reagan.

Further Reading

Friedman, Lawrence S. *The Cinema of Martin Scorsese*. New York: Continuum, 1998.

Hill, Anne E. *Ten American Movie Directors*. Berkeley Heights, N.J.: Enslow, 2003.

Keyser, Les. *Martin Scorsese*. New York: Twayne, 1992.

Thomas L. Erskine

See also Academy Awards; De Niro, Robert; Film in the United States.

■ Television in Canada

Definition Programs and series, both fictional and nonfictional, produced for or broadcast on Canadian television

During the 1970's, television was a powerful agent in building and maintaining Canadian identity and cohesion over a vast territory.

Television was introduced into Canada in 1952 and quickly became the country's fastest-growing industry. By the end of the 1950's, it had surpassed radio as the most popular electronic medium. The Canadian Broadcasting Corporation (CBC), established as a Crown Corporation in 1936, built an army of radio and television towers to take broadcasts to the farthest reaches of the country. Communications technology netted together the far reaches of Canadian territory, and television proved important for nation building and fostering national identification within Canada's ethnic and racial mosaic.

The CBC was funded primarily by the Canadian government, with the remainder of its revenue coming from program sales and commercial sponsorship. By Canadian law, broadcasting is "a public service" essential to "national identity and cultural sovereignty."

Rules and Regulations The Canadian Radio-Television Commission (CRTC), established in 1968 by the Broadcasting Act and renamed the Canadian Radio-Television and Telecommunications Commission in 1976, is the chief governing body for all communications in Canada and ensures that a large share of the CBC's programming is of Canadian content and origin. In 1970, the commission issued strict rules specifying that at least 60 percent of television programming in prime time was to be Canadian. At the same time, the CBC was losing large numbers of viewers to commercial television stations with mostly American fare.

The CRTC devoted much time throughout the 1970's to developing a regulatory framework for the cable industry. Fearing an American monopoly, the CRTC developed must-carry provisions so that Canadian television was included alongside American fare in cable packages. Efforts by the CRTC also resulted in limits to foreign ownership of Canadian broadcasting companies.

A dramatic shift occurred in Canadian broadcasting during the 1970's when the CRTC began licensing private stations in large metropolitan centers. Commercial television thrived in the 1960's and 1970's and chipped away at the preeminence of the CBC through intense audience fragmentation. The CBC responded by getting publicly funded programs on private television and increasing the content of Canadian material in CBC prime time. In 1978, the president of the CBC lamented that Canadian schoolchildren spent more hours viewing American television than learning in their Canadian classrooms.

News and Entertainment The media event of the decade occurred on October 17, 1977, when the CBC broadcast live proceedings from the Canadian parliament for the first time. News clips and documentaries were produced on a plethora of issues through the decade. For example, activists gained exposure for their protests against the Arctic seal hunt, and reports showed that phosphates, bacteria, and algae were choking fish and eutrophying the waters of the Great Lakes. The first news report of acid rain alerted the public to the environmental hazards of big industry. The Berger Report laid out the risks of pipeline construction, and television coverage allowed Canadians to debate its impact on the country's northern peoples. They also heard discussions about Bill 101, which mandated "French only," or unilingualism, in Quebec Province. In 1977, the year that CBC celebrated its twenty-fifth anniversary, Prime Minister Pierre Trudeau asked for an inquiry into the separatist bias of the CBC's French and English networks.

Canadian television produced the gamut of comedy, drama, theater, musicals, news shows, and documentaries. In the 1970's, *Friendly Giant* and *Mr. Dressup* won large audiences and eventual recognition as "CBC classics." Typical fare also included *The Bob McLean Show*, *Sesame Street*, and *Front Page Challenge*. The CBC offered *Ninety Minutes Live* with Rex Murphy covering Parliament. Broadcast media also brought an abundance of Canadian comedy, from rising comedian Rich Little to the *Royal Canadian Air Farce* parodies. Canadian pop stars Gordon Lightfoot and Anne Murray hosted television specials that attracted large audiences. Other events of the 1970's that received television coverage included the Montreal Expos playing the first major league baseball game in Canada on January 2, 1970, and the completion in 1976 of Toronto's CN Tower, a radio and television transmitting antenna and the world's tallest free-standing structure.

Impact The CBC, a public service monopoly with both English and French networks, remained the centerpiece of the Canadian broadcast industry during the 1970's. The licensing of private stations with mostly American fare posed a growing threat to the CBC, but it responded in unique and creative ways. Moreover, although television retained its Anglo dominance, the infusion of non-Europeans into Canadian society added diversity to television programming, as elements of immigrant culture were increasingly showcased in news segments and specials.

Subsequent Events By the late 1980's, the CBC's audience share had fallen to about 20 percent for English broadcasts and 30 percent for French broadcasts. In spite of setbacks, however, the CBC retained its position as the country's preeminent network and a champion of Canadian programming. By 1994, the Canadian content in CBC prime time was 85 percent, whereas for private stations it hung at 25 percent. The CBC archive is the country's main repository of films, tapes, photographs, manuscripts, and an electronic database of radio and television. The English-language materials are preserved in Toronto and the French ones in Montreal; additional holdings can be found at the National Archives in Ottawa as well as in several provincial facilities.

Further Reading

Collins, Richard. *Culture, Communication, and National Identity: The Case of Canadian Television*. Toronto: University of Toronto Press, 1990. Provides a history of television technology, marketing, and programming.

Rutherford, Paul. *When Television Was Young: Primetime Canada, 1952-1967*. Toronto: University of Toronto Press, 1990. Examines personalities, technologies, and programming for early Canadian television.

Smith, Anthony, and Richard Paterson, eds. *Television: An International History*. New York: Oxford University Press, 1998. Gives one chapter on the structure and philosophy of Canadian television.

Ann M. Legreid

See also Censorship in Canada; Children's television; Communications in Canada; Journalism in Canada; Radio; Television in the United States.

■ Television in the United States

Definition Programs and series, both fictional and nonfictional, produced for or broadcast on U.S. television

By the end of the 1970's, trends and fads that had typified television in its first two decades had faded and altered drastically, and the new forms and genres that would define the medium well into the twenty-first century had crystallized.

As television entered the 1970's, the medium was only slightly more than twenty years old. Many Americans—even young people—could still recall the first television set that their family ever owned. In that short amount of time, television had become the nation's primary source of entertainment and news, and many changes would occur during the 1970's.

Not Ready for Prime Time Most of the important changes that took place in American television programming in the 1970's involved prime time, the three hours between the evening meal and the eleven o'clock news. However, programming broadcast at other times of the day and night underwent significant alteration as well. For example, in 1971 daytime television saw the premiere on the American Broadcasting Company (ABC) of *All My Children,* the first soap opera to deal with sociopolitical topics such as the Vietnam War and drug addiction. In the mid-1970's, the National Broadcasting Company (NBC) began to broadcast *Wheel of Fortune,* a wordplay-oriented game show; it was destined to become an international sensation in later decades that freed the genre from the weekday morning dungeon into which it had been confined since the quiz show scandals of the 1950's. In children's programming, the gentle didacticism of the late 1960's phenomenon *Sesame Street* was reflected in two innovations on ABC: *Schoolhouse Rock!,* which used catchy pop-folk jingles to teach minilessons on mathematics, grammar, and history amid Saturday morning cartoons, and "Afterschool Specials," short films focusing on teen and preteen issues that were broadcast late on weekday afternoons.

Meanwhile, NBC brought important innovations to late-night programming. Having dominated this time period since the 1950's with *The Tonight Show,* the network decided to experiment with an even-later program in 1973, *The Tomorrow Show.* Tom Snyder, the host, used the relative freedom afforded by his early morning time slot of 1 to 2 A.M. to experiment with risqué, formerly taboo topics in depth, often devoting entire episodes to specific themes. Thus, the show pioneered the format later followed by the wildly popular talk shows of such hosts as Phil Donahue, Oprah Winfrey, and Jerry Springer. In the middle of the decade, NBC's experimentation with late-night programming spread to weekends as well, resulting in one of the longest-running shows in television history, *Saturday Night Live.* As *The Tomorrow Show* had done, *Saturday Night Live* took advantage of its late hour to indulge in bawdy social and political satire that would have raised eyebrows earlier in the evening. It thereby drew in millions of young viewers, a demographic group that network programmers had long assumed would be impossible to attract on Saturday nights, which had been in earlier decades a television wasteland of old reruns and older theatrical films. The name that NBC gave to its comic troupe *Saturday Night Live* clearly identified the network's canny exploitation of late-night hours: "The Not Ready for Prime Time Players."

Sports programming, however, did prove ready for a return to prime time. Football, except for weekends and holidays, had not been telecast on network prime-time television since the 1950's. Both the television industry and sports journalists were highly skeptical that Americans would want to watch football games on a weeknight. However, ABC's *Monday Night Football* was an immediate success, soon becoming a weekly ritual in millions of homes across the United States every autumn.

Fading Genres It was in prime-time programming that Americans saw the broadest and most obvious changes occurring in television in the 1970's. From the inception of the U.S. television industry in the 1940's, Westerns, variety shows, and anthology series had been prime-time staples, but the 1970's's saw the popularity of these genres wane.

In the late 1950's, the majority of highly rated shows were Westerns, but by the time the long-running *Gunsmoke* was canceled in 1975, it was the sole example of the genre. Dramatic anthology series such as *Studio One* and *The Twilight Zone* had been viewers' favorites and critics' darlings as well. However, when Rod Serling, the creator and chief writer of *The Twilight Zone*, tried to re-create the success of that program with the very similar *Night Gallery*, the show drew only mediocre ratings and little critical attention, and it was canceled after only two seasons.

Only three new variety shows drew much of an audience in the 1970's. Each was a music and comedy hour hosted by a male and female duo: *The Sonny and Cher Comedy Hour* (1971-1974), *The Captain and Tennille Show* (1976-1977), and *Donny and Marie* (1976-1979), starring the Osmond siblings. All were broadcast on ABC, and all were briefly very popular but faded fairly quickly. Even the venerable and long-running *Carol Burnett Show* disappeared in 1978. In the 1980's, only one mildly successful variety hour would appear on prime-time television, country singer Barbara Mandrell's show on NBC.

Dramatic Changes As these three classic television genres vanished, the remaining dominant forms—especially the crime drama and the situation comedy (sitcom)—underwent radical changes as both moved toward more realistic depictions of life in the United States in the 1970's. In the past, crime shows featuring the exploits of police officers, lawyers, and private investigators had been extremely popular with viewers, and several of them had drawn critical raves and professional awards with their supposed realism and sometimes quasi-documentary approaches—for example, *The Defenders*, *The Naked City*, *The Untouchables*, and *Dragnet*.

However, the "realism" of these programs was of a very restricted and selective sort, reflecting conservative, middle-class mores of the time. All protagonists were idealized heroes uncompromised by character defects or personal problems. They tended to be white men who sported neatly groomed hair, always wore a suit and tie, and never swore or used dialect or slang. Authority figures such as judges and high-ranking police officers were rarely corrupt or mistaken. The crimes involved unmitigated acts of cruelty or avarice, with few reflecting any shade of gray between absolute right and wrong. Violence was stylized and muted: No matter how many times victims were shot, they never bled.

In the 1970's, hit crime dramas such as *Baretta* and *Starsky and Hutch* played against these earlier traditions rather than along with them. The title charac-

Popular Prime-Time Family Programming in the 1970's

Title	*Airdates*	*Network*
*The Brady Bunch**	1969-1974	ABC
*The Partridge Family**	1970-1974	ABC
The Waltons	1972-1981	CBS
*The Six Million Dollar Man**	1973-1978	ABC
*Happy Days**	1974-1984	ABC
Little House on the Prairie	1974-1984	NBC
Welcome Back, Kotter	1975-1979	ABC
The Bionic Woman	1976-1978	ABC
Donny and Marie	1976-1979	ABC
The Muppet Show	1976-1981	Syndicated
Laverne and Shirley	1976-1983	ABC
Wonder Woman	1976 1977-1979	ABC CBS
The Hardy Boys/ Nancy Drew Mysteries	1977-1979	ABC
Eight Is Enough	1977-1981	ABC
CHiPs	1977-1983	NBC
Battlestar Galactica	1978-1979	ABC
The Incredible Hulk	1978-1982	CBS
Mork and Mindy	1978-1982	ABC
The Facts of Life	1978-1985	NBC
Diff'rent Strokes	1978-1986	NBC

*indicates the presence of a separate entry in *The Seventies in America* ters wore trendy fashions or scruffy T-shirts and jeans. They let their hair grow long or hang unkempt, and they swore and used street language. Often, they mistrusted their superiors and "the system" as much as the criminals whom they pursued. These protagonists had doubts, personal problems, and personality quirks, and the violence that they encountered, though never graphic, was more realistic and frightening than that of earlier decades. Series such as *Baretta* and *Starsky and Hutch* may seem dated and, at times, even laughable when viewed from the perspective of later decades, but critically acclaimed, grittily accurate crime programs of the 1980's and 1990's, such as *Hill Street Blues* and *NYPD Blue*, owe a debt to these 1970's programs for the first steps that they took toward realistic crime drama.

Real Comedy While the steps toward realism taken in crime shows were somewhat tentative, the innovations that occurred in the situation comedy in the 1970's were revolutionary. Like dramatic series, sitcoms before the 1970's were subject to restrictions. Language, behavior, and thematic content had to respect traditional, conservative morality—to such an extent that even married characters could not be shown sleeping together in one bed. As plot motivations, social and political issues were ignored in favor of classical comic devices such as verbal misunderstandings and crafty schemes by trickster figures.

These traditions were obliterated in the 1970's by a string of extremely popular sitcoms produced by two of the most important innovators in the history of television programming: Mary Tyler Moore and Norman Lear. Moore, in partnership with her then husband, Grant Tinker, produced both *The Mary Tyler Moore Show* and several others, most notably *The Bob Newhart Show*. These sitcoms engaged audiences with witty and sophisticated writing, excellent acting, and irreverence for sitcom conventions. For example, Mary Richards, the protagonist of *The Mary Tyler Moore Show*, rarely had a steady boyfriend and seldom seemed bothered by the lack. Moore's show regularly tackled issues that previous sitcoms could never have explored: drugs, anti-Semitism, adultery. One episode even depicted Mary humiliating herself by bursting into laughter during a funeral.

An even greater innovator was Lear, the producer whose groundbreaking *All in the Family* premiered in 1971. This hit series used comic conventions as old as ancient Greece and as recent as 1950's sitcoms—the grouchy old man stereotype and generational conflict—to examine candidly a long list of issues confronting America in the 1970's: Vietnam, Watergate, women's rights, gay rights, racism, abortion, and rape. The success of *All in the Family* led to a spate of successful issue-oriented comedies—many also created by Lear, such as *Sanford and Son*, *Maude*, and *Good Times*. Two other popular comedies of the decade reflected the new freedom and frankness that Lear's successes permitted: the satirical, pacifistic *M*A*S*H* and the sexually freewheeling *Three's Company*.

In the 1950's and 1960's, sitcoms tended to reflect American ideals—what Americans would like their families, neighborhoods, and workplaces to be like. From the 1970's onward, there would always be a second alternative in television comedy—realism.

Television Films and Miniseries Another important development in television in the 1970's was experimentation with new formats in order to tell stories too complex to fit neatly into a thirty- or sixty-minute program. In a sense, this experimentation had begun in the 1960's on NBC with the Western *The Virginian* and the journalism drama *The Name of the Game*, both of which had ninety-minute formats. *The Name of the Game* had premiered with the first-ever made-for-television film, a two-hour program of the same name. ABC soon began to produce made-for-television films, even scheduling them regularly on Tuesday nights as "Movies of the Week."

Soon, ABC took an even bolder step, developing a format that came to be called the "miniseries"—a limited run of two or more episodes broadcast over several evenings but telling a unified story. The first two of these miniseries, based on novels, were *QB VII* (1974) and *Rich Man, Poor Man* (1976). The high ratings and Emmy awards garnered by these series led to one of the major events in television history, the dramatization by ABC of Alex Haley's *Roots* (1977) as an epic miniseries. It not only drew record-breaking ratings and critical praise but also sparked a national discussion about slavery, history, and race relations and a nationwide fascination with genealogy.

The English Connection The new realism in sitcoms and the development of the miniseries in the 1970's were both part of a television trend of the times that was broad but subtle. In a very real sense, in the 1970's American television underwent what

American popular music had in the 1960's: a British invasion. Lear's breakthrough comedy *All in the Family* was based on an English sitcom, *Till Death Do Us Part,* and another of his hit series, *Sanford and Son,* starring the black comic Redd Foxx, was based on the English series *Steptoe and Son,* in which the analogue to the Foxx character was a Cockney dustman (garbage collector).

Three's Company, in which a young man pretends to be gay so that a conservative landlord will let him share an apartment with two female roommates, was based on yet another English comedy series, *A Man About the House.* In the case of *Three's Company,* all five of the principal characters—the cheeky young man, his two female roommates, the stuffy, tight-fisted landlord, and the landlord's neglected, sex-starved wife—were all drawn directly from *A Man About the House,* and some of the early episodes were basically remakes of episodes from the English original. When the American landlord and his wife, the Ropers, proved to be popular with viewers, executives at ABC decided to do exactly what English producers had done with the characters who had been the Ropers' prototypes on the English series—spin them off into a show of their own.

In like fashion, the development of the miniseries format in the 1970's owed a debt to the continued popularity in United States on the Public Broadcasting Service (PBS) of English series such as *The Forsythe Saga* (1967, but replayed in some parts of the United States in the 1970's), *The Six Wives of Henry VIII* (1970), *Elizabeth R* (1971), *Upstairs, Downstairs* (1971), and *I, Claudius* (1976). The earliest miniseries on ABC as well as NBC's *Holocaust* (1978), another hugely successful miniseries, all shared prominent traits with these British series. Like *The Forsythe Saga* and *I, Claudius,* the ABC programs were based on works of literature—and all of the American shows, like the British ones, told complex stories that dealt with two or more generations of a family experiencing the vagaries of history while undergoing intense internal conflicts among themselves.

Other Genres An important characteristic or trend that 1970's television maintained from the first few decades of the medium's history was its eclecticism. Viewers were presented each week with a smorgasbord of different formats and genres. In addition to crime dramas, comedies revolving around social and political issues, and miniseries chronicling family histories, other popular series of the 1970's included science fiction (*Star Trek, Battlestar Galactica, The Six Million Dollar Man,* and *The Bionic Woman*), fantasy (*Fantasy Island*), campy escapist action (*Charlie's Angels*), family drama (*The Waltons* and *Family*), sentimental family comedy (*The Brady Bunch*), nostalgia (*Happy Days*), and news magazines (*20/20* and *60 Minutes*). Furthermore, producers and programmers displayed throughout the 1970's great imagination in their willingness to explore the blending of genres, resulting in such unlikely hit series as a Western about a Daoist monk from China in the Old West (*Kung Fu*), a science-fiction comedy (*Mork and Mindy*), and even two comic soap operas (ABC's *Soap* and Lear's *Mary Hartman, Mary Hartman*).

Adding to the heady television variety of the decade was PBS, which carried out a major expansion of its programming in the 1970's, not only with adaptations of British literature on its popular *Masterpiece Theatre* and with creative children's programming such as *Sesame Street* but also in a groundbreaking documentary on family life in the 1970's, *An American Family.* PBS also introduced America to the wry, surreal comedy of the Monty Python comic troupe from England.

Programming Shifts One trend in American television that began in the 1970's can hardly be seen as positive: the tendency of network programmers to shuffle and revive their lineups continually. In the first two decades of television's existence as a mass medium, programmers and network executives gave series at least half a season and often an entire television season, from early in the autumn until late spring, to find an audience and thrive in the ratings. In 1966, when respected stage actress Tammy Grimes appeared in a sitcom that was canceled after only four weeks, a near scandal ensued, and the incident quickly became industry legend.

In the 1970's, however, the spectacular successes of various shows of varying genres and formats—the Lear and Moore comedies, miniseries such as *Roots* and *Holocaust,* escapist entries such as *Charlie's Angels*—drove programmers to search frantically and constantly for the "next big thing," the next ratings sensation. As a result, they began to reassign timeslots frequently and cancel programs quickly and abruptly if a series did not achieve immediate success. Gone were the days when American television viewers could expect their favorite programs to remain in the same time-slots for an entire season, and no longer could they know with certainty when—or if—their favorites would appear again. What happened to *The Tammy Grimes Show* in the 1960's became in the 1970's not an industry scandal but an industry standard practice.

Impact It is customary to speak of the 1950's as the golden age of American television. Following this metaphor, one could safely call the 1970's the silver age. Television programming of the 1950's is revered for its hard-hitting drama anthologies such as *Studio One* and its hilarious, inventive sitcoms such as *I Love Lucy.* The pioneering spirit of 1950's television was echoed in 1970's television programming, with its innovative comedies that dealt with social and political issues and its dramatic series and miniseries that treated realistically topics such as racism, government corruption, and violence.

Further Reading

Bedell, Sally. *Up the Tube: Prime-Time TV and the Silverman Years.* New York: Viking, 1981. Insightful and definitive biography of Fred Silverman, who worked as an executive at all three major television networks at various times during the 1970's and was responsible for much innovative programming.

Brooks, Tim, and Earle Marsh. *The Complete Directory to Prime Time Network and Cable TV Shows: 1946-Present.* 8th ed. New York: Ballantine, 2003. An indispensable reference work for research into prime-time American television—accessible, informative, exhaustive.

Stark, Steven D. *Glued to the Set.* New York: Free Press, 1997. Pithy analyses of some of the most popular television shows of the 1970's as well as of other decades.

TV Guide, editors of. *"TV Guide" Guide to TV: The Most Definitive Encyclopedia of Television.* New York: Barnes & Noble, 2004. A very accessible reference work by the editors of the premiere American television magazine. With an introduction by Adam West from the 1960's *Batman* series.

Thomas Du Bose

See also Academy Awards; *All in the Family*; *American Family, An*; Atari; *Battle of the Network Stars*; *Battlestar Galactica*; Belushi, John; *Brady Bunch, The*; *Carol Burnett Show, The*; *Charlie's Angels*; *Chico and the Man*; Children's television; Closed captioning; Communications in Canada; Communications in the United States; *Donahue*; *Family*; *Fat Albert and the Cosby Kids*; *Free to Be . . . You and Me*; *Get Christie Love*; *Happy Days*; *Hawaii Five-O*; Home Box Office; *Jeffersons, The*; Kaufman, Andy; *Love, American Style*; *Mary Hartman, Mary Hartman*; *Mary Tyler Moore Show, The*; *M*A*S*H*; *Maude*; Miniseries; *Mister Rogers' Neighborhood*; *Monday Night Football*; Monty Python; Muppets, The; *Partridge Family, The*; Police and detective shows; Public Broadcasting Service (PBS); *Room 222*; *Roots*; *Sanford and Son*; *Saturday Night Live*; *Schoolhouse Rock!*; Sitcoms; *Six Million Dollar Man, The*; *Star Trek*; Talk shows; *Taxi*; Television in Canada; *Three's Company*; Travolta, John; Variety shows; Video games; *White Shadow, The.*

■ 10

Identification Motion picture
Director Blake Edwards (1922-)
Date Released in 1979

Edwards's 10 *explores 1970's attitudes toward the sexual revolution through characters who epitomize liberated women and men who are threatened by them.*

In *10*, a critical and financial success, Blake Edwards critically evaluates the traditional norm of monogamous heterosexual relationships and finds them wanting. George Webber, played by Dudley Moore, is a successful Hollywood songwriter, who, at his fortieth birthday party, suffers from male menopause. More interested in voyeurism than in his own relationships, he fails to satisfy Samantha (Sam) Taylor (Julie Andrews) sexually, preferring television to sex. He falls in love with Jennifer (Bo Derek) when he sees her at her wedding, which would seem to make his pursuit of her impossible, but he nevertheless follows Jennifer and her husband to Mexico, where he saves her husband from drowning and finds himself in bed with Jennifer. However, he is no more successful with her, thanks to a series of comic interruptions, than he was with Sam. In fact, the notion of romantic love and eroticism (depicted by a *Playboy*-type shot of Jennifer's naked body) is undercut first by the comedy and then by some dramatic dialogue that leaves George disillusioned by Jennifer and on his way, with little enthusiasm, back to Sam. His own sexuality is undermined when he seeks advice from his black psychiatrist and his colleague Hugh, a homosexual, both of whom suggest that

George may have latent homosexual tendencies.

Sam and Jennifer are 1970's women, although they seem to be polar opposites. Sam is the no-nonsense businesswoman who insists on sex, rather than being seduced, and voices her displeasure at being unsatisfied. Her car license plate is SAM1, rendering her low on the ten-point ratings scale of women around which the film revolves. Jennifer has lived with her boyfriend for two years before their marriage, and at the wedding she looks bored with the proceedings. While her husband is in the hospital during their honeymoon, she is more than willing to have sex with a complete stranger. She does not have to be seduced romantically and seems more at home in the bedroom than in the kitchen. She, not George, is the aggressor. The film points out that marriage and commitment are not 1970's values and that the 1970's male seems intimidated and bumbling—symbolized by Moore's physical comedy—when confronted by liberated women.

Bo Derek, the star of 10, *walks by a theater in New York City playing her film.* (AP/Wide World Photos)

Impact Besides popularizing Maurice Ravel's *Bolero* (1928), the music that promises to signal the climax of George's liaison with Jennifer, Blake Edwards's sophisticated look at the evolving nature of gender roles and the precarious state of monogamous heterosexual relationships, to say nothing of marriage, seemed to capture the effect of the sexual revolution that occurred during the 1970's. It also prepared the way for the more sexually explicit films of the 1980's.

Further Reading

Lehman, Peter, and William Luhr. *Blake Edwards.* Athens: Ohio University Press, 1981.

Windeler, Robert. *Julie Andrews: A Life on Stage and Screen.* New York: Citadel, 1997.

Thomas L. Erskine

See also Film in the United States; Marriage and divorce; Sexual revolution.

■ Tennis

Definition Racket sport played in singles or pairs

During the 1970's, tennis became more popular with the American public because of the introduction of regularly televised matches, the bombardment of advertising, and a new breed of tennis star that gained prominence.

Everything changed in the world of competitive tennis in 1968. Prior to that year, only amateur tennis players could play in the major international competitions. Beginning in 1968, professional tennis players were allowed to compete in such prestigious tournaments as Wimbledon, the U.S. Open, the French Open, and the Australian Open. (The U.S., French, and Australian tournaments had the word "Open" attached to them only after the introduction of professionals into the mix.) These four tournaments are considered the Grand Slam events of tennis.

At the 1968 and 1969 Wimbledon tournaments, the great Australian player Rod Laver won the men's singles title. He had been barred from competing at the major tournaments for several years because of his status as a professional player. American Billie Jean King won the first "open" Wimbledon women's singles title in 1968. At the first U.S. Open of the same year, African American Arthur Ashe won the men's singles title in spectacular fashion. He became the first African American man to win a Grand Slam tournament. Tennis was poised to enter the 1970's with newfound vitality and appeal.

Big Money and Popular Male Players The first U.S. Open in 1968 had a total purse of $100,000, and ever-increasing amounts of prize money would be offered to tennis players during the 1970's. Professional tennis went through growing pains during this time, fraught with legal disputes and political posturing. The players realized that it was in their own best interest to organize. The men formed the Association of Tennis Professionals (ATP), and the women formed the Women's Tennis Association (WTA). Slowly but surely, professional players learned that it was necessary to speak with one voice when negotiating with sponsors and tournament officials.

The majority of male players of the early 1970's were products of the previous system. They had played by the established rules that had governed the sport of tennis for decades. Such American players as Ashe and Stan Smith were soft-spoken, well-behaved individuals who did not antagonize the tennis hierarchy. Veteran Australian players such as Laver, Ken Rosewall, John Newcombe, and Tony Roche believed in playing hard, but they never resorted to outbursts of temper.

As the popularity of the sport grew, television played an important role in presenting new players to the viewing audience and a more flamboyant and temperamental tennis star came onto the tennis scene. In the early 1970's, the Romanian player Ilie Nastase horrified many tennis fans with his extreme mood swings on the court. He personified the image of the temperamental artist rather than the steady, clean-cut traditional tennis player.

Jimmy Connors, a fiery American tennis player,

Jimmy Connors (left) and Arthur Ashe shake hands after Ashe's victory at Wimbledon in 1975. (AP/Wide World Photos)

created an even bigger sensation. He was aggressive and seemed to consider each match a war that he had to win at all costs. Connors won the 1974 U.S. Open, Wimbledon, and the Australian Open tournaments and was ranked number one in the world. He remained one of the top tennis players in the world for several years, winning the U.S. Open a total of five times during his illustrious career. In a stunning upset, though, the crafty veteran Ashe beat Connors in the 1975 Wimbledon men's singles final.

During the mid-1970's, the stoic Björn Borg from Sweden was one of the most dominant players on the tour. He won the Wimbledon men's singles title five years in a row, from 1976 to 1980. By the late 1970's, another brash young American tennis player climbed to the top ranks of the men's game. John McEnroe won his first of four U.S. Open men's singles titles in 1979. His fiery outbursts on the court became as legendary as his brilliance as a tennis player. During the 1970's, a new breed of champion emerged, to the chagrin of many veteran players and pundits alike.

Female Players Raise a Ruckus During the 1960's and early 1970's, Billie Jean King was at the top of her game. In addition to being a fierce competitor in singles, she was an extraordinary doubles player. King had learned to play tennis on the public courts of Long Beach, California. Never one to shy away from taking a stand on a social issue, she was an outspoken activist for women's rights. During the 1970's, King was instrumental in organizing the WTA. She was also active in helping to establish the women's professional circuit, and she voiced her opinion that women tennis players should receive an equitable share of the purse at all tennis tournaments. On September 20, 1973, King made history by competing against Bobby Riggs at the Houston Astrodome in what was advertized as the "Battle of the Sexes." More than thirty thousand people attended the event and watched King soundly defeat Riggs.

By the mid-1970's, the American Chris Evert had become the darling of the tennis world. Known for her precise two-handed backhand and a mental toughness second to none, she was ranked number one in the world for five years in a row, from 1974 to 1978. In 1976, she became the first woman to earn a million dollars. By the late 1970's, Evert would be challenged by American Tracy Austin and Czech Martina Navratilova for supremacy of the woman's game. Navratilova decided not to return to Czechoslovakia in 1975. She took up residence in the United States and became an American citizen in 1981. By 1979, Navratilova was ranked number one in the world. She and Evert would have many memorable matches against each other over the years.

Impact With the introduction of sponsors, televised matches, and popular tennis stars, tennis in the 1970's became much more than a mere country club sport. Millions of middle class suburbanites took up the game, and the racket used by Jimmy Connors or Chris Evert was mass-produced in order to satisfy the weekend tennis warrior. Because of the advertising and endorsement money that was made available to top tennis professionals, many of them became millionaires almost overnight. After all the decades in which tennis was a game played by the rich, now it was possible for someone to become wealthy by playing tennis. The sport of tennis grew during the 1970's into a professionally run commodity in which the sky was the limit. By the 1980's, tennis stars were reaping the multimillion-dollar rewards of the efforts made by the visionaries who fought to expand the sport in the late 1960's and 1970's.

Further Reading

Baltzell, E. Digby. *Sporting Gentlemen: Men's Tennis from the Age of Honor to the Cult of the Superstar.* New York: The Free Press, 1995. A splendid overview of the history of tennis.

Collins, Bud, and Zander Hollander, eds. *Bud Collins' Modern Encyclopedia of Tennis.* Garden City, N.Y.: Doubleday, 1980. Gives the reader a detailed account of all the major developments in the history of tennis.

Evans, Richard. *Open Tennis: 1968-1988.* Lexington, Mass.: Stephen Greene Press, 1989. Details how competitive tennis was altered forever with the introduction of professional tennis players into the premier tennis tournaments.

Wind, Herbert Warren. *Game, Set, and Match: The Tennis Boom of the 1960's and 70's.* New York: E. P. Dutton, 1979. Takes a detailed look at the seminal events that transformed competitive tennis during the 1960's and 1970's.

Jeffry Jensen

See also Ashe, Arthur; Battle of the Sexes; Connors, Jimmy; Evert, Chris; King, Billie Jean; Sports.

Terrorism

Definition Violent acts by individuals or groups seeking to influence public opinion or public policy

During the decade, the United States and Canada dealt with terrorist acts that emanated from a variety of "homegrown" and international sources.

Terrorism in the United States and Canada can be divided into roughly four categories: religious extremism, state-sponsored terrorism, secessionist violence, and domestic extremism, including antiabortion, animal rights, antiglobalization, and environmental groups, as well as a small but receptive audience for militia messages emanating from white supremacists. Because of their strong desire for attention and publicity, terrorists must use elements of drama, awe, and theater in order to be successful—in the eyes of terrorists, the more bizarre an act, including the number of casualties sustained, the greater the success of the terrorist campaign.

Many of the terrorist acts affecting the United States and Canada during this period were reactions to foreign policy in the course of dealing with radical and revolutionary groups around the world and often took place in foreign locales. In Latin America, the United States gave military and financial support to anticommunist governments, many of which brutally repressed their own people. Americans traveling to or living in these countries were sometimes killed by local terrorists opposing the U.S. support for their repressive government. Many of the governments fought back with state-sponsored terrorist campaigns of their own, apparently to frighten the citizens into submission to state authority. In 1979, in arguably the worst foreign act of terrorism against Americans, hundreds of armed Iranian students stormed the American embassy in Tehran and took fifty-three Americans as hostages. The young Islamic militants were infuriated by Mohammad Reza Shah Pahlavi's "modernization" policies and turned instead to the ultraconservative doctrine of the Ayatollah Khomeini and his religious extremism. The Ayatollah preached that the shah's program to modernize Iran was offensive to God and that the United States was both "the Great Satan" and the central source of the moral corruption spreading throughout the world.

Domestic Extremism Domestic or homegrown terrorists are those related to domestic issues and sectarian concerns. Domestic terrorism in the United States often was enacted by left-wing or right-wing groups. Right-wing extremism was represented by groups such as the Klu Klux Klan, Tax Rebels, militia patriots, and various antiabortionists and neo-Nazis. Many of these groups had their origin in the discrimination and prejudice that have historically accompanied immigrants to the United States.

American right-wing terrorist groups were dominated by a large segment of white supremacist, antigovernment militants who hated Jews, Asian Americans, black Americans, and others, whom they collectively referred to as "mud people." They were widely scattered around the country, with their largest support base in midwestern and southern states. These groups were referred to as terrorists because they often used the tactics of terror both to intimidate their victims and to pursue their various agendas. During this period, the Ku Klux Klan was the longest-running and best-known terrorist organization in the United States. It experienced a revival and continued to recruit thousands of members to fight the gains of civil rights legislation of the era. The Covenant, the Sword, and the Arm was another right-wing movement that often resorted to violence and was based in Arkansas.

Several left-wing terrorist organizations also emerged during this period. Many of these groups had their roots in the turbulent years of the 1960's and peaked during the 1970's. Their targets included military facilities, corporate establishments, and the U.S. Capitol Building. Fueled by similar social ferment, a wave of leftist-revolutionary, antigovernment terrorist acts were committed by small groups in European and Latin American countries. While in the United States, revolutionary terrorists soon dwindled to a handful of near dormant activists. In Europe, leftist terrorists were active for much longer, striking military targets as well as European civilians during this time. These groups of terrorists shared resources with one another and had a common agenda: to destroy the political, economic, and social order of the world's industrialized, capitalist nations in order to pave the way for a new, socialist-communist world order.

In the United States, this sentiment was manifested in several high-profile groups, among them the Black Panther Party, the Weather Underground, and the Armed Forces of National Liberation (FALN). The Black Panthers were an African American leftist and revolutionary group founded in the 1960's, which wanted to incite a violent revolution on behalf of black Americans. It continued its activities into the 1970's. The Weather Underground emerged from the student antiwar protests of the 1960's. As a small group living "underground" (in hiding from the law), it occasionally committed terrorist acts in pursuit of socialist revolution in the 1970's. Finally, a group supporting Puerto Rican nationalism and calling itself the FALN was believed to be responsible for a December, 1975, bombing at New York's La Guardia Airport that killed twelve people. The FALN conducted a series of bombings in New York City in the fall of 1974.

Canada's Experience Canada witnessed its own version of terrorism, although most incidents were generally minor and narrowly focused within particular communities. However, hundreds of terrorist incidents did occur during this period, orchestrated by a variety of actors from the radical Left and Right, including Quebec separatists, the Doukhobors, and single-issue players such as the Animal Liberation Front and antiabortion activists. The majority of these actions involved Quebec separatists and the Sons of Freedom, a subset of the Doukhobors. The Doukhobors, a Russian group that rejected secular government among other things, were the first of the imported or "émigré" terrorist groups to come into Canada. They witnessed a major revival after World War II and were quite active during the 1970's.

In Canada during the late 1960's and early 1970's, the Front de Libération du Québec (FLQ), which sought the secession of Quebec from Canada, embarked on numerous bombings and kidnappings and succeeded in murdering Quebec cabinet minister Pierre Laporte. The activities of the FLQ represent the most violent period of domestic terrorism in Canada. A domestic left-wing extremist group, Direct Action, was also believed to have formed in the 1970's with plans to bomb and maim its victims at several locations.

In the early 1970's, many other violent terrorist incidents were also recorded in Canada, although on a smaller scale than those of the FLQ. Canada served as a spillover of violence from conflicts in faraway places and became home to such groups as the Armenian Secret Army for the Liberation of Armenia, the Justice Commandos of the Armenian Genocide, and Sikh extremist groups, who protested against events in India and began to make their presence felt in Canadian territory.

Many incidents of international or émigré terrorism were recorded during this period. Most of these involved unsophisticated attacks with pipe bombs and Molotov cocktails on diplomatic sites; for example, the Cuban Consulate in Montreal received much unwelcome attention from Cuban expatriates during the 1960's and 1970's. Canadian Croatians protesting against developments in their native country of Yugoslavia attacked various locations in Canada. In a series of letter bomb campaigns orchestrated by Black September, a paramilitary Palestinian organization, in 1971 and 1972, some prominent Canadian Jews were among the intended targets. Palestinians also created a number of groups around the globe during the 1960's and 1970's that worked for the overthrow of Israel and freedom for their people. These satellite locations were meant to help with fund-raising activities, and those in Canada attempted to use their tactics to influence foreign policies that were favorable to the Palestinian cause.

Impact In comparison to other industrialized nations, the United States and Canada may have suffered least from the prevalent spate of terrorism following the ideological and religious turmoil of the 1960's. Among the major currents that drove terrorism in United States and Canada were deepening agitation for socialist reforms, racial inequality, and nationalism. Terrorist acts were therefore inspired and committed by domestic groups or greatly influenced by foreign sources that sought to change the policies of the government in their favor.

Further Reading

Adrryszewski, Tricia. *The Militia Movement in America: Before and After Oklahoma City.* Brookfield, Conn.: Millbrook Press, 1996. Chronicles the origin, development, and growth of the militia movement in the United States.

Carnes, Jim. *Us and Them: A History of Intolerance in America.* New York: Oxford University Press, 1996. A historical analysis of some of the origins and patterns of intolerance in the United States toward minorities and immigrants.

Chalmers, David M. *Hooded Americanism: The History of the Ku Klux Klan.* Durham, N.C.: Duke University Press, 1987. A historical perspective of the origin, development, and process of decline of the Ku Klux Klan.

Fridell, Ron. *Terrorism: Political Violence at Home and Abroad.* Hillside, N.J.: Enslow, 2001. A critical examination and comparison of the nature, processes, and growth of terrorism in the United States and overseas.

Gaines, Ann Graham. *Terrorism.* Broomal, Pa.: Chelsea House, 1998. A wide-ranging discussion of the various aspects of terrorism.

Garza, Hedda. *African Americans and Jewish Americans: A History of Struggle.* New York: Franklin Watts, 1995. A comparison of some similarities in the suffering of African Americans and Jewish Americans as a result of racial discrimination in the United States.

Austin Ogunsuyi

See also Black Panthers; Munich Olympics terrorism; October Crisis; Puerto Rican nationalism; Symbionese Liberation Army (SLA); Weather Underground.

■ Test-tube babies

Definition Method of reproduction in which fertilization of a human egg occurs in a laboratory dish

Place Oldham, England

The birth of a test-tube baby in Great Britain in 1978 following a successful in vitro fertilization (IVF) procedure transformed fertility treatment and provided hope to couples throughout the world.

Patrick Steptoe, an obstetrician at Oldham General Hospital in Oldham, England, and Robert Edwards, a Cambridge University physiologist, first met while attending the same scientific meeting in 1968. Steptoe had long been interested in problems of infertility and, in particular, had studied women who suffered from blockages of the Fallopian tubes. Edwards's specialties included the roles played by hormones in maturation of the ovaries and oocytes.

The first attempt at IVF occurred in the early 1970's. In 1963, Doris and John Del Zio had a baby. The pregnancy, however, had left scarring in Doris's Fallopian tubes, which resulted in an inability to produce further children. In September, 1973, the Del Zios requested their physician, William Sweeney of New York Hospital, to attempt external fertilization. On September 12, Sweeney withdrew follicular fluid from Doris Del Zio that contained a viable egg; the fluid was carried by John Del Zio to Presbyterian Hospital, where Landrum Shettles attempted an external fertilization using sperm from the husband.

Shettles had not initially obtained permission from the chairman of his department, and in any event, the sterility of the solution in which the fertilized egg was being incubated was in question. The experiment ended when the material was removed from the incubator the next day and eventually destroyed. The procedure itself was a failure, and the controversies resulting from the methodology threatened future research into the process.

A year later, Doris Del Zio filed a lawsuit against the hospital for "destruction of their property." Ironically, the "test tube death trial" reached Federal District Court at the same time that a more successful attempt at IVF was nearing completion.

Success for the Brown Family Like Doris Del Zio, Lesley Brown—a twenty-seven-year-old Bristol, England, resident—suffered from scarred Fallopian tubes. She and her husband, John, were referred to Steptoe in 1976 and discussed with him the possibility of another attempt at external fertilization. Following 1969, Steptoe and Edwards had collaborated in research into methods of obtaining viable oocytes and carrying out fertilization. Their only "success" out of some eighty attempts, however, was a single ectopic pregnancy in 1975, which had to be terminated.

By 1976, modifications in their procedures, including more rapid implantation of the fertilized egg, promised a greater chance of success. On November 10, 1977, Steptoe removed an egg from Lesley Brown and placed it in a sterile dish, and Edwards mixed sperm obtained from her husband with the egg to allow fertilization. Three days later an embryo in the eight-cell stage was implanted in Brown's uterus; the procedure was successful.

Hounded by the press, Brown spent the initial months of her pregnancy living with the Steptoe family or shuttling from house to house. In part, the media frenzy was of their own volition. A London tabloid, the *Daily Mail*, paid the equivalent of nearly $500,000 for exclusive rights to the story. The paper assigned reporters to follow the Browns twenty-four hours a day, including several who moved in with the husband. As the pregnancy progressed, Brown de-

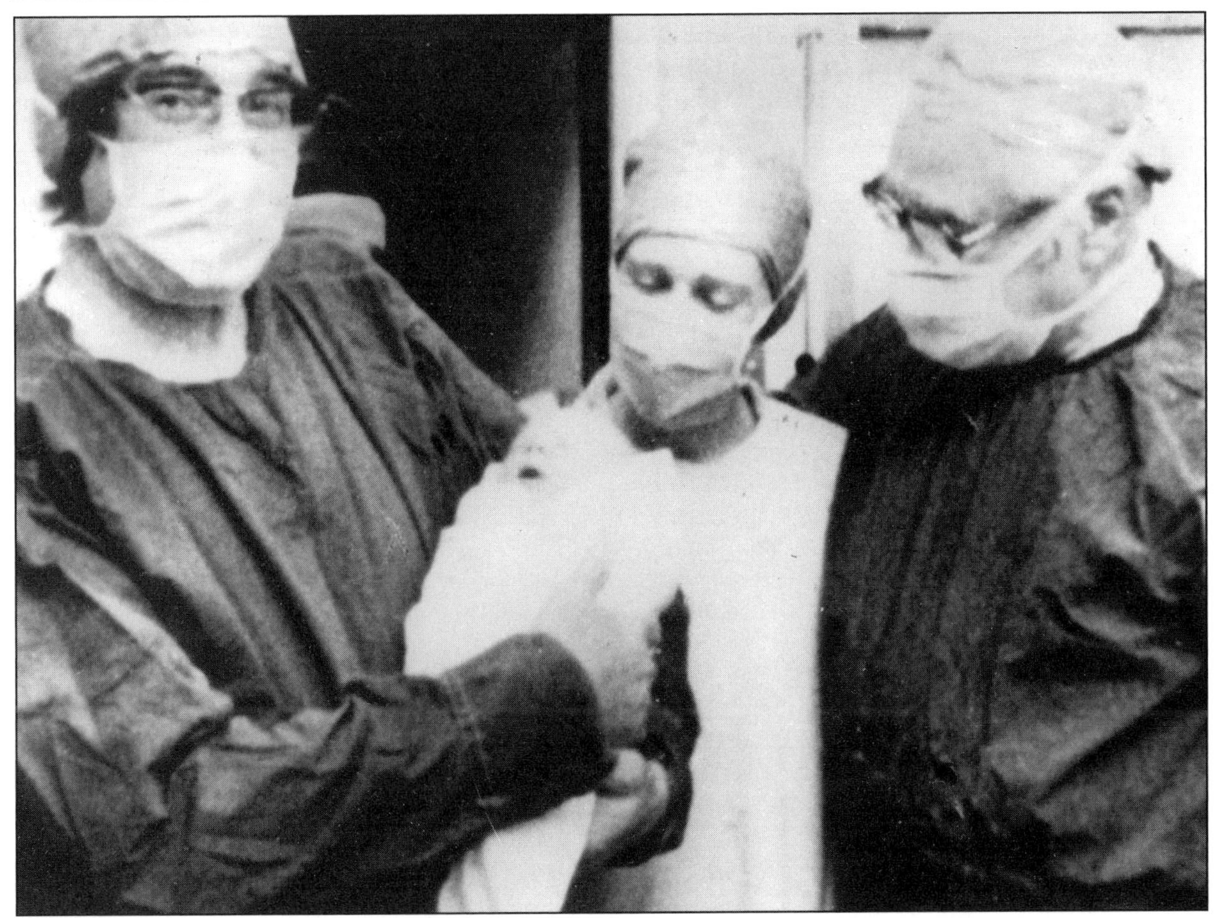

Dr. Robert Edwards holds Louise Brown, the world's first test-tube baby, on July 25, 1978, as Dr. Patrick Steptoe (right) looks on. (AP/ Wide World Photos)

veloped toxemia and elevated blood pressure, forcing her admittance to Oldham General Hospital for the final two months of the pregnancy. Fortunately, the baby developed normally. On July 25, 1978, Louise Joy Brown was successfully delivered by cesarean section. Weighing five pounds, twelve ounces, the baby was normal and healthy.

Impact The ability to carry out fertilization outside of a woman's body provided immediate hope to couples who wished to produce a child biologically rather than adopt one. The procedure developed by Steptoe and Edwards was quickly adapted by other clinics. As news of the success became widespread, thousands of women expressed the desire to undergo a similar procedure.

Subsequent Events Initially, most attempts at IVF were unsuccessful. Beginning in the 1980's, procedures for preparation and isolation of the eggs underwent modifications, as well as the fertilization and implantation methods themselves. Statistics have borne out the safety and success of the procedure. In the early twenty-first century, the success rate was approximately 30 percent, higher even than the fertilization rate of 20 percent that a healthy couple may achieve through intercourse in a normal month.

Four years after Louise Brown's birth, the family had a second baby named Natalie, who was also the result of IVF.

Further Reading

Bonnicksen, Andrea. *In Vitro Fertilization.* New York: Columbia University Press, 1989. Offers a history of IVF and discusses the role of public policies in regulation of the procedure.

Edwards, Robert, and Ruth Fowler. "Human Embryos in the Laboratory." *Scientific American* 223 (December, 1970): 44-54. A description and depiction of the early work dealing with regulation of oocyte maturation and isolation of the human egg.

Edwards, Robert, and Patrick Steptoe. *A Matter of Life.* New York: William Morrow, 1980. An autobiographical account of the research and procedure in the first successful IVF.

Henig, Robin. *Pandora's Baby: How the First Test Tube Babies Sparked the Reproductive Revolution.* New York: Houghton Mifflin, 2004. An examination of the history of IVF, with discussion of its implications and controversies.

Orr, Tamra. *Test Tube Babies: The Science of In Vitro Fertilization.* San Diego, Calif.: Blackbirch Press, 2003. High school level discussion of infertility and the role played by IVF in achieving pregnancy.

Richard Adler

See also Genetics research; Medicine; Ultrasonography.

■ Teton Dam collapse

The Event The earth-fill dam on the Teton River collapses just three days after it was filled to completion

Date June 5, 1976

Place Fremont County, Idaho

The dam's collapse was the first in the history of Bureau of Reclamation projects and caused extensive damage to several counties in Idaho.

The Bureau of Reclamation, responsible for the building of the Grand Teton Dam, decided to locate it on the Teton River, a tributary of the Snake River, in Fremont County, Idaho. The site was selected after extensive investigations were carried out by geologists from the United States Geological Survey (USGS) from 1932 to 1957. Though faults had been located in the area, the geologists determined that the level of seismic activity was very low and would not have an impact on the dam. They also assessed

This part of the Teton Dam collapsed in 1976, flooding parts of Idaho. (AP/Wide World Photos)

the nature of underlying rocks to evaluate the possibility of underground water losses from future reservoirs.

The construction of the 305-feet-high Grand Teton Dam began in 1972. It was earth-fill construction, comprising about ten million cubic yards of compacted fill composed of debris excavated from the reservoir mixed with sandy gravel, silt, and rock. In order to provide a solid footing, a trench approximately one hundred feet deep was excavated to reach solid rock that lay beneath a jointed overlay. Filling of the reservoir began on October 3, 1975; when it was completed on June 1, 1976, the reservoir contained 234,259 acre-feet of water and had the capacity to hold 288,256.

Problems with the dam were immediately apparent. By June 3, two small springs had developed downstream from the spillway. On June 4, another spring appeared. During the morning of June 5, major leaks were discovered that defeated all attempts to repair them. By 10:43 A.M., it became evident that the collapse of the dam was imminent and could not be avoided; residents downstream were advised to evacuate. At 11:57 A.M., the reservoir broke, sending a wall of debris-filled water down the Teton River Valley, severely damaging the towns of Wilford, Sugar City, and Rexburg. The next day, President Gerald R. Ford declared Bingham, Bonneville, Fremont, Jefferson, and Madison Counties federal disaster areas.

Impact The flood caused two billion dollars of property damage, washed out irrigation canals and Union Pacific railroad tracks, drowned thirteen thousand head of livestock, and killed eleven people. The Department of the Interior instituted two panels to examine the cause of the failure, one comprising members of the federal agencies that had sited and built the dam and one comprising independent experts not associated with the construction.

A subcommittee of the House of Representatives, chaired by California congressman Leo Ryan, held hearings on August 5, 1976, in order to evaluate the reports of these panels and the testimony of other expert witnesses such as geologists Robert Curry of the University of Montana and Marshall Corbett from Idaho State University. The consensus of opinion was that the design and construction of the dam were not at fault; the collapse was caused by the high permeability and porosity of the materials beneath the dam. The dam was never rebuilt. Its failure triggered the passage of the Reclamation Safety of Dams Act in 1978, which established stricter guidelines for the location and construction of dams.

Further Reading

Collier, Michael. *Dams and Rivers: A Primer on the Downstream Effects of Dams.* Denver: U.S. Geological Survey, Branch of Information Services, 1996.

Lowry, William R. *Dam Politics: Restoring America's Rivers.* Washington, D.C.: Georgetown University Press, 2003.

Denyse Lemaire and David Kasserman

See also Natural disasters.

■ Theater in Canada

Definition Live dramatic entertainment in a variety of languages and forms

In all parts of Canada during the 1970's, increasing development and excellence in theater brought critical approval from national and international sources and established permanent audiences.

Although some nationalist critics thought theater in Canada in the 1970's was not Canadian enough, the country continued to produce fine actors who made careers at home and abroad and built significant theatrical institutions. Notable playwrights and directors also emerged who made surprising new contributions to Canadian national identity. The economies of festival towns such as Stratford, and Niagara-on-the-Lake in Ontario flourished and developed new infrastructure because of the influx of theater audiences, while urban centers like Montreal, Toronto, Winnipeg, and Vancouver attracted new visitors because of the lively theatrical scene. Both subsidized and independent theater caught hold in every province across the vast, multicultural nation.

Fueled by an upsurge in French-speaking particularism, playwrights took francophone drama in new directions. Michel Tremblay's *Les Belles-sœurs* (pr. 1968; English translation, 1973) pioneered the use of *joual,* the common urban Québécois dialect. This innovation was used by Tremblay in 1970's plays that were popular in French-speaking countries as well as in English translation in Canada and elsewhere. Jean Barbeau, Réjean Ducharme, Jean-Claude Germain, Robert Gurik, Marie Laberge, and Jovette Marchessault were other French-speaking playwrights who wrote innovative works produced in the 1970's. Michel Garneau even made a notable translation of William Shakespeare's *Macbeth* into rural Québécois dialect in 1978.

English-language playwrights also broke new ground. David French's Mercer plays (pr. 1972-1988), James Reaney's Donnelly plays (pr. 1973-1975), and George F. Walker's Power plays (pr. 1977-1983) encouraged the development of a Canadian school of realistic drama during this era. Sharon Pollock's black comedy *A Compulsory Option* (pr. 1972), her historical play *Walsh* (pr. 1973), and her antinuclear *The Komagata Maru Incident* (pr. 1976) showed other directions for Canadian drama. George Ryga's *Grass and Wild Strawberries* (pr. 1969) dealt engagingly with the counterculture, but his *Captives of the Faceless Drummer* (pr. 1971) proved too controversial politically to be produced in the venue for which it was intended. Peter Colley's *I'll Be Back Before Midnight* (pr. 1978) was a solid thriller with a rural Canadian setting. Sheldon Rosen's *Ned and Jack* (pr. 1977) dealt with an actor, John Barrymore, as did John Murrell's *Memoir* (pr. 1978), about Sarah Bernhardt.

Toward the end of the 1970's, two popular and thoughtful plays dealt with the complexities of Canadian attitudes toward the world wars of the century. John Gray's *Billy Bishop Goes to War* (pr. 1978) concerned a real-life World War I air ace, and Murrell's *Waiting for the Parade* (pr. 1977) concerned women on the homefront in Alberta during World War II. Collective authorship produced such popular plays as Toronto Workshop Productions' *Ten Lost Years* (pr. 1977) about the Depression and, in Saskatoon, the 25th Street Theatre Centre's *Paper Wheat* (pr. 1977) about the development of grain cooperatives.

Theater Companies and Festivals All of Atlantic Canada had significant theater companies in the 1970's. The Mummers Troupe and Codco performed lively collective creations in Newfoundland, as did Theatre Newfoundland and Labrador in Corner Brook and the Rising Tide Theatre in St. John's. The large Confederation Centre of the Arts in Charlottetown, Prince Edward Island, filled with visitors seeing pastoral musicals with productions of local favorites such as *Anne of Green Gables* (pr. 1965) and *Johnny Belinda* (pr. 1968). Walter Learning's Theatre New Brunswick made live theater available to many communities, as did several companies serving the Acadian community. The Neptune Theatre in Halifax and the Mermaid Theatre in Wolfville were supplemented by a variety of experimental companies in Nova Scotia.

Quebec remained the center of French-speaking theater in Canada, with a variety of companies in Montreal, Quebec City, and elsewhere presenting both classics and daring modern plays, many of them relevant to the local experience. Theater in English also continued in Montreal, and plays were presented in both languages until the end of the decade at La Poudrière on Ile Ste-Helene.

Canada's foremost classical theater company continued to develop at Ontario's Stratford Shakespeare Festival under the direction of Jean Gascon and Robin Phillips, adding an experimental Third Stage. It featured stars like Maggie Smith and Brian Bedford as well as many Canadian actors and performers, such as Nicholas Pennell, who became Canada-centered for the remainder of their careers. The Blyth Festival developed Canadian plays, as did the Tarragon Theatre in Toronto. The Shaw Festival in Niagara-on-the-Lake opened a new festival theater in 1972 and continued to expand its production schedule. Toronto developed a lively cabaret scene where its Second City Company rivaled the Chicago original.

The Manitoba Theatre Centre in Winnipeg became the model for regional theaters in Canada and developed significant local talent, including actor Len Cariou. The Globe Theatre in Regina and the 25th Street Theatre in Saskatoon served Saskatchewan. Theatre Calgary, where Murrell developed as a playwright, and the Citadel Theatre in Edmonton established projects that brought theater to ever-wider audiences in Alberta. The Banff Centre continued to train young professionals in a variety of theatrical skills. Vancouver and Victoria established stable repertory theaters, and the Vancouver had a significant cabaret scene. Both professional and amateur companies served French, Ukrainian, and other special linguistic groups in western Canada. Amerindian and Inuit groups performed ritual dramas both for themselves and for interested outsiders.

Impact Theater in Canada in the 1970's provided not only cultural riches but also a significant economic boost for many communities and helped increase a sense of Canadian national identity.

Further Reading

Benson, Eugene, and L. W. Conolly, eds. *The Oxford Companion to Canadian Theatre.* Toronto: Oxford University Press, 1989. This volume has articles that cover the history of theater in Canada up to the end of the 1980's.

Pettigrew, John, and Jamie Portman. *Stratford: The First Thirty Years, 1953-1983.* Toronto: Macmillan, 1985. An excellent history of the beginning of Canada's foremost theater festival.

Wagner, Anton, ed. *Contemporary Canadian Theatre: New World Visions.* Toronto: Simon and Pierre, 1985. This interesting group of essays deals with many problematic aspects of the Canadian theater scene.

J. Quinn Brisben

See also Literature in Canada; Minorities in Canada; Theater in the United States.

■ Theater in the United States

Definition Live presentations of dramatic, comedic, or musical performances before an audience

Theatrical art during the 1970's took a radical turn, embracing postmodernism and poststructuralism, as well as many aspects of popular culture, including rock-and-roll music and new freedoms of expression. Women's issues and the issues of American minorities also were emphasized.

Theater in the United States throughout the 1970's tended to expand trends initiated in the late 1960's. In 1968, nudity and obscenity were introduced to the Broadway stage in the musical *Hair,* and in the following year, whole scenes were performed entirely in the nude in the 1969 musical *Oh! Calcutta!* These two works also presented audiences with the sounds and dances of the new rock-and-roll culture.

With the impetus provided by the late 1960's, Broadway theater became increasingly postmodern in the 1970's. As with postmodernism in literature and other media, the emphasis in theater was on the work as self-reflexive, calling attention to itself as theater and how it was made. A good example of this self-reflexivity is the extremely popular musical *A Chorus Line* (pr. 1975). The lead "character" of the work is actually the entire chorus line, members of which are in the process of auditioning for work. Each auditioning dancer is asked by the director to relate a story about his or her life. The production thus is created from the lives of its performers. In its construction, *A Chorus Line* may also be considered poststructuralist, in that it has not one story but several, and these may be interpreted and assembled by the audience in any manner that suits them at the moment. *A Chorus Line,* with music by Marvin Hamlisch, book by James Kirkwood and Nicholas Dante, and lyrics by Edward Kleban, won the 1976 Pulitzer Prize in drama.

Playwrights such as David Mamet and John Guare also embraced various aspects of postmodernism in Broadway presentations. However, the American theater was enlarging its base so that many of the most important new directions were happening in locales away from Broadway and in cities outside New York. In Chicago, the Second City Company headed by Mike Nichols and Elaine May was at the height of its fame and was matched in 1976 by the emergence of Steppenwolf Theater Company of Chicago, which featured John Malkovich among its performers. Also growing into maturity was the Free Southern Theater of New Orleans, which was devoted to black theatrical artists. In 1975, the Los Angeles Theater Center was founded as a venue committed to new plays, and in 1977, the Actors Theatre of Louisville won international acclaim by initiating the Humana Festival of new plays.

Other significant regional theaters were the Guthrie Theater of Minneapolis, the Kennedy Center for Performing Arts in Washington, D.C., and several Shakespearean summer theaters in states ranging from Ohio to Oregon, as well as the New York Shakespeare Festival in Central Park. While most of these groups were involved in traditional theatrical production, there did emerge a number of significant guerrilla theaters, which staged performances infused with political and at times subversive commentary and often used alternative theatrical techniques.

New Trends In October, 1971, the Company Theater of Los Angeles produced a work at the Guggenheim Museum of New York City called the James Joyce Memorial Liquid Theater. When spectators arrived, they were asked to divest themselves of as much clothing as they wished. They were then asked to close their eyes and were caressed, fondled, and kissed as they were led into a performance chamber where they were presented with sudden displays of nudity, made to participate in theater games, and in other ways treated to sensual stimulation. The James Joyce Memorial Liquid Theater became quite popular.

Other fringe groups, such as the Mabou Mimes of San Francisco and Richard Schechner's New York Performance Group, pushed the idea of "environmental theater" by using found space, communal development of story line and ritualized performance, and the inclusion of the audience in all parts of the production. While most environmental theater is unencumbered with traditional scenery and costume, it often involves the free intermix of media, including slides, cinema, and video. This mixing of media was to become a trademark of the theater of the 1970's and was taken to major artistic heights by the director Robert Wilson in productions such as that of Philip Glass's opera *Einstein on the Beach* (pr. 1976).

The extensive use of mixed media was also a favorite device of a new theatrical art form, performance art, in which individual performers might spend an evening painting their bodies or sticking pins in themselves. Perhaps the best known of such performers was Laurie Anderson in works such as *Automotive* in which she performed on a street to a musical score made up of automobile horns.

The new freedom of the theater in the 1970's can also be seen in the emergence of women playwrights and minority theaters. The black theater movement was supported by the founding of the Black Theater Alliance in 1971. The African American experience was explored in plays such as a revised 1970 production of *Purlie Victorious* (pr. 1961) by Ossie Davis, Ntozake Shange's *for colored girls who have considered suicide/ when the rainbow is enuf* (pr. 1975), and the musical *Raisin* (pr. 1973), an adaptation of Lorraine Hansberry's hit play *A Raisin in the Sun* (pr. 1959). The most popular black theater musical was Wil-

Nipsey Russell as the Tinman, Diana Ross as Dorothy, and Michael Jackson as the Scarecrow (left-right) in a scene from the film version of the Broadway musical The Wiz. *The 1970's saw several successful motion pictures based on theatrical sources.* (AP/Wide World Photos)

liam F. Brown and Charlie Smalls's *The Wiz*, (pr. 1975), which retold *The Wizard of Oz* story with "jive talk" and rock, gospel, and soul music.

Paralleling the rise of black theater was the emergence of a significant group of women playwrights, including Corinne Jacker, Joyce Carol Oates, Megan Terry, and Wendy Wasserstein. To meet new feminist interests, 110 theaters devoted to women's issues were established around the country by 1980, including the Off-Broadway venue the Women's Project of New York.

The growing prominence of gays and lesbians in society was also addressed directly during the 1970's in Ron Clark and Sam Bobrick's *Norman Is That You?* (pr. 1970) and David Rabe's *Streamers* (pr. 1976). A whole company devoted to gay subject matter was Charles Ludlam's Ridiculous Theater Company.

Taken as a whole, all of the emerging theatrical trends had powerful influences on the established American theater, especially on the musical.

Traditional Theater Responds to New Ideas The 1970's had many important productions that may be considered as traditional twentieth century realism. Neil Simon's works, such as *The Sunshine Boys* (pr. 1972), may be classified among the most typical of the traditional 1970's plays, as was the 1972 Pulitzer Prize-winning work, Jason Miller's *That Championship Season*, about a group of middle-age men reliving their year of a high-school basketball championship. Other playwrights prompted by the new freedoms of the fringe groups, such as Christopher Durang, David Mamet, Lanford Wilson, and Harold Pinter, mixed traditional realism with techniques ranging from experiments in story line to excessive obscenity in the presentation of seemingly normal people with various hidden secrets. Sam Shepard's 1979 work *Buried Child* is a good example of the liberties taken in the traditional theater. Shepard employs a tenuous story line to explore a young farmer's uncovering of the sordid secret history of his family.

Perhaps the most changed of all the traditional theatrical forms of the 1970's was the American musical. The 1970's saw a invasion of musicals from Great Britain led by the British composer Andrew Lloyd Webber, whose most important work, *Jesus Christ Superstar*, written with Tim Rice, opened in New York in 1971. Opening in 1972 was Jim Jacobs and Warren Casey's rock musical *Grease*. Both of these musicals followed in the footsteps of *Hair* in terms of pushing the limits of what was considered acceptable subject matter and "normal" music. They were received not only with considerable enthusiasm but also with great indignation on the part of some members of the establishment. Indeed, in 1972, *Hair* was banned in Boston and Chattanooga, Tennessee, because of nudity.

The major composer of American musicals in the 1970's was Stephen Sondheim, whose work *Company* was presented in 1970 under the direction of Harold Prince. Prince and Sondheim would go on to cooperate on four other productions in the 1970's: *Follies* (pr. 1971), *A Little Night Music* (pr. 1973), *Pacific Overtures* (pr. 1976), and *Sweeney Todd: The Demon Barber of Fleet Street* (pr. 1979). Each of these works was experimental in different ways, from the use of unorthodox tonalities and atonal music to the employment of the techniques of Japanese Kabuki theater.

A number of director-choreographers emerged during the 1970's, including Prince and Michael Bennett, the creator of *A Chorus Line*. Perhaps the most famous of the director-choreographers was Bob Fosse, whose major hit of the 1970's was *Chicago* (pr. 1975), with music by John Kander and lyrics by Fred Ebb. Fosse followed *Chicago* with *Dancin'* (pr. 1978). His innovations included slow, sinuous movement, especially hand movements and positions, accentuated by white gloves and derby hats.

There were many 1970's musicals that fell into the classic form perfected in the 1950's. Chief among these were Betty Comden and Adolph Green's hit *Applause* (pr. 1970), Peter Stone and Richard Rodgers's *Two by Two* (pr. 1970), and Charles Strouse and Martin Charnin's *Annie* (pr. 1977), based on the popular comic strip and featuring the popular song "Tomorrow."

With all the innovations in experimental theater. as well as the freedoms introduced into even the most traditional theatrical forms, there was also a major shift in acting styles. The predominant method acting of the Actors Studio was altered or abandoned completely in favor of new "transformational" techniques in which actors did not inhabit characters but saw themselves as elements in the total kinetic and vocal structure of the theater piece. Such an approach allowed both for more ritualistic presentations as well as for more experiments by playwrights with story-line structure and language style. Among the major actors using this acting approach were Kevin Kline, Bernadette Peters, Glenn Close, Meryl Streep, William Hurt, and Stockard Channing, all of whom would continue to be important actors in subsequent decades. It was also a common practice for established film stars to take a turn at theatrical productions. Among the most prominent of such stars was Lauren Bacall in *Applause*, Danny Kaye in *Two by Two*, Gwen Verdon in *Annie*, as well as Ingrid Bergman, Lily Tomlin, Christopher Reeve, and James Earl Jones in various other shows.

Impact The innovative spirit of the 1970's laid important groundwork for theater of future decades. New trends in theater—many falling under the terms postmodernism and poststructuralism—commenced in the previous decade and grew into maturity during this period. A number of fringe movements, including the James Joyce Memorial Liquid Theater, drew closer to the mainstream and exerted influence on even the most traditional playwrights. As a result, increasingly more innovations were made in dramatic structure and more liberties were taken in language and subject matter. Even the most traditional playwrights of the time ventured into unusual subject matter, including Neil Simon and his play *God's Favorite* (pr. 1974), a modern retelling of the biblical Job legend.

As theater away moved from a New York monopoly, Chicago rose in prominence, as did many U.S. locales. The classical Broadway musical of the 1960's continued, but the more popular musicals were those that presented the musical innovations of Stephen Sondheim or that embraced rock and roll. Other innovations in dance and visual manipulation were introduced into the musical by Bob Fosse. All theater was taught to embrace the use of various mixed media as introduced by the performance artists and brought to full exploitation by the director Robert Wilson. Of equal importance was the emergence of theater that represented minorities, bringing forth many new playwrights.

Further Reading

Brockett, Oscar G., and Franklin J. Hildy. *History of the Theatre.* 9th ed. Boston: Allyn and Bacon, 2002. A standard text in general theater history with an excellent section on American theater since 1968.

Loney, Glenn. *Twentieth Century Theatre.* Vol. 2. New York: Facts On File, 1983. A year-by-year, day-by-day listing of events occurring in the British, American, and Canadian theater from 1948 to 1979.

Wilmeth, Don B., and Christopher Bigsby, ed. *The Cambridge History of American Theatre.* Cambridge, England: Cambridge University Press, 2002. A current, extensive, and dependable history of American theater.

August W. Staub

See also Black Arts movement; Broadway musicals; *Chorus Line, A*; Durang, Christopher; *Grease*; *Jesus Christ, Superstar*; Mamet, David; Oates, Joyce Carol; Shange, Ntosake; Simon, Neil; Sondheim, Stephen; Theater in Canada; *Torch Song Trilogy*; Wilson, Lanford.

■ Thompson, Hunter S.

Identification American journalist
Born July 18, 1937; Louisville, Kentucky
Died February 20, 2005; Woody Creek, Colorado

Thompson developed a new style of journalism known as "gonzo" that reflected the cynicism and introspection of the 1970's.

Hunter S. Thompson began the 1970's as a journalist with a growing reputation, having risen to national prominence with the publication of *Hell's Angels* (1966), an exposé of the Northern California motorcycle underground. Influenced by the participatory journalism of Tom Wolfe and George Plimpton and the acerbic observations of H. L. Mencken, Thompson employed a freewheeling, highly personal reporting style that won the acclaim both of critics and of the burgeoning counterculture with which he identified.

Thompson created the gonzo style accidentally in early 1970 while covering the Kentucky Derby for *Scanlan's* magazine. Unable to meet his deadline, Thompson submitted pages of raw notes at the behest of his editor, who published them verbatim. The resulting article received critical acclaim, to the surprise of its dejected author. Titled "The Kentucky Derby Is Decadent and Depraved," it was a scathing work of social satire told in a spare, muscular prose that echoed beat poetry and the rhythms of rock music.

Thompson subsequently built on the success of the article with *Fear and Loathing in Las Vegas* (1971), an account of his drug-fueled exploits with Chicano activist Oscar Zeta Acosta, and a series of *Rolling Stone* magazine articles on the 1972 presidential campaign published in book form as *Fear and Loathing: On the Campaign Trail '72* (1973). Filled with harsh indictments of the social and political establishments and with often embellished tales of excess, these works exposed Thompson to a broader audience and enhanced his image as an eccentric but visionary antihero. The gonzo persona that Thompson cultivated was popularized even more in the mid-1970's by the character Uncle Duke—based on Thompson—in the Garry Trudeau comic strip *Doonesbury* and later, by the film *Where the Buffalo Roam* (1980).

Marital difficulties and the pressures of his newfound celebrity plagued Thompson for the remainder of the decade. Although he continued to write for *Rolling Stone* and numerous other publications, the quantity (and, some have argued, the quality) of his published work declined. His conspicuous consumption of alcohol and various illicit substances combined with his chaotic appearances on the college lecture circuit seemed to validate critics who dismissed Thompson as an irrelevant drug casualty. However, Thompson continued to receive critical acclaim and lucrative assignments and remained popular for his acerbic observations on politics, sports, and culture. *The Great Shark Hunt*, a compilation of Thompson articles from the 1960's and 1970's, was published in 1979.

Impact The gonzo journalism that Thompson created articulated the personal angst, social tensions, and political cynicism of the 1970's. His work and persona inspired a number of imitators in the 1970's and beyond, yet few were able to approximate his style and insight. Thompson continued to write for print and Internet publications into the twenty-first century but committed suicide in early 2005.

Further Reading

Carroll, E. Jean. *Hunter: The Strange and Savage Life of Hunter S. Thompson*. New York: Dutton, 1993.

Thompson, Hunter S. *The Great Shark Hunt: Strange Tales from a Strange Time*. New York: Simon & Schuster, 1979.

Whitmer, Peter O. *When the Going Gets Weird: The Twisted Life and Times of Hunter S. Thompson*. New York: Dutton, 1993.

Michael H. Burchett

See also *Doonesbury*; Elections in the United States, 1972; Journalism in the United States; "Me Decade"; New Journalism; Wolfe, Tom.

■ Three Mile Island

The Event A failure at a nuclear power plant causes a core meltdown accident

Date March 28-30, 1979

Place Middletown, Pennsylvania

The accident at Three Mile Island increased public fear and distrust about the safety of nuclear power plants.

At about 4:00 A.M. on March 28, 1979, Unit 2 of the Three Mile Island nuclear power plant, located near Harrisburg, Pennsylvania, experienced a failure in a nonnuclear section of the plant. This failure caused the main water pumps, which provided the water that cooled the steam turbine generators, to stop. The automatic control system immediately shut down the turbine generator and then the reactor itself. However, the lack of coolant caused the pressure in the nuclear portion of the plant to increase. In order to prevent that pressure from becoming excessive, the operator opened a pressure relief valve, which should have closed automatically when the pressure dropped. However, it failed to close, and cooling water poured out of the core into a section called the pressurizer. The lack of water caused the core of the reactor to heat up.

The instrument panel displayed confusing and contradictory information. No instrument showed the level of coolant in the core; instead, the water level in the pressurizer was displayed. Moreover, there was no indication that the valve was still open. Since the water level in the pressurizer was high, the operator assumed that there was sufficient water in the core, but as a result of this incorrect assumption, the operator reduced the flow of coolant through the core. This caused the nuclear fuel to overheat and melt.

Core meltdown is considered to be the most dangerous type of nuclear power accident. Although it was determined later that about one-half of the core melted, the Three Mile Island accident did not produce the most serious consequences feared by many experts. The hot nuclear fuel did not breach the containment building, which would have released a large amount of radioactive fission products into the environment.

The plant operator notified the Nuclear Regulatory Commission's regional office in Pennsylvania at 7:45 A.M. about the situation. The regional office sent a team of inspectors to the site. At 11:00 A.M., all

Demonstrators protest nuclear power in the wake of the Three Mile Island accident in 1979. (National Archives)

nonessential personnel were ordered off the plant site. Helicopters began sampling the atmosphere above the plant. Small amounts of radioactive gas were detected outside the boundaries of the plant by noon on March 28. However, by that evening the reactor appeared to be stable and cooling.

A new concern arose on the morning of March 30. Pressure started building in the primary cooling system. This pressure threatened to interrupt the flow of cooling water to the core. To relieve the pressure, the operator allowed a significant release of radiation from the auxiliary building of the plant. This release confused the government officials, who were not expecting it. Because of the uncertainty about the condition of the plant, Richard Thornburgh, the governor of Pennsylvania, recommended that pregnant women and preschool-age children—the people most vulnerable to radiation—evacuate from a zone within a 5-mile radius of the plant.

Detailed studies of the consequences of the accident were conducted by the Nuclear Regulatory Commission, the Environmental Protection Agency (EPA), the Department of Energy, and the state of Pennsylvania. They all concluded that the two million people who lived or worked near the plant were exposed to very little radiation from the accident. The average annual radiation exposure in that part of Pennsylvania from natural sources of radiation is 100 to 125 millirems. Persons in the counties near Three Mile Island were exposed to an average radiation dose of about 1 millirem as a result of the accident, with a person located right at the boundary of the plant receiving a dose of less than 100 millirems. Thus, all government agencies concluded that people in the community were not injured by the accident.

Impact The Nuclear Regulatory Commission concluded that "the accident was caused by a combination of personnel error, design deficiencies, and component failures." In an odd coincidence, a film called *The China Syndrome* (1979), featuring Jane Fonda as a television news reporter who uncovers a serious accident at a nuclear power plant, was released less than two weeks before the accident at Three Mile Island. The combination of the accident and the film resulted in a significant increase in the fear and distrust expressed by the public over the safety of nuclear power plants.

As a result of the accident, the Nuclear Regulatory Commission was asked to play a more direct role in the oversight of the management, training, and operation of nuclear power plants. The Nuclear Regulatory Commission increased its oversight and regulation of the nuclear industry, and it required a redesign of the monitoring equipment in all nuclear plants so the plant operators would have a clear indication of what is occurring at all times inside a reactor. However, the public's continuing fear of nuclear power plants has been a significant contributing factor to the fact that since the Three Mile Island accident, no new nuclear power plants have been built in the United States.

Subsequent Events Within weeks of the accident, a class-action suit was filed against the Metropolitan Edison Company, a subsidiary of General Public Utilities, on behalf of businesses and residents located within 25 miles of the Three Mile Island plant. More than two thousand personal injury claims were filed by people who claimed their health had suffered because they were exposed to radiation released during the accident. Over the next fifteen years, the case was heard by a variety of Pennsylvania courts. It was not until June, 1996, that judge Sylvia Rambo of the Pennsylvania District Court dismissed the lawsuits, ruling that the plaintiffs were not able to prove that they were exposed to doses of radiation that could cause health problems. This court ruling backed the claims of the Nuclear Regulatory Commission and the operator of the Three Mile Island plant that the amount of radioactive material released during the accident was insufficient to cause any harm to the public.

Further Reading

Hampton, Wilborn. *Meltdown: A Race Against Nuclear Disaster at Three Mile Island: A Reporter's Story.* Boston: Candlewick Press, 2001.

Osif, Bonnie A., Anthony J. Baratta, and Thomas W. Conkling. *TMI, Twenty-five Years Later: The Three Mile Island Nuclear Power Plant Accident and Its Impact.* University Park: Pennsylvania State University Press, 2004.

Walker, J. Samuel. *Three Mile Island: A Nuclear Crisis in Historical Perspective.* Berkeley: University of California Press, 2004.

George J. Flynn

See also Antinuclear movement; Disaster films; Fonda, Jane; Greenpeace; Science and technology; Silkwood, Karen.

■ Three's Company

Identification Television situation comedy
Date Aired from 1977 to 1984

One of television's highest-rated shows in the late 1970's, Three's Company *featured slapstick humor in stories about a man and two women living together as friends. The comedy reflected a new trend of cohabitation among young Americans and a growing acceptance of sexual themes in popular entertainment.*

The runaway success of *Three's Company*—a top-twenty hit from the airing of its second episode in 1977—showed that Americans were accepting the idea of young men and women living together platonically. The program seemed innocent in spite of its sexual innuendos because its characters were likeable (and never actually had sex), and its situations were punctuated by physical comedy.

Based on the British hit comedy *A Man About the House, Three's Company* featured John Ritter as Jack Tripper, a chef who pretended to be gay so that his landlord, Mr. Roper (Norman Fell), would let him share an apartment with "dumb blonde" Chrissy Snow (Suzanne Somers) and "smart brunette" Janet Wood (Joyce DeWitt). The plots often revolved around Jack's attempts to date women while the roommates struggled to hide his heterosexuality from Mr. Roper. Many episodes also featured Mrs. Roper (Audra Lindley) trying to get her unwilling husband into bed. While the program's comedy grew from sexually titillating situations and double entendres, the relationships between Jack, Chrissy, and Janet were like those of a caring, close-knit family that took care of one another.

Three's Company helped make American Broadcasting Company (ABC) the highest-rated television network on Tuesday nights from 1977 through 1980. Beginning in February, 1978, it was frequently the highest-rated show in its time slot, and it was the most-watched show on television in 1979. That year, ABC created a new show featuring the Ropers, and comedic actor Don Knotts joined the cast of *Three's Company* as the roommates' new landlord, Ralph Furley.

Critics panned *Three's Company* because of its sexually charged humor and particularly for its portrayal of Chrissy Snow as a stereotypical, scantily clad blonde. In spite of those who criticized her performance as mindless "jiggle," Somers's portrayal of Chrissy made her a major star. Newspaper and magazine stories about the show often focused on Somers, and she posed for countless magazine covers and pinup posters. Although Somers overshadowed her costars, Ritter became known as an accomplished comedian as the show's writers took advantage of his talent for slapstick and worked physical comedy into the plotlines.

Impact By showing three young people sharing an apartment in sexually tense situations but not hav-

Loni Anderson (left) guest stars on a 1978 episode of the sitcom Three's Company *with John Ritter, Suzanne Somers, and Joyce DeWitt.* (Hulton Archive/Getty Images)

ing sex, *Three's Company* provided role models for young people as they experimented with platonic cohabitation. The show's popularity and high ratings indicated that many Americans saw this new social phenomenon as a viable lifestyle, accepting it as a way of creating surrogate families and nontraditional but caring relationships based on friendship.

Further Reading

Mann, Chris. *Come and Knock on Our Door: A Hers and Hers and His Guide to "Three's Company."* New York: St. Martin's Press, 1998.

Marc, David. *Comic Visions: Television Comedy and American Culture.* 2d ed. Malden, Mass.: Blackwell, 1997.

Somers, Suzanne. *After the Fall: How I Picked Myself Up, Dusted Myself Off, and Started All Over Again.* New York: Crown, 1998.

Maureen Puffer-Rothenberg

See also Cohabitation; Sexual revolution; Sitcoms; Television in the United States.

■ Timber industry in Canada

Definition Employment, revenue, and forest products associated with the commercial harvest of mostly softwood species

In the 1970's, lumbering was the primary commercial activity in Canadian forests and an important sector in the Canadian economy. Canada led the world in wood exports—a rank that it has held for decades—and the United States was the largest single buyer.

Canada's commercial forestlands are located chiefly in the Provinces of British Columbia, Quebec, Ontario, New Brunswick, and Nova Scotia. More than 90 percent of this commercial forest consists of softwood species. About half of the total acreage is limited for commercial use by climate and terrain. The boreal softwoods form a thick band across central Canada, the largest forest region. Other forest regions are the Great Lakes and Acadian in the east and the Columbian, Coast, and Montane in the west. British Columbia has the highest-quality building timber and the highest annual harvest rate in Canada.

The greatest concentration of paper and pulp mills lies in southern Quebec. Newsprint for the U.S. market is the main product. Major paper and pulp industries also exist in places such as Newcastle, New Brunswick, and Liverpool, Nova Scotia. Grand Falls and Corner Brook, Newfoundland, are also heavily dependent on the pulpwood industries.

In the 1970's, as today, lumbering was mostly large scale and concentrated on the west-facing slopes of the coastal mountains. Many settlements were single-industry towns producing paper and pulp for the large California market. The best forest stands on the Canadian Shield were in the drainage basins of rivers that flow through Ontario and Quebec, and traditionally logs were sent on outflowing rivers to processing facilities on the coast. By the 1970's, logging trucks had begun to supplant rivers as the major mode of transportation. The boreal forests were generally harvested by clear-cutting, while cutting of the mixed forest on the southern Shield was done selectively.

Aboriginal issues, acid rain, insect pests, market fluctuations, and the environmental impacts of logging were some of the key challenges facing the Canadian timber industry through this decade.

Impact Canada has had a major logging industry for more than a century, but the rate of logging increased markedly in the 1970's, mostly as a result of increased demand from the United States. Large private companies harvested trees mostly on public lands, and the United States, Europe, and Japan were the chief buyers. The timber industry suffered a slump in the mid-1970's but recovered and reached an all-time high in 1988.

Further Reading

Gillis, R. Peter, and Thomas R. Roach. *Lost Initiatives: Canada's Forest Industries, Forest Policy, and Forest Conservation.* New York: Greenwood Press, 1986.

Robinson, J. Lewis. *Concepts and Themes in the Regional Geography of Canada.* Vancouver: Talonbooks, 1983.

Ann M. Legreid

See also Acid rain; Business and the economy of Canada; Canada and the United States; Environmental movement; International trade of Canada; Unions in Canada.

■ Title IX of the Education Amendments of 1972

Identification U.S. federal legislation
Date Enacted on June 23, 1972

Title IX served as the first legislation to protect gender equality in education and to prohibit use of federal funds that support discriminatory practices.

In 1970, women's rights became one more focus of the continuing Civil Rights movement of the previous two decades. As more women sought to pursue professional careers, greater attention was focused on the societal limitations that resulted in decreased opportunities and inequitable compensation. The culture of higher education became a target for advocacy groups that noted, among other things, sexual biases against women in colleges and universities. Even before Congress began its discussion of gender discrimination, many expert and politicians understood that women's economic disadvantages were often rooted in educational inequities.

Congressional Action Congressional hearings began in 1970, directed by the House Subcommittee on Education and chaired by Oregon representative Edith Green. Though these initial efforts were unable to influence the 1971 Education Amendments to eliminate gender-based discrimination, a year later, Senator Birch Bayh of Indiana introduced an amendment seeking to end "unjustified discrimination against women in the American educational system."

Subsequent House and Senate proposals followed, indicating a growing acceptance for action yet offering little consensus on how the goal of gender equity should be reached. The principal area of contention centered on whether or not a quota system would result, particularly regarding access to educational opportunity. Senator Bayh continued her efforts to support passage of public policy, firmly discouraging any notion of quotas and advancing merit as the sole criterion for access to educational opportunity. The final version of the legislation emerged only after assurances against quotas were written into the act.

Eventually, joint House and Senate proposals seeking to end sex discrimination resulted in Title IX legislation, which was enacted during the summer of 1972 by President Richard M. Nixon. In summary, it stated: "No person in the United States shall, on the basis of sex, be excluded from participation in, be denied the benefits of, or be subjected to discrimination under any educational program or activity receiving federal financial assistance."

Title IX was modeled on Title VI of the Civil Rights Act of 1964, in that federal funds could not support discriminatory practices. However, Title IX was limited in scope to education and necessitated institutions to establish grievance procedures to address concerns or complaints. The essence of the legislation was to ensure equitable opportunity and equivalent funding in all educational programs receiving federal financial funding, including athletics, physical education, and intramurals. Often, separate facilities, equipment, and limited resources had resulted in few school sport opportunities for women. Salaries for coaches of female teams were comparably small. When opportunities did exist for girls and women, practice and game scheduling was secondary to male teams.

Interpretations and Challenges The first significant amendment to Title IX occurred in 1974, sponsored by Senator Jacob Javits of New York. It became necessary to clarify whether Congress intended to regulate athletics, which had become one of the early points of contention among those in educational administration. Through the Javits Amendment, Congress authorized the Department of Health, Education, and Welfare (HEW) to issue regulations for implementation.

The spring and summer of 1975 brought unsuccessful attempts through proposed resolutions to either dismantle Title IX altogether or exclude revenue-producing sports (for example, football) from the criteria to determine institutional compliance. Nevertheless, on July 21, 1975, the HEW regulations prohibiting gender discrimination in intercollegiate athletics appeared, along with a three-year timetable for full institutional compliance.

A "presumed compliance" was acknowledged if there were basically equal per-capita resources dedicated to men and women athletes and a commitment to increased opportunity for females in the future. During that three-year period, however, HEW received almost one hundred complaints from more than fifty higher education institutions, necessitating further clarification and guidance for educational administrators. This ultimately led to a move to document "actual compliance." On December, 11, 1979, HEW's Office of Civil Rights issued a final policy interpretation on Title IX and intercollegiate athletics. Clarifying "equal opportunity" in the 1972 language, this interpretation introduced what became known as the "three-prong test," which asked three questions. Is the provision of opportunity for females substantially proportional to the institution's female enrollment? Is there a documented history and continued practice of providing increased athletic opportunity for women? Finally, does the institution meet full and effective accommodation of women's sport interest and ability? Only one of these had to be met to be in compliance, with the intention of moving toward the other goals.

Impact Between 1972 and 1995, female interscholastic athletic participation rose from one in twenty-seven enrolled to one in three. Moreover, during the 1970's, enrollment in college by women began to outpace men so that by the year 2000, women's athletic participation had increased at twice the rate of their undergraduate enrollment.

Subsequent Events The Association for Intercollegiate Athletics for Women, the leading sports governing body, gave way in the early 1980's to the National Collegiate Athletic Association (NCAA) and the National Association of Intercollegiate Athletics (NAIA) as they developed women's championship events. Despite a temporary setback with *Grove City v. Bell* (1984), the 1988 Civil Rights Restoration Act assured compliance by all institutions receiving federal funds, directly or indirectly. The 1992 Gender Equity study by the NCAA was followed by the 1994 Equity in Athletics Disclosure Act. Policy clarifications continued into the late 1990's, but the record of accomplishment was significant.

Further Reading

Carpenter, Linda, and R. Vivian Acosta. *Title IX*. Champaign, Ill: Human Kinetics, 2004. Written by two leading legal and sport professionals, the book summarizes the legislation, its societal impact, and its twenty-first century application.

Harter, Carol C. "Defending Title IX." *The Presidency*, Spring, 2003, 25-28. Reviews the key triumphs and remaining challenges confronting Title IX legislation in 2003.

Tungate, David E., and Daniel P. Orie. "Title IX Lawsuits." *Phi Delta Kappan*, April, 1998, 603-604. Outlines four key legal decisions involving university compliance with Title IX, including the landmark case of *Amy Cohen, et al. v. Brown University*, which the authors litigated.

P. Graham Hatcher

See also Congress, U.S.; Education in the United States; Feminism; Little League participation by girls; National Organization for Women (NOW); Sports; Women's rights.

■ *Torch Song Trilogy*

Identification A collection of three one-act plays
Author Harvey Fierstein (1954-)
Date Published in 1979; first performed in 1981

Torch Song Trilogy *was one of the most important gay plays of the decade. Its nonstop depictions and revelations of homosexual life were unsurpassed in American drama at the time of its initial performances.*

In 1978, a short one-act play titled *The International Stud* opened Off-Broadway, followed the next year by *Fugue in a Nursery* and *Widows and Children First*. All three plays—later published and performed together as *Torch Song Triology*—had at their center the trials and tribulations of a New York City drag queen named Arnold. Unabashedly the semiautobiographical and fantasized life of its author Harvey Fierstein, the play commanded popularity of a mainstream office from the beginning. Of most importance was the playwright's success in depicting homosexuals (herein, even a drag queen) in their kindred humanity to the straight American public. However, the play is not nearly so much about gay life as it is about family relations, love, and social placement.

The play also intermingles topics such as bisexuality, partner-swapping, casual sex, anonymous sex, gay adoption, female impersonation, and Jewish identity (particularly as the product of Jewish motherhood) in such a way as to suggest that there might be normative behaviors in all of these, albeit not readily apparent to outsiders. For 1970's audiences, this relentless attack on those who did not recognize homosexuals with dignity and respect was not only shocking and riveting but also depicted in order to provoke sympathy and acceptance on the part of those who saw the play. Perhaps the central event is the beating death of Alan, one of Arnold's lovers, by a mob of gay-bashers wielding baseball bats. Senseless, stupid bigotry, however, does not ultimately triumph in the play since the survivors do make peace with one another.

Impact Even more successful than another gay drama of the era, Mart Crowley's *The Boys in the Band* (1970), *Torch Song Trilogy* was among the earliest of literary works in the United States to attract and hold large numbers of mainstream viewers while always keeping gay life at its focus. Those seeing the play could, perhaps for the first time, entertain the idea that homosexuals were overwhelmingly like heterosexuals in their longings and attempts for happiness, fulfillment, and self-worth in life.

Subsequent Events These three one-act plays were not presented collectively and under their umbrella title until 1981; they debuted on Broadway in June, 1982. In 1983, Harvey Fierstein, who played Arnold, received Tony Awards both for best play and for best actor. A successful film version, starring Fierstein along with Anne Bancroft and Matthew Broderick, was released in 1988.

Further Reading

Galens, David. *Drama for Students: Presenting, Analysis, Context, and Criticism on Commonly Studied Dramas.* Vol. 6. Detroit: Gale Group, 1999.

Whited, Lana A. *"Torch Song Trilogy."* In *Masterplots*, edited by Frank N. Magill. Rev. 2d ed. Pasadena, Calif.: Salem Press, 2003.

Carl Singleton

See also Homosexuality and gay rights; National Lesbian and Gay Rights March of 1979; Sexual revolution; Theater in the United States.

■ Toxic shock syndrome

Definition Rare but potentially fatal disease caused by a bacterial toxin, usually streptococci and staphylococci

An epidemic of toxic shock syndrome was linked to a particular brand of tampon used by menstruating women.

While toxic shock syndrome was not strictly speaking a "new" disease, it was one about which the general public was unaware until the 1970's. The disease had been recognized since 1927 and generally had been reported as staphylococcal scarlet fever. Periodic reports in the literature from the 1940's and 1950's also described a disease that exhibited the same symptoms of severe shock, fever, and organ failure.

Between 1975 and 1977, a sudden outbreak occurred among a number of young men and women, with at least one death. Similar outbreaks were observed in populations of women between the ages of twenty and fifty, with mortality rates ranging from 5 to 15 percent. In 1978, James Todd and his coworkers linked the disease to toxin-producing strains of the bacterium *Staphylococcus aureus*. The following year, University of California at Los Angeles (UCLA) scientist Patrick Schlievert isolated the toxin itself and demonstrated that symptoms of the disease can be induced in animals using the material even in the absence of the microorganisms. The same toxin subsequently was shown to be produced by some strains of a second organism, *Streptococcus pyogenes*. The toxin would eventually acquire the name toxic shock syndrome toxin.

The disease historically was reported in both men and women, but a significant proportion of the newer victims diagnosed after the 1978 report involved menstruating women. This latest outbreak was eventually linked by the Centers for Disease Control (CDC) to the use of a particular type of tampon, the Rely brand manufactured by Proctor and Gamble. While some women who contracted the illness had used other brands, the majority from the CDC study—more than 70 percent—used this particular brand. The studies themselves proved controversial, since it never was established fully whether this brand proved a greater risk factor or whether tampon use in general placed women at greater risk.

Ironically, the marketing strategy for the new tampon was based upon its significant absorbency. Composed of beads manufactured from a form of polyacrylate, the tampon would actually dry and adhere to the vaginal wall. When removed, tearing or traumatization of tissue would sometimes result, providing an entry point for the organism.

Impact Between 1975 and 1980, more than four hundred cases of toxic shock syndrome were reported to the CDC, with a mortality rate of about 10 percent; the actual number of cases was probably much higher. Following the removal from the market of tampons comprised of polyacrylate, the incidence of toxic shock syndrome began to drop. Changes in uses of tampons were also implemented, principally a recommendation that women reduce or avoid their use entirely.

Subsequent Events As a result of the continued impact on sales, in 1986, Proctor and Gamble stopped the manufacture of the Rely brand of tampon. Consumers continued to be warned of the possibility of contracting toxic shock syndrome from tampon use. Though the epidemiology of the disease changed in the next decade, affecting both men and women, the disease never disappeared.

Further Reading

Garrett, Laurie. *The Coming Plague.* New York: Penguin Books, 1994.

Parker, James. *The Official Patient's Sourcebook on Toxic Shock Syndrome.* San Diego, Calif.: Icon Health, 2002.

Richard Adler

See also Cancer research; Genetics research; Legionnaires' disease; Medicine; Smallpox eradication.

■ Toys and games

Definition Action figures, playsets, dolls, videos, and role-playing games

Toys and games of the early 1970's reflected social attitudes of the later Vietnam War era as well as new developments in video and computer technology.

During the late 1960's and early 1970's, the established trends in post-World War II era toys underwent a gradual but significant shift in themes and character. The antimilitary sentiment that prevailed during the final years of the Vietnam War had a significant impact on the development and marketing of children's toys, especially those targeted at preteenage boys. Several already established toy lines, notably Mattel's Barbie doll and Hasbro's popular G.I. Joe action figures, were significantly redefined during this period.

Older and more conservative toy manufacturers were less successful; among them, the Marx Toy Company, whose output had consisted mainly of Western-themed and military toys sold through the Sears company stores. Marx classic playsets such as "Fort Apache" and "Battleground," which consisted of small plastic figures, vehicles, and lithographed tin buildings, had dominated the toy market throughout the 1950's and 1960's but slowly faded into oblivion following Louis Marx's retirement and subsequent sale of the company to Quaker Oats in 1972.

Dolls and Action Figures Mattel's eleven-inch Barbie doll, developed between 1956 and 1959 by Ruth Handler (wife of Mattel's cofounder Elliot Handler), continued to enjoy immense popularity among pre-teenage girls throughout the 1970's. It has been argued that the doll's phenomenal success stems from the fact that Barbie has a dual nature—a plaything and a miniature mannequin designed to display "grown-up" fashions. Clothing and accessories for Barbie paralleled fashion trends of the 1970's, with perhaps the most notable development being the introduction of the tanned Malibu Barbie. Whereas the clothing and accessory sets the 1960's Barbie had represented her as a nascent career girl (the airline stewardess and nurse sets were especially popular), the Barbie of the 1970's became a perpetual teenager and "fun-loving, light, and breezy." Consequently, the Barbie doll designs and accessories of the 1970's did not yet address the issues raised later by feminists concerning the sexism implicit in the doll's appearance or play scripts. Her unnaturally exaggerated anatomy, as well as her manufacturer's penchant for playing to unflattering gender stereotypes, did not surface as serious criticisms until the emergence of the women's movement.

In contrast, Hasbro's G.I. Joe, the toy credited with introducing the concept of an articulated "action figure" and essentially a 12-inch doll for boys, offers a clear example of shifting social attitudes during the 1970's. Following its introduction in 1964, G.I. Joe had remained a military character toy with uniforms, vehicles, weapons, and equipment representative of those in use during the Korean War. Later, as the marketing success of the toy became more realized, Hasbro elaborated upon the basic G.I. Joe figure by producing a multinational series of World War II soldiers (all without the trademark cheek scar) as well as an African American figure. A wide variety of military period sets followed. Then, beginning in 1970, as sales of military toys began to falter because of the unpopularity of the Vietnam War, Hasbro shifted the focus of their G.I. Joe line from "fighting men" to that of an "adventure team." The new nonmilitary focus is evident in figure sets such as "Hunt for the Pygmy Gorilla" (G.I. Joe as a hunter) and "Eight Ropes of Danger" (G.I. Joe as deep sea diver). In fact, some of these later sets were simply repackaged versions of earlier military releases. The blurring of focus occasioned by this shift away from his original military identity, as well as escalating production costs, eventually resulted in the expiration of the G.I. Joe line in 1978.

Similarly, in a final effort to boost its flagging sales, the Marx Toy Company created a series of eleven-inch articulated Western figures, hoping to capitalize upon the enduring popularity of television series such as *Bonanza* and *Gunsmoke*. While the resulting "Best of the West" figure line, aimed at both boys and girls, did its best to emulate Mattel and Hasbro's products, by the mid-1970's even the once popular Western theme had been played out.

Toy guns, which had been among the most popular of all postwar-era toys, declined notably in popularity throughout the 1970's. Historically, toy guns fall into three main categories: the ubiquitous cowboy pistol, which for several decades was the best-seller, and military and police weapons of various types. Interest in nearly all of these evaporated as a result of the Vietnam War abroad and escalating rates of violent urban crime at home.

Film and Television Tie-ins Probably the most powerful influence in the toy industry during the late 1970's was the release of George Lucas's film *Star Wars* (1977). As toy manufacturers scrambled to develop film merchandizing tie-ins in order to exploit its popularity, it soon became apparent that any licensed product associated with the *Star Wars* concept became an immediate best-seller. Sales of the Kenner Toy company's *Star Wars* product line alone were sufficient to make it the fifth largest toy company in the world.

The success of *Star Wars* also generated a positive halo effect for other space fantasy toys. Even the original *Star Trek* television series, which had been canceled in 1966 and had not yet gone into syndicated reruns, had its principal characters brought back to marketing life as eight-inch action figures by the Mego Toy Company. Mego had declined the license to produce the Star Wars toys, a decision that contributed directly to the company's eventual demise only a few years later.

Among the most important television tie-ins from this period were a line of puppets developed by Topper in 1971 based upon the principal characters from *Sesame Street*, the award-winning public television program directed at preschool children.

Role-Playing Games The idea of role-playing games—in which each player assumes the persona of an imaginary (sometimes nonhuman) character as defined by certain traits, abilities, and character flaws—became one of the iconic developments in gaming during the 1970's. The first of these games, Dungeons and Dragons (D&D), a fantasy-adventure epic set in a medieval sword-and-sorcery world, premiered in 1974. The game's coinventors, Gary Gygax and Dave Arneson, derived their basic general model from tabletop games of military strategy. The new role-playing games, however, placed relatively greater emphasis upon individual character development over time, as well as players' interactions; thus, while solitary versions of these games existed, most games were manifestly intended as being social in nature at every level. Role-playing games emphasized the imaginative adventure of the quest, rather than winning in the traditional sense. Furthermore, although benefits accrued from surviving skirmishes and completing a quest, the experience of the game could be quite satisfying, even for a character who was "killed" along the way.

The particulars of the role-playing game's story line, along with its plot complications, settings, and props, were set forth in detailed games scenarios, often many pages in length, which also contained rules governing players' movements and behaviors, such as hand-to-hand combat or the gathering and use of mundane or magical objects. Character's behaviors are mediated by rolls of dice, the results of which are indexed in interpretive statistical tables; for example, Player 1 attacks Player 2 with a sword and rolls a "3," miss, blade glances off helmet. Each boxed basic game included several basic adventure scenarios. In complex adventures, sometimes spanning several gaming sessions, the game's flow of events was managed by a designated "Dungeon Master," who directed nonplayer characters, initiated encounters, and acted as a referee.

In the first few years following its introduction, the popularity of D&D increased at nearly an exponential rate—at one time during the late 1970's, every U.S. nuclear submarine on active duty was running a D&D game. This amazing success surprised no one more than the game's inventors, who had anticipated a much more modest response. D&D was so effective at defining the new role-playing games genre that it became the basic template for scores of new games by other designers who explored nearly every conceivable historical period and fantasy world. Ironically, D&D's explosive success also hastened its demise. Over time, the competition from other games, in all the richness of their many variations, sliced away at D&D's target audience and, eventually, undercut the mass market profitability of role-playing games as a commercial enterprise.

Games and Technology Computer games predate the development of video games. As late as 1966, a large mainframe computer of the type usually found only on major university campuses was required to play a relatively simple joystick-controlled, plain-view computer game, such as *Space Wars*, which pitted two tiny "wire-model" spacecraft against each other in electronic space combat. Electronic engineer-inventor Ralph Baer is credited with the development of the first video game, created from hard-wired circuitry during the period from 1966 to 1969. Baer's creation, *Pong*, a minimalist electronic version of table tennis, enabled players to maneuver an electronic sliding "paddle" to strike a tiny electronic ball that rebounded back and forth across the television screen.

The first commercial video game, developed by the Magnavox Corporation, was *Odyssey*, which premiered in May, 1972. Like Baer's *Pong*, the *Odyssey* video game system had no microprocessors and no memory. In order to create the backgrounds for its various games, it was necessary for the players to attach colored acetate transparencies directly to the glass surface of the television screen, since the system was incapable of generating complex videographic imagery. By inserting one of the six game cartridges (and attaching the associated transparency), one of twelve different games could be played, including basketball, hockey, roulette, pass-kick football, a submarine invasion maze, and a shooting gallery.

Impact During the early 1970's, it was widely believed that continued economic affluence, combined with a parallel reduction in the number of hours in the workweek, would result in an increase in the amount of discretionary leisure time available to the average person. Consequently, hobby markets expanded to meet this need. In actuality, however, exactly the opposite occurred. Hardest hit were time-intensive hobbies, such as plastic model kit making, which had enjoyed popularity among teenage boys since the 1940's. Simultaneously, object-oriented playthings began to be replaced, first by games that allowed players to vicariously experience character roles, and later, by computer-video simulations that offered participants an increased sense of immediacy and excitement.

Further Reading

Dunnigan, James F. *The Complete Wargames Handbook.* New York: William Morrow, 1992. A comprehensive examination of military war games, with additional material on fantasy role-playing and computer games. Many useful appendices detailing related publications, an annotated game bibliography, and game publishers.

Heaton, Tom. *The Encyclopedia of Marx Action Figures.* Iola, Wis.: Krause, 1999. A comprehensive catalog of all major examples of the Marx Toy Company's articulated figure product line. Well illustrated in color.

Huxford, Sharon, and Bob Huxford. *Schroeder's Collectible Toys, Antique to Modern Price Guide.* Paducah, Ky.: Collector Books/Schroeder, 2004. Well-researched guidebook listing a wide variety of collectible toys. Contains background information on principal toy manufacturers and appendices listing dealers, Web sites, and collectors' newsletters, among other features.

Kent, Steven L. *The Ultimate History of Video Games.* Roseville, Calif.: Prima, 2001. An encyclopedic, sociohistorical study of the development of interactive gaming from its earliest forerunner, the pinball game, through the contemporary era.

Kline, Stephen. *Out of the Garden: Toys, TV, and Children's Culture in the Age of Marketing.* London: Verso, 1993. Examines in detail the concept of "character advertising," in which television programs become virtual commercials for the toys they represent and the broader sociocultural impact.

McDonough, Yona Zeldis. *The Barbie Chronicles.* New York: Touchstone/Simon & Schuster, 1999. A collection of essays and other writings that examine the sociological impact of Barbie from a variety of intellectual perspectives.

Larry Smolucha

See also Atari; Computers; Dungeons and Dragons; Fads; Hobbies and recreation; *Star Trek*; *Star Wars*; Video games.

■ Trail of Broken Treaties

The Event Native Americans make a protest caravan across the United States

Date Summer and fall, 1972

The focus of American Indian activism and nationalism was defined during a journey across the United States in 1972 to protest the fact that numerous historical treaties between the United States and Native Americans had been broken by the U.S. government. The protest caravan was followed, during the last week of the 1972 national presidential election, by an occupation of the Bureau of Indian Affairs (BIA) headquarters in Washington, D.C.

During the summer of 1972, Hank Adams, a leader of indigenous fishing rights struggles in Washington State, and Dennis Banks, a founder of the American Indian Movement (AIM), met in Denver to plan a Trail of Broken Treaties caravan. Banks, a Chippewa who was born on the Leech Lake Reservation in northern Minnesota in 1932, and Russell Means became familiar faces to television news viewers as the two most easily recognizable leaders of AIM. Participants in the Trail of Broken Treaties sought to marshal thousands of protesters across the United States to dramatize issues related to American Indian self-determination.

Caravans assembled in Seattle, a center of fishing-rights activism, and in San Francisco, the site of the American Indian occupation of Alcatraz Island between 1969 and 1971. The two groups merged in Minneapolis, the birthplace of AIM. Here, the group issued its Twenty Points, a document that sought to revive Native American sovereignty. Among other things, the Twenty Points advocated the repeal of the 1871 federal statute that ended treaty making, the restoration of treaty-making status to native nations, the establishment of a commission to review past treaty violations, the resubmission of unratified treaties to the Senate, and the elimination of all state jurisdiction over American Indian affairs.

The Trail of Broken Treaties caravan moved on to Washington, D.C. Upon its arrival on November 3, 1972, the protesters learned that there was not enough lodging. In his memoir *Ojibwe Warrior* (2004), Banks wrote that the marchers had not planned to take over the Bureau of Indian Affairs headquarters building at the conclusion of the Trail of Broken Treaties. However, the decision was made after the participants learned that the only lodg-

Native American activists occupy the Bureau of Indian Affairs buildings in Washington, D.C., on November 8, 1972, during the Trail of Broken Treaties march. (Library of Congress)

ing available to them in Washington, D.C., was a rat-infested church basement.

The protesters decided to stay in the BIA building for several hours until security guards sought to remove them forcibly. At that point, events turned violent. The protesters seized the building for six days as they asserted their demands that native sovereignty be restored and immunity be granted to all protesters. Files were seized and damage was done to the BIA building—AIM leaders asserted that federal agents had infiltrated the movement and had done most of the damage. On November 8, 1972, federal officials offered immunity and transportation home to the protesters. The offer was accepted and the crisis was resolved for the moment. A few months later, however, many of the same themes were sounded as AIM occupied the hamlet of Wounded Knee, South Dakota.

Impact The Trail of Broken Treaties, the occupation of Wounded Knee the following year, and another nationwide march, the Trail of Self-Determination in 1976, all served to raise awareness of Native American treaty rights throughout the United States. These events occurred during a decade when Native Americans were asserting their treaty rights, often in federal courts. For example, during this period Native Americans in Washington State obtained rights to half the salmon returning to Washington State coastal waters in *United States v. Washington* (1974), commonly called the Boldt decision. Native Americans in Maine argued for enforcement of the federal nonintercourse acts, which forbade land sales without approval of the federal government during the seventeenth and eighteenth centuries, resulting in settlements that restored land and provided cash for economic ventures.

Further Reading

Banks, Dennis, and Richard Erdoes. *Ojibwa Warrior: Dennis Banks and the Rise of the American Indian Movement.* Norman: University of Oklahoma Press, 2004.

Deloria, Vine, Jr. *Behind the Trail of Broken Treaties.* New York: Delacorte, 1974.

Bruce E. Johansen

See also American Indian Movement (AIM); Native Americans; Peltier, Leonard; Wounded Knee occupation.

■ Transportation

Definition The means of traveling from one place to another and its issues and effects

The 1970's was a period of significant change in transportation. A world energy crisis, the oil embargo, and a new national speed limit were just a few of the events that had an impact on transportation during this period.

The energy crisis in the early 1970's caused significant changes and innovations in American transportation. Mass urban transportation became somewhat more popular out of necessity because of the energy crisis, while the demand for smaller, more fuel-efficient import automobiles grew when fuel prices rose during the gasoline rationing periods.

A transportation fad also occurred during this period with the moped, whose popularity grew as a direct result of the gasoline shortages of the 1970's. As an alternative to the gas-guzzling vehicles of the day, they were mainly used by urban commuters and students for short, in-town trips. At the height of the moped craze, more than 125 different models were available in the United States. Like the moped, the Volkswagen Beetle also joined the "fad" category. The unique little German car with an air-cooled engine in the rear had been in production since the late 1940's. While the bulk of its appeal emerged from its unique styling, its fuel economy also played a role in its widespread popularity.

Domestic and Import Automobiles At the beginning of the decade, domestic automobile manufacturers were still producing the roomy and powerful "muscle cars" that had been popular during the 1960's. However, in 1973, the United States experienced a gas shortage caused when the members of the Organization of Petroleum Exporting Countries (OPEC) refused to ship oil to any nation that supported Israel in the conflict with Egypt; the United States supported Israel. The nationwide gasoline shortages were so severe that an odd-even system of rationing had to be instituted. Those with license plates ending with an even number could purchase gasoline on even-numbered days and those with odd-ending numbers on odd days. The shortages also caused the price of gasoline to increase substantially. Consumers complained so much that the United States government introduced legislation to try to force domestic automobile manufacturers to design and produce more fuel-efficient vehicles. Automobile manufacturers fought the legislation, and shortly, the gasoline supply and prices returned to normal and efficiency was much less an issue.

However, the ongoing worldwide energy crisis caused some consumers to look to smaller, more fuel-efficient import automobiles. The domestic automobile manufacturers did make some attempts to compete with the imports; for example, Ford tried in 1971 to gain a substantial share of the subcompact market with the Ford Pinto. Volkswagen and some Japanese imports dominated the subcompact market at this point, but before the 1970's were over, the Pinto had gained a sizable portion of the subcompact market. Nonetheless, the American love affair with larger and more powerful cars continued, as the enduring popularity of the gas-guzzling Pontiac Firebird demonstrated.

The import automobile manufacturers enjoyed a large share of the subcompact market in the United States at the start of the 1970's. In 1972, Honda introduced the Civic, followed by the Accord. Datsun (part of Nissan) had dominated the compact pickup market in the United States since 1965 and continued to do so throughout the 1970's. The Volkswagen Beetle also held a sizable share of the market. The common factor among these vehicles was their fuel efficiency, which made them appealing to U.S. consumers when fuel shortages drove operating costs substantially upward.

When domestic manufacturers did start to compete with the imports, the issue became one of quality. The imports had the distinction of higher quality in manufacturing methods, and the vehicles that were produced outperformed their domestic counterparts on a regular basis. The issues of economy and quality permitted the import manufacturers to maintain a large share of the U.S. automobile market throughout the 1970's. The Japanese manufacturers also heavily surveyed their American customers to find out what was important to them and then incorporated changes into their production runs. Domestic automobile manufacturers historically resisted changes, often citing cost as the main factor. Issues of quality and change would keep the import manufacturers ahead of the domestic manufacturers for many years.

Mass Transit and Commercial Transportation Urban mass transit in the form of buses, subways, and other passenger rail systems expanded slightly in the early 1970's in response to increased demand and gasoline shortages. There were 946 metropolitan transit systems in operation throughout the United States in the 1970's. Nearly all American urban transit systems were bus-only systems. The government encouraged commuters to utilize mass transit systems for many reasons, including the Clean Air Act of 1970. The use of urban mass transit systems had been in a steady decline since the peak was reached in the mid-1940's. The first year in nearly thirty years that there was in increase in passengers over the previous year was 1973.

With the interstate highway system in the United States completed prior to the 1970's, the major form of commercial transportation was tractor trailers, which moved virtually all freight from origin to destination within the country. Even rail- and water-bound freight reached its final destination on tractor trailers. During the 1970's, only 8 percent of freight was waterborne while just more than 15 percent was transported by rail.

Consumer Travel Trends In previous decades, air travel had showed steady growth, and by the 1970's, it was no longer a novelty or just for the wealthy. In 1970, Boeing Aircraft Company introduced the first jumbo jet—the Boeing 747. These jumbo jets could carry larger passenger and cargo loads for greater distances and do so more efficiently than other air-

The last original model Volkswagen Beetle was produced in West Germany on January 19, 1978. The U.S. automobile industry was dominated by small foreign imports during the decade. (AP/Wide World Photos)

liners of the time. Moreover, competition among the airlines for passengers increased, which brought fare prices down and allowed more Americans than ever to choose air travel as their method of traveling.

For budget-minded travelers, intercity bus services had established a complete nationwide route by 1976. Although there were many local and regional providers during the 1970's, Greyhound Corporation and Continental Trailways were the largest intercity bus companies.

For many Americans, however, the most popular form of travel in the 1970's was the automobile. Most American households owned at least one car and traveling at a self-designed pace with flexibility of schedule options was most appealing to them. Recreational vehicles (RVs) came into more use, often in the form of travel trailers and campers, which were towed behind a motor vehicle.

The passenger rail service had been in decline for nearly thirty years at the beginning of the 1970's. In 1970, the Amtrak system was created and supported through legislation passed by the Unites States government. Amtrak was given two goals: operate at a profit and maintain nationwide passenger rail service. These two objectives contradicted each other because, in order to remain a nationwide service, unprofitable routes had to be maintained at a loss. Small, yearly increases in number of passengers occurred throughout the 1970's, but the personal motor vehicle remained the most popular form of transportation.

The Strategic Petroleum Reserve and Unleaded Gas

As a result of the nationwide effects of the oil embargo of 1973-1974 on the transportation system, the United States government created the Strategic Petroleum Reserve in 1975. The purpose of the Strategic Petroleum Reserve, which has a capacity of 700 million barrels of oil (the largest emergency oil reserve in the world), is to supplement domestic oil production in the event of another embargo. The reserve is stored in natural salt domes deep under the earth in four locations near the Gulf of Mexico because of the proximity of oil refineries in the area. It is estimated that this reserve would last the United States about sixty days, with the single largest consumer being the transportation network.

Because of the toxic nature of lead and the fact that 200,000 tons a year of it was used in gasoline, the Environmental Protection Agency (EPA) mandated that, starting in 1975, American refineries gradually phase out lead in gasoline. Further, many new vehicles first appeared on the market in 1975 in the United States with catalytic converters installed in their exhaust systems. The catalytic converter is one component of a system designed to limit toxic emissions from motor vehicles. Gasoline containing lead can destroy a catalytic converter; therefore, these new vehicles required the use of unleaded gasoline.

Impact The worldwide energy crisis, gasoline shortages and rationing, and the populace gaining awareness of the impact that transportation had upon the environment all caused immediate and everlasting effects upon transportation. When domestic automobile manufacturers realized that Americans would indeed purchase imports because of the better fuel economy, they started building more efficient vehicles themselves. Imported vehicle sales in the United States remained strong throughout the 1970's largely because of their quality.

Many Americans abandoned large muscle cars in the name of economy and environment. While the fuel crisis would lead some to the mass transit system, a staggering exodus did not occur. Most consumers simply replaced their gas guzzlers with more fuel-efficient vehicles or simply added a moped to their garages. Commercial transportation also suffered because of the fuel shortages. Many truck carrier companies shut down operations permanently. The time period between the fuel price increase and when they eventually collected the surcharges that had been added to cover the extra costs of fuel was long enough that many operations could not be sustained.

Further Reading

Bureau of Transportation Statistics. Http://www.bts.gov. The federal Bureau of Transportation Statistics Web site contains a wealth of facts and figures related to transportation in the United States.

Meyer, John R., and Jose A. Gomez-Ibanez. *Autos, Transit, and Cities.* Cambridge, Mass.: Harvard University Press, 1981. A thorough study of urban mass transit and automobiles within major metropolitan areas. The 1970's transportation issues are thoroughly examined.

Nice, David C. *Amtrak: The History and Politics of a National Railroad.* Boulder, Colo.: Lynne Rienner, 1998. An extensive study of the Amtrak passenger rail system, including its founding and operation throughout the 1970's.

Rae, John B. *The Road and the Car in American Life.* Cambridge, Mass.: Massachusetts Institute of Technology Press, 1971. A broad survey of transportation in the United States, including information and statistics on automobiles, mass transit, and commercial transportation.

Reische, Diana, ed. *Problems of Mass Transportation.* New York: H. W. Wilson, 1970. Details the problems faced by the mass transit system in the United States at the beginning of the 1970's.

Smerk, George M. *Urban Mass Transportation.* Bloomington: Indiana University Press, 1974. Contains an extensive study of mass transit issues in the United States during the early 1970's.

Glenn S. Hamilton

See also Air bags; Aircraft; Airline Deregulation Act of 1978; Automobiles; Clean Air Act of 1970; Containerization; Energy crisis; Ford Pinto; Gas shortages; Jumbo jets; Mopeds; National Maximum Speed Limit; Oil embargo of 1973-1974; Roller skating; RVs; Skateboards.

■ Travolta, John

Identification American television and film actor

Born February 18, 1954; Englewood, New Jersey

As a multitalented acting icon of the 1970's, Travolta helped set popular trends and define a generation.

Expressing an interest in the theater at an early age, John Travolta took acting, dancing, and voice lessons as a child. In 1966, at the age of twelve, he made his theatrical debut in the Actors Studio production of *Who'll Save the Plowboy?* As a teenager, the young actor appeared in summer stock theater, supper club productions, and commercials. By the early 1970's, he was earning roles in television shows such as *The Rookies*, *Emergency!*, and *Medical Center.* In 1973, Travolta made his Off-Broadway debut in the play *Rain* and also toured with the musical *Grease.* His acting career continued to flourish with his performance in the Broadway play *Over Here!* (1974) and his motion-picture debut in *Devil's Rain* (1975).

By the mid-1970's, Travolta had earned widespread popularity with his role as high school troublemaker Vinnie Barbarino in the television situation comedy *Welcome Back, Kotter,* on the American Broadcasting Company (ABC), from 1975 to 1978. Other notable film roles that solidified his popularity included the made-for-television film *The Boy in the Plastic Bubble* (1976) and the Metro-Goldwyn-Mayer (MGM) film adaptation of the Stephen King novel *Carrie* (1976).

In 1977, Travolta's portrayal of Tony Manero in the Paramount film *Saturday Night Fever* catapulted the actor to icon status. The film not only epitomized the disco dance craze of the 1970's but also earned the actor his first Academy Award nomination as well as his first Golden Globe nomination for Best Actor. Taking on a similar role as Danny Zuko in the Paramount musical *Grease* (1978), Travolta firmly established himself as a megastar. The popularity of the film secured for both Travolta and his costar, Olivia Newton-John, a place in the history of American popular culture. His portrayal of Danny Zuko also earned him his second Golden Globe nomination for Best Actor.

In 1978, Travolta costarred in the Universal Studios film *Moment by Moment* with Lily Tomlin. The movie, which explored the intimate relationship between a younger man and an older woman, did not do well at the box office. His role in the film as a sensitive leading man was a dramatic departure from the super masculine characters that had brought him worldwide fame.

Impact John Travolta's portrayal of Tony Manero in *Saturday Night Fever* and Danny Zuko in *Grease* created a cultlike fan base for the star. These films and Travolta's characters had a significant impact on the popular culture of the 1970's. With a slightly different legion of fans for each film, they each helped to define a generation. While *Saturday Night Fever* sparked a disco dance craze and established fashion trends for young adults, *Grease* would become for many teenagers an identifying experience of their youth.

Further Reading

Andrews, Nigel. *Travolta: The Life.* New York: Bloomsbury, 1999.

Clarkson, Wensley. *John Travolta: Back in Character.* New York: Overlook Press, 1997.

Bernadette Zbicki Heiney

See also Academy Awards; Blockbusters; Disco; Fashions and clothing; Film in the United States; *Grease*; Leisure suits; Music; Platform shoes; *Saturday Night Fever*; Sitcoms; Television in the United States.

■ Trudeau, Pierre

Identification Prime minister of Canada, 1968-1979, 1980-1984
Born October 18, 1919; Montreal, Canada
Died September 28, 2000; Montreal, Canada

During the 1970's, Trudeau carried out social reforms, defended the unity of Canada against regional interests, and enhanced the authority of the federal government over the provinces.

Pierre Trudeau was in the middle of his first term in 1970, engaged in carrying out pledges made during the 1968 election to continue social reforms begun by his predecessor, Lester Pearson. His efforts were aided by the enthusiasm—commentators called it "Trudeaumania"—that he had aroused among voters during the campaign. In 1971, he succeeded both in ending discriminatory practices that had distorted the unemployment insurance program and in extending maternity benefits. He successfully brought into operation the Medicare program that Pearson had proposed but had been unable to make effective, and he also liberalized Canada's immigration and refugee policies.

Asserting that the federal government had a duty to ensure that Canadians would feel at home regardless of where they moved within the nation, Trudeau insisted that governmental services in French be available everywhere. However, he opposed special status for Quebec, arguing that all provinces were equal parts of Canada. Trudeau's stand angered Québécois nationalists, who desired autonomy or independence for their province, as well as leaders of the prairie provinces, who resented his language program as interference in their affairs. However, the program was popular with many non-Quebec voters.

October Crisis The Front de Libération du Québec (FLQ) had engaged in sporadic bombing of federal property during the 1960's, demanding that Quebec leave Canada. On October 5, 1970, a cell of the FLQ kidnapped James Cross, British trade commissioner in Montreal, and on October 10, another cell seized Pierre Laporte, the provincial minister of labor. When Quebec's premier requested help, Trudeau invoked the War Measures Act on October 16 and sent in the army. The next day, Laporte's body was found. More than four hundred people were arrested, with most released shortly thereafter. When Cross was freed in December, his captors were permitted to fly to Cuba; Laporte's assassins were caught and sent to prison. Trudeau won almost universal praise for his firm response to terrorism, and Quebec public opinion thereafter rejected the use of violence for political ends.

Canadian Independence Trudeau moved to assert Canadian independence in foreign affairs, in economic policy, and in cultural matters. In 1970, he opened diplomatic relations with communist China, angering U.S. president Richard M. Nixon, who would not be ready to follow suit for two more years. To reduce Canadian economic dependence on the United States, Trudeau organized a Canada Development Corporation in 1971 to finance Canadian businesses that desired to buy U.S.-controlled firms.

Canadian prime minister Pierre Trudeau walks with Barbra Streisand at a cultural event in 1970. (AP/Wide World Photos)

That same year, his administration enacted a rule that required 30 percent Canadian content on all radio stations.

Trudeau also strongly desired to end Canada's colonial dependency on Great Britain. The British 1867 North America Act, which had served as the constitution of Canada, required consent of Britain's Parliament to amendments. Trudeau proposed to replace it with a Canadian constitution that included a Charter of Rights and Freedoms, which guaranteed individual liberties and ensured group rights concerning language and education. He believed that he had achieved his objective when the June, 1971, conference of federal and provincial first ministers in Victoria, British Columbia, unanimously approved a constitution with an amending formula that reserved provincial veto rights and included a charter of rights interpreted by the Supreme Court. However, the agreement fell apart when the premier of Quebec, under intense criticism by separatists after he returned home, withdrew Quebec's consent. Trudeau continued to raise the constitutional issue throughout the 1970's.

Elections and Personal Life Deteriorating economic conditions in 1972, with unemployment and inflation rising, led to Trudeau's near defeat in the October vote. His Liberal Party ended with only two parliamentary seats more than the Conservatives, and Trudeau suddenly led a minority government, liable to defeat if the other parties combined against him. In 1974, believing that voters were more favorable, Trudeau dissolved Parliament; on July 8, he won a commanding majority.

In March, 1971, the fifty-one-year-old Trudeau married twenty-two-year-old Margaret Sinclair. At first, the marriage appeared to be a brilliant success; they quickly had three children, and Margaret's beauty and verve helped Trudeau during the 1974 campaign. However, the marriage collapsed when Margaret became publicly and flamboyantly unfaithful. The two separated in 1977 and were divorced in 1984.

Trudeau's popularity plummeted in the late 1970's. Economic problems worsened. Trudeau angered voters by imposing wage and price controls in October, 1975, after having ridiculed the Conservative leader when he suggested the controls a year earlier during the election campaign. Conservatives gained a plurality in the May, 1979, election, and Trudeau found himself out of office after eleven years as prime minister.

On November 21, 1979, Trudeau announced his resignation as leader of the Liberal Party and his retirement from politics. The situation changed drastically the next month. Conservative prime minister Joe Clark lost a vote of confidence on December 13, dissolved Parliament, and called a new election for February 18. After a show of reluctance, Trudeau agreed to resume the Liberal leadership. He would have another chance to advance his constitutional ideas.

Impact Trudeau's efforts made Canada a more equitable, tolerant, and pluralistic society than the country in which he grew up. His immigration reforms encouraged newcomers from outside Europe, altering the ethnic composition of the nation. By insisting on official bilingualism and appointing French speakers to major offices, Trudeau made Canada more congenial to people of French descent, while his resistance to Quebec nationalism strengthened the federal government. All Canadians benefited from Trudeau's social and health care reforms.

Further Reading

Clarkson, Stephen, and Christina McCall. *Trudeau and Our Times.* 2 vols. Toronto: McClelland & Stewart, 1990, 1994. A detailed narrative and analysis of Trudeau's political career.

Finkel, Alvin. *Our Lives: Canada After 1945.* Toronto: James Lorimer, 1997. Trudeau receives substantial attention in this social history of late twentieth century Canada.

Laforest, Guy. *Trudeau and the End of a Canadian Dream.* Translated by Paul Leduc Browne and Michelle Weinroth. Montreal: McGill-Queen's University Press, 1995. A bitterly critical review of the impact of Trudeau's federalism on hopes for a special position for Quebec.

Mann, Susan. *The Dream of Nation: A Social and Intellectual History of Quebec.* 2d ed. Montreal: McGill-Queen's University Press, 2002. Describes the evolution of Quebec nationalism, providing useful background of Trudeau's intellectual development concerning this issue.

See, Scott W. *The History of Canada.* Westport, Conn.: Greenwood Press, 2001. A brief narrative supplies historical perspective for Trudeau's career.

Milton Berman

See also Business and the economy in Canada; Canada and the British Commonwealth; Canada and the United States; Canadian Citizenship Act of 1977; Canadian Human Rights Act of 1977; Charter of the French Language; Clark, Joe; Elections in Canada; Foreign policy of Canada; Inflation in Canada; International trade of Canada; Minorities in Canada; Multiculturalism in Canada; October Crisis.

■ Tutankhamen traveling exhibit

The Event Artifacts from the tomb of the Egyptian king Tutankhamen traveled to several museums in the United States

Date November 17, 1976-April 15, 1979

The traveling exhibit of artifacts from the tomb of the Egyptian king Tutankhamen was a watershed event in providing Americans insight into the ancient world of Egypt. During the thirty months in which the exhibit traveled the country, millions of museumgoers became acquainted at first hand with the artistry, politics, and religion of a country that had, for nearly a century, been an object of mystery and fascination.

The immense popularity of the traveling exhibit featuring artifacts from King Tutankhamen's tomb was predictable. The American public had had its interest in Egypt whetted by Hollywood spectacles such as *Cleopatra* (1963) and *Land of the Pharoahs* (1955). The dark side of Egyptian burial rites had been dramatized in a series of horror movies such as *The Mummy* (1932), *The Mummy's Tomb* (1942), and *The Mummy's Curse* (1944). Many Americans were already familiar with the story of Howard Carter's 1922 discovery of Tutankhamen's tomb and the attendant string of deaths that supposedly had been brought about as a result of a mysterious ancient curse.

For nearly two years, Thomas Hoving, director of the Metropolitan Museum of Art in New York, worked with the Egyptian Organization of Antiquities and government authorities in Egypt and the United States to arrange for the transport of fifty-five artifacts from the tomb of the boy-king. The artifacts came to the United States by ship, under U.S. Navy escort.

The exhibit opened at the National Gallery of Art in Washington, D.C., on November 17, 1976, and it remained there for four months. Nearly one million people visited the exhibit in the nation's capital. It then moved to the Field Museum in Chicago, the New Orleans Museum of Art, the Los Angeles County Museum of Art, and the Seattle Art Museum, remaining at each location for approximately four months and drawing similar crowds. In December, 1978, the exhibit traveled to New York's Metropolitan Museum of Art, where it closed its tour on April 15, 1979. The various museums went to great lengths to present these Egyptian artifacts in a memorable setting: For example, the National Gallery built a replica of the entrance to the tomb in which the treasures were discovered, and the New Orleans Museum of Art painted the street leading to the museum's entranceway in a bright blue hue, mimicking the Nile River.

Impact The success of the exhibition signaled to museum directors around the world that it was possible to exchange artifacts and enhance the reputa-

Tutankhamen's golden death mask was one of the Egyptian artifacts on display during the 1970's traveling exhibit. (Library of Congress)

tion of individual museums by mounting displays that placed objects in context to tell a story about the past. In the decades following the Tutankhamen exhibition, dozens of similar exhibits from countries such as Russia and China were brought to the United States to entertain, educate, and awe a receptive public.

Further Reading

Hall, A. J. "Dazzling Legacy of an Ancient Quest: King Tut's Gold." *National Geographic* 151 (March, 1977): 292-311.

Prideaux, Tom. "Now It's Our Turn to Be Fascinated by Tut's Treasure." *Smithsonian* 7 (November, 1976): 42-51.

Reeves, C. N., and Nicholas Reeves. *The Complete Tutankhamun: The King, the Tomb, the Royal Treasure.* New York: W. W. Norton, 1990.

Laurence W. Mazzeno

See also Archaeology.

■ Twenty-sixth Amendment

Identification Constitutional amendment lowering the voting age in federal, state, and local elections from twenty-one to eighteen

Date Ratified on June 30, 1971

The ratification of the Twenty-sixth Amendment to the Constitution put an end to a long-festering controversy over what precise age properly determined civic and political maturity for U.S. citizens.

While the debate over granting the vote to eighteen-year-old citizens was long-standing, it gained impetus in the 1950's and 1960's—particularly in the wake of the Korean and Vietnam Wars. The peacetime draft under the Selective Service Act inducted, for the most part, males right out of high school. The point was made that, while these young men were obligated to serve in the military and were considered mature enough to participate in warfare, they were still being denied the right to participate in the

A clerk delivers instructions to an eighteen year old who has just registered to vote in 1971, following passage of the Twenty-sixth Amendment lowering the voting age requirement. (AP/Wide World Photos)

electoral process. The issue of nonrepresentation was succinctly expressed in Barry McGuire's popular 1965 song *Eve of Destruction*: "You're old enough to kill, but not for voting."

During the 1950's, President Dwight D. Eisenhower openly endorsed the idea, and the issue of lowering the voting age to eighteen became part of the general clamor for reform in the next decade. In 1970, Congress passed an amendment to the Voting Rights Act of 1965, mandating the lowering of the voting age to eighteen in federal, state, and local elections.

This move was challenged almost immediately in the courts, and on October 19, 1970, the case of *Oregon v. Mitchell* was argued before the Supreme Court. The Court ruled by a 5-4 vote, on December 21, 1970, that Congress was within its rights in lowering the age to eighteen in federal elections, under the Equal Protection Clause of the Fourteenth Amendment, but another 5-4 decision ruled that this did not extend constitutionally to state and local elections.

That decision left state and local electoral officials with a potentially nightmarish situation: Unless the voting age could be made uniform, there would have to be two separate voters' rolls, one for federal and one for state and local elections. Moreover, the additional cost and time that would have to be invested would be prohibitive. These factors undercut most of the opposition to lowering the voting age to eighteen in all elections.

Therefore, when an amendment to the Constitution was proposed in Congress on March 23, 1971, to make the voting age of eighteen a uniform standard in every election, the states were willing to resolve their quandary, accepting what became the Twenty-sixth Amendment. It was passed by Congress and ratified by the states in record time—slightly more than three months.

Impact The addition of a large block of younger voters certainly affected the strategies of both major political parties. The fears of conservatives, who had strongly opposed the change, proved unjustified: There was no sustained liberal trend during the rest of the decade or for years thereafter.

Further Reading

Keyssar, Alexander. *The Right to Vote: The Contested History of Democracy in the United States.* New York: Basic Books, 2000.

Peltason, J. W. *Understanding the Constitution.* New York: Holt, Rinehart and Winston, 1985.

Raymond Pierre Hylton

See also Congress, U.S.; Supreme Court decisions; Vietnam War.

Ultrasonography

Definition The reflection of high-frequency sound waves to image body structures

Ultrasonography provided a noninvasive method for analysis of disease and a means to monitor medical areas as diverse as fetal development, cardiac activity, and gallstones.

The principle behind ultrasonography was applied as early as the first decades of the twentieth century. The first echo-sounding device was in use shortly after the sinking of the *Titanic* in 1912. During World War I, it was applied in submarine detection.

The first medical applications of the procedure occurred during the 1940's and were primarily for therapeutic purposes rather than for diagnosis. Ultrasonic waves were used to destroy brain tissue for elimination of pain, as a treatment for rheumatoid arthritis, and for destruction of tumors. In 1947, however, Karl and Friedrich Dussik applied the process for the location of brain tumors, representing one of the first diagnostic applications.

The major application of ultrasonography during the 1970's was in the practice of fetal monitoring. A handheld transducer was placed on the abdomen of a pregnant woman, and high-frequency sound waves were passed through the tissue. A monitor was set up to produce a "real-time" image on the screen. The physician or technician could evaluate the fetus for any obvious physical abnormalities and for its position in the uterus.

Many of these advancements were carried out in Great Britain during this period. In particular, Dr. Peter Wells and Dr. Stuart Campbell were instrumental in advancing applications. The science of ultrasonography was officially acknowledged in 1977 with the formation of the British Medical Ultrasonography Society, an "offspring" of an earlier founded group. In 1972, Campbell had reported a diagnosis of anencephaly in a seventeen-week fetus and spina bifida in a fetus in 1975, the first applications of the procedure that led to the termination of pregnancies. In 1975, Campbell demonstrated the use of abdominal circumference for assessment of fetal growth. Previously, measurements of fetal diameters had been the parameter by which fetal weight was established; however, the measurement had limitations resulting from changes in the shape of the fetus.

Among the advances in ultrasonography during the 1970's was greater application of what was known as B-mode (or brightness) imaging. Brightness modulation is an imaging technique in which bright dots appear on an oscilloscope, the intensity of the image being determined by the strength of the signal. While the B-scan was initially developed some years earlier, also by the Campbell group, improved technology allowed for its greater sensitivity and wider application. In 1979, Margi Mantoni and Jan Fog Pederson in Denmark first observed the yolk sac around the fetus using B-mode ultrasonography.

Impact Improvements in technology associated with ultrasonography during the 1970's resulted in its increased use in diagnosis of disease for a wide range of medical applications. In particular, the discipline of obstetrics was able to apply the procedure as a means to assess fetal development.

Further Reading

England, Marjorie. *Life Before Birth.* 2d ed. St. Louis: Elsevier, 1996.

Meire, Hylton, and Pat Farrant. *Basic Ultrasound.* Indianapolis: John Wiley & Sons, 1995.

Richard Adler

See also Cancer research; CAT scans; Inventions; Medicine; Science and technology.

Unemployment in Canada

Definition The proportion of the Canadian labor force that is without work and seeking work

The high unemployment in Canada during the 1970's was mainly the consequence of monetary conditions, government policies, and an expanding labor force that surpassed

employment availability, successively altering the attitudes of the Canadian population.

The 1970's began with a period of growth in Canada due to the expansionary monetary and fiscal policies measures established by the federal government. However, policies from earlier decades were no longer sufficient to manage the escalating unemployment and inflation rates. Policy approaches that were intended to address the inflation problem had the corollary effect of increasing unemployment. Overall, the average unemployment rate for the decade was 6.7 percent, compared to 4.6 percent in the 1960's.

In 1975, the federal government adopted a policy of deliberately restraining economic growth in order to halt the rising inflation rate, which resulted in high unemployment in subsequent years. The total employment grew at a rate of 2.8 percent, whereas Canada's labor force grew at a rate of 3.9 percent as a result of the sustained growth in the number of working women and an increased amount of youths.

In 1971, the federal government modified the unemployment insurance program, which had been identified as a contributing factor to the higher unemployment rate. It is estimated that the liberalization of unemployment insurance benefits increased the unemployment rate by 0.8 percent and had the largest effect on youth unemployment. The unemployment policy changed at the end of 1979 to reduce the effects of the unemployment benefits on the economy.

The social changes of the 1960's helped increase the number of women seeking jobs during the 1970's. It became more acceptable for women to find employment outside the home and to take part in a dual-income household in order to maintain the living standards of the family. The participation rate of women in the labor force increased by an average of 10 percent from the 1960's. Although the unemployment rate among women was the highest in the population, the majority of working women found jobs in services, which coincided with an expansion of this sector.

The population aged fifteen to twenty-four grew during the decade, as the baby boom generation reached working age. Despite an increase in advanced academic participation, the number of youths seeking employment increased. The participation rate of youths in the labor force increased by 5.5 percent from the previous decade.

The attitude toward job attachment changed as youths and women entered the labor force. The young people had grown up in an era of prosperity, which caused their need for job security to decrease and their unemployment and job turnover rates to increase. In contrast, adult males remained responsible for households and required job security to sustain high living standards for their dependents.

Impact The high unemployment rates of the 1970's resulted in tighter control of the fiscal and monetary policies in Canada. Slow-growth policies combined with the rising numbers of women and youths entering the labor market were recognized as the primary reasons for the lack of employment opportunities.

Further Reading

Bryan, Ingrid A. *Economic Policies in Canada.* Toronto: Butterworth, 1982.

Statistics Canada. *Labour Force Annual Averages.* Ottawa, Ont.: Minister of Industry, 1996.

Sonya Pongratz

See also Business and the economy in Canada; Demographics of Canada; Foreign policy of Canada; Income and wages in Canada; Inflation in Canada; International trade of Canada; Unemployment in the United States; Unions in Canada; Women in the workforce.

■ Unemployment in the United States

Definition The proportion of the U.S. labor force that is without work and seeking work

Unemployment in the United States during the 1970's reached the highest level since prior to World War II. As a result, many workers and their families suffered major declines in their standards of living.

From 1966 to 1969, unemployment averaged 3.6 percent. However, during the 1970's, the rate was much higher, averaging 6.2 percent. One major reason was the recession of 1970 and the severe recession of 1973-1975. During recessions, economic activity declines, and workers lose their jobs, thereby increasing the rate of unemployment. By late 1970, the unemployment rate was 6.1 percent, compared with 3.5 percent at the beginning of the recession in December, 1969. Even as the recovery occurred in 1971 and 1972, the unemployment rate was slow to decline, averaging 5.7 percent during those two years.

During the early 1970's, the labor force was expanding rapidly as children born in the post-World War II baby boom were reaching the age of labor force entry. This meant that more teenagers were looking for jobs. Since teens generally have a higher unemployment rate than do older workers, overall unemployment rates rose as this age group became a higher proportion of the total labor force. Moreover, some firms were reluctant to hire previously laid-off workers until there was greater certainty that the economic expansion would be long lasting.

The 1973-1975 recession, which began in November, 1973, lasted until March, 1975. It was the most severe post-World War II recession. Industrial production declined almost 15 percent, and construction activity fell by 25 percent. Employment declined by 3.3 million jobs from October, 1974, until February, 1975. Three-fourths of the loss in jobs was in the manufacturing sector. In 1975, manufacturing unemployment was 10.9 percent, and joblessness reached 18 percent in construction. Before the recession ebbed in the spring of 1975, the unemployment rate rose to a post-World War II high of 9.2 percent.

Economic recovery during the 1976-1979 period was slow; there was virtually no economic growth in 1979 as the economy began its slide into a recession, which commenced in January, 1980. Unemployment averaged 6.7 percent from 1976 to 1979 as slow job creation meant that many workers who lost their jobs during the 1973-1975 recession had to compete with new entrants into the labor force for the limited number of additional jobs available.

Racial Differences in Unemployment During the 1970's, African American unemployment figures averaged 11.7 percent, compared with white unemployment figures of 5.6 percent; black unemployment rates were more than double white rates. The relative unemployment rate for black workers worsened during the decade. In 1970-1971, black joblessness rates were 86 percent higher than white rates, but by 1977-1979, black rates were 145 percent higher than white rates. Because black workers typically were concentrated heavily in construction and manufacturing as compared with white workers, these workers were affected more adversely by the high unemployment rates in those sectors following 1973.

Another factor responsible for the worsening unemployment rate among black Americans in the 1970's was the movement of jobs from the central core of big cities to the suburbs. White workers, who often lived in suburban areas, obtained most of these jobs while black workers, who often lacked transportation from their homes in the central city, could not share in this employment expansion. Moreover, during this period, there was a decline of employment in agriculture and other lower-skill industries. These occupations traditionally employed a large share of black workers.

Although the fact attracted only limited attention at the time, unemployment rates among the nation's 750,000 American Indians living on reservations averaged approximately 40 percent during the 1970's. This was the highest unemployment rate among any minority group. On some reservations, such as the Navajo, more than half of the workforce was unemployed or underemployed. High birthrates, coupled with swiftly falling death rates, added increasing population pressure to the already overburdened reservation economies. In addition, Indian agricultural employment, including the number of Indian-owned farm enterprises, declined steadily, and industrial development occurred too slowly to provide employment opportunities for those Native Americans displaced from agriculture.

International Outlook and Labor Surveys During the decade, unemployment rates in Japan, West Germany, Italy, and Sweden were only half those of U.S. figures. Australia and Great Britain had rates that were slightly lower than in the United States, while the Canadian unemployment rate was consistently higher than U.S. rates. At this time, many Western European countries had higher rates of economic growth and employment expansion than the United States, thereby resulting in low unemployment rates in those nations. Moreover, job turnover rates in the 1970's tended to be lower in Western Europe, and employment exchanges and job vacancy information were more effectively utilized in Western Europe than in the United States.

In 1976, Congress established the National Commission on Employment and Unemployment Statistics to examine systematically both the methods of data collection and the measurement of various labor force concepts utilized in the monthly unemployment survey. In late 1979, the commission completed its work. It recommended that the official measures of employment and unemployment remain unchanged. However, the commission recommended that the sample of households interviewed each month in the employment survey be increased from 60,000 to 100,000 in order to obtain more accurate unemployment data for states and local areas. Because of budget cuts during the Reagan administration, the Bureau of Labor Statistics was not able to implement this recommendation.

Impact A major impact of the unemployment of the 1970's was political. The high unemployment rates of the 1974-1976 period played a role in the defeat of President Gerald R. Ford by Jimmy Carter in the November, 1976, election. Moreover, the relatively high rates between 1977 and 1980 helped Ronald Reagan defeat President Carter in November, 1980.

Further Reading

Council of Economic Advisors. *Economic Report of the President.* Washington, D.C.: U.S. Government Printing Office, published annually. Highlights short-term and long-term economic trends for each year during the 1970's.

Ehrenberg, Ronald, and Robert Smith. *Modern Labor Economics: Theory and Public Policy.* 8th ed. Upper Saddle River, N.J.: Pearson Education, 2002. A comprehensive treatment of labor markets after World War II.

Kurian, George, ed. *Datapedia of the United States, 1970-2003.* Washington, D.C.: Bernan Press, 2004. Provides highly detailed labor force statistics for the U.S. economy.

Alan L. Sorkin

See also Business and the economy in the United States; Energy crisis; Equal Employment Opportunity Act of 1972; Income and wages in the United States; Inflation in the United States; Oil embargo of 1973-1974; Unemployment in Canada; Women in the workforce.

Unions in Canada

Definition Organizations representing Canadian workers in various sectors

Labor unions gained strength in Canada during the 1970's while they were losing clout in the United States. Their growing power led to many work stoppages as well as an increased role in national politics during this time.

By the start of the 1970's, labor unions already represented nearly 30 percent of all Canadian workers, mostly in government and manufacturing jobs. The Canadian economy was still enjoying relatively low inflation (around 2 percent per year) and low unemployment (3 to 5 percent), as well as strong international demand for its products. Although their rate of union membership was slightly higher than in the United States (28 percent), Canadian workers earned slightly less than their U.S. industrial counterparts. By 1975, Canadian wages in many industries were slightly higher than in the United States, as Canadian unions gained in strength and membership. By the end of the 1970's, 37 percent of all Canadian workers were union members, compared with only 24 percent of U.S. workers.

Canadian labor unions flourished during the 1970's, both as insurance against the ravages of inflation for their members and as a ready source of support for Quebec separationists. By 1975, unemployment compensation benefits covered 99 percent of Canadian workers—compared with 50 to 80 percent in Western Europe and 45 percent in Japan—relieving much of the sting of strikes and layoffs. Unemployment was already at 8.4 percent by 1975, but rapid price inflation and the rapidly eroding value of the Canadian dollar were just as important concerns for unions.

A labor union provided the bargaining clout that individual workers could not hope to achieve on their own, and during the inflationary 1970's this was a powerful enticement for workers. Before the Trudeau government instituted wage and price restraints in 1975 with the creation of the Anti-Inflation Board (AIB), labor union contracts with wage increases of 20 percent and more per year were not uncommon in an effort to keep workers' wages in line with inflation. When labor unions' demands were not met (or were later thwarted by the AIB), labor strikes and work stoppages became common occurrences.

Labor unions were also heavily courted by Quebec secession proponents, most notably Quebec premier René Lévesque's Parti Québécois. The separationist platform included mandatory dues checkoffs (automatic paycheck deductions from workers' checks, regardless of union membership) and union certification votes if 35 percent of an employer's workers request them. Following a labor conflict at at Robin Hood Multifoods Ltd. flour mill in Montreal in July, 1976, in which security guards escorting replacement workers shot at striking workers, injuring eight, Parti Québécois added an "anti-scab" bill to its proposal for secession.

Impact Labor unions enjoyed particularly strong support by workers in the 1970's. They were variously blamed for causing inflationary pressures in the Canadian economy and looked to for relief from the same inflation. As unions became more powerful, separatist factions in Quebec sought to solicit their support for secession from Canada.

Further Reading

"Canada's Economic Squeeze." *Business Week*, March 29, 1977, 60.

"The Price That Canada Pays for High Wages." *Business Week*, September 29, 1975, 80.

Betsy A. Murphy

See also Business and the economy in the United States; Inflation in Canada; International trade of Canada; Lévesque, René; Unemployment in Canada; Unions in the United States.

■ Unions in the United States

Definition Organizations representing U.S. workers in various sectors

As the U.S. economy began to reel from emerging global industrial competition during the 1970's, labor unions continued to decline in their overall percentage of the workforce from their postwar high of 35 percent. All regions of the country experienced change and economic instability during the decade, a fact that had a significant impact on unions.

Labor unions in the United States reached their peak of 35 percent of the labor force in the years immediately following World War II. By the end of the 1970's, however, they had fallen to a low of 25 percent. The decade produced an even more precipitous decline as American industrial sectors began to transform from a localized industrial model to one that featured globalization, outsourcing, a shift to a service-oriented workforce, and a decline in domestic manufacturing. Severe economic conditions during the 1970's, such as the Arab oil embargos and accompanying inflation, unemployment, and social dislocation, all combined to usher in a period of declining union membership and a decline in the political clout of organized labor. During the presidential election of 1972, the Vietnam War seemed to have an effect within the Democratic Party by pitting George Meany, the president of the AFL-CIO, against George McGovern, the Democratic Party's antiwar candidate.

The first major blow to the growth and strength of organized labor in the postwar era was the growth of foreign competition in manufacturing beginning in the 1960's. Japan and Germany and the rest of Europe, recovered from the war, were again becoming competitors with the United States in the world marketplace. In order to maintain their high levels of profit, the U.S. automobile, steel, electrical, textile, and rubber industries, among others, were forced into critical restructuring because of the competition from abroad. Plants began to close in the industrial Northeast and Midwest, ushering in the use of the phrase "Rust Belt" to describe states like Pennsylvania, Ohio, and Michigan as plant closures became a very common phenomenon in this region, and factories stood abandoned. As major steel plants and other manufacturing plants closed, industrialists scrambled to find a way to survive in the ever-increasing global economy.

World Financial Institutions and Globalization During the decade, U.S. corporations began to develop a new ability to move capital to various parts of the world without regard to national boundaries. This in turn allowed them to move their production operations to locations around the world to take advantage of significantly lower labor costs. They were aided in this effort by global economic institutions such as the World Trade Organization (WTO), the International Monetary Fund (IMF), and the World Bank. This globalization had significant effects on organized labor in the United States and workforces in other industrialized nations. It allowed business to pit workers in Third World countries against workers in the industrial nations. Some believed that many corporations had effectively created a "global hiring hall" that allowed them to move their operations to countries offering the lowest labor costs. Initially, some industries, such as the textile industry, had moved to the American South where organized labor had never fully penetrated. As union organizers followed these industries to the South, however, the companies then moved their operations offshore to avoid unions, eventually even fleeing locations such as Mexico and the Caribbean to seek even lower labor costs in Bangladesh or India.

As a response both to the economic crisis in the early part of the decade and to increased competition from abroad, corporations began to reject the "class compromise" that had existed between themselves and labor between the end of World War II and the beginning of the 1970's. Douglas Fraser, head of the United Automobile Workers (UAW), noted during the decade that industry, commerce, and finance leaders broke and discarded "the fragile, unwritten compact previously existing during a past period of growth and progress . . . [and they] have chosen to wage a one-sided class war." There was some truth to Fraser's words as during the decade, because as many as ten thousand permanent replacement workers were hired a year in place of workers fired for attempting to organize unions at various plants.

Population Shifts and New Jobs One of the other elements affecting labor in the United States during the decade was the population shift that accompanied the emergence of the Rust Belt in the Northeast and Midwest. The 1980 census showed the dramatic population shift from the Rust Belt to the Sun Belt area, notably California, Florida, Texas, and Arizona. The population shift also reflected significant economic realities. The growth of high-tech industries—computer, microchip, and electronic companies located in the Sun Belt—attracted more highly educated workers and college graduates. While massive unemployment was occurring in the East and Midwest, new, primarily nonunion jobs were being created in the Sun Belt.

The net effect of the population shift to this region and to suburban areas around major cites was to divide the working class along geographic, racial, and economic lines. Low-paid, minimum-wage earners became centered in the inner cities with very high unemployment rates, while those with significantly higher paying jobs relocated to the suburbs and to the Sun Belt.

At the same time that this population shift was occurring with the accompanying shift to high-tech jobs, there was also a shift from manufacturing jobs to service employment taking place across the country. Positions such as insurance agents, real estate brokers, sales personnel, consultant specialists in everything from advertising to personal fitness, and numerous other service occupations were replacing the traditional manufacturing jobs.

Public Sector Growth The only significant growth for labor unions during the decade was in the public sector. Teachers, firefighters, prison guards, highway patrol troopers, nurses and health care workers, and other government employees were beginning to organize into unions, sometimes into preexisting ones, such as Service Employees International Union (SEIU) and the American Federation of State, County, and Municipal Employees (AFSCME), or into new ones, such as teachers unions and municipal employee unions. Many states, such as California and Massachusetts, passed public sector labor laws modeled on the National Labor Relations Act during the decade, allowing for public employees to organize into unions and bargain collectively. Traditional industrial unions, including Teamsters, the UAW, and Chemical Workers, got into the act as well, vying to represent various bargaining units in the public sector as they sought to organize under the new laws. Ultimately, public sector union growth was the only bright spot for labor during the decade as membership in industrial unions continued to decline.

Minorities and Farmworkers The growth in these new public sector unions was accompanied by an increase in union membership by women and minorities. The previous model of industrial unions and skilled craft unions was decidedly weak on the notion of affirmative action. The leadership of all of the industrial and craft unions was almost universally white, with many of the leaders coming from white European ethnic backgrounds. Certainly, blacks Americans, Latinos, and women were in no way represented in union membership or leadership positions commensurate with their percentage of the labor force. Traditionally, the unskilled laborers unions were where minorities found a spot. Women fared better in the new teacher unions and hospital workers unions as they represented a significant percentage of the labor force in these occupations. Many of the women union leaders of subsequent decades emerged from this group of female union leaders in the service industries.

The only other high spot for labor during the decade was the success of union organizer César Chávez in getting Governor Jerry Brown and the California legislature to enact the Agricultural Labor Relations Act in 1976, allowing for California farmworkers to organize themselves legally into unions. California became the only state to date to have passed such a law. While it produced significant benefits for California farmworkers by putting the spotlight on California growers who cleaned up working conditions in the industry, the law had limited impact on the labor scene. Chávez's efforts to have similar legislation passed in other agricultural states met with no success. While the AFL-CIO brought Chávez's United Farm Workers (UFW) union under the AFL-CIO umbrella, the federation did not make an effort to have agricultural workers included under the National Labor Relations Act. This became a monumental task for the labor federation, which saw its political clout diminish significantly over the years.

Loss of Political Clout Early in the decade, AFL-CIO president Meany embroiled the labor federation in the first of many political confrontations with the Democratic Party, where labor had found its political home since its inception. In the midst of the Vietnam War and as a prelude to the Watergate scandal, the McGovern-Fraser Commission of the Democratic Party enacted new rules for the party's nominating procedures. Instead of back-room deals, the commission instituted reforms that would guarantee delegation spots for women and minorities at nominating conventions. Angered by these new rules that diminished labor's role in the nominating process, Meany's AFL-CIO boycotted the 1972 presidential election and refused to endorse the party nominee, George McGovern. Labor's support of the Vietnam War was in sharp contrast to the views of many Democrats. Thus, the war served to create a significant wedge between liberal Democrats and union members.

Regarding international politics, organized labor was alienated from much of the Democratic Party because of its support of national policy to support dictators in various parts of the world so long as they professed to be anticommunist. The AFL-CIO, through its four international bureaus, supported labor movements in Third World countries with funds provided by the U.S. government, leading to speculation that these institutes were working closely with the Central Intelligence Agency (CIA) in respective Third World countries.

The aftermath of this fissure between labor and the Democratic Party may have had something to do with labor's failure to pass any significant legislation during the decade. Even though labor had persuaded Congress in 1975 to overturn a 1951 Supreme Court ruling limiting picketing at construction sites, the bill was vetoed by President Gerald R. Ford. Later, with Jimmy Carter as president, labor confidently attempted to pass the legislation again, only to come up a few votes short in the Democratic-controlled House of Representatives. In 1978, labor again moved for a comprehensive Labor Law Reform Bill, endorsed by Carter, only to have it blocked by a Republican filibuster in the Senate. The bill had been designed to reverse labor defeats in the workforce by simplifying procedures for representation elections under the National Labor Relations Board (NLRB), by increasing the number of members of the board in order to speed up the processing of unfair labor charges, and by increasing penalties against employers found guilty of unfair labor practices.

These labor defeats came as union membership was declining. In order to stem the diminishing clout, labor chose to increase political activity at the expense of decreasing union membership. The size of labor's political lobbying force increased, as did political action committee (PAC) activities. This new aggressiveness at the end of the decade ushered in a period of instability and conflict for labor unions. The notion of unions collecting dues from members and then using much of these funds for political activities rather than on member support alienated not only some union members but also business executives. Citing already low-wage foreign labor competition, corporations felt emboldened in rolling back wages and opposing unions at home, as well as shipping jobs overseas.

Impact The realities of global competition, with the ability for manufacturers to relocate factories to countries with significantly lower labor costs because of global access to finances, brought about a significant decline in union membership. As factories began closing in the Rust Belt region, nonunion high-tech jobs in computers and electronics began to emerge in the Sun Belt and suburban regions of some major cities. The only area to see union growth was public sector jobs. Labor also began to see its political clout diminish within the Democratic Party.

Subsequent Events With the election of Ronald Reagan in 1980, labor was faced with the wave of conservatism that would increase the rate of decline for unions in the country. In addition to firing thousands of airline traffic controllers who went on strike early in his administration, Reagan appointed an unsympathetic NLRB, which, within the first two years, reversed twenty-nine NLRB precedential decisions that had favored labor. It was clear that business had been given the green light to "bash unions," according to a *Business Week* report of the time. The heyday of American labor was clearly coming to an end.

Further Reading

Breecher, Jeremy, and Tim Costello. "Labor's Day: The Challenge Ahead." *The Nation*, September 21, 1998.

Brody, David, ed. *The American Labor Movement.* New York: Harper & Row, 1971.

Crenson, Matthew A., and Benjamin Ginsberg. *Downsizing Democracy.* Baltimore: Johns Hopkins University Press, 2002.

Divine, Robert, et al. Rev. 6th ed. *America Past and Present.* New York: Longman, 2003.

Gershman, Carl. *The Foreign Policy of American Labor.* Beverly Hills, Calif.: Sage Publications, 1975.

Lopez, Steven Henry. *Reorganizing the Rust Belt.* Berkeley: University of California Press, 2004.

Smith, Jim. "The AFL-CIO's Last Cold Warrior." *Z Magazine*, July, 1995.

Raymond J. Gonzales

See also Automobiles; Business and economy in the United States; Chávez, César; Equal Employment Opportunity Act of 1972; Hard Hat Riot of 1970; Income and wages in the United States; International trade of the United States; Japan and North America; McGovern, George; Mexico and the United States; Oil embargo of 1973-1974; Unemployment in the United States; Unions in Canada; Women in the workforce.

■ United Nations

Identification International organization
Date Established in 1945
Place Headquartered in New York City

During the 1970's, the Cold War framed many issues at the forefront of the United Nations' agenda. The United States and its allies often found themselves at odds in the organization with the former Soviet Union and its allies.

During the decade of the 1970's, the United States was represented in the United Nations by a series of high-profile ambassadors. Between 1971 and 1973, future president George H. W. Bush was President Richard M. Nixon's choice for U.N. ambassador; Daniel Patrick Moynihan, a diplomat, academic, and later, a distinguished New York state senator, served as ambassador to the organization from 1975 to 1976; and civil rights leader Andrew Young served as U.N. ambassador under the Carter administration. The U.N. secretary-general during this time was Kurt Waldheim of Austria, who replaced Burma's U Thant in 1972 and served two terms until 1981, after which he was replaced by Javier Pérez de Cuéllar. Waldheim's reign in the United Nations later proved controversial. At the time that he served, it generally was not known that he had been accused of collaborating with the Nazis and had served as a lieutenant in the German army during World War II.

Extending Help to the Developing World If the 1970's was a time of progress for the United Nations on a number of fronts—economic, social, and peacekeeping—it was also one of growing confrontation in a politically and ideologically divided world. U.N. member states were polarized by the Cold War and generally fell into either the Western camp, headed by the United States, or the Soviet camp, headed by the Soviet Union. The Cold War, then, became the defining backdrop to most of the United Nations' actions during this decade.

By 1970, the United Nations had added as member states countries in Asia and Africa that had gained independence from their colonial powers in prior decades. The United Nations is generally hailed as having championed and facilitated the decolonization process from its inception in 1945. Many of these developing countries gravitated naturally to the Soviet camp, and all of them fell into what had come to be called the G-77, or Group of 77, a network of former colonies that banded together in the global arena to further their particular concerns. These concerns included economic development, attractive trade and aid terms from the developed world, and relief from debt, among other issues.

The United Nations Conference on Trade and Development (UNCTAD) was created by a General Assembly resolution in 1964 and served through the 1970's as a forum for the developing world to better its terms of trade with developed world countries. In a similar vein, in 1974, the G-77 called for the creation of a New International Economic Order (NIEO) that would further the economic needs and interests of the developing world in a global economic order that they claimed was set up to benefit the developed world. They charged that this unfair global economic order included fiscal and monetary organizations headed by the International Monetary Fund (IMF) and the World Bank.

Another major occurrence during this time was the debt crisis facing G-77 countries. Created in the 1970's by the confluence of the heavy borrowing of financial capital by these countries and the global oil crisis, the debt crisis necessitated negotiations by the United Nations and IMF, along with the United States and other creditor countries, to come up with debt repayment plans.

The United Nations responded to other problems facing the developing world with a series of international conferences throughout the 1970's, examining issues such as the environment, population, food, women's rights, human settlements, employment, desertification, and health. These conferences underlined the growing importance of the developing world to the United Nations and its agenda.

During this decade and indeed during most of the period of the Cold War, the G-77 was able to use tensions between the United States and the Soviet

Pope John Paul II bows before the United Nations General Assembly in 1979. (AP/Wide World Photos)

New Members Admitted to the United Nations During the 1970's

Year	Country
1970	Fiji
1971	Bahrain, Bhutan, Oman, Qatar, United Arab Emirates
1973	Bahamas, Federal Republic of Germany (West Germany), German Democratic Republic (East Germany)
1974	Bangladesh, Grenada, Guinea-Bissau
1975	Cape Verde, Comoros, Mozambique, Papua New Guinea, Sao Tome and Principe, Suriname
1976	Angola, Samoa, Seychelles
1977	Djibouti, Vietnam
1978	Dominica, Solomon Islands
1979	St. Lucia

Union to gain leverage for its demands. On many occasions, countries in the group, such as India, began to side more heavily and clearly with the Soviets on issues coming before the General Assembly and reaped economic and military rewards from the Soviets. Those that sided with the United States and its allies, such as Pakistan, also were rewarded with military and development assistance.

Apartheid, the Environment, the Middle East Apartheid in South Africa was another issue the United Nations tackled during the decade, with the United States, Great Britain, and France cooperating in 1977 in approving a Security Council-backed arms embargo as part of ongoing sanctions against the apartheid government. Indeed, the imposition of U.N.-sponsored sanctions on South Africa and the resulting fall of apartheid in the early 1990's could be viewed as one arena in which the developed and developing countries worked together to achieve a single goal.

The first U.N. conference addressing environmental issues was the United Nations Conference on the Human Environment, held in Stockholm, Sweden, in 1972. It made recommendations on issues ranging from natural resource management to pollution. It also established the United Nations Environment Program (UNEP) to monitor global environmental conditions.

Many of the security and peacekeeping concerns that the United Nations and United States were consumed with during this decade were in the Middle East. In 1973, after Egypt and Syria's attack on Israel, the Security Council authorized a United Nations Emergency Force (UNEF II) to supervise a cease-fire and act as a buffer between the two sides. All parties involved agreed that UNEF II was helpful in negotiating a peace settlement that culminated in the Camp David Accords between Israel and Egypt in 1978. In 1975, the U.N. General Assembly also voted to adopt Resolution 3237, conferring the status of observer to the Palestine Liberation Organization (PLO) in the Assembly and in other international U.N.-sponsored conferences. Since that time, the U.N. General Assembly has served as the forum for numerous diplomatic battles between the Israelis, the PLO, and their respective global allies.

Impact The decade of the 1970's was a critical one to the diplomatic directions that the United Nations took in later decades. It was one in which Cold War concerns reigned supreme, the G-77 established itself as a formidable group, and the concerns of the developing world took center stage.

Further Reading

Bennett, LeRoy, and James K. Oliver. *International Organizations: Principles and Issues.* 7th ed. Upper Saddle River, N.J.: Prentice Hall, 2002. This comprehensive volume examines and analyzes the activities of a number of important international governmental and nongovernmental organizations, focusing particularly on the evolution and workings of the United Nations. Covers its organization, structure, and operations, including critical and controversial issues like U.N. peacekeeping forces, human rights, and collective security.

Claude, Inis L., Jr. *Swords into Ploughshares: The Problems and Progress of International Organization.* 4th ed. New York: Random House, 1964. A classic work on the origin of the U.N. system and an examination of the various organs of the United Nations.

Garthoff, Raymond. *Détente and Confrontation.* Rev. ed. Washington, D.C.: Brookings Institution, 1994. This lengthy volume serves to explain diplomatic negotiations and various crises of the 1970's through the lens of U.S.-Soviet relations.

Jones, Bartlett C. *Flawed Triumphs: Andy Young at the United Nations.* Lanham, Md.: University Press of America, 1996. Details Andrew Young's tenure as secretary-general at the United Nations from 1977 to 1979.

Peterson, M. J. *The General Assembly in World Politics.* Boston: Unwin Hyman, 1986. Provides an in-depth look at the structure and function of the U.N. General Assembly.

Tinaz Pavri

See also Africa and the United States; Camp David Accords; China and the United States; Cold War; Energy crisis; Europe and North America; Foreign policy of Canada; Foreign policy of the United States; International trade of Canada; International trade of the United States; Israel and the United States; Japan and North America; Middle East and North America; Soviet Union and North America.

■ Up with People

Identification An organization that sponsored traveling youth troupes and uplifting song-and-dance performance events

Date Founded in 1965

Through their high-energy, easy-listening, upbeat music, the traveling youth troupes, or casts, promoted national moral rearmament, renewed patriotism, and a positive outlook on the United States. These values contrasted with the antiestablishment rhetoric, increasing secularism, racial unrest, hard-edged music, and leftist, antiwar politics of the 1960's and 1970's.

Up with People was founded in 1965 and operated as loosely organized local performance choirs until incorporated as a national educational and nonprofit organization in 1968. The phrase "Up with People" expressed the group's convictions, served as the title of its popular theme song, and was the name of the organization.

In the late 1960's, local and national traveling troupes of young people, most between seventeen and twenty-six years old, performed choreographed songs especially written for Up with People in such community venues as gymnasiums and auditoriums. By the 1970's, the organization was earning thirty million dollars per year and had five distinct, 150-member international casts touring the globe as goodwill ambassadors and recording albums of music. Both the American casts and the international casts were assigned accommodations with host families in the communities in which they performed in the hope of promoting goodwill and international understanding within those communities.

Up with People helped restore a positive spirit at the 1972 Munich Olympics following the shooting of the Israeli athletes, visited Northern Ireland during the tensions of 1974, was one of the first youth groups invited to the newly opened China in 1978, and headlined four Super Bowl halftime shows, including the memorable 1976 Super Bowl X American bicentennial production. The group also headlined Super Bowls XIV, XVI, and XX.

Impact More than twenty thousand young Up with People performers from seventy-nine countries traveled, studied, and visited with host families in thirty-eight countries following the group's founding. The group was one of several forces and organizations that countered the negative cultural and political feelings of the 1960's and 1970's. Ultimately, the group helped American youth appreciate and adopt traditional values in a turbulent time.

Subsequent Events Up with People was the first international youth group invited to the Soviet Union, in 1988. In the late 1990's, financial difficulties forced the casts to postpone touring for several years. The organization subsequently was revived in 2003 as the Worldsmart Leadership Program, with less emphasis on musical performance and increased emphasis on study, the development of leadership skills, and the promotion of international understanding. Several multinational, multicultural casts still travel throughout the United States, Canada, Europe, Japan, and Latin America.

Further Reading

Aven, Paula. "A Lively Organization: CEO Wants to Recharge Up with People." *Denver Business Journal,* January 22, 1999.

Sweeny, Patrick. "Up with People Getting Ready for a Comeback." *Denver Business Journal*, November 29, 2002.

Gordon Neal Diem

See also Bicentennial celebration; Hippies; Munich Olympics terrorism; Music; Olympic Games of 1972; Religion and spirituality in the United States.

■ Updike, John

Identification American novelist, poet, and essayist
Born March 18, 1932; Shillington, Pennsylvania

During the 1970's, Updike's fictional focus on the disintegration of middle-class marriages gained him a popular following and critical respect. He linked sexual infidelities with the demise of American religious faith and moral values.

Achieving fame with *Couples* in 1968, John Updike moved into the 1970's as a provocative narrator of American middle-class suburban life. Sexual promiscuity provides plot interest and thematic significance in his fiction. Stories about the Maples written throughout the decade fictionalize his own approaching marital breakup. First appearing in *Museums and Women* (1972), the Maples stories are collected for the 1979 publication *Too Far to Go: The Maples Stories*. Primarily focused on discord, the stories also affirm the ordinary fabric of married life. In these stories, however, critics noted a stylistic directness missing in his more elaborately metaphorical works.

In 1970, Updike showed a different novelistic approach in *Bech: A Book*, his witty story collection featuring a middle-aged Jewish novelist. In *Rabbit Redux* (1971), he returned to the central character of his famed *Rabbit Run* (1960) and narrated marital discord against a background of national unrest. *Buchanan Dying*, a closet drama, appeared in 1974 to lukewarm critical reception. Returning to fiction, he produced *A Month of Sundays* (1975), detailing the spiritual crisis of the Reverend Tom Marshfield, and a book of collected essays, *Picked-Up Pieces* (1975).

Impressions from a State Department that visit he made to African countries in 1973 figure prominently in *The Coup* (1978). *Marry Me: A Romance* appeared in 1976. His fourth collection of poems, *Tossing and Turning*, was published in 1977; the poems resemble his 1970's fiction in their sexual frankness and confessional tone. The last two years of the decade saw the publication of the Maples stories and a short-story collection titled *Problems* (1979).

Between the stories written in the late 1960's and early 1970's and those written near the end of the decade, a noticeable shift in tone occurs. The earlier stories' protagonists yearn for the lost innocence of youth; the later characters long for contentment in marriage. Updike carried forward his concerns with fidelity, infidelity, and quests for religious faith in his fictional publications of the next decade.

Impact John Updike's 1970's fiction led some critics to suggest that he made an American epic out of sex and guilt. He wrote these narratives during the decade of the countercultural revolution, and while such novels as *Couples* gained notoriety for sexual frankness, they also called attention to the loss of a moral center in the lives of affluent suburbanites. Although his characters do not openly rebel against American culture, their inability to form lasting relationships reflects a disillusionment mirroring their revolutionary counterparts.

Further Reading

Detweiler, Robert. *John Updike*. Rev. ed. Boston: Twayne, 1984.
MacNaughton, William R., ed. *Critical Essays on John Updike*. Boston: G. K. Hall, 1980.

Bes Stark Spangler

See also Literature in the United States; Poetry; Sexual revolution.

V

■ Van Halen

Identification American rock band
Date Formed in 1974

Eddie Van Halen's self-taught virtuoso guitar work, combined with dynamic lead vocalist David Lee Roth's showmanship, set the stage for Van Halen to become one of the most popular and influential bands of the late 1970's and early 1980's.

The Netherlands-born Van Halen brothers, Alex and Eddie, immigrated to the United States with their family in 1967. Their father, Jan Van Halen, was a Dutch bandleader and clarinet player, and the two boys took classical music lessons until their early teens. Once in the United States, they made the switch to rock and roll. Eddie started out playing drums, while Alex played guitar, but the two soon switched instruments and started putting together a band. The brothers were joined by flamboyant vocalist David Lee Roth and bass player Michael Anthony. The new band was initially called Mammoth but changed its name to Van Halen in 1974 when band members found out the first name was already in use.

Van Halen played hundreds of shows throughout Southern California and developed a small following in bars and nightclubs. They started out performing covers of popular songs, but as their fame increased, they were able to work more and more original material into the act. They started to attract the attention of record company executives. Their 1977 demo was financed by Gene Simmons, of KISS fame, who saw them perform and recommended the band to Warner Bros., where they were signed by Mo Ostin and Ted Templeman.

The band's debut album, the self-titled *Van Halen*, was released in 1978. Its first single, "Runnin' with the Devil," reached only eighty-four on the *Billboard* pop singles chart, and the follow up, a cover of the Kink's classic "You Really Got Me," barely broke through the Top 40 to reach number thirty-six. Nevertheless, based on strong word of mouth, touring, and radio support, the album went gold in three months and platinum in five. The next year, the band followed up with *Van Halen II*. This album contained "Dance the Night Away," which became Van Halen's first top-twenty single.

Impact Eddie Van Halen changed the way electric guitar was played, and the band set the bar higher for the hard-rock and heavy-metal artists that followed in the 1980's and 1990's.

Subsequent Events Three albums followed *Van Halen II* in quick succession: *Women and Children First*

Guitarist Eddie Van Halen performs with his band in Toronto in 1979. (Patrick Harbron/Landov)

(1980), *Fair Warning* (1981), and *Diver Down* (1982). However, it was not until 1984, with the album titled *1984*, that the band would reach superstardom. By then, David Lee Roth's burgeoning solo career had caused stress within the band, and Sammy Hagar replaced him as lead singer in 1985.

Further Reading

Chilvers, C. J. *The Van Halen Encyclopedia.* Lincoln, Nebr.: Writers Club Press, 2001.

Leonard, Hal. *"Guitar World" Presents Van Halen.* Milwaukee: Hal Leonard, 1997.

Prown, Pete, and H. P. Newquist. *Legends of Rock Guitar: The Essential Reference of Rock's Greatest Guitarists.* Milwaukee, Wis.: Hal Leonard, 1997.

P. S. Ramsey

See also Aerosmith; Cooper, Alice; Hard rock and heavy metal; Heart; KISS; Led Zeppelin; Music; Pink Floyd; Queen; Radio; Rush.

■ Variety shows

Definition Television programs made up of different kinds of acts, such as comedy skits, songs, and dance numbers

The television variety show of the 1970's continued the entertainment tradition enjoyed in previous decades by fans of the vaudeville stage show. They offered television viewers humor and music as well as insight into contemporary events and figures.

The television variety show is a technological variation of old-time vaudeville—stage entertainment that presented songs, dancing, magic acts, comedic skits, and sketches. Comedians and singers already popular for their work in other media were immediate draws on television and reached larger audiences in one evening than they ever could have on stage or even in film theaters.

The "flagship" of variety shows, *The Ed Sullivan Show*, started in 1948 under the name *The Toast of the Town* and set the standard for the 1970's variety show, even though its last broadcast was in 1971. Other shows that started before the decade but continued into the early and middle years of the 1970's were *The Dean Martin Show*, *Hee Haw*, *The Johnny Cash Show*, *The Red Skelton Show*, and *Rowan and Martin's Laugh-In*. These programs typically featured musical performances if the show's host was a singer and comedy when the host was a comedian.

The 1970's began to outgrow the desire for relevance that had powered many shows in the 1960's, such as the Smothers Brothers' controversial and irreverent program. While the comedy in the 1970's variety shows was sharper and more reality-based than that of earlier shows, there was still a decided bias toward the downright silly and ridiculous. For example, *Hee Haw* had blackouts, running gags that bordered on the maniacal, and one-liners with the banal humor of a ten-year-old jokester. *Rowan and Martin's Laugh-In* was silly, too, but its blackouts, sketches, and one-liners, delivered sometimes by the most unexpected celebrity—for example, when President Richard M. Nixon somberly said "Sock it to me?"—gave it a tremendous following during its five-year run.

Emphasis on Music and New Headliners Some variety shows were aimed at music lovers. *The Lawrence Welk Show*, which started in 1955, provided old-fashioned melodic dance tunes with which the audience was familiar, sung and played by competent, well-rehearsed musicians. Very popular, especially with middle-aged and older Americans, the show ran until 1971, followed by years in syndication. Popular singers and singing acts such as Julie Andrews, Tony Orlando and Dawn, the Captain and Tennille, and Andy Williams brought more up-to-date and popular music to the shows. The variety shows that emphasized music often spawned "spin-offs," such as *Donny and Marie*—the Osmond siblings who got their start after appearing on Andy Williams's show in the late 1960's and early 1970's. *The Sonny and Cher Comedy Hour* led to *Cher* and *The Sonny Comedy Hour*, while *The Captain and Tennille Show* grew out of the popularity of the duo's recordings. Julie Andrews, a British musical-comedy stage star known from her appearances in several popular films, offered high-quality singing and comedy with her show, which lasted one season.

Some African American artists also got their own variety shows. Comics especially got opportunities that had not been available earlier. Flip Wilson mounted a highly successful show that won an Emmy Award, while Redd Foxx and Sammy Davis, Jr., had short runs on television. One of the few African American women to get her own show was Barbara McNair, who had a short-lived syndicated show. Richard Pryor, considered one of the best comedians of all time, did five shows, but his comedic material

Sister-and-brother act Marie and Donny Osmond starred in one of the most popular television variety shows of the 1970's. (AP/Wide World Photos)

proved too controversial for the network and he chose not to continue.

Blockbuster Shows In 1975, the long-running *Saturday Night Live* started, broadcast at a late hour that freed the comics to try routines that would have been censored in prime time. The program was a showpiece for up-and-coming comedians that over the years produced stars such as Bill Murray, Jane Curtin, the Muppets, Eddie Murphy, Chevy Chase, Steve Martin, and countless others.

The Carol Burnett Show was another show that became an all-time favorite variety show with viewers. It was first telecast in 1967 and ran until 1979. It successfully drew viewers on Saturday nights, a major accomplishment since traditionally people did not stay at home on Saturday nights to watch television. A mixture of comedy sketches and occasional musical numbers, the show had something for just about everybody, and viewers enjoyed the gorgeous and outrageous costumes and a cast that worked well together and clearly enjoyed one another.

Impact Television variety shows enlightened audiences about issues of the day in a humorous, stimulating, and subtle way. They introduced young or unknown artists to vast audiences, paving the way for careers that, for many, lasted long after the 1970's ended. Most important, they provided generally inoffensive, intelligent, even nourishing entertainment to a generation of Americans (and others throughout the world) whose lives were unsettled by the Vietnam War, the civil rights upheavals, and the Watergate, oil, and Iranian hostage crises, as well as other political, social, and cultural transfigurations of the era.

Cable television networks such as Home Box Office (HBO) on cable television as well as increasing competition for audiences from specialty channels and commercial-free motion pictures made variety shows, with their familiar format of songs and skits and guest stars, seem stale. Therefore, by the end of the decade, most of the hit variety shows of the 1970's had disappeared from the air, with the notable exception of *Saturday Night Live.*

Further Reading

America A to Z: People, Places, Customs, and Culture. Pleasantville, N.Y.: Readers Digest, 1997. Articles on various aspects of American culture; covers *The Carol Burnett Show, Saturday Night Live,* and the vaudeville genre.

Brooks, Tim, and Earle Marsh. *The Complete Directory of Prime Time Network and Cable TV Shows.* 8th ed. New York: Ballantine, 2003. This source lists all the television shows broadcast since 1946. Casts, actual broadcast dates and times, and critiques and commentaries inform readers about each show.

Shales, Tom, and J. A. Miller. *Live from New York.* New York: Little, Brown, 2002. Provides a history of the variety show *Saturday Night Live.*

Jane L. Ball

See also *Carol Burnett Show, The*; Comedians; Martin, Steve; Nixon, Richard M.; Pryor, Richard; *Saturday Night Live*; Sitcoms; Television in the United States.

■ Video games

Definition Games played using an electronic device with a visual display

During the 1970's, the video game came of age and began to be mass-produced, marketed, and played by large numbers of people.

Prior to the 1970's, the few video games that were available were played only by hobbyists, game designers, and experimenters. During the 1970's, however, video games came into their own, both as an entertainment device and as a successful business enterprise. Many "firsts" in video game design, development, and marketing occurred.

Video games were designed for use in several venues. Arcade games were coin operated and placed in public spaces such as bars and shopping malls. Games for the home, in turn, were either battery-operated and handheld or managed from a tabletop console with connection to a larger video display, usually a television set.

Pioneers and Early Games In the early 1970's, a few pioneers, such as Ralph Baer and Nolan Bushnell, developed games in their spare time. Magnavox purchased the rights to a hockey video game from Baer in 1970, while Bushnell was refining a game called *Computer Space* in which a flying saucer and a spaceship battled. It was designed as a coin-operated game.

Many of the most famous video game companies were founded during this period. In 1972, Bushnell formed Atari in a room in his home. "Atari" is a Japanese word that means much the same as the term "check" in chess. Magnavox, known as a television manufacturer, began promoting its *Odyssey* video game in the early 1970's. The *Odyssey* game console was inspired by the work of Baer. The game, marketed for home use, allowed for a variety of tennis-like, hockeylike, and maze games. By the end of 1972, 100,000 units had been sold at about $150 each.

The classic game *Pong* was originally rejected by Bally/Midway. Therefore, its designer, Bushnell, began marketing it independently as a coin-operated game. Reportedly the games often malfunctioned simply because they were too full of quarters, attesting to their popularity.

Pong, as well as similar games called "*Pong*-clones," became popular in the mid-1970's, with about 100,000 in use by 1974. Another video game producer, Exidy, was founded in 1974 and first released *TV Pinball*. Atari expanded with the acquisition of Kee Games, which was producing games very similar to those of Atari. A problem of potential copyright infringement—a fairly common problem among game producers and designers—was solved by the companies' merging.

Mass Marketing and Concerns over Violence By 1975, Sears began to market Atari games widely. In the fall of 1975, Sears had sold all the *Pong* games that Atari could manufacture. Sears reportedly made forty million dollars in gross sales, and Atari made a three-million-dollar profit. Coleco introduced the Telstar Arcade for home use in 1975. By the end of 1975, more than fifty companies were manufacturing video games.

Also in the mid-1970's, *Breakout*, another video game that became a classic, reportedly was created in four days by Steve Jobs and Steve Wozniak—men later made famous in the development of Apple Computer. *Breakout* became the number-one game of the year.

In 1976, Warner Communications purchased Atari from Bushnell for $28 million. The company had been started only four years before with an initial investment of less than one thousand dollars. This serves as just one example of the rapid growth of the video game industry in the 1970's.

Ethical and Legal Battles Ethical controversy began to arise around the violent content of video games by the mid-1970's. An event that brought the issue to the public's attention was the release by Exidy of a coin-operated game based on the film *Death Race 2000* (1975). In this game, motor vehicles were steered over people in order to obtain points. It quickly was removed from the market, but many violent games continued to be developed.

With so many games being designed and many having similar features, there were numerous legal battles over ownership. Magnavox and Atari fought such a battle for three years over the similarities of Atari's *Pong* and Magnavox's *Odyssey*. The case was settled by making Atari a "prepaid licensee" of Magnavox for a fee of $700,000.

The Late 1970's By the late 1970's, the industry was beginning to identify and honor its pioneers. Bushnell and Baer were recognized for their historic contributions at the Gametronic Conference in San Francisco in 1977. Handheld video games were making as much as $22 million by this time.

In 1978, *Space Invaders*, another game that became a classic, was introduced by the Taito Corporation of Japan. *Space Invaders* became so popular that it began to move from bars and pool halls into mainstream restaurants, film theaters, and malls.

In 1979, *3D Tic Tac Toe*—reportedly the first game designed by a female game designer, Carol Shaw—was introduced. Also in 1979, a game called *Lunar Lander*, which allowed the player to attempt to pilot a lunar module, was not popular at first but used vector technology, which was a new innovation. It was later renamed *Asteroids* and became extremely popular with adult players.

Impact The 1970's served as the precocious "childhood" of the video game era. Hardware innovations occurring in the 1970's included handheld games with a liquid crystal display (LCD), the use of "dedicated chip" technology for home video games, the trackball, games with technology to keep a "high score" table, membrane keyboards, and vector display technology. Moreover, many classic games that became well known to game aficionados were developed in this decade. Hundreds of companies and games were created. Some survived only briefly; others disappeared in mergers. Competition among game developers and producers was fierce.

Controversies begun in the 1970's continued in later decades, including debates over the ethics of violent games and whether gaming makes children sedentary. Some of the classic games of this decade made a comeback a generation later, as youths who did not live in the 1970's became interested in video game history.

Further Reading

Burnham, Van. *Supercade: A Visual History of the Video Game Age, 1971-1984*. Boston: MIT Press, 2003. Provides chronologically organized capsule descriptions of games and essays as well as screen shots.

DeMaria, Rusel, and Johnny L. Wilson. *High Score! The Illustrated History of Electronic Games*. New York: McGraw Hill, 2002. Gives a well-illustrated history.

Kent, Stephen L. *The Ultimate History of Video Games: From "Pong" to Pokemon—The Story Behind the Craze That Touched Our Lives and Changed the World*. New York: Crown, 2001. Considered one of the best histories of the video game era; contains many little-known facts.

Wolf, Mark J. P. *The Medium of the Video Game*. Austin: University of Texas Press, 2002. Defines "video game" and studies it as a medium of popular culture.

Mary C. Ware

See also Apple Computer; Atari; Business and the economy in the United States; Computers; Inventions; LED and LCD screens; Microprocessors; Science and technology; Toys and games.

■ Videocassette recorders (VCRs)

Definition Devices that permit home viewers to record television shows

Date Introduced to the U.S. consumer market in 1976

The availability of VCRs allowed home viewers to tape television programming for the first time, as well as watch movies on video cassette, thereby fundamentally changing viewer expectations and entertainment industry practices.

In the 1970's, videocassette recorders and cable television changed the face of television forever. Pioneered in Japan, VCRs had been used in industrial, broadcast, and educational settings as early as 1966, but commercial video recorders did not become a significant part of the home-viewing landscape until a decade later. Sony's first commercial model appeared on the market in 1970, but because of price (more than one thousand dollars) and consumer skepticism, this VCR was not a success. Modification resulted in the first successful consumer VCR, Sony's Betamax, in 1976. Though expense remained an issue for the average consumer, prices soon dropped to affordable levels. JVC marketed its competing VHS format in 1976, and this type of VCR soon effectively dominated the market, with prices dropping to compete with Betamax at approximately four hundred dollars.

VCRs were capable of many uses. Previously, home viewers were restricted to the scheduling and censorship policies of local stations and networks. Consumers could "time-shift," that is, record a program and watch it later, and they could watch a program on one station while taping a competing show on another station. Broadcasters accustomed to controlling television scheduling were resistant at first, some even insisting that "record" buttons be removed from machines. VCR owners did not merely time-shift their programming but also added favorites to their personal libraries. Moreover, bootlegging, or copying videotaped material for others, was known to occur. As motion pictures became available for sale or rental, the copyright issue became ever murkier.

Eventually, the television and film industries reached compromises that not only allayed their fears of video "piracy" but also increased their revenues while pleasing home viewers. The massive growth of video rental stores allowed studios an additional, very successful "window" for marketing their product. The entertainment industry's awareness of a burgeoning collectors' market provided another satisfactory compromise: Expensive videocassettes of films were drastically reduced in price for purchase for what came to be known as the "sell-through" market. Finally, one of the biggest, and undoubtedly least expected, boons to the VCR industry came in the form of prerecorded pornographic films, which allowed people to watch X-rated fare in the privacy of their own homes, eliminating the stigma of going to see them in public and making film censorship much more difficult to impose.

Impact VCRs drastically altered the delivery of entertainment in the United States by vastly expanding home viewers' options, freeing them from the constraints of network and local programming, and forcing the television and motion picture industries to change day-to-day operations and their basic business philosophy.

Further Reading

Cohen, Henry B., with Bruce Apar. *The Home Video Survival Guide: How to Understand and Use Home Video, Electronic Games, and Game Computers.* New York: American Photographic Books, 1983.

Smith, Wendy A. *Video Fundamentals: A Practical Handbook for the Entry-Level Video User.* Englewood Cliffs, N.J.: Prentice-Hall, 1983.

Charles Lewis Avinger

See also Advertising; Censorship in Canada; Censorship in the United States; Communications in Canada; Communications in the United States; Film in Canada; Film in the United States; Home Box Office (HBO); Inventions; Pornography; Science and technology; Television in Canada; Television in the United States.

■ Vietnam Veterans Against the War

Identification Activist organization
Date Formed in 1967

Vietnam Veterans Against the War (VVAW) brought the credibility of combat veterans to the antiwar movement, addressed painful truths about the war, and provided veterans with psychological help.

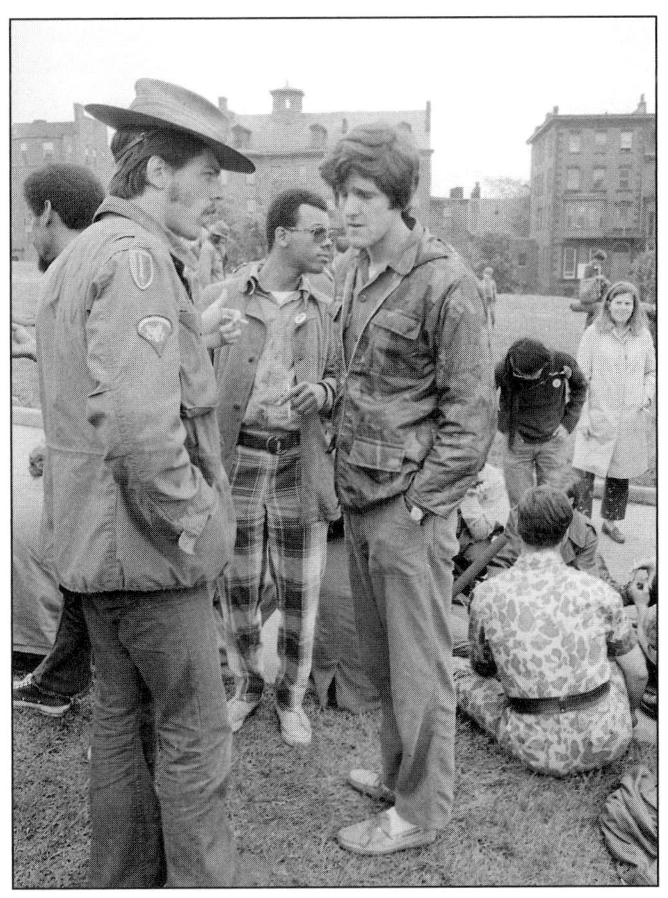

John F. Kerry (center), a future presidential candidate, talks with fellow members of Vietnam Veterans Against the War before a march in 1971. (AP/Wide World Photos)

VVAW was formed in New York City in 1967 and gained national attention in the early 1970's. Events such as the Kent State massacre in 1970 and President Richard M. Nixon's escalation of the war led VVAW to take action, starting with Operation Rapid American Withdrawal in 1970. This three-day march began in New Jersey and ended in Valley Forge, Pennsylvania, a site chosen in order to link Vietnam veterans to Revolutionary War soldiers. In early 1971, VVAW gathered in Detroit for the Winter Soldier Investigation. Participants discussed war crimes that veterans claimed they committed or observed; this set the stage for Operation Dewey Canyon III in April, 1971.

Dewey Canyon III took place in Washington, D.C., and was VVAW's defining event. Activities included testimony before the U.S. Congress and a memorial service for Vietnam casualties in Arlington National Cemetery. Former VVAW member John F. Kerry, later a U.S. senator and the Democratic presidential nominee in 2004, described the Winter Soldier Investigation to Congress in a speech that remained controversial in subsequent decades. A ceremony at the U.S. Capitol in which more than one thousand veterans disowned their medals and other service decorations was even more contentious.

In addition to antiwar activism, VVAW helped veterans heal psychologically. Gatherings called "rap groups" started in 1970 as forums for veterans to discuss experiences in Vietnam and on the homefront. The groups offered peer therapy at a time when many Americans avoided and stigmatized Vietnam veterans. Government and private counseling programs that followed the rap group model began appearing later in the 1970's.

VVAW remained a force for dissent in 1972 and 1973 by protesting at the Democratic and Republican National Conventions and during President Nixon's inauguration for a second term. The group also reached out to advocates for the rights of women, workers, and ethnic and racial minority groups.

When the Vietnam War ended in 1975, VVAW entered a phase with internal conflict over ideology and tactics. Membership and activity declined dramatically in the late 1970's, but the group survived and consistently opposed the U.S. government's post-Vietnam military actions.

Impact VVAW showed that peace activism was not confined to college campuses and kept pressure on a government that was simultaneously withdrawing from and escalating the Vietnam War. Some saw VVAW as patriotic; others saw it as treasonous and challenged the Winter Soldier Investigation testimony as well as the military records of VVAW members. In general, however, VVAW appears to have helped many veterans deal with their experiences during and after the war, both publicly and privately.

Further Reading

Hunt, Andrew E. *The Turning: A History of Vietnam Veterans Against the War.* New York: New York University Press, 1998.

Moser, Richard R. *The New Winter Soldiers: GI and Veteran Dissent During the Vietnam Era.* New Brunswick, N.J.: Rutgers University Press, 1996.

Ray Pence

See also Antiwar demonstrations; Cambodia invasion and bombing; Clemency for Vietnam draft evaders and deserters; *Coming Home*; Elections in the United States, 1972; Fall of Saigon; Kent State massacre; Nixon, Richard M.; POWs and MIAs; Vietnam War.

■ Vietnam War

Definition Armed conflict between communist and noncommunist forces in South Vietnam

Date United States involved from 1965 to 1975

After many frustrating years of attempting to maintain the existence of a noncommunist government in South Vietnam, the United States in 1973 agreed to end active participation in the war, and two years later, North Vietnam successfully unified all of Vietnam into a single communist country.

American involvement in Vietnam was an application of the Containment Policy, which was a longstanding commitment of U.S. foreign policy makers to stop the expansion of communism (also called Marxist-Leninism). Before 1954, the U.S. government financially supported French colonialism in Vietnam because Ho Chi Minh and other rebel leaders were dedicated communists. After 1954, Vietnam was "temporarily" divided into two countries, with the South having a noncommunist government and the North having a Marxist-Leninist system. The South Vietnamese confronted an insurgency of procommunist guerrilla fighters, called the Viet Cong.

Although most of the Viet Cong were poor peasants living in the South, many "volunteers" from the North were among the insurgents. Beginning in 1965, regular U.S. combat troops directly participated in the war, and U.S. bombers attacked North Vietnam on a massive scale.

In early 1968, the Viet Cong conducted large-scale offensive operations that convinced many Americans that the war was unwinnable. On March 31, President Lyndon B. Johnson announced the initiation of peace talks and a reduction in the bombing of the North. He also declared that he would not be a candidate in the presidential election of that year.

In May, peace negotiations began slowly in Paris. The Democrats nominated Hubert H. Humphrey, who hinted that he was not committed fully to defending South Vietnam's independence. Republican candidate Richard M. Nixon said that he had a plan for achieving an "honorable end" to the war but that he would not reveal its contents for fear of jeopardizing the Paris negotiations. Nixon's critics spoke despairingly of his "secret plan."

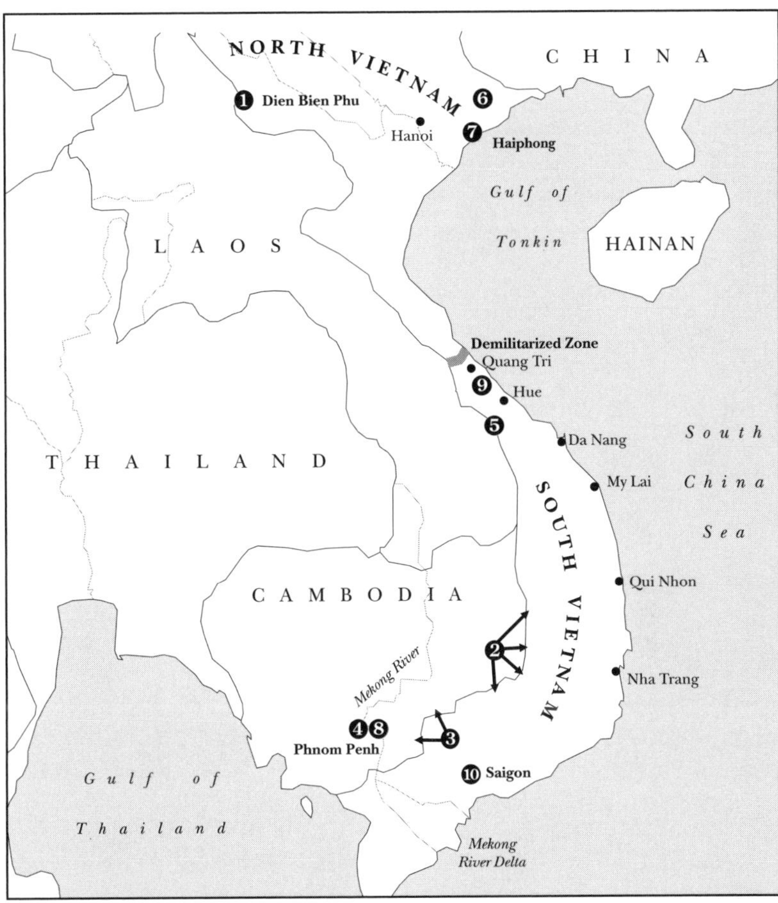

(1) France falls, 1954. (2) Tet Offensive, January, 1968. (3) Cambodian invasion, April-May, 1970. (4) Sihanouk falls, April, 1970. (5) Laotian incursion, February, 1971. (6) Areas of U.S. bombing, 1972. (7) Mining of Haiphong Harbor, May, 1972. (8) Lon Nol falls, April, 1975. (9) North Vietnamese offensive, spring, 1975. (10) South Vietnam surrenders, April 30, 1975.

Nixon's Vietnamization Policies When Nixon was inaugurated as president in January, 1969, public opinion was bitterly divided about the Vietnam issue. Approximately 550,000 U.S. troops were stationed in South Vietnam. About 33,000 American soldiers had already died in combat, and they were continuing to die at the rate of some 800 a month. Initially, the Nixon administration did not appear to depart significantly from the Vietnam policies of the last year of the Johnson administration. Adopting the label "Vietnamization," the new administration hoped to transfer most of the actual fighting from the Americans to the Republic of South Vietnamese, while continuing to provide financial and technological support for the war. In July, Nixon announced the so-called Nixon Doctrine, which supported extending the approach of Vietnamization throughout Asia. Nixon was not willing to abandon the long-standing goal of preserving a noncommunist government in South Vietnam. The North Vietnamese, in contrast, continued to demand the withdrawal of American troops from South Vietnam and the formation of a coalition government with the participation of the Viet Cong.

Nixon's most influential adviser was his assistant for national security, Henry Kissinger, a German-born professor of government at Harvard. From 1969 until 1972, Nixon and Kissinger's approach to Vietnamization included four main components. First, they tried to neutralize the domestic antiwar

Milestones in the Vietnam War During the 1970's

Year	*Date*	*Event*
1970	April 29-June 29	South Vietnamese troops invade Cambodia, pushing toward Viet Cong bases.
1971	February/March	South Vietnamese divisions enter Laos to attack enemy bases and unknowingly walk into a North Vietnamese trap. More than nine thousand South Vietnamese troops are killed or wounded and more than two-thirds of the South Vietnamese Army's armored vehicles are destroyed, as well as hundreds of U.S. helicopters and planes.
	November 12	President Richard M. Nixon announces that he will withdraw 45,000 troops from Vietnam by early 1972
1972	January	After the withdrawal of roughly two-thirds of American troops in two years, 133,000 U.S. servicemen remain in South Vietnam.
	March/April	North Vietnamese forces launch an aggressive attack and invasion of the South.
	July-September	The South, with U.S. air support, fights to recapture occupied territory and eventually retains control of the northern part of the Binh Dinh province.
	December 13	Peace talks in Paris between the North Vietnamese and the Americans break down.
1973	January 8	Peace talks resume in Paris.
	January 27	The Paris Peace Accords are signed by North Vietnam, South Vietnam, and the United States.
	March 30	The last American combat soldiers leave South Vietnam, although military advisers and Marines, who are protecting U.S. installations, remain.
1974	January	The North Vietnamese resupply and fortify their forces.
1975	January 6	The North Vietnamese take Phuoc Long City and the surrounding province, a violation of the Paris Peace Accords that produces no retaliation from the United States.
	March	Several North Vietnamese offensives succeed in capturing key cities and provinces in South Vietnam.
	April 27	Saigon is encircled by North Vietnamese troops.
	April 29	U.S. military helicopters begin an eighteen-hour evacuation of more than one thousand American civilians and almost seven thousand South Vietnamese refugees.
	April 30	Two U.S. Marines are killed in a rocket attack at Saigon's airport, becoming the last Americans to die in the Vietnam War. At dawn, the last Marines of the force guarding the U.S. embassy lift off. Hours later, North Vietnamese tanks roll into Saigon, ending the war.

movement by gradually withdrawing American troops. Second, they continued negotiations with both North Vietnam and the Soviet Union. Third, assuming that a "fourth-rate power" like North Vietnam would have a "breaking point," they accelerated the use of bombs and firepower in an effort to get Hanoi to make concessions at the bargaining table. The fourth component was the strengthening of the military and the government of the South Vietnamese Republic. Its army (or ARVN) was provided with the latest military equipment, improved training, and higher pay scales. ARVN forces were expanded to more than one million men. The country's air force became the fourth largest in the world.

As American troops withdrew from Vietnam, the morale declined among those who remained. With the growing antiwar movement at home, soldiers increasingly questioned whether they were fighting for a just cause. Racial tensions among soldiers were growing, with more and more incidents of "fraging," or attacks on officers by enlisted men. One government study found that about half of the American army personnel smoked marijuana, while one-fourth used stronger drugs such as heroin or opium.

Revelations about the My Lai massacre, in which more than two hundred Vietnamese civilians had been murdered in 1968, further inflamed passions. In 1970-1971, the courts-martial of Lieutenant William Calley and others kept the public from forgetting about the shocking incident. When Calley was sentenced to life imprisonment in March, 1971, many people thought that he was a scapegoat for a strategy of emphasizing body count. The widespread outcry prompted President Nixon to intervene. In August, Calley's sentence was reduced to twenty years, and three years later he was paroled for good behavior.

The Cambodian Incursion As early as the spring of 1969, Nixon ordered the bombing of border sanctuaries in Cambodia, which were used by North Vietnamese forces to launch attacks on South Vietnam. This controversial program was kept secret from the Congress and the American public for more than a year. However, the dropping of 110,000 tons of bombs succeeded only in driving the Viet Cong into other hiding places. In March, 1970, the U.S. supported a military coup in Cambodia, which was led by a pro-Western leader, General Lon Nol. In April, Nixon ordered a joint U.S.-ARVN military campaign in Cambodia with the objective of destroying Viet Cong bases. He spoke of the need to "show the enemy" that the United States was "still serious" in its opposition to communism in Southeast Asia.

Nixon defended the incursion in a nationalized televised speech, declaring that the world's most powerful nation could not act like a "pitiful helpless giant" without encouraging the "forces of totalitarianism and anarchy." The speech infuriated opponents of the war. A demonstration in Washington, D.C., attracted more than 100,000 people, and similar protests took place in most major cities. Students boycotted classes on hundreds of campuses, making it impossible for many universities to hold final examinations. On May 4, 1970, a peaceful protest at Kent State University in Ohio turned into a national tragedy. Members of the National Guard, nervous because of the earlier burning of a Reserve Officers' Training Corps (ROTC) building, fired on students, killing four and wounding ten others. Ten days later, in a confrontation at Jackson State University in Mississippi, police shot into a dormitory and killed two black students.

By the end of June, Nixon was obliged to pull all U.S. forces out of Cambodia without achieving his objectives. Most of the North Vietnamese troops had escaped and moved farther into Cambodia, where they increased their support for the Khmer Rouge, a radical organization of Cambodian communists dedicated to overthrowing Lon Nol's pro-U.S. government. Some historians believe that the dispersion of the North Vietnamese into the country helped the Khmer Rouge to acquire power, which would have tragic consequences a few years later.

Veterans' Response and the Pentagon Papers Antiwar demonstrations in the United States became larger and angrier in 1971. Vietnam Veterans Against the War (VVAW) were among the most vocal of the protesters. In Detroit, VVAW organizers held an investigation into the conduct of war, reporting a large number of atrocities and brutalities against Vietnamese civilians. On April 22, John F. Kerry, a spokesman for the VVAW, testified about the results of the investigation before a Senate committee hearing. Three days later, about 500,000 demonstrators arrived in Washington, D.C., to lobby the government against the war and threatened to shut down the government if Nixon did not end the war. Hundreds of veterans threw away their medals and ribbons. In early May, about forty thousand protesters blocked traffic and engaged in other acts of civil disobedience. Officials made more than twelve thousand arrests.

In June, *The New York Times* began to publish a secret study of the war, called the Pentagon Papers, which were leaked by researcher Daniel Ellsberg. The documents revealed that American policy makers had been highly skeptical about winning the war but had said otherwise in their public comments. When the Nixon administration tried to prevent their publication, the Supreme Court refused to support the administration's position. The Pentagon Papers encouraged people to question the government's credibility. A public opinion poll reported that 60 percent of the public believed that American entrance into the war had been a mistake and that 58 percent judged American policy to be immoral. However, opposition to the war was diffused by the continuing decrease of U.S. troops in Vietnam, which numbered less than 150,000 by the end of 1971.

The Paris Peace Accords During the presidential election year of 1972, Nixon and Kissinger continued to pursue a dual strategy of using military force while negotiating for a peace settlement. In the Easter Offensive of that year, approximately 120,000 North Vietnamese troops advanced within fifty miles of Saigon. By then, the United States had only 69,000 personnel and 10,000 combat troops in Vietnam, which meant that ARVN forces were virtually on their own. On May 8, faced with the prospects of a North Vietnamese victory, Nixon announced Operation Linebacker I, which included the heavy bombing of the North, the mining of Haiphong harbor, and a naval blockade. Although opposition to the war was growing, the majority of voters reacted unfavorably to Democratic candidate George McGovern's proposal to withdraw from the war without any further attempts to assist South Vietnam. Shortly before the elections in November, Kissinger announced that he believed that "peace is at hand." The announcement helped Nixon to win a landslide triumph.

After the election, however, the negotiations broke down, largely because the president of South Vietnamese, Nguyen Van Thieu, refused to consider any settlement that allowed North Vietnamese troops to stay in the South. On December 18, 1972,

American soldiers celebrate the end of U.S. involvement in the Vietnam War in 1973. (Library of Congress)

Nixon unleashed Linebacker II, often called the Christmas bombing, in which B-52 planes pounded both military and civilian targets of North Vietnam around the clock for twelve days. The two objectives of the massive bombings were to bring North Vietnamese negotiators back to the peace talks and to persuade Nguyen Van Thieu's government to compromise on terms for a cease-fire.

On January 23, 1973, Kissinger and Hanoi's senior negotiator, Le Duc Tho, initialed a peace settlement in Paris, and four days later, representatives of the four parties signed the formal peace accords. The terms included the withdrawal of all U.S. troops from Vietnam and the return of prisoners of war, both within sixty days. Although the agreement called for a cease-fire, it allowed the United States to continue to provide financial assistance and military hardware to South Vietnam, while it also permitted North Vietnamese troops to retain their strongholds in the South, a concession that constituted a major strategic threat to South Vietnamese survival. Secretary of State Kissinger was quoted as having said that his goal was to provide a "decent interval" before the fall of South Vietnam.

The Paris Peace Accords called for supervision of the cease-fire by an International Commission of Control and Supervision. The accords also provided for the establishment of a National Council of Reconciliation and Concord to organize and conduct elections in South Vietnam. On March 4, representatives from thirteen countries met in Paris and endorsed the settlement. By March 29, the exchange of the prisoners of war was complete, and the last of the American troops left to return home. Soon thereafter, however, both the South Vietnamese and Viet Cong violated the terms of the cease-fire, and fighting quickly resumed.

The Fall of South Vietnam Dispersed widely throughout the country, the South Vietnamese forces were stretched too thin to protect many strategic locations. Taking advantage of this situation, the Viet Cong and North Vietnamese soldiers expanded their control over outposts and hamlets in the Mekong Delta region. As the military situation deteriorated, the Watergate scandal made it impossible for the Nixon administration to persuade Congress to provide needed military supplies to the South Vietnamese. Angry about the continuing air campaign in Laos and Cambodia, Congress stopped all funding for the operations in June, 1973. Although the House of Representatives sustained Nixon's veto, public opinion compelled an end to the bombing.

In January, 1975, the North Vietnamese armies launched a large-scale offensive, and by the end of March, they controlled about two-thirds of the country. As the collapse of South Vietnam appeared to be near, Congress refused to authorize any additional military assistance, although it approved funds to evacuate Americans, as well as Vietnamese likely to face persecution.

On April 21, following a disastrous retreat by ARVN troops, President Nguyen Van Thieu resigned. On May 1, the Viet Cong took control of Saigon and soon renamed it Ho Chi Minh City. In a chaotic and confusing situation, U.S. helicopters evacuated Americans remaining in the city, along with 150,000 South Vietnamese. Lacking enough helicopters and time to evacuate all those wanting to leave, U.S. Marines had to beat back many desperate Vietnamese. The United States' longest war had ended in defeat.

Aftermath During the Vietnam War, about 56,800 Americans lost their lives, including 20,000 during Nixon's term of office. An additional 780 Americans were missing, and about 303,700 were seriously wounded. South Vietnam suffered about 254,300 troop deaths, while the deaths of North Vietnam and Viet Cong troops numbered about half a million. Between one and two million Vietnamese civilians died as a result of the war. The United States dropped about one million tons of bombs on North Vietnam and four million on South Vietnam, compared with two million tons of bombs dropped on Germany, Italy, and Japan during World War II.

In the aftermath of this costly and divisive war, Americans disagreed about why the richest country in the world had failed to prevail over a small nation composed mostly of poor peasants. Many supporters of the war blamed the media and the peace movement, and they argued that the military had been held back and not allowed to take advantage of its technological superiority. In contrast, critics of the war argued that policy makers had underestimated the force of Vietnamese nationalism and had misunderstood the dynamic nature of socialism. They further asserted that policy makers had harbored unrealistic and arrogant ideas about American military omnipotence. Regardless of their differing assessments, however, most Americans agreed that there should be "no more Vietnams."

Impact As a result of the war, Congress reasserted its authority over foreign policy. Congressional committees began to give greater scrutiny to executive requests for military budgets. In November, 1973, Congress enacted the War Powers Resolution over Nixon's veto. The law required the president to notify Congress within forty-eight hours of sending troops into a hostile region and required the president to withdraw the troops within sixty days unless Congress authorized them to remain. In the post-Vietnam years, Congress tended to be somewhat more skeptical about military interventions in other countries and covert operations by the Central Intelligence Agency (CIA).

Defeat in Vietnam did not mean an end to U.S. opposition to international communism. During the administration of President Gerald R. Ford, the United States continued to support authoritarian governments so long as they were anticommunist. This was true in South Korea, Taiwan, Iran, the Philippines, and much of Latin America. Even Jimmy Carter, who was president from 1977 to 1981, supported the Cold War consensus in places such as the Philippines and Iran, although he emphasized human rights and said he was not motivated by an "an inordinate fear of communism."

A large percentage of veterans were embittered by their experiences in Vietnam. Some resented the antiwar protesters and believed that the government had betrayed military personnel by not letting them fight to win. Other blamed the government for sacrificing the nation's youth in a useless or immoral conflict. Veterans frequently suffered from post-traumatic stress disorders. Beginning in the late 1970's, they suffered in disproportionate numbers from cancers and other illnesses. Most believed that Agent Orange, a widely used herbicide with dioxin, was the culprit, but it took the government more than a decade to recognize a linkage between the herbicide and the illnesses. In 1982, the unveiling of the Vietnam Veterans Memorial encouraged many veterans to believe that that the country was finally recognizing their heroic sacrifices.

Further Reading

Clodfelter, Mark. *The Limits of Airpower: The American Bombing of North Vietnam.* New York: Simon & Schuster, 1989. Demonstrates that the use of air power had great limitations in a guerrilla-type war.

Herring, George. *America's Longest War: The United States and Vietnam, 1950-1975.* 4th ed. New York: McGraw-Hill, 2001. An excellent textbook that includes the military, political, and diplomatic aspects of the war.

Hunt, Andrew. *The Turning: A History of Vietnam Veterans Against the War.* New York: New York University Press, 1999. Based on archives and interviews, the book tells about the motivations, activities, controversies, and influences of the disillusioned young men of an influential antiwar organization.

Isaacs, Arnold. *Vietnam Shadows: The War, Its Ghosts, and Its Legacy.* Baltimore: Johns Hopkins University Press, 1997. A former war correspondent's analysis of many aspects of the war, including "the Vietnam Syndrome," stories of soldiers missing in action (MIAs), and the conflicting memories and interpretations of the war.

Karnow, Stanley. *Vietnam: A History.* New York: Penguin, 1997. A standard and well-written account by a journalist who spent many of the war years in Vietnam.

Kimball, Jeffrey. *The Vietnam War Files: Uncovering the Secret History of Nixon-Era Strategy.* Lawrence: University Press of Kansas, 2003. Based on archival materials, Kimball argues that Nixon gave up the "madman theory" and that he and Kissinger cynically insisted on a peace that would give South Vietnam a "decent interval" for survival.

Stanton, Shelby. *The Rise and Fall of an American Army: U.S. Ground Troops in Vietnam, 1965-1973.* New York: Random House, 2003. An outstanding historical work of ground combat forces, battlefield by battlefield.

Takiff, Michael. *Brave Men, Gentle Heroes: Fathers and Sons in World War II and Vietnam.* New York: William Morrow, 2003. The contrasting personal experiences of participants in two wars that differed greatly in objectives and degrees of public support.

Terry, Wallace. *Bloods: An Oral History of the Vietnam War by Black Veterans.* New York: Ballantine Books, 1985. A fascinating collection of essays demonstrating a great diversity of experiences by African Americans who participated in the war.

Young, Marilyn, and John Fitzgerald, ed. *The Vietnam War: A History in Documents.* New York: Oxford

University Press, 2002. An excellent collection of important documents, although the commentary is one-sided in condemning U.S. policy.

Thomas Tandy Lewis

See also Antiwar demonstrations; Cambodia invasion and bombing; Central Intelligence Agency (CIA); Cold War; Détente; Elections in the United States, 1972; Fonda, Jane; Ford, Gerald R.; Foreign policy of the United States; Kissinger, Henry; McGovern, George; Nixon, Richard M.; Paris Peace Accords; Pentagon Papers; POWs and MIAs; Vietnam Veterans Against the War; War Powers Resolution of 1973.

■ Viking space program

Identification Missions to orbit and land on Mars
Date Viking 1 launched on August 20, 1975, and landed on Mars on July 20, 1976; Viking 2 launched on September 9, 1975, and landed on Mars on September 3, 1976

Though they failed to detect life, the two Viking spacecraft, in the most ambitious planetary missions to date, produced a detailed photographic map of the Martian surface and surprising new data on the planet's chemistry, geology, atmosphere, weather, and polar ice caps.

Conceived as part of the United States' bicentennial celebration in 1976, the two identical Viking spacecraft, each consisting of an orbiter and a lander, had as their scientific objectives the study of the topography, soil, and atmosphere of Mars and the search for life-forms there. Both spacecraft were launched successfully in 1975 and inserted into orbits around Mars in 1976.

Viking 1's orbiter sent vivid pictures of the planet more than 200 million miles back to Earth, where space scientists used them to select Chryse Planitia as an appropriate site for the first lander. Because of the cautious selection process, the lander touched down on Mars on July 20, 1976, the seventh anniversary of the first Moon landing, rather than on July 4, Independence Day. Over the next several months, the lander sent thousands of pictures back to Earth, revealing a rocky desert with windblown sand dunes. When the lander's robotic arm scooped up soil samples and analyzed them, scientists learned that Martian soil had an interesting chemistry but no biology.

Scientists passionately debated where Viking 2 was to land, some arguing for the safe choice of another flat plain and others arguing for the riskier choice of a canyon or mountain. Viking 2 landed safely on a plain, Utopia Planitia, much farther north than the Viking 1 site. Though similar in many ways to the first site, Utopia Planitia revealed channels that could have been the conduit for flowing water in the past. As with Viking 1, the biological experiments of Viking 2 confirmed that the Martian surface, unprotected by any ozone layer, was constantly bombarded with solar ultraviolet rays, rendering the soil sterile.

Impact The overwhelming success of the Viking space program ushered in a new age of space exploration. The data from the orbiters and landers provided scientists with their most extensive view of any extraterrestrial planet to that time. The orbiters generated more than 50,000 images, while the landers, which provided more than three million weather reports, sent 4,500 pictures of their environs back to Earth. Though Viking's instruments detected neither microorganisms nor organic molecules, scientists were pleased to discover that the Martian polar caps were composed mostly of water ice with a seasonal covering of solid carbon dioxide. The evidence that liquid water once existed on the Martian surface gave some scientists hope that life might yet be found on the red planet.

Further Reading

Crosswell, Ken. *Magnificent Mars.* New York: Free Press, 2003.
Hartman, William K. *A Traveler's Guide to Mars: The Mysterious Landscapes of the Red Planet.* New York: Workman, 2003.

Robert J. Paradowski

See also Apollo space program; Astronomy; Pioneer space program; Science and technology; Skylab; Space exploration; Voyager space program.

■ Village People, The

Identification Pop music band
Date Formed in 1976-1977

Formed to explore gay stereotypes to a disco beat, the Village People combined popular appeal and camp humor.

As with many pop bands, the Village People was first a concept, with group members recruited for established roles. French music producer-composer Jacques Morali and his business partner, Henri

Belolo, were inspired by costume-wearing residents of New York's Greenwich Village, including a male go-go dancer, Felipe Rose, wearing Native American regalia. Morali decided to form a group of handsome men wearing the costumes of gay sexual fantasy roles and singing disco songs with a homosexual subtext.

Earlier, explicitly gay, bisexual, and androgynous entertainment was limited to cult or avant-garde artists and works, such as David Bowie and *The Rocky Horror Picture Show.* However, the Village People arrived at disco's peak popularity and at a time when audiences enjoyed its catchy, hook-laden tunes whether in on the joke or not.

Stories about the band's formation vary, but the resulting group had six members: the American Indian (Rose), a cowboy (Randy Jones), a police officer (Victor Willis), a construction worker (David Hodo), a leather-wearing biker (Glenn Hughes), and the athlete-turned-sailor-or-soldier (Alexander Briley). Songwriters Phil Hurtt and Peter Whitehead provided material. Even before band members were chosen, Morali had a contract with Casablanca Records, then well known for promoting the career of disco diva Donna Summer.

Members of the Village People relax at a disco in 1979. (AP/Wide World Photos)

Morali had not expected popular success, but the band was immediately well received, as gay listeners enjoyed the group as "camp" and straight listeners enjoyed rollicking, fun disco. The group's first hit single was in Great Britain: "San Francisco" from their first album, *The Village People* (1977). Three other songs on that album paid homage to three other gay destinations: Hollywood, Greenwich Village, and Fire Island, New York. The group's album *Macho Man* (1978) sold more than one million copies, qualifying it as a gold record. Its title song was a Top 30 hit in the United States, and another single, "YMCA," reached number two in the United States and number one in Great Britain. "In the Navy" became another hit single in 1978.

Impact The group received phenomenal media coverage and popularity, notably defeating the Bee Gees for the 1978 Group of the Year Award at *Billboard* magazine's International Disco Forum. The group won further awards, but their popularity began to decline after 1978. As the group played Las Vegas and courted mainstream audiences, their camp stereotypes and humor began to seem self-mocking, and they lost their gay audience support. The music scene tired of disco, and the band's participation in the disastrous film *Can't Stop the Music* (1980) further lowered its popular standing.

Further Reading

Ferber, Lawrence. "The Village People." In *Popular Musicians*, edited by Steve Hochman. Pasadena, Calif.: Salem Press, 1999.

"The Village People: With a Bump, a Grind and a Wink, Disco's Macho Men Are Time-Warp Wonders." *People* 45, no. 24 (June 17, 1996): 60-61.

Bernadette Lynn Bosky

See also Bee Gees, The; Bowie, David; Disco; Discotheques; Homosexuality and gay rights; Music; *Rocky Horror Picture Show, The*; Summer, Donna.

■ Vonnegut, Kurt

Identification American novelist, playwright, and essayist

Born November 11, 1922; Indianapolis, Indiana

Vonnegut, a largely overlooked writer of science fiction, was suddenly catapulted into the public eye when his sixth novel, Slaughterhouse-Five, *was published in 1969.*

In 1943, Kurt Vonnegut enlisted in the United States Army and was captured the next year at the Battle of the Bulge. He was incarcerated as a prisoner of war in a meat locker (Slaughterhouse Five) in Dresden, Germany, and lived through the Allied firebombing that completely destroyed that city. In the opening chapter of *Slaughterhouse-Five: Or, The Children's Crusade, a Duty-Dance with Death,* the author addresses his audience and explains that the book, on which he had been working fitfully since his return to civilian life, had proved virtually impossible to write until the wife of an old army friend berated him not to romanticize the war. Vonnegut makes clear that his intentions are thoroughly antiwar. The book features straightforward war narrative mixed with time traveling and characters inhabiting an alien planet.

His next novel, *Breakfast of Champions: Or, Goodbye Blue Monday* (1973) was an overwhelming popular success but a critical disappointment that inaugurated a series of acidic reviews and slights for his remaining novels during the 1970's. The author's flippant tone, understated asides, and nonsensical drawings in *Breakfast of Champions* offered a nonthreatening introduction to the methods of postmodern fiction. The introduction of the author himself in the book's closing pages when he comes to free one of his principal characters from narrative servitude signaled a self-conscious metafictionality that other writers would explore in more depth in the ensuing decades. Vonnegut claimed at that time that he would never use the character of Kilgore Trout again, only to reprise the fictional alter ego in *Timequake* (1997).

His next novel, *Slapstick: Or, Lonesome No More!* (1976), was roundly dismissed, and 1979's *Jailbird* fared no better. His 1974 collection *Wampeters, Foma, and Granfalloons (Opinions)* brings together speeches,

Author Kurt Vonnegut (right) chats with producer and director Mark Robson in 1971. (AP/Wide World Photos)

reviews, and essays that solidified his reputation as a social satirist and critic of rampant technology and political mendacity.

Impact Kurt Vonnegut became extremely popular with young readers in the 1970's, an appreciation that began on college campuses where anti-Vietnam War sentiment was especially strong. *Slaughterhouse-Five*'s unequivocal criticism of governments, the military, and warfare in general resonated with a youth culture that was questioning many of the same institutions. The novel's popularity was significantly increased when George Roy Hill's feature film version was released in 1972.

Further Reading

Allen, William Rodney, ed. *Conversations with Kurt Vonnegut.* Jackson: University Press of Mississippi, 1988.

_______. *Understanding Kurt Vonnegut.* Columbia: University of South Carolina Press, 1991.

Broer, Lawrence R. *Sanity Plea: Schizophrenia in the Novels of Kurt Vonnegut.* 2d ed. Tuscaloosa: University of Alabama Press, 1994.

Klinkowitz, Jerome. *Kurt Vonnegut.* London: Methuen, 1982.

Merrill, Robert, ed. *Critical Essays on Kurt Vonnegut.* Boston: G. K. Hall, 1990.

David W. Madden

See also Antiwar demonstrations; Literature in the United States.

■ Voting Rights Act of 1975

Identification Legislation that extended and expanded the Voting Rights Acts of 1965 and 1970

Date Signed on August 6, 1975

This legislation furthered substantially the national effort to improve voter turnout among African Americans and other minority groups.

The Voting Rights Act first became law in 1965 (with an extension adopted in 1970), requiring federal clearance for changes in election laws in seven southern states and some northern counties, as well as a temporary ban on literacy tests for voter qualification. Though there was a significant increase in African American election turnout in many areas of the South after this legislation was passed, a great deal of discrimination remained. The proportion of African Americans eligible to vote and who were registered remained ten percentage points behind white registration. More than one-third of southern counties with majority African American populations did not have a single elected official at any level from the majority group.

Debate on extending the Voting Rights Act began in 1975. Democrats proposed a bill that would extend the act for ten years, as well as expanding its protections, and in June, it easily gained passage, by a vote of 341-70. The Senate passed the bill in July but with an amendment that would cut the extension from ten years to seven. Rather than risk a Senate filibuster on a Conference Report, the Democratic leadership in the House decided to vote on the Senate version, as amended. The House did approve the amended bill on July 28, and President Gerald R. Ford signed the bill on the tenth anniversary of the first Voting Rights Act.

The Voting Rights Act of 1975 was technically a group of amendments to the earlier acts. It extended federal voting protection to all or parts of ten new states not previously covered, including areas in the North and West. After the act of 1970, congressional investigation found that some Latinos and others were being discriminated against because of their inability to read or speak English. Therefore, in those states or in areas in which the federal government had authority, bilingual ballots became a requirement, and the temporary ban on literacy tests was made permanent. This legislation also extended voting protection to Latinos, Native Americans, and Asian Americans, in terms of the requirement for pre-clearance of voting changes. This legislation allowed individuals to sue in federal court to ask that voting registrars be sent to their area.

Impact The Voting Rights Acts, some of the most effective pieces of civil rights legislation ever enacted, provided the franchise to thousands of minority voters and had a significant impact on southern and national elections. The South had only seventy-two African American elected officials in 1965 but had almost two thousand by 1976.

Further Reading

Davidson, Chandler, and Bernard Grofman. *Quiet Revolution in the South: The Impact of the Voting Rights Act, 1965-1990.* Princeton, N.J.: Princeton University Press, 1994.

Thernstrom, Abigail. *Whose Votes Count? Affirmative*

Action and Minority Voting Rights. Cambridge, Mass.: Harvard University Press, 1987.

Thompson, Kenneth H. *The Voting Rights Act and Black Electoral Participation.* Washington, D.C.: Joint Center for Political Studies, 1982.

Eduardo Magalhães III

See also Affirmative action; African Americans; Racial discrimination.

■ Voyager space program

Identification Interplanetary exploration by robotic spacecraft

Date Voyager 2 launched on August 20, 1977; Voyager 1 launched on September 5, 1977

The two Voyager missions performed a Grand Tour of the outer solar system.

Planetary alignments that permit one spacecraft to visit several planets using gravity boosts to continue toward the next target are infrequent events. One such alignment existed in the late 1970's that would allow two spacecraft to conduct a reconnaissance of the outer solar system. One spacecraft could fly by Jupiter and Saturn and then be directed toward Pluto; another could fly by Jupiter, Uranus, and Neptune. This Grand Tour was projected to be expensive, but it was an opportunity that would not return for 176 years.

Planning the Missions The National Aeronautics and Space Administration (NASA) was given authorization only for a scaled-down Mariner Jupiter-Saturn mission in 1977. Two Mariner-class spacecraft were designed to encounter the Jovian and Saturnian systems carrying more sophisticated instrumentation than had the Pioneer 10 and 11 spacecraft. Despite a smaller budget authorization, NASA built spacecraft that could carry out a modified Grand Tour if they survived their Saturn encounters. Renamed Voyager, the plan was to fly Voyager 1 on a trajectory that included close encounters with Jupiter, Saturn, and Saturn's large moon Titan and to send Voyager 2 on a trajectory incorporating a Saturn encounter that could push the spacecraft toward Uranus, where it could be gravity-assisted toward Neptune. With dual spacecraft redundancy for Jupiter and Saturn, the primary mission objective, Voyager could not incorporate a Pluto encounter.

Because of the lower sunlight levels in the outer solar system, the Voyager spacecraft could not use solar panels. Instead, they were powered by radioisotope thermal generators, which transform heat produced by radioactive decay into electrical power. Each spacecraft carried a magnetometer, cosmic ray detector, plasma detector, infrared spectrometer and radiometer, low-energy charge particle detector, ultraviolet spectrometer, photopolarimeter, and both narrow-angle and wide-angle television cameras to investigate planetary magnetic fields, ring systems, planetary atmospheres, and the many moons around the outer planets.

Voyager 2 launched on August 20, 1977. Its slower trajectory required that it launch first, as the faster trajectory taken by Voyager 1 would make it encoun-

Voyager 2 is launched on August 20, 1977, from Cape Canaveral, Florida, on its mission to explore the outer planets of the solar system. (NASA)

ter Jupiter first. Voyager 1, virtually an identical twin to its sister ship, launched on September 5, 1977. The two spacecraft passed through the asteroid belt between Mars and Jupiter without incident, but both encountered significant problems, forcing control teams to work ingeniously to maintain each probe's science productivity. For example, Voyager 2's main radio receiver failed early in the mission.

Voyager 1 Mission Voyager 1 made its closest approach to Jupiter on March 5, 1979, at a distance of 280,000 kilometers. Voyager 1 discovered two new moons and a thin ring, identified active volcanoes on Io, and produced high-resolution images of Io, Europa, Ganymede, Callisto, and several smaller moons.

Jupiter's gravity directed Voyager 1 toward Saturn, and the spacecraft made its closest approach to the ringed planet on November 12, 1980. There, it produced high-resolution images of the complex structure within Saturn's ring system, discovered three new moons and dark spokes that appear above the ring plane, and produced data suggesting that small moonlets shepherd ring particles. Saturn's largest moon, Titan, revealed nothing of its surface. From 4,000 kilometers, Titan appeared shrouded in an obscuring thick atmosphere of nitrogen, methane, and argon.

Voyager 1 departed Saturn and headed above the ecliptic plane toward an encounter with the dwarf star AC+79 3888 in the constellation Camelopardus forty thousand years after launch. Both spacecraft carried special data records containing images and greetings from Earth that any extraterrestrial life should find decipherable.

Voyager 2 Mission Voyager 2 made its closest approach to Jupiter on July 9, 1979. It flew closer to the icy moon Europa than had Voyager 1, which had seen only streaks on an otherwise smooth, white spherical body. Voyager 2's Europa images resolved those streaks into a patchwork of cracks in the ice. This evidence supported notions that Europa could support an ocean underneath its thick ice and that even aquatic life might exist there.

Voyager 2 made its closest approach to Saturn on August 26, 1981, and experienced a problem with its science scan platform that required resolution for its research to continue. In January, 1986, Voyager 2 became the first spacecraft to investigate Uranus, and in August, 1989, it became the first spacecraft to study Neptune. Voyager 2 then headed out of the solar system, flying below the ecliptic plane toward a rendezvous with the star Sirius 358,000 years after launch. Both Voyager spacecraft continued to collect data as they were leaving the solar system.

Impact It is often said that these two spacecraft completed the first reconnaissance of the solar system; such a statement neglects the fact, however, that Pluto has yet to be examined up close by a robotic spacecraft. Nevertheless, it is correct to note that launch of the Voyager probes signaled the end of NASA's first golden age of planetary exploration.

The Voyager spacecraft were not the first to use planetary gravity assists to alter trajectory without propellant consumption. Mariner 10 accomplished that feat on its mission to Mercury. However, the Voyager probes incorporated gravity assists routinely in order to complete their complex missions.

Voyagers 1 and 2 followed the journeys of Pioneers 10 and 11 to Jupiter and Pioneer 11 to Saturn, but the scientific yield of the Voyager missions greatly exceeded the harvest from Pioneer flybys of those planets. The Voyager probes answered many questions but, like any good scientific investigation, generated far more questions than they answered. Voyager flyby data strongly influenced the design of the Galileo spacecraft that orbited Jupiter for years and the Cassini spacecraft that entered orbit around Saturn in summer, 2004.

Subsequent Events Both Voyager spacecraft continued transmitting data from the distant reaches of the solar system. It was estimated that onboard power would keep them reporting to Earth until 2013.

Further Reading

Greely, Ronald. *Planetary Landscapes.* 2d ed. New York: Chapman & Hall, 1994.

Morrison, David. *Voyages to Jupiter.* Washington, D.C.: U.S. Government Printing Office, 1980.

_______. *Voyages to Saturn.* Washington, D.C.: U.S. Government Printing Office, 1982.

Murray, Bruce. *Journey into Space.* New York: W. W. Norton, 1989.

David G. Fisher

See also Apollo space program; Astronomy; Pioneer space program; Science and technology; Skylab; Space exploration; Viking space program.

■ Walkman

Identification Portable stereo cassette player
Date Introduced in 1979

The introduction of the Walkman altered the way that the public listened to music. No longer bound by the limitations of the transistor radio of the 1950's or the "ghetto blasters" or "boom boxes" of the 1960's and early 1970's, the Walkman allowed individuals the ability to listen to music anywhere, anytime.

The portable stereo cassette player debuted on July 1, 1979. Originally introduced by the Sony Corporation as the Soundabout, it was renamed the Walkman and soon became a success, forever changing the way people listened to and experienced music. Akio Morita, cofounder and chairman of the Sony Corporation, is credited with the development of the Walkman. Morita was interested in designing a small, portable, high-fidelity tape player that could be paired with lightweight headphones. The result was the Walkman, offering the user a choice of musical selection combined with the freedom of portability.

Initially considered a novelty item, the Walkman later proved to be a huge product and a marketing success for Sony. The idea of being able to listen to music on demand appealed to music lovers everywhere. The first model available to consumers was the TPS-12. The compact blue-and-black cassette player included lightweight headphones and provided eight hours of high-quality sound on a single charge of batteries.

Impact The introduction and subsequent popularity of the Walkman has been called a cultural phenomenon. The design and portability of the Walkman initially appealed to young consumers, but its popularity soon spread to include a much wider audience. The Walkman took listening to music from the public arena and placed it squarely in the realm of personal experience. Listeners engaged in everyday mundane activities such as commuting, exercising, and housework could now complete these tasks accompanied by the soundtrack of their choice. Moreover, by allowing listeners to have a sense of isolation from their surroundings, the Walkman created a bubble of sound, giving the impression of a private space even in public. Finally, the Walkman was heralded as a symbol of Japan's skill not only in the field of technology but also in the areas of marketing and design. Sony single-handedly created a new market for portable stereo systems, which resulted in a marked increase in music listening.

Further Reading

Du Gay, Paul. *Doing Cultural Studies: The Story of the Sony Walkman.* Thousand Oaks, Calif.: Sage, 1997.

Kleinholz, L. "Happy Tenth Anniversary, Sony Walkman." *Radio-Electronics* 60, no. 10 (October, 1989): 72-73.

Patton, Phil. "Humming Off Key for Two Decades." *The New York Times,* July 29, 1999, p. G1.

Kelly C. Rhodes

See also Business and industry in the United States; Communications in the United States; Inventions; Music; Science and technology.

■ Wallace, George C.

Identification American politician
Born August 25, 1919; Clio, Alabama
Died September 13, 1998; Montgomery, Alabama

Alabama governor Wallace was an antiestablishment and populist national political candidate. His campaigns promoted national political party realignments and influenced national politics in subsequent decades.

George C. Wallace began his political career within the Alabama Democratic Party as a progressive liberal state representative and circuit court judge. His politics moved to the right after he lost his first bid for the Alabama governorship in 1958 to a conservative segregationist opponent. In 1962, he was elected governor on a pro-state's rights, pro-segregation, populist platform, earning the largest popular vote in Alabama gubernatorial history. In 1963, he stood on the schoolhouse steps in an unsuccessful attempt to block the admission of the first two African American students to the University of Alabama. His opposition to school desegregation propelled Wallace into his first presidential primary in 1964. His repeated reelection as governor of Alabama served as the base for his multiple attempts to seek election as president of the United States. He was elected governor in 1962, 1970, 1974, and 1982. Because of term limits, his wife was elected to serve as his surrogate in 1966.

Campaigns for the Presidency After a failed attempt at the presidency in 1964, which saw numerous Democrats transfer their support to Republican candidate Barry Goldwater, Wallace left the Democratic Party in 1968 to run for president as the candidate of the newly formed American Independent Party. He hoped to receive enough electoral votes to force the U.S. House of Representatives to make the final selection of the president, in accordance with the Constitution. He won ten million votes, 13 percent of the total votes cast, and carried five southern states, but Republican candidate Richard M. Nixon received enough electoral votes to be elected by the Electoral College.

President Nixon feared Wallace's popularity with southern and populist voters. He attempted to remove Wallace's political base by supporting Wallace's unsuccessful opponent in the 1970 Alabama gubernatorial election. The Internal Revenue Service (IRS) also investigated Wallace's campaign finances. These controversies kept Wallace's name in the national media. A Gallup poll showed Wallace to be the seventh-most-admired person in the United States, just ahead of the pope.

In 1972, Wallace entered the Democratic presidential primary race and scored an overwhelming victory in the Florida primary, defeating eleven other opponents and carrying every county in the state. In May, his aggressive campaign ended when Wallace was shot four times and paralyzed from the waist down by publicity seeker Arthur Bremer while Wallace was campaigning in Laurel, Maryland. Wallace's campaign momentum and an outpouring of sympathy subsequently lead to primary victories in Maryland, Michigan, Tennessee, and North Carolina and large vote totals in other primaries. He lost the nomination to George McGovern, who subsequently lost to Nixon. Wallace addressed the 1972 Democratic National Convention in Miami from a wheelchair.

George C. Wallace. (Library of Congress)

In 1975, Wallace announced his fourth run for the presidency. He dropped out of the race in June, 1976, after losing several southern primaries to former Georgia governor Jimmy Carter, who went on to win the presidency. Concerns about Wallace's health and his perceived helplessness were fanned by the press and stymied his campaign.

Political Realignment and Populism As a result of the fracture caused within the Democratic Party by Wallace's primary campaign in 1964, Republican presidential candidate Barry Goldwater carried many southern states. The Republican Party machines in the South, which had been struggling, received an infusion of energy and money and garnered power and respect within the national Republican Party. Some southern elected officials, such as South Carolina senator Strom Thurmond, shifted their registration to the Republican Party. Subsequently, the Republican Party mounted southern strategies in the

1968, 1972, and 1976 presidential elections, hoping that the schism between Wallace and the national Democratic Party would lead to victories for the Republican presidential candidate in those states and to the election of Republicans in statewide elections.

Except for his 1968 presidential run, Wallace remained a Democrat throughout his life, and he was a traditional public policy populist throughout most of his career. Wallace supported government education and health care programs for the poor and the working classes. He spoke out against the privileged rich, intellectuals, and federal bureaucrats. His administrations promoted public works and support for parks, education, and humanities, within the limited budget available in his poor state. He believed it should be the state government, not the national government, that provided public goods and services. It was his emphasis on state's rights and state responsibility that appealed to conservative voters outside the South.

Impact George Wallace's campaigns broke the century-old alliance between southern voters and the Democratic Party, allowing the southern states to become competitive two-party states. Southern Republicans eventually became dominant within the national Republican Party, both in the national legislature and in national political campaigns.

Subsequent Events In his 1982 gubernatorial race, Wallace repudiated his earlier segregationist views, saying he had been wrong about race, and he apologized to civil rights leaders. His election was supported by a coalition of African Americans, organized labor, and the education reform lobby. He carried all ten Alabama counties with majority African American populations. During his final term as governor between 1983 and 1987, Wallace appointed a record number of minorities to governmental positions.

Further Reading

Canfield, James Lewis. *A Case of Third Party Activism: The George Wallace Campaign Worker and the American Independent Party*. Lanham, Md.: University Press of America, 1984. Traces the third-party movement in the United States from its pinnacle of support with the Wallace presidential candidacy in 1968 through its declining years throughout the 1970's.

Carter, Dan T. *The Politics of Rage: George Wallace, the Origins of the New Conservatism, and the Transformation of American Politics*. Baton Rouge: Louisiana State University Press, 2000. Addresses Alabama and U.S. politics and government and party realignments.

Lesher, Stephan. *George Wallace: American Populist*. Reading, Mass.: Addison-Wesley, 1993. Discusses Wallace's appeal for populist voters and the Everyman.

Wallace, George, Jr. *The Wallaces of Alabama: My Family*. Chicago: Follett, 1975. Provides an autobiographical family portrait.

Gordon Neal Diem

See also African Americans; Conservatism in U.S. politics; Elections in the United States, 1972; McGovern, George; Racial discrimination.

■ Walt Disney World

Identification Resort and theme park
Date Opened on October 1, 1971
Place Orlando, Florida

Walt Disney World solidified the legacy of one of America's great creative geniuses and provided a setting for millions of visitors to envision the future, remember the past, and have a memorable entertainment experience.

Walt Disney World, the companion park to California's Disneyland, resulted from the creative mind of Walt Disney, who was intrigued with the technological advances of the space age. Having established himself as an American legend and developed major attractions for the New York World's Fair in 1964, Disney wanted to create a larger theme park and resort than Disneyland, which had opened in 1955.

Following an exhaustive nationwide search for the best location, Disney led the efforts in acquiring more than forty square miles of land in central Florida. Construction began in 1969 on the latest Magic Kingdom and two hotels. In what would become the largest private project in the world, Disney's "Imagineers" and nine thousand workers employed many new innovations in developing Walt Disney World, at an eventual cost of more than $400 million. Having died in 1966, Disney did not see his dream fulfilled, but the much-anticipated opening occurred in 1971, with twenty-six attractions and five thousand performers. The park was immensely popular, with more than ten million guests arriving in the first ten months.

Walt Disney World under construction in Orlando, Florida, on July 7, 1971. (AP/Wide World Photos)

Steady growth defined the next few years, as eleven new attractions were introduced by 1975. The original resort hotels were joined by a dozen more before the end of the decade. Entertainment milestones included the first Easter Parade in 1972, Donald Duck's fortieth birthday celebration in 1974, the bicentennial-themed America on Parade from 1975 to 1976, the large fireworks show Fantasy in the Sky and the Main Street Parade in 1977, and the fiftieth birthday celebration of Mickey Mouse in 1978. The Walt Disney Village emerged in 1975 as a gathering of residential, recreational, and commercial enterprises.

In 1975, plans were announced for the Experimental Prototype Community of Tomorrow (Epcot), the second phase of development at the site. Though different from Disney's original concept of a working future city, the park offered two themed areas, Future World and World Showcase. During construction, Epcot required ten thousand workers and had as its focal point Spaceship Earth, a large geodesic dome. Epcot opened on October 1, 1982, exactly eleven years after Walt Disney World.

Impact Walt Disney World grew to become one of the world's leading tourist destinations and transformed the central Florida area. Two of later additions were the theme parks Disney-MGM Studios and Disney's Animal Kingdom. Walt Disney World's unwavering commitment to customer satisfaction has set an enviable standard worldwide for high-quality entertainment and service. It has kept alive the spirit of imagination and wonder for people of all ages.

Further Reading

Barrett, Steven M. *Hidden Mickeys: A Field Guide to Walt Disney World's Best Kept Secrets.* Branford, Conn.: Intrepid Traveler, 2003.

Mongello, Louis A. *The Walt Disney World Trivia Book: Secrets, History, and Fun Facts Behind the Magic.* Branford, Conn.: Intrepid Traveler, 2004.

P. Graham Hatcher

See also Children's television; Film in the United States; Hobbies and recreation; Science and technology; Television in the United States.

■ Walters, Barbara

Identification Television journalist and personality

Born September 25, 1931; Boston, Massachusetts

Walters was the most visible and influential female broadcaster in the 1970's, blazing a career path for other women while attracting criticism for demeaning the quality of television news.

By 1970, reporter Barbara Walters was a household name, well known for her regular appearances on the National Broadcasting Company (NBC) network's *Today* show. Her public profile grew even more prominent during the 1970's. Walters continued to score exclusive interviews with U.S. president Richard M. Nixon, Cuban leader Fidel Castro, and other news makers. She was the first journalist to conduct a joint interview with Israeli prime minister Menachem Begin and Egyptian president Anwar Sadat. In 1971, she began hosting a daily talk show, *Not for Women Only.* The program garnered a large audience and was the forerunner to subsequent and popular daytime talk show programs such as *Donahue* and *Oprah.*

Many viewers admired Walters, considering this ambitious and hardworking broadcaster a model for women carving a niche in male-dominated professions. However, some television critics denounced her as an abrasive interviewer who spoke with a lisp. This criticism reached a crescendo in 1976, when Walters signed a one-million-dollar contract to co-anchor American Broadcasting Company's (ABC) evening news show and produce special programs. She became the highest-paid journalist in television history and the first woman to anchor a national network news program.

The contract announcement created an uproar among male journalists, who viewed Walters as a symbol of everything that was wrong with television news. They questioned why someone with her limited experience was worth a million dollars. To them, Walters was not a seasoned reporter but a chatty and shallow celebrity interviewer. Her con-

Barbara Walters smells a flower given to her by former coworkers Gene Shalit, Jim Hartz, and Lew Woods (left-right) after her departure from NBC's The Today Show *to become the coanchor of the* ABC Evening News. (AP/Wide World Photos)

tract, they argued, demonstrated how journalism was moving away from news and becoming entertainment. To add comedy to injury, Walters was parodied on the *Saturday Night Live* television show, with comedian Gilda Radner portraying a lisping newswoman named Baba Wawa.

ABC Evening News, with coanchors Walters and Harry Reasoner, debuted on October 4, 1976, initially drawing a large audience of curious viewers. However, neither the show nor Walters lived up to advance publicity, and ratings quickly plummeted. In 1978, Walters was demoted to reporter, and within a year, she was featured increasingly less on the program.

Walters concentrated on producing interview programs, with the first *Barbara Walters Special* airing on December 14, 1976. Three years later, she became a correspondent for *20/20,* a newsmagazine show.

Impact No other woman had a greater impact on television news during the 1970's than Barbara Walters. She overcame criticism to prove there was a place for women—and for her brand of celebrity interviews—in broadcast journalism. In succeeding decades, Walters continued producing her specials and appearing on *20/20.*

Bill Walton announces that he has signed a contract to play for the San Diego Clippers in 1979. (AP/Wide World Photos)

Further Reading

Marlane, Judith. *Women in Television News Revisited: Into the Twenty-first Century.* Austin: University of Texas Press, 1999.

Oppenheimer, Jerry. *Barbara Walters: An Unauthorized Biography.* New York: St. Martin's Press, 1990.

Rebecca Kuzins

See also *Donahue*; Journalism in the United States; *Saturday Night Live*; Talk shows; Television in the United States.

■ Walton, Bill

Identification American basketball player
Born November 5, 1952; La Mesa, California

Walton was a championship center on both the college and the professional level, and his unusual personality demonstrated that the counterculture had spread to basketball.

Bill Walton grew up in Southern California and played at Helix High School in La Mesa, California, from which he graduated in 1970. At Helix, Walton was an all-state center and was an obvious recruit for the neighboring University of California at Los Angeles (UCLA) under legendary coach John Wooden. Walton began his college career in 1970 and led UCLA to two championships as well as to consecutive undefeated seasons and a record eighty-eight consecutive wins. Widely considered the best college basketball team ever, UCLA was so good that Swen Nater, Walton's backup who barely played in college, had a long and successful professional career.

Walton was drafted first overall by the Portland Trail Blazers in 1974 and was immediately hailed as the savior of a franchise that had been plagued by unfortunate personnel moves and selfish players. By 1977, Portland was one of the dominant teams in the National Basketball Association (NBA). Walton was surrounded by a group of unselfish ensemble players—such as Bob Gross, Larry Steele, and Dave Twardzik—who knew to get Walton the ball and to play tough defense on the other side. He was also complemented by the fearsome strength of power forward Maurice Lucas. As a result, Portland upset the heralded Philadelphia 76ers for the 1977 NBA championship.

Far from the collegiate, crew-cut-bearing image of most white players in the NBA, Walton had long hair and looked like a prototypical hippie. Advised by activist Jack Scott, Walton took controversial political and social positions and proselytized for his vegetarian dietary habits. Walton seems perfect for liberal, laid-back Portland.

Unfortunately, Walton suffered a series of injuries to his foot, the climactic one marring a 1977-1978 season that had been even better than Portland's 1976-1977 championship season. The injury ended the Trail Blazers' chances of repeating and soured the relationship between Walton and Portland. In 1979, Walton was traded to the San Diego Clippers for Kevin Kunnert and Kermit Washington. This trade upset Clippers fans who felt their team gave up too much. Their apprehensions were justified as Walton, again slowed by injuries, played marginally through the length of his contract.

Impact Bill Walton was an athlete who challenged the conventional assumptions of the sports fan. Though committed to winning, he manifested a social conscience and a lifestyle independence that made him a symbol of the new age sports hero, one no longer tied to the clichés of past generations. As the nation swung back to more conventional modes of conduct, however, so did Walton.

Subsequent Events After a complicated series of foot surgeries in 1981, Walton returned to basketball. He joined the Boston Celtics and was able to contribute significantly to the team's title run in 1986. By this time, he had started to eat meat again and developed a more mainstream persona, one which aided him in becoming a respected and admired announcer for NBA telecasts during the 1990's and into the twenty-first century.

Further Reading

Halberstam, David. *The Breaks of the Game.* New York: Ballantine, 1983.

Stambler, Irwin. *Bill Walton, Super Center.* New York: Putnam, 1976.

Walton, Bill. *Nothing but Net: Just Give Me the Ball and Get Out of the Way.* New York: Hyperion, 1994.

Nicholas Birns

See also Basketball; Erving, Julius; Sports; Washington punching of Tomjanovich; Wooden, John.

War Powers Resolution of 1973

Identification U.S. federal legislation
Date Signed into law on November 7, 1973

Disturbed by its inability to guide the Vietnam War policy choices of President Richard M. Nixon, the U.S. Congress enacted Public Law 93-148—the War Powers Resolution—to enhance legislative control over all presidents. Only for a brief time, however, did it restrain presidential uses of military power.

Public opinion regarding American involvement in the Vietnam War sharply divided the nation after 1968. During April, 1970, without congressional authorization, President Nixon sent U.S. and allied South Vietnamese armed forces into neighboring and neutral Cambodia, attacking sanctuaries used by Vietnamese communist fighters there. Democratic Party leaders controlled both houses of Congress and opposed the Cambodian invasion. A series of legislative restrictions on the war were introduced, but most initiatives were blocked. In November, 1972, Nixon was reelected, defeating antiwar Democratic candidate George McGovern.

After the election, congressional investigations into the Watergate break-in and related scandals left the Nixon White House weakened. Long stalled in Congress, a war powers measure designed to curb presidential war making was passed. Nixon vetoed it on October 24, 1973. A further sharp decline in support for Nixon then took place, mostly sparked by his firing of Watergate Special Prosecutor Archibald Cox and others. In this context, Congress again took up the war powers proposal and overrode Nixon's veto: 284-185 in the House of Representatives and 75-18 in the Senate.

By this action, Congress asserted its coequal status with the presidency regarding decisions to go to war and sought to enable future Congresses to end long military campaigns conducted solely on presidential authority. Public Law 93-148 stated its purpose to be to "insure that the collective judgement of both the Congress and the President" guides decisions to use U.S. armed forces. Beyond traditional courtesies, it codified that Congress formally must be notified by the president within forty-eight hours if troops are sent into areas where hostilities are imminent. Its key provision demanded that unless Congress declared war or otherwise specifically authorized the use of force, any president may keep the troops in combat no longer than sixty days. A further thirty-day period was permitted for the safe withdrawal of troops.

Impact The War Powers Resolution was a reflection of widespread dissatisfaction with the Nixon presidency and the long Vietnam War. It helped induce his immediate successors, Gerald R. Ford and Jimmy Carter, to achieve a greater degree of cooperation with Congress in handling military matters relating to foreign policy. Consistent with the law, Congress was kept informed regarding the few and limited military rescue operations ordered by Ford; Carter chose to use means other than military force in pursuit of his objectives. The War Powers Resolution was never repealed, but when filing required reports with Congress, many presidents asserted their belief that the act unconstitutionally limited inherent presidential powers.

Further Reading

Fisher, Louis. *Presidential War Power.* Lawrence: University Press of Kansas, 1995.

Wormuth, Francis D., and Edwin B. Firmage. *To Chain the Dog of War: The War Power of Congress in History and Law.* Dallas: Southern Methodist University Press, 1986.

Gordon L. Bowen

See also Cambodia invasion and bombing; Committee to Re-elect the President (CRP); Congress, U.S.; Cox, Archibald; Elections in the United States, 1972; Fall of Saigon; Foreign policy of the United States; Kissinger, Henry; Nixon, Richard M.; Saturday Night Massacre; Vietnam War.

■ Washington punching of Tomjanovich

The Event Kermit Washington punches Rudy Tomjanovich during a professional basketball game

Date December 9, 1977

Washington's near fatal punch to the face of Tomjanovich caused the National Basketball Association (NBA) to remodel its image and rulebook.

During a game between the Los Angeles Lakers and the Houston Rockets, Kareem Abdul-Jabbar and Kevin Kunnert became involved in a scrap that quickly developed into a multiplayer melee which included Kermit Washington and others. Kermit Washington's back was turned to Rudy Tomjanovich, who had run from the other side of the court to help break up the fight. Tomjanovich arrived as Washington turned around. Believing that Tomjanovich was going to attack him, Washington threw a punch at him. The combination of Tomjanovich's momentum and Washington's strength had disastrous consequences.

Tomjanovich was nearly killed by the blow. He suffered spinal and brain injuries as well as multiple facial fractures. Washington received a sixty-day suspension and was permanently marked as a violent and dangerous man. He was targeted for derision by fans and was one of the league's most unpopular players. He became depressed and lost much of his effectiveness as a player whose style depended on gritty and rough play. Tomjanovich's playing career resumed the following season, but not with the same level of success as before the incident.

"The Punch," as it quickly became known, resonated around the country, not only because of its devastating effect on Tomjanovich but also because of its racial subtext. For some, the incident's significance rested upon Washington's being black and Tomjanovich's being white. Washington believed that the length of his suspension was race-based, as did his teammate Abdul-Jabbar. They believed that if Tomjanovich were black or Washington were white, then the incident would not have been as important to the public as it was.

The NBA, which had been suffering from declining attendance for several years prior to the incident, decided to revamp its rulebook and its marketing strategy as a result. New bylaws resulting in automatic suspensions for players who fought were put in place and strictly enforced. The league also added to its games a third referee, who would trail the players and be able to intervene quickly in case of trouble behind the ball in the backcourt, as had happened with Abdul-Jabbar and Kunnert. Most important, the league sought to cleanse its image, which resulted in new marketing techniques and a repackaging of professional basketball to the public.

Impact Although one of the league's ugliest incidents, "The Punch" ultimately helped the NBA rise as a worldwide phenomenon. It forced league officials to rethink its public image and make itself more palatable to a mainstream audience.

Further Reading

Feinstein, John. *The Punch: One Night, Two Lives, and the Fight That Changed Basketball Forever.* Boston: Little, Brown, 2002.

Tomjanovich, Rudy, with Robert Falkoff. *A Rocket at Heart: My Life and My Team.* New York: Simon & Schuster, 1997.

Michael Ezra

See also Basketball; Sports.

■ Water pollution

Definition Degradation of water quality by chemical or biological agents

Water pollution posed environmental and health problems for the United States in the 1970's. Although national legislation provided some remediation, new sources of pollution presented themselves so that the issue still remained at the end of the decade.

Historically, water pollution was one of the first forms of pollution dealt with by government. Early concerns were for safe drinking water although concern for ecosystem damage developed during the 1960's. During the 1970's, the U.S. Congress passed two pieces of legislation that provided for a comprehensive approach to the issue. This legislation also signaled a turn to a national rather than a state approach to water pollution. Overall, water quality had improved markedly by the end of the decade, but new water pollution issues were arising that would be difficult to address.

Sources Water pollution came from several sources during the decade. Conventionally six pollutants can be noted, although other forms of water pollution also exist. First, biochemical oxygen demand is a measure of oxygen in water; low amounts of oxygen are often indicative of sewage or other organic waste that depletes oxygen in water. Second, nutrients, such as phosphorus, promote life, but when present in too great an amount—from sewage or fertilizers—they lead to algae growth in bodies of water. Algae bloom and die, and when enough algae die, the resulting debris can fill up a lake and eventually turn it into a bog. This process, known as eutrophication, is a natural one, but this process can be shortened dramatically by the addition of nutrients. Third, a measure of acidity or alkalinity is pH. Water that is too acidic or too alkaline will not support life. A fourth form of pollution is suspended solids; for example, soil from agricultural operations. Oil spills provide a fifth form of pollution. Finally, bacteria, viruses, and protozoa are found in sewage and can cause numerous diseases, such as cholera, when they appear in drinking water.

Organic wastes from humans and animals continued to be a water quality problem in the 1970's. Runoff from cleared land fouled many streams and lakes with solid material as well as nutrients derived from fertilizers. Runoff from parking lots and streets often led oil and other chemicals to be deposited in nearby bodies of water. Chemical waste that was the by-product of industrial society also posed a major problem for streams, lakes, and groundwater. Industrial discharges or spills might include heavy metals such as mercury or lead as well as oil or solvents. Underground chemical and oil or gasoline tanks leaked at times, providing another form of water pollution that would go unnoticed for many years. Some pollutants entered groundwater supplies, posing long-term health problems.

Another type of chemicals, polychlorinated biphenyls (PCBs) found their way into water from industrial discharges or leaks from electrical equipment. Although banned in the 1970's, PCBs continued to be present from such sources as old electrical equipment. PCBs are highly toxic, posing potential cancer risks.

Finally, electric power generation that used water for cooling returned to streams water that was often much hotter than the existing flow. This kind of thermal pollution led to fish kills or the growth of certain types of algae.

Effects Water pollution posed a direct hazard to human health through contamination of drinking water. Water pollution also led to fish kills, harmed animal and plant life that came in contact with pollutants, and even led to silting up of streams. Human health was affected as pollutants moved up the food chain when people ate animal or plant matter that had been contaminated by polluted water.

Water pollution in its most obvious forms also created eyesores or produced noxious odors that destroyed the scenic value of some streams and lakes. Some pollutants, such as soil washed into streams, were easy to detect. However, many forms of chemical and organic pollution required sophisticated chemical analysis to detect. As the United States and

Canada continued to industrialize, the sources of water pollution expanded.

Water Pollution Control Act Amendments The continuing industrialization of American and Canadian society, combined with increasing use of chemical fertilizer and land clearing, had rendered the water in many streams and lakes dangerous to humans by 1960. National or state legislation had already addressed some of the impact of water pollution by 1970. However, there was an awareness, expressed by some of the participants at the first Earth Day in 1970, that more needed to be done. Throughout the decade, local environmental groups participated in stream and lake cleanups that removed the most obvious forms of pollution. Some activists also organized protests outside firms that were major polluters or even engaged in vandalism directed against polluters. However, local activism simply was not enough to clean up American water.

In 1972, Congress passed the Federal Water Pollution Control Act Amendments (FWPCAA), which amended 1948 legislation. The FWPCAA had the goal of restoring the biological, chemical, and physical integrity of water in the United States. The act required the ending of all discharges that were considered to be pollutants into navigable streams by 1985. Its goal was to return American water to drinkable or fishable quality. In 1972, only 30 percent of American waters were judged drinkable or fishable by one estimate, so it was clear that much needed to be done.

However, several drawbacks of the legislation emerged, including that it did not provide specific targets for all pollutants and it did not take the cost of combating pollution into consideration. Limits were placed on various forms of pollution based on existing technology with these targets to be achieved by 1977. The legislation also mandated that effluent discharges were to be controlled by the "best available" technology by 1983, a form of forcing technological progress. Some forms of pollution, most notably heavy metals, were not addressed. Most of the standards dealt with "point pollution" that came from specific discharge points such as a municipal waste treatment plant. Pollution that came from runoff from agriculture or industry, called nonpoint pollution because there is no specifically identifiable discharge point, was much harder to identify, and the legislation did little to address this form of pollution.

With the FWPCAA, Congress and the Environmental Protection Agency (EPA), which prepared many of the specific water quality standards, moved to set national water pollution standards and provided for enforcement with criminal and civil penalties. This approach was a change from the past as the national government now began to play a much larger role than it had in the past in setting standards and enforcement. The legislation also provided for grants to municipalities for the construction of sewage treatment plants but not to private entities.

However, the FWPCAA illustrates what has come to be called a "command and control" approach to pollution control. The national government "commanded" that a specific environmental problem be addressed. It tried to "control" behavior through inspections, permits, and criminal and civil penalties. It also tried to force technological development by mandating

A fisherman in 1971 holds up paper pulp sludge in the Hudson River that results when summer heat evaporates the water and leaves behind industrial waste and sewage. Legislation enacted during the 1970's attempted to stop such water pollution. (AP/Wide World Photos)

that technologies had to be developed to address water pollution problems. Such an approach did not always take into account other, nontechnological means of pollution control that might be more effective and less costly than technological "fixes." When technological solutions are rigidly specified, as the FWPCAA seemed to do, achieving compliance is costly.

Additional Legislation In 1977, Congress continued to press for action in dealing with water pollution with the passage of the Clean Water Act (CWA). The CWA followed essentially the same technology-based approach to effluent standards as the FWPCAA. It did use somewhat different criteria for establishing the conventional pollutants (organic matter, suspended solids, bacteria, and pH). Some deadlines were also modified. One means of dealing with discharge was through a process of establishing permits for dischargers. Initially the EPA administered this program, but gradually states took over this responsibility.

Other legislation also addressed water pollution. The Safe Drinking Water Act of 1974 provided specific standards for drinking water. The Resource Conservation and Recovery Act of 1976 indirectly addressed water pollution by regulating chemical and heavy metal pollution that often affected groundwater.

What Was Left Undone As indicated above, the FWPCAA did not address nonpoint pollution. Nonpoint pollution continued to be an important source of groundwater pollution in the late 1970's and beyond. Agricultural runoff, especially fertilizer residues, often led to oxygen depletion or algae growth in many streams and lakes. The inter-related nature of environmental problems is evident in one form of water pollution. Sulfur dioxide was a by-product of coal-burning electric power plants in the Midwest that entered the atmosphere from smokestack emissions. The sulfur dioxide reacted with hydrogen in the atmosphere and returned to lakes and streams in the Northeast and southern Canada as acid deposition. Acid deposition (acid rain) turned the water of many lakes acidic, killing all plant and fish life. A lake might look beautiful and clear, but it was dead when it was affected by acid deposition. The growth of strip mining of coal in the eastern United States, especially in Kentucky, also began to contribute to water pollution by the end of the decade. The water that gathered in abandoned strip mine pits was often acidic and contained heavy metals. The dams impounding this wastewater broke on occasion, leading to floods downstream of chemically fouled water.

The legislation of the 1970's addressed inland water. It was becoming apparent by the end of the decade, however, that near-coastal waters and estuaries were also becoming fouled by the same sources of water pollution. For example, fish kills generated by chemical pollution were starting to become an issue in Chesapeake Bay. Some estuaries experienced algae growth generated by agricultural runoff. In addition, oil spills from tankers and other ships often fouled large expanses of ocean water, leading to the death of marine life.

Impact The water pollution legislation of the 1970's made a start at controlling point pollution. Nonpoint pollution in various forms would become an increasingly important problem in the years ahead. Americans had become more sophisticated about the sources of water pollution by the end of the decade and continued to demand action.

Subsequent Events It has proven difficult to measure how much water quality was improved by the FWPCAA. Nonetheless, one estimate is that by 1994, 60 percent of American water had achieved drinkable or fishable standards. The grants program helped to control municipal sewage discharge. Because enforcement was difficult to achieve, however, other forms of pollution continued to be a problem, particularly those generated by nonpoint sources.

Further Reading

Freeman, A. Myrick, III. "Water Pollution Policy." In *Public Policies for Environmental Protection*, edited by Paul Portney. Washington, D.C.: Resources for the Future, 1990. Good summary of water pollution legislation in the 1970's and its impact.

Hill, Marquita. *Understanding Environmental Pollution.* Cambridge, England: Cambridge University Press, 1997. Good nontechnical introduction to the science of water pollution.

Montrie, Chad. *To Save the Land and People.* Chapel Hill: University of North Carolina Press, 2003. Addresses the impact of strip mining on water quality and community efforts at addressing the problem.

Peirce, J. Jeffrey, Ruth Werner, and P. Aarne Veslind.

Environmental Pollution and Control. 4th ed. Boston: Butterworth-Heineman, 1998. Includes a sophisticated analysis of forms of water pollution and means of control.

Rosenbaum, Walter. *Environmental Politics and Policy.* 6th ed. Washington, D.C.: CQ Press, 2004. Relates water pollution to other environmental issues.

John M. Theilmann

See also Acid rain; Air pollution; Earth Day; Environmental movement; Environmental Protection Agency (EPA); Great Lakes Water Quality Agreement of 1972; PCB ban; Safe Drinking Water Act of 1974.

■ Watergate

Identification The break-in at the Democratic National Headquarters in Washington, D.C.'s Watergate office complex and the resulting scandal

Date Break-in occurred on June 17, 1972

This seemingly unimportant event, unknown to President Richard M. Nixon when it occurred, led the president to the brink of impeachment and to resignation from the presidency as he attempted to cover up the event and was accused of obstruction of justice.

In June, 1972, Richard Nixon was within half a year of completing his first term as president of the United States and was considered the certain victor in the 1972 election. He had a substantial lead against his possible Democratic opponents, one of whom would be nominated to run against him during the upcoming Democratic National Convention. Nixon had a high approval rating, largely because of his effectiveness in foreign affairs.

On Saturday evening, June 17, 1972, a security guard at the Watergate office complex in Washington, D.C., called the police to report suspicious activities in the building. The three district police officers who answered the call found five men in the act of breaking into the suite occupied by the Democratic National Committee (DNC). The intruders, who wore rubber gloves, were attempting to install covert listening devices in DNC headquarters. They were arrested and booked on suspicion of burglary.

Among those arrested was James McCord, formerly of the Central Intelligence Agency (CIA), who was the security director of the Committee to Reelect the President (CRP), labeled CREEP by some Nixon detractors. Also arrested was Frank Sturgis, an American and former Cuban military officer, as well as three men who had fled communist Cuba. These three men had a total of $2,400 on their persons at the time of their arrests, and $3,500 more was later found in their rooms, presumably their payments from CRP.

The burglars were suspected of having CIA connections. On September 15, 1972, they were charged formally with burglary, wiretapping, and conspiracy. Two co-conspirators, E. Howard Hunt and G. Gordon Liddy, also were charged on that day after it was revealed that they had helped plan the break-in. Hunt, a former CIA employee, worked as a consultant to Nixon. Liddy, a former agent of the Federal Bureau of Investigation (FBI), had been a staff assistant to Nixon for the preceding year.

Nixon's Involvement Nixon, who was vacationing in south Florida, first learned of the Watergate break-in the morning after it happened, when he read about it in the *Miami Herald.* Initially, he dismissed the event as unimportant. The public would surely realize that, being so far ahead in the polls, he had no reason to order an illegal act of this sort. He clearly was not involved in it directly. He reasoned that any information its successful completion might have provided was information his presidential campaign did not need.

Nixon considered the break-in a prank that went awry and whose potential for damage was minimal. Upon learning that the Watergate burglars were associated with CRP, however, he became apprehensive that the break-in might have graver implications than he had originally thought. He was now forced to consider ways in which to deflect the public's attention from the event. This realization marked the first tentative step of his active participation in obstructing justice, the crime that eventually destroyed his presidency.

Nixon's aide, H. R. Haldeman, advised the president to control the damage by making the break-in look like an attempt of the ultraconservative anti-Castro participants to retaliate against George McGovern, Nixon's expected opponent in the 1972 election, for his proposal to reestablish diplomatic relations with Castro's Cuba. Nixon told Haldeman that probably the best way to get the Watergate Five to support this fiction was to give them money to cover their legal expenses and living costs. He told

Haldeman to use secret discretionary funds from CRP for this purpose. Haldeman suggested that the FBI could probably be diverted from investigating the break-in thoroughly by making it seem that it was a CIA operation.

Nixon, who maintained an Enemies List, had a notably paranoid disposition. He feared that his political enemies might learn about the break-in and use this information against him. He agreed with Haldeman that the FBI should be misled with the expectation that the matter of Watergate soon would fade from public view.

This conversation with Haldeman in the Oval Office on June 23, 1972, one week after the break-in, was the single most condemnatory piece of evidence pointing to the president's complicity in a plan to obstruct justice. It was recorded on a tape that ran during Nixon's entire meeting with Haldeman.

The Role of *The Washington Post* Bob Woodward, a local reporter for *The Washington Post*, grudgingly accepted a Saturday morning assignment to the hearing at which the Watergate burglars were arraigned. Little did he know how dramatically this hearing would affect his future life and that of Carl Bernstein, who, along with Woodward, investigated the Watergate break-in for the newspaper.

The first Watergate story appeared on the front page of *The Washington Post*'s Sunday edition but initially attracted little attention. The reporters were still unaware that there was a CIA connection with Watergate. However, in the months ahead, the investigative reporting of Woodward and Bernstein unraveled the complex intricacies of Watergate in such great and accurate detail that in 1973, their newspaper was awarded a Pulitzer Prize for its coverage. These reporters traced the money trail that established the bribery in which the White House had been complicit as it attempted to quash the Watergate investigation.

The White House Tapes Nixon anticipated writing a detailed memoir upon completing his presidency. In order to document many of the details that such a

The Watergate office complex in 1971. (*The Washington Post*; reprinted by permission of the D.C. Public Library)

Time Line of the Watergate Scandal

Year	*Date*	*Event*
1968	November 5	Richard M. Nixon is elected president of the United States.
1971	June 13	Portions of the Pentagon Papers, the Defense Department's secret history of Vietnam, are published in *The New York Times* and *The Washington Post.*
	September 3	A group created to stop leaks of White House information, nicknamed the "Plumbers' Unit," breaks into the office of the psychiatrist of Daniel Ellsberg, the man who leaked the Pentagon Papers, in an attempt to find information to discredit him.
1972	June 17	Five men are arrested in the middle of the night while trying to bug the offices of the Democratic National Committee at the Watergate hotel and office complex; one man claims that he used to work for the CIA.
	June/July	Reports emerge that a Republican security aide was among the Watergate burglars and that the burglars were employed by the Committee to Re-elect the President (CRP). Former attorney general John Mitchell, head of the Nixon reelection campaign, denies any link to the operation.
	August 1	The media discovers that a $25,000 cashier's check, allegedly earmarked for the Nixon campaign, wound up in the bank account of a Watergate burglar.
	August 29	According to Nixon, an investigation led by White House counsel John Dean shows that "no one in the White House staff, no one in this administration, presently employed, was involved in this very bizarre incident."
	September 29	*The Washington Post* reports that while serving as U.S. attorney general, Mitchell controlled a secret Republican fund used to finance widespread intelligence-gathering operations against Democrats.
	October 10	FBI agents find that Nixon's reelection effort included a widespread campaign of political spying and sabotage.
	November 7	Nixon is reelected in a landslide win.
1973	January 30	Former Nixon aides G. Gordon Liddy and James McCord are convicted of conspiracy, burglary, and wiretapping in the Watergate incident, while five others plead guilty.
	February	In order to investigate the Watergate break-in and allegations of spying and sabotage, the Senate establishes a Select Committee on Presidential Campaign Activities, chaired by Senator Sam Ervin.
	March	One of the burglars, McCord, tells U.S. District Judge John J. Sirica that he is being pressured to remain silent.
	April 20	Acting FBI director L. Patrick Gray resigns after admitting that he had destroyed Watergate evidence under pressure from Nixon aides.
	April 30	Nixon's top White House staffers, H. R. Haldeman and John Ehrlichman, as well as Attorney General Richard Kleindienst, resign over the growing scandal, and Dean is fired.

(continued)

Year	*Date*	*Event*
1973 *(cont.)*	May 18	Nationally televised hearings of the Senate committee begin, and Attorney General-designate Elliot Richardson chooses former solicitor general Archibald Cox as the Justice Department's special prosecutor for Watergate.
	June	Dean tells investigators that there was an ongoing cover-up within the White House and that Nixon was involved in approving "hush money" for the burglars. Meanwhile, a memo is found addressed to Ehrlichman that describes the plans to break in to the office of Ellsberg's psychiatrist.
	July 13	In his testimony before the Senate committee, White House aide Alexander Butterfield reveals that Nixon had taped all conversations inside the Oval Office since 1971.
	July 23	Nixon refuses to hand over the audiotapes from the Oval Office.
	October 20	In what was called the Saturday Night Massacre, Nixon fires Cox, and Richardson and Deputy Attorney General William Ruckelshaus resign. The event bolsters the demand among politicians and the American public for impeachment.
	November 17	Nixon declares "I am not a crook" and maintains his innocence.
	November/ December	The audiotapes are subpoenaed by the Senate committee, but an eighteen-minute gap exists in one tape.
1974	April 30	The White House releases more than 1,200 pages of audiotape transcripts.
	July 24	The Supreme Court rules that Nixon must hand over all audiotapes, rejecting the claim of executive privilege.
	July 24-30	The House Judiciary Committee approves three articles of impeachment: obstruction of justice, misuse of powers and violation of his oath of office, and failure to comply with House subpoenas.
	August 9	Nixon resigns.
	September 8	President Gerald R. Ford pardons Nixon.

memoir would involve, he had recording devices installed in the Oval Office in order to have a complete record of every transaction that took place there. These voice-activated devices captured in full everything that was said in the Oval Office, but Nixon had no idea that his tapes would ever be made public. He considered them his personal property.

Although the courts became deeply involved in Watergate after the indictment of the Watergate conspirators in September, 1972, Nixon quite handily won a second term as president by a landslide, garnering 60.7 percent of the popular vote, the second largest victory in history. He carried every state but Massachusetts.

However, the Watergate net was closing in on Nixon, who now engaged in desperate efforts to save his presidency. On March 19, 1973, McCord informed Judge John J. Sirica that the Watergate defendants were under political pressure to keep silent. Two days later, John Dean, a close adviser to the president, warned Nixon that "a cancer [is] growing on the presidency." The Watergate defendants were demanding hush money for their continued silence. On April 30, Nixon announced that Haldeman, John Ehrlichman, Dean, and Attorney General Richard Kleindienst had resigned. The Senate-appointed Watergate committee began its hearings on May 17.

It was not until July, 1973, however, that Alexander Butterfield, a former Nixon aide, revealed to the committee details about the taping system in the

Excerpt from the Oval Office tape of March 21, 1973, in which President Richard M. Nixon discusses with White House counsel John Dean the way in which "hush money"could be obtained for Watergate burglars:

NIXON: We could get that. On the money, if you need the money, you could get that. You could get a million dollars. You could get it in cash. I know where it could be gotten. It is not easy, but it could be done. But the question is, who would handle it? Any ideas on that?

Oval Office. This marked a significant milestone in the Watergate investigation. On July 23, Special Prosecutor Archibald Cox asked that the tapes be turned over to the committee. Nixon, claiming that the tapes were his personal property, refused to release them, causing a bitter tug-of-war between the Senate committee and the White House.

During this battle, Vice President Spiro T. Agnew was accused of tax evasion and eventually pleaded no contest to the indictment against him. He was fined ten thousand dollars and placed on probation for three years. His resignation from the vice presidency on October 10, 1973, temporarily deflected attention from the Watergate debacle. Nixon appointed Gerald R. Ford to replace Agnew.

The Saturday Night Massacre By late 1973, Nixon was sinking rapidly into the quagmire that Watergate was creating. He ordered Attorney General Elliot Richardson to fire Special Prosecutor Cox. Richardson refused, and in late October, 1973, Nixon himself fired the special prosecutor along with Richardson and his deputy, William Ruckelshaus, in what came to be called the Saturday Night Massacre.

Prior to this event, Nixon had battled ardently to keep the tapes from the Senate committee. He offered to provide edited transcripts of them and supervised the production of a 1,308-page transcript. The committee, however, would not retreat from its demand to receive the tapes, and on July 24, 1974, the Supreme Court, by a vote of 8-0, decreed that Nixon had to turn over sixty-four tapes to Special Prosecutor Leon Jaworski.

As early as October 23, 1973, twenty-one members of Congress had called for Nixon's impeachment. On March 1, 1974, seven former Nixon aides were indicted for crimes associated with Watergate, and Nixon himself was named as an unindicted co-conspirator. On May 9, 1974, the House Judiciary Committee began impeachment proceedings and, on July 27, voted 27-11 in favor of the first article of impeachment, obstruction of justice.

On August 5, Nixon was forced to release the transcript of the damning June 23, 1972, tape of his conversation with Haldeman. This so-called smoking gun transcript caused nearly all of Nixon's supporters to desert him, and on August 9, he resigned his presidency, convinced that he would be impeached if he did not leave office and equally convinced that he would be convicted in such an impeachment.

Impact Watergate initially left the American public severely disenchanted with government and with politics. The same public that had less than two years earlier returned Richard Nixon to a second term as president by the greatest landslide in American history now watched as a shamed and disgraced president was forced out of office and replaced by Gerald R. Ford, who had not been elected to the office of president, the first time in the nation's history that such a situation had occurred.

Despite the public consternation that the Watergate disaster evoked, most Americans, after reflecting on the matter, had to acknowledge that the system in place since the Founding Fathers fashioned a new nation based on a remarkably sound Constitution could deal effectively even with a situation as threatening to the nation's political stability as Watergate. It became evident that the United States was well equipped to maintain the sort of constitutional government that had, for more than two centuries, made it a beacon of liberty throughout the world. Many people surmised that this sad affair essentially would destroy the Republican Party, a prediction that did not hold.

Further Reading

Emery, Fred. *Watergate: The Corruption of American Politics and the Fall of Richard Nixon.* New York: Times Books, 1994. A comprehensive presentation of the Watergate scandal.

Fremon, David K. *The Watergate Scandal in American History.* Springfield, N.J.: Enslow, 1998. Directed to young adult readers, this book is especially valuable for its timeline.

Marquez, Heron. *Richard M. Nixon.* Minneapolis: Lerner, 2003. The brief section on Watergate is lucid and accurate. Recommended for young adults.

Nixon, Richard M. *In the Arena: A Memoir of Victory, Defeat, and Renewal.* New York: Simon & Schuster, 1990. Nixon's personal account of how he coped with the aftermath of Watergate.

_______. *RN: The Memoirs of Richard Nixon.* New York: Grosset & Dunlap, 1978. Nixon's own, admittedly biased, account of the Watergate scandal.

Schuman, Michael A. *Richard M. Nixon.* Springfield, N.J.: Enslow, 1998. Directed to an adolescent audience, Schuman's presentation of Watergate is brief but penetrating.

Summers, Anthony. *The Arrogance of Power: The Secret World of Richard Nixon.* New York: Viking Press, 2000. A thorough psycho-political assessment of Nixon.

R. Baird Shuman

See also Agnew, Spiro T.; *All the President's Men*; Cox, Archibald; Dean, John; Deep Throat; Ehrlichman, John; Elections in the United States, 1972; Enemies List; Ford, Gerald R.; Haldeman, H. R.; Liddy, G. Gordon, and E. Howard Hunt; Mitchell, John; Nixon, Richard M.; Nixon tapes; Nixon's resignation and pardon; Pentagon Papers; Saturday Night Massacre; Scandals; Sirica, John J.; Woodward, Bob, and Carl Bernstein.

■ Watkins Glen rock festival

The Event Approximately 600,000 fans attend a rock music festival
Date July 28, 1973
Place Watkins Glen, New York

The Watkins Glen festival signaled the end of Woodstock-era music festivals and the beginning of the commercialized popular music concerts of the "Me Decade."

The Watkins Glen festival took place during the declining years of the rock festival movement that began with the Monterey Pop Festival of 1967, peaked with the Woodstock festival of 1969, and took a sharp downward turn following the violence at the Rolling Stones' free 1969 Altamont concert near San Francisco. Unlike traditional music festivals that featured a large number of performers representing a variety of musical genres, the Watkins Glen festival featured only three bands—the Allman Brothers, the Band, and the Grateful Dead—that shared similar musical styles and a common audience. Watkins Glen also contrasted with the 1960's festivals in its lack of political overtones, reflecting a decline in political activism among American youth in the aftermath of the Vietnam conflict. However, the Watkins Glen festival was the largest music festival and one of the largest gatherings in American history.

Preparation for the event was meticulous. In compliance with state laws enacted after the Woodstock festival, promoters constructed a large campground with more than one thousand portable toilets, a dozen water wells, and a heliport. Neither the promoters nor racetrack officials anticipated more than 150,000 people. However, by Thursday, July 26, the campground already held more than 100,000 concertgoers, and highways leading into the venue were gridlocked with traffic jams stretching for dozens of miles. More than a quarter of a million young people had gathered at the racetrack by Friday evening. With 100,000 fans already gathered in front of the stage anticipating the start of the festival, what was planned as a test of the innovative digital sound system that evening became an impromptu concert when the performers decided to play extended sets. By Saturday, the day of the festival, approximately 600,000 people occupied the ninety-acre raceway grounds.

Impact The Watkins Glen festival was the last of the large rock festivals held in the United States during the 1970's. Despite its enormity, it never attained the cultural significance or lasting financial success of Woodstock, the largest of the 1960's festivals. The performances, although by most accounts inspired, failed to hold the attention of the sprawling audience, many of whom were out of viewing range of the stage. The limited number of performers and their penchant for lengthy improvisation exacerbated the apathy of the attendees, many of whom were either intoxicated or distracted by the general atmosphere of revelry. Rain and the death of a skydiver in a fiery accident further dulled the impact of the performances, which began to suffer as the musicians grew tired. Disagreements among the performers derailed plans for potentially lucrative record album and motion-picture releases.

Further Reading

McNally, Dennis. *A Long Strange Trip: The Inside History of the Grateful Dead.* New York: Broadway Books, 2003.

Santelli, Robert. *Aquarius Rising: The Rock Festival Years.* New York: Delacorte Press, 1980.

Michael H. Burchett

See also Band, The; Music.

■ Weather Underground

Identification A group of U.S. leftist revolutionaries

Date Formed in 1969 as the Weatherman

The Weather Underground bombed military and other symbols of American power to express their opposition to the war in Vietnam and to racism in the United States. Their politics were a mix of Marxism-Leninism and countercultural antiauthoritarianism, and they represented the extreme left of the U.S. student movement.

The Weather Underground was one of the factions that came out of the disintegration of the Students for a Democratic Society (SDS) during that organization's June, 1969, national convention in Chicago. Dedicated to the idea of armed revolution in the United States, the group originally was named Weatherman after the line "You don't need a weatherman to know which way the wind blows" from Bob Dylan's 1965 song "Subterranean Homesick Blues."

The first national action of the Weatherman took place in October, 1969, in Chicago. Under the rally cry Bring the War Home, approximately one thousand activists gathered in Chicago the week of October 7-13 with the intention of causing havoc. These protests became known as the Days of Rage and resulted in destruction that cost hundreds of thousands of dollars, 284 arrests, and dozens of injuries to police and activists.

Covert Activities After the Days of Rage ended, the Weatherman debated the usefulness of their street fighting tactics, with many members of the group arguing for an end to such tactics because they were "suicidal." This faction argued instead for the group to go underground and wage a campaign of bombings. After a national convention in December, 1969, known as the National War Council, this strategy was adopted, despite opposition from many in the organization and its allies.

On March 6, 1970, three members of the organization were killed when a bomb that they were building accidentally exploded, destroying the Greenwich Village townhouse in which they lived. Two other members escaped. The bomb was intended for a military ball in Fort Dix, New Jersey. After this incident, the remaining members of Weatherman disappeared underground and began a campaign of symbolic bombings of U.S. government and corporate buildings. Some of their targets included the Pentagon, the U.S. Capitol Building, various police stations, corrections offices, and banks. Each bombing was accompanied by a communiqué explaining the reasons for the attack and sent to newspapers. In addition, the attacks usually were preceded by a phone call that instructed police to empty the targeted building.

Weatherman began to call itself the Weather Underground in late 1970 in an attempt to be consciously nonsexist. This decision reflected the important role of women in the group and the growing influence of the 1970's feminist movement in the New Left. The group was the ongoing subject of a Federal Bureau of Investigation (FBI) manhunt, and many of its supporters were the targets of illegal surveillance. Members of the group, meanwhile, continued their existence underground, blending into the sympathetic countercultural communities that existed in most large U.S. cities and many college towns.

The support among the counterculture was the result of both the tendency of law enforcement to treat all those youths who adopted the counterculture lifestyle as potential enemies and the conscious strategy of the Weather Underground to organize these young people. This strategy took center stage over the summer of 1970 and went public that autumn when the Weather Underground helped counterculture guru Timothy Leary escape from a prison in California, where he was serving a sentence for possession of a small amount of marijuana. The Weather Underground then helped Leary go into exile in Algeria.

After the Weather Underground bombed the Pentagon on May 19, 1972, in protest of the renewed U.S. bombing of North Vietnam and the mining of its harbors, the group began to founder. Discussions about its future continued from 1973 through 1975. By this time, the group consisted of not more than a few dozen members, many of whom spent most of their time just trying to exist outside of society. The desire to end their underground existence was voiced by those who felt increasingly irrelevant politically. Furthermore, the war in Vietnam was winding down as the United States began withdrawing its forces. As fewer American personnel were sent to Vietnam, young people in the United States became less political.

Changes and Disintegration In 1975, the Weather Underground released a film that featured five of its members (with their faces hidden) in a conversation with the filmmaker about their politics and histories. The film had been preceded by the release of a manifesto explaining the Weather Underground's perception of the world in the mid-1970's. This manifesto, titled *Prairie Fire—The Politics of Revolutionary Anti-Imperialism,* was distributed throughout the United States. The release of the document was accompanied by the formation of an aboveground organization of Weather Underground supporters called the Prairie Fire Organizing Committee (PFOC). In January, 1976, the PFOC helped organize a conference to discuss the situation of the working class in the United States. This was the group's last major public action.

During the remaining months of its existence, the Weather Underground split into two factions—one in favor of continuing its bombing campaign and the other in favor of moving above ground to organize. The former faction, infiltrated by undercover California police, was arrested in 1977 for conspiring to bomb an antigay California state senator's office. The other faction disintegrated, and its members turned themselves in to or were discovered by law enforcement.

Impact The Weather Underground's impact was felt throughout most of U.S. society. Their use of bombings scared many Americans and helped feed the mainstream media's portrayal of the antiwar movement as being too radical. Their political commitment continued to inspire youthful activists of later decades.

Further Reading

Ayers, Bill. *Fugitive Days: A Memoir.* New York: Penguin, 2003. Ayers was a part of the Weather Underground leadership. His personal story reveals a little about the inner workings of the group and much about his personal motivation.

Jacobs, Ron. *The Way the Wind Blew: A History of the Weather Underground.* New York: Verso, 1997. A very readable history of the organization that emphasizes its politics. Written from a leftist perspective.

Varon, Jeremy. *Bringing the War Home: The Weather Underground, the Red Army Faction, and the Revolutionary Violence in the Sixties and Seventies.* Berkeley: University of California Press, 2004. Varon compares two of the best-known revolutionary groups of the 1960's and 1970's in Western society and examines their political and social motivations.

Ron Jacobs

See also Antiwar demonstrations; Black Panthers; Davis, Angela; Federal Bureau of Investigation (FBI); Feminism; Hearst, Patty; Hippies; Huston Plan; May Day demonstrations of 1971; Soledad Brothers; Symbionese Liberation Army (SLA); Terrorism; Vietnam War.

■ Welfare

Definition Public provision of cash, goods, or services to those in need

The 1970's witnessed disenchantment with governmental operation of social welfare programs, as well as the creation of new programs to assist persons facing economic and other hardships.

Introduced by the Nixon administration in 1969, the Family Assistance Plan (FAP) would have federalized the Aid to Families with Dependent Children (AFDC) program, the federal-state program created in 1935 to provide cash assistance primarily to poor widowed mothers. FAP was reintroduced to Congress in 1971 and withdrawn in 1972. It was proposed as a substitute for AFDC, replacing welfare with "workfare" and incorporating a negative income tax mechanism that set a minimum guaranteed income while encouraging people to work. Instead of FAP, Congress created the Supplemental Security Income (SSI) program, which transferred responsibility of poor, aged, blind, and disabled persons from their respective federal-state programs to the Social Security Administration as part of the Social Security Amendments of 1972.

The average monthly benefit for AFDC in 1996 dollars was $734 in 1970, and it declined to $523 by 1980. The number of families served, however, increased from 1,909, or 6.6 percent of U.S. families with children, in 1970 to 3,574, or 11.5 percent of U.S. families with children, by 1980. SSI payments varied by whether recipients owned their own home or resided in another's household or in an institution covered by Medicaid. In 1974, the benefit was set in 1996 dollars at $414 for a single individual living in his or her own home and at $621 for a couple, increasing respectively to $453 and $680 by 1980. In 1977, the Carter administration proposed a revised version of FAP, the Program for Better Jobs and Income, which also failed to find congressional support.

Increased Federal Spending Public welfare legislation enacted during the 1960's had enabled states to use federal funds to pay voluntary agencies 75 percent of services provided to public welfare recipients. During the 1970's, states took advantage of such provisions, thereby increasing federal outlays. In 1975, Congress placed a cap on such services with enactment of Title XX of the Social Security Amendments of 1974, which also initiated comprehensive social services programs directed toward achieving economic self-support and preventing dependence on government for assistance.

Federal expenditures for all income-tested programs increased throughout the 1970's. Medical benefits, primarily reflecting the Medicaid program created in 1965, nearly doubled in 1998 inflation-adjusted dollars from $12.9 billion in 1968 to $24.5 billion in 1973, increasing annually to reach $36.9 billion in 1979. Cash assistance, primarily for AFDC, increased from $23.6 billion in 1968 to $31.5 billion in 1973, peaking at $42.3 billion in 1997 and ending the decade at $38.1 billion. Food benefits, primarily food stamps, increased from $4.2 billion in 1968 to $14.2 billion in 1973 and steadily increasing to $23.3 billion in 1979.

Federal expenditures for services increased from $1.2 billion in 1968 to $6.2 billion in 1973, peaking at $8.7 billion in 1977 and ending the decade at $8.2 billion in 1979. As a share of the federal budget, medical assistance increased from 1.54 percent in 1968 to 3.18 percent in 1978; cash assistance went from 2.83 percent to 3.50 percent; food assistance from 0.50 percent to 1.86 percent; and services from 0.22 percent to 0.75 percent.

Welfare Legislation Congress also addressed the needs of low-skilled persons seeking employment. In 1974, it passed the Comprehensive Employment and Training Act (CETA), which initiated extensive job education and experience opportunities for unemployed people. As a result, federal outlays for job training increased in 1998 inflation-adjusted dollars from $3.5 billion in 1968 to $6.6 billion in 1975 to $24.4 billion, which included related public employment expenditures, in 1979.

Congress had also addressed child welfare in the 1970's. In 1971, it passed the Comprehensive Child Development Act to provide comprehensive, high quality day care and support services to all children. President Richard M. Nixon, however, vetoed the act. In 1974 Congress passed the Child Abuse Prevention and Treatment Act, which initiated financial assistance for demonstration programs for prevention, identification, and treatment of child abuse and neglect and established the National Center on Child Abuse and Neglect. In 1978, Congress passed the Child Abuse Prevention and Treatment and Adoption Reform Act, which extended the 1974 act and initiated new programs to encourage and improve adoptions.

Other legislation in the 1970's that benefited those in need and addressed the general welfare of the U.S. population included the Equal Employment Opportunity Act of 1972, the Health Maintenance Organization Act of 1973, the Education for All Handicapped Children Act of 1974, the Earned Income Tax Credit (EITC), and the Full Employment and Balanced Growth Act of 1978, which reaffirmed the right of all Americans to employment and asserted the federal government's responsibility to promote full employment, production and real income, balanced growth, and better economic policy planning and coordination.

Impact The 1970's served as a transition decade between the 1960's expansion of public responsibility and activist government and the 1980's erosion of confidence in government, especially in the federal government, to address many social problems. Despite its reaffirmation of the work ethic, Congress eventually ended the federal entitlement aspect of the AFDC program, and it increasingly sought ways to curtail escalating costs of programs targeting people in need, particularly costs associated with Medicaid, the federal-state administered program making health care available to low-income individuals and families. Despite Congress's commitment to a full-employment economy, the CETA program also was terminated, jettisoning public service jobs as an option for assisting low-income individuals seeking employment and brought subsequent spending for job training programs to pre-CETA levels. Congress brought under its auspices in the SSI program populations of poor persons deemed unable to compete in the labor market and provided them with higher levels of monthly income than those of AFDC recipients.

Further Reading

Axinn, June, and Mark Stern. *Social Welfare: A History of the American Response to Need.* 6th ed. Boston: Allyn & Bacon, 2004. This book provides original source material as well as summary, analysis, and commentary by Axinn and Stern.

Caputo, Richard K. *Welfare and Freedom American Style II: The Role of the Federal Government, 1941-1980.* Lanham, Md.: University Press of America, 1994. This book traces the contemporary development of social welfare and poverty programs in the United States. Contains an index and bibliography of original and secondary sources.

Patterson, James T. *America's Struggle Against Poverty in the Twentieth Century.* Cambridge, Mass.: Harvard University Press, 2000. Chronicles the development of poverty-related programs in the U.S. throughout the twentieth century. Contains an index and a resource section of archival sources and documents.

Richard K. Caputo

See also Child Abuse Prevention and Treatment Act of 1974; Conservatism in U.S. politics; Disability rights movement; Earned Income Tax Credit program; Education for All Handicapped Children Act of 1975; Equal Employment Opportunity Act of 1972; Liberalism in U.S. politics; Social Security Amendments of 1972; Unemployment in the United States.

■ White Night Riots

The Event Riots erupt over the verdict in the murder trial of Dan White
Date May, 1979
Place San Francisco

In a watershed moment in the struggle for gay rights akin to 1969's Stonewall Inn riots, the White Night Riots turned Americans' attention toward two unspoken and serious problems in U.S. society: discrimination against gays and hate crimes.

On November 27, 1978, Dan White—an antigay, conservative reactionary and a former San Francisco city supervisor, police officer, and firefighter—walked into the office of openly gay city supervisor Harvey Milk and shot him dead. Then, White continued his killing spree with the assassination of Mayor George Moscone. Afterward, White turned himself into a friend on the police force and confessed to the murders.

At trial, White's attorney Douglas Schmidt introduced the infamous "Twinkie defense" to justify his clients actions and the not-guilty plea. Schmidt charged that White's depression was heightened by his high-sugar diet of Coca-Cola and Twinkies snack cakes. Schmidt argued that White, mentally incapacitated by depression, was incapable of rational thought and, therefore, not guilty of premeditated murder. The jury accepted Schmidt's arguments and found White guilty of manslaughter, not murder, on May 21, 1979, and sentenced him to seven years.

After the gay community of the Castro District reacted strongly to the verdict, a fury of protests were ignited throughout San Francisco. The crowds at the outset were peaceful as they marched from the Castro District to City Hall, but as the evening wore on and riot police assembled, the crowd became violent. Despite the breaking of City Hall windows and burning of patrol cars, Chief of Police Charles Gain kept his officers in check and temporarily prevented a police counterriot. Afterward, Gain would be criticized for his actions, although his restraint prevented additional needless damage to property and persons. Nonetheless, almost two dozen protesters were arrested and litigation from the incident continued for almost a decade.

Later that evening, after the crowd had dispersed, some police officers went into the Castro District to enact revenge. Although gay men and women had been only a small portion of the crowd outside City Hall, they were the focus of the police department's rage. White's assassination of Milk was a hate crime, and the San Francisco Police Department had an antigay reputation. As such, the gay community of the Castro District formed a visible and easy target for police rage. In the ensuing police riot, officers moved unchecked through the Castro District, damaging property and hurting people.

Impact Named for the man whose actions triggered a community's outrage, the White Night Riots

Gay rights advocates in New York City protest the light sentence for Dan White, who assassinated San Francisco mayor George Moscone and Harvey Milk. In San Francisco, the anger escalated to violence called the White Night Riots. (AP/Wide World Photos)

marked a turning point in San Francisco and U.S. history. White's murder of the openly gay Milk, who had been a positive role model for gay Americans, shone a bright light on issues heretofore buried in the darkest recesses of the nation's collective closet: gay rights and hate crimes.

Subsequent Events Years later, litigation stemming from the police riot would continue to confront the city. Those who sued the city for civil rights violations and filed claims with their insurance companies continued to be the victims of ongoing discrimination when their suits were dismissed and their claims denied when the insurance companies contended that the police were not vandals. In shepherding the city through the difficult aftermath of the murders and riot, Mayor Dianne Feinstein, however, revitalized a political career that would eventually include election to the U.S. Senate.

Further Reading

Marcus, Eric. *Making Gay History: The Half-Century Struggle for Lesbian and Gay Equal Rights.* New York: Perennial, 2002.

Shilts, Randy. *The Mayor of Castro Street: The Life and Times of Harvey Milk.* Reprint. New York: St. Martin's Press, 1988.

Paul D. Gelpi, Jr.

See also Feinstein, Dianne; Homosexuality and gay rights; Milk, Harvey; Moscone, George; National Lesbian and Gay Rights March of 1979.

■ *White Shadow, The*

Identification Television drama series
Date Aired from 1978 to 1981

Although a comparatively short-lived entry in the long tradition of television series set in high schools, The White

Shadow *reflected the developing social awareness of its era to tackle themes previously ignored in television broadcasting.*

An hour-long drama series produced by Mark Tinker and Bruce Paltrow for Mary Tyler Moore (MTM) Enterprises and airing on the Columbia Broadcasting System (CBS) network, *The White Shadow* starred Ken Howard as Ken Reeves, a former professional basketball player whose playing career was ended by injury. The series began with him accepting an offer from a former college teammate, now a Los Angeles high school principal, to coach the boys' basketball team at Carver High School. The team's mostly black players are skeptical of Reeves's qualifications when he shows up on the court but are quickly won over when he trounces the team's top players in a game of one-on-two.

High schools have been popular settings for television series since at least 1952, when the popular radio series *Our Miss Brooks* moved to television. When *The White Shadow* began airing in 1978, it followed closely on the heels of several other series with superficially similar themes. Bill Cosby had earlier played a high school gym teacher and basketball coach in *The Bill Cosby Show* (1969-1971), but that series focused on amiable humor and rarely even acknowledged racial themes or serious social problems. In contrast, *Room 222* (1969-1974), set in a racially integrated Los Angeles high school, explored social issues. After that series ended, the genre arguably took a step backward with *Welcome Back, Kotter* (1975-1979), a low-brow comedy set in a Brooklyn high school that showcased the talents of standup comic Gabe Kaplan and future film star John Travolta.

Created by veteran television producer and basketball fan Paltrow, *The White Shadow* contained a great deal of basketball but was mostly about the pressures of growing up in the inner city. Most of Coach Reeves's players were African Americans and Latinos who cope with gang violence, poverty, academic pressures, and drugs. The show offered something new in television. Although humor pervaded the series, many of its episodes focused on realistically dark themes, and the series was unusual in not offering pat solutions to the problems that its characters confronted. Indeed, the show startled audiences in the last episode of its second season by having one of the basketball players shot to death as a bystander during a liquor store holdup.

In November, 1979, *Saturday Night Live* parodied the seriousness of *The White Shadow* in a sketch titled "The Black Shadow." Inverting the series' premise, that sketch featured former basketball star Bill Russell as a troubled black coach in a predominantly white high school whose basketball players help him work through his many personal problems.

Impact During its third and final season, *The White Shadow* turned to generally lighter themes, but it is still remembered for its efforts to address realistic problems and is considered a forerunner to such later series as *Hill Street Blues* and *St. Elsewhere.* Those shows involved many members of the creative team behind *The White Shadow,* including composer Mike Post, who wrote the music for *The White Shadow* with Pete Carpenter.

Further Reading

Gray, Herman. *Watching Race: Television and the Struggle for Blackness.* Minneapolis: University of Minnesota Press, 2004.

Hunt, Darnell M. *Channeling Blackness: Studies on Television and Race in America.* New York: Oxford University Press, 2004.

McNeil, Alex. *Total Television: A Comprehensive Guide to Programming from 1948 to the Present.* New York: Penguin Group, 1996.

R. Kent Rasmussen

See also *Room 222*; *Saturday Night Live*; Television in the United States.

■ Who, The

Identification British hard-rock band
Date Formed in 1963

The Who became one of the premier hard-rock acts in the United States during the 1970's.

At the beginning of the decade, the Who was still riding high on the success of their 1969 epic album *Tommy.* Lead guitarist and chief writer Pete Townshend had styled the work as a "rock opera," since the entire album spun a continuous musical tale about a traumatized deaf, dumb, and blind boy who happened to be a whiz at pinball. Competing with Townshend's wildly energetic, guitar-smashing performances was lead singer Roger Daltrey's considerable stage presence and Keith Moon's savage drum work. The most passive member of the quartet was bassist John "The Ox" Entwistle. Their efforts were not always consistent, but by the end of the 1970's, the band had generated a solid catalog of powerful and sophisticated hard rock.

The Who started the decade with *Who's Next*, released in 1971. Although Townshend harbored doubts about the material, many consider this album the band's finest work. In particular, "Baba O'Riley" had a cutting-edge synthesizer sound that became something of an anthem to hard-core rock devotees. Another cut, "Won't Get Fooled Again," generated enormous airplay and mocked antiestablishment baby boomers with lines like "meet the new boss, same as the old boss."

Two years later, the Who released another concept-opera album, *Quadrophenia*, a work about the 1960's mod scene in London that was not considered the equivalent of Townsend's first rock opera, although it contained notable melodies such as "Love Reign O'er Me." Other original work at mid-decade included a compilation titled *Odds and Sods* (1974) and *The Who by Numbers* (1975). The latter work was self-critical of the band, but its somewhat silly "Squeeze Box" found significant airplay.

The Who in 1976. (AP/Wide World Photos)

During the late 1970's, the band continued to suffer from its usual internal tensions: It had always comprised a fractious lot and was often on the brink of breakup. Townshend in particular struggled throughout the decade with depression, hearing damage, drinking, identity issues, and the sense that he was too old to fill his once familiar role of youth rebel. The other band members had experienced disappointment in a variety of solo music and film ventures, most of which proved unsuccessful save for a 1975 film version of *Tommy*, starring Daltrey, Eric Clapton, Elton John, and Tina Turner, which generated good box-office returns.

The Who also managed to pull together one more chart-topping album before the end of the decade. *Who Are You* appeared in 1978 and rose to number two in the U.S. charts. Driven by its hit title song, the work showed much of the old drive, energy, and intelligence that had characterized the Who's music ten years earlier.

Impact Unfortunately, the last years of the decade brought two significant events. Keith Moon died of a drug overdose at age thirty-one in 1978. However, the rest of the band chose not to break up its famous stage act and hired Moon's friend Kenney Jones as a replacement. In spite of an enormously successful tour, the decade ended with an even greater tragedy. On December 3, 1979, at Cincinnati's Riverfront Coliseum, eleven fans were trampled to death, and scores were injured during a stampede at a sold-out concert. The event, caused by a flawed seating arrangement, shocked both the American general public and horrified the band members themselves. They would soldier on for a few years into the 1980's, but Moon's loss and Townshend's increasing preoccupation with solo work would mean that a final break would not be long in coming.

Further Reading

Fletcher, Tony. *Dear Boy: The Life of Keith Moon.* London: Omnibus Press, 1999.

Guiliano, Geoffry. *Behind Blue Eyes: The Life of Pete Townshend.* London: Cooper Square Press, 2002.

Schaffner, Nicholas. *The British Invasion.* New York: McGraw-Hill, 1982.

Roger Pauly

See also Hard rock and heavy metal; Music; Progressive music.

■ Wiccan movement

Definition Revival of an ancient mystery religion in American popular culture

The permissive attitudes in American culture during the late 1960's and early 1970's helped foster a renewed interest in alternative neopagan religions, including the "Old Religion" of "magick-working," or Wicca.

Modern Wicca—this Old English term is preferred in order to avoid the negative implications arising from the more bias-laden "witchcraft"—can be traced most directly to the seminal writings of Gerald Gardner, a British amateur folklorist who became converted to Wicca in later life after being introduced to its system of beliefs by supposedly authentic practitioners. Along with his partner Doreen Valiente, Gardner both elucidated and elaborated upon established Wiccan beliefs and principles in his books *Witchcraft Today* (1954) and *The Meaning of Witchcraft* (1959). Gardnerian Wicca, as it has been called, became the template for most later groups, especially those arising during the 1970's. This form of Wicca, in general, is a nature-based mystery religion emphasizing spiritual exploration and fulfillment, environmental stewardship (with animistic overtones), and attainment of individual harmony with intrapersonal and transcendental forces.

Modern forms of Wicca attracted the attention of feminists seeking an alternative to the male-dominated teachings and sacerdotal organization of Orthodox Christianinty and Judaism. In contrast to the gods of these religions, the principal Wiccan deities are dualistic, represented as a goddess (the embodiment of Nature) and her consort, a stag-horned god representing the Hunter and inspired by the Celtic deity Cernunnos. In formal rites, the goddess usually predominates, although both aspects are held to be complimentary and of equal importance. Various forms of homeopathic-sympathetic magic, based upon the manipulation of shared resemblances between dissimilar things, plays a significant role. The ethical underpinnings of Wiccan beliefs are evidenced in the "Wiccan Rede," which states "An it harm none, do what thou wilt," as well as the "Threefold Principle," which holds that the consequences of any spell will return thrice magnified to the spellcaster.

The distorted portrayal of witches in books and films of the late 1960's and the 1970's, such as *Rosemary's Baby* (1968) and *The Exorcist* (1973), prompted extremists wrongly to deride Wicca as a thinly disguised form of Satanism. This falsehood, spread largely through misinterpretation or plain ignorance of historical facts, resulted in isolated instances of persecution of Wiccans during this period, sometimes taking violent form. These unfortunate events led to the establishment of the Witchcraft Anti-defamation League and, later, the Aquarian Anti-defamation League (AADL), created to protect the rights of persons who practice alternative religions.

Impact Popular interest in the various New Age movements of the 1970's resulted in the creation of recognized Wiccan nature sanctuaries, the oldest and most successful of which, Circle Sanctuary, is located in Mount Horeb, Wisconsin. Because of the small size and secretive nature of the covens, however, Wicca remained a fragmented collection of loosely affiliated sects and individual practitioners, each espousing a personal interpretation of essential rites and beliefs. This modern Wicca more closely resembles a shared system of metaphysics rather than a formalized religion.

Further Reading

Adler, Margot. *Drawing Down the Moon: Witches, Druids, Goddess-Worshipers, and Other Pagans in America Today.* New York: Viking Press, 1979.

Buckland, Raymond. *The Complete Book of Witchcraft.* St. Paul, Minn.: Llewellyn, 2004.

Larry Smolucha

See also Castaneda, Carlos; Feminism; New Age movement; Religion and spirituality in the United States.

■ Wilder, Gene

Identification American actor, screenwriter, and director

Born June 11, 1933; Milwaukee, Wisconsin

A successful but not widely celebrated stage actor, Wilder rose to international prominence in the 1970's in a string of popular comedies.

Gene Wilder's interest in acting and comedy led at fifteen to parts in local theater in Milwaukee. After his graduation from the University of Iowa in 1955, he studied at the Old Vic Theatre School in Bristol, England, and returned to the United States and served in the military. In 1961, he began studying at the famed Actors Studio in New York, which led to parts on Broadway, one of which, in *The Complaisant Lover* (1961), earned him the Clement Derwent Award. A small part in the film *Bonnie and Clyde* (1967) and his supporting role in Mel Brooks's *The Producers* (1968), which brought an Academy Award nomination, marked him as a rising comic star.

Gene Wilder (right) with Cleavon Little in a scene from the motion picture Blazing Saddles. (Hulton Archive/Getty Images)

During the 1970's, Wilder appeared in his most successful and enduring films. They began with a dual role in *Start the Revolution Without Me* (1970) and as the threatening, yet benign, candy manufacturer in *Willy Wonka and the Chocolate Factory* (1971). He had a small part in Woody Allen's film version of *Everything You Always Wanted to Know About Sex but Were Afraid to Ask* (1972) and reteamed with old friend Brooks in the wildly popular *Blazing Saddles* (1974). The same year, the two worked again in *Young Frankenstein*, which starred Wilder and inaugurated his screenwriting career. In 1975, he directed and starred in *The Adventure of Sherlock Holmes' Smarter Brother* and found even greater commercial success with costar Richard Pryor in *Silver Streak* (1976).

Impact Gene Wilder worked with some of the most successful directors in Hollywood—Woody Allen, Mel Brooks, Arthur Hiller—and established himself as box-office gold with one successful comedy after another. He specialized in parodic treatments of older films or cinematic genres, and he displayed a remarkable comedic range, moving from wry, understated characterizations to wildly frenetic neurotics who could barely control their emotions. Wilder was also in the forefront of the popular "buddy" genre in films with Richard Pryor. In an era of cinematic auteurs, Wilder further distinguished himself with films such as *The Adventure of Sherlock Holmes' Smarter Brother* and *The World's Greatest Lover* (1977).

Further Reading

Chase, Chris. "Gene Wilder's Plans Include Gilda Radner." *The New York Times*, June 4, 1982, p. C12.

"A Quiet Battle: Actor Gene Wilder, Who Nursed Gilda Radner, Confronts Cancer Himself." *People Weekly* 53, no. 7 (February 21, 2000): 60.

Stuart, Mel, and Josh Young. *Pure Imagination: The Making of "Willy Wonka and the Chocolate Factory."* New York: St. Martin's Press, 2002.

Wilder, Gene. *Kiss Me Like a Stranger: My Search for Love and Art.* New York: St. Martin's Press, 2005.

David W. Madden

See also Allen, Woody; *Blazing Saddles*; Brooks, Mel; Comedians; *Everything You Always Wanted to Know About Sex but Were Afraid to Ask*; Film in the United States; Pryor, Richard; *Young Frankenstein.*

■ Wilson, Lanford

Identification American playwright
Born April 13, 1937; Lebanon, Missouri

Wilson came to maturity as a playwright during the 1970's, bringing forth plays that employ unique time sequences and create disparate but compelling characters.

The 1970's saw the production of fourteen Lanford Wilson plays—six one-acts and an opera libretto for Tennessee Williams's *Summer and Smoke* (pr. 1971). With *Lemon Sky* (pr. 1970), Wilson began to mature, producing scripts suitable for full-length presentation. Wilson's career burgeoned with *Hot l Baltimore* (pr. 1973), which ran for 1,166 Off-Broadway performances and received the New York Drama Critics Circle Award. It became a television series in 1975.

Marking a capstone in Wilson's career, *Talley's Folly* (pr. 1979) received a Pulitzer Prize in the late 1970's. Meanwhile, Wilson produced *Victory on Mrs. Dandywine's Island* (pr. 1973), *The Mound Builders* (pr. 1975), *Brontosaurus* (pr. 1977), and *Fifth of July* (pr. 1978).

Wilson's plays lack unified and compelling plots. Rather, as in *Hot l Baltimore*, they often present groups of unrelated characters who find themselves thrust together in tense situations. Wilson often permits the drama to evolve almost accidentally. His greatest strength is in shaping enticing and convincing characters. These characters, a hodgepodge of pimps, priests, whores, professors, drag queens, and others, who, on the surface, have little in common, sometimes talk simultaneously, creating dual or triple dialogue. The time lines in Wilson's plays are often blurred, but such blurring is a calculated part of his inventive technique. Characters drift in and out of the plays, sometimes spawned by other characters' imaginations or memories.

The loss-of-innocence theme that has intrigued literary greats such as Nathaniel Hawthorne, Mark Twain, Tennessee Williams, William Inge, Robert Anderson, James Agee, and John Steinbeck also fascinated Wilson, who considered himself a product of American counterculture. He frequently focused on the American heartland and on the disintegration of American families, culling from his experience in his own family unit, which dissolved with his parents' divorce when he was five. He treats the effects of this divorce in *Lemon Sky*.

The family is also central to most of Wilson's plays. Families, however, usually are not represented as the wholesome units people mistakenly assume them to be. Wilson highlighted realistically the dysfunctions of families and, as in *Hot l Baltimore*, constructed surrogate families for those who have spurned familial support.

Impact Lanford Wilson's apprenticeship in his first decade of writing yielded during the 1970's to more realistic and conventional plays than his earlier experimental efforts. During the 1970's, the author matured into a significant and influential American playwright, becoming an undisputed force in American theater.

Further Reading

Barnett, Gene A. *Lanford Wilson*. Boston: Twayne, 1987.

Bryer, Jackson R., ed. *Lanford Wilson: A Casebook*. New York: Garland, 1994.

Dean, Anne M. *Discovery and Invention: The Urban Plays of Lanford Wilson*. Rutherford, N.J.: Fairleigh Dickinson University Press, 1994.

R. Baird Shuman

See also Literature in the United States; Theater in the United States.

■ Wolfe, Tom

Identification American author and essayist
Born March 02, 1931; Richmond, Virginia

Wolfe pioneered the New Journalism movement in literature, which he used to chronicle, in colorful verbiage, many aspects of the decade's culture, including hippie life, the Black Panther movement, and the world of astronauts.

Tom Wolfe. (Hulton Archive/Getty Images)

Tom Wolfe is best known for his writing style, which he developed by adding to traditional nonfiction writing techniques more often used in fiction—for example, dialogue and attention to minute detail. After achieving success with several books that employed aspects of what was to become New Journalism—including *The Kandy-Kolored Tangerine-Flake Streamline Baby* (1965) and *The Electric Kool-Aid Acid Test* (1968)—Wolfe began to write in detail about this new writing style.

He authored *The New Journalism* in 1973, in which he included his definition of this genre, rules for its application, and an anthology of works that fit this definition by his contemporaries, including authors such as Truman Capote and Norman Mailer. He included his own commentary on each piece. The term "New Journalism" has been variously defined, but in general, it can be considered as factual writing (nonfiction) enlivened by the type of detail and human interest usually presented in fictional works.

Wolfe wrote many articles and books in the 1970's: *Radical Chic and Mau-Mauing the Flak Catchers* (1970), *The Painted Word* (1975), *Mauve Gloves and Madmen, Clutter and Vine, and Other Stories, Sketches, and Essays* (1976), and one of his most famous, *The Right Stuff* (1979). These books enlightened readers about such diverse topics as the Black Panthers, the history of art, and the culture of the Mercury astronauts. He coined many phrases that became part of the American vocabulary, including, "the right stuff," "radical chic," "the Me Decade," and "good ol' boy."

Impact During the 1970's, Tom Wolfe became a chronicler of American popular culture. He attracted controversy as he described, "warts and all," a variety of aspects of American life. In later decades, New Journalism evolved into what was called literary journalism, and Wolfe received renewed attention as the forerunner of one of the era's most successful journalistic styles.

Further Reading

Bloom, Harold. *Tom Wolfe: Modern Critical Views.* Langhorne, Pa.: Chelsea House, 2000.

Scura, Dorothy. *Conversations with Tom Wolfe.* Jackson: University Press of Mississippi, 1990.

Mary C. Ware

See also Journalism in the United States; Literature in the United States; Mailer, Norman; "Me Decade"; New Journalism; "Radical Chic."

■ Woman Warrior, The

Identification Feminist mythic-autobiographical novel

Author Maxine Hong Kingston (1940-)

Date Published in 1976

Uniting American individualism with a Chinese urge toward cultural identity, The Woman Warrior: Memoirs of a Girlhood Among Ghosts *was embraced by feminist writers of the 1970's as an unprecedented attempt at creating a way of reading and writing by a Chinese American woman.*

In *The Woman Warrior,* Maxine Hong Kingston's personal issue of identity informs her imaginative accounts of her immigrant parents' culture. Kingston also struggles with her family's habit of not telling the whole story. In piecing together her history, Kingston is an adventurous—some would say distorting—reteller both of Chinese myths and of family history because her cultural and familial mythology challenges Chinese traditions of male dominance as well as Western stereotypes.

From the time of its publication and culminating in a series of articles in the 1990's, *The Woman Warrior* has been denounced by some critics, most notably playwright Frank Chin. Chin and others complain that the novel does not meet the expectations of its autobiographical genre, that it does not present a positive image of the Chinese and Chinese American communities, particularly males, and that it distorts Chinese sources, especially the ballad of Fa Mulan, an ancient woman warrior legend that Kingston imaginatively rewrote. These critics dismissed Kingston's novel as being aligned with Western tastes that have an Orientalist agenda in the dominant American culture.

Other 1970's critics regarded the novel as a watershed work of ethnic feminist writing that challenges conventions and standards of ethnic representation. They also suggested that the Kingston denigrators wrote out of the same misogynist loyalty to patriarchal systems that has moved any critic in any age to dismiss an innovative work by a woman. Kingston maintains that her novel is not intended to be a textbook for educating white readers, but rather as a personal search for integrity by a woman of two cultures.

Impact Although *The Woman Warrior* became one of the most controversial novels in twentieth century literature, it also remains one of the most frequently taught books in higher education by a living writer, and it continues to be a central focus of Asian and feminist studies. Proponents of the book take a feminist postmodern view, suggesting that writing need not be restricted rigidly to the set of genre conventions created by a Western system. Opposing views show ways in which Kingston's work may lead to misunderstanding Chinese culture, some drawing on the critical stance of widely known theorist Michel Foucault, who demands that evaluation of literature be deeply situated in the cultural setting.

Further Reading

Chin, Frank. "Come All Ye Asian American Writers of the Real and the Fake." In *The Big Aiiieee! An Anthology of Chinese American and Japanese American Literature*, edited by Jeffrey Paul Chan, et. al. New York: Meridian, 1974.

Kingston, Maxine Hong. *The Woman Warrior.* New York: Vintage, 1976.

Lim, Shirley G. *Approaches to Teaching Kingston's "The Woman Warrior."* New York: Brodart, 1991.

Suzanne Araas Vesely

See also Asian Americans; China and the United States; Feminism; Literature in the United States.

■ Women in the military

Definition Wide integration of women into the armed forces

The decision by Congress and President Richard M. Nixon to increase the number of women in the military and expand career opportunities hitherto denied them changed not only the gender composition of the armed forces, but also many of the policies regarding assignment, training, and deployment for combat missions.

A unique confluence of events led to a series of decisions made during the 1970's to permit women to enter the military in larger numbers and to work in specialties traditionally considered off limits to women. First, the unpopularity of the Vietnam War led President Nixon and his military advisers to explore the feasibility of creating an all-volunteer force. Their initial studies demonstrated that it would be impossible to staff such a force without allowing greater numbers of women to fill positions throughout the ranks; they could not be restricted to traditional jobs in the medical and administrative fields. At the same time, leaders of the women's movement were lobbying Congress and the public to accept women as equals in all occupations and professions. During the first five years of the decade, laws and regulations were changed to permit women to join the Reserve Officers' Training Corps (ROTC); to enlist for specialties such as supply, motor maintenance, and demolitions; and to be admitted at the three military service academies.

Problems and Challenges Leaders of the four branches of the service, both uniformed and civilian, and many members of Congress were initially hostile to increasing the numbers of women and assigning them to specialties considered beyond their capabilities. When pressure began to mount for change, service leaders developed numerous regulations regarding enlistment and assignment criteria that worked against mandates for change. All of the services immediately developed "combat exclusion" policies prohibiting women from serving in specialties that would put them in the direct line of fire during combat. Hence, women could not fly fighter jets, serve aboard ships, or be assigned as ground troops in infantry or field artillery. Because these were the specialties that produced most of the generals and admirals, it would still be difficult for women to achieve full equality within the services; nevertheless, for years these rules remained in place. The services also attempted to retain high physical and strength standards geared toward male physiology but were eventually mandated to develop job-specific criteria for strength and stamina that permitted women to hold positions previously denied to them simply because of social stereotyping.

The services also were forced to deal with issues such as pregnancy, child care, and joint assignments of military couples. Before the 1970's, service women who married were required to resign. During the decade, that rule was struck down, as was the one requiring women who became pregnant to leave active service. These policies were replaced by sensible regulations regarding time off for pregnancy and child care—the latter applied to fathers as well as mothers—and making the military more accommodating for women who wished to pursue a career. All of the services found it necessary to review their policies on fraternization and develop sensible rules regarding relationships between individuals of different ranks. Various experiments were tried to replace separate basic and advanced training for women with integrated training that would better expose female recruits to the wide array of specialties in which they would now be permitted to serve.

While there was much controversy over the change in the law regarding admission to the service academies, the real watershed in providing full career opportunities for women in the military came in 1976, when the first women entered the academies at West Point, Annapolis, and Colorado Springs. The first female cadets faced significant discrimination from classmates and even from some officers and staff, but their persistence demonstrated that women could survive the rigors of academy life and prepare for military careers that could allow the best of them to reach the highest levels of the Army, Navy, Air Force, and Marines.

In 1975, a woman at West Point models one of the uniforms that would be available for female cadets admitted to the military academy the following year. (AP/Wide World Photos)

Impact The initial resistance to integrating women more fully into all the services led to numerous forms of discrimination that on occasion diminished the ability of units in one or another of the military services to carry out missions. Long-established social stereotyping continued to affect male service members' willingness to accept women as equal partners in defending the nation in armed conflict. Nevertheless, the performance of women in high-stress situations demonstrated that they could handle jobs traditionally reserved for men, and during the 1980's, restrictions on combat service were loosened so that by the advent of the Persian Gulf War in 1991, women were assigned to virtually every specialty except infantry.

Further Reading

Harris, Beverly C., Zita M. Simutis, and Melissa Meyer Gantz. *Women in the Army: An Annotated Bibliography.* Alexandria, Va.: U.S. Army Research Institute for the Behavioral and Social Sciences, 2002. Provides excellent summaries of books and articles published during the 1970's through 2000. An introduction offers a historical overview of women's roles in the Army.

Herres, Robert T., et al. *The Presidential Commission on the Assignment of Women in the Armed Forces.* Washington, D.C.: Government Printing Office, 1992. Comprehensive documentation of the work of a panel commissioned to evaluate the success of the armed forces' efforts to integrate women more fully into all of the services. Provides personal assessments from many individuals who were instrumental in the effort.

Holm, Jeanne. *Women in the Military: An Unfinished Revolution.* Rev. ed. Novato, Calif.: Presidio Press, 1992. Written by the general who led Air Force efforts to integrate women into that service during the 1970's. Extensive analysis of the political, sociological, and moral issues that arose as a result of the effort. Updated to describe continuing progress through the period of the Persian Gulf War in 1991.

Stiehm, Judith Hicks, ed. *It's Our Military, Too! Women and the U.S. Military.* Philadelphia: Temple University Press, 1996. Collection of essays by women in military professions and higher education examining issues of gender discrimination, homosexuality, and political climate that have affected women's full integration into military service in the United States.

Laurence W. Mazzeno

See also Affirmative action; Equal Employment Opportunity Act of 1972; Feminism; National Organization for Women (NOW); Women in the workforce; Women's rights.

■ Women in the workforce

Definition Women employed in a specific activity or enterprise during a specific period

The 1970's propelled women into changing the fabric of the American workforce. New patterns of labor market involvement by women emerged, and with increased female labor market activity, substantial changes in family responsibilities developed, which in turn affected many different aspects of the American family.

In 1970, only 43 percent of women age sixteen and older participated in the workforce, and they earned approximately half of what men earned but their income accounted for almost 27 percent of their family's total income. However, the infusion of several legislative changes during the decade marked the beginning of significant workforce changes in general, especially for women. For example, in order to stop the discrimination of women in the workplace, the Equal Pay Act of 1970 gave women the right to equal pay for a job similar in nature to one that was held by a man. Several major court cases further defined and strengthened the Equal Pay Act. *Schultz v. Wheaton Glass Co.* (1970) (1970) ruled that jobs needed to be "substantially equal" but not "identical" in order to fall under the Equal Pay Act. This case prevented employers from changing job titles for men and adding more duties in order to justify a man's higher pay. The second court case was *Corning Glass Works v. Brennan* (1974), which was heard in the U.S. Supreme Court. The ruling in this case stated that employers cannot justify paying women lower wages because of the "going market rate." Wage differentials were not to be in place and considered acceptable just because men were not willing to work for a lower rate.

Title VI of the Civil Rights Act of 1964, which prohibited discrimination based on race, color, and national origin, was the basis for Title IX of the Education Amendments of 1972, which further prohibited sex discrimination in federally assisted education programs. Furthermore, Section 504 of the Rehabilitation Act of 1973 prohibited disability discrimination, and the Age Discrimination Act of 1975 prohibited age discrimination. Finally, the Pregnancy Discrimination Act of 1978 forbid employers from discriminating against workers based on pregnancy, childbirth, or related medical conditions. The act made it is illegal for employers to treat pregnancy differently than any other temporary medical disability.

NOW and Trade Union Involvement The women's liberation movement flourished in the 1970's and gained momentum as it spread, increasing opportunities for girls and women in numerous arenas. The National Organization for Women (NOW) was formed in order to fight for women's rights and was a significantly large women's group. Among its many goals, it worked to begin organizing women in the factories. The group tended to draw attention to the real problems of this era. One of the most significant problems was that a woman's income was not the same as that of a man's even though her work was the same.

Female membership in trade unions increased by 60 percent during the 1970's. During this same period, male membership had an increase of only 19 percent. Even in the union environment, women were still in the lower segment of the paid jobs, partly because of their lack of industrial muscle. Male-dominated management within the unions meant that the industries could still find ways for differentials to be made between male and female pay scales.

Careers and Education The acceleration of the postindustrial economy and legislative changes helped propel the growth of female employment by approximately 44 percent during the decade. However, millions of women continued to find themselves locked in low-wage jobs because they lacked the education to escape menial work in manufacturing or service industries. In 1970, the impact of marriage and motherhood on women's workforce participation rates was strikingly evident. At that time, women's participation reached its initial peak at ages twenty to twenty-four, dropped at ages twenty-five to thirty-four, and then gradually rose to a second peak between ages forty-five and fifty-four, before tapering off permanently. In 1970, 64 percent of all females were married in their twenties. It was traditionally believed that women should take "women's" jobs that did not require extensive education and that they would leave these jobs once they found the right man to marry.

Women consistently suffered sexual harassment and filled less desirable jobs. The majority of women who worked during the decade were employed in clerical positions, factory work, retail sales, and service jobs. Secretaries, bookkeepers, and typists accounted for a large portion of women clerical workers. Women in factories often worked as machine operators, assemblers, and inspectors. Many women in service jobs worked as waitresses, cooks, hospital attendants, cleaning women, and hairdressers. However, as the decade continued, the rapidly expanding public and commercial sectors emerged as a low-wage "ghetto," replacing unskilled labor in households, agriculture commerce, and manufacturing.

It has been understood historically that the movement of women into the labor force as well as into higher-paying occupations has gone hand-in-hand with their pursuit of higher education. During this decade, antidiscrimination laws helped open university doors for women. The number of women entering professional programs in U.S. colleges increased substantially around 1970. Fields such as fine arts and foreign languages were more common for female college graduates in the early 1970's. In 1970, women received 43 percent of all bachelor's degrees conferred. Of these degrees, less than 1 percent in engineering went to women, and only 9 percent of business degrees went to women. Through the 1970's, however, women advanced in management and administration by 60 percent, and the number of women in law multiplied fivefold. The number of women in dentistry, veterinary medicine, and medicine increased 65 percent.

Impact In 1970, wives' earnings accounted for almost 27 percent of their families' median incomes. However, despite their increased presence in the workforce, most women still had primary responsi-

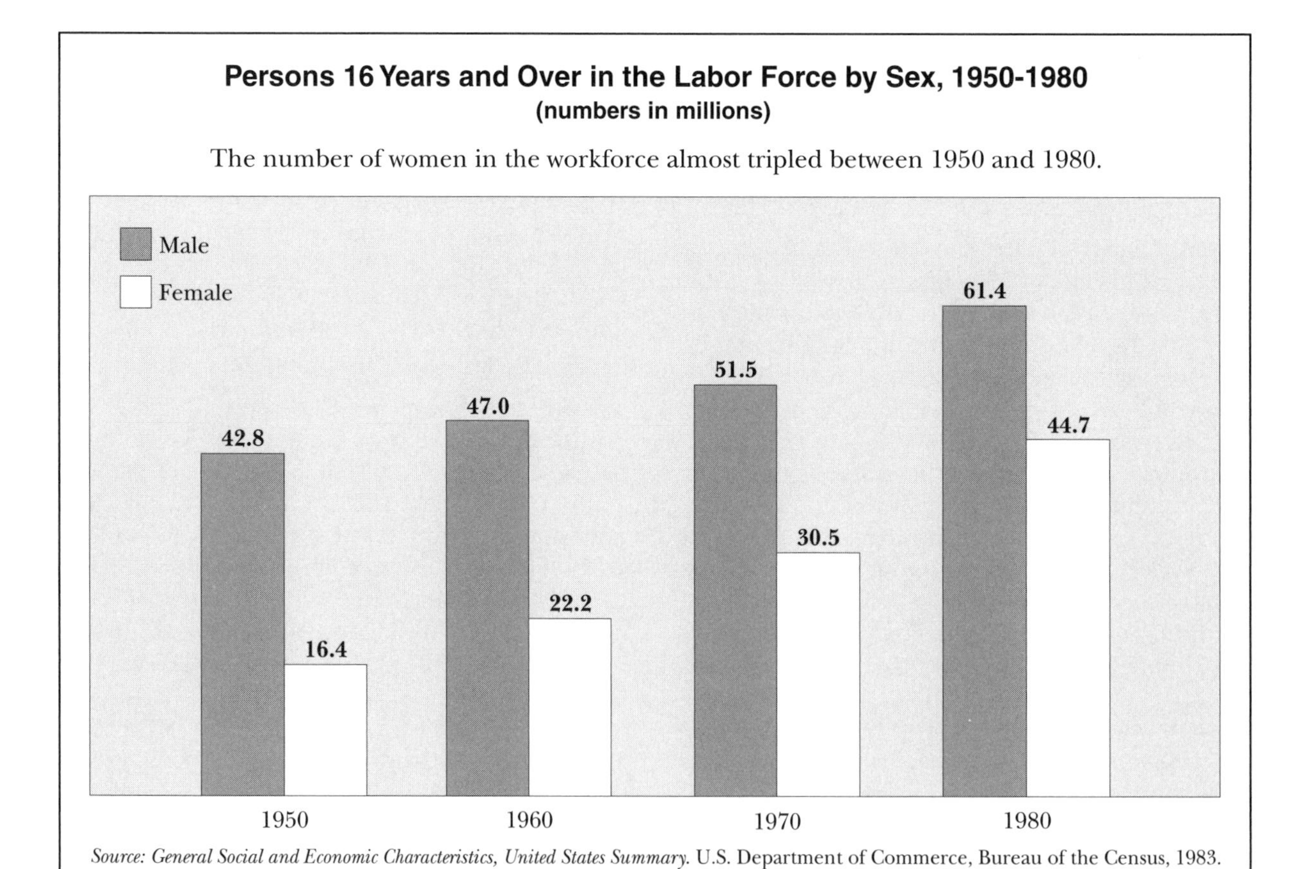

Source: General Social and Economic Characteristics, United States Summary. U.S. Department of Commerce, Bureau of the Census, 1983.

Lionne Kim Brown, the first female trader at Chicago's Midwest Stock Exchange, at work in 1974. The decade saw women enter the workforce in large numbers and in a variety of fields. (AP/ Wide World Photos)

bility for housework and family care and struggled with work-life balance. In the late 1970's, men with an employed wife spent only about 1.4 hours a week more on household tasks than those whose wife was a full-time homemaker. However, because of the strides made during the decade, a significantly greater proportion of women participated in the American workforce, and women's careers changed considerably.

Subsequent Events Because of the significantly greater portion of women in the workforce, women made considerable inroads into managerial occupations. Between 1972 and 2002, the proportion of managerial jobs held by women more than doubled, increasing from 20 percent to 46 percent. Despite the movement of many women into managerial and professional jobs, however, they remained concentrated in clerical and service jobs by the early twenty-first century. Nearly one-half of women workers were employed in three occupational groups—sales (retail and personal services,) services, and administrative support—compared with about one-fifth of male workers. The ratio of women's to men's earnings rose 63 percent between 1979 and 2002. However, despite the fact that women made substantial progress in gender equality, a study in the late 1990's by a Cornell University labor economist provided dramatic evidence that the economic status of less-educated women had deteriorated. Therefore, although the 1970's were the beginning of notable progress in the workforce for women, several decades later, considerably more progress needed to be made.

Further Reading

Albelda, Randy, and Chris Tilly. *Glass Ceilings and Bottomless Pits, Women's Work, Women's Poverty.* Cambridge, Mass.: South End Press, 1997. Using an economic perspective, the book compares the tenuous roles of women in managerial occupations with those held by women on welfare.

Deckard, Barbara Sinclair. *The Women's Movement: Political, Socioeconomic, and Psychological Issues.* 3d ed. New York: Harper & Row, 1983. Examines the processes that women went through in their equality struggles and looks at the changing roles of women in society as well as how women themselves have changed.

Kittay, Eva Feder. *Love's Labor: Essays on Women, Equality, and Dependency.* London: Routledge, 1998. Explores two federal policies enacted during the 1990's—welfare reform and family leave—to discuss how women are continuously hindered in their professional careers by issues of family dependency.

Padavic, Irene, and Barbara Reskin. *Women and Men at Work.* Rev. ed. Thousand Oaks, Calif.: Pine Forge Press, 2002. Examines the role that gender has played historically in work environments.

Joy Portillo

See also Affirmative action; Age Discrimination Act of 1975; Equal Employment Opportunity Act of 1972; Equal Rights Amendment (ERA); Feminism; Income and wages in Canada; Income and wages in the United States; National Organization for Women (NOW); Pregnancy Discrimination Act of 1978; Title IX of the Education Amendments of 1972; Unemployment in Canada; Unemployment in the United States; Unions in Canada; Unions in the United States; Women in the military; Women's rights.

■ Women's rights

Definition The movement to attain equal rights for women in Canada and the United States

The 1970's witnessed both striking successes and profound failures in the attainment of women's rights, as this decade became a staging ground for the struggle for women's liberation.

Several events and political movements provided the catalyst for the second wave of the women's rights movement in the United States. In 1961, President John F. Kennedy, whose record of appointing women to government positions was worse than those of both of his predecessors, established the President's Commission on the Status of Women. Eleanor Roosevelt chaired the commission, and although she died in November, 1962, the commission issued its report to honor her birthday on October 11, 1963. The report did not endorse passage of the Equal Rights Amendment (ERA) because several commission members hoped to retain labor movement support. With the support of labor unions, however, it did result in the passage of the Equal Pay Act of 1963. In 1963, Kennedy created the Citizen's Advisory Council on the Status of Women to stop sex discrimination in the workplace.

In a move similar to Kennedy's, Canadian prime minister Lester Pearson established the Royal Commission on the Status of Women in 1967, chaired by journalist Florence Bird. The Bird Commission, as it was termed, concluded after interviewing women throughout the nation that Canadian women wanted equality and the right to choose whether they were to give birth. In 1969, Minister of Justice Pierre Trudeau ushered in a law that legalized birth control and that made abortion legal under somewhat restrictive circumstances. That same year, Toronto women picketed a bikini contest, arguing that women were objectified and treated as less than human in such events.

Betty Friedan wrote a best-selling book in 1963, *The Feminine Mystique*, striking a chord among millions of women who were told that their main purposes in life consisted of being wives, mothers, and homemakers. Friedan had served on the President's Commission and was well aware of the aimlessness and discontent felt by postwar women who lacked careers and direction in their lives. Her publisher had initially printed only two thousand copies believing that there would be little interest in the book, but within ten years, Friedan's book had sold more than three million copies.

Moreover, the Civil Rights movement of the 1960's and the courage of women such as Rosa Parks and Fannie Lou Hamer became a catalyst for the women's liberation movement. American women were also activated by Title VII of the Civil Rights Act of 1964, which prohibited employment discrimination on the basis not only of race but also of sex. Executive Order 11246 strengthened this law by establishing a policy of affirmative action. Mary King and Casey Hayden wrote one of the first documents of the second wave of women's liberation, linking it directly to the African American struggle for civil rights in the United States. They used the language of black oppression to describe the status of women in the movement, that of second-class citizens.

In June, 1966, a group of fifteen women, including Friedan and Congresswoman Martha Griffiths, met to discuss their frustration over the federal government's unwillingness to enforce Title VII of the 1964 Civil Rights Act. The National Organization for Women (NOW), a a feminist organization, was conceived during this meeting. Shortly after its formation, NOW leaders issued a mission statement that contained the new organization's purpose of establishing "full equality for women, in fully equal partnership with men." Within two years, dissension within NOW, caused partly by NOW's controversial Bill of Rights, had created new organizations on both ends of the political spectrum. One of these new organizations was the Women's Equity Action League (WEAL), created created by Elizabeth Boyer in Cleveland, Ohio, in 1968.

The student-led antiwar movement, with its socialist stance, provided the initial ideology of the women's liberation movement of the late 1960's, although that ideology was to be challenged and radically modified. The emerging ideology of women's liberation was contained in a plethora of books and articles written by theorists such as Shulamith Firestone, Germaine Greer, Kate Millett, Juliet Mitchell, Mary Daly, and Robin Morgan, among others.

Women's liberation groups took an activist stance in the closing years of the 1960's. On January 15, 1968, Women Strike for Peace organized an all-woman protest against the war in Vietnam, calling themselves the Jeanette Rankin Brigade. In January, 1970, a group of women took control of the male-dominated leftist newspaper, the *Rat*, and put together a special issue on the paper's negative attitude toward "women's issues." In the spring of 1970, women staffers at *Newsweek*, *Time*, and the National Broadcasting Company (NBC) network filed sex discrimination charges against their respective media agencies. Radical and liberal women's groups led a sit-in at the *Ladies Home Journal* with the result that the women were allowed to publish an eight-page supplement in a future issue that would address women's rights issues such as consciousness-raising.

Direct Political Action in the 1970's Political action on the part of organized women began in the late 1960's, and in 1971, the National Women's Caucus was founded in the United States. In 1968, Shirley Chisholm was the first African American woman elected to the House of Representatives, while Rosemary Brown became the first black woman to be elected to a Canadian legislature in 1972.

In 1970, Canadian women protested the limited abortion law by organizing an Abortion Caravan that traveled from Vancouver to Ottawa. Young women chained themselves to the gallery in Parliament to protest the law. The Bird Commission issued its report during these upheavals, with 167 recommendations, including day care for children, more equal treatment of aboriginal women, and equal pay for equal work for women. The report was at first treated with derision and then tabled, but it was resurrected within the year as a result of the protests of women across the country.

In 1970, Therese Casgrain became the first woman in Quebec appointed to the Senate. While in the Quebec Senate, she supported the right of women to serve on juries in Quebec. After a public protest, eight Quebec women were jailed for protesting the all-male jury law. Quebec juries were sexually integrated in 1971. The Canada Labour Code was amended that year to prohibit sex discrimination and to reinforce equal pay for equal work. Women were also given a seventeen-week maternity leave.

Educational Advances in the 1970's At the beginning of the 1970's, women's rights groups in the United States focused their energies on women's second-class status in higher education. These groups also called attention to the inculcation of sex roles in elementary and high schools, but their main target was at the higher education level. Women began insisting on programs in women's studies, and during the decade, more than three hundred colleges developed such programs. While most of them offered only a certificate, more than fifty offered a baccalaureate degree in women's studies.

In the mid-1970's, academic professionals founded the National Women's Studies Association, an organization dedicated to establishing and supporting women's studies programs in colleges and universities in the United States. Many institutions of higher learning offered space, often called women's centers or resource centers, with modest budgets and small staffs. Such centers sponsored guest speakers, disseminated information on their respective and

Women's rights activists display signs at the statue of Admiral Farragut in downtown Washington, D.C., in 1970. (AP/Wide World Photos)

neighboring campuses, published newsletters, and maintained contact with other women's centers in the United States and Canada.

Women's educational attainments in the United States changed dramatically during this decade. The percentage of U.S. women below age twenty-four who received a baccalaureate degree increased from 19.7 percent in 1970 to almost 30 percent in 1980. The number of women pursuing and receiving graduate degrees increased dramatically also. Almost as many women as men received master's degrees in 1980, and the gap between men and women receiving doctorates also narrowed the ratio, standing at 2.5 to 1 in 1980. Women also began pursuing different academic programs in the 1970's, many switching from fields such as education and social work to business, mathematics, and the physical and biological sciences. Women began to enter professional fields such as medicine, law, theology, and veterinary medicine in ever increasing numbers throughout the 1970's.

Despite these impressive gains, however, women still faced discrimination in higher education—in funding, athletic scholarships, and fellowships and teaching assistantships. The Education Amendments Act of 1972 forced colleges and universities to examine their practices, and federal pressure urged them to end restrictive quotas and to admit women on the same basis as men. Women athletes faced a variety of discriminatory practices, ranging from having to buy needed equipment to having to pay their own way to athletic events. The U.S. Department of Health, Education, and Welfare urged compliance with Title IX of the Education Amendments Act, forcing many colleges and universities to restructure their athletic programs for women.

Women faculty at institutions of higher learning also faced discrimination. Under the Education Amendments Act, schools agreed to recruit women for vacancies and to adjust salary and rank to reflect a more equitable arrangement. Unfortunately, the law could not force compliance or keep women faculty and athletics directors from being dismissed for "cause," a term that covered a wide variety of reasons for dismissal or denial of tenure.

Canadian universities also began developing women's studies programs in the 1970's. In 1973, Pauline Jewett, president of Simon Fraser University in Burnaby, became the first woman president of a coeducational Canadian university. She later became a member of the Canadian Parliament.

Legislative Decisions, Supreme Court Rulings

Many U.S. women's organizations, most notably NOW, focused on passage of the Equal Rights Amendment in 1970. The amendment was first proposed in 1925, but Congress had never passed it. After its reintroduction by Congresswoman Martha Griffiths in 1971, both the House and Senate had passed it by the spring of 1972. It then went to the states for ratification. By the end of the following year, thirty states had ratified the amendment, eventually followed by five more.

Opponents of the ERA, most notably right-wing publicist Phyllis Schlafly, immediately attacked the amendment on the grounds that it would legalize homosexuality, require that women be drafted, lead to unisex public restrooms, and ultimately destroy the American family. By 1975, support for the ERA had slowed, with the thirty-fifth and last state, Indiana, ratifying it in 1977. Although NOW, WEAL, and other organizations tried to rally state support, its ten-year deadline approached in 1979. Women's rights leadership was able to secure a three-year extension of time from Congress but was unable to secure approval from any of the remaining fifteen states. When the final deadline approached in 1982, the ERA was still lacking the approval of three states required to make the necessary thirty-eight for ratification.

Despite the failure of fifteen states to ratify the ERA during the 1970's, state legislatures as well as Congress passed laws that improved the status of women. In 1972, the Equal Pay Act was extended to cover executive, administrative, professional, and traveling sales employees, and two years later, this protection was afforded to federal, state, and local government employees. In 1972, Congress offered protection to federal, state, and local government employees and those employed by educational institutions under Title VII of the Civil Rights Act of 1964. Title IX of the Educational Amendments of 1972 forbade sex discrimination in educational institutions. The 1974 Equal Credit Opportunity Act forbade creditors from discriminating against applicants on the basis of sex or marital status, thus allowing married and nonmarried women to establish credit. States that had ratified the ERA passed laws or adopted reforms that tended to equalize the sexes before the law. If an existing law provided benefit to one sex, it was most often extended to the other, and if an existing law proved a burden to one sex, it was often removed.

Marriage and family laws were amended during the decade, with the old doctrine of *femme couvert* being discontinued. In most states, a wife's property rights became identical to those of her husband. Property exemptions on the death of a spouse were extended equally to husband and wife, moving the state of marriage toward a partnership of equals. Divorce and dissolution laws also became more equitable, especially in states that had approved the ERA, with some states adopting no-fault divorce. Child support and child custody were often determined as mutually responsible decisions. The Uniform Parentage Act of 1973 addressed the problem of illegitimacy by determining that all biological parents would have potential rights in their children, regardless of their sex or marital status.

In 1971, the Supreme Court made a major departure in favor of women's rights in the case of *Reed v. Reed.* Using the equal protection clause of the Constitution, the Court ruled that when heirs were equally entitled to administer a decedent's estate, men could no longer be given preference over women. In 1973, the Court ruled in *Frontiero v. Richardson* that a female lieutenant in the U.S. Air Force had the right to claim her husband as a dependent in the same way that men could claim their wives as dependents regardless of whether they were in fact dependent on them for financial support. The Court declared in this case that "sex," like "race" was a "suspect classification." In the years following the *Frontiero* decision, however, the Court gradually retreated from its ruling, strengthening the argument for an Equal Rights Amendment so that women's equality would not be dependent on the Court's opinions.

Without doubt, the most controversial U.S. Supreme Court ruling of the era was the 1972 decision of *Roe v. Wade.* The decision began in Dallas, Texas, where the defendant known as Roe brought suit against district attorney, Henry Wade, stating that he had no right to prevent her from having an abortion. Roe won in the lower court, and the Supreme Court upheld that ruling, refusing to define the point at which life begins and upholding a woman's right to privacy before the point of viability. The most outspoken critic of the decision, the Roman Catholic Church, was supported by many state and national right-to-life organizations following the Court's decision.

In 1975, the Canadian Parliament amended eleven laws that provided equality for women, and overt discrimination against women immigrants was removed from the Citizenship Act in 1978. By the end of the 1970's, Canadian women were lobbying Parliament for women's rights inclusion in the proposed new Charter of Human Rights. Their efforts resulted in a victory for women's rights in the charter that was enacted in 1982.

Impact Advances made by American women in the 1970's were significant, and they paved the way for even more achievements in the decades to follow. Although the ERA was not ratified by the necessary number of states, by the early 1980's women were able to enter almost any profession or occupation they wished. Although one might argue that the Canadian women's movement was partially inspired by events in the United States, women's rights, including the right to terminate a pregnancy, eventually proved to be more firmly established in Canada.

Subsequent Events By the end of the 1970's and early 1980's, women were able to enter the service academies of West Point, Annapolis, the Air Force Academy, and any others they wished, and women became airline and fighter pilots. Ivy League institutions opened their doors to women, and in 1981, Sandra Day O'Connor became the first woman appointed to the United States Supreme Court. In 1983, astronaut Sally Ride became the first woman to travel in space, and in 1984, Geraldine Ferraro became the female nominee for vice president of the United States. In 1985, Wilma Mankiller became the first woman to be elected principal chief of the Cherokee Nation.

The Canadian women's rights movement became arguably the most successful in the entire world. Under the 1982 Canadian Charter of Rights and Freedoms, women's rights were redefined in Canada. The charter protects individual rights, preventing the passage of laws that interfere with human rights or the rights of any man or woman. The charter did for Canadian women what many American women hoped that the Equal Rights Amendment would do for them—protect them against reactionary executives, legislators, or Supreme Court justices. Kim Campbell served in the highest political office in Canada, as prime minister in 1993. Many women in the United States do not expect to see a woman president elected within the next several decades.

Time Line of the Women's Movement in the 1970's

Year	*Notable Event*	*Significance*
1970	Women's Strike for Equality is held	Organized by feminist Betty Friedan, the day commemorated the fiftieth anniversary of women's gaining the right to vote.
	The National Organization for Women (NOW) stages demonstrations at local telephone companies in fifteen cities across the country	The protest called attention to AT&T's discriminatory practices toward women in hiring, promotions, fringe benefits, and executive appointments. The company and NOW battled these issues for several more years.
1971	The National Women's Political Caucus (NWPC) is organized at a conference attended by some two thousand women	Caucus attendees hoped to field women candidates, influence both parties to support women, and organize women at state and local levels.
1972	The Equal Rights Amendment (ERA) is passed by Congress and sent to individual states for ratification	The ERA stated that "Equality of rights under the law shall not be denied or abridged by the United States or by any State on account of sex."
	Barbara Jordan, a Democrat from Texas, is elected to the House of Representatives	Jordan becomes the first African American woman elected to Congress from a southern state.
	U.S. House Representative Shirley Chisholm declares her candidacy for the U.S. presidency	Chisholm becomes the first black woman to run for president in the primary of one of the two major parties. She was endorsed by NOW, and NOW members worked to organize her campaign in many states.
	The Supreme Court rules on *Eisenstadt v. Baird*	The decision establishes that the right to privacy encompasses an unmarried person's right to use contraceptives.
	NOW initiates action against sexism in elementary school textbooks	A leading publisher of textbooks, Scott Foresman and Co., soon publishes a booklet titled *Guidelines for Improving the Image of Women in Textbooks.*
	NOW pressures and convinces the U.S. Census Bureau to revise fifty-two sexist job titles	The move calls attention to the ways in which words and language can be sexist.
	Title IX of the Education Amendments is passed	Title IX prohibits sex discrimination in all aspects of education programs that receive federal support and helps open athletic participation to women.
1973	U.S. Supreme Court rules on *Roe v. Wade*	The decision declares that the Constitution protects women's right to terminate an early pregnancy, thus making abortion legal in the United States.
	Ms. magazine begins publication	Gloria Steinem, the editor of *Ms.*, becomes a leading journalist and media personality for the women's movement. The publication reaches a circulation of 350,000 within one year.

(continued)

Year	*Notable Event*	*Significance*
1973 *(cont.)*	Billie Jean King beats Bobby Riggs in the "Battle of the Sexes" tennis tournament	Watched by millions of people on television, King's win becomes a symbolic victory for all female athletes.
	Civil Service Commission eliminates height and weight requirements for employment	The decision opens fire fighting, police force, and park service jobs to women.
	Our Bodies, Ourselves is published	The book is the first on women's health issues to be conceived of, and written by, women.
	The Supreme Court rules on *Pittsburgh Press v Pittsburgh Commission on Human Relations*	The decision outlaws sex-segregated help-wanted ads in newspapers, which opens the way for women to apply for jobs previously limited to men and offering better pay and advancement opportunities.
	Introduced in Congress by Representative Bella Abzug and confirmed by Congress and President Richard M. Nixon, Women's Equality Day is established	Feminists and women's groups celebrate in parks and streets nationwide and commemorate the fifty-third anniversary of women's suffrage.
	Singer, songwriter Helen Reddy wins a Grammy Award for her hit song "I Am Woman"	The song was the first explicitly feminist song to become a gold record, and it became an unofficial anthem of the feminist movement.
	The National Black Feminist Organization is established	The group adds minority representation to the women's movement.
1974	The Equal Credit Opportunity Act is passed	The decision outlaws discrimination in consumer credit practices on the basis of sex, race, marital status, and other categories.
	U.S. Supreme Court rules on *Cleveland Board of Education v. LaFleur*	The decision determines it is illegal to force pregnant women to take maternity leave on the assumption that they are incapable of working in their physical condition.
	Little League admits girls for the first time	Allowing girls "in deference to a change in social climate," the league nonetheless creates a softball branch specifically for girls in order to keep them away from baseball.
	The Women's Educational Equity Act is passed	The decision funds the development of nonsexist teaching materials and model programs that encourage full educational opportunities for women.
	Ella Grasso is elected governor of Connecticut	Grasso becomes the first woman governor in the United States elected in her own right.
	Eleven women are ordained as the first female priests of the Episcopal Church	The move challenges the denomination's rules and practices as well as two thousand years of male dominance of the Christian priesthood.
1975	U.S. Supreme Court rules on *Taylor v. Louisiana*	The decision denies states the right to exclude women from juries.

(continued)

Year	*Notable Event*	*Significance*
1975 *(cont.)*	The United Nations' World Conference on International Women's Year is held in Mexico City	A ten-year Plan of Action is developed, which covers education, employment, population control, and child marriages, among other topics. It is criticized by many, however, for not condemning overall sexism.
	Mothers' Day of Outrage attracts four thousand pro-choice demonstrators to the Vatican Embassy in Washington, D.C.	The Eastern Region chapter of NOW organizes the event in order to publicize the amount of money that the Catholic Church had spent to enforce compulsory pregnancy.
1976	The United Nations' Decade for Women begins	This pronouncement brings more of an international focus to the movement.
	U.S. military academies open admission to women	The integration of the military is a major step for the movement.
	Nebraska becomes the first state to outlaw marital rape	The groundbreaking law sets a precedence for other states.
1977	In Houston, Texas, the first National Women's Conference is held	Organized by Abzug, the conference delegates publish a twenty-five-point Plan of Action.
	The National Women's Studies Association is founded	The association helps pave the way for the introduction of the field of women's studies into liberal arts curriculum.
	Indiana becomes the last state to ratify the ERA	Three more states are needed to make the amendment law, an effort that ultimately is unsuccessful.
1978	The Pregnancy Discrimination Act is passed	The decision bans employment discrimination against pregnant women.
	The National Coalition Against Domestic Violence forms	The coalition brings together shelters and other organizations in order to publicize the issue.
	The first Take Back the Night march is staged in San Francisco	Thousands of women across the country soon stage their own similar events against violence.
	In San Francisco, feminist artist Judy Chicago debuts her art exhibit titled *The Dinner Party*, which honors notable women in history	The exhibit draws record-setting attendance as well as angry reviews.
	More than 100,000 people march in Washington, D.C., in support of the ERA and to demand an extension of the time line to get it ratified	The crowds, which snarl city traffic and encompass the entire Capitol Mall, emphasize that a majority of Americans support passage of the ERA.
	The U.S. House of Representatives votes to extend until June 30, 1982, the ratification deadline for the ERA; the Senate follows a few months later	The extension is only half of the seven years that had been requested in the original bill, however, and many blame this fact for the ERA's eventual failure.

(continued)

Year	Notable Event	Significance
1979	NOW launches a new National ERA Campaign	The campaign is in response to increasing recision threats in the embattled states and is designed to rally ERA supporters in ratified and unratified states; activists defeat ERA recision efforts in thirteen states by the end of the year.
	Sonia Johnson, founder of Mormons for ERA, gains support from feminists nationwide for her "trial" by the Mormon Church because of her support of the ERA	The Johnson case calls further attention to the sexism of male hierarchy in many religions; Johnson is excommunicated at the end of the year.

Further Reading

Berkeley, Kathleen C. *The Women's Liberation Movement in America.* Westport, Conn.: Greenwood Press, 1999. This volume explores the philosophies, goals, and tactics of the women's liberation movement of the 1960's and 1970's.

Lunardini, Christine A. *Women's Rights: Social Issues in American History Series.* Phoenix, Ariz.: Oryx Press, 1996. Provides an overview of more than three hundred years of American women's history. It also provides short biographic profiles of women from Anne Hutchinson to Wilma Mankiller, as well as a chronology of women's history from 1607 to 1993.

Rebick, Judy. *Ten Thousand Roses: The Making of a Feminist Revolution.* Toronto: Penguin Books Canada, 2005. This book spans four decades of Canadian feminist history. More than one hundred women who participated in the Canadian women's revolution discuss the roles that they played in the feminist movement.

Rosen, Ruth. *The World Split Open: How the Modern Women's Movement Changed America.* New York: Penguin Books, 2000. Rosen's book is a history of the women's liberation movement in the United States and the backlash that followed that movement. The author concludes that the women's movement had profoundly changed American culture by the end of the twentieth century and had inspired women in many parts of the globe to challenge patriarchal authority.

Yvonne Johnson

See also Abortion rights; Affirmative action; Canadian Human Rights Act of 1977; Chisholm, Shirley; Education in Canada; Education in the United States; Equal Employment Opportunity Act of 1972; Equal Rights Amendment (ERA); Feminism; Marriage and divorce; National Organization for Women (NOW); Pregnancy Discrimination Act of 1978; *Roe v. Wade*; Steinem, Gloria; Women in the military; Women in the workforce.

■ Wonder, Stevie

Identification African American singer, composer, and musician

Born May 13, 1950; Saginaw, Michigan

As one of the most creative personalities in the popular music field during the 1970's, Wonder participated fully in the movement away from commercially driven "hit singles" to an emphasis on the long-playing (LP) record as an extended form. He was equally popular with African American and general audiences and blended his love songs with messages advocating social harmony, justice, and spirituality.

Stevie Wonder began the 1970's with the release of the album *Signed, Sealed and Delivered.* He had already achieved international fame as a child prodigy, recording a string of hit records for the successful Motown label. As he entered adulthood at the turn of the decade, Wonder began to expand musically as well, writing more of his own material and experimenting with new sounds. Motown had supplied him with a recording contract and gave him access to its studio musicians and arrangers that provided Motown recordings a characteristic style that remained a consistent musical backdrop for its famous vocalists. While Wonder did not reject these resources, he began layering other elements in his music and incorporating contrasting sections.

His next album, *Where I'm Coming From,* was released in 1971. In contrast to his earlier work, all of the music was written by Wonder in collaboration with Syreeta Wright, whom he had married in 1970. After Wonder's first contract with Motown expired, he immersed himself in the latest recording technology and electronic instruments favored by progressive rock bands. The resulting album, *Music of My Mind* (1972), was very popular and featured Wonder taking advantage of multiple recording tracks so that he could provide his own instrumental accompaniment. Similar techniques were used on the next album, *Talking Book,* released the same year. This album included the song "You Are the Sunshine of My Life," which became one of Wonder's most popular songs.

In 1973, Wonder released *Innervisions,* an album with a wide range of musical styles and themes that included the song "Higher Ground." He was severely injured in a car accident later that year but soon returned to creative activity with the production of *Fulfillingness' First Finale,* released in 1974. This album won five Grammy Awards. Wonder finished the decade with three more albums: *Songs in the Key of Life* (1976), *Looking Back* (1977), and *Stevie Wonder's Journey Through the Secret Life of Plants* (1979).

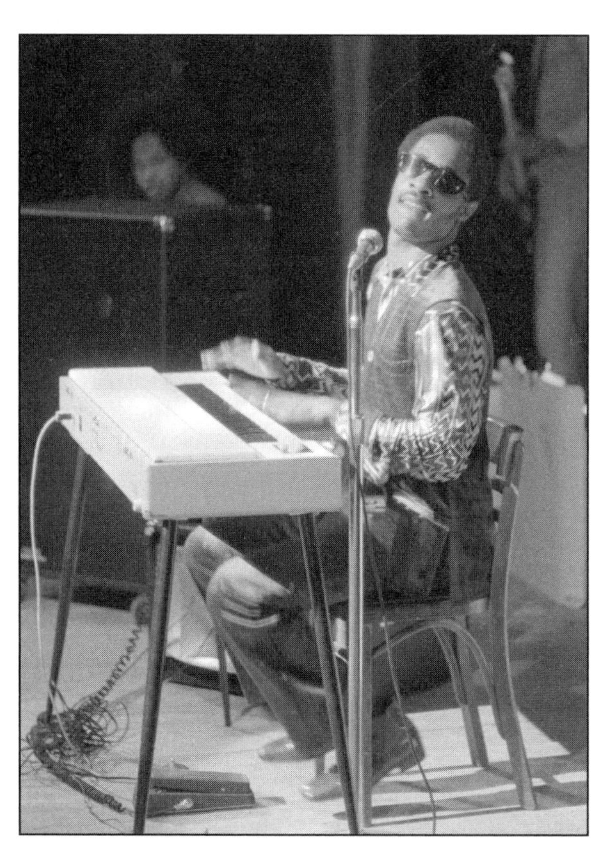

Stevie Wonder. (AP/Wide World Photos)

Impact Although Stevie Wonder continued to record and perform after this period, the 1970's were especially productive years in which he defined himself artistically by creating some of his finest music and providing future generations of musicians and listeners with a rich legacy of songs and inspiration. He strongly asserted the spiritual, political, and environmental values of his generation without resorting to drugs or confrontation, and he influenced millions of people who enjoyed his music.

Further Reading

Horn, Martin E. *Innervisions: The Music of Stevie Wonder.* Bloomington, Ind.: 1stBooks Library, 2000.

Swenson, John. *Stevie Wonder.* New York: Harper & Row, 1986.

Werner, Craig Hansen. *Higher Ground: Stevie Wonder, Aretha Franklin, Curtis Mayfield, and the Rise and Fall of American Soul.* New York: Crown, 2004.

John Myers

See also African Americans; Music; Radio; Singer-songwriters; Soul music.

■ Wooden, John

Identification American basketball coach, mentor, and humanitarian

Born October 14, 1910; Hall, Indiana

The success of University of California Los Angeles (UCLA) men's basketball teams under Wooden in the early to mid-1970's is credited with promoting the national popularity of men's college basketball and the extensive television coverage of the sport.

John Wooden's UCLA basketball teams are recognized as being among the great athletic dynasties in sports history. The teams won the National Collegiate Athletic Association (NCAA) championship in 1970, 1971, 1972, 1973, and 1975. UCLA's record for 1970 to 1975 was 171 wins and 10 losses.

In 1948, Wooden was hired as head coach of the UCLA men's basketball team. His coaching at this institution became one of the most incredible athletic success stories ever. During his twenty-seven seasons at UCLA, his teams won 316 games and lost 68. They also won ten NCAA championships in twelve

John Wooden. (AP/Wide World Photos)

years, including seven in a row from 1966 to 1973. He had four undefeated seasons, and his teams won the conference championship nineteen times and had a record streak of winning eighty-eight consecutive games. Some of the great players that Wooden recruited and coached include Kareem Abdul-Jabbar, Bill Walton, Keith Wilkes, Henry Bibby, Lucius Allen, Sidney Wicks, and Gail Goodrich.

The teams Coach Wooden coached lived his character-development philosophy, which helped lead to his historical success and forever influenced coaches and players at all levels of sport.

Impact In forty seasons of coaching basketball and baseball at the high school and college levels, John Wooden's teams had 885 wins and 203 losses, a .813 winning percentage. The National Basketball Hall of Fame inducted Coach Wooden in 1960 as a player and in 1972 as a coach, making him the first person ever to receive both honors.

He also received the 1977 Reagan Distinguished American Award and years later, in 2003, the Presidential Medal of Freedom from President George W. Bush.

Subsequent Events Wooden made a significant contribution to the coaching profession by publishing and promoting *The John Wooden Pyramid of Success* (2000), wherein his philosophy of and practical guide to coaching offered insight to other coaches and athletic administrators regarding the responsibility that organized school athletics has and can make to the student-athlete's character and maturity development.

Further Reading

Bjarkman, Peter C. *Hoopla: A Century of College Basketball.* New York: McGraw-Hill, 1996.

Johnson, Neville, with John Wooden. *The John Wooden Pyramid of Success: The Ultimate Guide to Life, Leadership, Friendship and Love Created by the Greatest Coach in the History of Sports.* Los Angeles: Cool Titles, 2000.

Wooden, John, with Jack Tobin. *They Call Me Coach.* Chicago: Contemporary Books, 2004.

Alan P. Peterson

See also Basketball; Sports; Walton, Bill.

■ Woodward, Bob, and Carl Bernstein

Identification Investigative reporters for *The Washington Post*

Carl Bernstein

Born: February 14, 1944; Washington, D.C.

Bob Woodward

Born: March 26, 1943; Geneva, Illinois

Woodward and Bernstein wrote a series of articles that revealed the involvement of the Nixon White House in the break-in at the Watergate office complex and its subsequent cover-up. Their continuing work between 1972 and 1974 spurred investigations by the Senate Select Committee on Presidential Election Activities and the House Judiciary Committee and contributed to the resignation of President Richard M. Nixon on August 9, 1974.

On June 17, 1972, Bob Woodward received a phone call from Barry Sussman, the city editor of *The Washington Post,* and learned that the offices of the Democratic National Committee at the Watergate had been burglarized, and five men had been arrested. Woodward was assigned the story, and at the arraignment on June 18, he learned that James McCord, one of those arrested, was a former consultant for the Central Intelligence Agency (CIA). During the next two days, Woodward was able to connect the break-in to E. Howard Hunt, a White House aide. Within a week *Washington Post* editor Ben Bradlee had teamed Woodward with Carl Bernstein.

During the months that followed, Woodward and Bernstein pursued every lead from the Committee to Re-elect the President (CRP), the Justice Department, the CIA, and the White House. Multiple sources and inquiries resulted in new revelations during 1972 and 1973. Woodward had an inside source known only as Deep Throat, who clarified information and provided further direction for the investigation. Through diligence and hard work, the reporters were able to implicate Attorney General John Mitchell in both the break-in and the cover-up that was being orchestrated by the Nixon White House. They also revealed the illegal involvement of the Federal Bureau of Investigation (FBI), the CIA, and White House aides H. R. Haldeman, John Ehrlichman, and John Dean. Woodward and Bernstein also revealed the White House Enemies List, the conspiracy to discredit and ruin Senator Ted Kennedy, and the use of Internal Revenue Service (IRS) audits to harass political enemies. Their work assisted the investigation conducted by the Senate Select Committee on Presidential Election Activities that was led by senators Sam Erwin and Russell Baker.

The Washington Post received the Pulitzer Prize in 1973 for outstanding journalism. In 1974, Woodward and Bernstein published *All the President's Men*, an account of their investigation; it served as an important contribution to history and investigative journalism. In 1976, they coauthored *The Final Days*, which provides a detailed description and analysis of the last months of the Nixon presidency.

Impact The legacy of Bob Woodward and Carl Bernstein included awakening the American media to its responsibilities in investigative journalism and reminding American politicians that no one, including the president, is above the law. This exercise of

Carl Bernstein (left) and Bob Woodward in 1973. (AP/Wide World Photos)

responsible journalism was dependent upon the courage and principles of Katharine Graham, owner of *The Washington Post,* editor Ben Bradlee, and Woodward and Bernstein themselves.

Further Reading

Hamill, Adrian. *Deep Truth: The Lives of Bob Woodward and Carl Bernstein.* Secaucus, N.J.: Carol, 1993.

Woodward, Bob, and Carl Bernstein. *All the President's Men.* 2d ed. New York: Simon & Schuster, 1994.

_______. *The Final Days.* Reprint ed. Cutchogue, N.Y.: Buccaneer Books, 1994.

William T. Walker

See also Agnew, Spiro T.; *All the President's Men;* Central Intelligence Agency (CIA); Cox, Archibald; Dean, John; Deep Throat; Ehrlichman, John; Elections in the United States, 1972; Erwin, Sam; Federal Bureau of Investigation (FBI); Journalism in the United States; Haldeman, H. R.; Liddy, G. Gordon, and E. Howard Hunt; Mitchell, John; Nixon, Richard M.; Pentagon Papers; Saturday Night Massacre; Sirica, John J.; Watergate.

■ Wounded Knee occupation

The Event Native Americans activists stage an occupation to protest broken treaties and the purported corruption of the federal Bureau of Indian Affairs (BIA)

Date February 28-May 7, 1973

Place Pine Ridge Indian Reservation, Wounded Knee, South Dakota

The tiny hamlet of Wounded Knee, the site at which more than two hundred Sioux and others were massacred in 1890, became a symbolic site again as members of the American Indian Movement (AIM) occupied the site during 1973. They quickly were confronted by armored troops and police.

The seventy-one-day occupation of Wounded Knee began on February 28, 1973. On March 11, 1973, AIM members declared their independence as the Oglala Sioux Nation, defining its boundaries according to the Treaty of Fort Laramie, signed in 1868. At one point, federal officials considered an armed attack on the camp, but the plan ultimately was discarded. Dennis Banks and Russell Means, AIM's best-known leaders, stated that they would hold out until the U.S. Senate Foreign Relations Committee had reviewed all broken treaties and the corruption of the BIA had been exposed to the world. After much gunfire and negotiation, AIM's occupation of Wounded Knee ended on May 7, 1973.

Providing food for a community of several hundred people under siege was a continual problem. Some food was smuggled through police lines, but fresh meat was acquired on the hoof. Writing in his memoir, *Ojibwe Warrior* (2004), Banks noted that occupants of Wounded Knee rustled cattle from local ranches. Most of the AIM leaders were urban people, however, who had to learn quickly how to process meat straight from the animal.

Pine Ridge tribal police supported tribal chairman Richard Wilson, an Oglala Lakota, against the occupiers of Wounded Knee. From the early 1970's until his defeat for the chairman's office by Al Trimble in 1976, Wilson outfitted a tribal police force that was often called the Goon Squad. This police force, which understood "goon" to mean "Guardians of the Oglala Nation," was financed with money from the federal government. The local context of the occupation included an effort to confront publicly Wilson's policies, which often favored non-Native American ranchers, farmers, and corporations.

Political Context The struggle between AIM and Wilson also was taking place within the realm of tribal politics. Wilson had a formidable array of supporters on the reservation, many of whom criticized AIM for being urban-based and insensitive to reservation residents' needs.

When Wilson sought reelection in 1974, Means challenged him. In the primary, Wilson trailed Means, 667 votes to 511. Wilson won the final election over Means by fewer than two hundred votes in balloting, which the U.S. Commission on Civil Rights later found to be permeated with fraud.

The Commission on Civil Rights recommended a new election, which was not held; Wilson answered his detractors by increasing assaults on his opponents, examples of which were described in a chronology of more than sixty murders between 1973 and 1976 kept by the Wounded Knee Legal Defense-Offense Committee. One of the Goons' favorite weapons was the automobile; officially, automobile deaths could be reported as traffic accidents. Between 1973 and 1976, Pine Ridge experienced a

A flyer in New York City asks for support during the occupation of Wounded Knee, South Dakota, by members of the American Indian Movement (AIM). (Library of Congress)

higher per-capita murder rate than any U.S. urban area.

Aftermath Following the occupation of Wounded Knee, Banks and Means were charged with three counts of assault on federal officers, one charge each of conspiracy and one each of larceny. The men, facing five charges each, could have been sentenced to as many as eighty-five years in prison. For several months in 1974, a year after the occupation of Wounded Knee, the defense and prosecution presented their cases in a St. Paul, Minnesota, federal court.

On September 16, Judge Fred J. Nichol dismissed all the charges. The judge said that Federal Bureau of Investigation (FBI) agents had lied repeatedly during the trial while under oath and had often furnished defense attorneys with altered documents. Judge Nichol said that R. D. Hurd, the federal prosecutor, had deliberately deceived the court. "The Federal Bureau of Investigation," said Judge Nichol, "has stooped to a new low." To the chagrin of the judge and jurors, however, the Justice Department responded by presenting Hurd with an award for "superior performance" during the trial.

Impact The occupation of Wounded Knee by Native American activists had a profound impact on non-Indians, as news of the conflict spread worldwide through the media. The occupation had a major effect on American culture: A book by Dee Brown about the history of oppression at Wounded Knee, titled *Bury My Heart at Wounded Knee* (1970), also became an international best-seller. At the 1973 Academy Awards, held as Wounded Knee was being occupied, Marlon Brando refused to accept his Academy Award in order to protest the treatment of American Indians.

Unrest continued at Pine Ridge for several years after the 1973 occupation. More than sixty people, many of them AIM members, were murdered in factional violence between 1973 and 1976. In June, 1975, two FBI agents and one Native American man died in a shootout at the Jumping Bull Ranch, west of Wounded Knee, for which Leonard Peltier later was convicted on what his defenders contend was falsified evidence. By the early twenty-first century, Peltier continued to serve a life sentence.

Further Reading

Banks, Dennis, and Richard Erdoes. *Ojibwa Warrior: Dennis Banks and the Rise of the American Indian Movement.* Norman: University of Oklahoma Press, 2004. A lively, personal account of the Wounded Knee occupation by one of its leaders.
Churchill, Ward, and Jim Vander Wall. *Agents of Repression: The FBI's Secret War Against the Black Panther Party and the American Indian Movement.* Boston: South End Press, 1990. Detail on the FBI's

attempts during the 1970's to destroy AIM during and after the occupation of Wounded Knee.

Johansen, Bruce E., and Roberto F. Maestas. *Wasi'chu: The Continuing Indian Wars.* New York: Monthly Review Press, 1979. Context describing the situation at Pine Ridge before and after the Wounded Knee Occupation.

Josephy, Alvin, Jr. *Red Power: The American Indians Fight for Freedom.* New York: McGraw-Hill, 1971. Provides context on the social movement that gave birth to the occupation at Wounded Knee.

Matthiessen, Peter. *In the Spirit of Crazy Horse.* New York: Viking, 1991. An account of the many political murders at Pine Ridge after the Wounded Knee occupation.

Bruce E. Johansen

See also American Indian Movement (AIM); Brando, Marlon; Federal Bureau of Investigation (FBI); Littlefeather, Sacheen; Native Americans; Peltier, Leonard; Trail of Broken Treaties.

■ Wyeth, Andrew

Identification American realist painter
Born July 12, 1917; Chadds Ford, Pennsylvania

During the 1970's, Wyeth was one of the United States' most popular and celebrated living artists. Beginning in 1971, he worked secretly with a model named Helga to create an extraordinary set of more than 240 works of art.

As the 1970's began, Andrew Wyeth was already famous for his watercolor and tempera paintings of people and rural landscapes. *Christina's World* (1948) was one of his most popular and familiar paintings. In 1963, Wyeth was the first painter to receive the Presidential Medal of Freedom, and his 1967 exhibit at the Whitney Museum in New York City set new attendance records.

During the 1970's, more honors followed. In 1970, Wyeth became the first living artist to have an exhibition at the White House, and in 1976, he became the first living American artist to have a retrospective exhibit at the Metropolitan Museum. In 1977, Wyeth was elected to the French Academie des Beaux-Arts, and the Soviet Academy of the Arts granted him an honorary membership in 1978.

Although Wyeth was possibly the most successful American artist at the time, some critics discounted Wyeth's traditional, realistic style of painting and subject matter—nostalgic characters and rural settings—which were outside of the abstract art movement or other prominent trends in the field, including environmental art and pop art. Abstract or "nonrepresentational" art focused on forms and colors for their own sake, rather than using them to represent nature or recognizable objects.

However, unknown to anyone else, even to his wife, Wyeth had a secret model from 1971 through 1985. Helga Testorf was a German immigrant who worked for Karl Kuener, Wyeth's neighbor in Chadds Ford, Pennsylvania. In 1971, she was thirty-two years old and a married mother of four. She posed clothed and in the nude, in the studio and outdoors, and in shadow and sunlight. Previously, Wyeth had done very few nude studies. He created more than 240 "Helga pictures" in pencil, watercolor, drybrush, and tempera.

Impact The 1970's were pivotal years in Wyeth's life and career. With a new direction and a model-collaborator, Wyeth created works displaying remarkable technical versatility. Never before in American art had there been such continuous, intensive studies of an individual subject, over the course of so many years.

In 1986, the Helga pictures were revealed to the public and immediately became a sensation in the art world, as well as a media event. The Helga revelation appeared on the front page of *The New York Times* and the covers of *Newsweek* and *Time.* The National Gallery of Art arranged a national tour of the works from 1987 to 1989. Considered among his greatest works, the Helga series solidified Wyeth's reputation as one of America's foremost artists.

Further Reading

Meryman, Richard. *Andrew Wyeth: A Secret Life.* New York: HarperCollins, 1998.

Wilmerding, John, and Andrew Wyeth. *Andrew Wyeth: The Helga Pictures.* New York: H. N. Abrams, 1987.

Wyeth, Andrew. *Andrew Wyeth: Autobiography.* Boston: Bulfinch Press, 1998.

Alice Myers

See also Art movements; Feminist art; Hockney, David; Pop art.

■ Young, Andrew

Identification African American civil rights leader who became a congressman and an ambassador
Born March 12, 1932; New Orleans, Louisiana

Young became one of the most important African American political leaders of the decade in a number of arenas.

In 1970, Andrew Young, already well known as an aide to Martin Luther King, Jr., in the Southern Christian Leadership Conference (SCLC), left that group for a try at electoral politics. He wrote that as civil rights organizations and alliances began to disintegrate, "I became convinced that our participation in the political system was all the more imperative."

He campaigned for the U.S. House of Representatives in Georgia's Fifth District, centered on Atlanta. He won the Democratic primary, but Republican Fletcher Thompson won the general election after smearing Young by associating him with the militant Black Panther movement, which cost Young nearly all the white vote. The 1970 census caused redistricting, which left the district 38 percent African American. Young was better known locally thanks to his work on Atlanta's Community Relations Commission and had the support of liberal whites such as Stuart Eisenstadt and Georgia governor Jimmy Carter. Young won the general election in 1972, sharing with Barbara Jordan the honor of being the first southern African American in Congress since Reconstruction.

Young became a member of the Banking Committee and the powerful Rules Committee. He worked for human rights in Africa and all over the world. He made trips to Africa, the Caribbean, and Asia, sponsored Urban Mass Transit legislation, and helped Atlanta mayor Maynard Jackson, Jr., get funding for Hartsfield Airport. Young had hoped to become the first African American speaker of the house but found insufficient support. Although his majority increased with each election, he decided to shift his efforts to the 1976 presidential campaign of Governor Carter. He defended Carter against attacks and advised him in many areas.

President Carter appointed Young permanent representative to the United Nations with cabinet rank; the Senate overwhelmingly confirmed him. He greatly improved relations with African countries and firmly opposed racism in South Africa and Rhodesia (later called Zimbabwe). His informal diplomatic approach pleased Third World diplomats but disturbed traditionalists. He helped settle civil wars in Africa and worked for the Panama Canal treaty. In 1979, Young met informally with a representative of the Palestine Liberation Organization (PLO) as part of a campaign to get Arab countries to recognize Israel. When Israel and many Jewish Americans protested, Young resigned, and Carter accepted his resignation. Young returned to Atlanta, where he soon became a candidate for mayor, a post he won in 1981.

Impact Andrew Young became one of the first African Americans to wield real institutional power nationally and internationally.

Further Reading

DeRoche, Andrew J. *Andrew Young: Civil Rights Ambassador.* New York: SR Books, 2003.

Young, Andrew. *An Easy Burden: The Civil Rights Movement and the Transformation of America.* New York: HarperCollins, 1996.

J. Quinn Brisben

See also African Americans; Black Panthers; Carter, Jimmy; Chisholm, Shirley; Congress, U.S.; Jackson, Maynard, Jr.; Jordan, Barbara; Liberalism in U.S. politics; Racial discrimination; United Nations.

■ *Young Frankenstein*

Identification American comic film
Director Mel Brooks (1926-   )
Date Released in 1974

A spoof on American horror films, Young Frankenstein *became known as one of the best exercises in genre satire in world cinema.*

Produced and directed by Mel Brooks from a screenplay he wrote with his star, Gene Wilder, who plays Dr. Frankenstein, this affectionate parody of the Frankenstein films released by Universal Studios during the 1930's and 1940's was a major hit in the early 1970's. Brooks lovingly and painstakingly re-creates the look of James Whale's classic films *Frankenstein* (1931) and *Bride of Frankenstein* (1935) by using carefully reconstructed, near-identical sets and employing a number of actual props from the original films. Brooks's cinematographer, Gerald Hirschfeld, earned an Academy Award nomination for his use of vintage-looking, black-and-white film and 1930's-style, expressionist camera angles.

The plot follows closely those of Whale's films, and a number of scenes—the creation of the monster and his encounters with a little girl, a blind hermit, and the inevitable throng of hysterical villagers—mirror scenes in the earlier films, though Brooks's versions are suffused with slapstick and sight gags. Much of the film's humor foregrounds the sexual tensions implicit in Mary Shelley's 1818 novel and the studio adaptations of it; for example, references to the monster's large male organ as a "schvanstucker" and scenes in which the monster or his creator demonstrate their sexual prowess by causing their partners to burst into arias from operettas during intercourse.

Beyond bawdy humor, however, most of the film's funniest moments come from other traditional comic devices such as wordplay and unexpected turns of events. Some of *Young Frankenstein*'s biggest laughs come from characters bickering about how to pronounce "Frankenstein" and "Igor." When the assistant nervously moans "Werewolf!" upon hearing a distant lupine howl, Frankenstein points and announces, "There wolf." When the housekeeper, played by Cloris Leachman, explains that she had been involved romantically with the original Dr. Frankenstein, the dramatic buildup of the dialogue cues the audience to expect blunt language in her ultimate admission, but instead the woman spits out the banal "He vass my boyfriend!" When scientist and his creation appear at a scholarly conference, they present not a dry lecture but a song-and-dance number, "Puttin' on the Ritz." Finally, when the monster meets a little girl (whose counterpart is drowned in the Universal original), the scene ends not in death but in a ridiculous sight gag: The child flies through the air into her bedroom after being bounced off a seesaw.

Impact With its likable characters, coherent plot, and excellent cast, which includes Peter Boyle as the monster, Teri Garr and Marty Feldman as lab assistants, and Madeline Kahn as the scientist's haughty fiancé, *Young Frankenstein* avoids the pitfalls that weaken many satires of film genres, which often degenerate into a disjunct series of poorly developed comic sketches. One of the best comic films of the 1970's, it demonstrates the decade's ability to reflect fondly on the past without necessarily descending into sentiment and extreme nostalgia.

Further Reading

Sinyard, Neil. *The Films of Mel Brooks.* New York: Bookthrift, 1988.

Svehla, Gary J., and Susan Svehla. *We Belong Dead: Frankenstein on Film.* Baltimore: Midnight Marquee Press, 1997.

Thomas Du Bose

See also *Blazing Saddles*; Brooks, Mel; Film in the United States; Wilder, Gene.

Z

■ *Zen and the Art of Motorcycle Maintenance*

Identification Autobiographical travelogue
Author Robert M. Pirsig (1928-)
Date Published in 1974

Pirsig's book accomplished a philosophical and literary balancing act, which resulted in a significant number of devotees throughout the country. It received mostly rave reviews and was eventually published in twenty-three languages.

Zen and the Art of Motorcycle Maintenance recounts a motorcycle trip west taken by Robert M. Pirsig and his eleven-year-old son, Chris. They began in Minnesota, accompanied by a married couple on a separate motorcycle. The foursome traversed the Dakotas and reached Bozeman, Montana, where the couple turned back as planned. Pirsig and Chris proceeded through Idaho and Oregon before heading south to San Francisco.

Interspersed throughout the travelogue are chautauquas, or elucidations, regarding the dichotomy between the classical and romantic divisions of Western thought. Woven into the chautauquas are references to the author's persona before his mental breakdown—the brilliant, self-driven Phaedrus, named after a character in a Platonic dialogue. Phaedrus Pirsig had dared to rail against the classical object's separation from the romantic subject as promoted by Aristotelian logic. As a solution to this separation, the creator melds with the creation in a Zen-like existence, while his model becomes the upkeep of his motorcycle during the westward trek. With each carburetor adjustment, each cleaning of the spark plugs, Pirsig's dual personality merges toward becoming a unity.

The third theme of this story relates to the salvaging of the Pirsigs' father-son relationship. The formerly insane parent, his philosophical obsession notwithstanding, had been approachable and was able to relate to his offspring. However, the shock-treatment survivor, while now declared mentally competent, is aloof and often stares into space. Chris misses the crazy dad with whom he could converse. By San Francisco, the father realizes that he does also. The return trip promises a brighter day.

Impact Readers have described *Zen and the Art of Motorcycle Maintenance* as "life changing." During the mid-1970's, Americans were still absorbing the cultural changes begun in the 1960's. Many in the West were finding fulfillment in Eastern philosophies. That Robert M. Pirsig found a way to bridge the hemispheres remains a major contribution.

Further Reading

DiSanto, Ronald, and Thomas Steele. *Guidebook to "Zen and the Art of Motorcycle Maintenance."* New York: Perennial Press, 1990.

Pirsig, Robert. *Lila: An Inquiry into Morals.* New York: Bantam, 1991.

Jim Heaney

See also Buddhism; Literature in the United States; Religion and spirituality in the United States.

■ Zodiac killer

Identification Serial killer
Date Active between 1966 and 1978

Although the brutal murders officially attributed to the Zodiac killer took place between 1968 and 1969, he inspired enormous fear in the citizens of Northern California throughout the 1970's, as he remained at large and continued to send threatening letters to the press.

The identity of the Zodiac killer is one of the great unsolved crimes of the twentieth century. Between December, 1968, and October, 1969, the Zodiac murdered six people in Northern California. He killed his first two victims at a lover's lane in Vallejo, California, in December, 1968, and six months later, the killer murdered a couple at another area lover's lane. In September, 1969, he struck again, this time attacking a couple at Lake Berryessa in Napa County, killing the woman and wounding her boyfriend. The killer's last-known victim was a cab driver murdered in San Francisco the following month.

In August, 1969, San Francisco Bay Area newspapers began receiving letters from a person claiming responsibility for these murders, referring to himself as the Zodiac. The letters were marked with the same symbol that was seen on the killer's sweatshirt in the Lake Berryessa attack, giving credence to the author's claims. Portions of these letters consisted of coded messages, which the writer demanded that the paper publish. Although professional code breakers failed to crack the code, a pair of amateurs was able to decipher his messages. Several of the letters contained pieces of the murdered cab driver's bloody shirt, providing further proof that the author was the killer. He warned that he would kill again, threatening to attack a schoolbus full of children, which resulted in buses being staffed with armed guards for several months. Although the Zodiac claimed to have killed seventeen people in all, police were able to positively connect only one other crime to him, the 1966 death of a Riverside, California, woman. Newspapers continued to receive messages from the killer as late as 1978, with a total of twenty-one messages.

Impact The Zodiac killer was a prototype of the modern serial killer. Whatever his motive for murder, his desire for recognition and publicity was just as important to him. He was one of the first murderers to stage-manage his own "image," which had a huge impact upon serial killers in the 1970's, such as Ted Bundy.

In the attempts to solve one of the most frustrating unsolved crimes in history, countless theories on the Zodiac have been put forward, and many possible suspects have been suggested, but the case remains open. The Zodiac killer inspired several films, the best known of which is *Dirty Harry* (1971), starring Clint Eastwood.

Further Reading

Graysmith, Robert. *Zodiac.* New York: St. Martin's Press, 1986.

_______. *Zodiac Unmasked: The Identity of America's Most Elusive Serial Killer Revealed.* New York: Berkley, 2002.

Mary Virginia Davis

See also Berkowitz, David; Bundy, Ted; Death penalty; Gilmore, Gary; Manson Family.

■ Entertainment: Major Films

The one hundred titles listed here are a representative sampling of 1970's films that are regarded as significant because of their box-office success, their Academy Award honors, or their critical reputations. Entries here that include "*See also* main entry" have a full essay in *The Seventies in America*. All references to awards refer to the Academy Awards given by the Academy of Motion Picture Arts and Sciences.

1970

Airport (Universal; *dir.*, George Seaton) This adaptation of Arthur Hailey's best-selling novel focuses on an airport manager (played by Burt Lancaster) trying to keep his facility functioning during a snowstorm and a pilot (Dean Martin) whose passengers include a mad bomber (Van Heflin). Helen Hayes won a Best Supporting Actress award as an eccentric passenger.

Diary of a Mad Housewife (Universal; *dir.*, Frank Perry) A New York housewife (Carrie Snodgress) bored with her life and with her self-pitying, insensitive attorney husband (Richard Benjamin) has an affair with a narcissistic womanizer (Frank Langella).

Five Easy Pieces (BBS/Columbia; *dir.*, Bob Rafelson) An oil field worker (Jack Nicholson) heads back to his family home in the Northwest with his girlfriend (Karen Black). Her crassness clashes with his cultured family's snobbery, and he seduces his brother's fiancé (Susan Anspach). The confrontation between the hero and a waitress is one of the most famous scenes in film history.

The Great White Hope (Twentieth Century-Fox; *dir.*, Martin Ritt) This adaptation of Howard Sackler's Broadway hit presents Jack Johnson (James Earl Jones), the first black heavyweight boxing champion, and his efforts to be his own man in the United States in 1910. He is forced to leave the country and fight in Cuba because of his affair with a white woman (Jane Alexander).

Joe (Canon; *dir.*, John G. Avildsen) Peter Boyle received his career break in this controversial low-budget film about a reactionary New York factory worker who develops an odd friendship with a middle-class advertising executive (Dennis Patrick). United in their hatred of hippies, the pair searches for the executive's daughter (Susan Sarandon, in her first film).

Little Big Man (Cinema Center 100/National General; *dir.*, Arthur Penn) Jack Crabb (Dustin Hoffman), a 121-year-old survivor of the Little Big Horn, recalls his life as an orphan adopted by a tribe of Cheyenne led by Old Lodge Skins (Chief Dan George). This comic, violent adaptation of Thomas Berger's acclaimed novel examines such topics as racism, identity, and the myth of the American West.

Love Story (Paramount; *dir.*, Arthur Hiller) One of the most popular soap operas of all time depicts the ill-fated romance between a wealthy Harvard student (Ryan O'Neal) and a Radcliffe student (Ali MacGraw) with a blue-collar background. *See also* main entry.

M*A*S*H (Twentieth Century-Fox; *dir.*, Robert Altman) Basis of the long-running television series, this black comedy satirizes the Vietnam War era through the exploits of two army doctors (Elliott Gould and Donald Sutherland) during the Korean War. Deliberately anachronistic, it treats death, religion, and race with an antiestablishment attitude. *See also* main entry.

Patton (Twentieth Century-Fox; *dir.*, Franklin J. Schaffner) This biography of the World War II general Patton (George C. Scott) provides a sympathetic look at his often controversial behavior. It gained additional fame when Scott rejected an Academy Award for his performance. Its other awards included Best Picture and Best Director. *See also* main entry.

Woodstock (Warner Bros.; *dir.*, Michael Wadleigh) The documentary of the famous three-day 1969 music festival presents it both as a sociological event and as a record of performances by such acts as Joan Baez, Joe Cocker, Jimi Hendrix, and the Who. Coedited by a young Martin Scorsese, it received an Academy Award for Best Documentary.

1971

Billy Jack (National Student Film/Warner Bros; *dir.*, Tom Laughlin) A half-Native American Vietnam veteran (Tom Laughlin) skilled in martial arts comes to the aid of a progressive school whose minority students are the targets of local bigots. This surprise hit led to three less successful sequels.

Carnal Knowledge (Avco Embassy; *dir.*, Mike Nichols) The sexual exploits of two friends are followed from the 1940's to the 1970's. The marriage of Sandy (Art Garfunkel) to his college sweetheart (Candice Bergen) leaves him unfulfilled, and the womanizing Jonathan (Jack Nicholson) marries his mistress (Ann-Margret) only after she attempts suicide.

A Clockwork Orange (Stanley Kubrick/Warner Bros.; *dir.*, Stanley Kubrick) Futurist punk Alex (Malcolm McDowell) roams London with his thuggish friends until he is given a psychological treatment to cure his violent behavior. This adaptation of the Anthony Burgess novel was controversial for its depiction of sex and violence. *See also* main entry.

Dirty Harry (Warner Bros.; *dir.*, Don Siegel) Clint Eastwood became a superstar for his portrayal of vicious San Francisco policeman Harry Callahan. Harry's rules-bending pursuit of a psychotic killer (Andrew Robinson) led some critics to call the film fascist. Its success resulted in four sequels.

The French Connection (Twentieth Century-Fox; *dir.*, William Friedkin) Tough cop Popeye Doyle (Gene Hackman) will stop at nothing to capture a French drug smuggler (Fernando Rey). This fast-paced, fact-based action thriller includes a car-subway chase through the streets of New York. It won five awards, including Best Picture, Best Actor, and Best Director. *See also* main entry.

Harold and Maude (Paramount; *dir.*, Hal Ashby) This cult favorite presents a suicidal young man (Bud Cort) who appalls his family and psychiatrist by falling in love with a seventy-nine-year-old free spirit (Ruth Gordon). *See also* main entry.

Klute (Warner Bros.; *dir.*, Alan J. Pakula) Jane Fonda won her first Academy Award for her portrayal of an upscale Manhattan prostitute being stalked by one of her customers and unexpectedly falling in love with a private investigator (Donald Sutherland).

The Last Picture Show (BBS/Columbia; *dir.*, Peter Bogdanovich) In the small-town Texas of 1951, high school senior Sonny (Timothy Bottoms) has an affair with his football coach's wife (Cloris Leachman), while his friend Duane (Jeff Bridges) falls for the spoiled, rich Jacy (Cybill Shepherd). The two boys also learn about life from a philosophical pool-hall owner (Ben Johnson). Leachman and Johnson won Academy Awards for their supporting roles.

McCabe and Mrs. Miller (Warner Bros.; *dir.*, Robert Altman) John McCabe (Warren Beatty) arrives in the new frontier town of Presbyterian Church to open a gambling casino and brothel with the help of the prostitute Mrs. Miller (Julie Christie). As with *M*A*S*H*, Altman uses the past to comment on the present, in this case violence, corporate greed, and the role of the individual in society.

Shaft (Roger Lewis/Sterling Silliphant/MGM; *dir.*, Gordon Parks) African American private detective John Shaft (Richard Roundtree) is hired by a Harlem crime boss (Moses Gunn) to find his daughter, who may have been kidnapped by the Mafia. The film was the most commercially successful of the blaxploitation genre.

1972

Cabaret (ABC/Allied Artists; *dir.*, Bob Fosse) This adaptation of the Broadway musical drawn from stories by Christopher Isherwood is set in 1930's Berlin as cabaret performer Sally Bowles (Liza Minnelli) observes the rise of the Nazis. It won eight Academy Awards, including ones for Fosse, Minnelli, and supporting actor Joel Grey.

The Candidate (Warner Bros., *dir.*, Michael Ritchie) A liberal, activist California lawyer (Robert Redford), the son of a former governor (Melvyn Douglas), is convinced by a campaign manager (Peter Boyle) to run against an incumbent U.S. senator (Don Porter). Former Eugene McCarthy speechwriter Jeremy Larner's screenplay received an Academy Award.

Deliverance (Warner Bros., *dir.*, John Boorman) Four middle-class men (Burt Reynolds, Jon Voight, Ned Beatty, and Ronny Cox) take a canoe trip down a dangerous river in the Georgia backwoods and encounter violent hillbillies. James Dickey appears as a sheriff in this adaptation of his novel. *See also* main entry.

Fritz the Cat (Steve Krantz/Cinemation/American International; *dir.*, Ralph Bakshi) Robert Crumb's underground comic book became the first X-rated animated film portraying a feline college student's adventures with sex and drugs in 1960's New York.

The Godfather (Paramount; *dir.*, Francis Ford Coppola) The saga of the Mafia family headed by Don Vito Corleone (Marlon Brando) in the years following World War II became an enormous critical and commercial success. It won Best Picture and Best Actor and introduced the world to Al Pacino. *See also* main entry.

The Heartbreak Kid (Palomar/Twentieth Century-Fox; *dir.*, Elaine May) On his honeymoon, Lenny Cantrow (Charles Grodin) falls in love with beautiful Kelly (Cybill Shepherd). After leaving his bride (Jeannie Berlin), he encounters his new love's hostile father (Eddie Albert). The witty screenplay is by Neil Simon.

Lady Sings the Blues (Paramount; *dir.*, Sidney J. Furie) Pop singer Diana Ross made her film debut as legendary jazz singer Billie Holiday. The film depicts Holiday's struggles in the segregated society of the 1930's, as well as her use of illegal drugs.

Last Tango in Paris (Franco London/PEA/United Artists; *dir.*, Bernardo Bertolucci) A guilt-ridden American (Marlon Brando) in Paris is tormented by his estranged wife's suicide and enters into a sadomasochistic relationship with a young woman (Maria Schneider). The film was one of the decade's most controversial because of its sex scenes. *See also* main entry.

The Poseidon Adventure (Twentieth Century-Fox; *dir.*, Ronald Neame) A tidal wave overturns an ocean liner, and a minister (Gene Hackman) tries to lead the ten survivors to safety.

Sounder (Twentieth Century-Fox; *dir.*, Martin Ritt) A black mother (Cicely Tyson) in 1930's Louisiana struggles after her husband (Paul Winfield) is sent to prison for stealing a loaf of bread. Their oldest son (Kevin Hooks) sets out to find where his father is being held in this examination of poverty, racism, and injustice.

1973

American Graffiti (Universal; *dir.*, George Lucas) This nostalgic look at a simpler time follows the exploits of Curt (Richard Dreyfuss), Steve (Ron Howard), and their teenage friends on the last night of summer in 1962. *See also* main entry.

The Exorcist (Warner Bros.; *dir.*, William Freidkin) A young priest (Jason Miller) fails to help a girl (Linda Blair) who may be possessed by the devil and calls in an exorcist (Max von Sydow). *See also* main entry.

The Last Detail (Columbia; *dir.*, Hal Ashby) Veteran sailors Billy "Bad Ass" (Jack Nicholson) and Mule (Otis Young), escorting a bumbling seaman (Randy Quaid) to prison, decide to show the young man a final good time. The comic but bittersweet film is famous for its proliferation of profanity.

Mean Streets (TPS/Warner Bros.; *dir.*, Martin Scorsese) Scorsese established himself as a major director with this look at young small-time hoodlums in New York's Little Italy. The film, which also boosted the careers of Harvey Keitel and Robert De Niro, became highly influential because of its visual style, the use of rock and roll on the soundtrack, and its treatment of male camaraderie and sudden eruptions of violence.

The Paper Chase (Twentieth Century-Fox; *dir.*, James Bridges) A naïve Harvard law student (Timothy Bottoms) falls for the sophisticated daughter (Lindsay Wagner) of his tyrannical professor (John Houseman). Houseman, a veteran producer in his second acting role, won a Best Supporting Actor award and later starred in the television series based on the film.

Paper Moon (Paramount; *dir.*, Peter Bogdanovich) A con man (Ryan O'Neal) and a nine-year-old orphan (Tatum O'Neal) travel through the Midwest of 1936. Tatum O'Neal won a Best Supporting Actress award as the precocious little girl who smokes and swears.

Serpico (Paramount; *dir.*, Sidney Lumet) Undercover officer Frank Serpico (Al Pacino) risks his life to expose police corruption in New York. With long hair and a beard, Pacino offers one of the most distinctive of his lonely outsider characters.

The Sting (David Brown/Universal; *dir.*, George Roy Hill) Hill, Paul Newman, and Robert Redford reteam after *Butch Cassidy and the Sundance Kid* (1969) in this comic yarn about con artists running a scam on a Chicago mobster (Robert Shaw). The year's highest-grossing film won seven Academy Awards, including Best Picture, Best Director, and Best Adapted Score for Marvin Hamlisch's famous use of Scott Joplin's ragtime music.

Walking Tall (Cinerama; *dir.*, Phil Karlson) Tennessee sheriff Buford Pusser (Joe Don Baker) fights gambling, prostitution, and bootlegging. The low-budget unexpected hit spawned two sequels and a television series.

The Way We Were (Rastar/Columbia; *dir.*, Sydney Pollack) This old-fashioned romance follows an unlikely couple, a radical political activist (Barbra Streisand) and a quiet "big man on campus" (Robert Redford), from the 1930's through World War II and into the anticommunist hysteria of postwar Hollywood. The film's music won two Academy Awards.

1974

Alice Doesn't Live Here Anymore (Warner Bros.; *dir.*, Martin Scorsese) After her husband dies, an unfulfilled woman (Ellen Burstyn) leaves her New Mexico home with her young son (Alfred Lutter III) to try to begin a singing career in California, only to become a waitress in Arizona. The film features eleven-year-old Jodie Foster as a flamboyant tomboy.

Blazing Saddles (Warner Bros.; *dir.*, Mel Brooks) A black sheriff (Cleavon Little) cleans up a town with the help of a washed-up gunfighter (Gene Wilder). This often crude spoof became Hollywood's highest-grossing Western. *See also* main entry.

Chinatown (Paramount; *dir.*, Roman Polanski) This stylish evocation of *film noir* of the past depicts a private investigator (Jack Nicholson) in 1937 Los Angeles who uncovers a complex plot of political corruption, incest, and murder. Robert Towne's original screenplay won an Academy Award. *See also* main entry.

The Conversation (Paramount; *dir.*, Francis Ford Coppola) A San Francisco surveillance expert (Gene Hackman) recording the conversations of a young couple (Cindy Williams and Frederic Forrest) becomes suspicious of the motives of his mysterious client (Robert Duvall). With its detailed portrayal of sound-recording devices, the film offers one of the decade's most original and distinctive treatments of paranoia.

Death Wish (Paramount; *dir.*, Michael Winner) After his wife is murdered and his daughter brutally raped, a liberal New York architect (Charles Bronson) becomes a vigilante. The film established Bronson as a major box-office force and led to four sequels.

The Godfather, Part II (Francis Ford Coppola/Paramount; *dir.*, Francis Ford Coppola) The saga of Michael Corleone (Al Pacino) continues as the gangster becomes estranged from his brother (John Cazale) and wife (Diane Keaton). Flashbacks show how young Vito Corleone (Robert De Niro) began his crime empire. The film won seven awards, including Best Picture, Best Director, and Best Supporting Actor for De Niro. *See also* main entry.

Hearts and Minds (BBS/Rainbow/Warner Bros.; *dir.*, Peter Davis) News footage of the Vietnam War is juxtaposed with interviews with participants, opponents, and proponents. The controversial film won an Academy Award for Best Documentary.

The Towering Inferno (Twentieth Century-Fox/Warner Bros.; *dir.*, John Guillermin) The world's tallest building catches on fire the night that it opens. The era's most successful disaster epic won three Academy Awards. Its all-star cast includes Paul Newman, Steve McQueen, Faye Dunaway, William Holden, Fred Astaire, and O. J. Simpson.

A Woman Under the Influence (Faces; *dir.*, John Cassavetes) The suburban wife (Gena Rowlands) of a construction worker (Peter Falk) experiences a nervous breakdown. The most popular of Cassavetes' seemingly improvised films is a showcase for his wife's performance.

Young Frankenstein (Crossbow/Gruskoff/Venture/Twentieth Century-Fox; *dir.*, Mel Brooks) Brooks followed *Blazing Saddles* with a wittier spoof, as the grandson (Gene Wilder) of the infamous scientist creates a new monster (Peter Boyle). Cinematographer Gerald Hirschfeld perfectly captures the black-and-white look of 1930's horror films. *See also* main entry.

1975

Barry Lyndon (Warner Bros.; *dir.*, Stanley Kubrick) This tale of the adventures of a social climber (Ryan O'Neal) in eighteenth century Europe was dismissed by many as slow, overly mannered, and pretentious but was seen as a ravishing visual spectacle by others. It won four Academy Awards, including one for John Alcott's cinematography.

Dog Day Afternoon (Artists Entertainment Complex/Warner Bros.; *dir.*, Sidney Lumet) Lumet and Al Pacino followed *Serpico* with another true crime tale as a bisexual man (Pacino) tries to rob a Brooklyn bank to finance a sex-change operation for his transvestite lover (Chris Sarandon).

Jaws (Universal; *dir.*, Steven Spielberg) A police chief (Roy Scheider), a fisherman (Robert Shaw), and a scientist (Richard Dreyfuss) battle a human-eating shark near an Atlantic coast resort. The film's enormous success changed the way films are marketed and distributed. *See also* main entry.

The Man Who Would Be King (Columbia; *dir.*, John Huston) Sean Connery and Michael Caine portray British soldiers in nineteenth century India who go to Afghanistan in search of riches. Huston's old-fashioned entertainment is based on a Rudyard Kipling story.

Nashville (Paramount; *dir.*, Robert Altman) Altman follows twenty-four characters around the country-music capital for five days to comment on celebrity, politics, and power. The ironic anthem "It Don't Worry Me" won an Academy Award for its composer and singer, Keith Carradine.

One Flew over the Cuckoo's Nest (Fantast/United Artists; *dir.*, Milos Forman) Free spirit Randle P. McMurphy (Jack Nicholson) is tamed by Nurse Ratched (Louise Fletcher) in an Oregon mental institution. This adaptation of the Ken Kesey novel won awards for Best Picture, Best Director, Best Actor, and Best Actress. *See also* main entry.

The Rocky Horror Picture Show (Twentieth Century-Fox; *dir.*, Jim Sharman) Susan Sarandon and Barry Bostwick play a young couple whose car breaks down during a storm. They take refuge in the isolated mansion of Dr. Frank N. Furter (Tim Curry). The first transsexual rock musical is most notable as a vehicle for audience participation. *See also* main entry.

Shampoo (Columbia; *dir.*, Hal Ashby) Beverley Hills hairdresser George Roundy (Warren Beatty) is having affairs with Jack Warden's wife (Lee Grant) and mistress (Julie Christie) and is also seduced by his daughter (Carrie Fisher). Beatty, spoofing his real-life image as a ladies' man, is forced to pose as a homosexual in order to deceive Warden further. Grant won the award for Best Supporting Actress.

Three Days of the Condor (Paramount; *dir.*, Sydney Pollack) Central Intelligence Agency (CIA) operative Joseph "the Condor" Turner (Robert Redford), on the run from assassins in New York, enlists the aid of photographer Kathy Hale (Faye Dunaway) and comes to believe that his employers are out to kill him. Arguably one of the best American spy films, it reflects the paranoia of the Watergate era.

The Wind and the Lion (MGM/United Artists; *dir.*, John Milius) President Theodore Roosevelt (Brian Keith) sends in the Marines when an Arab chieftain (Sean Connery) kidnaps an American woman (Candice Bergen) and her children. Meanwhile, Germans land in North Africa to try to turn the situation to their advantage.

1976

All the President's Men (Warner Bros; *dir.*, Alan J. Pakula) Screenwriter William Goldman received one of the film's four Academy Awards for turning the true story of how *The Washington Post* covered Watergate into an engrossing detective film. Robert Redford and Dustin Hoffman play reporters Bob Woodward and Carl Bernstein, and Jason Robards won the Best Supporting Actor award as editor Ben Bradlee. *See also* main entry.

The Bad News Bears (Paramount; *dir.*, Michael Ritchie) Coach Morris Buttermaker (Walter Matthau) turns a gang of Little League rejects into winners with the help of a female pitcher (Tatum O'Neal). One of several sports films directed by Ritchie, it uses profanity to counterbalance its message about accepting one another's differences.

Bound for Glory (United Artists; *dir.*, Hal Ashby) This biography of politically progressive folk singer Woody Guthrie (David Carradine) won two Academy Awards, including one for Haskell Wexler's cinematography, which beautifully evokes Depression-era America.

Carrie (United Artists; *dir.*, Brian De Palma) A repressed high-school student (Sissy Spacek) dominated by her religious-fanatic mother (Piper Laurie) discovers that she has telekinetic powers and wreaks havoc on her cruel classmates at the prom. De Palma scored his first big hit with this Stephen King adaptation.

Harlan County, USA (Cabin Creek; *dir.*, Barbara Kopple) This chronicle of a thirteen-month coal-miners' strike in Kentucky during 1973-1974 won the award for Best Documentary.

Marathon Man (Paramount; *dir.*, John Schlesinger) A Columbia University graduate student and marathoner (Dustin Hoffman) is pursued by a Nazi war criminal (Laurence Olivier) because of information thought to have been passed on by his secret-agent brother (Roy Scheider). The dental torture scene is a classic.

Network (MGM/United Artists; *dir.*, Sidney Lumet) Screenwriter Paddy Chayefsky's satire of the corruption of network television won awards for Original Screenplay, Actor (Peter Finch), Actress

(Faye Dunaway), and Supporting Actress (Beatrice Straight). *See also* main entry.

The Omen (Twentieth Century-Fox; *dir.*, Richard Donner) Capitalizing on the success of *The Exorcist,* this horror classic led to two sequels. The American ambassador (Gregory Peck) to Great Britain replaces his dead baby with a child who turns out to be the Antichrist. Jerry Goldsmith's score, featuring a chanting chorus, won an Academy Award.

Rocky (United Artists; *dir.*, John G. Avildsen) Inspired by the characters played by Marlon Brando in *On the Waterfront* and Paul Newman in *Somebody Up There Likes Me,* screenwriter-star Sylvester Stallone created Rocky Balboa, a mediocre Philadelphia boxer who unexpectedly wins a shot at the heavyweight championship. The film won three Academy Awards, including Best Picture and Best Director, and it was followed by three sequels. *See also* main entry.

Taxi Driver (Columbia; *dir.*, Martin Scorsese) New York cab driver Travis Bickle (Robert De Niro) is disgusted by the city's decadence and decides to rescue a young runaway-turned-prostitute (Jodie Foster). Scorsese and cinematographer Michael Chapman create an indelible view of New York as a neon hell, aided immeasurably by the final score of the great composer Bernard Herrmann. *See also* main entry.

1977

Annie Hall (United Artists; *dir.*, Woody Allen) Allen's most critically and commercially successful film looks at the up-and-down relationship of a comedian (Allen) and an aspiring singer (Diane Keaton). It won awards for Best Picture, Best Actress, Best Director, and Best Original Screenplay. *See also* main entry.

Close Encounters of the Third Kind (Columbia; *dir.*, Steven Spielberg) Spielberg's meditation on the fascination with intelligent life in outer space focuses on the experiences of Everyman Richard Dreyfuss with extraterrestrial forces. *See also* main entry.

The Goodbye Girl (MGM/Warner Bros.; *dir.*, Herbert Ross) A divorced mother (Marsha Mason) and her daughter (Quinn Cummings) are forced to share their New York apartment with an eccentric actor (Richard Dreyfuss). Neil Simon's screenplay blends comedy, romance, and sentiment.

Julia (Twentieth Century-Fox; *dir.*, Fred Zinnemann) Playwright Lillian Hellman (Jane Fonda) visits her childhood friend (Vanessa Redgrave), an opponent of fascism in 1930's Vienna. Redgrave and Jason Robards, as Hellman's lover, Dashiell Hammett, won Academy Awards.

Killer of Sheep (no distributor; *dir.*, Charles Burnett) A black man (Henry Sanders) working in a Los Angeles slaughterhouse tries to resolve his strained relationship with his family. Burnett began the film while a university student and shot it over several years. Little seen at the time, the film became a classic of African American cinema.

The Late Show (Warner Bros.; *dir.*, Robert Benton) An aging Los Angeles detective (Art Carney) and a would-be actress (Lily Tomlin) with a missing cat team up to solve a complicated murder mystery. Benton's *film noir* tribute was neglected at the time, but its reputation has increased.

Saturday Night Fever (Paramount; *dir.*, John Badham) John Travolta became a star as a Brooklyn native who hangs out with his aimless buddies but truly lives only on the dance floor. The film is dominated by its hugely popular disco soundtrack. *See also* main entry.

Smokey and the Bandit (Universal; *dir.*, Hal Needham) The Bandit (Burt Reynolds) bets eighty thousand dollars that he can transport a shipment of beer from Texarkana, Texas, to Atlanta within twenty-eight hours. His efforts are hindered by Sheriff Buford T. Justice (Jackie Gleason).

Star Wars (Twentieth Century-Fox; *dir.*, George Lucas) Luke Skywalker (Mark Hamill) is advised by Obi-Wan Kenobi (Alec Guinness) in his confrontation with the evil Darth Vader. Lucas's science-fiction epic helped create the special-effects-driven blockbuster genre and won seven Academy Awards. *See also* main entry.

The Turning Point (Twentieth Century-Fox; *dir.*, Herbert Ross) Meeting old friend Anne Bancroft, an aging ballerina, for the first time in many years makes Shirley MacLaine wonder about having chosen marriage over her ballet career. Her daughter (Leslie Browne) then has a chance to become the star that she never was.

1978

Coming Home (United Artists; *dir.*, Hal Ashby) When her husband (Bruce Dern) goes to Vietnam, a woman (Jane Fonda) volunteers to work at a veterans' hospital, meets a bitter paraplegic (Jon Voight), and begins to reevaluate her unreflective life. Fonda, Voight, and the screenplay by Waldo Salt and Robert C. Jones won Academy Awards. *See also* main entry.

Days of Heaven (Bert Schneider/Harold Schneider/Paramount; *dir.*, Terrence Malick) In the Texas of the early 1900's, lovers Bill (Richard Gere) and Abby (Brooke Adams) pose as brother and sister to entice a wealthy, sickly farmer (Sam Shepherd) into marrying her. Malick's film is crammed with Biblical and mythical allusions. Ennio Morricone provides a stirring score, and the magnificent cinematography of Nestor Almendros won an Academy Award.

The Deer Hunter (EMI/Universal; *dir.*, Michael Cimino) Three friends (Robert De Niro, Christopher Walken, and John Savage) go to Vietnam, are taken prisoner by the Viet Cong, and are forced to play Russian roulette. The film won five awards, including Best Picture, Best Director, and Best Supporting Actor for Walken. *See also* main entry.

Grease (Paramount; *dir.*, Randal Kleiser) One of the most popular film versions of a Broadway musical features John Travolta, Olivia Newton-John, and Stockard Channing as 1950's high-school students. *See also* main entry.

The Last Waltz (United Artists; *dir.*, Martin Scorsese) This documentary about the Band's final concert in 1976 captures a period when rock performers were beginning to take a nostalgic look back at the recent past. Guest performers include Bob Dylan, Van Morrison, and Muddy Waters.

Midnight Express (Casablanca/Columbia; *dir.*, Alan Parker) Based on a true story, the film depicts the experiences of young American (Brad Davis) who tries to smuggle hashish out of Turkey and is thrown into a prison whose inmates are constantly beaten, raped, and otherwise abused. It won awards for Giorgio Moroder's score and Oliver Stone's adapted screenplay.

National Lampoon's Animal House (ABC/Twentieth Century-Fox/Universal; *dir.*, John Landis) Students rejected by other early 1960's fraternities end up at Delta House, where "Bluto" Blukarsky (John Belushi) leads them in food fights and other antics. *See also* main entry.

Pretty Baby (Paramount; *dir.*, Louis Malle) E. J. Bellocq (Keith Carradine) photographs the prostitutes in the Storyville section of New Orleans in the 1910's and falls in love with the twelve-year-old daughter (Brooke Shields) of Hattie (Susan Sarandon). The film was controversial for treating a child as a sex object.

Superman (Warner Bros.; *dir.*, Richard Donner) Christopher Reeve stars as the Man of Steel, and Margot Kidder is Lois Lane. The film also features Gene Hackman as the evil Lex Luthor and Marlon Brando as Superman's father.

An Unmarried Woman (Twentieth Century-Fox; *dir.*, Paul Mazursky) The best-known feminist film of the decade presents a New York woman (Jill Clayburgh) whose husband (Michael Murphy) leaves her for a younger woman. Clayburgh finds her true self with the help of artist Saul (Alan Bates).

1979

Alien (Brandywine/Twentieth Century-Fox; *dir.*, Ridley Scott) One by one, the crew of the spaceship *Nostromo* become victims of a bloodthirsty, fast-growing alien until only Ripley (Sigourney Weaver) and the ship's cat are left. The film's special effects won an Academy Award. *See also* main entry.

All That Jazz (Columbia/Twentieth Century-Fox; *dir.*, Bob Fosse) A choreographer/director (Roy Scheider) edits a film, organizes a Broadway musical, juggles his love life, and contemplates death. Fosse's autobiographical film, inspired by Federico Fellini's *8 1/2* (1963), won four Academy Awards.

Apocalypse Now (United Artists; *dir.*, Francis Ford Coppola) Loosely based on Joseph Conrad's 1902 novel *Heart of Darkness*, Coppola's controversial look at Vietnam follows an Army captain (Martin Sheen) as he journeys upriver into Cambodia in order to assassinate Colonel Kurtz (Marlon Brando), a renegade Green Beret. It won two awards, including one for Vittorio Storaro's cinematography. *See also* main entry.

Being There (Lorimar/United Artists; *dir.*, Hal Ashby) A simpleton (Peter Sellers) who spends most of his time watching television accidentally becomes a confidant of a wealthy adviser (Melvyn Douglas) to the U.S. president (Jack Warden). Douglas won an Academy Award, and Sellers gives his last great performance.

The Black Stallion (United Artists; *dir.*, Carroll Ballard) Alec Ramsey (Kelly Reno) is rescued from a sinking ship by an Arabian stallion. When they return to Alec's hometown, the horse is cared for by a trainer (Mickey Rooney) who also turns Alec into a jockey. Perhaps the best children's film of the decade.

Breaking Away (Twentieth Century-Fox; *dir.*, Peter Yates) Four recent high-school graduates (Dennis Christopher, Dennis Quaid, Daniel Stern, and Jackie Earle Haley) in Bloomington, Indiana, are considered, as "townies," outcasts by the Indiana University students. They enter the university's annual bicycle race to prove their worth. Steve Tesich's original screenplay won an Academy Award.

The China Syndrome (IPC/Columbia; *dir.*, James Bridges) A television reporter (Jane Fonda) and her cameraman (Michael Douglas) witness a mishap at the local nuclear power plant. A harried engineer (Jack Lemmon) narrowly averts disaster. The film opened three weeks before a real-life accident at Three Mile Island.

Kramer vs. Kramer (Stanley R. Jaffe/Columbia; *dir.*, Robert Benton) After his wife (Meryl Streep) leaves him to "find herself," a New York advertising agency art director (Dustin Hoffman) loses his job because of the strain of caring for his young son (Justin Henry). The film won five awards: Best Picture, Best Actor, Best Supporting Actress, Best Director, and Best Adapted Screenplay. *See also* main entry.

Manhattan (United Artists; *dir.*, Woody Allen) A television writer (Allen) is dissatisfied with his work and feels guilty about his affair with a high-school student (Mariel Hemingway). He dumps her for the neurotic lover (Diane Keaton) of his best friend (Michael Murphy). Meanwhile, his ex-wife (Meryl Streep), a lesbian, has written a book about their marriage. The film is perhaps Allen's best balance between comedic and serious themes.

10 (Orion/Warner Bros.; *dir.*, Blake Edwards) A successful songwriter (Dudley Moore) grows dissatisfied with his life and becomes infatuated with a beautiful young woman (Bo Derek). *See also* main entry.

Michael Adams

Entertainment: Academy Awards

A title or name followed by an asterisk (*) indicates the presence of a full-length essay within *The Seventies in America.*

1970

Best Picture: *Patton*
Best Actor: George C. Scott, *Patton*
Best Actress: Glenda Jackson, *Women in Love*
Best Supporting Actor: John Mills, *Ryan's Daughter*
Best Supporting Actress: Helen Hayes, *Airport*
Best Director: Franklin J. Schaffner, *Patton*
Best Original Screenplay: Francis Ford Coppola and Edmund H. North, *Patton*
Best Adapted Screenplay: Ring Lardner, Jr., *M*A*S*H*
Best Cinematography: Freddie Young, *Ryan's Daughter*

1971

Best Picture: *The French Connection**
Best Actor: Gene Hackman, *The French Connection**
Best Actress: Jane Fonda*, *Klute*
Best Supporting Actor: Ben Johnson, *The Last Picture Show*
Best Supporting Actress: Cloris Leachman, *The Last Picture Show*
Best Director: William Friedkin, *The French Connection**
Best Original Screenplay: Paddy Chayefsky, *The Hospital*
Best Adapted Screenplay: Ernest Tidyman, *The French Connection**
Best Cinematography: Oswald Morris, *Fiddler on the Roof*

1972

Best Picture: *The Godfather**
Best Actor: Marlon Brando*, *The Godfather**
Best Actress: Liza Minnelli, *Cabaret*
Best Supporting Actor: Joel Grey, *Cabaret*
Best Supporting Actress: Eileen Heckart, *Butterflies Are Free*
Best Director: Bob Fosse, *Cabaret*
Best Original Screenplay: Jeremy Larner, *The Candidate*
Best Adapted Screenplay: Mario Puzo and Francis Ford Coppola, *The Godfather**
Best Cinematography: Geoffrey Unsworth, *Cabaret*

1973

Best Picture: *The Sting*
Best Actor: Jack Lemmon, *Save the Tiger*
Best Actress: Glenda Jackson, *A Touch of Class*
Best Supporting Actor: John Houseman, *The Paper Chase*
Best Supporting Actress: Tatum O'Neal, *Paper Moon*
Best Director: George Roy Hill, *The Sting*
Best Original Screenplay: Davis S. Ward, *The Sting*
Best Adapted Screenplay: William Peter Blatty, *The Exorcist**
Best Cinematography: Sven Nykvist, *Cries and Whispers*

1974

Best Picture: *The Godfather, Part II**
Best Actor: Art Carney, *Harry and Tonto*
Best Actress: Ellen Burstyn, *Alice Doesn't Live Here Anymore*
Best Supporting Actor: Robert De Niro*, *The Godfather, Part II**
Best Supporting Actress: Ingrid Bergman, *Murder on the Orient Express*
Best Director: Francis Ford Coppola, *The Godfather, Part II**
Best Original Screenplay: Robert Towne, *Chinatown**
Best Adapted Screenplay: Mario Puzo and Francis Ford Coppola, *The Godfather, Part II**
Best Cinematography: Fred Koenekamp and Joseph Biroc, *The Towering Inferno*

1975

Best Picture: *One Flew over the Cuckoo's Nest**
Best Actor: Jack Nicholson*, *One Flew over the Cuckoo's Nest**
Best Actress: Louise Fletcher, *One Flew over the Cuckoo's Nest**
Best Supporting Actor: George Burns, *The Sunshine Boys*
Best Supporting Actress: Lee Grant, *Shampoo*
Best Director: Milos Forman, *One Flew over the Cuckoo's Nest**
Best Original Screenplay: Frank Pierson, *Dog Day Afternoon*

Best Adapted Screenplay: Lawrence Hauben and Bo Goldman, *One Flew over the Cuckoo's Nest**
Best Cinematography: John Alcott, *Barry Lyndon*

1976

Best Picture: *Rocky**
Best Actor: Peter Finch, *Network**
Best Actress: Faye Dunaway*, *Network**
Best Supporting Actor: Jason Robards, *All the President's Men**
Best Supporting Actress: Beatrice Straight, *Network**
Best Director: John G. Avildsen, *Rocky**
Best Original Screenplay: Paddy Chayefsky, *Network**
Best Adapted Screenplay: William Goldman, *All the President's Men**
Best Cinematography: Haskell Wexler, *Bound for Glory*

1977

Best Picture: *Annie Hall**
Best Actor: Richard Dreyfuss,* *The Goodbye Girl*
Best Actress: Diane Keaton, *Annie Hall**
Best Supporting Actor: Jason Robards, *Julia*
Best Supporting Actress: Vanessa Redgrave, *Julia*
Best Director: Woody Allen*, *Annie Hall**
Best Original Screenplay: Woody Allen and Marshall Brickman, *Annie Hall**
Best Adapted Screenplay: Alvin Sargent, *Julia*
Best Cinematography: Wilmos Zsigmond, *Close Encounters of the Third Kind**

1978

Best Picture: *The Deer Hunter**
Best Actor: Jon Voight, *Coming Home**
Best Actress: Jane Fonda*, *Coming Home**
Best Supporting Actor: Christopher Walken, *The Deer Hunter**
Best Supporting Actress: Maggie Smith, *California Suite*
Best Director: Michael Cimino, *The Deer Hunter**
Best Original Screenplay: Nancy Dowd, Waldo Salt, and Robert C. Jones, *Coming Home**
Best Adapted Screenplay: Oliver Stone, *Midnight Express*
Best Cinematography: Nestor Almendros, *Days of Heaven*

1979

Best Picture: *Kramer vs. Kramer**
Best Actor: Dustin Hoffman*, *Kramer vs. Kramer**
Best Actress: Sally Field*, *Norma Rae*
Best Supporting Actor: Melyvn Douglas, *Being There*
Best Supporting Actress: Meryl Streep*, *Kramer vs. Kramer**
Best Director: Robert Benton, *Kramer vs. Kramer**
Best Original Screenplay: Steve Tesich, *Breaking Away*
Best Adapted Screenplay: Robert Benton, *Kramer vs. Kramer**
Best Cinematography: Caleb Deschanel, *The Black Stallion*

Entertainment: Major Broadway Plays and Awards

This list contains all Broadway plays that ran for at least one full month between January 1, 1970, and December 31, 1979, and that had total runs of at least two hundred performances. It also includes plays with shorter runs that received major awards. An asterisk (*) next to a title or personage indicates that a full essay exists on the topic within *The Seventies in America.*

Plays Opening in 1969

Oh! Calcutta! (opened June 17, 1969) 1,314 performances

No Place to Be Somebody (opened September 9, 1969) 39 performances
1970 Pulitzer Prize: Charles Gordone (playwright)

Butterflies Are Free (opened October 21, 1969) 1,128 performances
1970 Tony Awards: Best Featured Actress in a Play, Blythe Danner

Coco (opened December 18, 1969) 329 performances
1970 Tony Awards: Best Featured Actor in a Musical, René Auberjonois

Last of the Red Hot Lovers (opened December 28, 1969) 706 performances

Plays Opening in 1970

Child's Play (opened February 17, 1970) 342 performances
1970 Tony Awards: Best Actor, Fritz Weaver; Best Featured Actor, Ken Howard; Best Director, Joseph Hardy

Purlie (opened March 15, 1970) 688 performances
1970 Tony Awards: Best Actor in a Musical, Cleavon Little; Best Featured Actress in a Musical, Melba Moore

Applause (opened March 26, 1970) 896 performances
1970 Tony Awards: Best Musical, Betty Comden and Adolph Green (book), Charles Strous (music), Lee Adams (lyrics), and Joseph Kipness and Lawrence Kasha (producers); Best Actress in a Musical, Lauren Bacall; Best Direction of a Musical, Ron Field

Borstal Boy (opened March 31, 1970) 143 performances
1970 Tony Awards: Best Play, Frank McMahon (playwright) and Michael McAloney and Burton C. Kaiser (producers)
1970 New York Drama Critics Circle Award: Best Play, Frank McMahon

Company (opened April 26, 1970) 705 performances
1971 Tony Awards, Best Musical, Harold Prince (producer); Best Book of a Musical, George Furth; Best Original Score, Stephen Sondheim*; Best Lyrics, Stephen Sondheim*; Best Direction of a Musical, Harold Prince
New York Drama Critics Circle Award: Best Musical, Stephen Sondheim and George Furth

The Rothschilds (opened October 19, 1970) 507 performances
1971 Tony Awards: Best Actor in a Musical, Hal Linden; Best Featured Actor in a Musical, Keene Curtis

Paul Sills's Story Theater (opened October 26, 1970) 243 performances
1971 Tony Awards: Best Featured Actor in a Play, Paul Sand

Sleuth (opened November 12, 1970) 1,222 performances
1971 Tony Awards: Best Play, Anthony Shaffer (playwright) and Helen Bonfils, Morton Gottlieb, and Michael White (producers)

Home (opened November 17, 1970) 110 performances
1971 New York Drama Critics Circle Award: Best Play, David Storey (playwright)

The Gingerbread Lady (opened December 3, 1970) 193 performances
1971 Tony Awards: Best Actress in a Play, Maureen Stapleton

The Me Nobody Knows (opened December 18, 1970) 378 performances

Plays Opening in 1971

No, No, Nanette (opened January 19, 1971) 861 performances
1971 Tony Awards: Best Actress in a Musical, Helen Gallagher; Best Featured Actress in a Musical, Patsy Kelly

A Midsummer Night's Dream (opened January 20, 1971) 62 performances (revival)
1971 Tony Awards: Best Direction of a Play, Peter Brook

The School for Wives (opened February 16, 1971) 120 performances
1971 Tony Awards: Best Actor in a Play, Brian Bedford

And Miss Reardon Drinks a Little (opened February 25, 1971) 108 performances
1971 Tony Awards: Best Featured Actress in a Play, Rae Allen

Follies (opened April 4, 1971) 522 performances
1972 Tony Awards: Best Actress in a Musical, Alexis Smith; Best Direction of a Musical, Michael Bennett and Harold Prince
New York Drama Critics Circle Award: Best Musical, Stephen Sondheim* and James Goldman

Lenny (opened May 26, 1971) 453 performances
1972 Tony Awards: Best Actor in a Play, Cliff Gorman

Jesus Christ Superstar (opened October 12, 1971) 711 performances

Ain't Supposed to Die a Natural Death (opened October 20, 1971) 325 performances

The Prisoner of Second Avenue (opened November 11, 1971) 798 performances
1972 Tony Awards: Best Featured Actor in a Play, Vincent Gardenia; Best Direction of a Play, Mike Nichols

Twigs (opened November 14, 1971) 289 performances
1972 Tony Awards: Best Actress in a Play, Sada Thompson

Two Gentlemen of Verona (opened December 1, 1971) 613 performances
1972 Tony Awards: Best Musical, the New York Shakespeare Festival and Joseph Papp (producers)
New York Drama Critics Circle Award: Best Musical, Galt MacDermot and John Guare

Inner City (opened December 19, 1971) 97 performances
1972 Tony Awards: Best Featured Actress in Musical, Linda Hopkins

Plays Opening in 1972

Grease (opened February 14, 1972) 3,388 performances

Sticks and Bones (opened March 1, 1972) 246 performances
1972 Tony Awards: Best Play, David Rabe (playwright) and Joseph Papp (producer); Best Featured Actress in a Play, Elizabeth Wilson

A Funny Thing Happened on the Way to the Forum (opened March 30, 1972) 156 performances
1972 Tony Awards: Best Actor in a Musical, Phil Silvers; Best Featured Actor in a Musical, Larry Blyden

Sugar (opened April 9, 1972) 505 performances

Don't Bother Me, I Can't Cope (opened April 19, 1972) 1,065 performances

That Championship Season (opened September 14, 1972) 700 performances
1973 Tony Awards: Best Play, Jason Miller (playwright) and Joseph Papp (producer); Best Direction of a Play, A. J. Antoon
1973 Pulitzer Prize: Jason Miller
1973 New York Drama Critics Circle Award: Best Play, Jason Miller

6 Rms Riv Vu (opened October 17, 1972) 247 performances

Pippin (opened October 18, 1972) 1,944 performances
1973 Tony Awards: Best Actor in a Musical, Ben Vereen; Best Direction of a Musical, Bob Fosse

Butley (opened October 31, 1972) 135 performances
1973 Tony Awards: Best Actor in a Play, Alan Bates

The Last of Mrs. Lincoln (opened December 12, 1972) 63 performances
1973 Tony Awards: Best Actress in a Play, Julie Harris; Best Featured Actress in a Play, Leora Dana

The Sunshine Boys (opened December 20, 1972) 538 performances

Plays Opening in 1973

A Little Night Music (opened February 25, 1973) 601 performances
1973 Tony Awards: Best Musical, Harold Prince (producer); Best Book of a Musical, Hugh Wheeler; Best Original Score, Stephen Sondheim*; Best Actress in a Musical, Glynis Johns; Best Featured Actress in a Musical, Patricia Elliott
New York Drama Critics Circle Award: Best Musical, Hugh Wheeler and Stephen Sondheim*

The Changing Room (opened March 6, 1973) 192 performances
1973 Tony Awards: Best Featured Actor in a Play, John Lithgow
1973 New York Drama Critics Circle Award: Best Play, David Storey (playwright)

Irene (opened March 13, 1973) 594 performances
1973 Tony Awards: Best Featured Actor in a Musical, George S. Irving

Seesaw (opened March 18, 1973) 296 performances
1973 Tony Awards: Best Featured Actor in a Musical, Tommy Tune

The River Niger (opened March 27, 1973) 162 performances
1973 Tony Awards: Best Play, Joseph A. Walker (playwright) and the Negro Ensemble Company (producers)

Cyrano (opened May 13, 1973) 49 performances
1973 Tony Awards: Best Actor in a Musical, Christopher Plummer

Raisin (opened October 18, 1973) 847 performances
1974 Tony Awards: Best Musical, Robert Nemiroff (producer); Best Actress in a Musical, Virginia Capers

Good Evening (opened November 14, 1973) 438 performances

The Good Doctor (opened November 27, 1973) 208 performances
1974 Tony Awards: Best Featured Actress in a Play, Frances Sternhagen

Find Your Way Home (opened December 13, 1973) 135 performances
1974 Tony Awards: Best Actor in a Play, Michael Moriarty

A Moon for the Misbegotten (opened December 29, 1973) 313 performances
1974 Tony Awards: Best Actress in a Play, Colleen Dewhurst; Best Featured Actor in a Play, Ed Flanders; Best Direction of a Play, José Quintero

Plays Opening in 1974

Lorelei (opened January 27, 1974) 320 performances

Over Here! (opened March 6, 1974) 341 performances
1974 Tony Awards: Best Featured Actress in a Musical, Janie Sell

Candide (opened March 10, 1974) 740 performances (revival)
1974 Tony Awards: Best Book of a Musical, Hugh Wheeler; Best Direction of a Musical, Harold Prince
New York Drama Critics Circle Award: Best Musical, Hugh Wheeler

My Fat Friend (opened March 31, 1974) 288 performances

Thieves (opened April 7, 1974) 313 performances

My Sister, My Sister (opened April 30, 1974) 238 performances

Short Eyes (opened May 23, 1974) 80 performances
1975 Tony Awards: Best Play, Miguel Pinero (playwright) and Joseph Papp (producer)
New York Drama Critics Circle Award: Best American Play, Miguel Pinero

The Magic Show (opened May 28, 1974) 1,920 performances

Gypsy (opened September 23, 1974) 120 performances
1975 Tony Awards: Best Actress in a Musical, Angela Lansbury

Absurd Person Singular (opened October 8, 1974) 591 performances

Equus (opened October 14, 1974) 1,209 performances
1974 Tony Awards: Best Play, Peter Shaffer (playwright) and Kermit Bloomgarden and Doris Cole Abrahams (producers); Best Direction of a Play, John Dexter
New York Drama Critics Circle Award: Best Play, Peter Shaffer

Sherlock Holmes (opened November 12, 1974) 471 performances

Sizwe Banzi Is Dead (opened November 13, 1974) 159 performances
1975 Tony Awards: Best Actor in a Play, John Kani and Winston Ntshona

The Island (opened November 24, 1974) 52 performances
1975 Tony Awards: Best Actor in a Play, John Kani and Winston Ntshona

In Praise of Love (opened December 10, 1974) 200 performances

All Over Town (opened December 29, 1974) 233 performances

Plays Opening in 1975

The Wiz (opened January 5, 1975) 1,672 performances
1975 Tony Awards: Best Musical, Ken Harper (producer); Best Original Score, Charlie Smalls; Best Featured Actor in a Musical, Ted Ross; Best Featured Actress in a Musical, Dee Dee Bridgewater; Best Direction of a Musical, Geoffrey Holder

Shenandoah (opened January 7, 1975) 1,050 performances
1975 Tony Awards: Best Book of a Musical, James Lee Barrett, Peter Udell, and Philip Rose; Best Actor in a Musical, John Cullum

The Ritz (opened January 10, 1975) 398 performances
1975 Tony Awards: Best Featured Actress in a Play, Rita Moreno

Dance with Me (opened January 23, 1975) 396 performances

Seascape (opened January 26, 1975) 63 performances
1975 Tony Awards: Best Featured Actor in a Play, Frank Langella
1975 Pulitzer Prize: Edward Albee

Same Time, Next Year (opened March 14, 1975) 1,453 performances

Chicago (opened June 3, 1975) 936 performances

*A Chorus Line** (opened July 25, 1975) 6, 137 performances
1976 Tony Awards: Best Musical, Joseph Papp (producer); Best Book of a Musical, James Kirkwood and Nicholas Dante; Best Original Score, Marvin Hamlisch (music), Edward Kleban (lyrics); Best Direction of a Musical, Michael Bennett; Best Actress in a Musical, Donna McKechnie; Best Featured Actor in a Musical, Sammy Williams; Best Featured Actress in a Musical, Carole Bishop
New York Drama Critics Circle Award: Best Musical, Michael Bennett (choreographer and director); James Kirkwood and Nicholas Dante (book); Marvin Hamlisch (music); Edward Kleban (lyrics)
1976 Pulitzer Prize: Michael Bennett, James Kirkwood, and Nicholas Dante

Me and Bessie (opened October 22, 1975) 453 performances

Yentl (opened October 23, 1975) 223 performances

Travesties (opened October 30, 1975) 156 performances
1976 Tony Awards: Best Play, Tom Stoppard (playwright) and David Merrick, Doris Cole Abrahams, and Bury Fredrik (producers); Best Actor in a Play, John Wood

New York Drama Critics Circle Award: Best Play, Tom Stoppard

Kennedy's Children (opened November 3, 1975) 72 performances
1976 Tony Awards: Best Featured Actress in a Play, Shirley Knight

Very Good Eddie (opened December 21, 1975) 304 performances

Sweet Bird of Youth (opened December 29, 1975) 48 performances
1976 Tony Awards: Best Actress in a Play, Irene Worth

The Royal Family (opened December 30, 1975) 233 performances
1976 Tony Awards: Best Direction of a Play, Ellis Rabb

Plays Opening in 1976

Pacific Overtures (opened January 11, 1976) 193 performances
New York Drama Critics Circle Award: Best Musical, Stephen Sondheim* (music and lyrics), John Weidman (book), and Hugh Wheeler (additional material)

Mrs. Warren's Profession (opened February 18, 1976) 55 performances
1976 Tony Awards: Best Featured Actor in a Play, Edward Herrmann

Bubbling Brown Sugar (opened March 2, 1976) 766 performances

My Fair Lady (opened March 25, 1976) 377 performances (revival)
1976 Tony Awards: Best Actor in a Musical, George Rose

Streamers (opened April 25, 1976) 478 performances
New York Drama Critics Circle Award: Best American Play, David Rabe

The Belle of Amherst (opened April 28, 1976) 116 performances
1977 Tony Awards: Best Actress in a Play, Julie Harris

Threepenny Opera (opened May 1, 1976) 306 performances

The Runner Stumbles (opened May 18, 1976) 396 performances

California Suite (opened June 10, 1976) 445 performances

Godspell (opened June 17, 1976) 527 performances

Guys and Dolls (opened July 21, 1976) 239 performances (revival)

for *colored girls who have considered suicide/ when the rainbow is enuf* (opened September 15, 1976) 742 performances
1977 Tony Awards: Best Featured Actress in a Play, Trazana Beverley

Oh! Calcutta! (opened September 24, 1976) 5,959 performances (revival)

The Robber Bridegroom (opened October 9, 1976) 145 performances
1977 Tony Awards: Best Actor in a Musical, Barry Bostwick

Comedians (opened November 28, 1976) 145 performances
1977 Tony Awards: Best Featured Actor in a Play, Jonathan Pryce

Sly Fox (opened December 14, 1976) 495 performances

Your Arms Too Short to Box with God (opened December 22, 1976) 429 performances
1977 Tony Awards: Best Featured Actress in a Musical, Delores Hall

Plays Opening in 1977

Otherwise Engaged (opened February 2, 1977) 309 performances
1977 New York Drama Critics Circle Award: Best Play, Simon Gray (playwright)

Mummenschanz (opened March 30, 1977) 1,326 performances

The Shadow Box (opened March 31, 1977) 315 performances
1977 Tony Awards: Michael Cristofer (playwright) and Allan Francis, Ken Marsolais, Lester Osterman, and Leornard Soloway (producers)
1977 Pulitzer Prize: Michael Cristofer

I Love My Wife (opened April 17, 1977) 857 performances
1977 Tony Awards: Best Featured Actor in a Musical, Lenny Baker; Best Direction of a Musical, Gene Saks

Side by Side by Sondheim (opened April 18, 1977) 384 performances

Annie (opened April 21, 1977) 2,377 performances
1977 Tony Awards: Best Musical, Lewis Allen, Mike Nichols, Irwin Meyer, and Stephen R. Friedman (producers); Best Book of a Musical, Thomas Meehan; Best Actress in a Musical, Dorothy Loudon
New York Drama Critics Circle Award: Best Musical, Charles Strouse (music); Martin Charnin (lyrics); Thomas Meehan (book); Mike Nichols (producer)

The Basic Training of Pavlo Hummel (opened April 24, 1977) 117 performances
1977 Tony Awards: Best Actor in a Play, Al Pacino*

The King and I (opened May 2, 1977) 695 performances (revival)

Gemini (opened May 21, 1977) 1,819 performances

Beatlemania (opened May 26, 1977) 1,006 performances

The Gin Game (opened October 6, 1977) 517 performances
1978 Tony Awards: Best Actress in a Play, Jessica Tandy
1978 Pulitzer Prize: Donald L. Coburn (playwright)

Dracula (opened October 20, 1977) 925 performances (revival)

The Act (opened October 29, 1977) 233 performances
1978 Tony Awards: Best Actress in a Musical, Liza Minnelli

Chapter Two (opened December 4, 1977) 857 performances
1978 Tony Awards: Best Featured Actress in a Play, Ann Wedgeworth

Plays Opening in 1978

On the Twentieth Century (opened February 19, 1978) 449 performances
1978 Tony Awards: Best Book of a Musical, Betty Comden and Adolph Green; Best Actor in a Musical, John Cullum; Best Featured Actor in a Musical, Kevin Kline

Deathtrap (opened February 26, 1978) 1,793 performances

Timbuktu! (opened March 1, 1978) 221 performances

The Effect of Gamma Rays on Man-in-the-Moon Marigolds (opened March 14, 1978) 16 performances
1971 Pulitzer Prize: Paul Zindel (playwright)

Dancin' (opened March 27, 1978) 1,774 performances

Da (opened May 1, 1978) 697 performances
1978 Tony Awards: Best Play, Hugh Leonard (playwright) and Lester Osterman, Marilyn Strauss, and Marc Howard (producers); Best Actor in a Play, Barnard Leonard; Best Featured Actor in a Play, Lester Rawlins; Best Direction of a Play, Melvin Bernhardt
New York Drama Critics Circle Award: Best Play, Hugh Leonard

Ain't Misbehavin' (opened May 9, 1978) 1,604 performances
1978 Tony Awards: Best Musical, Emanuel Azenberg, Dasha Epstein, the Shubert Organization, Jane Gayno, and Ron Dante (producers); Best Featured Actress in a Musical, Nell Carter; Best Direction of a Musical, Richard Maltby, Jr.
New York Drama Critics Circle Award: Best Musical, Emanuel Azenberg, Dasha Epstein, the Shubert Organization, Jane Gayno, and Ron Dante

Runaways (opened May 13, 1978) 274 performances

Tribute (opened June 1, 1978) 212 performances

The Best Little Whorehouse in Texas (opened June 19, 1978) 1,584 performances
1979 Tony Awards: Best Featured Actor in a Musical, Henderson Forsythe; Best Featured Actress in a Musical, Carlin Glynn

Eubie! (opened September 20, 1978) 439 performances

The Crucifer of Blood (opened September 28, 1978) 236 performances

Plays Opening in 1979

Wings (opened January 28, 1979) 113 performances
1979 Tony Awards: Best Actress in a Play, Constance Cummings

They're Playing Our Song (opened February 11, 1979) 1,011 performances

Whoopee! (opened February 14, 1979) 204 performances

Sweeney Todd (opened March 1, 1979) 557 performances
1979 Tony Awards: Best Musical, Richard Barr, Charles Woodward, Robert Fryer, Mary Lea Johnson, and Martin Richards (producers); Best Book of a Musical, Hugh Wheeler; Best Score, Stephen Sondheim*; Best Actor in a Musical, Len Cariou; Best Actress in a Musical, Angela Lansbury; Best Direction of a Musical, Harold Prince
New York Drama Critics Circle Award: Best Musical, Stephen Sondheim* and Hugh Wheeler

Bedroom Farce (opened March 29, 1979) 276 performances
1979 Tony Awards: Best Featured Actor in a Play, Michael Gough; Best Featured Actress in a Play, Joan Hickson

Whose Life Is It Anyway? (opened April 17, 1979) 223 performances
1979 Tony Awards: Best Actor in a Play, Tom Conti

The Elephant Man (opened April 19, 1979) 916 performances
1979 Tony Awards: Best Play, Bernard Pomerance (playwright) and Richmond Crinkley, Elizabeth I. McCann, and Nelle Nugent (producers); Best Actress in a Play, Carole Shelley; Best Direction of a Play, Jack Hofsiss
1979 New York Drama Critics Circle Award: Best Play, Bernard Pomerance

Peter Pan (opened September 6, 1979) 554 performances (revival)

On Golden Pond (opened September 12, 1979) 424 performances

Evita (opened September 25, 1979) 1,567 performances
1979 Tony Awards: Best Musical, Robert Stigwood (producer); Best Book of a Musical, Tim Rice; Best Original Score, Andrew Lloyd Webber (music) and Tim Rice (lyrics); Best Actress in a Musical, Patti LuPone; Best Featured Actor in a Musical, Mandy Patinkin; Best Direction of a Musical, Harold Prince

Sugar Babies (opened October 8, 1979) 1,208 performances

Romantic Comedy (opened November 8, 1979) 396 performances

Strider (opened November 14, 1979) 214 performances

Bent (opened December 2, 1979) 241 performances

Oklahoma! (opened December 13, 1979) 293 performances (revival)

Entertainment: Most-Watched U.S. Television Shows

This list shows the top-ten U.S. television programs of each October-April season, as ranked by the Nielsen Media Company. The ratings in the right column indicate the average percentage of American homes with televisions watching each show. For example, during the 1970-1971 season, 29.6 percent of all American homes with a television watched *Marcus Welby, M.D.*, on the evenings that it was broadcast. Titles followed by an asterisk (*) indicate that the program has its own full-length essay within *The Seventies in America.*

1970-1971

Rank	Program	Network	Rating
1.	*Marcus Welby, M.D.*	ABC	29.6
2.	*The Flip Wilson Show*	NBC	27.9
3.	*Here's Lucy*	CBS	26.1
4.	*Ironside*	NBC	25.7
5.	*Gunsmoke*	CBS	25.5
6.	*ABC Movie of the Week*	ABC	25.1
7.	*Hawaii Five-O* *	CBS	25.0
8.	*Medical Center*	CBS	24.5
9.	*Bonanza*	NBC	23.9
10.	*The F.B.I.*	ABC	23.0

1971-1972

Rank	Program	Network	Rating
1.	*All in the Family* *	CBS	34.0
2.	*The Flip Wilson Show*	NBC	28.2
3.	*Marcus Welby, M.D.*	ABC	27.8
4.	*Gunsmoke*	CBS	26.0
5.	*ABC Movie of the Week*	ABC	25.6
6.	*Sanford and Son* *	NBC	25.2
7.	*Mannix*	CBS	24.8
8.	*Funny Face*	CBS	23.9
	Adam-12	NBC	23.9
10.	*The Mary Tyler Moore Show* *	CBS	23.7

1972-1973

Rank	Program	Network	Rating
1.	*All in the Family* *	CBS	33.3
2.	*Sanford and Son* *	NBC	27.6
3.	*Hawaii Five-O* *	CBS	25.2
4.	*Maude* *	CBS	24.7
5.	*Bridget Loves Bernie*	CBS	24.2
	The NBC Sunday Mystery Movie	NBC	24.2
7.	*The Mary Tyler Moore Show* *	CBS	23.6
	Gunsmoke	CBS	23.6
9.	*The Wonderful World of Disney*	NBC	23.5
10.	*Ironside*	NBC	23.4

1973-1974

Rank	Program	Network	Rating
1.	*All in the Family* *	CBS	31.2
2.	*The Waltons*	CBS	28.1
3.	*Sanford and Son* *	NBC	27.5
4.	*M*A*S*H* *	CBS	25.7
5.	*Hawaii Five-O* *	CBS	24.0
6.	*Maude* *	CBS	23.5
7.	*Kojak*	CBS	23.3
	The Sonny and Cher Comedy Hour	CBS	23.3
9.	*The Mary Tyler Moore Show* *	CBS	23.1
	Cannon	CBS	23.1

1974-1975

Rank	Program	Network	Rating
1.	*All in the Family* *	CBS	30.2
2.	*Sanford and Son* *	NBC	29.6
3.	*Chico and the Man* *	NBC	28.5
4.	*The Jeffersons* *	CBS	27.6
5.	*M*A*S*H* *	CBS	27.4
6.	*Rhoda*	CBS	26.3
7.	*Good Times*	CBS	25.8
8.	*The Waltons*	CBS	25.5
9.	*Maude* *	CBS	24.9
10.	*Hawaii Five-O* *	CBS	24.8

1975-1976

Rank	Program	Network	Rating
1.	*All in the Family* *	CBS	30.1
2.	*Rich Man, Poor Man*	ABC	28.0
3.	*Laverne and Shirley*	ABC	27.5
4.	*Maude* *	CBS	25.0
5.	*The Bionic Woman*	ABC	24.9
6.	*Phyllis*	CBS	24.5
7.	*Sanford and Son* *	NBC	24.4
	Rhoda	CBS	24.4
9.	*The Six Million Dollar Man*	ABC	24.3
10.	*ABC Monday Night Movie*	ABC	24.2

1976-1977

Rank	Program	Network	Rating
1.	*Happy Days* *	ABC	31.5
2.	*Laverne and Shirley*	ABC	30.9
3.	*ABC Monday Night Movie*	ABC	26.0
4.	*M*A*S*H* *	CBS	25.9
5.	*Charlie's Angels* *	ABC	25.8
6.	*The Big Event*	NBC	24.4
7.	*The Six Million Dollar Man*	ABC	24.2
8.	*ABC Sunday Night Movie*	ABC	23.4
	Baretta	ABC	23.4
	One Day at a Time	CBS	23.4

1977-1978

1. *Laverne and Shirley*	ABC	31.6
2. *Happy Days* *	ABC	31.4
3. *Three's Company* *	ABC	28.3
4. *60 Minutes* *	CBS	24.4
Charlie's Angels *	ABC	24.4
All in the Family *	CBS	24.4
7. *Little House on the Prairie*	CBS	24.1
8. *Alice*	CBS	23.2
*M*A*S*H* *	CBS	23.2
10. *One Day at a Time*	CBS	23.0

1978-1979

1. *Laverne and Shirley*	ABC	30.5
2. *Three's Company* *	ABC	30.3
3. *Mork and Mindy*	ABC	28.6
Happy Days *	ABC	28.6
5. *Angie*	ABC	26.7
6. *60 Minutes* *	CBS	25.5
7. *M*A*S*H* *	CBS	25.4
8. *The Ropers*	ABC	25.2
9. *All in the Family* *	CBS	24.9
Taxi *	ABC	24.9

1979-1980

1. *60 Minutes* *	CBS	28.4
2. *Three's Company* *	ABC	26.3
3. *That's Incredible*	ABC	25.8
4. *Alice*	CBS	25.3
*M*A*S*H* *	CBS	25.3
6. *Dallas*	CBS	25.0
7. *Flo*	CBS	24.4
8. *The Jeffersons* *	CBS	24.3
9. *The Dukes of Hazzard*	CBS	24.1
10. *One Day at a Time*	CBS	23.0

Entertainment: Emmy Awards

The categories and titles of the Emmy Awards changed almost every year. This list contains a selection of the television awards generally considered to be the most important. Programs followed by an asterisk (*) are subjects of their own full-length essays within *The Seventies in America.*

1970-1971

Outstanding Series—Drama: *The Bold Ones: The Senator* (NBC)
Outstanding Series—Comedy: *All in the Family** (CBS)
Outstanding Single Program—Drama or Comedy: *The Andersonville Trial* (PBS)
Outstanding Variety Series—Musical: *The Flip Wilson Show* (NBC)
Outstanding Variety Series—Talk: *The David Frost Show* (syndicated)
Outstanding New Series: *All in the Family**
Outstanding Continued Performance by an Actor in a Leading Role in a Dramatic Series: Hal Holbrook, *The Bold Ones: The Senator* (NBC)
Outstanding Continued Performance by an Actress in a Leading Role in a Dramatic Series: Susan Hampshire, *The First Churchills* (PBS)
Outstanding Continued Performance by an Actor in a Leading Role in a Comedy Series: Jack Klugman, *The Odd Couple* (ABC)
Outstanding Continued Performance by an Actress in a Leading Role in a Comedy Series: Jean Stapleton, *All in the Family** (CBS)
Outstanding Performance by an Actor in a Supporting Role in Drama: David Burns, *The Price* (NBC)
Outstanding Performance by an Actress in a Supporting Role in Drama: Margaret Leighton, *Hamlet* (NBC)
Outstanding Performance by an Actor in a Supporting Role in Comedy: Edward Asner, *The Mary Tyler Moore Show** (CBS)
Outstanding Performance by an Actress in a Supporting Role in Comedy: Valerie Harper, *The Mary Tyler Moore Show** (CBS)
Outstanding Directorial Achievement in Drama: Daryl Duke, "The Day the Lion Died," *The Bold Ones: The Senator* (NBC)
Outstanding Directorial Achievement in Comedy: Jay Sandrich, "Toulouse Lautrec Is One of My Favorite Artists," *The Mary Tyler Moore Show** (CBS)
Outstanding Directorial Achievement in Variety or Music: Mike Warren, *Rowan and Martin's Laugh-In* (NBC)

1971-1972

Outstanding Series—Drama: *Elizabeth R* (PBS)
Outstanding Series—Comedy: *All in the Family** (CBS)
Outstanding Single Program—Drama or Comedy: *Brian's Song* (ABC)
Outstanding Variety Series—Musical: *The Carol Burnett Show** (CBS)
Outstanding Variety Series—Talk: *The Dick Cavett Show* (ABC)
Outstanding New Series: *Elizabeth R* (PBS)
Outstanding Continued Performance by an Actor in a Leading Role in a Dramatic Series: Peter Falk, *Columbo* (NBC)
Outstanding Continued Performance by an Actress in a Leading Role in a Dramatic Series: Glenda Jackson, *Elizabeth R* (PBS)
Outstanding Continued Performance by an Actor in a Leading Role in a Comedy Series: Carroll O'Connor, *All in the Family** (CBS)
Outstanding Continued Performance by an Actress in a Leading Role in a Comedy Series: Jean Stapleton, *All in the Family** (CBS)
Outstanding Performance by an Actor in a Supporting Role in Drama: Jack Warden, *Brian's Song* (ABC)
Outstanding Performance by an Actress in a Supporting Role in Drama: Jenny Agutter, *The Snow Goose* (NBC)
Outstanding Performance by an Actor in a Supporting Role in Comedy: Edward Asner, *The Mary Tyler Moore Show** (CBS)
Outstanding Performance by an Actress in a Supporting Role in Comedy (tie): Valerie Harper, *The Mary Tyler Moore Show** (CBS); Sally Struthers, *All in the Family** (CBS)
Outstanding Achievement by a Performer in Music or Variety: Harvey Korman, *The Carol Burnett Show** (CBS)
Outstanding Directorial Achievement in Drama: Alexander Singer, "The Invasion of Kevin Ireland," *The Bold Ones: The Lawyers* (ABC)
Outstanding Directorial Achievement in Comedy: John Rich, "Sammy's Visit," *All in the Family** (CBS)

Outstanding Directorial Achievement in Comedy/ Variety or Music: Art Fisher, *The Sonny and Cher Comedy Hour* (ABC)

1972-1973

Outstanding Series—Drama: *The Waltons* (CBS)
Outstanding Series—Comedy: *All in the Family** (CBS)
Outstanding Single Program—Drama or Comedy: *A War of Children* (CBS)
Outstanding Variety Musical Series: *The Julie Andrews Hour* (ABC)
Outstanding New Series: *America* (NBC)
Outstanding Continued Performance by an Actor in a Leading Role (Drama Series—Continuing): Richard Thomas, *The Waltons* (CBS)
Outstanding Continued Performance by an Actress in a Leading Role (Drama Series—Continuing): Michael Learned, *The Waltons* (CBS)
Outstanding Continued Performance by an Actor in a Leading Role in a Comedy Series: Jack Klugman, *The Odd Couple* (ABC)
Outstanding Continued Performance by an Actress in a Leading Role in a Comedy Series: Mary Tyler Moore, *The Mary Tyler Moore Show** (CBS)
Outstanding Performance by an Actor in a Supporting Role in a Drama: Scott Jacoby, *That Certain Summer* (ABC)
Outstanding Performance by an Actress in a Supporting Role in a Drama: Ellen Corby, *The Waltons* (CBS)
Outstanding Performance by an Actor in a Supporting Role in a Comedy: Ted Knight, *The Mary Tyler Moore Show** (CBS)
Outstanding Performance by an Actress in a Supporting Role in a Comedy: Valerie Harper, *The Mary Tyler Moore Show** (CBS)
Outstanding Achievement by a Supporting Performer in Music or Variety: Tim Conway, *The Carol Burnett Show** (CBS)
Outstanding Directorial Achievement in Drama: Jerry Thorpe, "An Eye for an Eye," *Kung Fu* (ABC)
Outstanding Directorial Achievement in Comedy: Jay Sandrich, "It's Whether You Win or Lose," *The Mary Tyler Moore Show** (CBS)
Outstanding Directorial Achievement in Comedy/ Variety: Bob Fosse, *Liza with a "Z"* (NBC)
Outstanding Directorial Achievement in Variety or Music: Bill Davis, *The Julie Andrews Hour* (ABC)

1973-1974

Outstanding Series—Drama: *Upstairs, Downstairs* (PBS)
Outstanding Series—Comedy: *M*A*S*H* * (CBS)
Outstanding Musical/Variety Series: *The Carol Burnett Show** (CBS)
Outstanding Limited Series: *Columbo* (NBC)
Outstanding Special—Drama or Comedy: *The Autobiography of Miss Jane Pittman* (CBS)
Outstanding Comedy/Variety, Variety, or Music Special: *Lily* (CBS)
Outstanding Children's Special: *Free to Be... You and Me** (ABC)
Best Lead Actor in a Drama Series: Telly Savalas, *Kojak* (CBS)
Best Lead Actress in a Drama Series: Michael Learned, *The Waltons* (CBS)
Best Lead Actor in a Comedy: Alan Alda, *M*A*S*H** (CBS)
Best Lead Actress in a Comedy: Mary Tyler Moore, *The Mary Tyler Moore Show** (CBS)
Best Supporting Actor in Drama: Michael Moriarty, *The Glass Menagerie* (ABC)
Best Supporting Actress in Drama: Joanna Miles, *The Glass Menagerie* (ABC)
Best Supporting Actor in Comedy: Rob Reiner, *All in the Family** (CBS)
Best Supporting Actress in Comedy: Cloris Leachman, *The Mary Tyler Moore Show** (CBS)
Best Supporting Actor in Comedy/Variety, Variety, or Music: Harvey Korman, *The Carol Burnett Show** (CBS)
Best Supporting Actress in Comedy/Variety, Variety, or Music: Brenda Vaccaro, *The Shape of Things* (CBS)
Best Directing in Drama: Robert Butler, *The Blue Knight*, Part III (NBC)
Best Directing in Comedy: Jackie Cooper, "Carry on, Hawkeye," *M*A*S*H** (CBS)
Best Directing in Variety or Music: Dave Powers, "The Australia Show," *The Carol Burnett Show** (CBS)
Best Directing in Comedy/Variety, Variety, or Music: Dwight Hemion, *Barbra Streisand . . . and Other Musical Instruments* (CBS)

1974-1975

Outstanding Drama Series: *Upstairs, Downstairs* (PBS)
Outstanding Comedy Series: *The Mary Tyler Moore Show** (CBS)

Outstanding Music/Variety Series: *The Carol Burnett Show** (CBS)
Outstanding Limited Series: *Benjamin Franklin* (CBS)
Outstanding Special—Drama or Comedy: *The Law* (NBC)
Outstanding Comedy/Variety or Music Special: *An Evening with John Denver* (ABC)
Outstanding Lead Actor in a Drama Series: Robert Blake, *Baretta* (ABC)
Outstanding Lead Actress in a Drama Series: Jean Marsh, *Upstairs, Downstairs* (PBS)
Outstanding Lead Actor in a Comedy Series: Tony Randall, *The Odd Couple* (ABC)
Outstanding Lead Actress in a Comedy Series: Valerie Harper, *Rhoda* (CBS)
Outstanding Continuing Performance by a Supporting Actor in a Drama Series: Will Geer, *The Waltons* (CBS)
Outstanding Continuing Performance by a Supporting Actress in a Drama Series: Ellen Corby, *The Waltons* (CBS)
Outstanding Continuing Performance by a Supporting Actor in a Comedy Series: Edward Asner, *The Mary Tyler Moore Show** (CBS)
Outstanding Continuing Performance by a Supporting Actress in a Comedy Series: Betty White, *The Mary Tyler Moore Show** (CBS)
Outstanding Directing in a Drama Series: Bill Bain, *Upstairs, Downstairs* (PBS)
Outstanding Directing in a Comedy Series: Gene Reynolds, *M*A*S*H** (CBS)
Outstanding Directing in a Comedy/Variety or Music Series: Dave Powers, *The Carol Burnett Show** (CBS)

1975-1976

Outstanding Drama Series: *Police Story* (CBS)
Outstanding Comedy Series: *The Mary Tyler Moore Show**
Outstanding Comedy/Variety or Music Series: *NBC's Saturday Night** (NBC)
Outstanding Limited Series: *Upstairs, Downstairs, Masterpiece Theatre* (PBS)
Outstanding Special—Drama or Comedy: *Eleanor and Franklin* (ABC)
Outstanding Comedy/Variety or Music Special: *Gypsy in My Soul* (CBS)
Outstanding Lead Actor in a Drama: Peter Falk, *Columbo* (NBC)
Outstanding Lead Actress in a Drama: Michael Learned, *The Waltons* (CBS)
Outstanding Lead Actor in a Comedy: Jack Albertson, *Chico and the Man** (NBC)
Outstanding Lead Actress in a Comedy: Mary Tyler Moore, *The Mary Tyler Moore Show** (CBS)
Outstanding Continuing Performance by a Supporting Actor in a Drama: Anthony Zerbe, *Harry O* (ABC)
Outstanding Continuing Performance by a Supporting Actress in a Drama: Ellen Corby, *The Waltons* (CBS)
Outstanding Continuing Performance by a Supporting Actor in a Comedy: Ted Knight, *The Mary Tyler Moore Show** (CBS)
Outstanding Continuing Performance by a Supporting Actress in a Comedy: Betty White, *The Mary Tyler Moore Show** (CBS)
Outstanding Continuing or Single Performance by a Supporting Actor in Variety or Music: Chevy Chase, *NBC's Saturday Night** (NBC)
Outstanding Continuing or Single Performance by a Supporting Actress in Variety or Music: Vicki Lawrence, *The Carol Burnett Show** (CBS)
Outstanding Directing in a Drama Series: David Greene, *Rich Man, Poor Man* (ABC)
Outstanding Directing in a Comedy Series: Gene Reynolds, *M*A*S*H** (CBS)
Outstanding Directing in a Comedy/Variety or Music Series: Dave Wilson, *NBC's Saturday Night** (NBC)

1976-1977

Outstanding Drama Series: *Upstairs, Downstairs* (PBS)
Outstanding Comedy Series: *The Mary Tyler Moore Show** (CBS)
Outstanding Comedy/Variety or Music Series: *Van Dyke and Company* (NBC)
Outstanding Limited Series: *Roots** (ABC)
Outstanding Special—Drama or Comedy (tie): *Eleanor and Franklin: The White House Years* (ABC); *Sybil* (NBC)
Outstanding Special—Comedy/Variety or Music: *The Barry Manilow Special* (ABC)
Outstanding Lead Actor in a Drama Series: James Garner, *The Rockford Files* (NBC)
Outstanding Lead Actress in a Drama Series: Lindsay Wagner, *The Bionic Woman* (ABC)
Outstanding Lead Actor in a Comedy Series: Carroll O'Connor, *All in the Family** (CBS)
Outstanding Lead Actress in a Comedy Series: Beatrice Arthur, *Maude** (CBS)

Outstanding Continuing Performance by a Supporting Actor in a Drama Series: Gary Frank, *Family** (ABC)

Outstanding Continuing Performance by a Supporting Actress in a Drama Series: Kristy McNichol, *Family** (ABC)

Outstanding Continuing Performance by a Supporting Actor in a Comedy Series: Gary Burghoff, *M*A*S*H** (CBS)

Outstanding Continuing Performance by a Supporting Actress in a Comedy Series: Mary Kay Place, *Mary Hartman, Mary Hartman** (syndicated)

Outstanding Continuing or Single Performance by a Supporting Actor in Variety or Music: Tim Conway, *The Carol Burnett Show** (CBS)

Outstanding Continuing or Single Performance by a Supporting Actress in Variety or Music: Rita Moreno, *The Muppet Show* (syndicated)

Outstanding Directing in a Drama Series: David Green, *Roots*, Part I* (ABC)

Outstanding Directing in a Comedy Series: Alan Alda, *M*A*S*H** (CBS)

Outstanding Directing in Comedy/Variety or Music Series: Dave Powers, *The Carol Burnett Show** (CBS)

1977-1978

Outstanding Drama Series: *The Rockford Files* (NBC)

Outstanding Comedy Series: *All in the Family** (CBS)

Outstanding Comedy/Variety or Music Series: *The Muppet Show* (syndicated)

Outstanding Limited Series: *Holocaust* (NBC)

Outstanding Special—Drama or Comedy: *The Gathering* (ABC)

Outstanding Special—Comedy/Variety or Music: *Bette Midler—Ol' Red Hair Is Back* (NBC)

Outstanding Children's Special: *Halloween Is Grinch Night* (ABC)

Outstanding Lead Actor in a Drama Series: Edward Asner, *Lou Grant* (CBS)

Outstanding Lead Actress in a Drama Series: Sada Thompson, *Family** (ABC)

Outstanding Lead Actor in a Comedy Series: Carroll O'Connor, *All in the Family** (CBS)

Outstanding Lead Actress in a Comedy Series: Jean Stapleton, *All in the Family** (CBS)

Outstanding Continuing Performance by a Supporting Actor in a Drama Series: Robert Vaughn, *Washington: Behind Closed Doors* (ABC)

Outstanding Continuing Performance by a Supporting Actress in a Drama Series: Nancy Marchand, *Lou Grant* (CBS)

Outstanding Continuing Performance by a Supporting Actor in a Comedy Series: Rob Reiner, *All in the Family** (CBS)

Outstanding Continuing Performance by a Supporting Actress in a Comedy Series: Julie Kavner, *Rhoda* (CBS)

Outstanding Continuing Performance by a Supporting Actor in Variety or Music: Tim Conway, *The Carol Burnett Show** (CBS)

Outstanding Continuing Performance by a Supporting Actress in Variety or Music: Gilda Radner, *Saturday Night Live** (NBC)

Outstanding Directing in a Drama: Marvin J. Chomsky, *Holocaust* (NBC)

Outstanding Directing in a Comedy: Paul Bogart, *All in the Family** (CBS)

Outstanding Directing in Comedy/Variety or Music: Dave Powers, *The Carol Burnett Show** (CBS)

1978-1979

Outstanding Drama Series: *Lou Grant* (CBS)

Outstanding Comedy Series: *Taxi** (ABC)

Outstanding Limited Series: *Roots: The Next Generation* (ABC)

Outstanding Drama or Comedy Special: *Friendly Fire* (ABC)

Outstanding Comedy/Variety or Music Program: *Steve and Eydie Celebrate Irving Berlin* (NBC)

Outstanding Children's Program: *Christmas Eve on Sesame Street* (PBS)

Outstanding Lead Actor in a Drama Series: Ron Liebman, *Kaz* (CBS)

Outstanding Lead Actress in a Drama Series: Mariette Hartley, *The Incredible Hulk* (CBS)

Outstanding Lead Actor in a Comedy Series: Carroll O'Connor, *All in the Family** (CBS)

Outstanding Lead Actress in a Comedy Series: Ruth Gordon, *Taxi** (ABC)

Outstanding Supporting Actor in a Drama Series: Stuart Margolin, *The Rockford Files* (NBC)

Outstanding Supporting Actress in a Drama Series: Kristy McNichol, *Family** (ABC)

Outstanding Supporting Actor in Comedy, Comedy/Variety, or Music Series: Robert Guillaume, *Soap* (ABC)

Outstanding Supporting Actress in a Comedy, Comedy/Variety, or Music Series: Sally Struthers, *All in the Family** (CBS)

Outstanding Directing in a Drama Series: Jackie Cooper, *The White Shadow** (CBS)

Outstanding Directing in Comedy, Comedy/Variety, or Music Series: Noam Pitlik, "The Harris Incident," *Barney Miller* (ABC)

1979-1980

Outstanding Drama Series: *Lou Grant* (CBS)

Outstanding Comedy Series: *Taxi** (ABC)

Outstanding Limited Series: *Edward and Mrs. Simpson* (syndicated)

Outstanding Drama or Comedy Special: *The Miracle Worker* (NBC)

Outstanding Variety or Music Program: *IBM Presents Baryshnikov on Broadway* (ABC)

Outstanding Children's Program: *Benji at Work* (ABC)

Outstanding Lead Actor in a Drama Series: Edward Asner, *Lou Grant* (CBS)

Outstanding Lead Actress in a Drama Series: Barbara Bel Geddes, *Dallas* (CBS)

Outstanding Lead Actor in a Comedy Series: Richard Mulligan, *Soap* (ABC)

Outstanding Lead Actress in a Comedy Series: Cathryn Damon, *Soap* (ABC)

Outstanding Supporting Actor in a Drama: Stuart Margolin, *The Rockford Files* (NBC)

Outstanding Supporting Actress in a Drama: Nancy Marchand, *Lou Grant* (CBS)

Outstanding Supporting Actor in a Comedy, Variety, or Music Series: Henry Morgan, *M*A*S*H** (CBS)

Outstanding Supporting Actress in a Comedy, Variety, or Music Series: Loretta Swit, *M*A*S*H** (CBS)

Outstanding Directing in a Drama Series: Roger Young, "Cop," *Lou Grant* (CBS)

Outstanding Directing in a Comedy Series: James Burrows, "Louie and the Nice Girl," *Taxi** (ABC)

■ Legislation: Major U.S. Legislation

Year	Legislation	Significance
1970	Clean Air Amendments	Established deadlines for reduction of hazardous emissions from new automobiles; required each state to establish an air quality program; authorized funds for air quality research.
1970	Occupational Safety and Health Act	Created the Occupational Safety and Health Review Commission within the Department of Labor; authorized the secretary of labor to establish and enforce national safety standards; permitted federal inspections and investigations of working conditions; funded research on occupational safety and health training programs.
1970	Racketeer Influenced and Corrupt Organizations (RICO) Act	Enacted as Title IX of the Organized Crime Control Act, it toughened penalties for criminal acts performed as part of an ongoing criminal organization, such as extortion, blackmail, or witness intimidation.
1970	Postal Reorganization Act	Created an independent U.S. Postal Service to operate the nation's postal system.
1970	Legislative Reorganization Act	Created a Joint Committee on Congressional Operations; increased size of congressional staff; required that all committee roll-call votes be made public; revised other committee procedures.
1970	Rail Passenger Service Act	Established the National Railroad Passenger Corporation (Amtrak) to operate a nationwide rail system; authorized the Interstate Commerce Commission to promulgate rail passenger regulations.
1970	Poison Prevention Packaging Act	Provided for special packaging regulations for household goods that were potentially dangerous to children.
1971	Federal Election Campaign Act	Limited the amount of money a candidate for president, vice president, or Congress could spend on political advertising; required full disclosure of campaign contributions and expenditures.
1971	Economic Stabilization Act Amendments	Extended the president's authority to control prices, wages, rents, and salaries; broadened the president's stabilization authority to include control of finance charges, interest rates, and corporate dividends.
1971	Emergency Loan Guarantee Act	Guaranteed up to $250 million in commercial bank loans to forestall bankruptcy of Lockheed Aircraft Corporation.
1971	Alaska Native Claims Settlement Act	Furnished natives of Alaska with land and mineral rights; provided funds from federal grants and mineral revenues.
1972	Title IX of Education Amendments	Prohibited discrimination on the basis of gender in any federally funded education activity.
1972	Noise Control Act	Imbued the Environmental Protection Agency (EPA) with the primary role in reducing environmental noise; allowed the EPA to set standards for controlling noise emanating from construction and transportation.
1972	Great Lakes Water Quality Control Act	Encouraged cooperation between the United States and Canada to reduce pollution in Lake Erie and the international section of the St. Lawrence River.

Year	Legislation	Significance
1972	Consumer Product Safety Act	Created Consumer Product Safety Commission to set standards for a variety of consumer products.
1972	Federal Environmental Pesticide Control Act	Broadened governmental authority to control pesticides.
1972	Marine Mammal Protection Act	Established a permanent moratorium on most hunting, capturing, or killing of any marine mammal.
1972	Coastal Zone Management Act	Started program for federal government management, protection, development, and restoration of the nation's coastal resources.
1972	U.S.-Soviet Strategic Arms Limitation Talks (SALT)	Authorized presidential acceptance of a five-year interim agreement between the United States and the Soviet Union to limit offensive nuclear weapons.
1972	Social Security Amendments	Created the Supplemental Security Income program to assist needy disabled, blind, and aged persons; assigned responsibility for the program to the Social Security Administration.
1973	Endangered Species Act	Strengthened federal authority to protect endangered species of fish, plants, and wildlife; encouraged creation of state conservation and management programs to protect threatened species; established federal criminal penalties for violation of regulations dealing with endangered species.
1973	War Powers Resolution	Required the president to consult and notify Congress in instances where American armed forces were sent into a hostile situation abroad; limited the time U.S. troops could be used in overseas hostile operations unless extended by Congress.
1973	Federal Aid Highway Act	Authorized funds for a national system of interstate and defense highways over a five-year period; furnished federal funds for an urban highway system; allowed the federal secretary of transportation to approve mass transit projects.
1973	Comprehensive Employment and Training Act	Provided federal block grants to states and local governments for job training and public sector employment; created a National Commission for Manpower Policy to identify manpower goals and needs; consolidated manpower programs established by previous laws.
1974	Child Abuse Prevention and Treatment Act	Furnished federal funding to states in support of prevention, assessment, investigation, and treatment of child abuse; established the Office of Child Abuse and Neglect and the National Clearinghouse on Child Abuse and Neglect Information.
1974	Parens Patriae Act	Established the Office of Juvenile Justice and Delinquency Prevention to oversee programs that emphasize community-based treatment and prevention of youth crime; eliminated court authority over status offenders.
1974	Safe Drinking Water Act	Directed the Environmental Protection Agency to develop national drinking water standards for state groundwater and pollution control programs.
1974	Privacy Act	Permitted inspection and revision of files contained in certain federal agencies.

Year	Legislation	Significance
1974	Employee Retirement Income Security Act (ERISA)	Required firms that provided pension funds for employees to adhere to federal rules; allowed persons not covered by a pension plan to create individual retirement accounts.
1974	Legal Services Corporation Act	Established the Legal Services Corporation as an independent agency to provide legal assistance to the poor.
1974	Congressional Budget and Impoundment Act	Created House and Senate Budget Committees to analyze the president's budget and set spending priorities; started the Congressional Budget Office to provide members of Congress with budget information; changed start of fiscal year from July 1 to October 1; tightened control over the impoundment of funds by the executive branch.
1974	Federal Energy Administration Act	Reorganized certain functions of the federal government into a temporary Federal Energy Administration to manage short-term fuel shortages.
1974	Energy Reorganization Act	Established Energy Research and Development Administration to direct federal research of energy; abolished Atomic Energy Commission.
1974	Equal Credit Opportunity Act	Prohibited discrimination in credit transactions based on gender or marital status.
1974	Freedom of Information Amendments	Mandated deadlines for agency responses to document requests; required agencies to publish a uniform set of fees for document requests and to release an annual report on all decisions to withhold information.
1975	Speedy Trial Act	Allowed for dismissal of charges against defendants accused of federal crimes if their trials did not begin within one hundred days of arrest.
1975	Age Discrimination Act	Forbade discrimination based on age in programs or activities that receive federal financial assistance.
1975	Indian Self-Determination and Education Assistance Act	Granted the secretaries of the interior and health and human services authority to furnish contracts and grants to Native American tribes and organizations for delivery of federal services.
1975	Trade Act	Authorized the president to enter into trade agreements with other nations for the purpose of reducing trade barriers; required corrective action whenever the United States had a large balance of payments surplus or deficit; established a congressional approval procedure for trade agreements.
1975	Voting Rights Act Amendments	Extended the Voting Rights Act of 1965 for an additional seven years; made permanent the national ban on literacy tests; mandated bilingual education under certain circumstances; broadened the law's coverage to include Alaskan natives, Asian Americans, Native Americans, and Spanish-speaking Americans.

Year	Legislation	Significance
1975	Education for All Handicapped Children Act	Required each state to provide a free and appropriate education for all disabled children between ages three and twenty-one within a three-year period; established a new grant formula for determining which states would receive federal assistance in meeting the educational needs of the handicapped; provided states with incentive grants for education of preschool disabled children between three and five years old.
1975	Energy Policy and Conservation Act	Granted the president standby authority to deal with energy emergencies; promoted energy conservation and efficiency in order to reduce consumption.
1975	Tax Reduction Act	Provided individual and business tax cuts; increased business tax credits; reduced oil and gas depletion allowances; curbed foreign oil benefits.
1976	Copyright Law	Revised federal copyright law through defining criteria for protection, expanding protection, and extending the duration of protection.
1976	Tax Reform Act	Repealed and revised obsolete provisions in the tax code.
1976	Government in the Sunshine Act	Required all government agencies and commissions headed by two or more people to open their meetings to public scrutiny during official business; provided procedures for court redress to open a meeting.
1976	National Emergencies Act	Provided for a congressional review of national emergencies declared by the president; created procedures for terminating national emergencies.
1976	Fishery Conservation and Management Act	Established a fishery conservation zone by extending the existing twelve-mile exclusive zone to two hundred miles off coasts.
1976	Equal Credit Opportunity Amendments	Amended 1974 act by banning credit discrimination on the basis of race, color, religion, or national origin.
1976	Toxic Substances Control Act	Announced national policy that manufacturers should develop adequate data on environmental effects of chemicals; directed the Environmental Protection Agency to establish standards for testing chemicals; regulated or banned certain chemicals.
1976	Federal Land Policy and Management Act	Consolidated almost three thousand public land laws into a single statute that defined Bureau of Land Management (BLM) authority; directed the secretary of the interior to manage BLM lands and develop land use plans for those areas.
1976	Resource Conservation and Recovery Act	Authorized expenditures for solid waste programs for three years; directed the Environmental Protection Agency (EPA) to review solid waste regulations every three years; required the EPA to establish waste safety standards and publish guidelines.
1977	Tax Reduction and Simplification Act	Revised the standard deduction for individual and joint tax returns; adjusted tax tables and rates.

Year	Legislation	Significance
1977	Clean Air Act Amendments	Extended existing automobile emission standards through 1979 model year; delayed the deadline for cities to meet national clean air standards; established new air quality standards for national parks, recreation areas, wilderness areas, and national monuments; required federal agencies to conduct studies on air pollution; created the National Commission on Air Quality.
1977	Department of Energy Act	Established the cabinet-level Department of Energy; consolidated most existing energy programs within the new department; abolished three energy agencies and transferred functions to the new department.
1977	Surface Mining Control and Reclamation Act	Created an Office of Surface Mining Reclamation and Enforcement within the Department of the Interior to administer the act's regulatory and reclamation programs, monitor state programs, and furnish grants and technical assistance; set environmental protection standards for all major coal surface mining operations; protected certain lands from surface mining.
1977	Community Reinvestment Act	Required federal supervisory agencies to make sure that local financial institutions take into consideration the credit needs of the entire community when they apply for deposit facilities.
1978	Airline Deregulation Act	Scheduled deregulation of commercial air traffic and the phasing out of the Civilian Aeronautics Board by 1985; created new services and routes by airlines; granted flexibility in raising and lowering fares; furnished assistance to airline employees adversely affected by the new law.
1978	American Indian Religious Freedom Act	Made it national policy to protect and preserve the traditional religions of American Indians, Eskimos, Aleuts, and Native Hawaiians, including access to sites, use and possession of sacred objects, and freedom to worship through ceremonials and traditional rites; directed various departments and agencies to evaluate their procedures for protecting Native American religious rights and practices.
1978	Age Discrimination in Employment Act Amendments	Raised permissible mandatory retirement age for most nonfederal workers from sixty-five to seventy; removed age ceiling of seventy for most federal employees.
1978	International Banking Act	Subjected foreign banks operating in the United States to the federal bank regulatory system.
1978	Civil Service Reform Act	Created an independent Office of Personnel Management to administer and enforce civil service statutes within the executive branch; established a Merit Systems Protection Board to adjudicate appeals of employees or applicants from federal jobs; started merit pay for federal employees; allowed increased management flexibility in firing employees; began a Senior Executive Service.
1978	Federal District and Circuit Judges Act	Added 152 new federal judgeships, including 117 at the district court level and 35 at the circuit court of appeals level.

Year	Legislation	Significance
1978	Revenue Act	Provided for $18.7 billion in tax cuts; allowed taxpayers over age fifty-five a one-time capital gains tax exclusion for sale of personal residences.
1978	Ethics in Government Act	Established the Office of Government Ethics to develop rules and regulations pertaining to conflicts of interest in the executive branch; institutionalized public financial disclosure requirements adopted by Congress in 1977; barred former executive branch employees from representing anyone before their former agencies for one year after leaving office.
1978	Full Employment and Balanced Growth Act	Also known as the Humphrey-Hawkins Act. Announced that it was the policy of the federal government to promote full employment, increased real income, balanced growth, a balanced budget, growth in productivity, an improved balance of trade, and price stability; established procedures for congressional review of the president's annual economic report and biannual reports of the Federal Reserve Board; prohibited discrimination in any of the act's programs.
1978	Pregnancy and Sex Discrimination Prohibition Act	Forbade discrimination in every aspect of employment on the basis of pregnancy, childbirth, and related medical conditions; required employers to carry disability and health insurance plans that covered pregnant workers; mandated that employers provide sick leave and disability to women recovering from an abortion.
1978	Presidential Records Act	Declared that as of 1981 most of the records of presidents and vice presidents would become public property at the end of their tenure in office.
1978	Bankruptcy Reform Act	Authorized Congress to establish permanent bankruptcy judgeships, which would replace temporary positions in the federal district courts; made the term of bankruptcy judges fourteen years.
1978	National Energy Conservation Act	Required utilities to inform consumers about energy conservation devices; mandated efficiency standards for major home appliances; provided grants for hospitals and schools to install energy-saving equipment; offered subsidies to low-income families for home conservation investments.
1978	Energy Tax Act	Furnished tax credits to both homeowners and businesses for installing certain energy conservation equipment; imposed penalties on automobiles with low fuel economy.
1978	Power Plant and Industrial Fuels Use Act	Necessitated use of coal by new industries and utilities; required existing utility plants using oil or gas to switch to coal by 1990; allowed the federal secretary of energy to provide exemptions to these requirements in some cases.
1978	National Gas Policy Act	Allowed for price controls on newly discovered natural gas until 1985; permitted special pricing categories for industrial and residential users of gas; prohibited installation of new decorative outdoor gaslights, with current ones being eliminated within three years.

Year	Legislation	Significance
1978	Nuclear Nonproliferation Act	Prohibited U.S. government from exporting nuclear material unless assurances were received by other nations that it was not being used in weapons production; stipulated conditions under which exports of nuclear material would be banned.
1978	Foreign Intelligence Surveillance Act	Created legal standards and procedures for obtaining electronic surveillance warrants for national security purposes; established new special courts to hear requests for electronic surveillance used to obtain foreign intelligence information within the United States; specified that certain district courts could hear appeals; exempted certain National Security Agency surveillance from warrant requirements.
1979	Department of Education Organization Act	Merged more than 150 education-related programs into a new cabinet-level Department of Education, which would foster equal educational opportunities, encourage increased involvement in education, and assist public and private groups in improving education.
1979	Panama Canal Act	Established Panama Canal Commission as an agency of the federal government to operate and maintain the Panama Canal through 1999; required that all funds collected by the commission would be deposited in the federal Treasury; started a civil service system for canal employees.
1979	Trade Agreements Act	Streamlined procedures for resolving complaints considered under U.S. countervailing duty law; provided for faster investigations and impositions of penalties for violations of duty laws or antidumping statutes; established a new system of customs valuation.
1979	Taiwan Relations Act	Stipulated that it would be national policy to preserve and promote friendly relations with Taiwan, including those in trade, transportation, and cultural links; pledged arms sales to Taiwan; promised that the United States would take action in the event of an attack on Taiwan.
1979	Special International Security Assistance Act	Approved arms sales to Israel and Egypt; provided Egypt with economic assistance and low-interest loans.
1979	Veterans' Health Care Amendments	Authorized the Veterans Administration (VA) to furnish outpatient counseling and mental health services for Vietnam War veterans and dental services for certain of those veterans; established pilot programs for preventive health care and treatment for veterans suffering from drug and alcohol problems; prohibited construction or renovation of certain VA facilities based on cost.

Samuel B. Hoff

■ Legislation: U.S. Supreme Court Decisions

Year	Case	Significance
1970	*Bachellar v. State of Maryland*	A unanimous Court overturned the disorderly conduct convictions of demonstrators protesting U.S. involvement in the Vietnam War. The guilty verdicts resulted merely because the protesters' views had offended onlookers.
1970	*Boys Markets, Inc. v. Retail Clerks Union*	Justice William Brennan wrote the majority opinion that held that an employer could get a court order to end a strike if the strike violated a no-strike clause in the employees' union contract. This 5-3 decision overturned the Court's 1962 *Sinclair v. Refining Co. v. Atkinson* decision, in which Justice Brennan wrote the dissenting opinion.
1970	*Danridge v. Williams*	In a 5-4 decision, the Court ruled that a Maryland welfare regulation limiting the maximum amount of Aid to Families with Dependent Children funding did not violate the federal Social Security Act.
1970	*Lewis v. Martin*	In a 6-3 decision, the Court ruled that California welfare officials could not cut off welfare payments to dependent children because there was a man living in the house with the mother, unless there was proof that the man actually contributed to the child's support.
1970	*Oregon v. Mitchell*	The Court upheld Congress's lowering of the minimum voting age from twenty-one to eighteen for federal elections. This 5-4 decision also upheld amendments to the federal Voting Rights Act banning the use of literacy tests as a qualification for voting and prohibiting residency requirements of more than thirty days in order to be eligible to vote in presidential elections.
1970	*Rowan v. U.S. Post Office Department*	The Court upheld a federal law permitting householders to have their names removed from mailing lists to receive unsolicited advertisements.
1970	*Schacht v. United States*	The Court held that the arrest and conviction of an actor for wearing a military uniform as part of a skit protesting the Vietnam War was an unconstitutional restraint on his or her First Amendment right of free speech.
1970	*Turner v. Fouche*	A unanimous Court ruled that a Georgia county's system of selecting members for its board of education was racially discriminatory.
1970	*United States v. Interstate Commerce Commission*	The U.S. Department of Justice challenged a proposed merger of the Great Northern Railway Co. and the Northern Pacific Railway Co. because it believed that the merger would create a monopoly. In a unanimous decision, the Court upheld the merger, ruling that any anticompetitive effects would be overcome by savings and benefits to the public and railway employees.

Year	Case	Significance
1970	*Walz v. Tax Commission of the City of New York*	In a 5-4 decision, the Court ruled that the tax exemption for religious organizations did not violate the religious freedom clause of the First Amendment.
1970	*Welsh v. United States*	In a 5-3 decision, the Court ruled that a draftee could be exempt from military service if he had strong moral or ethical objections to the Vietnam War in any form. The Court held that a man no longer had to claim religious convictions in order to be granted an exemption as a conscientious objector.
1970	*Winship, In re*	The Court ruled unconstitutional a state law permitting a lower standard of proof in juvenile proceedings. In a 5-3 decision, the Court held that juveniles, like adults, are constitutionally entitled, under the due process clause of the Fourteenth Amendment, to proof beyond a reasonable doubt when they are charged with a crime.
1971	*Blount v. Rizzi*	A unanimous Court declared unconstitutional two federal laws that allowed U.S. Post Office officials to prevent the delivery of obscene materials. Justice Brennan, writing for the majority, held that the 1890 and 1960 federal laws were a form of government censorship.
1971	*Cohen v. California*	In a 5-to-4 decision, the Court overturned the thirty-day sentence of a man convicted of disturbing the peace for displaying a four-letter vulgarity in public. The Court ruled that the wording on the man's jacket was symbolic speech and protected under the First Amendment.
1971	*Graham v. Richardson*	In a unanimous decision, the Court struck down an Arizona law that prevented immigrants from receiving welfare benefits.
1971	*Griggs v. Duke Power Company*	In a unanimous decision, the Court ruled that a North Carolina power company's job requirements of a high school diploma and a satisfactory intelligence test score discriminated against African Americans. The Court held that both requirements were not significantly related to job performance and, therefore, perpetuated the effects of the employer's past racial discrimination.
1971	*Harris v. New York*	In a 5-4 vote, the Court ruled that voluntary statements made by defendants who were not properly warned of their constitutional rights at the time of their arrests still may be used against them in court if they take the witness stand in their own defense and contradict their earlier statements. This decision allowed the use of confessions that were extracted in violation of the Miranda rule to be used for a limited purpose.

Year	Case	Significance
1971	*New York Times Co. v. United States*	This Court decision denied the Nixon administration's request for a court order barring continued publication of newspaper articles based on classified documents, known as the Pentagon Papers, detailing the history of U.S. involvement in Vietnam. In a 6-3 vote, with each justice writing a separate opinion, the Court ruled that the government failed to justify sufficiently the need for imposing such a restraint on the press.
1971	*Swann v. Charlotte-Mecklenburg Board of Education*	A unanimous Court ruled that school busing, racial balance ratios, and gerrymandered school districts were permissible, temporary methods of integrating southern public schools.
1971	*Wyman v. James*	In a 6-3 decision, the Court upheld the right of welfare caseworkers to enter recipients' homes in order to check on their eligibility to receive funds.
1972	*Branzburg v. Hayes*	In a 5-4 vote, the Court ruled that the First Amendment guarantee of freedom of the press did not protect journalists from being held in contempt if they refuse to provide information to grand juries concerning a crime.
1972	*Furman v. Georgia, Jackson v. Georgia, Branch v. Texas*	In a 5-4 decision, the Court struck down all state death penalty laws for their arbitrary and discriminatory application. Especially in the South, a death sentence was likelier if the defendant was black and the victim was white. With each justice writing a separate opinion, the Court held that the death penalty laws were a form of cruel and unusual punishment. Chief Justice Warren Burger, who voted with the minority, noted that states could bring back the death penalty if they passed laws with clear guidelines that narrowly defined which crimes would warrant the death sentence.
1973	*Frontiero v. Richardson*	In an 8-1 decision, the Court struck down as discriminatory a federal law that automatically allowed a male member of the armed service to claim his spouse as a dependent, but a female could not receive this benefit unless she could show that her spouse depended on her for more than one-half of his support.
1973	*Keyes v. Denver School District No. 1*	In a 7-1 vote, the Court required Denver public schools to desegregate. This was the first time the Court had recognized that segregated public schools throughout the United States had the same responsibility to desegregate as the segregated public schools in the South.
1973	*Miller v. California*	In its first major obscenity ruling since its 1957 *Roth v. United States* decision, the Court gave the states more power to regulate obscene material. Rather than establishing a national standard, the Court in a 5-4 vote left it up to each community to decide what sexually explicit material would be deemed obscene and illegal.

Year	Case	Significance
1973	*Roe v. Wade*	Known as the landmark case that legalized abortion nationwide, the Court struck down a Texas law that made it a crime to perform an abortion unless a woman's life was at stake. In its ruling, the Court recognized for the first time that the constitutional right to privacy also includes a woman's decision of whether or not to terminate her pregnancy. The decision set a legal precedent that affected more than twenty subsequent Court cases involving restrictions on access to abortion.
1974	*Geduldig v. Aiello*	In a 6-3 vote, the Court ruled that California was not guilty of sexual discrimination when it excluded from its disability insurance program women unable to work because of pregnancy-related disabilities.
1974	*Lau v. Nichols*	In this 5-4 decision, the Court held that the failure of the San Francisco school system to provide English-language instruction to non-English-speaking students of Chinese ancestry violated the Civil Rights Act of 1964, which banned discrimination based on race, color, or national origin in any program receiving federal financial assistance.
1974	*Milliken v. Bradley*	In this school desegregation decision, the Court ruled 5-4 against a plan to desegregate the urban school system in Detroit, Michigan, by busing black students across district lines to the white schools in the surrounding counties.
1974	*United States v. Nixon*	The Court held that President Richard M. Nixon must comply with a subpoena for tapes of certain White House conversations, sought for evidence in the investigation of the June, 1972, break-in at the Democratic National Headquarters in the Watergate office complex.
1975	*Albemarle Paper Co. v. Moody*	The Court determined in a 7-1 vote that a North Carolina paper company had to award back pay to African American employees it discriminated against with its seniority program. The Court ruled that a company's seniority program was illegal if it locked racial minorities and women into lower-paying jobs while white males moved up into better-paying positions.
1975	*Bigelow v. Virginia*	The Court ruled that commercial advertising enjoys some First Amendment protection. In a 7-2 vote, the Court reversed the conviction of a newspaper editor for violating a Virginia law by publishing an advertisement that included information on legal abortions available in New York.
1975	*Nebraska Press Association v. Stuart*	The Court ruled that a judge's order prohibiting the media from publishing information regarding a multiple murder trial in Lincoln County, Nebraska, was a violation of the First Amendment. This unanimous Court decision all but eliminated protective "gag" orders directed against the media.

Year	Case	Significance
1976	*General Electric v. Gilbert*	In this sex discrimination case, the Court ruled that employed women do not have a legal right to disability benefits when they are absent from work for pregnancy. In a 6-3 decision, the Court held that a General Electric Company health plan was not sexually discriminatory, even though it provided no sick pay for women absent from work because of pregnancy.
1976	*Gregg v. Georgia*	In a complex ruling, the Court restored to states the right to execute convicted murderers, four years after ruling that the death penalty was unconstitutional in its 1972 *Furman v. Georgia* decision. In a 7-2 vote, the Court upheld laws in Georgia, Texas, and Florida that made the death penalty applicable only to individuals convicted of first-degree murder.
1976	*Pasadena Board of Education v. Spangler*	In this school desegregation decision, the Court ruled 6-2 that school districts cannot be required to change busing programs year by year to keep up with racial shifts in their population. The school district in Pasadena, California, was one of many school districts that found segregation recurring as white residents moved out of the district and African Americans or other minority residents moved in after it initiated a court-ordered busing program.
1976	*Runyon v. McCrary*	With this 7-2 decision, the Court extended its ban on racially segregated schools to include private academies as well as public schools. The Court held that federal law prohibits private schools from excluding qualified children solely because they are African American. The case arose from a lawsuit filed by the parents of black children who were excluded from Virginia private schools solely on racial grounds.
1976	*Virginia State Board of Pharmacy v. Virginia Citizens Consumer Council*	In a 7-2 decision, the Court ruled that a Virginia law prohibiting the advertising of prescription drug prices violated the First Amendment. The Court held that commercial advertisers are entitled to the same First Amendment right to free speech as newspapers and magazines in their news and editorial columns.
1977	*Ingraham v. Wright*	In a 5-4 Court decision, the Court ruled that teachers did not need parental consent to impose corporal punishment even if the punishment was so excessive that it caused severe injuries. The case arose when the parents of two boys sued school officials in Dade County, Florida, after the boys were beaten so severely with flat wooden paddles that they needed medical attention. The Court determined that the Eighth Amendment protection against cruel and unusual punishment was meant for criminals in detention, not for pupils in the classroom.

Year	Case	Significance
1977	*International Brotherhood of Teamsters v. United States*	This Court decision insulated the job-seniority system from lawsuits by persons who suffered racial bias in employment before the passage of the 1964 Civil Rights Act. By a 7-2 vote, the Court held that workers could not be given extra seniority to correct bias against them prior to 1964 if the seniority system itself was racially neutral. However, the Court said that extra seniority could be awarded to minority-group workers for job bias committed after enactment of the 1964 law. The federal government had filed suit against a nationwide trucking company because it believed that the company's seniority system discriminated against African Americans and Spanish-surnamed persons and perpetuated the effects of past discrimination.
1977	*Linmark Associates, Inc. v. Township of Willingboro*	The Court struck down a township ordinance prohibiting the posting of real estate "For Sale" and "Sold" signs for the purpose of stemming what the township perceived as the flight of white homeowners from a racially integrated community. A unanimous Court held that the ordinance violated the First Amendment's free speech guarantee.
1978	*Federal Communications Commission v. Pacifica Foundation*	The Court ruled that broadcasters could be fined for airing sexually explicit material during the day, when children were part of the listening audience. This 5-4 ruling upheld the Federal Communication Commission's authority to regulate the broadcasting of indecent, but not obscene, material to a "safe harbor" time period when children were least likely to hear it. The issue arose after a father complained that his young son had heard a comedian's monologue about seven "dirty words" in a daytime broadcast by a New York radio station.
1978	*Nixon v. Warner Communications, Inc.*	In a 7-2 decision, the Court denied broadcasters and recording companies the right to copy, broadcast, and sell excerpts of the White House tapes that had been played during the Watergate trial and resulted in President Nixon's resignation and the criminal convictions of four presidential aides. The Court concluded that networks had no constitutional right to reproduce and sell the tapes.
1978	*Regents of the University of California v. Bakke*	In this reverse discrimination case, the Court held that a state medical school's use of quotas to increase the number of minority students as part of a special admissions program violated the 1964 Civil Rights Act. In its 5-4 decision, the Court ruled that affirmative action plans generally are acceptable but that racial quotas are sometimes inappropriate.
1978	*Sears, Roebuck & Co. v. San Diego County District Council of Carpenters*	The Court held that employers could have striking union members arrested for trespassing if they picketed on private property. The case arose when a carpenter union set up a picket line on a private sidewalk next to a California Sears, Roebuck & Co. store.

Year	Case	Significance
1978	*Zurcher v. The Stanford Daily*	The Court ruled that a police search of a university student paper's newsroom for evidence in the investigation of a crime did not violate the newspaper's Fourth Amendment rights against unlawful search and seizure. With this 5-3 decision, the Court established a precedent that allowed police to search newspapers and other innocent third parties in order to obtain evidence about a crime.
1979	*Columbus Board of Education v. Penick, Dayton Board of Education v. Brinkman*	In these school desegregation decisions, the Court ruled that northern segregated school systems were required to integrate just as were segregated schools in the South. In 7-2 and 5-4 votes, the Court upheld systemwide busing orders for Columbus and Dayton, Ohio. The Ohio decisions came at a time of widespread northern segregation, with almost one-third of the African American students in large northern industrial states attending virtually all-black schools. These decisions also confirmed the Court's 1973 precedent in *Keyes v. Denver School District No. 1* that approved citywide busing in Denver in order to end intentional school segregation.
1979	*Davis v. Passman*	The Court held that congressional employees have as much right as other workers to sue their bosses for racial or sexual discrimination. Shirley Davis sued U.S. representative Otto Passman of Louisiana for sex discrimination after he fired her as his deputy administrative assistant because he preferred a man in that position. With this 5-4 decision, the Court went against Congress's long-standing practice of exempting itself from many laws that other U.S. citizens were required to obey.
1979	*Gannett Co. v. DePasquale*	In a 5-4 vote, the Court determined that the media and the public did not have a constitutional right to attend a criminal trial. The Court upheld a judge's order closing a pretrial hearing of a murder trial to the public in order to avoid publicity that would be prejudicial to the two defendants and, thus, violate their right to a fair trial.
1979	*Gladstone v. Village of Bellwood*	The Court held 7-2 that homeowners and their local governments could sue real estate agents for race discrimination if they steer customers into certain neighborhoods on the basis of their race.
1979	*Herbert v. Lando*	In a 6-3 decision, the Court confirmed the right of plaintiffs to ask questions about a reporter's state of mind when suing for libel. Writing the majority opinion, Justice Byron White ruled that retired Lieutenant Colonel Anthony Herbert could ask questions about the thoughts, opinions, and editing decisions of the producers of the Columbia Broadcasting System (CBS) network's *60 Minutes* in his attempt to prove that the news program's story about him was false and damaged his reputation.

Year	Case	Significance
1979	*Orr v. Orr*	In a 6-3 vote, the Court ruled that state laws barring husbands from collecting alimony from their former wives amounted to sex discrimination. The immediate effect of the *Orr* decision was to overturn the Alabama law, as well as similar laws in ten other states, that allowed women, but not men, to receive alimony as part of divorce settlements.
1979	*Smith v. Daily Mail Publishing Co.*	The Court ruled that a West Virginia law that made it illegal to publish, without written the approval of the juvenile court, the name of a youth charged with a crime violated the First Amendment. The case arose after two newspapers published articles identifying by name a fourteen-year-old youth who had been arrested for allegedly killing another youth, after learning the juvenile's identity through the use of routine reporting techniques.
1979	*United Steelworkers of America v. Weber*	In this reverse discrimination case, the Court supported the use of quotas to correct racial imbalance in traditionally segregated jobs. In its 5-2 decision, the Court upheld a factory's affirmative action program designed to increase the number of minority employees in areas where they had been traditionally underrepresented. The Court ruled that Brian Weber, a white Louisiana factory worker, was not a victim of racial bias when he was excluded from an on-the-job training program designed for African Americans.

Eddith A. Dashiell

Literature: Best-Selling U.S. Books

1970 Fiction

1. *Love Story,* Erich Segal
2. *The French Lieutenant's Woman,* John Fowles
3. *Islands in the Stream,* Ernest Hemingway
4. *The Crystal Cave,* Mary Stewart
5. *Great Lion of God,* Taylor Caldwell
6. *QB VII,* Leon Uris
7. *The Gang That Couldn't Shoot Straight,* Jimmy Breslin
8. *The Secret Woman,* Victoria Holt
9. *Travels with My Aunt,* Graham Greene
10. *Rich Man, Poor Man,* Irwin Shaw

1970 Nonfiction

1. *Everything You Always Wanted to Know About Sex but Were Afraid to Ask,* David Reuben
2. *The New English Bible*
3. *The Sensuous Woman,* "J"
4. *Better Homes and Gardens Fondue and Tabletop Cooking*
5. *Up the Organization,* Robert Townsend
6. *Ball Four,* Jim Bouton
7. *American Heritage Dictionary of the English Language,* William Morris
8. *Body Language,* Julius Fast
9. *In Someone's Shadow,* Rod McKuen
10. *Caught in the Quiet,* Rod McKuen

1971 Fiction

1. *Wheels,* Arthur Hailey
2. *The Exorcist,* William P. Blatty
3. *The Passions of the Mind,* Irving Stone
4. *The Day of the Jackal,* Frederick Forsyth
5. *The Betsy,* Harold Robbins
6. *Message from Malaga,* Helen MacInnes
7. *The Winds of War,* Herman Wouk
8. *The Drifters,* James A. Michener
9. *The Other,* Thomas Tryon
10. *Rabbit Redux,* John Updike

1971 Nonfiction

1. *The Sensuous Man,* "M"
2. *Bury My Heart at Wounded Knee,* Dee Brown
3. *Better Homes and Gardens Blender Cookbook*
4. *I'm OK, You're OK,* Thomas Harris
5. *Any Woman Can!,* David Reuben
6. *Inside the Third Reich,* Albert Speer
7. *Eleanor and Franklin,* Joseph P. Lash
8. *Wunnerful, Wunnerful!,* Lawrence Welk
9. *Honor Thy Father,* Gay Talese
10. *Fields of Wonder,* Rod McKuen

1972 Fiction

1. *Jonathan Livingston Seagull,* Richard Bach
2. *August, 1914,* Aleksandr Solzhenitsyn
3. *The Odessa File,* Frederick Forsyth
4. *The Day of the Jackal,* Frederick Forsyth
5. *The Word,* Irving Wallace
6. *The Winds of War,* Herman Wouk
7. *Captains and the Kings,* Taylor Caldwell
8. *Two from Galilee,* Majorie Holmes
9. *My Name Is Asher Lev,* Chaim Potok
10. *Semi-Tough,* Dan Jenkins

1972 Nonfiction

1. *The Living Bible,* Kenneth Taylor
2. *I'm OK, You're OK,* Thomas Harris
3. *Open Marriage,* Nena and George O'Neill
4. *Harry S. Truman,* Margaret Truman
5. *Dr. Atkins' Diet Revolution,* Robert C. Atkins
6. *Better Homes and Gardens Menu Cookbook*
7. *The Peter Prescription,* Laurence J. Peter
8. *A World Beyond,* Ruth Montgomery
9. *Journey to Ixtlan,* Carlos Castaneda
10. *Better Homes and Gardens Low-Calorie Desserts*

1973 Fiction

1. *Jonathan Livingston Seagull,* Richard Bach
2. *Once Is Not Enough,* Jacqueline Susann
3. *Breakfast of Champions,* Kurt Vonnegut
4. *The Odessa File,* Frederick Forsyth
5. *Burr,* Gore Vidal
6. *The Hollow Hills,* Mary Stewart
7. *Evening in Byzantium,* Irving Shaw
8. *The Matlock Paper,* Robert Ludlum
9. *The Billion Dollar Sure Thing,* Paul E. Erdman
10. *The Honorary Consul,* Graham Greene

1973 Nonfiction

1. *The Living Bible,* Kenneth Taylor
2. *Dr. Atkins' Diet Revolution,* Robert C. Atkins
3. *I'm OK, You're OK,* Thomas Harris
4. *The Joy of Sex,* Alex Comfort
5. *Weight Watchers Program Cookbook,* Jean Nidetch

6. *How to Be Your Own Best Friend,* Mildred Newman et al.
7. *The Art of Walt Disney,* Christopher Finch
8. *Better Homes and Gardens Canning Cookbook*
9. *Alastair Cooke's America,* Alastair Cooke
10. *Sybil,* Flora R. Schreiber

1974 Fiction

1. *Centennial,* James A. Michener
2. *Watership Down,* Richard Adams
3. *Jaws,* Peter Benchley
4. *Tinker, Tailor, Sailor, Spy,* John le Carré
5. *Something Happened,* Joseph Heller
6. *The Dogs of War,* Frederick Forsyth
7. *The Pirate,* Harold Robbins
8. *I Heard the Owl Call My Name,* Margaret Craven
9. *The Seven Percent Solution,* John J. Watson, M.D., and Nicholas Meyer, ed.
10. *The Fan Club,* Irving Wallace

1974 Nonfiction

1. *The Total Woman,* Marabel Morgan
2. *All the President's Men,* Carl Bernstein and Bob Woodward
3. *Plain Speaking: An Oral Biography of Harry S. Truman,* Merle Miller
4. *More Joy: A Lovemaking Companion to "The Joy of Sex,"* Alex Comfort
5. *Alastair Cooke's America,* Alastair Cooke
6. *Tales of Power,* Carlos Castaneda
7. *You Can Profit from a Monetary Crisis,* Harry Browne
8. *All Things Bright and Beautiful,* James Herriot
9. *The Bermuda Triangle,* Charles Berlitz with J. Manson Valentine
10. *The Memory Book,* Harry Lorayne and Jerry Lucas

1975 Fiction

1. *Ragtime,* E. L. Doctorow
2. *The Moneychangers,* Arthur Hailey
3. *Curtain,* Agatha Christie
4. *Looking for Mister Goodbar,* Judith Rossner
5. *The Choirboys,* Joseph Wambaugh
6. *The Eagle Has Landed,* Jack Higgins
7. *The Greek Treasure,* Irving Stone
8. *The Great Train Robbery,* Michael Crichton
9. *Shogun,* James Clavell
10. *Humboldt's Gift,* Saul Bellow

1975 Nonfiction

1. *Angels: God's Secret Agents,* Billy Graham
2. *Winning Through Intimidation,* Robert Ringer
3. *TM: Discovering Energy and Overcoming Stress,* Harold H. Bloomfield
4. *The Ascent of Man,* Jabob Bronowski
5. *Sylvia Porter's Money Book,* Sylvia Porter
6. *Total Fitness in Thirty Minutes a Week,* Laurence E. Morehouse and Leonard Gross
7. *The Bermuda Triangle,* Charles Berlitz with J. Manson Valentine
8. *The Save Your Life Diet,* David Reuben
9. *Bring on the Empty Horses,* David Niven
10. *Breach of Faith: The Fall of Richard Nixon,* Theodore H. White

1976 Fiction

1. *Trinity,* Leon Uris
2. *Sleeping Murder,* Agatha Christie
3. *Dolores,* Jacqueline Susann
4. *Storm Warning,* Jack Higgins
5. *The Deep,* Peter Benchley
6. *1876,* Gore Vidal
7. *Slapstick: Or, Lonesome No More!,* Kurt Vonnegut
8. *The Lonely Lady,* Harold Robbins
9. *Touch Not the Cat,* Mary Stewart
10. *A Stranger in the Mirror,* Sidney Sheldon

1976 Nonfiction

1. *The Final Days,* Carl Bernstein and Bob Woodward
2. *Roots,* Alex Haley
3. *Your Erroneous Zones,* Dr. Wayne W. Dyer
4. *Passages: The Predictable Crises of Adult Life,* Gail Sheehy
5. *Born Again,* Charles W. Colson
6. *The Grass Is Always Greener over the Septic Tank,* Erma Bombeck
7. *Angels: God's Secret Agents,* Billy Graham
8. *Blind Ambition: The White House Years,* John Dean
9. *The Hite Report: A Nationwide Study of Female Sexuality,* Shere Hite
10. *The Right and the Power: The Prosecution of Watergate,* Leon Jaworski

1977 Fiction

1. *The Silmarillion,* J. R. R. Tolkien
2. *The Thorn Birds,* Colleen McCullough

3. *Illusions: The Adventures of a Reluctant Messiah,* Robert Bach
4. *The Honourable Schoolboy,* John le Carré
5. *Oliver's Story,* Erich Segal
6. *Dreams Die First,* Harold Robbins
7. *Beggarman, Thief,* Irwin Shaw
8. *How to Save Your Own Life,* Erica Jong
9. *Delta of Venus: Erotica,* Anaïs Nin
10. *Daniel Martin,* John Fowles

1977 Nonfiction

1. *Roots,* Alex Haley
2. *Looking Out for Number One,* Robert Ringer
3. *All Things Wise and Wonderful,* James Herriot
4. *Your Erroneous Zones,* Dr. Wayne W. Dyer
5. *The Book of Lists,* David Wallechinski, Irving Wallace, and Amy Wallace
6. *The Possible Dream: A Candid Look at Amway,* Charles Paul Conn
7. *The Dragons of Eden: Speculation of the Evolution of Human Intelligence,* Carl Sagan
8. *The Second Ring of Power,* Carlos Castaneda
9. *The Grass Is Always Greener over the Septic Tank,* Erma Bombeck
10. *The Amityville Horror,* Jay Anson

1978 Fiction

1. *Chesapeake,* James A. Michener
2. *War and Remembrance,* Herman Wouk
3. *Fools Die,* Mario Puzo
4. *Bloodlines,* Sidney Sheldon
5. *Scruples,* Judith Katz
6. *Evergreen,* Belva Plain
7. *Illusions: The Adventures of a Reluctant Messiah,* Robert Bach
8. *The Holcroft Covenant,* Robert Ludlum
9. *Second Generation,* Howard Fast
10. *Eye of the Needle,* Ken Follett

1978 Nonfiction

1. *If Life Is a Bowl of Cherries, What Am I Doing in the Pits?,* Erma Bombeck
2. *Gnomes,* Wil Huygen and Rien Poortvliet
3. *The Complete Book of Running,* James Fixx
4. *Mommie Dearest,* Christina Crawford
5. *Pulling Your Own Strings,* Dr. Wayne W. Dyer
6. *RN: The Memoirs of Richard Nixon,* Richard Nixon
7. *The Distant Mirror: The Calamitous Fourteenth Century,* Barbara Tuchman
8. *Faeries,* Brian Froud and Alan Lee
9. *In Search of History: A Personal Adventure,* Theodore H. White
10. *The Muppet Show Book,* The Muppet People

1979 Fiction

1. *The Matarese Circle,* Robert Ludlum
2. *Sophie's Choice,* William Styron
3. *Overload,* Arthur Hailey
4. *Memories of Another Day,* Harold Robbins
5. *Jailbird,* Kurt Vonnegut
6. *The Dead Zone,* Stephen King
7. *The Last Enchantment,* Mary Stewart
8. *The Establishment,* Howard Fast
9. *The Third World War: August, 1985,* General Sir John Hackett et al.
10. *Smiley's People,* John le Carré

1979 Nonfiction

1. *Aunt Erma's Cope Book,* Erma Bombeck
2. *The Complete Scarsdale Medical Diet,* Herman Townower, M.D., and Samm Sinclair Baker
3. *How to Prosper During the Coming Bad Years,* Howard J. Ruff
4. *Cruel Shoes,* Steve Martin
5. *The Pritikin Program for Diet and Exercise,* Nathan Pritikin and Patrick McGrady, Jr.
6. *White House Years,* Henry Kissinger
7. *Lauren Bacall by Myself,* Lauren Bacall
8. *The Brethren: Inside the Supreme Court,* Carl Bernstein and Bob Woodward
9. *Restoring the American Dream,* Robert Ringer
10. *The Winner's Circle,* Charles Paul Conn

■ Literature: Major Literary Awards

Nobel Prizes in Literature

1970: Aleksandr Solzhenitsyn, Soviet Union
1971: Pablo Neruda, Chile
1972: Heinrich Böll, West Germany
1973: Patrick White, Australia
1974: Eyvind Johnson, Sweden
Harry Edmund Martinson, Sweden
1975: Eugenio Montale, Italy
1976: Saul Bellow, United States
1977: Vicente Aleixandre, Spain
1978: Isaac Bashevis Singer, United States (born in Poland)
1979: Odysseus Elytis, Greece

Pulitzer Prizes

1970

Fiction: *Collected Stories* by Jean Stafford
Drama: *No Place to Be Somebody* by Charles Gordone
History: *Present at the Creation: My Years in the State Department* by Dean G. Acheson
Biography: *Huey Long* by T. Harry Williams
Poetry: *Untitled Subjects* by Richard Howard

1971

Fiction: No award
Drama: *The Effect of Gamma Rays on Man-in-the-Moon Marigolds* by Paul Zindel
History: *Roosevelt: The Soldier of Freedom* by James MacGregor Burns
Biography: *Robert Frost: The Years of Triumph, 1915-1938* by Lawrance Thompson
Poetry: *The Carrier of Ladders* by William S. Merwin

1972

Fiction: *Angle of Repose* by Wallace Stegner
Drama: No award
History: *Neither Black Nor White* by Carl N. Degler
Biography: *Eleanor and Franklin* by Joseph P. Lash
Poetry: *Collected Poems* by James Wright

1973

Fiction: *The Optimist's Daughter* by Eudora Welty
Drama: *That Championship Season* by Jason Miller
History: *People of Paradox: An Inquiry Concerning the Origins of American Civilization* by Michael Kammen
Biography: *Luce and His Empire* by W. A. Swanberg
Poetry: *Up Country* by Maxine Kumin

1974

Fiction: No award
Drama: No award
History: *The Americans: The Democratic Experience* by Daniel J. Boorstin
Biography: *O'Neill, Son and Artist* by Louis Sheaffer
Poetry: *The Dolphin* by Robert Lowell

1975

Fiction: *The Killer Angels* by Michael Shaara
Drama: *Seascape* by Edward Albee
History: *Jefferson and His Time, Vols. I-V* by Dumas Malone
Biography: *The Power Broker: Robert Moses and the Fall of New York* by Robert Caro
Poetry: *Turtle Island* by Gary Synder

1976

Fiction: *Humboldt's Gift* by Saul Bellow
Drama: *A Chorus Line* by Michael Bennett, James Kirkwood, and Nicholas Dante
History: *Lamy of Santa Fe* by Paul Horgan
Biography: *Edith Wharton: A Biography* by R. W. B. Lewis
Poetry: *Self-Portrait in a Convex Mirror* by John Ashbery

1977

Fiction: No award
Drama: *The Shadow Box* by Michael Cristofer
History: *The Impending Crisis, 1841-1867* by David M. Potter and finished posthumously by Don E. Fehrenbacher
Biography: *A Prince of Our Disorder: The Life of T. E. Lawrence* by John E. Mack
Poetry: *Divine Comedies* by James Merrill

1978

Fiction: *Elbow Room* by James Alan McPherson
Drama: *The Gin Game* by Donald L. Coburn
History: *The Visible Hand: The Managerial Revolution in American Business* by Alfred D. Chandler, Jr.
Biography: *Samuel Johnson* by Walter Jackson Bate
Poetry: *Collected Poems* by Howard Nemerov

1979

Fiction: *The Stories of John Cheever* by John Cheever
Drama: *Buried Child* by Sam Shepard
History: *The Dred Scott Case* by Don E. Fehrenbacher
Biography: *Days of Sorrow and Pain: Leo Baeck and the Berlin Jews* by Leonard Baker
Poetry: *Now and Then* by Robert Penn Warren

National Book Awards

1970

Fiction: *Them* by Joyce Carol Oates
Arts and Letters: *An Unfinished Woman* by Lillian Hellman
History and Biography: *Huey Long* by T. Harry Williams
Science, Philosophy, and Religion: *Gandhi's Truth: On the Origins of Militant Nonviolence* by Erik H. Erikson
Children's Literature: *A Day of Pleasure: Stories of a Boy Growing up in Warsaw* by Isaac Bashevis Singer
Translation: *Castle to Castle* by Louis-Ferdinand Celine, translated by Ralph Manheim

1971

Fiction: *Mr. Sammler's Planet* by Saul Bellow
Arts and Letters: *Cocteau* by Francis Steegmuller
History and Biography: *Roosevelt: The Soldier of Freedom* by James MacGregor Burns
The Sciences: *Science in the British Colonies of America* by Raymond Phineas Stearns
Children's Literature: *The Marvelous Misadventures of Sebastian* by Lloyd Alexander
Translation: *Saint Joan of the Stockyards* by Bertolt Brecht, translated by Frank Jones

1972

Fiction: *Flannery O'Connor: The Complete Stories* by Flannery O'Connor
Arts and Letters: *The Classical Style: Haydn, Mozart, Beethoven* by Charles Rosen
Biography: *Eleanor and Franklin* by Joseph P. Lash
History: *Ordeal of the Union Series, Vols. 7-8* by Allan Nevins
The Sciences: *The Blue Whale* by George L. Small
Philosophy and Religion: *Righteous Empire: The Protestant Experience in America* by Martin E. Marty
Contemporary Affairs: *The Last Whole Earth Catalog: Access to Tools* by Stewart Brand
Children's Literature: *The Slightly Irregular Fire Engine: Or, the Hithering Trithering Djinn* by Donald Barthelme
Translation: *Chance and Necessity: An Essay on the Natural Philosophy of Modern Biology* by Jacques Monad, translated by Austryn Wainhouse

1973

Fiction: *Chimera* by John Barth
Arts and Letters: *Diderot* by Arthur M. Wilson
Biography: *George Washington: Anguish and Farewell (1793-1799)* by James Thomas Flexner
History: *The Children of Pride* by Robert Manson Myers
The Sciences: *The Serengeti Lion: A Study of Predator-Prey Relations* by George B. Schaller
Philosophy and Religion: *A Religious History of the American People* by Sydney E. Ahlstrom
Contemporary Affairs: *Fire in the Lake: The Vietnamese and the Americans in Vietnam* by Frances FitzGerald
Children's Literature: *The Farthest Shore* by Ursula K. LeGuin
Translation: *The Aeneid of Virgil*, translated by Allen Mandelbaum

1974

Fiction: *A Crown of Feathers and Other Stories* by Isaac Bashevis Singer
Arts and Letters: *Deeper into the Movies* by Pauline Kael
Biography: *Malcolm Lowry* by Douglas Day
History: *Macauley: The Shaping of the Historian* by John Clive
The Sciences: *Life: The Unfinished Experiment* by S. E. Luria
Philosophy and Religion: *Edmund Husserl: Philosopher of Infinite Tasks* by Maurice Natanson
Contemporary Affairs: *The Briar Patch* by Murray Kempton
Children's Literature: *The Court of the Stone Children* by Eleanor Cameron
Translation: *The Confessions of Lady Nijo*, translated by Karen Brazell

1975

Fiction: *Dog Soldiers* by Robert Stone
Arts and Letters: *Marcel Proust* by Roger Shattuck
Biography: *The Life of Emily Dickinson* by Richard Sewall
History: *The Ordeal of Thomas Hutchinson* by Bernard Bailyn

The Sciences: *Interpretation of Schizophrenia* by Silvano Arieti
Philosophy and Religion: *Anarchy, State, and Utopia* by Robert Nozick
Contemporary Affairs: *All God's Dangers: The Life of Nate Shaw* by Theodore Rosengarten
Children's Literature: *M. C. Higgins, the Great* by Virginia Hamilton
Translation: *The Agony of Christianity and Essays on Faith* by Miguel de Unamuno, translated by Anthony Kerrigan

1976

Fiction: *JR* by William Gaddis
Arts and Letters: *The Great War and Modern Memory* by Paul Fussell
History: *The Problem of Slavery in an Age of Revolution: 1770-1823* by David B. Davis
Contemporary Affairs: *Passage to Ararat* by Michael J. Arlen
Children's Literature: *Bert Breen's Barn* by Walter D. Edmonds
Translation: No award

1977

Fiction: *The Spectator Bird* by Wallace Stegner
Biography and Autobiography: *Norman Thomas: The Last Idealist* by W. A. Swanberg
History: *World of Our Fathers* by Irving Howe
Contemporary Thought: *The Uses of Enchantment: The Meaning and Importance of Fairy Tales* by Bruno Bettelheim
Children's Literature: *The Master Puppeteer* by Katherine Paterson
Translation: *Master Tung's Western Chamber Romance: A Chinese Chantefable*, translated by Li-li Ch'en
Special Merit: *Roots* by Alex Haley

1978

Fiction: *Blood Tie* by Mary Lee Settle
Biography and Autobiography: *Samuel Johnson* by M. Jackson Bate
History: *The Path Between the Seas: The Creation of the Panama Canal. 1870-1914* by David McCullough
Contemporary Thought: *Winners and Losers: Battles, Retreats, Gains, Losses, and Ruins from a Long War* by Gloria Emerson
Children's Literature: *The Views from the Oak: The Private World of Other Creatures* by Judith and Herbert Kohl
Translation: *In the Deserts of This Earth* by Richard and Clara Winston, translated by Uwe George

1979

Fiction: *Going After Cacciato* by Tim O'Brien
Biography and Autobiography: *Robert Kennedy and His Times* by Robert M. Schlesinger, Jr.
History: *Intellectual Life in the Colonial South, 1585-1763* by Richard Beale Davis
Contemporary Thought: *The Snow Leopard* by Peter Matthiessen
Children's Literature: *The Great Gilly Hopkins* by Katherine Paterson
Translation: *The Complete Posthumous Poetry* by César Vallejo, translated by Clayton Eshleman and José Rubia Barcía

Newbery Medal for Best Children's Book of the Year

1970: *Sounder* by William H. Armstrong
1971: *Summer of the Swans* by Betsy Byars
1972: *Mrs. Frisby and the Rats of Nimh* by Robert C. O'Brien
1973: *Julie of the Wolves* by Jean Craighead George
1974: *The Slave Dancer* by Paula Fox
1975: *M. C. Higgins, the Great* by Virginia Hamilton
1976: *The Grey King*, by Susan Cooper
1977: *Roll of Thunder, Hear My Cry* by Mildred D. Taylor
1978: *Bridge to Terabithia* by Katherine Paterson
1979: *The Westing Game* by Ellen Raskin

Canadian Library Association Book of the Year for Children

1970: *Sally Go Round the Sun*, Edith Fowler
1971: *Cartier Discovers the St. Lawrence*, William Toye
1972: *Mary of Mile Eighteen*, Ann Blades
1973: *The Marrow of the World*, Ruth Nichols
1974: *The Miraculous Hind*, Elizabeth Cleaver
1975: *Alligator Pie*, Dennis Lee
1976: *Jacob Two-Two Meets the Hooded Fang*, Mordecai Richler
1977: *Mouse Woman and the Vanished Princesses*, Christie Harris
1978: *Garbage Delight*, Dennis Lee
1979: *Hold Fast*, Kevin Major

■ Music: Popular Musicians

Groups and performers followed by an asterisk (*) are subjects of their own entries in *The Seventies in America.*

Act	Members	Notable 1970's Songs	Notable Facts
Abba	Anni-Frid "Frida" Synni-Lyngstad-Fredriksson-Andersson, Benny Andersson, Bjorn Ulvaeus, Agnetha Faltskog	"Fernando," "Dancing Queen," "Take a Chance on Me"	The name "Abba" is an acronym of the member's first names: Anni-Frid, Benny, Bjorn, and Agnetha.
Aerosmith*	Steven Tyler, Jo Perry, Brad Whitford, Joey Kramer, Tom Hamilton	"Dream On," "Sweet Emotion," "Walk This Way"	Aerosmith covered the Beatles' song "Come Together" for the 1978 film *Sgt. Pepper's Lonely Hearts Club Band.*
The Allman Brothers Band	Duane Allman, Gregg Allman, Dickey Betts, Berry Oakley, Butch Trucks, Jai Johanny Johanson, Chuck Leavell, Lamar Williams, Warren Haynes, Allen Woody	"Ramblin' Man," "Midnight Rider," "Crazy Love"	Duane Allman and Oakley died in separate motorcycle accidents in the early 1970's.
America	Gerry Beckley, Dewey Bunnell, Dan Peek	"Ventura Highway," "Sister Golden Hair," "Horse with No Name"	America won a Grammy Award for Best New Artist in 1972.
Bachman-Turner Overdrive	Randy Bachman, Robbie Bachman, Tim Bachman, Jim Clench, Blair Thornton, C. F. Turner	"Let It Ride," "Taking Care of Business," "You Ain't Seen Nothing Yet"	Randy Bachman was originally a member of the Guess Who.
Bad Company	Raymond "Boz" Burrell, Mick Ralphs, Paul Rodgers, Simon Kirke	"Feel Like Makin' Love," "Good Lovin' Gone Bad," "Rock and Roll Fantasy"	Rodgers would later become the lead vocalist for the 1980's supergroup the Firm, which also featured Led Zeppelin guitarist Jimmy Page.
The Bay City Rollers	Eric Faulkner, Alan Longmuir, Derek Longmuir, Leslie McKeown, Stuart Wood, Ian Mitchell, Duncan Faure	"I Only Want to Be with You," "Saturday Night," "You Made Me Believe in Magic"	Originally known as the Saxons, the Bay City Rollers selected its new name by sticking a pin in a map of the United States. It landed in Bay City, Michigan.

Act	Members	Notable 1970's Songs	Notable Facts
The Bee Gees*	Barry Gibb, Maurice Gibb, Robin Gibb	"Jive Talkin'," "Stayin' Alive," "Night Fever"	Prior to taking the disco world by storm in 1977 with the best-selling soundtrack to *Saturday Night Fever,* the Bee Gees enjoyed a series of hit singles during the late 1960's.
George Benson		"This Masquerade," "The Greatest Love of All," "On Broadway"	Benson received a Best Pop Instrumental Performance Grammy Award in 1976 for "This Masquerade."
Boston	Tom Scholz, Barry Goudreau, Brad Delp, Fran Sheehan, Sib Hashian, Jim Masdea	"More than a Feeling," "Piece of Mind," "Don't Look Back"	The band's 1976 debut album, *Boston,* was one of the fastest-selling debut albums in history.
David Bowie*		"Changes," "Fame," "Space Oddity"	Bowie's real name is David Jones, but he changed it professionally to avoid confusion with Davy Jones of the Monkees.
Bread	David Gates, James Griffin, Michael Botts, Larry Knechtel, Robb Royer	"Make It with You," "If," "Everything I Own"	Gates had a solo hit in 1978 with the title song from the film *The Goodbye Girl.*
Jackson Browne		"Running on Empty," "Doctor My Eyes," "The Load Out/Stay"	Browne toured briefly with the Nitty Gritty Dirt Band, who also recorded several of his songs on their first two records.
Glenn Campbell		"By the Time I Get to Phoenix," "Rhinestone Cowboy," "Country Boy (You've Got Your Feet in L.A.)"	Prior to his solo career, Campbell was a popular session musician, backing up artists such as Bobby Darin, Rick Nelson, and the Monkees.
Captain and Tennille	Daryl Dragon, Toni Tennille	"Love Will Keep Us Together," "Do That to Me One More Time," "Muskrat Love"	The hit single "Love Will Keep Us Together" was written by 1960's singer-songwriter Neil Sedaka.
The Carpenters*	Karen Carpenter, Richard Carpenter	"Close to You," "We've Only Just Begun," "Rainy Days and Mondays"	The Carpenters won a Grammy Award for Best New Artist in 1970.

Act	Members	Notable 1970's Songs	Notable Facts
The Cars	Ric Ocasek, Elliot Easton, Greg Hawkes, Benjamin Orr, David Robinson	"My Best Friend's Girl," "Just What I Needed," "Let's Go"	The Cars later made innovative music videos that helped establish the popularity of cable television's MTV.
Harry Chapin		"Cat's in the Cradle," "Taxi," "I Wanna Learn a Love Song"	Chapin died in an automobile accident on July 16, 1981.
Cheap Trick	Robin Zander, Bun E. Carlos, Rick Nielsen, Tom Petersson, John Brandt	"Surrender," "Dream Police," "I Want You to Want Me"	One of the early names that the band used was Sick Man of Europe.
Cher		"Gypsys, Tramps and Thieves," "Half-Breed," "Dark Lady"	Cher teamed with husband Sonny Bono in a hit variety television series titled *The Sonny and Cher Show*, which aired from 1971 to 1977.
Chic	Nile Rodgers, Bernard Edwards, Tony Thompson, Norma Jean Wright, Alfa Anderson	"Dance, Dance, Dance (Yowsah, Yowsah, Yowsah)" "Good Times," "Le Freak"	Founding members Rodgers and Edwards went on to become well-known producers who worked with such artists as Madonna, David Bowie, Rod Stewart, and Tina Turner.
Chicago	Peter Cetera, Robert Lamm, Lee Loughnane, James Pankow, Walter Parazaider, Danny Seraphine, Terry Kath	"If You Leave Me Now," "Wishing You Were Here," "25 or 6 to 4"	The original name of the band was Chicago Transit Authority; it was shortened in 1970 at the request of the real Chicago Transit Authority.
Eric Clapton		"After Midnight," "Layla," "I Shot the Sheriff"	In addition to his stellar solo career, Clapton has been a member of the following bands: the Yardbirds, John Mayall's Bluesbreakers, Cream, and Blind Faith.
Joe Cocker		"The Letter," "You Are So Beautiful," "She Came in Through the Bathroom Window"	A film version of Cocker's "Mad Dogs and Englishman" tour was released in 1971.
Natalie Cole		"This Will Be," "Sophisticated Lady," "I've Got Love on My Mind"	Cole won a Grammy Award for Best New Artist in 1975.

Act	Members	Notable 1970's Songs	Notable Facts
The Commodores	William King, Jr., Thomas McClary, Ronald LaPread, Walter "Clyde" Orange, Milan Williams, James, Dean "J. D." Nicholas, Lionel Richie, Jr.	"Brick House," "Easy," "Three Times a Lady," "Sail On"	Richie left the group in 1982 for a successful solo career.
Alice Cooper*		"School's Out," "Eighteen," "No More Mr. Nice Guy"	Cooper, whose real name is Vincent Damon Furnier, helped pioneer "shock rock."
Creedence Clearwater Revival	John Fogerty, Doug Clifford, Thomas Fogerty, Stuart Cook	"Lookin' out My Back Door," "Travelin' Band," "Who'll Stop the Rain"	Creedence Clearwater Revival originally performed as the Golliwogs.
Jim Croce		"You Don't Mess Around with Jim," "Bad, Bad Leroy Brown," "Time in a Bottle"	Croce died in a plane crash on September 20, 1973.
Crosby, Stills, Nash, and Young	David Crosby, Stephen Stills, Graham Nash, Neil Young	"Ohio," "Teach Your Children," "Our House"	The song "Ohio" was inspired by the National Guard shootings at Kent State University in 1970.
John Denver*		"Take Me Home, Country Roads," "Rocky Mountain High," "Sunshine on My Shoulders"	Denver died in a plane crash on October 12, 1997.
Neil Diamond		"Solitary Man," "I Am, I Said," "Song Sung Blue"	Diamond composed the soundtrack for the 1973 film *Jonathan Livingston Seagull.*
Doobie Brothers	Jeffrey Baxter, John Hartman, Keith Knudson, Michael McDonald, Tiran Porter, Patrick Simmons, David Shogren, Tom Johnston	"Long Train Runnin'," "Black Water," "What a Fool Believes"	The Doobie Brothers, who are not actually related, took the term "doobie" from a slang term for a joint.
The Doors	Jim Morrison, Robbie Krieger, Ray Manzarek, John Densmore	"Love Her Madly," "Riders on the Storm," "Gloria"	The Doors are said to have taken their name from the title of a 1954 book by Aldous Huxley, *The Doors of Perception.*
The Eagles*	Don Felder, Glenn Frey, Don Henley, Bernie Leadon, Randy Meisner, Joe Walsh	"Best of My Love," "Lyin' Eyes," "Hotel California"	The Eagles started out as members of Linda Ronstadt's band.

Act	Members	Notable 1970's Songs	Notable Facts
Earth, Wind, and Fire*	Philip Bailey, Larry Dunn, Johnny Graham, Ralph Johnson, Al McKay, Fred White, Maurice White, Verdine White, Andrew Woolfolk, Don Whitehead	"Shining Star" "Boogie Wonderland," "Got to Get You into My Life"	Earth, Wind, and Fire won five Grammy Awards between 1975 and 1979.
Electric Light Orchestra	Jeff Lynne, Bev Bevan, Richard Tandy, Kelly Groucutt, Mik Kaminski, Melyvn Gale, Hugh McDowell	"Do Ya," "Don't Bring Me Down," "Sweet Talkin' Woman"	The lineup for the Electric Light Orchestra (also known as ELO) changed constantly throughout the band's tenure.
Roberta Flack		"Where Is the Love," "The First Time Ever I Saw Your Face," "Killing Me Softly with His Song"	Flack is a former teacher with a master's degree in music education.
Fleetwood Mac*	Lindsey Buckingham, Mick Fleetwood, Christine McVie, John McVie, Stevie Nicks	"Say You Love Me," "Dreams," "Go Your Own Way"	Fleetwood Mac began as a British blues band and made the gradual shift to pop during the mid-1970's with the addition of California duo Buckingham and Nicks.
Foreigner	Mick Jones, Ian McDonald, Dennis Elliott, Al Greenwood, Edward Gagliardi, Lou Gramm	"Feels Like the First Time," "Cold as Ice," "Hot Blooded"	Vocalist Gramm would later have a top-ten solo hit with "Midnight Blue" in 1987.
Peter Frampton		"Show Me the Way," "Do You Feel Like We Do," "I'm in You"	Frampton was once of member of the British band Humble Pie.
Marvin Gaye*		"What's Going On," "Let's Get It On," "Mercy, Mercy Me"	Gaye died on April 1, 1984, of a gunshot wound inflicted by his father.
Grand Funk Railroad	Mark Farner, Dennis Bellinger, Don Brewer, Craig Frost, Mel Shacher	"We're an American Band," "The Loco-Motion," "Some Kind of Wonderful"	This band from Flint, Michigan, received minimal radio air play and critical support yet consistently performed to sold-out venues through the early to mid-1970's.
Al Green		"Let's Stay Together," "Here I Am (Come and Take Me)," "Tired of Being Alone"	Green made the shift from soul to gospel music in 1978 with his release *The Belle Album.*

Act	Members	Notable 1970's Songs	Notable Facts
Heart*	Ann Wilson, Nancy Wilson, Steve Fossen, Roger Fisher, Mike Fisher, Howard Leese, Michael Derosier, Mark Andes, Denny Carmassi	"Magic Man," "Barracuda," "Straight On"	After 1978, Heart faded in popularity but experienced a resurgence with four top-ten hits in the mid-1980's.
Michael Jackson		"Got to Be There," "Ben," "Don't Stop 'Til You Get Enough"	Jackson's career was transformed from child star to adult performer in 1979 with the release of his album *Off the Wall*.
The Jackson 5	Jermaine Jackson, Michael Jackson, Toriano "Tito" Jackson, Marlon Jackson, Sigmund "Jackie" Jackson	"I'll Be There," "ABC," "Dancin' Machine"	The Jackson 5 were favorites on national television variety programs and were featured in their own cartoon series.
Billy Joel*		"Piano Man," "Just the Way You Are," "She's Always a Woman"	Billy Joel's 1972 solo debut, *Cold Spring Harbor*, was mastered at the wrong speed and remained a collector's item until it was re-released in 1984.
Elton John*		"Crocodile Rock," "Bennie and the Jets," "Philadelphia Freedom"	In November, 1977, John announced that he was retiring from live performing; the break only lasted fifteen months.
KC and the Sunshine Band	Harry Wayne "KC" Casey, Richard Finch, Jerome Smith, Robert Johnson	"Get Down Tonight," "That's the Way (I Like It)," "(Shake, Shake, Shake) Shake Your Booty"	In 1979, Casey recorded a duet with Teri DeSario called "Yes, I'm Ready," that reached number two on the *Billboard* charts.
Carole King		"I Feel the Earth Move," "It's Too Late," "Jazzman"	King and husband Gerry Goffin wrote many hit singles for other artists in the early to mid-1960's, including "Will You Love Me Tomorrow" by the Shirelles and "Up on the Roof" by the Drifters.
KISS*	Gene Simmons, Paul Stanley, Peter Criss, Ace Frehley	"Rock and Roll All Night," "Detroit Rock City," "Beth"	Prior to KISS, Simmons financed a demo recording for Van Halen and was instrumental in getting them signed to Warner Bros. Records.

Act	Members	Notable 1970's Songs	Notable Facts
Gladys Knight and the Pips	Gladys Knight, Merald "Bubba" Knight, Brenda Knight, Edward Patten, William Guest, Elenor Guest, Langston George	"Neither One of Us (Wants to Be the First to Say Goodbye)," "Midnight Train to Georgia," "You're the Best Thing That Ever Happened to Me"	Knight later participated in Dionne Warwick's 1985 all-star charity recording of the Burt Bacharach/Carole Bayer Sager song "That's What Friends Are For."
Led Zeppelin*	Jimmy Page, Robert Plant, John Paul Jones, John Bonham	"Whole Lotta Love," "Immigrant Song," "Stairway to Heaven"	Led Zeppelin was the first band to have six albums on the *Billboard* charts simultaneously.
John Lennon		"Instant Karma! (We All Shine On)," "Imagine," "Whatever Gets You Thru the Night"	"Whatever Gets You Thru the Night" was a collaboration with Elton John.
Gordon Lightfoot		"If You Could Read My Mind," "Carefree Highway," "The Wreck of the *Edmund Fitzgerald*"	In the late 1960's, artists such as Johnny Cash, Judy Collins, and Harry Belafonte recorded Lightfoot's songs.
Lynyrd Skynyrd	Ronnie Van Zandt, Allen Collins, Gary Rossington, Leon Wilkeson, Billy Powell, Bob Burns, Artimus Pyle, Steve Gaines, Cassie Gaines, Larry Jungstrom, Ed King	"Free Bird," "Sweet Home Alabama," "What's Your Name"	Ronnie Van Zandt, Steve Gaines, and Cassie Gaines died in a plane crash on October 17, 1977.
Paul McCartney and Wings	Paul McCartney, Denny Laine, Linda McCartney, Denny Seiwell, Henry McCullough, Jimmy McCulloch, Geoff Britton, Joe English	"Live and Let Die," "Band on the Run," "Listen to What the Man Said"	McCartney and his wife, Linda, had a number-one single in 1971 with "Uncle Albert/Admiral Halsey."
Barry Manilow*		"Mandy," "I Write the Songs," "Copacabana (at the Copa)"	Manilow, whose real name is Barry Alan Pincus, wrote and performed advertising jingles and accompanied Bette Midler early in the decade.
Bob Marley and the Wailers*	Bob Marley, Aston Barrett, Carlton Barrett, Rita Marley, Marcia Griffiths, Judy Mowatt	"No Woman, No Cry," "Get Up, Stand Up," "Jamming"	Marley died of cancer on May 11, 1981.
The Steve Miller Band	Steve Miller, Ben Sidran, Tim Davis, Jesse Ed Davis	"Fly Like an Eagle," "Jet Airliner," "Jungle Love"	Miller broke his neck in a 1972 car accident and was sidelined for nearly two years.

Act	Members	Notable 1970's Songs	Notable Facts
Van Morrison		"Domino," "Wild Night," "Crazy Love"	Morrison formed a group called Them in the 1960's; its 1966 hit "Gloria" would later be covered by the Doors.
Anne Murray		"Snowbird," "Danny's Song," "You Needed Me"	Kenny Loggins wrote Murray's second hit single, "Danny's Song."
Olivia Newton-John		"Let Me Be There," "I Honestly Love You," "Have You Never Been Mellow"	Newton-John starred in the hit 1978 film *Grease* with John Travolta, which led to the duo's number-one hit single "You're the One That I Want."
Tony Orlando and Dawn	Tony Orlando, Telma Hopkins, Joyce Vincent-Wilson	"Knock Three Times," "Tie a Yellow Ribbon 'Round the Ole Oak Tree," "He Don't Love You (Like I Love You)"	The multiracial trio hosted a variety series from 1974 to 1976.
The Osmonds	Donny Osmond, Alan Osmond, Wayne Osmond, Merrill Osmond, Jay Osmond, Marie Osmond, Jimmy Osmond	"One Bad Apple," "Going Home," "Down by the Lazy River"	The Osmonds made their television debut on *The Andy Williams Show* in 1962, and *The Donnie and Marie Show* was popular during its network run from 1976 to 1979.
Parliament-Funkadelic	George Clinton, Bernie Worrell, William "Bootsy" Collins, various	"One Nation Under a Groove," "Flashlight," "(Not Just) Knee Deep"	More than fifty musicians performed as part of the band's lineup during the 1970's.
Dolly Parton		"I Will Always Love You," "Jolene," "Here You Come Again"	Parton was the first female country singer to have her own syndicated television show, *Dolly!*, which aired in 1976.
Queen*	Freddie Mercury, Brian May, Roger Taylor, John Deacon	"Bohemian Rhapsody," "We Will Rock You/We Are the Champions," "Somebody to Love"	On its first American tour, Queen was the opening act for Mott the Hoople.
Helen Reddy*		"I Am Woman," "Delta Dawn," "Angie Baby"	Reddy's first hit single was "I Don't Know How to Love Him," from the musical *Jesus Christ Superstar.*

Act	Members	Notable 1970's Songs	Notable Facts
Kenny Rogers		"Lucille," "The Gambler," "You Decorated My Life"	Rogers is a former member of the New Christy Minstrels and the First Edition.
The Rolling Stones	Mick Jagger, Keith Richards, Bill Wyman, Mick Taylor, Charlie Watts, Ron Wood	"Brown Sugar," "Angie," "Miss You"	The Rolling Stones established their own, self-titled record label in 1971.
Linda Ronstadt		"When Will I Be Loved," "You're No Good," "Blue Bayou"	Ronstadt originally recorded with the band the Stone Poneys.
Santana	Carlos Santana, various	"Black Magic Woman," "Oye Como Va," "Evil Ways"	Santana appeared at the 1969 Woodstock festival during the same month that its self-titled debut album was released.
Bob Seger and the Silver Bullet Band	Bob Seger, Drew Abbott, Chris Campbell, Robyn Robbins, Alto Reed, Charlie Allen Martin	"Night Moves," "Still the Same," "We've Got Tonight"	The band's 1976 live album, *Live Bullet*, went quadruple platinum despite never having a top-ten single prior to its release.
Carly Simon		"Anticipation," "You're So Vain," "Nobody Does It Better"	Simon won a Grammy Award for Best New Artist in 1972.
Paul Simon		"Loves Me Like a Rock," "Fifty Ways to Leave Your Lover," "Slip Slidin' Away"	Simon would go on to win a Grammy Award for Album of the Year for his 1986 release, *Graceland*.
Simon and Garfunkel	Paul Simon, Art Garfunkel	"Bridge over Troubled Water," "The Boxer," "Cecilia"	Simon and Garfunkel's final studio album, *Bridge over Troubled Water*, was released in 1970.
Sly and the Family Stone	Sly Stone, Cynthia Robinson, Freddie Stone, Larry Graham, Jr., Greg Errico, Jerry Martini, Rosie Stone	"Thank You Falettinme Be Mice Elf Agin," "Family Affair," "Everybody Is a Star"	Sly Stone's real name is Sylvester Stewart.
The Spinners	Bobbie Smith, Pervis Jackson, Billy Henderson, Henry Fambrough, Phillip Wynne	"I'll Be Around," "Could It Be I'm Falling in Love," "The Rubberband Man"	After he left the band in 1977, lead vocalist Wynne toured with Parliament-Funkadelic.

Act	Members	Notable 1970's Songs	Notable Facts
Bruce Springsteen*		"Born to Run," "Badlands," "Prove It All Night"	Springsteen appeared on the covers of *Time* and *Newsweek* during the same week in October, 1975.
Steely Dan	Walter Becker, Donald Fagen, Denny Dias, Jeff Baxter, Jim Hodder, David Palmer	"Reelin' in the Years," "Rikki Don't Lose That Number," "Peg"	Steely Dan stopped touring in 1974 and did not hit the road again until twenty years later.
Rod Stewart		"Maggie May," "Tonight's the Night (Gonna Be Alright)," "Do Ya Think I'm Sexy?"	Stewart was once a member of the Jeff Beck Group and the Faces.
Styx	Chuck Panozzo, John Panozzo, Dennis DeYoung, Tommy Shaw, James Young, John Curulewski	"Come Sail Away," "Babe," "Lady"	Styx released two concept albums in the early 1980's, *Paradise Theater* and *Kilroy Was Here.*
Donna Summer*		"Love to Love You Baby," "McArthur Park," "Bad Girls"	Summer's real name is LaDonna Andre Gaines.
James Taylor		"Fire and Rain," "You've Got a Friend," "Handy Man"	Taylor and then-wife Carly Simon recorded a remake of "Mockingbird" in 1974.
The Temptations	Otis Williams, Melvin Franklin, Eddie Kendricks, Paul Williams, Dennis Edwards, Damon Harris, Richard Street	"Papa Was a Rolling Stone," "Just My Imagination (Running Away with Me)," "Ball of Confusion (That's What the World Is Today)"	The Temptations were formed in the early 1960's as a merger of two local Detroit groups, the Primes and the Distants.
Three Dog Night	Danny Hutton, Chuck Negron, Cory Wells, Mike Allsup, Jimmy Greenspoon, Joe Schermie, Floyd Sneed	"Mama Told Me (Not to Come)," "Joy to the World," "Just an Old Fashioned Love Song"	Three Dog Night released eleven top-ten singles between 1969 and 1975.
Van Halen*	Eddie Van Halen, Alex Van Halen, David Lee Roth, Michael Anthony	"Dance the Night Away," "Runnin' with the Devil," "Jamie's Cryin'"	Sammy Hager replaced Roth as lead vocalist starting with the band's 1986 release *5150.*
The Village People*	Victor Willis, Felipe Rose, Alex Briley, David Hodo, Glenn Hughes	"Y.M.C.A.," "In the Navy," "Macho Man"	The Village People was a concept band, conceptualized and assembled by French producer Jacques Morali.

Act	Members	Notable 1970's Songs	Notable Facts
War	Papa Dee Allen, Harold Brown, B. B. Dickerson, Leroy "Lonnie" Jordan, Charles Miller, Lee Oskar, Howard Scott	"Low Rider," "Why Can't We Be Friends?" "Summer"	Animals' vocalist Eric Burdon was a strong champion of the band and performed with it during the late 1960's and early 1970's.
Dionne Warwick		"I'll Never Fall in Love Again," "Then Came You," "I'll Never Love This Way Again"	Warwick's 1974 hit single, "Then Came You," was sung with the Spinners.
Barry White		"Never, Never Gonna Give Ya Up," "You're the First, the Last, My Everything," "It's Ecstasy When You Lay Down Next to Me"	Over the course of his career, White produced or performed on 106 gold and 41 platinum albums.
The Who*	Roger Daltrey, Pete Townshend, Keith Moon, John Entwistle, Kenney Jones	"Baba O'Riley," "Who Are You," "Won't Get Fooled Again"	Moon died in 1978, and Jones took over on drums.
Stevie Wonder*		"You Are the Sunshine of My Life," "Superstition," "Sir Duke"	Wonder had his first hit single in 1963 while still in his early teens.
ZZ Top	Billy Gibbons, Dusty Hill, Frank Beard	"La Grange," "Tush," "Cheap Sunglasses"	Beard is the only member of the trio who does not have a beard.

P. S. Ramsey

■ Music: Grammy Awards

This list includes winners of Grammy Awards in major categories. "Album of the Year" awards the artist who performed the album. "Record of the Year" awards the producer and artist, while "Song of the Year" awards the songwriter. An asterisk (*) following a name or group indicates the presence of a full-length entry in *The Seventies in America.*

1970

Album of the Year: *Bridge over Troubled Water,* Simon and Garfunkel

Record of the Year: "Bridge over Troubled Water," Art Garkunkel, Paul Simon, and Roy Halee (producers), Simon and Garfunkel (artists)

Song of the Year: "Bridge over Troubled Water," Paul Simon (songwriter), Simon and Garfunkel (artists)

Best New Artist: The Carpenters*

Best Contemporary Vocal Performance, Female: "I'll Never Fall in Love Again," Dionne Warwick

Best Contemporary Vocal Performance, Male: "Everything Is Beautiful," Ray Stevens

Best Contemporary Vocal Performance by a Duo, Group, or Chorus: "Close to You," The Carpenters*

Best Contemporary Song: "Bridge over Troubled Water," Paul Simon (songwriter), Simon and Garfunkel (artists)

Best R&B Vocal Performance, Female: "Don't Play That Song," Aretha Franklin

Best R&B Vocal Performance, Male: "The Thrill Is Gone," B. B. King

Best R&B Vocal Performance by a Duo, Group, or Chorus: "Didn't I (Blow Your Mind This Time)," The Delfonics

Best R&B Song: "Patches," General Johnson and Ronald Dunbar (songwriters), Clarence Carter (artist)

Best Country Vocal Performance, Female: "Rose Garden," Lynn Anderson

Best Country Vocal Performance, Male: "For the Good Times," Ray Price

Best Country Vocal Performance by a Duo, Group, or Chorus: "If I Were a Carpenter," Johnny Cash and June Carter

Best Country Song: "My Woman, My Woman, My Wife," Marty Robbins (songwriter and artist)

Best Jazz Performance—Small Group or Soloist with Small Group: *Alone,* Bill Evans

Best Jazz Performance—Large Group or Soloist with Large Group: *Bitches Brew,* Miles Davis

1971

Album of the Year: *Tapestry,* Carole King

Record of the Year: "It's Too Late," Carole King and Lou Adler (producers), Carole King (artist)

Song of the Year: "You've Got a Friend," Carole King (songwriter and artist)

Best New Artist: Carly Simon

Best Pop Vocal Performance, Female: *Tapestry,* Carole King

Best Pop Vocal Performance, Male: "You've Got a Friend," James Taylor

Best Pop Vocal Performance by a Duo or Group: *The Carpenters,* The Carpenters*

Best R&B Vocal Performance, Female: "Bridge over Troubled Water," Aretha Franklin

Best R&B Vocal Performance, Male: "A Natural Man," Lou Rawls

Best R&B Vocal Performance by a Duo or Group: "Proud Mary," Ike and Tina Turner

Best R&B Song: "Ain't No Sunshine," Bill Withers (songwriter and artist)

Best Country Vocal Performance, Female: "Help Me Make It Through the Night," Sammi Smith

Best Country Vocal Performance, Male: "When You're Hot, You're Hot," Jerry Reed

Best Country Vocal Performance by a Duo or Group: "After the Fire Is Gone," Conway Twitty and Loretta Lynn

Best Country Song: "Help Me Make It Through the Night," Kris Kristofferson (songwriter and artist)

Best Jazz Performance by a Soloist: *The Bill Evans Album,* Bill Evans

Best Jazz Performance by a Big Band: *New Orleans Suite,* Duke Ellington

1972

Album of the Year: *The Concert for Bangla Desh,* Billy Preston, Bob Dylan, Eric Clapton, George Harrison, Klaus Voormann, Leon Russell, Ravi Shankar, and Ringo Starr

Record of the Year: "The First Time Ever I Saw Your Face," Joel Dorn (producer), Roberta Flack (artist)

Song of the Year: "The First Time Ever I Saw Your Face," Ewan MacColl (songwriter), Roberta Flack (artist)
Best New Artist: America
Best Pop Vocal Performance, Female: "I Am Woman," Helen Reddy*
Best Pop Vocal Performance, Male: "Without You," Harry Nilsson
Best Pop Vocal Performance by a Duo or Group: "Where Is the Love," Donny Hathaway and Roberta Flack
Best R&B Vocal Performance, Female: "Young, Gifted, and Black," Aretha Franklin
Best R&B Vocal Performance, Male: "Me and Mrs. Jones," Billy Paul
Best R&B Vocal Performance by a Duo or Group: "Papa Was a Rolling Stone," The Temptations
Best R&B Song: "Papa Was a Rolling Stone," Barrett Strong and Norman Whitfield (songwriters), The Temptations (artist)
Best Country Vocal Performance, Female: "Happiest Girl in the Whole USA," Donna Fargo
Best Country Vocal Performance, Male: *Charley Pride Sings Heart Songs*, Charley Pride
Best Country Vocal Performance by a Duo or Group: "Class of '57," The Statler Brothers
Best Country Song: "Kiss an Angel Good Mornin'," Ben Peters (songwriter), Charley Pride (artist)
Best Jazz Performance by a Soloist: *Alone at Last*, Gary Burton
Best Jazz Performance by a Group: *First Light*, Freddie Hubbard
Best Jazz Performance by a Big Band: *Toga Brava Suite*, Duke Ellington

1973

Album of the Year: *Innervisions*, Stevie Wonder*
Record of the Year: "Killing Me Softly with His Song," Joel Dorn (producer), Roberta Flack (artist)
Song of the Year: "Killing Me Softly with His Song," Charles Fox and Norman Gimbel (songwriters), Roberta Flack (artist)
Best New Artist: Bette Midler
Best Pop Vocal Performance, Female: "Killing Me Softly with His Song," Roberta Flack
Best Pop Vocal Performance, Male: "You Are the Sunshine of My Life," Stevie Wonder*
Best Pop Vocal Performance by a Duo, Group, or Chorus: "Neither One of Us (Wants to Be the First to Say Goodbye)," Gladys Knight and the Pips
Best R&B Vocal Performance, Female: "Master of Eyes," Aretha Franklin
Best R&B Vocal Performance, Male: "Superstition," Stevie Wonder*
Best R&B Vocal Performance by a Duo, Group, or Chorus: "Midnight Train to Georgia," Gladys Knight and the Pips
Best R&B Song: "Superstition," Stevie Wonder* (songwriter and artist)
Best Country Vocal Performance, Female: "Let Me Be There," Olivia Newton-John
Best Country Vocal Performance, Male: "Behind Closed Doors," Charlie Rich
Best Country Vocal Performance by a Duo or Group: "From the Bottle to the Bottom," Kris Kristofferson and Rita Coolidge
Best Country Song: "Behind Closed Doors," Kenny O'Dell (songwriter), Charlie Rich (artist)
Best Jazz Performance by a Soloist: *God Is in the House*, Art Tatum
Best Jazz Performance by a Group: *Supersax Plays Bird*, Supersax
Best Jazz Performance by a Big Band: *Giant Steps*, Woody Herman

1974

Album of the Year: *Fulfillingness' First Finale*, Stevie Wonder*
Record of the Year: "I Honestly Love You," John Farrar (producer), Olivia Newton-John (artist)
Song of the Year: "The Way We Were," Alan Bergman, Marilyn Bergman, and Marvin Hamlisch (songwriters), Barbra Streisand (artist)
Best New Artist: Marvin Hamlisch
Best Pop Vocal Performance, Female: "I Honestly Love You," Olivia Newton-John
Best Pop Vocal Performance, Male: *Fulfillingness' First Finale*, Stevie Wonder*
Best Pop Vocal Performance by a Duo, Group, or Chorus: "Band on the Run," Paul McCartney and Wings
Best R&B Vocal Performance, Female: "Ain't Nothing Like the Real Thing," Aretha Franklin
Best R&B Vocal Performance, Male: "Boogie On, Reggae Woman," Stevie Wonder*
Best R&B Vocal Performance by a Duo, Group, or Chorus: "Tell Me Something Good," Rufus
Best R&B Song: "Living for the City," Stevie Wonder* (songwriter and artist)

Best Country Vocal Performance, Female: "Love Song," Anne Murray
Best Country Vocal Performance, Male: "Please Don't Tell Me How the Story Ends," Ronnie Milsap
Best Country Vocal Performance by a Duo or Group: "Fairytale," The Pointer Sisters
Best Country Song: "A Very Special Love Song," Bill Sherrill and Norris Wilson (songwriters), Charlie Rich (artist)
Best Jazz Performance by a Soloist: *First Recordings!*, Charlie Parker
Best Jazz Performance by a Group: *The Trio*, Joe Pass, Niels Pedersen, and Oscar Peterson
Best Jazz Performance by a Big Band: *Thundering Herd*, Woody Herman

1975

Album of the Year: *Still Crazy After All These Years*, Paul Simon
Record of the Year: "Love Will Keep Us Together," Daryl Dragon (producer), Captain and Tennille (artist)
Song of the Year: "Send in the Clowns," Stephen Sondheim* (songwriter), Judy Collins (artist)
Best New Artist: Natalie Cole
Best Pop Vocal Performance, Female: "At Seventeen," Janis Ian
Best Pop Vocal Performance, Male: "Still Crazy After All These Years," Paul Simon
Best Pop Vocal Performance by a Duo, Group, or Chorus: "Lyin' Eyes," The Eagles*
Best R&B Vocal Performance, Female: "This Will Be," Natalie Cole
Best R&B Vocal Performance, Male: "Living for the City," Ray Charles
Best R&B Vocal Performance by a Duo, Group, or Chorus: "Shining Star," Earth, Wind, and Fire*
Best R&B Song: "Where Is the Love," Betty Wright, Harry Wayne Casey, Richard Finch, and Willie Clarke (songwriters), Roberta Flack (artist)
Best Country Vocal Performance, Female: "I Can't Help It (If I'm Still in Love with You)," Linda Ronstadt
Best Country Vocal Performance, Male: "Blue Eyes Cryin' in the Rain," Willie Nelson
Best Country Vocal Performance by a Duo or Group: "Lover Please," Kris Kristofferson and Rita Coolidge
Best Country Song: "(Hey, Won't You Play) Another Somebody Done Somebody Wrong Song," Chris Moman and Larry Butler (songwriters), B. J. Thomas (artist)
Best Jazz Performance by a Soloist: *Oscar Peterson and Dizzy Gillespie*, Dizzy Gillespie
Best Jazz Performance by a Group: *No Mystery*, Chick Corea and Return to Forever
Best Jazz Performance by a Big Band: *Images*, Michel LeGrand and Phil Woods

1976

Album of the Year: *Songs in the Key of Life*, Stevie Wonder* (artist and producer)
Record of the Year: "This Masquerade," Tommy LiPuma (producer), George Benson (artist)
Song of the Year: "I Write the Songs," Bruce Johnson (songwriter), Barry Manilow* (artist)
Best New Artist: Starland Vocal Band
Best Pop Vocal Performance, Female: *Hasten Down the Wind*, Linda Ronstadt
Best Pop Vocal Performance, Male: *Songs in the Key of Life*, Stevie Wonder*
Best Pop Vocal Performance by a Duo, Group, or Chorus: "If You Leave Me Now," Chicago
Best R&B Vocal Performance, Female: "Sophisticated Lady (She's a Different Lady)," Natalie Cole
Best R&B Vocal Performance, Male: "I Wish," Stevie Wonder*
Best R&B Vocal Performance by a Duo, Group, or Chorus: "You Don't Have to Be a Star (to Be in My Show)," Billy Davis, Jr., and Marilyn McCoo
Best R&B Song: "Lowdown," Boz Scaggs and David Paich (songwriters), Boz Scaggs (artist)
Best Country Vocal Performance, Female: *Elite Hotel*, Emmylou Harris
Best Country Vocal Performance, Male: "(I'm a) Stand by My Woman Man," Ronnie Milsap
Best Country Vocal Performance by a Duo or Group: "The End Is Not in Sight (The Cowboy Tune)," Amazing Rhythm Aces
Best Country Song: "Broken Lady," Larry Gatlin (songwriter and artist)
Best Jazz Vocal Performance: *Fitzgerald and Pass . . . Again*, Ella Fitzgerald
Best Jazz Performance by a Soloist: *Basie and Zoot*, Dizzy Gillespie
Best Jazz Performance by a Group: *The Leprechaun*, Chick Corea
Best Jazz Performance by a Big Band: *The Ellington Suites*, Duke Ellington

1977

Album of the Year: *Rumours*, Fleetwood Mac*
Record of the Year: "Hotel California," Bill Szymczyk (producer), The Eagles* (artist)
Song of the Year (tie): "Love Theme from A Star Is Born," Barbra Streisand and Paul Williams (songwriters), Barbra Streisand (artist); "You Light up My Life," Joe Brooks (songwriter), Debbie Boone (artist)
Best New Artist: Debbie Boone
Best Pop Vocal Performance, Female: "Love Theme from A Star Is Born," Barbra Streisand
Best Pop Vocal Performance, Male: "Handy Man," James Taylor
Best Pop Vocal Performance by a Group: "How Deep Is Your Love," The Bee Gees*
Best R&B Vocal Performance, Female: "Don't Leave Me This Way," Thelma Houston
Best R&B Vocal Performance, Male: *Unmistakably Lou*, Lou Rawls
Best R&B Vocal Performance by a Duo, Group, or Chorus: "Best of My Love," The Emotions
Best R&B Song: "You Make Me Feel Like Dancing," Leo Sayer and Vini Poncia (songwriters), Leo Sayer (artist)
Best Country Vocal Performance, Female: "Don't It Make My Brown Eyes Blue," Crystal Gayle
Best Country Vocal Performance, Male: "Lucille," Kenny Rogers
Best Country Vocal Performance by a Duo or Group: "Heaven's Just a Sin Away," The Kendalls
Best Country Song: "Don't It Make My Brown Eyes Blue," Richard Leigh (songwriter), Crystal Gayle (artist)
Best Jazz Vocal Performance: *Look to the Rainbow*, Al Jarreau
Best Jazz Performance by a Soloist: *The Giants*, Oscar Peterson
Best Jazz Performance by a Group: *The Phil Woods Six—Live from the Showboat*
Best Jazz Performance by a Big Band: *Prime Time*, Count Basie

1978

Album of the Year: *Saturday Night Fever*, various artists
Record of the Year: "Just the Way You Are," Billy Joel* and Phil Ramone (producers), Billy Joel (artist)
Song of the Year: "Just the Way You Are," Billy Joel* (songwriter and artist)
Best New Artist: Taste of Honey
Best Pop Vocal Performance, Female: "You Needed Me," Anne Murray
Best Pop Vocal Performance, Male: "Copacabana (at the Copa)," Barry Manilow*
Best Pop Vocal Performance by a Duo or Group: *Saturday Night Fever*, The Bee Gees*
Best R&B Vocal Performance, Female: "Last Dance," Donna Summer*
Best R&B Vocal Performance, Male: "On Broadway," George Benson
Best R&B Vocal Performance by a Duo, Group, or Chorus: "All in All," Earth, Wind, and Fire*
Best R&B Song: "Last Dance," Paul Jabara (songwriter), Donna Summer* (artist)
Best Country Vocal Performance, Female: "Here You Come Again," Dolly Parton
Best Country Vocal Performance, Male: "Georgia on My Mind," Willie Nelson
Best Country Vocal Performance by a Duo or Group: "Mamas, Don't Let Your Babies Grow Up to Be Cowboys," Willie Nelson and Waylon Jennings
Best Country Song: "The Gambler," Don Schlitz (songwriter), Kenny Rogers (artist)
Best Jazz Vocal Performance: *All Fly Home*, Al Jarreau
Best Jazz Performance, Soloist: *Montreaux '77—* Oscar Peterson
Best Jazz Performance, Group: *Friends*, Chick Corea
Best Jazz Performance, Big Band: *Live in Munich*, Mel Lewis and Thad Jones

1979

Album of the Year: *52nd Street*, Billy Joel*
Record of the Year: "What a Fool Believes," Ted Templeman (producer), The Doobie Brothers (artist)
Song of the Year: "What a Fool Believes," Kenny Loggins and Michael McDonald (songwriters), The Doobie Brothers (artist)
Best New Artist: Rickie Lee Jones
Best Pop Vocal Performance, Female: "I'll Never Love This Way Again," Dionne Warwick
Best Pop Vocal Performance, Male: *52nd Street*, Billy Joel*
Best Pop Vocal Performance by a Duo, Group, or Chorus: "Minute by Minute," The Doobie Brothers
Best Rock Vocal Performance, Female: "Hot Stuff," Donna Summer*
Best Rock Vocal Performance, Male: "Gotta Serve Somebody," Bob Dylan

Best Rock Vocal Performance by a Duo or Group: "Heartache Tonight," The Eagles*

Best R&B Vocal Performance, Female: "Déjà Vu," Dionne Warwick

Best R&B Vocal Performance, Male: "Don't Stop 'til You Get Enough," Michael Jackson

Best R&B Vocal Performance by a Duo or Group: "After the Love Is Gone," Earth, Wind, and Fire*

Best R&B Song: "After the Love Is Gone," Bill Champlin, David Foster, and Jay Graydon (songwriters), Earth, Wind, and Fire* (artist)

Best Disco Recording: "I Will Survive," Dino Fekaris and Freddie Perren (producers), Gloria Gaynor (artist)

Best Country Vocal Performance, Female: "Blue Kentucky Girl," Emmylou Harris

Best Country Vocal Performance, Male: "The Gambler," Kenny Rogers

Best Country Vocal Performance by a Duo or Group: "The Devil Went down to Georgia," The Charlie Daniels Band

Best Country Song: "You Decorated My Life," Bob Morrison and Debbie Hupp (songwriters), Kenny Rogers (artist)

Best Jazz Fusion Performance, Vocal or Instrumental: *8:30*, Weather Report

Best Jazz Vocal Performance: *Fine and Mellow*, Ella Fitzgerald

Best Jazz Performance by a Soloist: *Jousts*, Oscar Peterson

Best Jazz Performance by a Group: *Duet*, Chick Corea and Gary Burton

Best Jazz Performance by a Big Band: *Duke Ellington at Fargo, 1940 Live*, Duke Ellington

Sports: Winners of Major Events

Athletes whose names appear with an asterisk (*) are subjects of their own full-length essays within *The Seventies in America.*

Major League Baseball

World Series

1970: Baltimore Orioles (American League) 4, Cincinnati Reds (National League), 1
1971: Pittsburgh Pirates (NL) 4, Baltimore Orioles (AL) 3
1972: Oakland A's (AL) 4, Cincinnati Reds (NL) 3
1973: Oakland A's (AL) 4, New York Mets (NL) 3
1974: Oakland A's (AL) 4, Los Angeles Dodgers (NL) 1
1975: Cincinnati Reds (NL) 4, Boston Red Sox (AL) 3
1976: Cincinnati Reds (NL) 4, New York Yankees (AL) 0
1977: New York Yankees (AL) 4, Los Angeles Dodgers (NL) 2
1978: New York Yankees (AL) 4, Los Angeles Dodgers (NL) 2
1979: Pittsburgh Pirates (NL) 4, Baltimore Orioles (AL) 3

All-Star Games

1970: National League 5, American League 4 (12 innings)
1971: American League 6, National League 4
1972: National League 4, American League 3 (10 innings)
1973: National League 7, American League 1
1974: National League 7, American League 2
1975: National League 6, American League 3
1976: National League 7, American League 1
1977: National League 7, American League 5
1978: National League 7, American League 3
1979: National League 7, American League 6

American League Most Valuable Players

1970: Boog Powell, Baltimore Orioles
1971: Vida Blue, Oakland A's
1972: Dick Allen, Chicago White Sox
1973: Reggie Jackson*, Oakland A's
1974: Jeff Burroughs, Texas Rangers
1975: Fred Lynn, Boston Red Sox
1976: Thurman Munson, New York Yankees
1977: Rod Carew, Minnesota Twins
1978: Jim Rice, Boston Red Sox
1979: Don Baylor, California Angels

National League Most Valuable Players

1970: Johnny Bench*, Cincinnati Reds
1971: Joe Torre, St. Louis Cardinals
1972: Johnny Bench*, Cincinnati Reds
1973: Pete Rose*, Cincinnati Reds
1974: Steve Garvey, Los Angeles Dodgers
1975: Joe Morgan, Cincinnati Reds
1976: Joe Morgan, Cincinnati Reds
1977: George Foster, Cincinnati Reds
1978: Dave Parker, Pittsburgh Pirates
1979: Keith Hernandez, St. Louis Cardinals

American League Rookies of the Year

1970: Thurman Munson, New York Yankees
1971: Chris Chambliss, Cleveland Indians
1972: Carlton Fisk, Boston Red Sox
1973: Al Bumbry, Baltimore Orioles
1974: Mike Hargrove, Texas Rangers
1975: Fred Lynn, Boston Red Sox
1976: Mark Fidrych, Detroit Tigers
1977: Eddie Murray, Baltimore Orioles
1978: Lou Whitaker, Detroit Tigers
1979: John Castino, Milwaukee Twins; Alfredo Griffin, Toronto Blue Jays

National League Rookies of the Year

1970: Carl Morton, Montreal Expos
1971: Earl Williams, Atlanta Braves
1972: Jon Matlack, New York Mets
1973: Gary Matthews, San Francisco Giants
1974: Bake McBride, St. Louis Cardinals
1975: John Montefusco, San Francisco Giants
1976: Butch Metzger, San Diego Padres; Pat Zachry, Cincinnati Reds
1977: Andre Dawson, Montreal Expos
1978: Bob Horner, Atlanta Braves
1979: Rick Sutcliffe, Los Angeles Dodgers

National Basketball Association (NBA)

Championships

1970: New York Knicks 4, Los Angeles Lakers 3
1971: Milwaukee Bucks 4, Baltimore Bullets 0
1972: Los Angeles Lakers 4, New York Knicks 1
1973: New York Knicks 4, Los Angeles Lakers 1
1974: Boston Celtics 4, Milwaukee Bucks 3
1975: Golden State Warriors 4, Washington Bullets 0
1976: Boston Celtics 4, Phoenix Suns 2
1977: Portland Trail Blazers 4, Philadelphia 76ers, 2
1978: Washington Bullets 4, Seattle SuperSonics 3
1979: Seattle SuperSonics 4, Washington Bullets 1

NBA Most Valuable Players

1970: Willis Reed, New York Knicks
1971: Kareem Abdul-Jabbar, Milwaukee Bucks
1972: Kareem Abdul-Jabbar, Milwaukee Bucks
1973: Dave Cowens, Boston Celtics
1974: Kareem Abdul-Jabbar, Milwaukee Bucks
1975: Bob McAdoo, Buffalo Braves
1976: Kareem Abdul-Jabbar, Los Angeles Lakers
1977: Kareem Abdul-Jabbar, Los Angeles Lakers
1978: Bill Walton*, Portland Trail Blazers
1979: Moses Malone, Houston Rockets

NBA Rookies of the Year

1970: Lew Alcindor, Milwaukee Bucks
1971: Geoff Petrie, Trail Blazers, and Dave Cowens, Boston Celtics (tie)
1972: Sidney Wicks, Portland Trail Blazers
1973: Bob McAdoo, Buffalo Braves
1974: Ernie DiGregorio, Buffalo Braves
1975: Keith Wilkes, Golden State Warriors
1976: Alvan Adams, Phoenix Suns
1977: Adrian Dantley, Buffalo Braves
1978: Walter Davis, Phoenix Suns
1979: Phil Ford, Kansas City Kings

College Basketball

National Collegiate Athletic Association (NCAA) Championships

1970: UCLA 80, Jacksonville 69
1971: UCLA 68, Villanova 62
1972: UCLA 81, Florida State 76
1973: UCLA 87, Memphis State 66
1974: NC State 76, Marquette 64
1975: UCLA 92, Kentucky 85
1976: Indiana 86, Michigan 68
1977: Marquette 67, North Carolina 59
1978: Kentucky 94, Duke 88
1979: Michigan State 75, Indiana State 64

National Invitational Tournament (NIT)

1970: Marquette 65, St. John's 53
1971: North Carolina 84, Geogia Tech 66
1972: Maryland 100, Niagara, 69
1973: Virginia Tech 92, Notre Dame 91
1974: Purdue 97, Utah 81
1975: Princeton 80, Providence 69
1976: Kentucky 71, North Carolina Charlotte 67
1977: St. Bonaventure 94, Houston 91
1978: Texas 101, NC State 93
1979: Indiana 53, Purdue 52

Professional Football

National Football League (NFL) Championships

1970: Baltimore Colts 16, Dallas Cowboys 13
1971: Dallas Cowboys 24, Miami Dolphins 3
1972: Miami Dolphins 14, Washington Redskins 7
1973: Miami Dolphins 24, Minnesota Vikings 7
1974: Pittsburgh Steelers 16, Minnesota Vikings 6
1975: Pittsburgh Steelers 21, Dallas Cowboys 17
1976: Oakland Raiders 32, Minnesota Vikings 14
1977: Dallas Cowboys 27, Denver Broncos 10
1978: Pittsburgh Steelers 35, Dallas Cowboys 31
1979: Pittsburgh Steelers 31, Los Angeles Rams 19

NFL Most Valuable Players

1970: John Brodie, San Francisco 49ers
1971: Alan Page, Minnesota Vikings
1972: Larry Brown, Washington Redskins
1973: O. J. Simpson*, Buffalo Bills
1974: Ken Stabler, Oakland Raiders
1975: Fran Tarkenton, Minnesota Vikings
1976: Bert Jones, Baltimore Colts
1977: Walter Payton*, Chicago Bears
1978: Terry Bradshaw, Pittsburgh Steelers
1979: Earl Campbell, Houston Oilers

Canadian Football League (CFL) Gray Cup Winners

1970: Montreal Alouettes 23, Calgary Stampeders 10
1971: Calgary Stampeders 14, Toronto Argonauts 11
1972: Hamilton Tiger Cats 13, Saskatchewan Roughriders 10
1973: Ottawa Rough Riders 22, Edmonton Eskimos 18
1974: Montreal Alouettes 20, Edmonton Eskimos 7
1975: Edmonton Eskimos 9, Montreal Alouettes 8
1976: Ottawa Rough Riders 23, Saskatchewan Roughriders 20
1977: Montreal Alouettes 41, Edmonton Eskimos 6
1978: Edmonton Eskimos 20, Montreal Alouettes 13
1979: Edmonton Eskimos 17, Montreal Alouettes 9

College Football

Heisman Trophy Winners

1970: Jim Plunkett, Stanford
1971: Pat Sullivan, Auburn
1972: Johnny Rodgers, Nebraska
1973: John Cappelleti, Pennsylvania State
1974: Archie Griffin, Ohio State
1975: Archie Griffin, Ohio State
1976: Tony Dorsett, Pittsburgh
1977: Earl Campbell, Texas
1978: Billy Sims, Oklahoma
1979: Charles White, University of Southern California

National Hockey League (NHL)

Stanley Cup Winners

1970: Boston Bruins 4, St. Louis Blues 0
1971: Montreal Canadiens 4, Chicago Blackhawks 3
1972: Boston Bruins 4, New York Rangers 2
1973: Montreal Canadiens 4, Chicago Blackhawks 2
1974: Philadelphia Flyers 4, Boston Bruins 2
1975: Philadelphia Flyers 4, Buffalo Sabres 2
1976: Montreal Canadiens 4, Philadelphia Flyers 0
1977: Montreal Canadiens 4, Boston Bruins 0
1978: Montreal Canadiens 4, Boston Bruins 2
1979: Montreal Canadiens 4, New York Rangers 1

Hart Memorial Trophy (NHL MVP)

1970: Bobby Orr*, Boston Bruins
1971: Bobby Orr*, Boston Bruins
1972: Bobby Orr*, Boston Bruins
1973: Bobby Clarke, Philadelphia Flyers
1974: Phil Esposito, Boston Bruins
1975: Bobby Clarke, Philadelphia Flyers
1976: Bobby Clarke, Philadelphia Flyers
1977: Guy Lafleur*, Montreal Canadiens
1978: Guy Lafleur*, Montreal Canadiens
1979: Bryan Trottier, New York Islanders

NHL Rookies of the Year (began in 1973)

1973: Terry Caffery, New England Whalers
1974: Mark Howe, Houston Aeros
1975: Anders Hedberg, Winnipeg Jets
1976: Mark Napier, Toronto Toros
1977: George Lyle, New England Whalers
1978: Kent Nilsson, Winnipeg Jets
1979: Wayne Gretzky, Indianapolis Racers

Boxing

World Heavyweight Champions

1968-1970: Cassius Clay (Muhammad Ali)*
1970-1973: Joe Frazer
1973-1974: George Foreman
1974-1978: Muhammad Ali*
1978: Leon Spinks
1978-1979: Muhammad Ali*

Auto Racing

Indianapolis 500 Winners

1970: Al Unser
1971: Al Unser
1972: Mark Donohue
1973: Gordon Johncock
1974: Johnny Rutherford
1975: Bobby Unser
1976: Johnny Rutherford
1977: A. J. Foyt
1978: Al Unser
1979: Rick Mears

Tennis

Major Tournament Champions

Year	Australian Open	French Open	Wimbledon	U.S. Open
Men				
1970	Arthur Ashe*	Jan Kodes	John Newcombe	Ken Rosewall
1971	Ken Rosewall	Jan Kodes	John Newcombe	Stan Smith
1972	Ken Rosewall	Andrés Gimeno	Stan Smith	Ilie Nastase
1973	John Newcombe	Ilie Nastase	Jan Kodes	John Newcombe
1974	Jimmy Connors*	Björn Borg	Jimmy Connors*	Jimmy Connors*
1975	John Newcombe	Björn Borg	Arthur Ashe*	Manuel Orantes
1976	Mark Edmondson	Adriano Panatta	Björn Borg	Jimmy Connors*
1977	Roscoe Tanner (January); Vitas Gerulaitis (December)	Guermillo Vilas	Björn Borg	Guermillo Vilas
1978	Guermillo Vilas	Björn Borg	Björn Borg	Jimmy Connors*
1979	Guermillo Vilas	Björn Borg	Björn Borg	John McEnroe
Women				
1970	Margaret Court	Margaret Court	Margaret Court	Margaret Court
1971	Margaret Court	Evonne Goolagong	Evonne Goolagong	Billie Jean King*
1972	Virginia Wade	Billie Jean King*	Billie Jean King*	Billie Jean King*
1973	Margaret Court	Margaret Court	Billie Jean King*	Margaret Court
1974	Evonne Goolagong	Chris Evert*	Chris Evert*	Billie Jean King*
1975	Evonne Goolagong	Chris Evert*	Billie Jean King*	Chris Evert*
1976	Evonne Goolagong Cawley	Sue Barker	Chris Evert*	Chris Evert*
1977	Kerry Reid (January); Evonne Goolagong Cawley (December)	Mimi Jausovec	Virginia Wade	Chris Evert*
1978	Chris O'Neil	Virginia Ruzici	Martina Navratilova	Chris Evert*
1979	Barbara Jordan	Chris Evert*	Martina Navratilova	Tracy Austin

Golf

Major Tournament Champions (Men)

Year	British Open	Professional Golf Association (PGA) Championship	The Masters	U.S. Open
1970	Jack Nicklaus*	Dave Stockton	Billy Casper	Tony Jacklin
1971	Lee Trevino	Jack Nicklaus*	Charles Coody	Lee Trevino
1972	Lee Trevino	Gary Player	Jack Nicklaus*	Jack Nicklaus*
1973	Tom Weiskopf	Jack Nicklaus*	Tommy Aaron	Johnny Miller
1974	Gary Player	Lee Trevino	Gary Player	Hale Irwin
1975	Tom Watson	Dave Stockton	Jack Nicklaus*	Lou Graham
1976	Johnny Miller	Lanny Wadkins	Raymond Floyd	Jerry Pate
1977	Tom Watson	John Mahaffey	Tom Watson	Hubert Green
1978	Jack Nicklaus*	David Graham	Gary Player	Andy North
1979	Seve Ballesteros	Jack Nicklaus*	Fuzzy Zoeller	Hale Irwin

Major Tournament Champions (Women)

Year	U.S. Open	Ladies Professional Golf Association (LPGA) Championship
1970	Donna Caponi	Shirley Englehorn
1971	JoAnne Carner	Kathy Whitworth
1972	Susie Berning	Kathy Ahern
1973	Susie Berning	Mary Mills
1974	Sandra Haynie	Sandra Haynie
1975	Sandra Palmer	Kathy Whitworth
1976	JoAnne Carner	Betty Burfeindt
1977	Hollis Stacy	Chako Higuchi
1978	Hollis Stacy	Nancy Lopez*
1979	Jerilyn Britz	Donna Caponi

Horse Racing

Triple Crown Races

Year	Kentucky Derby	Preakness	Belmont Stakes
1970	Dust Commander	Personality	High Echelon
1971	Canonero II	Canonero II	Pass Catcher
1972	Riva Ridge	Bee Bee Bee	Riva Ridge
1973	Secretariat*	Secretariat*	Secretariat*
1974	Cannonade	Little Current	Little Current
1975	Foolish Pleasure	Master Derby	Avatar
1976	Bold Forbes	Elocutionist	Bold Forbes
1977	Seattle Slew	Seattle Slew	Seattle Slew
1978	Affirmed	Affirmed	Affirmed
1979	Spectacular Bid	Spectacular Bid	Coastal

Time Line

Additional dates on legislation, U.S. Supreme Court cases, films, television shows, plays, literature, popular music, and sports can be found in other appendices.

1970

International events: (Jan. 12) Biafra surrenders, ending the Nigerian civil war. (Jan. 15) Muammar al-Qaddafi is proclaimed premier of Libya. (Mar. 18) Lon Nol ousts Prince Norodom Sihanouk of Cambodia. (Jun. 9) Yassar Arafat becomes the leader of the Palestine Liberation Organization (PLO). (Jun. 18) Edward Heath is elected prime minister of the United Kingdom. (Sept. 3) Salvador Allende wins the presidential election in Chile. (Oct. 9) The Khmer Republic is proclaimed in Cambodia. (Oct. 13) Canada and the People's Republic of China establish diplomatic relations. (Oct. 17) Anwar Sadat officially becomes the president of Egypt.

Government and politics: The Nixon administration briefly approves the Huston Plan, a scheme to unify intelligence agencies for spying on Americans illegally. La Francophonie, a consortium of French-using states and governments that includes Quebec, is established. (Sept. 29) The U.S. Congress gives President Richard Nixon authority to sell arms to Israel.

Military and war: (Apr. 29) The United States invades Cambodia to search for Viet Cong soldiers. (May 4) Four students at Kent State University in Ohio are killed by the National Guard at an antiwar demonstration. (May 8) In the Hard Hat Riot, helmeted construction workers attack Vietnam War protesters in New York City's financial district. (Sept. 7) An antiwar rally in Valley Forge, Pennsylvania, is attended by future presidential candidate John F. Kerry and actors Jane Fonda and Donald Sutherland. (Nov. 17) Lieutenant William Calley goes on trial for the My Lai massacre.

Society: Charles A. Reich's *The Greening of America,* which explains the generation gap, is published. The Gray Panthers, a civil rights organization for older and retired Americans, is formed. (May) The U.S. government shuts off power and stops water supplies to the Native Americans occupying Alcatraz Island. (Jul. 6) California passes the first no-fault divorce law. (Aug. 7) At a hearing for the Soledad Brothers, Jackson's brother attempts an armed rescue; the resulting shootout kills four. (Aug. 21) The Canadian organization National Indian Brotherhood is founded. (Aug. 26) The Women's Strike for Equality, organized by Betty Friedan, commemorates the fiftieth anniversary of women's right to vote.

Business and economics: (Dec. 29) The Occupational Safety and Health Act (OSHA) is signed into law.

Transportation and communications: (Jan. 12) The Boeing 747 becomes the first jumbo jet in commercial service. (Feb. 24) National Public Radio (NPR) is founded. (Mar. 25) The Concorde makes its first supersonic flight. (Sept. 11) The Ford Pinto is introduced. (Oct.) The Public Broadcasting Service (PBS) begins operations.

Science and technology: Intel releases the first successful microprocessor. (Apr. 11) Apollo 13 launches for the Moon; it returns to Earth a week later when an explosion forces the crew to abort the mission.

Environment and health: The Clean Air Act establishes levels of pollution for sulfur dioxide, carbon monoxide, nitrogen oxides, particulates, and ozone. Congress passes the Resource Recovery Act to encourage recycling. Canada bans commercial fishing in Lake St. Clair and Lake Erie. (Apr. 22) The first Earth Day is celebrated. (Dec. 2) The Environmental Protection Agency (EPA) begins operation.

Arts and literature: FICTION: *Jonathan Livingston Seagull* (Richard Bach); *Deliverance* (James Dickey); *The Collected Works of Billy the Kid* (Michael Ondaatje). MUSICALS: *Company* (Stephen Sondheim); *Purlie* (Ossie Davis); *Applause* (Betty Comden and Adolph Green). (Jan. 1) Construction begins on Paolo Soleri's Arcosanti in Arizona. (Jun. 8) Tom Wolfe publishes the essay "Radical Chic." (Oct. 8) Soviet author Alexander Solzhenitsyn is named winner of the Nobel Prize in Literature.

Popular culture: The motion pictures *Love Story* and *Patton* are released. The musical television series *The Partridge Family* debuts. ALBUMS: *Let It Be* (The Beatles); *Close to You* (The Carpenters); *Bitches*

Brew (Miles Davis); *Bridge over Troubled Water* (Simon and Garfunkel); *Moondance* (Van Morrison). The Beatles, the Monkees, and Simon and Garfunkel break up. Aerosmith, Genesis, Styx, Weather Report, and Earth, Wind, and Fire form. (Jan. 25) Robert Altman's film *M*A*S*H* premieres. (Sept. 18) Guitarist Jimi Hendrix dies in London of a drug overdose. (Sept. 19) *The Mary Tyler Moore Show* goes on the air. (Oct. 4) Singer Janis Joplin dies of a heroin overdose at a Hollywood motel. (Oct. 26) Gary Trudeau's comic strip *Doonesbury* first appears.

Sports: Margaret Court wins the Grand Slam of women's tennis. (Jan. 11) The Kansas City Chiefs defeat the Minnesota Vikings in Superbowl IV. (Jan. 16) Curt Flood files a lawsuit challenging baseball's reserve clause. (Apr. 5) Bobby Orr becomes the first defenseman in the National Hockey League to lead in scoring. (May 8) New York Knicks defeat the Los Angeles Lakers in seven games in the National Basketball Association (NBA) Finals. (Sept. 3) Football coach Vince Lombardi dies in Washington, D.C. (Sept. 21) *Monday Night Football* premieres. (Oct. 15) The Baltimore Orioles win the World Series over the Cincinnati Reds.

Crime: (Mar. 5) The Weatherman terrorist group bombs a building in New York City. (Oct. 5) The Front de Libération du Québec (FLQ) kidnaps British trade commissioner James Cross in Montreal. (Oct. 10) Quebec cabinet minister Pierre Laporte is also kidnapped by the FLQ; he is found murdered a week later. (Oct. 15) The Racketeer Influenced and Corrupt Organizations (RICO) Act is signed. (Dec. 3) Police negotiate the release of Cross, and Canada grants five FLQ terrorists safe passage to Cuba.

1971

International events: (Jan.) The Singapore Conference becomes the first Commonwealth Heads of Government Meeting (CHOGM) held outside the United Kingdom. The Nixon administration ends the arms embargo against South Africa for its support for the overthrow of Angola's socialist-leaning government.

Government and politics: President Richard Nixon institutes his Enemies List of perceived political opponents of his administration. (May 31) *Time* magazine puts Georgia governor Jimmy Carter on its cover as a symbol of the changing South. (Jun. 13) Daniel Ellsberg leaks photocopied excerpts from the Pentagon Papers to *The New York Times.* (Jun. 30) The Twenty-sixth Amendment is ratified, lowering the voting age to eighteen. (Sept. 3) The White House "Plumbers' Unit" breaks into the office of Ellsberg's psychiatrist.

Military and war: (May 3-5) Antiwar protesters attempt to disrupt government activity in Washington, D.C., resulting in the largest mass detentions in U.S. history. (Nov. 12) President Nixon announces that he will withdraw 45,000 troops from Vietnam by early 1972.

Society: The Reverend Jesse Jackson founds Operation PUSH. (Feb. 9) A 6.6 earthquake kills sixty-five people in Southern California. (Apr. 20) In *Swann v. Charlotte-Mecklenburg Board of Education,* the U.S. Supreme Court unanimously approves the use of mandatory busing for desegregation. (Aug. 21) Soledad Brother George Jackson is shot by a guard at San Quentin. (Dec. 18) The Alaska Native Claims Settlement Act gives Inuits surface rights to their lands.

Business and economics: President Nixon establishes the Wage and Price Control Board. Docutel installs the first fully functioning bank automatic teller machine (ATM). The Supreme Court of Canada decides that only the federal government has jurisdiction of trade between provincial markets. (Sept.-Nov.) Workers at General Motors go on strike.

Transportation and communications: Department of Transportation secretary John Volpe announces that manufacturers must install passive restraining devices in new vehicles. The Amtrak rail service is created by the federal government and takes over intercity passenger operations. The Federal Communications Commission (FCC) sends telegrams to radio stations advising them not to play music glorifying drug use, with a reminder that their broadcast licenses could be revoked.

Science and technology: The digital watch, the floppy disk, the pocket calculator, and the videocassette recorder (VCR) are invented. (Feb. 5) Apollo 14 lands on the Moon in the Fra Mauro region, which had been the designated Apollo 13 landing site. (Jul. 29) Apollo 15 lands on the Moon. (Nov. 14) The Mariner 9 probe arrives at Mars and becomes the first artificial object to orbit another planet.

Environment and health: The international environmental group Greenpeace is founded. Keep America Beautiful begins its "Crying Indian" antilitter campaign. A court places restrictions on the building of a nuclear power plant at Chesapeake Bay. Health laws put limits on the amount of allowable exposure to asbestos. The Lead-Based Paint Poison Prevention Act of 1971 prohibits the application of lead-based paint in cooking, drinking, and eating utensils. (Jan. 1) All cigarette ads are banned from television and radio. (Jul. 26) Reporter James Reston publishes a landmark front-page article in *The New York Times* on acupuncture.

Arts and literature: Construction begins on San Francisco's Embarcadero, a series of modern high-rises. Artist Faith Ringgold helps establish the art collective Where We at Together Black Women in New York. Artists Judy Chicago and Miriam Schapiro start a feminist art program at CalArts in Los Angeles. Addison Gayle edits the essay collection *The Black Aesthetic*, which defines the Black Arts movement. FICTION: *The Autobiography of Miss Jane Pittman* (Ernest J. Gaines); *The Bell Jar* (Sylvia Plath); *The Exorcist* (William Peter Blatty); *Rabbit Redux* (John Updike); *St. Urbain's Horseman* (Mordecai Richler); *The Winds of War* (Herman Wouk). MUSICALS: *Follies* (Stephen Sondheim); *Godspell* (Stephen Schwartz). (Oct. 12) The rock opera *Jesus Christ Superstar* debuts on Broadway.

Popular culture: The blaxploitation film *Shaft* is released. The allegorical Western *McCabe and Mrs. Miller*, directed by Robert Altman, opens. *A Clockwork Orange* is released but is soon banned in several countries. The film *The French Connection* is released. The motion picture *Harold and Maude* provokes controversy. The Canadian film *Mon Oncle Antoine* is released. ALBUMS: *L.A. Woman* (The Doors); *What's Going On?* (Marvin Gaye); *All Things Must Pass* (George Harrison); *Aqualung* (Jethro Tull); *Pearl* (Janis Joplin); *Tapestry* (Carole King); *American Pie* (Don McLean); *Who's Next* (The Who). The bands the Eagles and Queen form. (Jan. 12) The controversial sitcom *All in the Family* first airs. (Aug. 1) The benefit Concert for Bangla Desh is held at Madison Square Garden. (Oct. 1) Walt Disney World opens in Orlando, Florida.

Sports: (Jan. 17) The Baltimore Colts beat the Dallas Cowboys in Superbowl V. (Apr. 30) Lew Alcindor leads the Milwaukee Bucks to the National Basketball Association (NBA) championship over the Baltimore Bullets; later that year, he changes his name to Kareem Abdul-Jabbar. (Jun. 15) A black woman, Cheryl White, becomes the first female jockey. (Jul. 7) Negro League players are given full membership in the Baseball Hall of Fame. (Sept. 20) The American League approves the move of the Washington Senators to Texas to become the Rangers. (Sept. 26) Ernie Banks retires from baseball. (Oct. 13) The first night game in World Series history is played; the Pittsburgh Pirates later take the Series in seven games over the Baltimore Orioles. Women's basketball reduces the number of players on a side from six to five.

Crime: (Sept. 9-13) Inmates riot and take over Attica State Prison in New York; thirty-nine people are killed.

1972

International events: (Jan. 4) Kurt Waldheim is named Secretary General of the United Nations. (Jan. 11) East Pakistan gains its independence and takes the name Bangladesh. (Feb. 21-28) President Richard Nixon visits the People's Republic of China and meets with Mao Zedong. (May 22) Ceylon becomes the Republic of Sri Lanka. (Jun. 25) Juan Peron is elected president of Argentina.

Government and politics: Barbara Jordan, a Democrat from Texas, becomes the first African American woman elected to Congress from a southern state. (Jan. 25) African American Congresswoman Shirley Chisholm announces her candidacy for U.S. president. (Feb. 15) The Committee to Re-elect the President (CRP) is formed. (Jun. 17) Five White House operatives are arrested for breaking into the offices of the Democratic National Committee in the Watergate office complex. (Jun. 23) President Nixon and White House chief of staff H. R. Haldeman are taped talking about using the Central Intelligence Agency (CIA) to obstruct the Federal Bureau of Investigation (FBI) probe into the Watergate break-in. (Nov. 7) Republican incumbent Nixon defeats Democratic Senator George McGovern for the U.S. presidency.

Military and war: (May 26) President Nixon and Soviet leader Leonid Brezhnev sign the SALT I and Anti-Ballistic Missile (ABM) treaties in Moscow. (Jun.) President Nixon announces that no new draftees will be sent to Vietnam. (Aug. 11-12) The last U.S. ground troops are withdrawn from Vietnam. (Dec. 13) Peace talks in Paris between North Vietnam and the United States break down.

Society: Alex Comfort's *The Joy of Sex* is published. The first video game, *Pong*, is created. (Jan.) Gloria Steinem's feminist periodical *Ms.* magazine begins publication. (Mar. 22) Congress passes the Equal Rights Amendment (ERA) and Hawaii becomes the first state to ratify it. (Jun. 3) Sally Priesand becomes the first female rabbi in the United States. (Jun. 4) Black activist Angela Davis is found not guilty of murder. (Nov. 5) Following the protest caravan called the Trail of Broken Treaties, a group of Native Americans occupies the Bureau of Indian Affairs (BIA).

Business and economics: The Supplemental Security Income (SSI) benefit is added to Social Security. (Jun. 26) Nolan Bushnell and Ted Dabney found Atari. (Jul.) A major strike by half a million workers for AT&T ends. (Oct. 27) The Consumer Product Safety Act is passed.

Transportation and communications: (Nov. 9) The Anik A-1 communication satellite is launched.

Science and technology: (Feb. 1) The first scientific handheld calculator is introduced. (Mar. 2) The Pioneer 10 spacecraft is launched. (Apr. 16) Apollo 16 is launched. (Dec. 7) Apollo 17, the last manned lunar mission, is launched.

Environment and health: The Great Lakes Water Quality Agreement is signed by Canada and the United States. CAT scans and MRI scans are invented. (Oct. 27) The Noise Control Act is signed into law. (Dec. 31) The ban on the widespread use of the pesticide DDT in the United States begins.

Arts and literature: Hunter S. Thompson publishes *Fear and Loathing in Las Vegas*. Margaret Atwood's *Survival: A Thematic Guide to Canadian Literature* and Farley Mowat's *A Whale for the Killing* are published. FICTION: *My Name Is Asher Lev* (Chaim Potok); *Watership Down* (Richard Adams). MUSICALS: *Grease* (Jim Jacobs and Warren Casey); *Pippin* (Stephen Schwartz). (Sept. 14) *That Championship Season*, a play written by Jason Miller, opens on Broadway.

Popular culture: Francis Ford Coppola's Mafia epic *The Godfather* is released. The motion picture *Deliverance* opens. The sexually explicit film *Last Tango in Paris* is released. The children's program *Fat Albert and the Cosby Kids* and the sitcom *Sanford and Son* go on the air. ALBUMS: *The Rise and Fall of Ziggy Stardust and the Spiders from Mars* (David Bowie); *Machine Head* (Deep Purple); *Will the Circle Be Unbroken* (The Nitty Gritty Dirt Band); *Fragile* (Yes); *Harvest* (Neil Young). The children's album *Free to Be . . . You and Me* is released. The rock group KISS forms. (Sept. 12) *Maude*, a spinoff of *All in the Family*, first airs. (Sept. 17) The television series *M*A*S*H* debuts.

Sports: (Jan. 16) The Dallas Cowboys crush the Miami Dolphins, 24-3, in Superbowl VI. (Feb. 3-13) The Winter Olympic Games are held in Sapporo, Japan. (May 7) The Los Angeles Lakers defeat the New York Knicks in five games in the National Basketball Association (NBA) Finals. (Jun. 23) Title IX of the Education Amendments promotes gender equality in education, including sports programs. (Aug. 26-Sept. 11) The Summer Olympic Games are held in Munich, West Germany. (Sept. 1) Bobby Fischer defeats Boris Spassky to become the first American chess champion. (Oct. 22) The Oakland Athletics win the World Series in seven games over the Cincinnati Reds. (Dec. 31) Baseball legend Roberto Clemente dies in a plane crash while delivering supplies to earthquake victims in Nicaragua.

Crime: (May 15) Alabama governor George Wallace is shot and paralyzed at a political rally. (Jun. 29) The U.S. Supreme Court rules that the death penalty is unconstitutional. (Sept. 5-6) Eleven Israeli athletes are killed after members of the Arab terrorist group Black September invade the Olympic Village in Munich.

1973

International events: (Jan. 17) Ferdinand Marcos becomes President for Life of the Philippines. (Sept. 11) The government of Chile is overthrown in a military coup. (Sept. 15) King Gustav VI Adolf of Sweden dies and is succeeded by Carl XVI Gustav. (Oct. 6) The Yom Kippur War begins when Egypt and Syria attack Israel.

Government and politics: (Feb.) The Senate establishes the Select Committee on Presidential Campaign Activities, chaired by Senator Sam Ervin, to investigate the Watergate break-in. (Aug. 22) National security adviser Henry Kissinger is named secretary of state. (Oct. 10) Vice President Spiro T. Agnew resigns, pleading no contest to charges of income tax evasion. (Oct. 20) Attorney General Elliot Richardson and Deputy Attorney General William Ruckelshaus refuse President Richard Nixon's order to dismiss Watergate special prosecutor Archibald Cox and resign in what is called the Saturday Night Massacre. (Dec. 6) The House of Representatives confirms Gerald R. Ford as vice president of the United States.

Military and war: (Jan. 27) The Paris Peace Accords are signed, ending U.S. military involvement in the Vietnam War. (Aug. 15) The United States stops its bombing of Cambodia. (Nov. 7) The War Powers Resolution is signed into law.

Society: Jews for Jesus, an evangelical group of Christian Jews, is founded. (Jan. 22) The U.S. Supreme Court hands down a decision in the abortion case *Roe v. Wade.* (Feb. 28-May 7) Native Americans activists occupy the Pine Ridge Indian Reservation in Wounded Knee, South Dakota. (Mar. 15) The Mississippi River begins to flood, eventually inundating millions of acres. (Dec. 15) The American Psychiatric Association removes homosexuality as an illness from the second edition of the *Diagnostic and Statistical Manual of Mental Disorders* (DSM-II).

Business and economics: (Oct. 17) Arab countries begin an oil embargo of pro-Israeli countries. (Nov. 16) President Nixon signs legislation authorizing construction of the Alaska Pipeline.

Transportation and communications: The first reduction standards for leaded gasoline are issued. Bar codes are invented.

Science and technology: (Apr. 5) Pioneer 11 is launched. (May 14) Skylab, the first U.S. space station, is sent into orbit. (Nov. 3) The National Aeronautics and Space Administration (NASA) launches the Mariner 10 probe.

Environment and health: *Our Bodies, Ourselves* is published by the Boston Women's Health Collective. (Dec. 28) The Endangered Species Act is signed into law.

Arts and literature: Erica Jong's controversial comic novel *Fear of Flying* is published. Thomas Pynchon's novel *Gravity's Rainbow* examines twentieth century history. FICTION: *Breakfast of Champions* (Kurt Vonnegut, Jr.); *Evening in Byzantium* (Irwin Shaw); *Sula* (Toni Morrison). MUSICALS: *A Little Night Music* (Stephen Sondheim); *Raisin* (Robert Nemiroff and Charlotte Zaltzberg). (May 4) Construction of the Sears Tower is completed.

Popular culture: The horror film *The Exorcist* premieres. The 1950's-era film *American Graffiti* is released. The educational segments *Schoolhouse Rock!* begin airing. *The Six Million Dollar Man* premieres on television. ALBUMS: *Goodbye Yellow Brick Road* (Elton John); *Band on the Run* (Paul McCartney and Wings); *The Dark Side of the Moon* (Pink Floyd); *Innervisions* (Stevie Wonder). Helen Reddy wins a Grammy for her hit song "I Am Woman." The rock groups Journey and AC/DC form. (Jan.-Apr.) The documentary television series *An American Family* is broadcast. (Jul. 28) Approximately 600,000 fans attend the Watkins Glen rock festival in New York.

Sports: (Jan. 14) In Super Bowl VII, the Miami Dolphins edge the Washington Redskins. (Jan. 22) George Foreman knocks out Joe Frazier to become heavyweight boxing champion. (Apr. 6) The designated hitter is first used in the American League. (May 10) The New York Knicks defeat the Los Angeles Lakers in five games in the National Basketball Association (NBA) Finals. (Jun. 9) Secretariat becomes the first Triple Crown winner since 1948. (Sept. 20) Tennis champion Billie Jean King defeats Bobby Riggs in the Battle of the Sexes. (Oct. 21) In the World Series, the Oakland Athletics beat the New York Mets in seven games.

Crime: (Nov. 6) The Symbionese Liberation Army (SLA) murders Marcus Foster, school superintendent for Oakland, California.

1974

International events: (Apr. 10) Golda Meir resigns as prime minister of Israel. (May 18) India successfully detonates its first nuclear weapon. (Jul. 3) Canada demands that its territorial waters be extended to 200 nautical miles.

Government and politics: (Jan. 14) Jules Léger is sworn in as Governor General of Canada. (Jul. 24-30) The House Judiciary Committee approves articles of impeachment against President Richard Nixon. (Aug. 9) Nixon resigns the presidency. (Sept. 8) President Gerald R. Ford pardons Nixon from any criminal wrongdoing that he may have committed while in office.

Military and war: (Sept. 16) The Presidential Clemency Board is established for Americans who deserted from the U.S. military or avoided conscription illegally.

Society: (Jan. 21) The U.S. Supreme Court decides the case *Lau v. Nichols*, establishing educational rights for non-English-speaking students. (Jan. 31) The Child Abuse Prevention and Treatment Act is signed into law. (Apr. 3-4) Multiple tornadoes strike parts of the United States and Canada in what is termed the Jumbo Tornado Outbreak. (Jul. 30) French is named the official language of government and business in Quebec. (Dec.) The Privacy Act is enacted to prevent unwarranted invasion of privacy by the government.

Business and economics: The Equal Credit Opportunity Act outlaws discrimination in consumer credit practices. (Mar. 18) Most members of the Organization of Petroleum Exporting Countries (OPEC) end a five-month oil embargo against the United States, Europe, and Japan. (Sept. 2) The Employee Retirement Income Security Act (ERISA) is signed.

Transportation and communications: A National Maximum Speed Limit of fifty-five miles per hour is established on highways and interstates.

Science and technology: (Feb. 8) The last crew of Skylab returns to Earth after eighty-four days in space.

Environment and health: F. Sherwood Rowland and Mario Molina warn that chlorofluorocarbons (CFCs) are destroying the ozone layer. (Nov. 13) Union activist Karen Silkwood is killed in a mysterious car accident while investigating workplace safety violations. (Dec. 16) The Safe Drinking Water Act mandates contaminant standards in the United States.

Arts and literature: Bob Woodward and Carl Bernstein publish *All the President's Men*, an account of their investigation into the Watergate break-in. Robert M. Pirsig's autobiographical travelogue *Zen and the Art of Motorcycle Maintenance* is published. FICTION: *Carrie* (Stephen King); *Centennial* (James A. Michener); *Look at the Harlequins!* (Vladimir Nabokov); *The Other Side of Midnight* (Sidney Sheldon); *Tinker, Tailor, Soldier, Spy* (John le Carré). (Jun. 29) Soviet ballet dancer Mikhail Baryshnikov defects in Toronto. (Oct. 14) Peter Shaffer's play *Equus* opens.

Popular culture: Roman Polanski's film *Chinatown* opens. Mel Brooks's spoofs *Blazing Saddles* and *Young Frankenstein* are released. The 1950's nostalgia series *Happy Days* debuts. The detective series *Get Christie Love* features an African American woman in the central role. The series *Chico and the Man* goes on the air. The talk show *Donahue* premieres on television. ALBUMS: *Waterloo* (Abba); *High Voltage* (AC/DC); *Endless Summer* (Beach Boys); *Let's Get It On* (Marvin Gaye). The bands the Ramones and Van Halen form. (Jan. 5) The role-playing game Dungeons and Dragons is first marketed commercially.

Sports: Frank Robinson becomes the first African American manager in Major League Baseball. (Jan. 13) The Miami Dolphins defeat the Minnesota Vikings and repeat as Super Bowl champions. (May 12) The Boston Celtics win the National Basketball Association (NBA) Finals in seven games over the Milwaukee Bucks. (Apr. 8) Hank Aaron hits his 715th home run, breaking Babe Ruth's record. (Oct. 17) The Oakland Athletics defeat the Los Angeles Dodgers in five games to win the World Series. (Oct. 30) Muhammad Ali regains the world heavyweight boxing title by knocking out George Foreman in the Rumble in the Jungle in Zaire. (Dec. 26) Little League officials decide to allow girls to participate.

Crime: (Feb. 4) Publishing heir Patty Hearst is kidnapped by the Symbionese Liberation Army (SLA). (Apr.) Hearst and the other members of the SLA rob a bank in San Francisco.

1975

International events: (Feb. 11) Margaret Thatcher becomes leader of the Conservative Party in the United Kingdom. (Mar. 25) King Faisal of Saudi Arabia is killed by his mentally disturbed nephew. (Apr. 17) Pol Pot names himself the prime minister of the Democratic Republic of Kampuchea (Cambodia). (May 12) The Cambodian navy seizes the SS *Mayaguez*, an American merchant ship. (Nov. 22) Juan Carlos is crowned king of Spain after the death of dictator Francisco Franco.

Government and politics: (Jan. 1) John Mitchell, H. R. Haldeman, and John D. Ehrlichman are found guilty of the Watergate cover-up. (Jan. 8) Ella T. Grasso becomes the governor of Connecticut, the first woman in the United States to serve as governor without succeeding her husband. (Sept. 5) Manson Family member Lynette

"Squeaky" Fromme attempts to assassinate President Gerald Ford and is arrested. (Sept. 22) A mentally unstable woman named Sara Jane Moore also tries unsuccessfully to shoot President Ford.

Military and war: (Jan. 6) North Vietnamese troops take Phuoc Long City and the surrounding province, violating the Paris Peace Accords. (Apr. 30) North Vietnamese forces conquer Saigon and end the war as the last Americans are evacuated from Vietnam.

Society: (Jan. 4) The Indian Self-Determination and Education Assistance Act is passed. (Jun. 27) The Quebec Charter of Human Rights and Freedoms is passed. (Aug. 6) A Voting Rights Act extending and expanding the legislation of 1965 and 1970 is signed into law. (Nov. 11) The James Bay and Northern Quebec Agreement is signed by the Canadian government. (Nov. 28) The Age Discrimination Act prohibiting age discrimination in any federally funded program, benefit, or activity is signed into law. (Nov. 29) The Education for All Handicapped Children Act is enacted.

Business and economics: (Jan. 1) Product labels in Canada use the metric system. (Mar. 29) The Earned Income Tax Credit program is enacted.

Transportation and communications: The National Transportation Safety Board (NTSB) becomes an independent agency. (Jan.) The first microcomputer, the Altair 8800, is released.

Science and technology: The laser printer and the microchip are introduced. (Jul. 17) Three American astronauts and two Soviet cosmonauts meet in space when their Apollo and Soyuz spacecraft dock. (Aug. 20) Viking 1 is sent on its mission to Mars. (Sept. 9) The Viking 2 spacecraft is launched.

Environment and health: Ernest Callenbach's utopian novel *Ecotopia* is published. The Hazardous Materials Transportation Act is passed. Ultrasound imaging is invented.

Arts and literature: FICTION: *Dhalgren* (Samuel R. Delany); *Looking for Mr. Goodbar* (Judith Rossner); *Ragtime* (E. L. Doctorow); *Shogun* (James Clavell). MUSICALS: *Chicago* (John Kander and Fred Ebb); *The Wiz* (William F. Brown and Charlie Smalls); *Shenandoah* (James Lee Barrett, Peter Udell, and Philip Rose). (Apr. 2) The CN Tower in Toronto is named the world's tallest free-standing structure. (Jul. 25) Marvin Hamlisch and Edward Kleban's *A Chorus Line* opens on Broadway.

Popular culture: Mood rings and pet rocks are introduced. The film *One Flew over the Cuckoo's Nest,* starring Jack Nicholson, is released. The cult classic *The Rocky Horror Picture Show* opens. The late-night comedic series *Saturday Night Live* premieres. ALBUMS: *Welcome to My Nightmare* (Alice Cooper); *Desperado* (The Eagles); *Wish You Were Here* (Pink Floyd); *Born to Run* (Bruce Springsteen); *Love to Love You Baby* (Donna Summer).

Sports: Bobby Unser is victorious in the Indianapolis 500. (Jan. 12) The Pittsburgh Steelers win Super Bowl IX over the Minnesota Vikings. (May 25) The Golden State Warriors sweep the Washington Bullets in the National Basketball Association (NBA) Finals. (Oct. 1) In the Thrilla in Manila, Muhammad Ali defeats Joe Frazier to keep the boxing heavyweight championship. (Oct. 22) In the World Series, the Cincinnati Reds beat the Boston Red Sox in seven games.

Crime: (Jan.) The Speedy Trial Act becomes law. (Jul. 30) Labor leader Jimmy Hoffa disappears after having lunch with Mafia figures. (Sept.) Patty Hearst and two members of the Symbionese Liberation Army (SLA) are arrested. (Dec. 29) A bomb at LaGuardia Airport in New York City kills eleven people.

1976

International events: The United Nations' Decade for Women begins. (Jan. 8) Zhou Enlai, the premier of the People's Republic of China, dies. (Mar. 18) Harold Wilson resigns as prime minister of the United Kingdom. (Mar. 24) Military forces depose Argentine president Isabel Perón. (Apr. 5) Jim Callaghan is named prime minister of the United Kingdom. (Jul. 2) North Vietnam and South Vietnam form the Socialist Republic of Vietnam.

Government and politics: (May 11) President Gerald Ford signs the Federal Election Campaign Act. (Jul. 4) The United States marks its bicentennial with numerous celebrations. (Nov. 2) Democratic candidate Jimmy Carter defeats Republican incumbent Ford to win the U.S. presidency.

Military and war: Military academies in the United States admit women for the first time.

Society: *The Hite Report,* a book about female sexuality, is published. Gail Sheehy's pop psychology work *Passages* is a best-seller. The first National

Women's Conference is held. Indiana becomes the last state to ratify the Equal Rights Amendment (ERA), leaving the measure three states short. (Aug. 5) An Immigration Act is passed establishing new ground rules for migration into Canada. (Dec. 27) The cohabitation case *Marvin v. Marvin* is decided by the California Supreme Court.

Business and economics: Bill Gates and Paul Allen found Microsoft. (Apr. 1) Apple Computer is founded by Steve Jobs and Steve Wozniak. (Oct. 19) A revised Copyright Act extends protection in the United States for an additional twenty years.

Transportation and communications: (Jan. 21) The Concorde makes its first commercial flight. (Jul. 1) The National Air and Space Museum opens in Washington, D.C.

Science and technology: Videocassette recorders (VCRs) are introduced to the U.S. consumer market. (Jul. 20) Viking 1 lands on Mars. (Sept. 3) The Viking 2 spacecraft lands on Mars.

Environment and health: The Sagebrush Rebellion protests federal public land policies in the West. Use of the food coloring red dye no. 2 is banned in the United States because of health concerns. (Jun. 5) The Teton Dam in Idaho collapses shortly after its completion. (Jul.) A deadly pneumonia outbreak occurs at an American Legion convention in Philadelphia and is termed Legionnaires' disease.

Arts and literature: Maxine Hong Kingston's autobiographical novel *The Woman Warrior* is published. Humorist Erma Bombeck publishes *The Grass Is Always Greener over the Septic Tank.* FICTION: *1876* (Gore Vidal); *Ordinary People* (Judith Guest); *Roots* (Alex Haley). (Apr. 25) David Rabe's *Streamers* opens on Broadway. (Jun. 10) Neil Simon's play *California Suite* debuts. (Nov. 17) The Tutankhamen traveling exhibit begins its journey to museums across the United States.

Popular culture: Martin Scorsese's critically acclaimed film *Taxi Driver* stars Robert De Niro. The satiric motion picture *Network* is released. The film version of *All the President's Men,* Bob Woodward and Carl Bernstein's Watergate exposé, opens. Sylvester Stallone's boxing film *Rocky* is released. The premium cable service Home Box Office (HBO) is introduced nationwide. The soap opera spoof *Mary Hartman, Mary Hartman* premieres on television. The controversial series *Family* goes on the air. ALBUMS: *Hotel California* (The Eagles); *Frampton Comes Alive!* (Peter Frampton); *Songs in the Key of Life* (Stevie Wonder). Influential rock group the Band dissolves. The Village People form. (Apr. 23) Punk rock group the Ramones releases its first album. (Nov.) The first television special *Battle of the Network Stars* airs.

Sports: Free agency is instituted in baseball. (Jan. 18) In Super Bowl X, the Pittsburgh Steelers edge the Dallas Cowboys. (Feb. 4-15) The Winter Olympic Games are held in Innsbruck, Austria. (Jun. 6) The Boston Celtics defeat the Phoenix Suns in six games in the National Basketball Association (NBA) Finals. (Jul. 17-Aug. 1) The Summer Olympic Games are held in Montreal, Canada. (Sept. 2-15) The first Canada Cup world hockey tournament takes place. (Oct. 21) In the World Series, the Cincinnati Reds sweep the New York Yankees.

Crime: (Mar. 20) Patty Hearst is found guilty of a bank robbery in San Francisco. (Jul. 15-17) Three men kidnap a busload of children and their driver in Chowchilla, California. (Jul. 29) The Son of Sam serial killer claims his first victim.

1977

International events: (Jun. 6-9) Jubilee celebrations in the United Kingdom celebrate twenty-five years of Elizabeth II's reign. (Jun. 15) Spain holds democratic elections after more than forty years of dictatorship. (Jul. 22) Communist leader Deng Xiaoping regains power in China. (Nov. 19) Egyptian president Anwar Sadat becomes the first Arab leader to make an official visit to Israel.

Government and politics: (Aug. 4) President Jimmy Carter signs legislation creating the Department of Energy. (Sept. 7) President Carter and General Omar Torrijos Herrera sign the Panama Canal treaties.

Military and war: (Jan. 21) President Carter pardons Vietnam War draft dodgers. (Sept. 21) A nuclear nonproliferation pact is signed by the United States, the Soviet Union, and thirteen other countries.

Society: (Jan.) Women are allowed to serve as ordained clergy in the Episcopal Church for the first time. (Feb. 15) The Canadian Citizenship Act takes effect. (Jul. 14) The Canadian Human Rights Act of 1977, extending protections in Canada, is passed. (Aug. 26) The Charter of the French Language, or Bill 101, is passed in Quebec.

Business and economics: (Jun. 20) The Alaska Pipeline becomes operational.

Transportation and communications: The space shuttle *Enterprise* is used for a variety of ground and flight tests.

Science and technology: (Aug. 20) The Voyager 2 spacecraft is launched. (Sept. 5) Voyager 1 is launched.

Environment and health: Congress creates the Federal Energy Regulatory Commission. The Clean Air Act is amended. (Jan. 18) Scientists identify the bacteria that cause Legionnaire's disease. (Sept. 11) The last natural infection of smallpox is reported in Somalia.

Arts and literature: Jim Fixx publishes *The Complete Book of Running*. FICTION: *Oliver's Story* (Erich Segal); *The Shining* (Stephen King); *Song of Solomon* (Toni Morrison); *Terms of Endearment* (Larry McMurtry); *The Thorn Birds* (Colleen McCullough). (Feb. 2) Simon Gray's play *Otherwise Engaged* premieres on Broadway. (Apr. 21) The popular musical *Annie* opens.

Popular culture: The motion picture *Saturday Night Fever* becomes a cultural sensation. Woody Allen's critically acclaimed *Annie Hall* is released. Steven Spielberg's science-fiction film *Close Encounters of the Third Kind* opens. *Three's Company* goes on the air. The discotheque Studio 54 opens in New York City. The Rubik's cube is invented. ALBUMS: *Heroes* (David Bowie); *Rumours* (Fleetwood Mac); *The Stranger* (Billy Joel); *Exodus* (Bob Marley and the Wailers); *Bat out of Hell* (Meat Loaf); *Cat Scratch Fever* (Ted Nugent); *Never Mind the Bollocks, Here's the Sex Pistols* (The Sex Pistols). (Jan. 23-30) The landmark television miniseries *Roots* airs. (May 25) George Lucas's space epic *Star Wars* debuts in theaters. (Aug. 16) Elvis Presley is found dead at his home, Graceland.

Sports: Janet Guthrie becomes the first woman to qualify for the Indianapolis 500. Major League Baseball expansion teams the Seattle Mariners and the Toronto Blue Jays debut. In horse racing, Seattle Slew wins the Triple Crown. (Jan. 9) The Oakland Raiders defeat the Minnesota Vikings in Super Bowl XI. (Jun. 5) The Portland Trail Blazers win the National Basketball Association (NBA) Finals in six games over over the Philadelphia 76ers. (Oct. 1) Soccer star Pelé plays his final game, the first half for the New York Cosmos and the second for Brazilian club FC Santos. (Oct. 18) In the World Series, the New York Yankees defeat the Los Angeles Dodgers. (Dec. 9) Kermit Washington of the Los Angeles Lakers punches Rudy Tomjanovich of the Houston Rockets during a basketball game, almost killing him.

Crime: (Jul. 13-14) A massive blackout takes place in New York City, accompanied by considerable looting and other crimes. (Aug. 11) David Berkowitz, serial killer known as the Son of Sam, is arrested in New York City.

1978

International events: (Mar. 3) Rhodesia attacks Zambia. (Mar. 16) Israel invades Lebanon. (Jun. 23) Tito is named president for life in Yugoslavia. (Sept. 17) The Camp David Accords are signed by Egyptian president Anwar Sadat and Israeli prime minister Menachem Begin and witnessed by U.S. president Jimmy Carter. (Sept. 28) John Paul I dies thirty-three days after being named pope. (Oct. 1) Vietnam attacks Cambodia. (Oct. 16) Polish cardinal Karol Jósef Wojtyla becomes Pope John Paul II.

Government and politics: (Jun. 6) California voters support Proposition 13, which rolls back property taxes. (Dec. 4) Dianne Feinstein becomes the first female mayor of San Francisco.

Military and war: The motion pictures *Coming Home* and *The Deer Hunter* call attention to the effect of the Vietnam War on veterans and their loved ones.

Society: More than 100,000 people march in Washington, D.C., demanding an extension for the attempted ratification of the Equal Rights Amendment (ERA). The first Take Back the Night march takes place in San Francisco to protest violence. Judith Martin's syndicated Miss Manners column is published in newspapers for the first time. (Jun. 9) The Mormon Church announces that it is lifting its priesthood ban on African American men. (Jun. 28) In the decision *Regents of the University of California v. Bakke,* the U.S. Supreme Court rules that race can be a factor in university admissions but limits the implementation of affirmative action programs. (Aug. 11) The American Indian Religious Freedom Act is adopted.

Business and economics: (Jan. 1) The Copyright Act of 1976 takes effect. (Oct. 31) The Pregnancy Discrimination Act mandates equal treatment by employers of their workers affected by "pregnancy, childbirth, or related medical conditions."

Transportation and communications: (Oct. 24) The Airline Deregulation Act is passed.

Science and technology: (May 20) Pioneer 12 is launched into space. (Jul. 25) Louise Brown, the first "test-tube baby," is born. (Aug. 8) The Pioneer 13 spacecraft launches.

Environment and health: The public learns that the Love Canal neighborhood in Niagara Falls, New York, was used as a chemical dumping ground. The United States prohibits the manufacture of aerosol sprays propelled by chlorofluorocarbons (CFCs). Lead paint is banned by the U.S. Consumer Product Safety Commission.

Arts and literature: Feminist artist Judy Chicago shows her art exhibit *The Dinner Party.* FICTION: *Chesapeake* (James A. Michener); *Eye of the Needle* (Ken Follett); *A Swiftly Tilting Planet* (Madeleine L'Engle); *War and Remembrance* (Herman Wouk); *The World According to Garp* (John Irving). MUSICALS: *On the Twentieth Century* (Betty Comden and Adolph Green); *The Best Little Whorehouse in Texas* (Larry F. King). (Feb. 26) The thriller *Deathtrap* opens on Broadway. (Mar. 14) Paul Zindel's play *The Effect of Gamma Rays on Man-in-the-Moon Marigolds* premieres. (May 9) *Ain't Misbehavin'*, based on the music of Fats Waller, opens.

Popular culture: The musical *Grease* becomes a blockbuster film. John Landis's hit comedy *National Lampoon's Animal House* is released. The science-fiction series *Battlestar Galactica* debuts. The sitcom *Taxi* goes on the air. The dramatic series *The White Shadow* premieres. ALBUMS: *Running on Empty* (Jackson Browne); *Birth of the Cool* (Miles Davis); *Van Halen* (Van Halen); *The Gambler* (Kenny Rogers). Rock groups the Knack, the Beastie Boys, the Pretenders, and Social Distortion form. (Apr. 22) The Blues Brothers, Jake and Elwood Blues (John Belushi and Dan Aykroyd), make their first appearance on *Saturday Night Live.*

Sports: Affirmed captures the Triple Crown of horse racing; Alydar finishes second in all three contests. (Jan. 15) In Super Bowl XII, the Dallas Cowboys triumph over the Denver Broncos. (Feb. 15) Leon Spinks takes the world heavyweight boxing title from Muhammad Ali. (Jun. 7) The Washington Bullets beat the Seattle SuperSonics in seven games in the National Basketball Association (NBA) Finals. (Aug. 3-12) The Commonwealth Games are held in Edmonton, Alberta, Canada. (Sept. 15) Ali recovers the boxing title from Spinks. (Oct. 17) In the World Series, the New York Yankees defeat the Los Angeles Dodgers in six games.

Crime: (Feb. 15) Escaped serial killer Ted Bundy is captured in Florida. (Nov. 18) Jim Jones and his People's Temple cult engage in a mass murder-suicide in Jonestown, Guyana, that kills more than nine hundred. (Nov. 27) Former San Francisco supervisor Dan White assassinates Mayor George Moscone and Supervisor Harvey Milk, a gay activist.

1979

International events: (Jan. 16) The shah of Iran flees his country. (Feb. 11) The Ayatollah Khomeini seizes power in Iran. (Apr. 11) Ugandan dictator Idi Amin is overthrown. (May 4) Margaret Thatcher becomes prime minister of the United Kingdom. (Oct. 1) Control of the Panama Canal passes from the United States to Panama. (Nov. 4) American employees of the U.S. embassy in Tehran, Iran, are taken hostage. (Dec.) The Soviet Union invades Afghanistan.

Government and politics: (Jan. 19) Former U.S. attorney general John Mitchell is released from federal prison. (Jun. 4) Joe Clark becomes the prime minister of Canada, replacing Pierre Trudeau.

Military and war: Francis Ford Coppola's controversial Vietnam War epic *Apocalypse Now* hits theaters. (Jun. 18) The nuclear arms control treaty SALT II is signed by the United States and the Soviet Union.

Society: (May) The White Night Riots erupt in San Francisco over the lenient sentence given to Dan White in the murders of Mayor George Moscone and openly gay city supervisor Harvey Milk. (Oct. 14) The National Lesbian and Gay Rights March in Washington, D.C., commemorates the tenth anniversary of the Stonewall Inn riots.

Business and economics: VisiCalc becomes the first spreadsheet program.

Transportation and communications: The Walkman portable stereo cassette player is introduced. The cell phone is invented. (Mar. 25) The space shuttle *Columbia* arrives in Florida to be prepared for its first launch.

Science and technology: (Mar. 5) Voyager I flies by Jupiter. (Jul. 11) The Skylab space station reenters Earth's atmosphere; pieces fall into the Pacific Ocean and the Australian Outback. (Sep. 1) Pioneer 11 becomes the first spacecraft to visit Saturn.

Environment and health: (Mar. 28-30) A failure at the Three Mile Island nuclear power plant results in a core meltdown. (Apr. 19) The United States announces a ban on polychlorinated biphenyls (PCBs). (Oct. 26) The worldwide eradication of smallpox is announced.

Arts and literature: Christopher Lasch's sociohistorical critique *The Culture of Narcissism* is published. Tom Wolfe's *The Right Stuff* describes the beginnings of the U.S. astronaut program. FICTION: *The Dead Zone* (Stephen King); *The Executioner's Song* (Norman Mailer); *Kindred* (Octavia Butler); *Sophie's Choice* (William Styron). MUSICALS: *Sweeney Todd* (Stephen Sondheim); *Evita* (Andrew Lloyd Webber and Tim Rice); *Sugar Babies* (Ralph G. Allen and Harry Rigby). (Apr. 19) The play *The Elephant Man* opens on Broadway.

Popular culture: The science-fiction horror film *Alien* is released. The film *Kramer vs. Kramer* examines the effects of divorce. *Star Trek: The Motion Picture* is released, ten years after the television series was canceled. Blake Edwards's film *10* stars Dudley Moore and Bo Derek. The single "Rapper's Delight" by the Sugar Hill Gang marks the commercial birth of hip-hop. ALBUMS: *Highway to Hell* (AC/DC); *Dream Police* (Cheap Trick); *London Calling* (The Clash); *Tusk* (Fleetwood Mac); *Off the Wall* (Michael Jackson); *52nd Street* (Billy Joel); *The Wall* (Pink Floyd).

Sports: (Jan. 21) The Pittsburgh Steelers edge the Dallas Cowboys in Super Bowl XIII. (Jun. 1) The Seattle SuperSonics take the National Basketball Association (NBA) Finals in five games over the Washington Bullets. (Jun. 22) The World Hockey Association folds; the Edmonton Oilers, Winnipeg Jets, Quebec Nordiques, and Hartford Whalers move to the National Hockey League (NHL). (Jul. 12) The promotional event Disco Demolition Night at Comiskey Park forces the cancellation of the second game in a doubleheader between the Chicago White Sox and the Detroit Tigers. (Oct. 17) In the World Series, the Pittsburgh Pirates defeat the Baltimore Orioles in seven games.

Crime: (Feb. 1) Patty Hearst is released from prison after her sentence is commuted by President Carter.

Tracy Irons-Georges

■ Bibliography

This bibliography lists books containing substantial material about a wide variety of topics pertaining to the 1970's. Additional works, and especially works on narrower subjects, can be found in the "Further Readings" notes at the end of every essay in *The Seventies in America.*

Books are listed under the following seven categories:

1. General Works

Bailey, Beth, and David Farber, eds. *America in the Seventies.* Lawrence: University Press of Kansas, 2004. Nine writers examine different cultural currents in the United States, including music, advertising, and the bicentennial celebrations.

Carroll, Peter N. *It Seemed Like Nothing Happened: America in the 1970's.* Reprint. New Brunswick, N.J.: Rutgers University Press, 1990. Provides a general history of the 1970's. In opposition to the common view that "nothing happened" during this decade, Carroll shows how the decade was filled with significant events, including Watergate, Richard M. Nixon's resignation, and Jimmy Carter's election. He also brings in international events such as the *Mayaguez* incident, Camp David Accords, and the Iranian hostage crisis.

Frum, David. *How We Got Here: The 70's—The Decade That Brought You Modern Life, for Better or Worse.* New York: Basic Books, 2000. This book looks at how modern life was shaped by the 1970's. It includes a consideration of many of the cultural phenomena of the period and concludes that the 1970's were much more transformative than the 1960's.

McQuaid, Kim. *The Anxious Years: America in the Vietnam-Watergate Era.* New York: Basic Books, 1989. McQuaid views Vietnam as the most important issue in the 1960's and 1970's, seeing it as the event that both allowed the rise of Nixon and permanently changed the Democratic Party.

Slocum-Schafer, Stephanie A. *America in the Seventies.* Syracuse, N.Y.: Syracuse University Press, 2003. Offers a broad overview of foreign policy, presidential administrations, social movements, and cultural issues.

2. Foreign Policy and Events

Clift, Arthur Denis. *With Presidents to the Summit.* Fairfax, Va.: George Mason University Press, 1993. Written by a former member of the National Security Council during this era, the book details the summits held by, and related foreign policy decisions of, Presidents Nixon, Ford, and Carter.

Gardner, Lloyd. *A Covenant with Power: America and World Order from Wilson to Reagan.* New York: Oxford University Press, 1984. This book examines the foundations of modern U.S. foreign policy. While not especially focused on the 1970's, it does deal directly with the foreign policies of Nixon and Carter and provides important historical context from which a better understanding of 1970's can be gained.

Kaufman, Edy. *Crisis in Allende's Chile: New Perspectives.* New York: Praeger, 1988. This book reexamines the overthrow of Chilean leader Salvador Allende in 1973. It reappraises the roles of the U.S. and other foreign governments as well as the actions of the Chilean military.

Kutler, Stanley I. *Encyclopedia of the Vietnam War.* New York: Macmillan Library Reference USA, 1996. A comprehensive history of the Vietnam War presented in alphabetical entries and overview essays.

Litwak, Robert S. *Détente and the Nixon Doctrine: American Foreign Policy and the Pursuit of Stability, 1969-1976.* New York: Cambridge University Press, 1984. Litwak looks at the way in which Nixon struggled to balance two foreign policy approaches that seemed, at times, to be in opposition.

Olmsted, Kathryn. *Challenging the Secret Government:*

The Post-Watergate Investigations of the CIA and FBI. Chapel Hill: University of North Carolina Press, 1996. This book examines why the CIA and FBI were not reshaped following Watergate. Investigations were undertaken, which Olmsted details, but no serious changes were made and the press ceased being zealous in its investigations. Olmsted explains why and how this happened.

Schulzinger, Robert. *Henry Kissinger: Doctor of Diplomacy.* New York: Columbia University Press, 1989. Schulzinger's well-researched analysis looks at both the accomplishments and the failures of Kissinger, noting his huge ego and how he promised more than he delivered at times.

Sick, Gary. *All Fall Down: America's Tragic Encounter with Iran.* New York: Random House, 1985. This book details the Iran hostage crisis and gives an insider's view of the revolution and U.S. response; Sick was the Iran expert for the National Security Council during the Carter administration.

3. Politics and Politicians

Ambrose, Stephen. *Nixon—Volume Two: The Triumph of a Politician, 1962-1972.* New York: Simon & Schuster, 1989. Ambrose paints a picture of the ten-year period in Nixon's life from his loss in the California's governor's race and his withdrawal from politics to his reelection to a second term as president. The book details his resurrection in politics, successful 1968 campaign, efforts in Vietnam, creation of détente with the Soviet Union, his marginally successful domestic policies, and the Watergate scandal.

Blum, John Morton. *Years of Discord: American Politics and Society, 1961-1974.* New York: W. W. Norton, 1991. Blum surveys U.S. politics from the inauguration of John F. Kennedy to the resignation of Nixon. He focuses on political history but also brings in some of the other events of the period, such as the counterculture and its impact on politics.

Bourne, Peter G. *Jimmy Carter: A Comprehensive Biography from Plains to Post-presidency.* New York: Scribner, 1997. Bourne, a friend who worked with Carter, details Carter's family history and explains Carter's early years in great detail. He also discusses Carter's meteoric rise to presidential candidate and president. The book also covers Carter's post-presidential efforts.

Cannon, James M. *Time and Chance: Gerald Ford's Appointment with History.* New York: HarperCollins, 1994. Cannon, an adviser to Ford, goes from Ford's boyhood through his presidency and, from a personal perspective, sheds light on why Ford was selected and why he pardoned Nixon, among many other topics.

Carter, Jimmy. *An Hour Before Daylight: Memoirs of a Rural Boyhood.* New York: Simon & Schuster, 2001. Carter's memoirs of his childhood, which detail the people who shaped his early life, and the oppressive segregation, never questioned, which permeated the South.

Colodny, Len, and Robert Gettlin. *Silent Coup: The Removal of a President.* New York: St. Martin's Press, 1991. This book defends Nixon and his role in the Watergate scandal more than most books on the topic. It suggests that several key people played a large role in removing Nixon and that Nixon was tricked into most of the mistakes that he made.

Emery, Fred. *Watergate: The Corruption of American Politics and the Fall of Richard Nixon.* New York: Times Books, 1994. Emery tackles two of the central myths about Watergate: that it was just a minor act of typical political spying and that Nixon did nothing worse than any other president but just got caught.

Green, John R. *The Limits of Power: The Nixon and Ford Administrations.* Bloomington: Indiana University Press, 1992. This book covers the eight years between Nixon's first election and Ford leaving office as the only president never elected as either president or vice president. He paints a familiar picture of Nixon as being limited by Watergate and shows Ford's mishandling of the pardon issue.

Greene, John Robert. *The Presidency of Gerald R. Ford.* Lawrence: University Press of Kansas, 1995. Greene presents Ford as a decent man who was not presidential material and details the burdens that Ford had to carry, both those of his own making and those of the period.

Hoff, Joan. *Nixon Reconsidered.* New York: Basic Books, 1994. Hoff emphasizes the radical programs of Nixon, which have been overshadowed by Watergate.

Kulter, Stanley I. *The Wars of Watergate: The Last Crisis of Richard Nixon.* New York: Knopf, 1990. Kulter paints a historical picture of the Watergate crisis and provides good insight and analysis into the personalities of the event.

Morris, Kenneth Earl. *Jimmy Carter, American Moralist.* Athens: University of Georgia Press, 1996. Morris examines how Carter tried to rule through morals, especially in the realm of foreign policy. He suggests that Carter failed because he lacked an ability to connect with the American people at a political level and lacked a workable plan to govern domestic affairs.

Moynihan, Daniel P. *The Politics of a Guaranteed Income: The Nixon Administration and the Family Assistance Plan.* New York: Random House, 1973. This book, written by Nixon aide and a later senator, details Nixon's Family Assistance Plan and its failure to be passed. This plan would have guaranteed all people a minimum level of income and radically restructured welfare.

Nixon, Richard. *RN: The Memoirs of Richard Nixon,* with a new introduction. New York: Simon & Schuster, 1990. One of Nixon's efforts to rehabilitate himself, this book is a political autobiography of Nixon and reveals a very complex man.

Parmet, Herbert. *Richard Nixon and His America.* Boston: Little, Brown, 1990. This work reflects favorably on Nixon, as might be expected as Nixon granted Parmet access to his private papers and granted interviews. Parmet focuses more on Nixon's political successes and foreign policy triumphs than on Watergate.

Reeve, Richard. *President Nixon: Alone in the White House.* New York: Simon & Schuster, 2002. This book presents a picture of Nixon as a man who was always alone and trusting no one, which Reeve attributes to Nixon's paranoia.

4. Economics

Conway, H. M., L. L. Liston, and J. Saul. *New Industries of the Seventies.* Atlanta: Conway, 1978. A general overview of American industry during the decade, giving information on size, cost, employment, and location.

Hartshorn, J. E. *Oil Trade: Politics and Prospects.* New York: Cambridge University Press, 1993. This book examines the rise and fall of OPEC power and compares the control of the world oil market by OPEC with that of previous controlling groups.

Patterson, James T. *America's Struggle Against Poverty in the Twentieth Century.* Cambridge, Mass.: Harvard University Press, 2000. This book tries to explain why the wealthy United States has historically had a sizable percentage of its people living in poverty. He surveys the efforts of each administration from Lyndon B. Johnson through Bill Clinton to tackle poverty.

Tsai, Hui-Liang. *Energy Shocks and the World Economy: Adjustment Policies and Problems.* Westport, Conn.: Greenwood, 1989. Examines the way in which national economies adjust to external developments and discusses the energy crises of the 1970's in depth.

5. Women and Minorities

Cruikshank, Margaret. *The Gay and Lesbian Liberation Movement.* New York: Routledge, 1992. Cruikshank produces a history of the gay and lesbian struggle for rights in the United States. Unlike many other works, she fully integrates the history of women into this struggle and includes the themes of ideas, political power, and sexual freedom.

Davis, Flora. *Moving the Mountain: The Women's Movement in America Since 1960.* New York: Touchstone, 1991. Profiles women's rights activists and examines the resulting changes in laws and institutions as well as the assumptions, prejudices, and unspoken rules governing a woman's place in American society that occurred because of their efforts.

Hartman, Susan M. *From Margin to Mainstream: Women and American Politics Since 1960.* New York: Knopf, 1989. This book looks at how women of all races and classes have participated in politics between 1960 and the late 1980's and what their different political concerns have been.

Kaiser, Charles. *The Gay Metropolis, 1940-1996.* Boston: Houghton Mifflin, 1997. Kaiser examines how the gay culture of New York City influenced the city's general culture and U.S. culture as a whole.

San Miguel, Guadalupe. *Brown, Not White: School Integration and the Chicano Movement in Houston.* College Station: Texas A&M University Press, 2001. Although focused on a specific locale, Houston, the book presents good contextual information about the rise of the Chicano movement in the United States during the 1970's.

Shilts, Randy. *The Mayor of Castro Street: The Life and Times of Harvey Milk.* New York: St. Martin's Press, 1982. This book surveys the life and death of the first openly gay elected politician in the United States. It also discusses the changes in San Francisco politics that enabled Milk's election, the development of gay culture in San Francisco, and the changes in gay life between the Stonewall Inn riots and the White Night Riots.

Sitkoff, Harvard. *The Struggle for Black Equality, 1954-1992.* New York: Hill & Wang, 1993. This work surveys the four decades following the landmark *Brown* case in the Civil Rights movement.

Skrentny, John D. *The Minority Rights Revolution.* Cambridge, Mass.: Belknap Press of Harvard University Press, 2002. Focuses on how the Civil Rights movement and the gains made by African Americans inspired several minority groups to work toward change by the late 1960's and early 1970's.

Wandersee, Winifred. *On the Move: American Women in the 1970's.* Boston: Twayne, 1988. This book focuses on radical groups and the National Organization for Women (NOW) as well as the larger concerns of women, including education and the working world. It also looks at Americans' reaction to the rising profile of women.

6. Culture and Entertainment

Braunstein, Peter. *Imagine Nation: The American Counterculture of the 1960's and 70's.* New York: Routledge, 2001. Fourteen essays detail the significant impact that the counterculture had on mainstream culture in the United States early in the decade. Their theme is the rejection by mainly young but also older people of prevailing political, social, and cultural norms through experimentation with drugs, sex, music, and identity to construct alternative ways of life.

Champ, Hamish. *One Hundred Best Selling Albums of the 70's.* New York: Barnes and Noble Books, 2004. Provides thorough details of the best-selling albums of the decade, as determined by sales awards from the Recording Industry Association of America (RIAA), including cover and sleeve artwork, production credits, and track listings.

Epstein, Dan. *Twentieth Century Pop Culture: The Seventies.* Philadelphia: Chelsea House, 2001. Includes a year-by-year chronology of events related to popular culture and focuses on television programs, actors, and music, among other topics.

Inness, Sherrie A., ed. *Disco Divas: Women and Popular Culture in the 1970's.* Philadelphia: University of Pennsylvania Press, 2003. This book examines popular culture in the 1970's and examines how images of women were changing in the media, which in turn changed the public conception of a woman's "proper" role. Among the topics considered are *Charlie's Angels,* cookbooks, and cheerleaders.

Kent, Stephen A. *From Slogans to Mantras: Social Protest and Religious Conversion in the Late Vietnam War Era.* Syracuse, N.Y.: Syracuse University Press, 2001. The 1960's and 1970's saw a rise in alternative churches such as Scientology and the Reverend Moon's Unification Church. Kent explains why this occurred and locates much of it in the failure of the political protest movements.

Malanga, Gerald. *Resistance to Memory: Portraits from the Seventies.* Text by Ben Maddow and Thurston Moore. Santa Fe, N. Mex.: Arena, 1998. Brings together Malanga's portraits of numerous cultural, artistic, literary, and musical personalities from the decade.

Miller, Stephen Paul. *The Seventies Now: Culture As Surveillance.* Durham, N.C.: Duke University Press, 1999. An examination of 1970's culture and how it was changing, including art, literature, music, cinema, and behavior of the period.

Shulman, Bruce J. *The Seventies: The Great Shift in American Culture, Society, and Politics.* Cambridge, Mass.: Da Capo Press, 2002. This book discusses a great deal of the cultural currents of the era, from the pop psychology of *Jonathan Livingston Seagull* to tennis great Billie Jean King. He also discusses the various political events of the decade, including the presidents and the energy crisis.

Sigoloff, Marc. *Films of the Seventies: A Filmography of American, British, and Canadian Films, 1970-1979.* Jefferson, N.C.: McFarland, 2000. An encyclopedic reference book that lists one thousand films from the decade and listings of cast and credits, awards won, and a summary of the plot, among other details.

Waldrep, Sheldon, ed. *Seventies: Age of Glitter in Popular Culture.* New York: Routledge, 2000. Waldrep's book is divided into five sections: "Re/Defining the Seventies," "Identifying Genres," "Fashioning the Body," "Queering the Seventies," and "Talking Music."

7. Miscellaneous

Bartley, Numan V. *The New South, 1945-1980.* Baton Rouge: Louisiana State University Press, 1995. This work discusses the postwar era in the South and covers a variety of areas, focusing on political and economic changes and the regional impact of the Civil Rights movement.

DiCanio, Margaret B. *Encyclopedia of American Activism: 1960 to the Present.* Santa Barbara, Calif.: ABC-Clio, 1998. An accessible reference guide of the people, events, movements, organizations, and issues associated with activist movements in the late twentieth century.

Kelner, Joseph, and James Munves. *The Kent State Coverup.* New York: Harper & Row, 1988. This book deals with the Kent State shootings, when Ohio National Guardsmen killed four war protesters and wounded nine. No one was officially responsible, so the families sued, and the book focuses on this trial.

Patterson, James T. *Grand Expectations: Postwar America, 1945-1974.* New York: Oxford University Press, 1996. Focuses on the three decades following the end of World War II and their mix of great optimism and great turmoil.

Woodward, Bob, and Scott Armstrong. *The Brethren: Inside the Supreme Court.* New York: Simon & Schuster, 1979. This book looks at the first six years of the Burger Court, from 1969 to 1975, looking at the fourteen justices who served for at least part of (if not all) of that time. It examines the internal tensions of the Court, noting how the decisions were often as much the product of personalities as they were of law.

Scott A. Merriman

Web Sites

In selecting the following Web sites, efforts have been made to identify the sites of broadest interest to readers and to those most useful in providing additional links. Attention has also been given to representatives examples of more specialized sites, such as pages on individuals personages and events.

Overviews of the Decade

Stuck in the '70's
http://www.stuckinthe70s.com

This site uses nostalgia and the site owner's personal reflection to examine the decade and complies several articles and links that are relevant to the 1970's. Its focus is primarily popular culture and includes topics such as television programs, fads, recipes and cookbooks, toys, and teen idols.

Welcome to the 1970's
http://www2.lhric.org/pocantico/century/1970s.htm

A site created and maintained by junior high students, it offers a thorough and chronological selection of links that take the user to Web sites of individual events and personages from the era.

Politics and Politicians

AmericanPresident.org
Http://www.americanpresident.org/history/richardnixon/biography/campaignsandelections.common.shtml

This site, maintained by the University of Virginia, provides a thorough treatment of Nixon. It provides good information on his early years, significant events during his presidency, key figures in his cabinet as well as his staff and advisers, a biography of First Lady Pat Nixon, and postpresidential activities.

Gerald R. Ford Library and Museum
http://www.ford.utexas.edu

This site details the activities and holdings of the Ford Library in Ann Arbor, Michigan, and the Ford Museum in Grand Rapids, Michigan. The site also presents a biography of Ford, a description of the libraries holdings, information for researchers, a list of available grants, and other information of interest to both the beginning history student and the more advanced scholar.

Jimmy Carter Library and Museum
http://www.jimmycarterlibrary.org

This site, which is administered by the National Archives and Record Administration, presents a great deal of information about Carter for the student and the historian. For the student, it presents a detailed biography of Carter (and one of First Lady Rosalyn Carter) and presents many photos of him. For the historian, it presents information about the library and the collections that are open to researchers.

Nixon Era Times
http://www.watergate.com

This site, based at Mountain State University in West Virginia, focuses on the whole presidency of Richard Nixon but has a special focus on Watergate.

Nixon Presidential Materials
http://www.archives.gov/nixon/index.html

This is a well-designed site that gives access to a wide array of Nixon's presidential materials. It has in-depth information about the infamous Watergate audiotapes, biographical information about Nixon and his family, and an administration time line, among many other features. Among the newer releases are twenty thousand pages of transcripts of Henry Kissinger's phone calls.

Presidential Elections, 1972
http://www.multied.com/elections/1972.html

This site contains information on the 1972 election. It includes the popular and electoral vote totals and a state-by-state breakdown of the vote, along with a short overview of the election.

Presidential Elections, 1976
http://www.multied.com/elections/1976.html

This site contains information on the 1976 election. It includes the popular and electoral vote totals, information on the two nominating conventions, and a state-by-state breakdown of the vote.

Revisiting Watergate
http://www.washingtonpost.com/wp-srv/national/longterm/watergate/front.htm

This site was created by *The Washington Post*, the newspaper that spearheaded the Watergate investigation. Among the resources here are a photo gallery; a video interview with Ben Bradlee, who was the editor at the time; and stories from the era. For historians interested in a deeper look or interested in doing some in-depth research, an archive of documents is also available, which includes transcripts from some of the Nixon tapes.

Richard Nixon Library and Birthplace
http://www.nixonfoundation.org

This library, the only presidential library to be privately funded and run, holds many of the personal papers of Nixon and is coordinated with his birthplace museum. Of particular interest to casual researchers is the six volumes of his public presidential papers, held and produced by the National Archives, but that are now available online at the Richard Nixon library. His presidential papers are held at the National Archives.

Foreign Policy

Camp David Accords
http://www.jimmycarterlibrary.org/documents/campdavid/index.html

This site, part of the Jimmy Carter Library, presents the basic documents that made up the Camp David Accords. It also has an article assessing the success and failures of the Camp David Accords twenty-five years later in 2003.

Documents on the Middle East
http://www.yale.edu/lawweb/avalon/mideast/mideast.htm#1970

This collection, from the Avalon Project at Yale University, presents in time-line form many of the documents related to American foreign policy in the Middle East during the 1970's. Some of the more well-known documents presented include Resolution 338 in 1973, dealing with the Yom Kippur War, and the Camp David Accords of 1978.

Mayaguez Takeover and Hostage Crisis
http://www.usmm.org/mayaguez.html

This site describes the seizure of the U.S. cargo ship *Mayaguez*, the successful release of the hostages, the retaking of the ship, and the problems encountered when American forces tried to storm the area in which they thought the hostages were held.

Trials

Charles Manson Trial
http://www.law.umkc.edu/faculty/projects/ftrials/manson/manson.html

Manson was convicted in 1971 of murdering seven people in the infamous Tate-LaBianca murders. What made the murders unusual is that Manson did not kill the people himself but had his followers do it for him. Manson was sentenced to death but still is in prison, and the site details the murders, the trial, and Manson's life in prison.

My Lai Trial
http://www.law.umkc.edu/faculty/projects/ftrials/mylai/mylai.htm

This site deals with the My Lai trial, which was held in 1970. The trial grew out of a massacre in Vietnam, where troops commanded by Lieutenant William Calley killed up to five hundred unarmed civilians. Calley was sentenced to life in prison at hard labor, but wound up serving only three and a half years, much of it in house arrest.

Civil Rights and Women's Rights

"Ghosts of the Second Wave": 51 Historic Photographs of the 1977 National Women's Conference in Houston, Texas
www.lindagriffith.com/IWYcaptionsmain.html

This site contains more than fifty photos documenting the National Women's Conference, which submitted a plan of action to the 1978 Congress. The plan called for, among other things, full support of *Roe v. Wade* and implementation of the Equal Rights Amendment (ERA). The pictures are annotated, and the plan's text is also available.

National Latino Communications Center
www.chicano.nlcc.com

This site provides links to films and information about the 1970's Chicano civil rights movement. While the site is focused on a variety of different issues relating to Latino Americans, it does provide some good Chicano civil rights information.

National Organization for Women (NOW)
www.now.org/history/history.html

This site provides a brief history of NOW, which was founded in 1966. The organization became very active in the 1970's, arguing for the ERA and for women's rights. The site details what NOW has fought for in the past and what it is advocating now.

Roe v. Wade
http://edition.cnn.com/SPECIALS/1998/roe.wade

A site created by CNN as a special report dealing with the landmark Supreme Court decision on its twenty-fifth anniversary. Included here is a profile of Norma McCorvey (Jane Roe), stories of women who at first wanted abortions but changed their minds, and a discussion of the personal and legal stories behind *Roe v. Wade*. A relatively comprehensive and neutral site.

Environment

Earth Day
http://www.earthday.net

This site details the history of Earth Day from 1970 into the twenty-first century and discusses how environmental protest has changed. The site also links to various people involved in the movement and the organizations supporting it.

Love Canal at Twenty-five
http://ublib.buffalo.edu/libraries/asl/exhibits/lovecanal.html

This site covers the Love Canal, arguably the best-known environmental story of the 1970's. The online exhibit provides maps, tells the story, provides copies of reports, provides a bibliography, links to related sites, and discusses twenty-fifth anniversary reminisces.

Three Mile Island
www.pbs.org/wgbh/amex/three

This site is from the Public Broadcasting Service (PBS) series titled *The American Experience* and uses information from the specific program about Three Mile Island. One can order the film through a link, and the site provides background, an enhanced transcript, maps, a teacher's guide, and an interactive time line. One of the more interesting things is a description of how a nuclear reactor works.

United States Environmental Protection Agency (EPA)
http://www.epa.gov/history

This site presents the history of the EPA, which was created in 1970. The site surveys the various administrators who have led the EPA and includes biographies of them and presents important news articles and press releases from the agency's history as well as discussions of issues with which the EPA has been involved.

Culture and Entertainment

American Cultural History, 1970-1979
http://kclibrary.nhmccd.edu/decade70.html

This site presents basics facts about the culture of the decade and provides short summaries of events and personages within art, literature, technology, music, films, education, and fashion. In each area, books are listed for further research, along with links to other Web sites on the topic.

Canadian Broadcasting Corporation
http://cbc.radio-canada.ca/history/1970s.shtml

Provides a time line of the history of the Canadian Broadcasting Corporation and its programming during the 1970's, among other decades.

Crazy Fads
http://www.crazyfads.com/70s.htm

This site links to discussions and images of fads that were popular during the decade, including streaking, video games, and platform shoes.

Encyclopedia of Television
www.museum.tv/archives/etv/index.html

This site is maintained by the Museum of Broadcast Communications, and the archives section is devoted to individual television programs, people, and events in television history. Pages on specific programs offer cast lists, production credits, programming history, and other background information.

Fashion-Era
http://www.fashion-era.com/1970s.htm

Provides detailed information about fads and trends in fashion during the decade, including ethnic fashion, the influence of disco, skirt lengths, and punk fashion, among other topics.

Filmsite.org
www.filmsite.org/70'sintro.html

This site provides a good history of film during the 1970's. It lists the Academy Award winners of each year and links to the top-ten box office draws of the 1970's. It also details the history of film and explains why the 1970's were a great decade for film making and profiles the film directors who got their start during the decade.

Hickok Sports
www.Hickoksports.com

A personal site containing more than three thousand pages of information, including extensive information on the histories of all the major sports at both the amateur and professional levels. Useful for identifying champions, award winners, and record-setters for the decade.

Institute for the Study of Evangelicals
http://www.wheaton.edu/isae/defining_evangelicalism.html

This site provides a definition of evangelicalism, an important part of the 1970's as evangelical Christianity grew in importance and interest. It provides definitions, with paragraphs of explanation, of a number of related terms, including evangelicalism and fundamentalism, and also provides a number of related short essays, including "Evangelicalism and the Media" and "How Many Evangelicals Are There?"

Internet Broadway Database
www.ibdb.com

This site is maintained by the League of American Theatres and Producers and provides a wealth of information on Broadway productions from the decade.

Internet Movie Database
www.imdb.com

A rich site maintained by online company Amazon.com that contains detailed cast and production credits and reviews many thousands of motion pictures, including nearly all feature films and documentaries of the decade.

Super Seventies Rock Site
http://www.superseventies.com

This site provides a wealth of information about the decade, all through the lens of popular culture and music. Links take users to information about the top one hundred singles of the decade and the greatest album covers, lists lyrics to popular songs, and profiles "superstars" of the era, among many other topics.

Scott A. Merriman

Glossary

This list is a representative collection of words and phrases that were either first used or gained prominence during the 1970's in the United States. (n. = noun; adj. = adjective; adv. = adverb; v. = verb; exp. = expression)

AC/DC, adj. Bisexual.
ageism, n. Prejudice against someone because of their age.
angel dust, n. The drug phencyclidine (PCP); originally prescribed by veterinarians for use in animals, it became popular with teenagers because it gave users the illusion of invincibility and an indifference to pain.
AOR, n. Album-oriented rock.
awesome, adj. Excellent or impressive.

babe, n. An attractive person.
baby blues, n. Blue eyes.
bad, adj. Good.
badass, n. A mean person.
bag, v. To steal.
bag job, n. A burglary.
bail out, v. To help someone get out of trouble.
ball-buster, n. A woman who takes away a man's sense of self-worth; also called a castrating female.
bananas, adj. Crazy, as in "My talking drove him bananas."
Barbie Doll, n. A person without a thought in his or her head.
bazongas, n. Female breasts.
be there or be square, v. To attend an important occasion or else be considered an outcast.
bean counter, n. Someone who works with numbers, such as an accountant.
beat the socks off, v. To defeat a person or team by a large margin.
bells and whistles, n. The items of a project or invention that serve little purpose other than to be flashy.
big enchilada, n. The boss.
big picture, n. The large situation or overview, as opposed to the small details.
biofeedback, n. A process by which someone can modify a body function, such as blood pressure.
black hole, n. A theoretical hole found in outer space created by a star collapsing in on itself.
blahs, n. The blues or low spirits.
bleep, n. A term used instead of a vulgar word, as in "He is an arrogant bleep."
body language, n. A person's gestures that communicate a feeling.
bogart, v. To hold onto something greedily.
bogue, n. An imitation.
boob tube, n. Television.
boogy or boogie, v. To dance
boom box, n. A portable music system primarily played on city streets with the volume turned up.
boot up, v. To start up the operating system of a computer.
boss, n. Fantastic.
bottomless, adj. Being naked from the waist down.
bubble gum, n. A form of rock music that appeals to young teenagers because of its simplistic or inane phrasings.
buckle your seat belts, v. To prepare for whatever may happen, especially trouble.
bug out, v. To leave in a hurry.
bummer, n. A disappointing experience.
burn artist, n. A dope dealer who cheats those to whom he sells.
burnout, n. A person who no longer has the ability to go on.
bust your hump, v. To work very hard.

can't win for losing, adj. Unable to succeed no matter what one tries.
chairperson, n. A gender-neutral term for the individual presiding over a meeting.
chill, v. To relax.
choirboy, n. Someone thought to be innocent or naïve.
clean, adj. Not in possession of or addicted to drugs.
climb the wall, v. To become very anxious or panicky.
clone, n. A copy or imitation of the real item; also a person who does everything as someone else would.
cold rodder, n. Someone who races snowmobiles.
computernik, n. A computer expert.
conceptual art, n. An art style whereby the concept or meaning is all-important.
conehead, n. Someone who is considered to be an intellectual.
copasetic, adj. Satisfactory.

counterculture, n. A culture that rejects mainstream or conventional social values.

crapshoot, n. A gamble with little chance of success.

crash and burn, v. To fail completely.

creative accounting, n. Imaginative bookkeeping that is employed to cover up fraud.

crossover, n. A deliberate move from playing one style of music to another.

Deadhead, n. A person who is a devoted fan of the rock group the Grateful Dead.

decriminalize, v. To remove criminal penalties.

déjà vu all over again, n. The same situation occurring repeatedly.

demo, n. A political demonstration.

designated driver, n. Someone who has chosen not to drink alcohol in order to be in a position to drive home anyone who has consumed too much alcohol.

designer jeans, n. Skintight jeans that have a designer label on the back pocket.

dig, v. To like or appreciate.

dingbat, n. A person considered to be ignorant or unsophisticated.

disco, n. A music style with a strong rhythmic beat making it perfect for dancing.

ditsy or **ditzy**, adj. Silly or frivolous.

dog it, v. To do badly or to not do one's best.

doobie, n. A marijuana cigarette.

dude, n. A guy.

dy-no-mite, n. A term for fabulous, made famous by the actor Jimmie Walker in the television series *Good Times.*

earth art, n. An art form that incorporates the natural environment into the finished piece.

factoid, n. Something that is taken for fact, but may or may not be true.

fall between the cracks, v. To be overlooked or forgotten.

fast on your feet, v. To be prepared or skillful at handling any eventuality.

fat Albert, n. A type of guided bomb.

fat, dumb, and happy, adj. Contented as a cow.

flake out, v. To fail.

foxy, adj. Attractive or sexy.

fragging, n. The tossing of a fragmentary grenade at a superior officer who is considered not to have his subordinates' best interests at heart.

freebase, v. To inhale the smoke from cocaine that has been heated.

fuzzbuster, n. A device that can detect the signals from police radar.

gasohol, n. A fuel for automobiles made up of nine parts unleaded gasoline and one part alcohol.

get behind, v. To support or approve of.

get down, v. To let go or abandon one's inhibitions.

gnarly, adj. Great; can also mean the opposite.

godfather, n. The person in authority, such as the head of a crime family; made famous by Mario Puzo's novel and the 1972 film of the same name.

gonzo journalism, n. A journalistic style that relies on exaggeration to make its point; made famous by the American author Hunter S. Thompson.

good ole boy, n. A male from the South who believes in the traditional values of the region.

grasshopper, n. A person who smokes marijuana.

greenhouse effect, n. A warming of Earth and its lower atmosphere caused by an increase in carbon dioxide.

gross, n. Disgusting.

gross out, v. To offend someone.

guilt trip, n. A mindset whereby someone is preoccupied with feelings of guilt.

hang, v. To stay or wait with someone.

hang a louie, v. To turn left.

hang loose, v. To remain relaxed.

hatchback, n. A style of automobile in which the rear window and trunk open as one.

haul ass, v. To start moving.

head shop, n. A store that primarily sells drug paraphernalia and related items.

headbanger, n. A fan of heavy metal music.

headcase, n. An eccentric or possibly insane person.

heavy, adj. A serious matter, as in "That is one heavy issue."

high-wire act, n. A precarious or dangerous plan of action.

hold onto your hat, v. To prepare for whatever may happen.

homie or **homey**, n. An African American term for a good friend.

hot pants, n. Extremely short shorts.

hotline, n. A service whereby callers can talk about personal problems without identifying themselves.

humongous, adj. Very large.
hunk, n. A good-looking man.
hype, n. An over-the-top advertisement.

If it ain't broke, don't fix it, exp. If something is working properly, then just leave it alone.
in the trenches, adv. In the office or workplace.
instant replay, n. A review of something that has already happened, such as a play in football.
It ain't over till the fat lady sings, exp. Until something (such as a game) is truly finished, the possibility remains that the outcome can be altered.
item, n. A couple currently involved in a relationship.
IUD, n. Intrauterine device used as a contraceptive.

Jesus freak, n. A person who belongs to a group in which Bible study, preaching on the street, and communal living are promoted.
jiggle TV, n. Television programming that sought popularity by casting young, sexually attractive female actors in prominent roles, such as *Charlie's Angels* and *Three's Company*.
jive turkey, n. A disagreeable person.
joanie or **joany**, adj. Old-fashioned in a tedious or boring way.
job bank, n. A job placement service that can be accessed by a computer.
jock, n. An athlete.
joint custody, n. Custody given to both parents after a divorce.
juice head, n. Someone who has a tendency to drink too much alcohol on a regular basis.
jump your bones, v. To have sex.
junk food, n. A food item that has very little or no nutritional value.

kazoo or **gazoo**, n. The buttocks or ass, as in "a pain in the kazoo."
keen, adj. Great.
keep on truckin', v. To continue or carry on.
kick the tires, v. To make a cursory inspection.
kidvid, n. Television programming geared toward children.
kosher, adj. Proper.

laid back, adj. Relaxed.
later, adv. Farewell or good-bye for now.
launder, v. To put illegal money into an honest enterprise in order to make the money legal.
lean and mean, adj. Ambitious in a desperate sort of way.
leisure suit, n. A suit worn at informal occasions that has a shirtlike jacket and a matching pair of slacks.
Let's blow this taco stand, exp. Let's leave.
letter bomb, n. An explosive that is mailed in an envelope to the intended victim.
like there's no tomorrow, adv. Behaving in a reckless manner, as in "He was drinking whiskey like there's no tomorrow."
lit up, adj. Drunk.
living will, adj. A person's written statement requesting that he or she not be kept alive by artificial means after he or she has suffered a disabling illness or accident.
loaded, adj. Under the influence of illegal drugs.
local yokel, n. The police officer of a town or city.
loose cannon, n. A person who cannot be counted on to behave properly and therefore will more than likely do something irresponsible.
love affair, n. A strong attraction for something, as in "He has a love affair with his car."

Ma Bell, n. The nickname for the Bell Telephone system.
macho, adj. Referring to a man who wishes to prove his masculinity by being aggressive.
mainline, v. To inject a drug (such as heroin) into a vein.
make the rounds, v. To pass around.
marathon, n. An extended session in which the members of a group hope for self-enlightenment.
mau-mau, v. To harass or intimidate.
maxi-skirt, n. A long skirt.
Me Decade, n. The 1970's preoccupation with self-growth; coined by the American author Tom Wolfe.
megafamily, n. A group of unrelated people—including men, women, and children—who have decided to live together in a communal manner.
mellow out, v. To relax or calm down.
meltdown, n. A disaster.
men's lib, n. Men's liberation.
metal head, n. A fan of heavy metal music.
Mickey Mouse around, v. To waste time, as in "With the deadline coming up, this is no time to Mickey Mouse around."
mind the store, v. To look after things and keep things running smoothly.

mindf—, v. To brainwash or confuse someone.
Mister Clean, n. An honest man who is above suspicion.
motor, v. To perform well without any unnecessary effort.
motormouth, n. Someone who is very talkative.
munchies, the, n. An incredible desire to eat after smoking marijuana.

neat, adj. Wonderful.
nerd, n. A dullard or tedious person.
new boy, n. Someone who is a beginner or novice.
nickel and dime, v. To remove in small amounts at a time until there is nothing left.
nuke, v. To destroy civilization with a nuclear device.
nut job, n. A disturbed or crazy person.

off the ground, adj. Running or in operation, as in "We need to find a way to get this business idea off the ground."
old lady, n. A girlfriend or wife.
old man, n. A boyfriend or husband.
on his case, adv. Paying very close attention to what someone is doing.
on the sauce, adj. Drinking alcohol.
OPEC, n. Organization of Petroleum Exporting Countries.
out of the closet, adj. Openly gay.
Ozzie and Harriet, n. A very middle-class couple.

page turner, n. A book so gripping that the reader cannot put it down.
palimony, n. The division of assets after an unmarried couple has separated.
payback, n. Revenge.
pissing contest, n. A confrontational encounter in which each person attempts to outdo the other.
plastic credit, n. Credit obtained through the use of credit cards.
play games, v. To toy with someone's emotions.
pop wine, n. A wine that has been flavored with fruit juice.
pre-owned, adj. An item that is used, such as an automobile.
primo, adj. First-class.
psychobabble, n. To talk about one's innermost feelings using convoluted jargon.
pull the plug, v. To commit suicide.
pump up, v. To exaggerate the importance of something.
punch your lights out, v. To beat up someone severely.
punk rock, n. A loud and extremely defiant form of rock music.
putz around, v. To fool around aimlessly.

rabbit died, the, exp. Confirmation that a woman is pregnant.
rad, adj. Admirable.
rebirthing, n. A form of therapy whereby someone's breathing is controlled in order to relive the experience of birth.
recycle, v. To reuse items or materials.
rent-a-cop, n. A security guard.
repo man, n. Someone who is employed to take repossession of an automobile.
right-on, adj. Admirable, as in "He was a right-on kind of guy."
right stuff, the, n. Possessing such qualities as heroism; a phrase made popular by the American author Tom Wolfe in his book of the same name.
ring someone's bell, v. To bring someone to a climax sexually.
rip off, v. To steal.
rope-a-dope, n. A boxing strategy in which a fighter remains against the ropes and absorbs his opponent's punches until the opponent becomes exhausted and vulnerable to a counterattack; this strategy was successfully employed by Muhammad Ali in his 1974 fight against George Foreman.

score, v. To take possession of or buy.
screw around with, v. To mess or tinker with.
sexism, n. A prejudice based on gender, especially a prejudice against women.
sexploitation, n. The exploitation of sex, primarily in film.
shine on, v. To reject someone.
sick-out, n. An unauthorized action whereby employees call in sick in order to show their displeasure with work conditions.
Silicon Valley, n. South of San Francisco within the Santa Clara Valley; so named because of the number of manufacturers of silicon computer chips that are located there.
six-hundred-pound gorilla, n. A powerful entity that is larger than life.
skinny-dipping, n. Swimming in the nude.
skyjack, v. To hijack an airplane.
Skylab, n. An American space laboratory.

skytel, n. An intimate hotel where passengers of private or chartered aircraft stay.
slam dunk, v. To dunk a basketball with ferocious authority.
slide, v. To give, as in "Slide him the photograph."
slimeball, n. An extremely disagreeable person.
smell blood, v. To get excited at the impeding demise of an opponent.
smokey, n. A police officer.
smoking gun, n. A valuable piece of evidence.
snazz the place, v. To improve or enhance a location.
snuff film, n. A motion picture in which a person is actually killed.
Sock it to me, exp. Strike or attack me; popularized on the television series *Laugh-In*.
south of the border, adj. A failed attempt at doing something, as in "His performance was truly south of the border."
spazz out, v. To become violently upset.
speed bump, n. A manufactured hump in a road that forces traffic to slow down.
split, v. To leave.
squeaky-clean, adj. Very clean or without blemish.
squeeze, n. A sweetheart.
stonewall, v. To block or put impediments in the way of further action.
streak, v. To run through a public area naked.
street worker, n. A concerned adult who wishes to help troubled teenagers.
stun gun, n. A pistol that fires small pellets for the purpose of stunning someone.
Sun Belt, n. The southwest region of the United States.
sweat bullets, v. To worry.
sweat-hog, n. A physically disgusting person.

Tap City, adj. Broke.
theme park, n. An amusement park based on an overriding idea or set of ideas.
thunder thighs, n. Extremely thick thighs.
tight, adj. Being a very close or good friend.
Tinseltown, n. The entertainment culture of Los Angeles, especially Hollywood.
totally clueless, adj. Ignorant.
trash, v. To vandalize or damage.
tripsit, v. To stay with someone who is under the influence of LSD.
tubular, adj. Fantastic or great.
turkey-shoot, n. Something that is extremely easy.
twist slowly in the wind, v. To suffer prolonged humiliation.

up front, adj. Truthful.

veggieburger, n. A burger that uses a vegetable patty instead of a meat patty.
vision center, n. A place of business where someone can get all vision needs met.

wacko, adv. Crazy, as in "The prisoner went wacko on me."
warmed over, adj. Something derivative or repeated with no thought of originality.
water bed, n. A bed that has a plastic mattress filled with water.
Watergate, n. A scandal.
wedgie or **wedgy**, n. A prank whereby someone's underwear is pulled up by another person.
where the action is, n. A place at the center of excitement or the latest of trends.
whistle blower, n. An employee who shares information with authorities about criminal or dubious activities of the company.
wicked, adj. Excellent.
wired, adj. Under the influence of drugs.
workaholic, n. Someone who works extended hours beyond what is required by the employer.
wrap, v. To finish or complete a project, as a film.

You can't fight city hall, exp. It is impossible to take on the establishment and hope to win.
youngblood, n. A young African American male.

zebra, n. A sports referee who wears a striped shirt as a uniform.
zipless f—, adj. A brief sexual encounter; popularized by American author Erica Jong in her 1973 novel *Fear of Flying*.
zorse, n. The offspring of a male horse and a female zebra.

Jeffry Jensen

List of Entries by Category

Subject Headings Used in List

African Americans

Art & Architecture

Asian Americans

Business

Canada

Court Cases

Crime & Punishment

Disasters

Economics

Education

Affirmative action
Busing
Education for All Handicapped Children Act of 1975
Education in Canada
Education in the United States
Lau v. Nichols
Metric system conversion
Missions of the College Curriculum
Regents of the University of California v. Bakke
Schoolhouse Rock!
Sesame Street
Swann v. Charlotte-Mecklenburg Board of Education
Title IX of the Education Amendments of 1972

Energy Issues

Alaska Pipeline
Antinuclear movement
Automobiles
Energy crisis
Gas shortages
Mopeds
Nader, Ralph
National Maximum Speed Limit
Oil embargo of 1973-1974
Three Mile Island
Transportation

Environmental Issues

Acid rain
Agriculture in Canada
Agriculture in the United States
Air pollution
Chlorofluorocarbon ban
Clean Air Act of 1970
DDT ban
Earth Day
Ecotopia
Endangered Species Act of 1973
Environmental movement
Environmental Protection Agency (EPA)
Great Lakes Water Quality Agreement of 1972
Green Revolution
Greenpeace
Keep America Beautiful
Leaded gasoline ban
Love Canal
PCB ban
Recycling movement
Safe Drinking Water Act of 1974
Sagebrush Rebellion
Water pollution

Film

Academy Awards
Alien
All the President's Men
Allen, Woody
American Graffiti
Annie Hall
Apocalypse Now
Beatty, Warren
Belushi, John
Blaxploitation films
Blazing Saddles
Blockbusters
Brando, Marlon
Brooks, Mel
Carlin, George
Cheech and Chong
Chinatown
Clockwork Orange, A
Close Encounters of the Third Kind
Comedians
Coming Home
De Niro, Robert
Deer Hunter, The
Deliverance
Disaster films
Dreyfuss, Richard
Dunaway, Faye
Eastwood, Clint
Exorcist, The
Field, Sally
Film in Canada
Film in the United States
Fonda, Jane
French Connection, The
Godfather films
Grease
Harold and Maude
Hoffman, Dustin
Horror films
Jaws
Kaufman, Andy
Kramer vs. Kramer
Last Tango in Paris
Love Story
Martin, Steve
Mon Oncle Antoine
Monty Python
Muppets, The
National Lampoon's Animal House
Network
Nicholson, Jack
One Flew over the Cuckoo's Nest
Pacino, Al
Patton
Pryor, Richard
Public Broadcasting Service (PBS)
Redford, Robert
Reynolds, Burt
Rocky
Rocky Horror Picture Show, The
Saturday Night Fever
Science-fiction films
Special effects
Spielberg, Steven
Star Trek
Star Wars
Streep, Meryl
Taxi Driver
10
Travolta, John
Wilder, Gene
Young Frankenstein

Health & Medicine

Acquired immunodeficiency syndrome (AIDS)
Acupuncture
Air pollution
Anorexia nervosa
Antinuclear movement
Artificial sweeteners
Asbestos ban
Cancer research
CAT scans
Child product safety laws
Chlorofluorocarbon ban
Cigarette advertising ban
Clean Air Act of 1970
Consumer Product Safety Act of 1972
DDT ban
Environmental movement
Environmental Protection Agency (EPA)
Fitness movement
Genetics research
Great Lakes Water Quality Agreement of 1972
Health care in Canada
Health care in the United States
Legionnaires' disease
Love Canal

Military & War

Music

Native Americans

People

Eagleton, Thomas F.
Eastwood, Clint
Ehrlichman, John
Ervin, Sam
Erving, Julius
Evert, Chris
Falwell, Jerry
Feinstein, Dianne
Field, Sally
Fischer, Bobby
Fonda, Jane
Ford, Gerald R.
Gaye, Marvin
Gilmore, Gary
Giovanni, Nikki
Grasso, Ella
Haldeman, H. R.
Hamill, Dorothy
Hearst, Patty
Hockney, David
Hoffman, Dustin
Jackson, Maynard, Jr.
Jackson, Reggie
Jenner, Bruce
Joel, Billy
John, Elton
John Paul II
Johnson, Sonia
Jordan, Barbara
Kaufman, Andy
Kennedy, Ted
King, Billie Jean
King, Stephen
Kissinger, Henry
Knievel, Evel
Koch, Ed
Lafleur, Guy
Léger, Jules
Levesque, René
Liddy, G. Gordon, and E. Howard Hunt
Littlefeather, Sacheen
Lopez, Nancy
McGovern, George
Mailer, Norman
Mamet, David
Manilow, Barry
Marley, Bob
Martin, Steve
Michener, Roland
Milk, Harvey
Mitchell, John
Mitchell, Joni
Morrison, Toni
Moscone, George
Mowat, Farley
Muldowney, Shirley
Nader, Ralph
Nicholson, Jack
Nicklaus, Jack
Nixon, Richard M.
Oates, Joyce Carol
Orr, Bobby
Pacino, Al
Palmer, Jim
Payton, Walter
Pelé
Peltier, Leonard
Presley, Elvis
Pryor, Richard
Reagan, Ronald
Reddy, Helen
Redford, Robert
Reynolds, Burt
Rich, Adrienne
Richler, Mordecai
Robbins, Harold
Robertson, Pat
Rockefeller, Nelson
Rose, Pete
Roy, Gabrielle
Ryan, Claude
Ryan, Nolan
Schreyer, Edward
Segal, George
Shange, Ntozake
Shaw, Irwin
Silkwood, Karen
Simon, Neil
Simpson, O. J.
Sirica, John J.
Sondheim, Stephen
Spielberg, Steven
Spitz, Mark
Springsteen, Bruce
Steinem, Gloria
Streep, Meryl
Summer, Donna
Thompson, Hunter S.
Travolta, John
Trudeau, Pierre
Updike, John
Vonnegut, Kurt
Wallace, George C.
Walters, Barbara
Walton, Bill
Wilder, Gene
Wilson, Lanford
Wolfe, Tom
Wonder, Stevie
Wooden, John
Woodward, Bob, and Carl Bernstein
Wyeth, Andrew
Young, Andrew

Politics & Government

Agnew, Spiro T.
Bicentennial celebration
Byrne, Jane
Canadian Citizenship Act of 1977
Canadian Human Rights Act of 1977
Carter, Jimmy
Central Intelligence Agency (CIA)
Charter of the French Language
Chisholm, Shirley
Chrétien, Jean
Clark, Joe
Committee to Re-elect the President (CRP)
Congress, U.S.
Conservatism in U.S. politics
Cox, Archibald
Daley, Richard J.
Dean, John
Eagleton, Thomas F.
Ehrlichman, John
Elections in Canada
Elections in the United States, midterm
Elections in the United States, 1972
Elections in the United States, 1976
Enemies List
Equal Rights Amendment (ERA)
Ervin, Sam
Federal Bureau of Investigation (FBI)
Federal Election Campaign Act of 1971 and amendments
Feinstein, Dianne
Ford, Gerald R.
Francophonie, La
Grasso, Ella
Haldeman, H. R.
Huston Plan
Jackson, Maynard, Jr.
Jordan, Barbara
Kennedy, Ted
Kissinger, Henry
Koch, Ed
Léger, Jules
Levesque, René
Liberalism in U.S. politics

Popular Culture

Religion & Spirituality

Science & Technology

Sexuality

Social Issues

Sports

Television

Theater & Dance

Transportation

Women's Issues

The Seventies in America

Photo Index

Personages Index

Page numbers in **boldface** type indicate full articles devoted to the topic.

Subject Index

Page numbers in **boldface** type indicate full articles devoted to the topic.